DOCUMENTS ON
INTERNATIONAL AFFAIRS
1963

DOCUMENTS ON
INTERNATIONAL AFFAIRS
1963

SELECTED AND EDITED
BY
D. C. WATT, JAMES MAYALL
AND
CORNELIA NAVARI

Published for
THE ROYAL INSTITUTE OF
INTERNATIONAL AFFAIRS
by
OXFORD UNIVERSITY PRESS
LONDON NEW YORK TORONTO
1973

Oxford University Press, Ely House, London W. 1 X 4AH

GLASGOW NEW YORK TORONTO MELBOURNE WELLINGTON
CAPE TOWN IBADAN NAIROBI DAR ES SALAAM ADDIS ABABA
DELHI BOMBAY CALCUTTA MADRAS KARACHI LAHORE DACCA
KUALA LUMPUR SINGAPORE HONG KONG TOKYO

ISBN 0 19 214818 4

*Printed in Great Britain
at the University Press, Oxford
by Vivian Ridler
Printer to the University*

CONTENTS

II. THE MIDDLE EAST

III. THE FAR EAST

PREFACE

LIKE its predecessors, this volume of *Documents on International Affairs* has been edited in conjunction with the *Survey of International Affairs* by the team responsible for writing the *Survey*. The documents here printed have been arranged in sections, which broadly correspond to the arrangement of the chapters in the forthcoming volume of the *Survey* for 1963.

Editorial practice remains the same as in the previous volumes. A few documents which date back to the end of 1962 or forward to the beginning of 1964 have been printed where these mark the most logical beginning and end points to the chapters and sections concerned. Documents have been printed in the sections to which the bulk of their contents is relevant, but where they cover more than one major theme this is indicated in the chronological list of documents at the end of the volume.

Like the *Survey* this is the last of the annual volumes of *Documents* to be published by Chatham House. The editors would like to thank all those who have assisted in the production of this volume, and in particular the staffs of the Chatham House Library and Press Library for their endless patience in dealing with numerous obscure inquiries.

The editorial work on this volume was greatly aided by a grant from the Social Science Research Council to whom we should like to express our gratitude.

D. C. WATT
JAMES MAYALL
CORNELIA NAVARI

December 1971

SOURCE ABBREVIATIONS

Cmnd, Cmd, C.	Command papers (London, H.M.S.O.)
Current Documents	*American Foreign Policy: Current Documents* (U.S.A., Department of State, Washington, D.C.)
Documents	*Documents on International Affairs* (Oxford University Press for the Royal Institute of International Affairs)
Documents on Disarmament	*Documents on Disarmament* (Washington, United States Arms Control and Disarmament Agency)
D.S.B.	Department of State Bulletin
G.A.O.R.	United Nations, *General Assembly Official Records*
H.C. deb.	House of Commons Debates (Hansard)
La Documentation Française	*Articles et Documents* (Paris, Ministère des Affaires Etrangères)
N.Y. Times	*New York Times*
O.A.U.	*Organization of African Unity*
O.A.S.	Organization of American States
Public Papers, 1963	Public Papers of the Presidents of the United States, 1963 (Washington, D.C., 1964)
S.C.O.R.	United Nations, *Security Council Official Records*
S.W.B.	*Summary of World Broadcasts* (British Broadcasting Corporation monitoring service)
Y.U.N. 1963	*Year Book of the United Nations, 1963* (United Nations, New York, 1964)

I. RELATIONS BETWEEN THE GREAT POWERS

A. THE WESTERN ALLIANCE

(a) *General Statements of American Policy*

Annual message of President Kennedy to the United States Congress on the State of the Union, 14 January 1963[1] (extract)

. . . Turning to the world outside, it was only a few years ago—in Southeast Asia, Africa, Eastern Europe, Latin American, even outer space—that communism sought to convey the image of a unified, confident, and expanding empire, closing in on a sluggish America and a free world in disarray. But few people would hold to that picture today.

In these past months we have reaffirmed the scientific and military superiority of freedom. We have doubled our efforts in space, to assure us of being first in the future. We have undertaken the most far-reaching defense improvements in the peacetime history of this country. And we have maintained the frontiers of freedom from Viet-Nam to West Berlin.

But complacency or self-congratulation can imperil our security as much as the weapons of tyranny. A moment of pause is not a promise of peace. Dangerous problems remain from Cuba to the South China Sea. The world's prognosis prescribes, in short, not a year's vacation for us, but a year of obligation and opportunity.

Four special avenues of opportunity stand out: the Atlantic Alliance, the developing nations, the new Sino-Soviet difficulties, and the search for world-wide peace.

First, how fares the grand alliance? Free Europe is entering into a new phase of its long and brilliant history. The era of colonial expansion has passed; the era of national rivalries is fading; and a new era of interdependence and unity is taking shape. Defying the old prophecies of Marx, consenting to what no conqueror could ever compel, the free nations of Europe are moving toward a unity of purpose and power and policy in every sphere of activity.

For 17 years this movement has had our consistent support, both political and economic. Far from resenting the new Europe, we regard her as a welcome partner, not a rival. For the road to world peace and freedom is still long, and there are burdens which only full partners can share—in supporting the common defense, in expanding world trade, in aligning our balance of payments, in aiding the emergent nations, in concerting political and economic policies, and in welcoming to our common effort other industrialized nations, notably Japan, whose remarkable economic and political development of the 1950's permits it now to play on the world scene a major constructive role.

[1] *Public Papers, 1963*, pp. 15–19.

No doubt differences of opinion will continue to get more attention than agreements on action, as Europe moves from independence to more formal interdependence. But these are honest differences among honorable associates —more real and frequent, in fact, among our Western European allies than between them and the United States. For the unity of freedom has never relied on uniformity of opinion. But the basic agreement of this alliance on fundamental issues continues.

The first task of the alliance remains the common defense. Last month Prime Minister Macmillan and I laid plans for a new stage in our long cooperative effort, one which aims to assist in the wider task of framing a common nuclear defense for the whole alliance.

The Nassau agreement[1] recognizes that the security of the West is indivisible, and so must be our defense. But it also recognizes that this is an alliance of proud and sovereign nations, and works best when we do not forget it. It recognizes further that the nuclear defense of the West is not a matter for the present nuclear powers alone—that France will be such a power in the future— and that ways must be found without increasing the hazards of nuclear diffusion, to increase the role of our other partners in planning, manning, and directing a truly multilateral nuclear force within an increasingly intimate NATO alliance. Finally, the Nassau agreement recognizes that nuclear defense is not enough, that the agreed NATO levels of conventional strength must be met, and that the alliance cannot afford to be in a position of having to answer every threat with nuclear weapons or nothing.

We remain too near the Nassau decisions, and too far from their full realization, to know their place in history. But I believe that, for the first time, the door is open for the nuclear defense of the alliance to become a source of confidence, instead of a cause of contention.

The next most pressing concern of the alliance is our common economic goals of trade and growth. This Nation continues to be concerned about its balance-of-payments deficit, which, despite its decline, remains a stubborn and troublesome problem. We believe, moreover, that closer economic ties among all free nations are essential to prosperity and peace. And neither we nor the members of the European Common Market are so affluent that we can long afford to shelter high cost farms or factories from the winds of foreign competition, or to restrict the channels of trade with other nations of the free world. If the Common Market should move toward protectionism and restrictionism, it would undermine its own basic principles. This Government means to use the authority conferred on it last year by the Congress[2] to encourage trade expansion on both sides of the Atlantic and around the world.

Second, what of the developing and non-aligned nations? They were shocked by the Soviets' sudden and secret attempt to transform Cuba into a nuclear striking base—and by Communist China's arrogant invasion of India. They have been reassured by our prompt assistance to India, by our support through the United Nations of the Congo's unification, by our patient search for disarmament, and by the improvement in our treatment of citizens and visitors

---

[1] *Documents, 1962*, pp. 482–4.
[2] The Trade Expansion Act, approved 11 October 1962; see *Current Documents, 1962*, pp. 1383–96.

whose skins do not happen to be white. And as the older colonialism recedes, and the neo-colonialism of the Communist powers stands out more starkly than ever, they realize more clearly that the issue in the world struggle is not communism versus capitalism, but coercion versus free choice.

They are beginning to realize that the longing for independence is the same the world over, whether it is the independence of West Berlin or Viet-Nam. They are beginning to realize that such independence runs athwart all Communist ambitions but is in keeping with our own—and that our approach to their diverse needs is resilient and resourceful, while the Communists are still relying on ancient doctrines and dogmas.

Nevertheless it is hard for any nation to focus on an external or subversive threat to its independence when its energies are drained in daily combat with the forces of poverty and despair. It makes little sense for us to assail, in speeches and resolutions, the horrors of communism, to spend $50 billion a year to prevent its military advance—and then to begrudge spending, largely on American products, less than one-tenth of that amount to help other nations strengthen their independence and cure the social chaos in which communism always has thrived.

I am proud—and I think most Americans are proud—of a mutual defense and assistance program, evolved with bipartisan support in three administrations, which has, with all its recognized problems, contributed to the fact that not a single one of the nearly fifty U.N. members to gain independence since the Second World War has succumbed to Communist control.

I am proud of a program that has helped to arm and feed and clothe millions of people who live on the front lines of freedom.

I am especially proud that this country has put forward for the 60's a vast cooperative effort to achieve economic growth and social progress throughout the Americas—the Alliance for Progress.

I do not underestimate the difficulties that we face in this mutual effort among our close neighbors, but the free states of this hemisphere, working in close collaboration, have begun to make this alliance a living reality. Today it is feeding one out of every four school age children in Latin America an extra food ration from our farm surplus. It has distributed 1·5 million school books and is building 17,000 classrooms. It has helped resettle tens of thousands of farm families on land they can call their own. It is stimulating our good neighbors to more self-help and self-reform—fiscal, social, institutional, and land reforms. It is bringing new housing and hope, new health and dignity, to millions who were forgotten. The men and women of this hemisphere know that the alliance cannot succeed if it is only another name for United States hand-outs —that it can succeed only as the Latin American nations themselves devote their best effort to fulfilling its goals.

This story is the same in Africa, in the Middle East, and in Asia. Wherever nations are willing to help themselves, we stand ready to help them build new bulwarks of freedom. We are not purchasing votes for the cold war; we have gone to the aid of imperiled nations, neutrals and allies alike. What we do ask —and all that we ask—is that our help be used to best advantage, and that their own efforts not be diverted by needless quarrels with other independent nations.

Despite all its past achievements, the continued progress of the mutual assistance program requires a persistent discontent with present performance. We have been reorganizing this program to make it a more effective, efficient instrument—and that process will continue this year.

But free world development will still be an uphill struggle. Government aid can only supplement the role of private investment, trade expansion, commodity stabilization, and, above all, internal self-improvement. The processes of growth are gradual—bearing fruit in a decade, not a day. Our successes will be neither quick nor dramatic. But if these programs were ever to be ended, our failures in a dozen countries would be sudden and certain.

Neither money nor technical assistance, however, can be our only weapon against poverty. In the end, the crucial effort is one of purpose, requiring the fuel of finance but also a torch of idealism. And nothing carries the spirit of this American idealism more effectively to the far corners of the earth than the American Peace Corps.

A year ago, less than 900 Peace Corps volunteers were on the job. A year from now they will number more than 9,000—men and women, aged 18 to 79, willing to give 2 years of their lives to helping people in other lands.

There are, in fact, nearly a million Americans serving their country and the cause of freedom in overseas posts, a record no other people can match. Surely those of us who stay at home should be glad to help indirectly; by supporting our aid programs; by opening our doors to foreign visitors and diplomats and students; and by proving, day by day, by deed as well as word, that we are a just and generous people.

Third, what comfort can we take from the increasing strains and tensions within the Communist bloc? Here hope must be tempered with caution. For the Soviet–Chinese disagreement is over means, not ends. A dispute over how best to bury the free world is no grounds for Western rejoicing.

Nevertheless, while a strain is not a fracture, it is clear that the forces of diversity are at work inside the Communist camp, despite all the iron disciplines of regimentation and all the iron dogmatisms of ideology. Marx is proven wrong once again: for it is the closed Communist societies, not the free and open societies which carry within themselves the seeds of internal disintegration.

The disarray of the Communist empire has been heightened by two other formidable forces. One is the historical force of nationalism—and the yearning of all men to be free. The other is the gross inefficiency of their economies. For a closed society is not open to ideas of progress—and a police state finds that it cannot command the grain to grow.

New nations asked to choose between two competing systems need only compare conditions in East and West Germany, Eastern and Western Europe, North and South Viet-Nam. They need only compare the disillusionment of Communist Cuba with the promise of the Alliance for Progress. And all the world knows that no successful system builds a wall to keep its people in and freedom out—and the wall of shame dividing Berlin is a symbol of Communist failure.

Finally, what can we do to move from the present pause toward enduring peace? Again I would counsel caution. I foresee no spectacular reversal in Communist methods or goals. But if all these trends and developments can persuade the Soviet Union to walk the path of peace, then let her know that all free nations will journey with her. But until that choice is made, and until the world can develop a reliable system of international security, the free peoples have no choice but to keep their arms nearby.

This country, therefore, continues to require the best defense in the world—a defense which is suited to the sixties. This means, unfortunately, a rising defense budget—for there is no substitute for adequate defense, and no 'bargain basement' way of achieving it. It means the expenditure of more than $15 billion this year on nuclear weapons systems alone, a sum which is about equal to the combined defense budgets of our European Allies.

But it also means improved air and missile defenses, improved civil defense, a strengthened anti-guerrilla capacity and, of prime importance, more powerful and flexible non-nuclear forces. For threats of massive retaliation may not deter piecemeal aggression—and a line of destroyers in a quarantine, or a division of well-equipped men on a border, may be more useful to our real security than the multiplication of awesome weapons beyond all rational need.

But our commitment to national safety is not a commitment to expand our military establishment indefinitely. We do not dismiss disarmament as merely an idle dream. For we believe that, in the end, it is the only way to assure the security of all without impairing the interests of any. Nor do we mistake honorable negotiation for appeasement. While we shall never weary in the defense of freedom, neither shall we ever abandon the pursuit of peace.

In this quest, the United Nations requires our full and continued support. Its value in serving the cause of peace has been shown anew in its role in the West New Guinea settlement, in its use as a forum for the Cuban crisis, and in its task of unification in the Congo. Today the United Nations is primarily the protector of the small and the weak, and a safety valve for the strong. Tomorrow it can form the framework for a world of law—a world in which no nation dictates the destiny of another, and in which the vast resources now devoted to destructive means will serve constructive ends.

In short, let our adversaries choose. If they choose peaceful competition, they shall have it. If they come to realize that their ambitions cannot succeed—if they see their 'wars of liberation' and subversion will ultimately fail—if they recognize that there is more security in accepting inspection than in permitting new nations to master the black arts of nuclear war—and if they are willing to turn their energies, as we are, to the great unfinished tasks of our own peoples— then, surely, the areas of agreement can be very wide indeed: a clear understanding about Berlin, stability in Southeast Asia, an end to nuclear testing, new checks on surprise or accidental attack, and, ultimately, general and complete disarmament.

For we seek not the worldwide victory of one nation or system but a worldwide victory of man. The modern globe is too small, its weapons are too destructive, and its disorders are too contagious to permit any other kind of victory.

To achieve this end, the United States will continue to spend a greater portion of its national production than any other people in the free world. For 15 years no other free nation has demanded so much of itself. Through hot wars and cold, through recession and prosperity, through the ages of the atom and outer space, the American people have never faltered and their faith has never flagged. If at times our actions seem to make life difficult for others, it is only because history has made life difficult for us all.

But difficult days need not be dark. I think these are proud and memorable days in the cause of peace and freedom. We are proud, for example, of Major Rudolf Anderson who gave his life over the island of Cuba. We salute Specialist James Allen Johnson who died on the border of South Korea. We pay honor to Sergeant Gerald Pendell who was killed in Viet-Nam. They are among the many who in this century, far from home, have died for our country. Our task now, and the task of all Americans is to live up to their commitment.

My friends: I close on a note of hope. We are not lulled by the momentary calm of the sea or the somewhat clearer skies above. We know the turbulence that lies below, and the storms that are beyond the horizon this year. But now the winds of change appear to be blowing more strongly than ever, in the world of communism as well as our own. For 175 years we have sailed with those winds at our back, and with the tides of human freedom in our favor. We steer our ship with hope, as Thomas Jefferson said, 'leaving Fear astern.'

Today we still welcome those winds of change—and we have every reason to believe that our tide is running strong. With thanks to Almighty God for seeing us through a perilous passage, we ask His help anew in guiding the 'Good Ship Union.'

Special message of President Kennedy to the United States Congress on Free World Defence and Assistance Programs, 2 April 1963[1] (extract)

. . . III. OBJECTIVES FOR IMPROVEMENT

In a changing world, our programs of mutual defense and assistance must be kept under constant review. My recommendations herein reflect the work of the Clay Committee,[2] the scrutiny undertaken by the new Administrator of the Agency for International Development, and the experience gained in our first full year of administering the new and improved program enacted by the Congress in 1961. There is fundamental agreement throughout these reviews: that these assistance programs are of great value to our deepest national interest— that their basic concepts and organization, as embodied in the existing legislation, are properly conceived—that progress has been made and is being made in translating these concepts into action—but that much still remains to be done to improve our performance and make the best possible use of these programs.

In addition, there is fundamental agreement in all these reviews regarding six key recommendations for the future.

Objective No. 1: To apply stricter standards of selectivity and self-help in aiding developing countries. This objective was given special attention by the Committee to Strengthen the Security of the Free World, (The Clay Report),

---

[1] *Public Papers, 1963*, pp. 294–303.

[2] *The Scope and Distribution of United States Military and Economic Assistance Programs: Report to the President of the United States from the Committee to Strengthen the Security of the Free World, March 20, 1963* (Washington, GPO, 1963); for extract, see *Current Documents, 1963*, pp. 1148–63.

which estimated that the application of such criteria could result in substantial savings in selected programs over the next one to three years.

Considerable progress has already been made along these lines. While the number of former colonies achieving independence has lengthened the total list of countries receiving assistance, 80% of all economic assistance now goes to only 20 countries; and military assistance is even more narrowly concentrated. The proportion of development loans, as contrasted with outright grants, has increased from 10% to 60%. We have placed all our development lending on a dollar repayable basis; and this year we are increasing our efforts, as the Clay Committee recommended, to tailor our loan terms so that interest rates and maturities will reflect to a greater extent the differences in the ability of different countries to service debt.

In the Alliance for Progress in particular, and increasingly in other aid programs, emphasis is placed upon self-help and self-reform by the recipients themselves, using our aid as a catalyst for progress and not as a handout. Finally, in addition to emphasizing primarily economic rather than military assistance, wherever conditions permit, we are taking a sharp new look at both the size and purpose of those local military forces which receive our assistance. Our increased stress on internal security and civic action in military assistance is in keeping with our experience that in developing countries, military forces can have an important economic as well as protective role to play. For example, in Latin America, in fiscal year 1963, military assistance funds allocated for the support of engineer, medical and other civic action type units more than doubled.

Objective No. 2: To achieve a reduction and ultimate elimination of U.S. assistance by enabling nations to stand on their own as rapidly as possible. Both this nation and the countries we help have a stake in their reaching the point of self-sustaining growth the point where they no longer require external aid to maintain their independence. Our goal is not an arbitrary cutoff date but the earliest possible 'take off' date—the date when their economies will have been launched with sufficient momentum to enable them to become self-supporting, requiring only the same normal sources of external financing to meet expanding capital needs that this country required for many decades.

For some, this goal is near at hand, insofar as economic assistance is concerned. For others, more time will be needed. But in all cases, specific programs leading to self-support should be set and priorities established—including those steps which must be taken by the recipient countries and all others who are willing to help them.

The record clearly shows that foreign aid is not an endless or unchanging process. Fifteen years ago our assistance went almost entirely to the advanced countries of Europe and Japan—today it is directed almost entirely to the developing world. Ten years ago most of our assistance was given to shoring up military forces and unstable economies—today this kind of aid has been cut in half, and our assistance goes increasingly toward economic development. There are still, however, important cases where there has been no diminution in the Communist military threat, and both military and economic aid are still required. Such cases range from relatively stabilized frontiers, as in Korea and Turkey, to areas of active aggression, such as Vietnam.

Objective No. 3: To secure the increased participation of other industrialized nations in sharing the cost of international development assistance. The United States is no longer alone in aiding the developing countries, and its proportionate share of the burden is diminishing. The flow of funds from other industrialized countries—now totaling on the order of $2 billion a year—is expected to continue; and we expect to work more closely with these other countries in order to make the most effective use of our joint efforts. In addition, the international lending and technical assistance agencies—to which we contribute heavily— have expanded the schedule and scope of their operations; and we look forward to supplementing those resources selectively in conjunction with increased contributions from other nations. We will continue to work with our allies, urging them to increase their assistance efforts and to extend assistance on terms less burdensome to the developing countries.

Objective No. 4: To lighten any adverse impact of the aid program on our own balance of payments and economy. A few years ago, more than half of U.S. economic aid funds were spent abroad, contributing to the drain on our dollars and gold. Of our current commitments, over eighty percent will be spent in the United States, contributing to the growth of our economy and employment opportunities. This proportion is rising as further measures are being taken to this end. I might add that our balance of payments position today is being significantly helped by the repayment of loans made to European countries under the Marshall Plan and by the Export-Import Bank. I am confident that in the future, as income in the less developed countries rises, we will similarly benefit from the loans we are now making to them.

Our economy is also being helped by the expansion of commercial exports to countries whose present growth and prosperity were spurred by U.S. economic assistance in earlier years. Over the last decade, our exports to Western Europe and the United Kingdom have more than doubled, and our exports to Japan have increased four-fold. Similarly, we can look forward to a future widening of trade opportunities in those countries whose economic development we are currently assisting.

In addition, our Food for Peace Program is increasingly using our agricultural commodities to stimulate the economic growth of developing nations and to assist in achieving other U.S. foreign policy goals. As the economies of developing nations improve, we are encouraging them to shift from foreign currency to cash sales or to dollar credit sales for these commodities.

The relative burden of our assistance programs has been steadily reduced— from some two percent of our national product at the beginning of the Marshall Plan to seven-tenths of one percent today—from 11·5 percent of the Federal Budget in 1949 to 4 percent today.

Although these figures indicate that our aid programs cost, in relative terms, considerably less today then they did ten or fifteen years ago, we are continuing our efforts to improve the effectiveness of these programs and increase the return on every dollar invested. Personnel, procedures, and administration are being improved. A number of field missions have been closed, scaled down or merged into embassies or regional offices. These efforts toward greater efficiency and economy are being accelerated under the new Administrator.

Objective No. 5: To continue to assist in the defense of countries under threat of external and internal Communist attack. Our military assistance program has been an essential element in keeping the boundary of Soviet and Chinese military power relatively stable for over a decade. Without its protection the substantial economic progress made by underdeveloped countries along the Sino-Soviet periphery would hardly have been possible. As these countries build economic strength, they will be able to assume more of the burden of their defense. But we must not assume that military assistance to these countries—or to others primarily exposed to subversive internal attack—can be ended in the foreseeable future. On the contrary, while it will be possible to reduce and terminate some programs, we should anticipate the need for new and expanded programs.

India is a case in point. The wisdom of earlier U.S. aid in helping the Indian subcontinent's considerable and fruitful efforts toward progress and stability can hardly now be in question. The threat made plain by the Chinese attack on India last Fall may require additional efforts on our part to help bolster the security of this crucial area, assuming these efforts can be matched in an appropriate way by the efforts of India and Pakistan.

But overall, the magnitude of military assistance is small in relation to our national security expenditures; in this fiscal year it amounts to about 3% of our defense budget. 'Dollar for dollar', said the Clay Committee with particular reference to the border areas, 'these programs contribute more to the security of the free world than corresponding expenditures in our defense appropriations . . . These countries are providing more than two million armed men ready, for the most part, for any emergency.' Clearly, if this program did not exist, our defense budget would undoubtedly have to be increased substantially to provide an equivalent contribution to the Free World's defense.

Objective No. 6: To increase the role of private investment and other non-Federal resources in assisting developing nations. In recent months, important new steps have been taken to mobilize on behalf of this program the competence of a variety of non-governmental organizations and individuals in this country. Cooperatives and savings and loan associations have been very active in establishing similar institutions abroad, particularly in Latin America. Our land grant and other universities are establishing better working relationships with our programs to assist overseas rural development. Already there are thirty-seven U.S. universities and land grant institutions at work in Latin America, for example, with a substantial increase expected during the coming year. Public and private leaders from the State of California are exploring with their counterparts in Chile how the talents and resources of a particular state can be more directly channeled toward assisting a particular country. Labor unions, foundations, trade associations, professional societies and many others likewise possess skills and resources which we are drawing upon increasingly—in order to engage in a more systematic and meaningful way, in this vital nation-building process, the whole complex of private and public institutions upon which our own national life depends. For at the heart of the modernization process lies the central problem of creating, adapting and improving the institutions which any modern society will need.

IV. PRIVATE INVESTMENT

The primary new initiative in this year's program relates to our increased efforts to encourage the investment of private capital in the under-developed countries. Already considerable progress has been made fostering U.S. private investment through the use of investment guaranties—with over $900 million now outstanding—and by means of cost-sharing on investment surveys, loans of local currencies, and other measures provided under existing law. During the first half of this fiscal year alone, $7·7 million in local currencies have been loaned to private business firms.

I believe much more should be done, however, both administratively through more vigorous action by the Agency for International Development, and legislatively by the Congress. Administratively, our Ambassadors and Missions abroad, in their negotiations with the less developed countries, are being directed to urge more forcefully the importance of making full use of private resources and improving the climate for private investment, both domestic and foreign. In particular, I am concerned that the investment guaranty program is not fully operative in some countries because of the failure of their governments to execute the normal inter-governmental agreements relating to investment guaranties.

In addition, the Agency for International Development will also strengthen and enlarge its own activities relating to private enterprise—both its efforts to assist in the development of vigorous private economies in the developing countries, and its facilities for mobilizing and assisting the capital and skills of private business in contributing to economic development.

Legislatively, I am recommending the following:

(a) An amendment to the Internal Revenue Code for a trial period to grant U.S. taxpayers a tax credit for new investments in developing countries, which should also apply to some extent to reinvestments of their earnings in those countries. Such a credit, by making possible an increased rate of return, should substantially encourage additional private investment in the developing countries. The U.S. businessmen's committee for the Alliance for Progress has recommended the adoption of such a measure.

(b) Amendments in the investment guaranty provisions of the Foreign Assistance Act designed to enlarge and clarify the guaranty program.

Economic and social growth cannot be accomplished by governments alone. The effective participation of an enlightened United States businessman, especially in partnership with private interests in the developing country, brings not only his investment but his technological and management skills into the process of development. His successful participation in turn helps create that climate of confidence which is so critical in attracting and holding vital external and internal capital. We welcome and encourage initiatives being taken in the private sector in Latin America to accelerate industrial growth and hope that similar cooperative efforts will be established with other developing countries.

V. THE ALLIANCE FOR PROGRESS

In a special sense, the achievements of the Alliance for Progress in the coming years will be the measure of our determination, our ideals, and our wisdom. Here in this hemisphere, in this last year, our resourcefulness as a people was challenged in the clearest terms. We moved at once to resist the threat of aggressive nuclear weapons in Cuba, and we found the nations of Latin America at our side. They, like ourselves, were brought to a new awareness of the danger of permitting the poverty and despair of a whole people to continue long anywhere in this continent.

Had the needs of the people of Cuba been met in the pre-Castro period—their need for food, for housing, for education, for jobs, above all, for a democratic responsibility in the fulfillment of their own hopes—there would have been no Castro, no missiles in Cuba, and no need for Cuba's neighbors to incur the immense risks of resistance to threatened aggression from that island.

There is but one way to avoid being faced with similar dilemmas in the future. It is to bring about in all the countries of Latin America the conditions of hope, in which the peoples of this continent will know that they can shape a better future for themselves, not through obeying the inhuman commands of an alien and cynical ideology, but through personal self-expression, individual judgment, and the acts of responsible citizenship.

As Americans, we have long recognized the legitimacy of these aspirations; in recent months we have been able to see, as never before, their urgency and, I believe, the concrete means for their realization.

In less than two years, the 10 year program of the Alliance for Progress has become more than an idea and more than a commitment of governments. The necessary initial effort to develop plans, to organize institutions, to test and experiment has itself required and achieved a new dedication—a new dedication to intelligent compromise between old and new ways of life. In the long run, it is this effort and not the threat of Communism—that will determine the fate of freedom in the Western Hemisphere.

These years have not been easy ones for any group in Latin America. A similar change in the fundamental orientation of our own society would have been no easier. The difficulty of the changes to be brought about makes all the more heartening the success of many nations of Latin America in achieving reforms which will make their fundamental economic and social structures both more efficient and more equitable.

Some striking accomplishments, moreover, are already visible. New housing is being expanded in most countries of the region. Educational facilities are growing rapidly. Road construction, particularly in agricultural areas, is accelerating at a rapid pace. With U.S. funds, over two million text books are being distributed to combat the illiteracy of nearly half of the 210 million people of Latin America. In the countries of the Alliance for Progress, the diets of eight million children and mothers are being supplemented with United States Food for Peace, and this figure should reach nearly 16 million by next year.

In trouble-ridden Northeast Brazil, under an agreement with the State of Rio Grande do Norte, a program is underway to train three thousand teachers, build one thousand classrooms, ten vocational schools, eight normal schools, and four teacher training centers. A $30 million slum clearance project is underway in Venezuela. In Bogota, Colombia, the site of the old airport is becoming a new city for 71 thousand persons who are building their own homes with support from the Social Progress Trust Fund.

This year I received a letter from Senor Argemil Plazas Garcia, whom I met in Bogota upon the dedication of an Alianza housing project. He writes: 'Today I am living in the house with my thirteen children, and we are very happy to be free of such poverty and no longer to be moving around like outcasts. Now we have dignity and freedom . . . My wife, my children and I are writing you this humble letter, to express to you the warm gratitude of such Colombian friends who now have a home in which they can live happily.' Of even greater long-range importance, a number of beginnings in self-help and reforms are now evident.

Since 1961, eleven Latin American countries—Argentina, Bolivia, Brazil, Colombia, Chile, Costa Rica, the Dominican Republic, El Salvador, Mexico, Panama, and Venezuela—have made structural reforms in their tax systems. Twelve countries have improved their income tax laws and administration.

New large scale programs for improved land use and land reform have been undertaken in Venezuela, the Dominican Republic and two states in Brazil. More limited plans are being carried out in Chile, Colombia, Panama, Uruguay and Central America.

Six Latin American countries—Colombia, Chile, Bolivia, Honduras, Mexico, and Venezuela—have submitted development programs to the panel of experts of the Organization of American States. The panel has evaluated and reported on the first three and will soon offer its views on the balance.

Viewed against the background of decades of neglect—or, at most, intermittent bursts of attention to basic problems—the start that has been made is encouraging. Perhaps most significant of all is a change in the hearts and minds of the people—a growing will to develop their countries. We can only help Latin Americans to save themselves. It is for this reason that the increasing determination of the peoples of the region to build modern societies is heartening. And it is for this reason that responsible leadership in Latin America must respond to this popular will with a greater sense of urgency and purpose, lest aspirations turn into frustrations and hope turn into despair. Pending reform legislation must be enacted, statutes already on the books must be enforced, and mechanisms for carrying out programs must be organized and invigorated. These steps are not easy, as we know from our own experience, but they must be taken.

Our own intention is to concentrate our support in Latin America on those countries adhering to the principles established in the Charter of Punta del Este, and to work with our neighbors to indicate more precisely the particular policy changes, reforms and other self-help measures which are necessary to make our assistance effective and the Alliance a success. The Clay Committee recommendation that we continue to expand our efforts to encourage economic integration within the region and the expansion of trade among the countries of Latin America has great merit. The determination of the Central American Presidents to move boldly in this direction impressed me greatly during my recent meeting with them in San Jose, Costa Rica;[1] and the Agency for International Development has already established a regional office in Central America, is giving support to a regional development bank and has participated in regional trade conferences.

A beginning has been made in the first two years of the Alliance; but the job that is still ahead must be tackled with continuing urgency. Many of the ingredients for a successful decade are at hand, and the fundamental course for the future is clear. It remains for all parties to the Alliance to provide the continuous will and effort needed to move steadily along that course.

[1] See pp. 486–8 below.

VI. THIS YEAR'S AUTHORIZING LEGISLATION

Translating the foregoing facts and principles into program costs and appropriations, based on the application of the standards set forth above and affirmed by the Clay Committee, yields the following results:

First, upwards of $200 million of economic assistance funds now available are expected to be saved and not used in the present fiscal year, and upwards of $100 million of these unused funds will remain available for lending in the future;

Second, in addition to the savings carried forward into next year, close review has indicated a number of reductions that can be made in the original budget estimates for economic and military assistance without serious damage to the national interest.

Together these factors permit a reduction in the original Budget estimates from $4·9 billion to $4·5 billion. This amount reflects anticipated reductions in military and economic assistance to a number of countries, in line with these standards and recommendations, and unavoidable increases to others. The principal net increases proposed in 1964 appropriations are the following:

—an additional $325 million for lending in Latin America—$125 million through the Agency for International Development and $200 million through the Social Progress Trust Fund, administered for the United States by the Inter-American Development Bank (for which no appropriation was needed in fiscal year 1963 because a two-year appropriation had been made the year before);

—an additional $85 million for lending elsewhere in the world, mostly in countries such as India, Pakistan, and Nigeria which are meeting those high standards of self-help and fiscal and economic progress which permit our aid to be directed toward ultimate full self-support;

—an additional $80 million for military aid, including the increased requirements for India (but still far below the fiscal 1961 level); and

—an additional $50 million for the contingency fund, which provides a flexibility indispensable to our security. We cannot ignore the possibility that new threats similar to those in Laos or Vietnam might arise in areas which now look calm, or that new opportunities will open up to achieve major gains in the cause of freedom. Foreign aid policy can no more be static than foreign policy itself.

I believe that it is necessary and desirable that these funds be provided by the Congress to meet program needs and to be available for program opportunities. Funds which are not required under the increasingly selective program and performance standards of our assistance programs will, as in this year, not be spent or committed.

The legislative amendments which I am forwarding herewith carry forward the basic structure and intent of the Foreign Assistance Act of 1961, as amended. No fundamental changes in this legislative structure now appear to be required.

One relatively minor change I am proposing is for a separate authorization for the appropriation of funds to assist American schools and hospitals abroad. A number of these schools sponsored by Americans have been most successful in the developing countries in providing an education built upon American standards. Until now some assistance has been made available to these schools from general economic aid funds, but this is becoming increasingly inappropriate. Separate authorization and appropriations would be used to help these schools carry out long-term programs to establish themselves on a sounder financial footing, becoming gradually independent, if at all possible, of U.S. Government support.

Finally, I am requesting the Congress in this legislation to amend that section of the Trade Expansion Act which requires the denial of equal tariff treatment to imports from Poland and Yugoslavia. It is appropriate that this amendment should be incorporated in this Bill since it is my conviction that trade and other forms of normal relations constitute a sounder basis than aid for our future relationship with these countries.

VII. CONCLUSION

In closing, let me again emphasize the overriding importance of the efforts in which we are engaged.

At this point in history we can look back to many successes in the struggle to preserve freedom. Our nation is still daily winning unseen victories in the fight against communist subversion in the slums and hamlets, in the hospitals and schools, and in the offices of governments across a world bent on lifting itself. Two centuries of pioneering and growth must be telescoped into decades and even years. This is a field of action for which our history has prepared us, to which our aspirations have drawn us, and into which our national interest moves us.

Around the world cracks in the monolithic apparatus of our adversary are there for all to see. This, for the American people, is a time for vision, for patience, for work and for wisdom. For better or worse, we are the pacesetters. Freedom's leader cannot flag or falter, or another runner will set the pace.

We have dared to label the Sixties the Decade of Development. But it is not the eloquence of our slogans, but the quality of our endurance, which will determine whether this generation of Americans deserves the leadership which history has thrust upon us.

Address by President Kennedy at American University, Washington, 10 June 1963[1]

It is with great pride that I participate in this ceremony of the American University, sponsored by the Methodist Church, founded by Bishop John Fletcher Hurst, and first opened by President Woodrow Wilson in 1914. This is a young and growing university, but it has already fulfilled Bishop Hurst's enlightened hope for the study of history and public affairs in a city devoted to the making of history and to the conduct of the public's business. By sponsoring this institution of higher learning for all who wish to learn, whatever their color or their creed, the Methodists of this area and the Nation deserve the Nation's thanks, and I commend all those who are today graduating.

Professor Woodrow Wilson once said that every man sent out from a

---

[1] *Public Papers, 1963*, pp. 459–64.

university should be a man of his nation as well as a man of his time, and I am confident that the men and women who carry the honor of graduating from this institution will continue to give from their lives, from their talents, a high measure of public service and public support.

'There are few earthly things more beautiful than a university,' wrote John Masefield, in his tribute to English universities—and his words are equally true today. He did not refer to spires and towers, to campus greens and ivied walls. He admired the splendid beauty of the university, he said, because it was 'a place where those who hate ignorance may strive to know, where those who perceive truth may strive to make others see.'

I have, therefore, chosen this time and this place to discuss a topic on which ignorance too often abounds and the truth is too rarely perceived—yet it is the most important topic on earth: world peace.

What kind of peace do I mean? What kind of peace do we seek? Not a Pax Americana enforced on the world by American weapons of war. Not the peace of the grave or the security of the slave. I am talking about genuine peace, the kind of peace that makes life on earth worth living, the kind that enables men and nations to grow and to hope and to build a better life for their children—not merely peace for Americans but peace for all men and women—not merely peace in our time but peace for all time.

I speak of peace because of the new face of war. Total war makes no sense in an age when great powers can maintain large and relatively invulnerable nuclear forces and refuse to surrender without resort to those forces. It makes no sense in an age when a single nuclear weapon contains almost ten times the explosive force delivered by all of the allied air forces in the Second World War. It makes no sense in an age when the deadly poisons produced by a nuclear exchange would be carried by wind and water and soil and seed to the far corners of the globe and to generations yet unborn.

Today the expenditure of billions of dollars every year on weapons acquired for the purpose of making sure we never need to use them is essential to keeping the peace. But surely the acquisition of such idle stockpiles—which can only destroy and never create—is not the only, much less the most efficient, means of assuring peace.

I speak of peace, therefore, as the necessary rational end of rational men. I realize that the pursuit of peace is not as dramatic as the pursuit of war—and frequently the words of the pursuer fall on deaf ears. But we have no more urgent task.

Some say that it is useless to speak of world peace or world law or world disarmament—and that it will be useless until the leaders of the Soviet Union adopt a more enlightened attitude. I hope they do. I believe we can help them do it. But I also believe that we must reexamine our own attitude—as individuals and as a Nation—for our attitude is as essential as theirs. And every graduate of this school, every thoughtful citizen who despairs of war and wishes to bring peace, should begin by looking inward—by examining his own attitude toward the possibilities of peace, toward the Soviet Union, toward the course of the cold war and toward freedom and peace here at home.

First: Let us examine our attitude toward peace itself. Too many of us think it is impossible. Too many think it unreal. But that is a dangerous, defeatist belief. It leads to the conclusion that war is inevitable—that mankind is doomed —that we are gripped by forces we cannot control.

We need not accept that view. Our problems are manmade—therefore, they can be solved by man. And man can be as big as he wants. No problem of human destiny is beyond human beings. Man's reason and spirit have often solved the seemingly unsolvable—and we believe they can do it again.

I am not referring to the absolute, infinite concept of universal peace and good will of which some fantasies and fanatics dream. I do not deny the value of hopes and dreams but we merely invite discouragement and incredulity by making that our only and immediate goal.

Let us focus instead on a more practical, more attainable peace—based not on a sudden revolution in human nature but on a gradual evolution in human institutions—on a series of concrete actions and effective agreements which are in the interest of all concerned. There is no single simple key to this peace—no grand or magic formula to be adopted by one or two powers. Genuine peace must be the product of many nations, the sum of many acts. It must be dynamic, not static, changing to meet the challenge of each new generation. For peace is a process—a way of solving problems.

With such a peace, there will still be quarrels and conflicting interests, as there are within families and nations. World peace, like community peace, does not require that each man love his neighbor—it requires only that they live together in mutual tolerance, submitting their disputes to a just and peaceful settlement. And history teaches us that enmities between nations, as between individuals, do not last forever. However fixed our likes and dislikes may seem, the tide of time and events will often bring surprising changes in the relations between nations and neighbors.

So let us persevere. Peace need not be impracticable, and war need not be inevitable. By defining our goal more clearly, by making it seem more manageable and less remote, we can help all peoples to see it, to draw hope from it, and to move irresistibly toward it.

Second: Let us reexamine our attitude toward the Soviet Union. It is discouraging to think that their leaders may actually believe what their propagandists write. It is discouraging to read a recent authoritative Soviet text on *Military Strategy* and find, on page after page, wholly baseless and incredible claims—such as the allegation that 'American imperialist circles are preparing to unleash different types of wars . . . that there is a very real threat of a preventive war being unleashed by American imperialists against the Soviet Union . . . [and that] the political aims of the American imperialists are to enslave economically and politically the European and other capitalist countries . . . [and] to achieve world domination . . . by means of aggressive wars.'

Truly, as it was written long ago: 'The wicked flee when no man pursueth.' Yet it is sad to read these Soviet statements—to realize the extent of the gulf between us. But it is also a warning—a warning to the American people not to fall into the same trap as the Soviets, not to see only a distorted and desperate view of the other side, not to see conflict as inevitable, accommodation as impossible, and communication as nothing more than an exchange of threats.

No government or social system is so evil that its people must be considered as lacking in virtue. As Americans, we find communism profoundly repugnant as a negation of personal freedom and dignity. But we can still hail the Russian people for their many achievements—in science and space, in economic and industrial growth, in culture and in acts of courage.

Among the many traits the peoples of our two countries have in common, none is stronger than our mutual abhorrence of war. Almost unique, among the major world powers, we have never been at war with each other. And no nation in the history of battle ever suffered more than the Soviet Union suffered in the course of the Second World War. At least 20 million lost their lives. Countless millions of homes and farms were burned or sacked. A third of the nation's territory, including nearly two thirds of its industrial base, was turned into a wasteland—a loss equivalent to the devastation of this country east of Chicago.

Today, should total war ever break out again—no matter how—our two countries would become the primary targets. It is an ironic but accurate fact that the two strongest powers are the two in the most danger of devastation. All we have built, all we have worked for, would be destroyed in the first 24 hours. And even in the cold war, which brings burdens and dangers to so many countries, including this Nation's closest allies—our two countries bear the heaviest burdens. For we are both devoting massive sums of money to weapons that could be better devoted to combating ignorance, poverty, and disease. We are both caught up in a vicious and dangerous cycle in which suspicion on one side breeds suspicion on the other, and new weapons beget counter-weapons.

In short, both the United States and its allies, and the Soviet Union and its allies, have a mutually deep interest in a just and genuine peace and in halting the arms race. Agreements to this end are in the interests of the Soviet Union as well as ours—and even the most hostile nations can be relied upon to accept and keep those treaty obligations, and only those treaty obligations, which are in their own interest.

So, let us not be blind to our differences—but let us also direct attention to our common interests and to the means by which those differences can be resolved. And if we cannot end now our differences, at least we can help make the world safe for diversity. For, in the final analysis, our most basic common link is that we all inhabit this small planet. We all breathe the same air. We all cherish our children's future. And we are all mortal.

Third: Let us reexamine our attitude toward the cold war, remembering that we are not engaged in a debate, seeking to pile up debating points. We are not here distributing blame or pointing the finger of judgment. We must deal with the world as it is, and not as it might have been had the history of the last 18 years been different.

We must, therefore, persevere in the search for peace in the hope that con-structive changes within the Communist bloc might bring within reach solutions which now seem beyond us. We must conduct our affairs in such a way that it becomes in the Communists' interest to agree on a genuine peace. Above all, while defending our own vital interests, nuclear powers must avert those confrontations which bring an adversary to a choice of either a humiliating retreat or a nuclear war. To adopt that kind of course in the nuclear age would be evidence only of the bankruptcy of our policy—or of a collective death-wish for the world.

To secure these ends, America's weapons are nonprovocative, carefully controlled, designed to deter, and capable of selective use. Our military forces are committed to peace and disciplined in self-restraint. Our diplomats are instructed to avoid unnecessary irritants and purely rhetorical hostility.

For we can seek a relaxation of tensions without relaxing our guard. And, for our part, we do not need to use threats to prove that we are resolute. We do not need to jam foreign broadcasts out of fear our faith will be eroded. We are unwilling to impose our system on any unwilling people—but we are willing and able to engage in peaceful competition with any people on earth.

Meanwhile, we seek to strengthen the United Nations, to help solve its financial problems, to make it a more effective instrument for peace, to develop it into a genuine world security system—a system capable of resolving disputes on the basis of law, of insuring the security of the large and the small, and of creating conditions under which arms can finally be abolished.

At the same time we seek to keep peace inside the non-Communist world, where many nations, all of them our friends, are divided over issues which weaken Western unity, which invite Communist intervention or which threaten to erupt into war. Our efforts in West New Guinea, in the Congo, in the Middle East, and in the Indian sub-continent, have been persistent and patient despite criticism from both sides. We have also tried to set an example for others—by seeking to adjust small but significant differences with our own closest neighbors in Mexico and in Canada.

Speaking of other nations, I wish to make one point clear. We are bound to many nations by alliances. Those alliances exist because our concern and theirs substantially overlap. Our commitment to defend Western Europe and West Berlin, for example, stands undiminished because of the identity of our vital interests. The United States will make no deal with the Soviet Union at the expense of other nations and other peoples, not merely because they are our partners, but also because their interests and ours converge.

Our interests converge, however, not only in defending the frontiers of freedom, but in pursuing the paths of peace. It is our hope—and the purpose of allied policies—to convince the Soviet Union that she, too, should let each nation choose its own future, so long as that choice does not interfere with the choices of others. The Communist drive to impose their political and economic system on others is the primary cause of world tension today. For there can be no doubt that, if all nations could refrain from interfering in the self-determination of others, the peace would be much more assured.

This will require a new effort to achieve world law—a new context for world discussions. It will require increased understanding between the Soviets and ourselves. And increased understanding will require increased contact and communication. One step in this direction is the proposed arrangement for a direct line between Moscow and Washington, to avoid on each side the dangerous delays, misunderstandings, and misreadings of the other's actions which might occur at a time of crisis.

We have also been talking in Geneva about other first-step measures of arms control, designed to limit the intensity of the arms race and to reduce the risks of accidental war. Our primary long-range interest in Geneva, however, is general and complete disarmament—designed to take place by stages, permitting parallel political developments to build the new institutions of peace which would take the place of arms. The pursuit of disarmament has been an effort of this Government since the 1920's. It has been urgently sought by the past three administrations. And however dim the prospects may be today, we intend to continue this effort—to continue it in order that all countries, including our own, can better grasp what the problems and possibilities of disarmament are.

The one major area of these negotiations where the end is in sight, yet where a fresh start is badly needed, is in a treaty to outlaw nuclear tests. The conclusion of such a treaty, so near and yet so far, would check the spiraling arms race in one of its most dangerous areas. It would place the nuclear powers in a position to deal more effectively with one of the greatest hazards which man faces in 1963, the further spread of nuclear arms. It would increase our security—it would decrease the prospects of war. Surely this goal is sufficiently important to require our steady pursuit, yielding neither to the temptation to give up the whole effort nor the temptation to give up our insistence on vital and responsible safeguards.

I am taking this opportunity, therefore, to announce two important decisions in this regard.

First: Chairman Khrushchev, Prime Minister Macmillan, and I have agreed that high-level discussions will shortly begin in Moscow looking toward early agreement on a comprehensive test ban treaty.[1] Our hopes must be tempered with the caution of history—but with our hopes go the hopes of all mankind.

Second: To make clear our good faith and solemn convictions on the matter, I now declare that the United States does not propose to conduct nuclear tests in the atmosphere so long as other states do not do so. We will not be the first to resume. Such a declaration is no substitute for a formal binding treaty, but I hope it will help us achieve one. Nor would such a treaty be a substitute for disarmament, but I hope it will help us achieve it.

Finally, my fellow Americans, let us examine our attitude toward peace and freedom here at home. The quality and spirit of our own society must justify and support our efforts abroad. We must show it in the dedication of our own lives—as many of you who are graduating today will have a unique opportunity to do, by serving without pay in the Peace Corps abroad or in the proposed National Service Corps here at home.

But wherever we are, we must all, in our daily lives, live up to the age-old faith that peace and freedom walk together. In too many of our cities today, the peace is not secure because freedom is incomplete.

It is the responsibility of the executive branch at all levels of government—local, State, and National—to provide and protect that freedom for all of our citizens by all means within their authority. It is the responsibility of the legislative branch at all levels, wherever that authority is not now adequate, to make it adequate. And it is the responsibility of all citizens in all sections of this country to respect the rights of all others and to respect the law of the land.

All this is not unrelated to world peace. 'When a man's ways please the Lord,' the Scriptures tell us, 'he maketh even his enemies to be at peace with him.' And is not peace, in the last analysis, basically a matter of human rights— the right to live out our lives without fear of devastation—the right to breathe air as nature provided it—the right of future generations to a healthy existence?

[1] See pp. 170-2 below.

While we proceed to safeguard our national interests, let us also safeguard human interests. And the elimination of war and arms is clearly in the interest of both. No treaty, however much it may be to the advantage of all, however tightly it may be worded, can provide absolute security against the risks of deception and evasion. But it can—if it is sufficiently effective in its enforcement and if it is sufficiently in the interests of its signers—offer far more security and far fewer risks than an unabated, uncontrolled, unpredictable arms race.

The United States, as the world knows, will never start a war. We do not want a war. We do not now expect a war. This generation of Americans has already had enough—more than enough—of war and hate and oppression. We shall be prepared if others wish it. We shall be alert to try to stop it. But we shall also do our part to build a world of peace where the weak are safe and the strong are just. We are not helpless before that task or hopeless of its success. Confident and unafraid, we labor on—not toward a strategy of annihilation but toward a strategy of peace.

Speech by the Secretary of Defence, Mr. McNamara, to the Economic Club of New York, 18 November 1963[1]

Before long this administration will be presenting, once again, the details of a proposed national defense budget for the consideration of the Congress and the public. Given the importance of these matters, their complexities and uncertainties and the existence of real differences of opinion, a degree of controversy is inevitable, and even desirable.

Some controversies, however, reveal underlying differences in perspective that scarcely suggest the participants are living in the same world. Within the past few weeks some critics have suggested that we have literally hundreds of times more strength than we need; others have accused us of risking the whole future of the Nation by engaging in unilateral disarmament. I would like to believe that criticisms bracketing our policy in that fashion prove it to be rational and sound. But a discrepancy of that order cannot be reassuring. Rather, it indicates that we have failed to convey to some part of our audience even the broadest outlines, as we see them, of the problems that our military strategy and force structure are meant to address.

I believe we should be able to move from controversy on that scale toward consensus in military affairs, not always on details or components of our policies but at least on an appreciation of the major national security problems confronting us, on the broad alternative paths to their solution, and on the dominant goals, obstacles, costs, and risks affecting choice. My purpose in speaking to you this evening is to help move in this direction.

As a prelude, then, to the coming season of debate, I should like to identify and discuss some basic matters on which a considerable degree of consensus seems to me both possible and desirable, although by no means assured.

These include those overall comparative strengths and weaknesses of the opposing military alliances that form the bold relief in the strategic environment. In short, they are the considerations that seem to have relatively long-term significance compared to the annual budget cycle.

[1] *D.S.B.*, 16 December 1963, pp. 914–21.

Matters of that degree of permanence tend to be stamped on our minds as being unchanging and unchangeable, the unquestioned framework of daily and yearly policymaking. Yet these factors of which I shall speak do change—more swiftly and more profoundly than our picture of them tends to change. Indeed, I believe it is just the fact that over the last decade this topography has changed—while many maps have not—that accounts for some apparently irreconcilable controversies.

Let me recall the earlier period briefly, for comparison. The strategic landscape at the outset of the fifties was dominated by two outstanding features. One was the practical U.S. monopoly of deliverable strategic nuclear weapons. The other was the Soviet Union and Communist China's virtual monopoly of ground force on the continents of Europe and Asia.

Both of these determinants of Western military policy had changed considerably by the end of the Korean war. The Soviets had produced atomic explosions and had created a sizable nuclear delivery capability against Europe, while NATO ground forces had expanded rapidly and military operations in Korea had greatly tarnished the significance of Chinese Communist superiority in numbers. But the old notions of monopoly persisted as shortcut aids to thinking on policy matters. And they were not so misleading as they came later to be. Soviet armed forces approaching 5 million men still heavily outweighed the NATO forces in Europe; and Soviet delivery capability against the U.S. was dwarfed by that of SAC [Strategic Air Command]. Moreover, tactical nuclear weapons were being heralded as a new nuclear monopoly for the West.

Even as these earlier notions of monopolies grew obsolete, ideas about the feasibility of alternative policies continued to reflect them. So did ideas about how wars might be fought. Nuclear operations, both strategic and tactical, by the U.S. in response to Soviet aggression against our allies were considered to be virtually unilateral. Hence it was supposed the problem of credibility of the U.S. response would scarcely arise, even in the case of relatively limited Soviet aggressions. Western reliance upon nuclear weapons, in particular strategic systems, both to deter and to oppose nonnuclear attack of any size seemed not only adequate but also unique in its adequacy.

That sort of situation is convenient for policymakers. It makes policy easy to choose and easy to explain. Perhaps that is why throughout most of the fifties, while the Soviets under various pressures decreased their ground forces and the NATO allies built theirs up, and while the Soviets acquired a massive nuclear threat against Europe and laid the groundwork for a sizable threat against the U.S., the picture underlying most policy debate remained that appropriate to 1949. It was a picture of a Communist Goliath in conventional strength facing a Western David, almost naked of conventional arms but alone possessed of a nuclear sling.

Toward the end of that decade the prospect that the Soviets would acquire intercontinental ballistic missiles at a time when our strategic forces consisted almost entirely of bombers focused our attention and our budget even more sharply than before upon our strategic forces. The urgency of the problem of deterring the most massive of attacks was a new reason for thinking that the West could spare neither resources nor thought to deal more specifically with lesser threats. The most urgent task was to provide for deterrence of massive aggression by assuring the survival under any attack of forces at least adequate, in the calculations of a potential attacker, to destroy his society in retaliation. It was now not the assurance of continued nuclear superiority that preempted the attention of policymakers but, on the contrary, the struggle to maintain it.

But it is time for the maps to change by which policy is charted and justified. The old ones, which assumed a U.S. nuclear monopoly, both strategic and tactical, and a Communist monopoly of ground combat strength, are too far removed from reality to serve as even rough guides. Neither we nor our allies can afford the crudities of maps that tell us that old policies are still forced upon us, when a true picture would show important new avenues of necessity and choice.

What most needs changing is a picture of ourselves and of the Western alliance as essentially at bay, outmanned and outgunned except for nuclear arms no longer exclusively ours. We should not think of ourselves as forced by limitations of resources to rely upon strategies of desperation and threats of vast mutual destruction, compelled to deal only with the most massive and immediate challenges, letting lesser ones go by default. It would be a striking historical phenomenon if that self-image should be justified. We are the largest member of an alliance with a population of almost 450 million people, an aggregate annual product which is fast approaching a trillion dollars, and a modern and diverse technological base without parallel, facing the Soviet Union and its European satellites with their hundred million fewer people and an aggregate output no more than half that of the West.

And quite apart from ignoring the underlying strengths of the West, the outdated picture I have described takes no account of the military capabilities in being that our investments over the last decade, and specifically in the last few years, have bought for us. If new problems put strong claims on our attention and our resources today, it is very largely because we have come a large part of the way that is feasible toward solving some old ones.

Let me summarize the current status of the balance of strategic nuclear forces, that part of the military environment that has preoccupied our attention for so long. In strictly relative numerical terms, the situation is the familiar one. The U.S. force now contains more than 500 operational long-range ballistic missiles—Atlas, Titan, Minuteman, Polaris—and is planned to increase to over 1,700 by 1966. There is no doubt in our minds and none in the minds of the Soviets that these missiles can penetrate to their targets. In addition the U.S. has Strategic Air Command bombers on air alert and over 500 bombers on quick-reaction ground alert. By comparison, the consensus is that today the Soviets could place about half as many bombers over North America on a first strike. The Soviets are estimated to have today only a fraction as many intercontinental missiles as we do. Furthermore, their submarine launched ballistic missiles are short range and generally are not comparable to our Polaris force. The Soviets pose a very large threat against Europe, including hundreds of intermediate- and medium-range ballistic missiles. This threat is today and will continue to be covered by the clear superiority of our strategic forces.

The most wishful of Soviet planners would have to calculate as a certainty that the most effective surprise attack they could launch would still leave us with the capability to destroy the attacker's society. What is equally pertinent is that the relative numbers and survivability of U.S. strategic forces would permit us to retaliate against all the urgent Soviet military targets that are subject to attack, thus contributing to the limitation of damage to ourselves and our allies.

Deterrence of deliberate, calculated attack seems as well assured as it can be, and the damage-limiting capability of our numerically superior forces is, I believe, well worth its incremental cost. It is a capability to which the smaller forces of the Soviet Union could not realistically aspire. That is one reason, among others, why I would not trade our strategic posture for that of the Soviets at any point during the coming decade.

But given the kind of force that the Soviets are building, including submarine, launched missiles beyond the reach of our offensive forces, the damage which the Soviets could inflict on us and our allies, no matter what we do to limit it, remains extremely high.

That has been true for our allies ever since the middle and late fifties. Soviet acquisition of a sizable delivery capability against the U.S., and more significantly their acquisition of relatively protected forces, submarine-launched or hardened, has been long and often prematurely heralded. Its arrival at last merely dramatizes the need to recognize that strategic nuclear war would, under all foreseeable circumstances, be bilateral—and highly destructive to both sides.

Larger budgets for U.S. strategic forces would not change that fact. They could have only a decreasing incremental effect in limiting somewhat the damage that the U.S. and its allies could suffer in a general nuclear war. In short, we cannot buy the capability to make a strategic bombing campaign once again a unilateral prospect.

That must, I suggest, be accepted as one of the determinants affecting policy. Another is that the same situation confronts the Soviet leaders, in a way that is even more intensely confining. In fact, enormous increases in Soviet budgets would be required for them to achieve any significant degree of damage-limiting capability. The present Soviet leaders show no tendency to challenge the basis of the U.S. strategic deterrent posture by such expenditures.

In the last 2 years alone we have increased the number of nuclear warheads in the strategic-alert forces by 100 percent. During that period we have more than doubled the megatonnage of the strategic-alert forces. The fact that further increases in strategic-force size will at last encounter rapidly diminishing returns —which is largely an effect of the very large investments the U.S. has made in this area—should be reflected in future budgets. The funding for the initial introduction of missiles into our forces is nearing completion. We can anticipate that the annual expenditure on strategic forces will drop substantially and level off well below the present rate of spending. This is not to rule out the possibility that research now in progress on possible new technological developments, including the possibility of useful ballistic missile defenses, will require major new expenditures. In any event, there will be recurring costs of modernization.

In the field of tactical nuclear weapons, the picture is in important respects similar. The U.S. at present has in stockpile, or planned for stockpile, tens of thousands of nuclear explosives for tactical use on the battlefield, in anti-submarine warfare, and against aircraft. They include warheads for artillery, battlefield missiles, demolition munitions, bombs, depth charges, air-to-air missiles, and surface-to-air missiles. The consensus is that the U.S. is presently substantially superior in design, diversity, and numbers in this class of weapons.

This is an indispensable superiority, as we can readily understand if we consider how our problems of strategic choice would be altered if the tables were reversed and it were the Soviet Union which held a commanding lead in this field. Nevertheless, what we have is superiority, not monopoly, and even if tactical nuclear warfare can be limited, below some ill-defined threshold of strategic exchange, the key fact is that if the West initiates such warfare in the future, it must be expected to be bilateral in any theater which engaged the Soviet Union. Again, we cannot buy back a monopoly, or the assurance of unilateral use.

Finally, there is the area of what we call our general-purpose forces. Within the last 2 years we have increased the number of our combat-ready Army divisions by about 45 percent, from 11 to 16. There has been a 30-percent increase in the number of tactical air squadrons, a 75-percent increase in airlift capabilities, and a 100-percent increase in ship construction and conversion to modernize the fleet.

But it is not only force size that matters. The key to the effective utilization of these forces is combat readiness and mobility.

The most recent demonstration of our ability to reinforce our troops presently stationed in Europe occurred last month in Operation Big Lift, the first of a series of planned large-scale, worldwide exercises. For the first time in military history, an entire division was airlifted from one continent to another. That movement could never have been accomplished without a massive increase in our airlift capability, which is still being expanded. (It will have risen 400 percent between 1961 and 1967.) It required the development of new techniques to preposition combat equipment, of which we have two extra division sets now in Europe. It called for new techniques in military training and administration to make sure that units are really ready to move out on a moment's notice. This exercise, in which some 16,000 airmen and soldiers and more than 350 planes took part, is directly relevant to the needs of Europe, where it brought a seventh division to join the six that are to remain in place. It is also relevant to the ability of the U.S. to fulfill its policy commitments worldwide, swiftly and in effective strength.

But, it might be asked, what is the significance of all this for the realistic security problems of the United States and its allies? To what contingencies are these forces expected to contribute, and how effective might they be, measured against the strength of opposing forces? How meaningful is it to talk of 16 or 20 or 30 divisions in opposing the ground armies of the Soviet Union and Communist China?

Such questions are often meant to be merely rhetorical, in view of the supposed masses of Communist troops. The fact is that they are serious, difficult questions, to which I shall suggest some tentative answers. But it is difficult to encourage realistic discussions of specific contingencies so long as the shadow of the Communist horde hangs unchallenged over the debate. The actual contingencies that seem to be to me most likely and most significant are not those which would involve all, or even a major part, of the Soviet bloc or Chinese Communist armed forces, nor do they all involve Europe. Hence, aggregate figures of armed strength of NATO and the Warsaw Pact nations are not immediately relevant to them. But it is useful to make these overall comparisons precisely because misleading or obsolete notions of these very aggregates often produce an attitude of hopelessness toward any attempt to prepare to meet Communist forces in ground combat, however limited in scope.

The announced total of Soviet armed forces for 1955 was indeed a formidable 5·75 million men. Today that figure has been cut to about 3·3 million; the Warsaw Pact total, including the Soviets, is only about 4·5 million. Against that, it is today the members of NATO whose active armed forces number over 5 million. The ground forces of NATO nations total 3·2 million, of which 2·2 million men are in Europe, as against the Soviet ground combat forces' total of about 2 million men, and a Warsaw Pact total of about 3 million. Both the Soviet Union and the U.S. forces of course include units stationed in the Far East. In Central Europe, NATO has more men, and more combat troops, on the ground than does the bloc. It has more men on the ground in West Germany than the bloc does in East Germany. It has more and better tactical aircraft, and these planes on the average can carry twice the pay-load twice as far as the Soviet counterparts.

These facts are hard to reconcile with the familiar picture of the Russian Army as incomparably massive. The usual index cited to support that picture is numbers of total active divisions, and the specific number familiar from the past is 175 divisions in the Soviet Army.

This total, if true, would indeed present a paradox. The Soviet ground forces are reliably estimated to be very close to 2 million men, compared to about 1 million for the U.S. How is it that the Soviets can muster ten times the number of active, combat-ready, fully manned divisions than the United States has manned, with only twice as many men on active duty? The answer is simply that they do not. Recent intensive investigation has shown that the number of active Soviet divisions that are maintained at manning levels anywhere close to combat readiness is less than half of the 160–175 figure.

What remains is a large number, but even that is misleading. For one thing, U.S. divisions have about twice as many men in the division unit and its immediate combat-supporting units as comparable Soviet divisions. A U.S. mechanized division has far more personnel in maneuvering units, far more in armored cavalry, far more engineers, far more signals, far more light armored personnel carriers, and far more aircraft available in support than Soviet divisions. In addition to longer staying power, much of the U.S. man-power and equipment margin is muscle that would make itself felt on D-Day. If, on the other hand, we were to reorganize along Soviet lines, we could display far greater numbers of divisions comparable to those of the Soviets.

The Soviet combat-ready force remains a formidable one. Moreover, the Russians do have a powerful mobilization capability; in particular, they have a large number of lightly manned or cadre divisions to be filled out on mobilization. Still, this reality remains strikingly different from our accustomed maps of it.

I do not wish to suggest that such aggregate comparisons are by themselves a valid index to military capabilities. But they are enough to suggest the absurdity, as a picture of the prevailing military strengths on which new efforts might build, of David-and-Goliath notions borrowed from 1949.

None of this is to say that NATO strength on the ground in Europe is adequate to turn back without nuclear weapons an all-out surprise nonnuclear attack.

But that is not in any case the contingency toward which the recent and future improvements in the mobility and capabilities of U.S. general-purpose forces are primarily oriented. Aggression on that scale would mean a war about the future of Europe and, as a consequence, the future of the U.S. and the U.S.S.R. In the face of threats of that magnitude, our nuclear superiority remains highly relevant to deterrence. The Soviets know that even non-nuclear aggression at that high end of the spectrum of conflict so threatens our most vital interests that we and our allies are prepared to make whatever response may be required to defeat it, no matter how terrible the consequences for our own society.

The probability that the Soviet leaders would choose to invoke that exchange seems to me very low indeed. They know well what even the Chinese Communist leaders must recognize upon further reflection: that a nuclear war would mean destruction of everything they have built up for themselves during the last 50 years.

If we were to consider a spectrum of the possible cases of Communist aggression, then, ranging from harassment, covert aggression, and indirect challenge at one end of the scale to the massive invasion of Western Europe or a full-scale nuclear strike against the West at the other end, it is clear that our nuclear superiority has been and should continue to be an effective deterrent to aggression at the high end of the spectrum. It is equally clear, on the other hand, that at the very low end of the spectrum a nuclear response may not be fully credible and that nuclear power alone cannot be an effective deterrent at this level in the future any more than it has been in the past.

The fact is that at every level of force the alliance in general, and the U.S. Armed Forces in particular, have greater and more effective strength than we are in the habit of thinking we have—and with reasonable continued effort we can have whatever strength we need. I have spoken already of strategic weapons, where the great superiority of the United States is the superiority also of the alliance. In tactical nuclear weapons a parallel superiority exists—and while many of our allies share with us in manning the systems which would use these tactical warheads in the hour of need, it is not unfair to point out that, even more than in the strategic field, the tactical nuclear strength of the alliance is a contribution of the United States. That strength has been increased, on the ground in Europe, by more than 60 percent in the last 2 years. Today the thousands of U.S. warheads deployed on the Continent for the immediate defense of Europe have a combined explosive strength more than 10,000 times the force of the nuclear weapons used to end the Second War. Tactical nuclear strength the alliance has today, and we have provided it.

But neither we nor out allies can find the detonation of such weapons—and their inevitable bilateral exchange—an easy first choice. At the lower end of the spectrum, therefore, we also need strong and ready conventional forces. We have done our part here, and we continue to believe it just—and practicable—for our partners to do theirs.

The most difficult questions arise over the best means for meeting a variety of dangerous intermediate challenges in many parts of the world: those which threaten the possibility of sizable conflict while still not raising the immediate issue of the national survival of ourselves or of any member of our alliances. Conflicts might arise out of Soviet subversion and political aggression backed up by military measures in non-NATO areas in Europe, Latin America, the Middle East, and Africa. There is a range of challenges that could arise from Communist China and its satellites in the Far East and in Southeast Asia. Most dangerously, approaching the upper end of the spectrum, there is the possibility of limited Soviet pressures on NATO territory itself, along the vast front running from Norway to Greece and Turkey. Both the flanks and the center contain potential targets. And always, of course, there are the contingencies that could arise in relation to Berlin.

It is difficult to say just how probable any of these circumstances might be, although they must be regarded as more likely than still larger aggressions. What one can say is that if any of these more likely contingencies should arise, they would be highly dangerous. Inaction, or weak action, could result in a serious setback, missed opportunity, or even disaster. In fact, if either a nuclear exchange or a major Soviet attack should occur, it would most likely arise from a conflict on a lesser scale which Western capabilities had failed to deter and which an inadequate Western response had failed to curb in time.

Since World War II, the expansionist impulse of the Communist bloc is clear, but equally clear is its desire to avoid direct confrontation with the military forces of the free world. In Greece, in Berlin, and in Cuba, Communists have probed for military and political weakness; but when they have encountered resistance, they have held back. Not only Communist doctrine has counseled this caution, but respect for the danger that any sizable, overt conflict would lead to nuclear war. It would follow that no deterrent would be more effective against these lesser and intermediate levels of challenge than the assurance that such moves would certainly meet prompt, effective military response by the West. That response could confront the Soviets with frustration of their purposes unless they chose themselves to escalate the conflict to a nuclear exchange or to levels that made nuclear war highly probable—a choice they are unlikely to make in the face of our destructive power.

The basis for that particular assurance cannot be systems in development, or weapons in storage depots, or reserves that must be mobilized, trained, and equipped, or troops without transport. We need the right combination of forward deployment and highly mobile combat-ready ground, sea, and air units, capable of prompt and effective commitment to actual combat, in short, the sort of capability we are increasingly building in our forces.

This capability requires of us—as of our allies—a military establishment that is, in the President's words, lean and fit. We must stop and ask ourselves, before deciding whether to add a new and complex weapon system to our inventory, whether it is really the most effective way to do the job under the rigorous conditions of combat. We must examine constantly the possibilities for combining functions, particularly in weapons that could be used by two or more services. Given this tough-minded sense of reality about the requirements of combat readiness, it should be possible for the United States not only to maintain but to expand this increased strength without overall increases in our defense budget. As our national productivity and our gross national product expand, the defense budget therefore need not keep pace. Indeed, it appears likely that measured in relative—and perhaps even absolute—terms, the defense budget will level off and perhaps decline a little. At the same time, we are continuing the essential effort to reduce the impact of defense spending on our balance of payments. We have already brought this figure down from $2·7 billion in fiscal year 1961 to $1·7 billion for fiscal year 1963, and we shall continue to reduce it, without reducing the combat ground forces deployed in Europe and while strengthening our overall combat effectiveness.

And it must be our policy to continue to strengthen our combat effectiveness. I do not regard the present Communist leaders as wholly reckless in action. But recent experience, in Cuba and, on a lesser scale, in Berlin, has not persuaded me that I can predict with confidence the sorts of challenges that Communist leaders will come to think prudent and profitable. If they were again to mis-calculate as dangerously as they did a year ago, it would be essential to confront them, wherever that might be, with the full consequences of their action: the certainty of meeting immediate, appropriate, and fully effective military action.

All of our strengths, including our strategic and tactical nuclear forces, con-tributed last year, and they would contribute in similar future situations, to the effectiveness of our response, by providing a basis for assurance that the Soviets would not dangerously escalate or shift the locale of the conflict. But above all, in order to fashion that response and to promise the Soviets local defeat in case of actual ground conflict, we had to use every element of the improvements in combat readiness and mobility that had been building over the preceding year and a half, including combat divisions, air transport, and tactical air. And the last ingredient was also there: the will to use those forces against Soviet troops and equipment.

Let us not delude ourselves with obsolete images into believing that our nuclear strength, great as it is, solves all of our problems of national security, or that we lack the strength to meet those problems that it does not solve. In the contingencies that really threaten—the sort that have occurred and will occur again—we and our allies need no longer choose to live with the sense or the reality of inferiority to the Soviet bloc in relevant, effective force. Let us be fully aware of the wide range of our military resources and the freedom they can give us to pursue the peaceful objectives of the free world without fear of military aggression.

(b) *The United States, Britain, Germany and N.A.T.O.*

Address by the United States Under Secretary of State, Mr. Ball, to the Princeton Alumni Association, Washington, 26 April 1963[1] (extract)

. . . The massive deterrent nuclear power which the United States has built serves more than our narrow national interests. We hold that force as trustee for the security of free men and free institutions everywhere. The manner in which we manage and discharge that trusteeship will have a direct bearing on our chances of survival.

Our choice in the matter is conditioned by the fact that the NATO alliance

[1] *D.S.B.*, 13 May 1963, pp. 736–9.

is composed principally of nations that are individually small in relation to the magnitudes of the nuclear age. Collectively, the European members of the alliance are a reservoir of vast talents and resources, but political power is still divided among national governments. Although they have made great strides toward unity, they have not yet established common political institutions to which they can entrust the power to make common decisions of war or peace, of life or death. If the momentum toward unity continues, such institutions may well come into being some day, but they do not exist now—and that makes the problem of nuclear management much more complicated.

For if the effective nuclear defense of the free world is, in fact, indivisible, then how can the indivisibility of that defense be secured within the present political framework and in such a way as to promote useful progress within that framework?

In seeking an answer we should start, I think, by recognizing that there are basically only three ways in which the Atlantic nations can manage their nuclear defense.

One way would be the continuance of the present situation. Today the effective management and control of the free world's nuclear defense are predominantly in the hands of the United States. Since the bulk of free-world nuclear power is thus under the control of one government, and that government is our own, we Americans are satisfied that the power will be responsibly used to defend and protect the vital interests of the free world.

But we cannot assume that all members of the Atlantic alliance will be forever content to accept this as a permanent solution. I am not suggesting that the United States is regarded as irresponsible or untrustworthy, for I think that our nation and our Government enjoy an almost unparalleled degree of trust on the part of our allies. But it is only natural that vigorous peoples should wish to play an effective role in their own defense, and, if no alternative is provided, the political pressures for the multiplication of national nuclear deterrent systems will make themselves felt.

This is, I think, very likely to happen if we simply let nature take its course. In one country after another these pressures may become irresistible. Moreover, the process will feed upon itself, since the decision to build a national deterrent in one country will almost certainly increase pressures for a similar decision in others.

Such a course would reflect the natural desire of patriotic peoples to make a self-respecting contribution to the strength of the Western deterrent. Nonetheless, it would start us down a road beset with dangers.

First, the development of national nuclear systems, by one nation and then another, could not help but heighten the feelings of mistrust within the alliance. At the same time it would increase the tensions between the free world and the bloc.

Second, the multiplication of national deterrents would multiply the chance that, at some point, nuclear weapons might fall under the control of an irresponsible government.

Third, the multiplication of national deterrents would render progressively more difficult the achievement of an ultimate agreement to control or limit nuclear armament.

But if the proliferation of national deterrents is full of dangers, then what is the alternative?

Quite obviously the alternative to concentrating nuclear power under one government or proliferating power among many must lie in some arrangement for the pooling of effort on a basis of international management and control. We have, therefore, made known our willingness to join our NATO partners, if they wished, in attempting to design and build a new multilateral force that could supplement the national forces already in existence.

Since such a force would be intended to serve the purposes of free-world defense, it should be organized within the framework of the Western alliance. To represent a truly international force, it has seemed to us that it should meet four conditions:

First, it should be assigned to NATO by the participating countries—which may be four, five, or six in number—and not by any one country.

Second, it should not be predominantly based on the soil of any one nation.

Third, it should be managed and operated by nationals of all participating countries in such a way as to be unavailable for withdrawal to serve the national uses of any participating government.

Fourth, the use of the force should be politically controlled by a collective decision of the participating nations.

It was with these considerations in mind that this administration has maintained and elaborated the concept of a multilateral sea-based MRBM [medium-range ballistic missile] force, first put forward by the Eisenhower administration.[1]

This multilateral force, as it has been conceived, would be designed to meet the four requirements I have just described.

First, the principle would be recognized that it was a force collectively assigned to NATO by the participants—not by a single nation-state—and all the participating nations would share in the costs of creating and maintaining it.

Second, it would be sea-based, consisting of Polaris-type missiles mounted on surface ships. Thus, the force would be deployed in international waters and not on the soil of any nation.

Third, it would be committed to NATO, and the ships themselves would be manned by mixed crews of nationals of the participating nations. The force could clearly, therefore, not be withdrawn to serve the purposes of any one member nation or government. The U.S. Navy has indicated that an efficient first-class force can be created in this fashion.

Fourth, political control would be exercised through some form of executive body representing the participating nations. The United States would, of course, be one of the participating nations and would, like other major participants, have an authoritative voice in any decisions concerning the use of the force.

We wish to go forward with such a force only if it is strongly desired by our allies and if they are willing to pay the greater part of its costs. We are now in the process of ascertaining Allied views. Before any final action is taken, whatever specific proposal emerges from this consultation will, of course, be submitted to the Congress for approval.

At the moment it appears likely that several major European countries will be interested in the development of a multilateral force along the lines I have discussed. They see it as an effective way of deploying MRBM's in the European

[1] Presented to the meeting of the N.A.T.O. Council, Paris, December 1960; see *Documents, 1960*, pp. 131–3.

area and thus offsetting Soviet MRBM's arrayed against Europe, while at the same time enhancing Allied cohesion and avoiding the divisive concerns attendant on national manning and ownership of nuclear-tipped strategic missiles. They also see it as a way of securing self-respecting and effective participation in strategic nuclear deterrence on a basis of essential equality among the nuclear and nonnuclear participating countries. And they see in such a nuclear association with the United States a means of reinforcing the assurance that we will remain deeply involved in the nuclear defense of Europe.

The multilateral force represents a novel approach to a novel, yet essentially practical, problem. There is no doubt that nuclear weapons could most easily be managed and controlled by a single government. But unless our allies will continue indefinitely to accept exclusive nuclear management by the United States, such an ideal solution cannot be achieved. For the dilemma in which we find ourselves is that Western political institutions have not evolved in pace with the advance of our technology.

When we face the problem squarely, it seems clear enough that there can be no perfect answer to the management of the nuclear power of the West until the West has achieved a far greater political unity than it possesses today. But events will not wait, and in this imperfect world we must deal with conditions as we find them. I see little future in letting nature take its course, and there is no use pretending that the problem does not exist.

The kind of multilateral force I have described has much to commend it. Not only is it the best means of dealing with the nuclear problem in the present political framework; it is also a means of promoting gradual and constructive evolution within that framework. The multilateral force would offer the great advantage of a further opportunity to work toward greater unity in Europe and closer partnership between Europe and the United States.

The striking progress achieved toward these goals in the past decade and a half has, to a considerable extent, come about from necessity—from the fact that governments were required to cope with specific and immediate problems in Europe and the Atlantic area. And as we seek to cope with the problem of nuclear management, I have no doubt that we shall, of necessity, make further strides toward a greater political unity in the years ahead.

For it will not be abstract principle but importunate necessity—the urgent need to get hard things done in order that we may survive and flourish—that will move us toward the attainment of that ultimate objective of which Woodrow Wilson spoke with such controlled passion—the 'universal dominion of right by such a concert of free peoples as shall bring peace and safety to all nations and make the world itself at last free.'[1]

Communiqué of the N.A.T.O. Council, Ottawa, 24 May 1963[2]

The North Atlantic Council met in Ministerial Session in Ottawa from 22nd to 24th May, 1963.

[1] Quotation from President Wilson's address of 2 April 1917, before the U.S. Congress for a declaration of war against Germany; text in *The Public Papers of Woodrow Wilson: War and Peace*, Baker and Dodd (eds.) (New York, 1927), vol. I, pp. 6–16.
[2] *D.S.B.*, 10 June 1963, pp. 895–6.

In their review of the international situation, the Ministers emphasized that in the world of today peace is indivisible. The enduring character of the North Atlantic Alliance, founded on the principles of interdependence and common defence, constitutes a basic guarantee for the maintenance of peace.

The Council noted with regret that the Soviet Union had so far shown little interest in seeking equitable solutions for outstanding problems.

With regard to Germany and Berlin, the threat has not disappeared. Thanks to the firm attitude maintained by the West, however, developments detrimental to the interests of Berlin and the Alliance have been effectively discouraged. In this connection, the Alliance abides by the terms of its declaration of 16th December, 1958, on Berlin.[1]

Outside the treaty area too, tensions and difficulties continue to exist which have a profound effect on the Alliance. Soviet military personnel remain in Cuba; and the situation there, with its repercussions in the region generally, still gives cause for concern. Ministers also expressed their disquiet over recent events in Laos, and stressed the importance of sustained efforts to secure respect for the Geneva Agreements.[2]

The Ministers reaffirmed the importance, in building a peaceful world, of progress towards general and complete disarmament by stages and under effective international control. In this connection, they noted that agreement in principle had been reached between the United States and the U.S.S.R. on measures to improve communications designed to reduce the risk of war by accident or miscalculation.[3] They expressed the hope that the Soviet Union's attitude would evolve sufficiently to permit genuine progress to be made on key disarmament questions.

The growing scope and complexity of the problems facing the Alliance make it imperative for the Council to ensure that its political consultations are as prompt and effective as they can be made. The Ministers noted the progress already achieved in this direction and expressed their determination to secure still further improvements.

The Ministers discussed NATO defence policy and approved the steps taken to organize the nuclear forces assigned or to be assigned to the Supreme Allied Command Europe (SACEUR).

These include notably:

(A) Assignment of the United Kingdom V-Bomber force and three U.S. Polaris submarines to SACEUR;

(B) Establishment by SACEUR on his staff of a deputy responsible to him for nuclear affairs;

(C) Arrangements for broader participation by officers of NATO member countries in nuclear activities in Allied Command Europe and in co-ordination of operational planning at Omaha;

(D) Fuller information to national authorities both political and military.

Ministers welcomed these measures to increase the effectiveness of the nuclear capability at the disposal of the Alliance and to improve co-ordination and control of its nuclear deterrent forces.

---

[1] Text in *Documents, 1958*, pp. 373–4.   [2] Texts in *Documents, 1962*, pp. 753–61.
[3] See pp. 164–6 below.

The Ministers recognized the need to achieve a satisfactory balance between nuclear and conventional arms. They directed the Council in permanent session to undertake, with the advice of the NATO military authorities, further studies of the inter-related questions of strategy, force requirements and the resources available to meet them.

The Council noted progress made in the implementation of earlier resolutions concerning the defence problems of Greece and reaffirmed its interest in the effective application of these resolutions.[1]

The North Atlantic Alliance seeks peace. It deplores the diversion into the military field of resources which might be used for the betterment of mankind, and in particular for increased efforts to raise living standards in developing countries. But the Free World remains faced with a continuing threat and the members of the North Atlantic Alliance have both the right and the duty to protect their freedom and independence.

The next Ministerial Meeting will be held in Paris in December 1963.

Communiqué issued by President Kennedy and the Federal German Chancellor, Dr. Adenauer, Bonn, 24 June 1963[2]

The President of the United States of America, John F. Kennedy, visited Bonn on June 23 and 24 and held talks with leaders of the Federal Republic of Germany. He had a private visit with Federal President Lübke, and on June 24 met privately with Chancellor Adenauer for detailed discussions on the general international situation. The President and Chancellor were later joined by Secretary of State Rusk, Vice-Chancellor Erhard and the Federal Minister of Foreign Affairs, Schröder, as well as other officials and advisers of the two Governments.

President Kennedy and Chancellor Adenauer discussed European integration, relations between the European Community and other nations of Europe, progress toward the achievement of the Atlantic partnership, and the problems of Berlin and German reunification. In this connection, they had an exchange of views on Western policy toward the Soviet Union and the countries of Eastern Europe.

The President and the Chancellor were in agreement that the two Governments would continue their close collaboration in the task of developing genuine unity among the nations of Europe and fostering an integrated European Community in close partnership with the United States. On questions of economics and trade, both in their multilateral and bilateral aspects, the President and the Chancellor reaffirmed their agreement on basic aims; among these matters they stressed in particular the need for stronger participation in world trade by the developing countries. They agreed that the strength of the Free World rests in common policies and common aims pursued jointly by all the nations dedicated to establishing peace in freedom.

The Federal Government shares the view of the United States and other allied powers that controlled disarmament and agreement on the cessation of atomic

---

[1] See *Documents, 1962*, pp. 440–2 and 443–4.
[2] *D.S.B.*, 22 July 1963, pp. 117–18.

weapons tests[1] would constitute an important step toward the avoidance of a dangerous armaments race.

The exchange of views confirmed full agreement of the principle that the North Atlantic Alliance continues to be a major instrument for the maintenance of freedom, and the President and the Chancellor agreed that every effort will be made to strengthen common defense planning and joint operation of NATO defense forces.

The President and the Chancellor discussed the proposed multilateral sea-borne MRBM force.[2] The multilateral organisation is considered a good instrument for serving all members of the Alliance in combining their defense efforts. They reaffirmed their agreement to use their best efforts to bring such a force into being. They also agreed that discussions about the principal questions involved in the establishment of such a force should be pursued with other interested Governments.

They reaffirmed the commitment of their two Governments to the right of self-determination, as embodied in the United Nations Charter, and to the achievement of German reunification in peace and freedom. They agreed that the freedom of Berlin will be preserved by every necessary means, and that the two Governments would seek every opportunity to counter the inhuman effects of the Wall. They also agreed that the two Governments would continue to seek to reduce tension through international understanding.

Peace and freedom are prerequisites for overcoming the obstacles that still prevent the greater part of mankind from enjoying full participation in social and economic development. The President and the Chancellor affirmed that the Governments of the United States and the Federal Republic of Germany are determined to assume their part in these tasks in the context of the free world's strategy of peace.

The discussions took place in a spirit of frankness and cordiality. These meetings have shown full agreement between the two Governments in assessing the international situation, and have once again demonstrated the close and friendly relations which exist between the two countries.

Address by President Kennedy in the Paulskirche, Frankfurt, 25 June 1963[3]

I am most honored, Mr. President, to be able to speak in this city before this audience, for in this hall I am able to address myself to those who lead and serve all segments of a democratic system—mayors, governors, members of cabinets, civil servants, and concerned citizens. As one who has known the satisfaction of the legislator's life, I am particularly pleased that so many members of your Bundestag and Bundesrat are present today, for the vitality of your legislature has been a major factor in your demonstration of a working democracy, a democracy worldwide in its influence. In your company also are several of the authors of the Federal Constitution who have been able through their own political service to give a new and lasting validity to the aims of the Frankfurt Assembly.

[1] See pp. 170–2 below.　　　　[2] See pp. 28–31 above.
[3] *Public Papers, 1963*, pp. 516–21.

One hundred and fifteen years ago a most learned Parliament was convened in this historic hall. Its goal was a united German Federation. Its members were poets and professors, lawyers and philosophers, doctors and clergymen, freely elected in all parts of the land. No nation applauded its endeavors as warmly as my own. No assembly ever strove more ardently to put perfection into practice. And though in the end it failed, no other building in Germany deserves more the title of 'cradle of German democracy.'

But can there be such a title? In my own home city of Boston, Faneuil Hall —once the meeting-place of the authors of the American Revolution—has long been known as the 'cradle of American liberty.' But when, in 1852, the Hungarian patriot Kossuth addressed an audience there, he criticized its name. 'It is,' he said, 'a great name—but there is something in it which saddens my heart. You should not say "American liberty." You should say "liberty in America." Liberty should not be either American or European—it should just be "liberty."'

Kossuth was right. For unless liberty flourishes in all lands, it cannot flourish in one. Conceived in one hall, it must be carried out in many. Thus, the seeds of the American Revolution had been brought earlier from Europe, and they later took root around the world. And the German Revolution of 1848 transmitted ideas and idealists to America and to other lands. Today, in 1963, democracy and liberty are more international than ever before. And the spirit of the Frankfurt Assembly, like the spirit of Faneuil Hall, must live in many hearts and nations if it is to live at all.

For we live in an age of interdependence as well as independence—an age of internationalism as well as nationalism. In 1848 many countries were indifferent to the goals of the Frankfurt Assembly. It was, they said, a German problem. Today there are no exclusively German problems, or American problems, or even European problems. There are world problems—and our two countries and continents are inextricably bound together in the tasks of peace as well as war.

We are partners for peace—not in a narrow bilateral context but in a framework of Atlantic partnership. The ocean divides us less than the Mediterranean divided the ancient world of Greece and Rome. Our Constitution is old and yours is young, and our culture is young and yours is old, but in our commitment we can and must speak and act with but one voice. Our roles are distinct but complementary—and our goals are the same: peace and freedom for all men, for all time, in a world of abundance, in a world of justice.

That is why our nations are working together to strengthen NATO, to expand trade, to assist the developing countries, to align our monetary policies and to build the Atlantic Community. I would not diminish the miracle of West Germany's economic achievements. But the true German miracle has been your rejection of the past for the future—your reconciliation with France, your participation in the building of Europe, your leading role in NATO, and your growing support for constructive undertakings throughout the world.

Your economic institutions, your constitutional guarantees, your confidence in civilian authority, are all harmonious with the ideals of older democracies. And they form a firm pillar of the democratic European Community.

But Goethe tells us in his greatest poem that Faust lost the liberty of his soul when he said to the passing moment: 'Stay, thou art so fair.' And our liberty, too, is endangered if we pause for the passing moment, if we rest on our achievements, if we resist the pace of progress. For time and the world do not stand still. Change is the law of life. And those who look only to the past or the present are certain to miss the future.

The future of the West lies in Atlantic partnership—a system of cooperation, inter-dependence, and harmony whose peoples can jointly meet their burdens and opportunities throughout the world. Some say this is only a dream, but I do not agree. A generation of achievement—the Marshall plan, NATO, the Schuman plan, and the Common Market—urges us up the path to greater unity.

There will be difficulties and delays. There will be doubts and discouragement. There will be differences of approach and opinion. But we have the will and the means to serve three related goals—the heritage of our countries, the unity of our continents, and the interdependence of the Western alliance.

Some say that the United States will neither hold to these purposes nor abide by its pledges—that we will revert to a narrow nationalism. But such doubts fly in the face of history. For 18 years the United States has stood its watch for freedom all around the globe. The firmness of American will, and the effectiveness of American strength, have been shown, in support of free men and free government, in Asia, in Africa, in the Americas, and, above all, here in Europe. We have undertaken, and sustained in honor, relations of mutual trust and obligation with more than 40 allies. We are proud of this record, which more than answers doubts. But in addition these proven commitments to the common freedom and safety are assured, in the future as in the past, by one great fundamental fact—that they are deeply rooted in America's own self-interest. Our commitment to Europe is indispensable—in our interest as well as yours.

It is not in our interest to try to dominate the European councils of decision. If that were our objective, we would prefer to see Europe divided and weak, enabling the United States to deal with each fragment individually. Instead we have and now look forward to a Europe united and strong—speaking with a common voice—acting with a common will—a world power capable of meeting world problems as a full and equal partner.

This is in the interest of us all. For war in Europe, as we learned twice in 40 years, destroys peace in America. A threat to the freedom of Europe is a threat to the freedom of America. That is why no administration—no administration—in Washington can fail to respond to such a threat—not merely from good will but from necessity. And that is why we look forward to a united Europe in an Atlantic partnership—an entity of interdependent parts, sharing equally both burdens and decisions, and linked together in the tasks of defense as well as the arts of peace.

This is no fantasy. It will be achieved by concrete steps to solve the problems that face us all: military, economic, and political. Partnership is not a posture but a process—a continuous process that grows stronger each year as we devote ourselves to common tasks.

The first task of the Atlantic Community was to assure its common defense. That defense was and still is indivisible. The United States will risk its cities to defend yours because we need your freedom to protect ours. Hundreds of thousands of our soldiers serve with yours on this continent, as tangible evidence

of that pledge. Those who would doubt our pledge or deny this indivisibility
—those who would separate Europe from America or split one ally from another
—would only give aid and comfort to the men who make themselves our
adversaries and welcome any Western disarray.

The purpose of our common military effort is not war but peace—not the
destruction of nations but the protection of freedom. The forces that West
Germany contributes to this effort are second to none among the Western European nations. Your nation is in the front line of defense—and your divisions,
side by side with our own, are a source of strength to us all.

These conventional forces are essential, and they are backed by the sanction of
thousands of the most modern weapons here on European soil and thousands
more, only minutes away, in posts around the world. Together our nations have
developed for the forward defense of free Europe a deterrent far surpassing the
present or prospective force of any hostile power.

Nevertheless, it is natural that America's nuclear position has raised questions
within the alliance. I believe we must confront these questions—not by turning
the clock backward to separate nuclear deterrents—but by developing a more
closely unified Atlantic deterrent, with genuine European participation.

How this can best be done, and it is not easy—in some ways [it is] more difficult
to split the atom politically than it was physically, but how this can best be
done is now under discussion with those who may wish to join in this effort.
The proposal before us is for a new Atlantic force. Such a force would bring
strength instead of weakness, cohesion instead of division. It would belong to all
members, not one, with all participating on a basis of full equality. And as Europe
moves towards unity, its role and responsibility, here as elsewhere, would and
must increase accordingly.

Meanwhile, there is much to do. We must work more closely together on
strategy, training, and planning. European officers from NATO are being
assigned to the Strategic Air Command Headquarters in Omaha, Nebr. Modern
weapons are being deployed here in Western Europe. And America's strategic
deterrent—the most powerful in history—will continue to be at the service of the
whole alliance.

Second: Our partnership is not military alone. *Economic* unity is also imperative—not only among the nations of Europe, but across the wide Atlantic.

Indeed, economic cooperation is needed throughout the entire free world.
By opening our markets to the developing countries of Africa, Asia, and Latin
America, by contributing our capital and our skills, by stabilizing basic prices,
we can help assure them of a favorable climate for freedom and growth. This is
an Atlantic responsibility. For the Atlantic nations themselves helped to awaken
these peoples. Our merchants and our traders ploughed up their soils—and their
societies as well—in search of minerals and oil and rubber and coffee. Now we
must help them gain full membership in the 20th century, closing the gap between
rich and poor.

Another great economic challenge is the coming round of trade negotiations.
Those deliberations are much more important than a technical discussion of
trade and commerce. They are an opportunity to build common industrial and
agricultural policies across the Atlantic. They are an opportunity to open up
new sources of demand, to give new impetus to growth, and make more jobs

and prosperity, for our expanding populations. They are an opportunity to recognize the trading needs and aspirations of other free world countries, including Japan.

In short, these negotiations are a test of our unity. While each nation must naturally look out for its own interests, each nation must also look out for the common interest—the need for greater markets on both sides of the Atlantic —the need to reduce the imbalance between developed and underdeveloped nations—and the need to stimulate the Atlantic economy to higher levels of production rather than to stifle it by higher levels of protection.

We must not return to the 1930's when we exported to each other our own stagnation. We must not return to the discredited view that trade favors some nations at the expense of others. Let no one think that the United States—with only a fraction of its economy dependent on trade and only a small part of that with Western Europe—is seeking trade expansion in order to dump our goods on this continent. Trade expansion will help us all. The experience of the Common Market—like the experience of the German Zollverein—shows an increased rise in business activity and general prosperity resulting for all participants in such trade agreements, with no member profiting at the expense of another. As they say on my own Cape Cod, a rising tide lifts all the boats. And a partnership, by definition, serves both partners, without domination or unfair advantage. Together we have been partners in adversity—let us also be partners in prosperity.

Beyond development and trade is monetary policy. Here again our interests run together. Indeed there is no field in which the wider interest of all more clearly outweighs the narrow interest of one. We have lived by that principle, as bankers to freedom, for a generation. Now that other nations—including West Germany —have found new economic strength, it is time for common efforts here, too. The great free nations of the world must take control of our monetary problems if those problems are not to take control of us.

Third and finally: Our partnership depends on common *political* purpose. Against the hazards of division and lassitude, no lesser force will serve. History tells us that disunity and relaxation are the great internal dangers of an alliance. Thucydides reported that the Peloponnesians and their allies were mighty in battle but handicapped by their policy-making body—in which, he related 'each presses its own ends . . . which generally results in no action at all . . . they devote more time to the prosecution of their own purposes than to the consideration of the general welfare—each supposes that no harm will come of his own neglect, that it is the business of another to do this or that—and so, as each separately entertains the same illusion, the common cause imperceptibly decays.'

Is this also to be the story of the Grand Alliance? Welded in a moment of imminent danger, will it disintegrate into complacency, with each member pressing its own ends to the neglect of the common cause? This must not be the case. Our old dangers are not gone beyond return, and any division among us would bring them back in doubled strength.

Our defenses are now strong—but they must be made stronger. Our economic goals are now clear—but we must get on with their performance. And the greatest of our necessities, the most notable of our omissions, is progress toward unity of political purpose.

For we live in a world in which our own united strength will and must be our first reliance. As I have said before, and will say again, we work toward the day when there may be real peace between us and the Communists. We will not be second in that effort. But that day is not yet here.

We in the United States and Canada are 200 million, and here on the European side of the Atlantic alliance are nearly 300 million more. The strength and unity of this half-billion human beings are and will continue to be the anchor of all freedom, for all nations. Let us from time to time pledge ourselves again to our common purpose. But let us go on, from words to actions, to intensify our efforts for still greater unity among us, to build new associations and institutions on those already established. Lofty words cannot construct an alliance or maintain it—only concrete deeds can do that.

The great present task of construction is here on this continent where the effort for a unified free Europe is under way. It is not for Americans to prescribe to Europeans how this effort should be carried forward. Nor do I believe that there is any one right course or any single final pattern. It is Europeans who are building Europe.

Yet the reunion of Europe, as Europeans shape it—bringing a permanent end to the civil wars that have repeatedly wracked the world—will continue to have the determined support of the United States. For that reunion is a necessary step in strengthening the community of freedom. It would strengthen our alliance for its defense. And it would be in our national interest as well as yours.

It is only a fully cohesive Europe that can protect us all against the fragmentation of our alliance. Only such a Europe will permit full reciprocity of treatment across the ocean, in facing the Atlantic agenda. With only such a Europe can we have a full give-and-take between equals, an equal sharing of responsibilities, and an equal level of sacrifice. I repeat again—so that there may be no misunderstanding—the choice of paths to the unity of Europe is a choice which Europe must make. But as you continue this great effort, undeterred by either difficulty or delay, you should know that this new European greatness will be not an object of fear, but a source of strength, for the United States of America.

There are other political tasks before us. We must all learn to practice more completely the art of consultation on matters stretching well beyond immediate military and economic questions. Together, for example, we must explore the possibilities of leashing the tensions of the cold war and reducing the dangers of the arms race. Together we must work to strengthen the spirit of those Europeans who are now not free, to reestablish their old ties to freedom and the West, so that their desire for liberty and their sense of nationhood and their sense of belonging to the Western Community over hundreds of years will survive for future expression. We ask those who would be our adversaries to understand that in our relations with them we will not bargain one nation's interest against another's and that the commitment to the cause of freedom is common to us all.

All of us in the West must be faithful to our conviction that peace in Europe can never be complete until everywhere in Europe, and that includes Germany, men can choose, in peace and freedom, how their countries shall be governed, and choose—without threat to any neighbor—reunification with their countrymen.

I preach no easy liberation and I make no empty promises; but my country-men, since our country was founded, believe strongly in the proposition that all men shall be free and all free men shall have this right of choice.

As we look steadily eastward in the hope and purpose of new freedom, we must also look—and evermore closely—to our trans-Atlantic ties. The Atlantic Community will not soon become a single overarching superstate. But practical steps toward stronger common purpose are well within our means. As we widen our common effort in defense, and our threefold cooperation in economics, we shall inevitably strengthen our political ties as well. Just as your current efforts for unity in Europe will produce a stronger voice in the dialog between us, so in America our current battle for the liberty and prosperity of all of our citizens can only deepen the meaning of our common historic purposes. In the far future there may be a great new union for us all. But for the present, there is plenty for all to do in building new and enduring connections.

In short, the words of Thucydides are a warning, not a prediction. We have it in us, as 18 years have shown, to build our defenses, to strengthen our econo-mies, and to tighten our political bonds, both in good weather and in bad. We can move forward with the confidence that is born of success and the skill that is born of experience. And as we move, let us take heart from the certainty that we are united not only by danger and necessity, but by hope and purpose as well.

For we know now that freedom is more than the rejection of tyranny—that prosperity is more than an escape from want—that partnership is more than a sharing of power. These are, above all, great human adventures. They must have meaning and conviction and purpose—and because they do, in your country now and in mine, in all the nations of the alliance, we are called to a great new mission.

It is not a mission of self-defense alone—for that is a means, not an end. It is not a mission of arbitrary power—for we reject the idea of one nation dominating another. The mission is to create a new social order, founded on liberty and justice, in which men are the masters of their fate, in which states are the servants of their citizens, and in which all men and women can share a better life for themselves and their children. That is the object of our common policy.

To realize this vision, we must seek a world of peace—a world in which peoples dwell together in mutual respect and work together in a mutual regard—a world where peace is not a mere interlude between wars, but an incentive to the creative energies of humanity. We will not find such a peace today, or even tomorrow. The obstacles to hope are large and menacing. Yet the goal of a peaceful world—today and tomorrow—must shape our decisions and inspire our purposes.

So we are all idealists. We are all visionaries. Let it not be said of this Atlantic generation that we left ideals and visions to the past, nor purpose and deter-mination to our adversaries. We have come too far, we have sacrificed too much, to disdain the future now. And we shall ever remember what Goethe told us—that the 'highest wisdom, the best that mankind ever knew' was the realiza-tion that 'he only earns his freedom and existence who daily conquers them anew.'

Communiqué issued by President Kennedy and the Prime Minister of Great Britain, Mr. Macmillan, Birch Grove, 30 June 1963[1]

During the past two days President Kennedy and Prime Minister Macmillan have held their seventh meeting to discuss current problems. Their talks have taken place at Prime Minister Macmillan's home in Sussex and followed on President Kennedy's visit to Germany and Eire.

The United States Secretary of State, Mr. Rusk, Lord Home, British Foreign Secretary, Mr. Duncan Sandys, Secretary of State for Commonwealth Relations and Secretary of State for the Colonies, Lord Hailsham, Lord President of the Council, Mr. Thorneycroft, Minister of Defence, and Mr. Heath, Lord Privy Seal, took part in the talks at various times.

During some twelve hours of discussion the President and the Prime Minister began by hearing reports from Lord Home and Mr. Rusk about conversations which the two Ministers had held in London during the previous two days. The topics covered included Laos and the Far Eastern situation, the position in the Middle East, the problems of NATO and the Western Alliance and the effort for a test ban treaty. President Kennedy and the Prime Minister took note in particular of the situation in Laos and expressed their concern at the frequent breaches of the Geneva Agreement of 1962[2] and at the failure of certain parties to the Agreement to carry out their obligations under it. They agreed to continue to work closely together for the preservation of peace in Laos and the independence and neutrality of that country. They also agreed to continue close general cooperation in the Far East, particularly in regard to the problems of Viet Nam. As regards the Middle East, the President and the Prime Minister agreed on the importance of the efforts made by the United Nations in working towards conciliation in the Yemen and pledged their support to the Secretary-General.[3]

The President and the Prime Minister were agreed on their policy of continuing to help India by providing further military aid to strengthen her defences against the threat of renewed Chinese Communist attack. They were impressed by the importance to the economic progress and defence of both India and Pakistan of whose anxieties they were fully aware, of an honourable and equitable settlement of the outstanding differences between the two countries; they stood ready to help in any way which might be desired by both countries.

President Kennedy and the Prime Minister then reviewed the problems of the Western Alliance, especially in regard to NATO. They noted with satisfaction the decisions reached at the recent NATO meeting in Ottawa[4] which implemented the concept which they had themselves set out at their meeting at Nassau in December 1962,[5] by which a number of powers assigned some or all of their present and future forces to NATO Command.

With regard to the future they took note of the studies now under way in NATO for review of the strategic and tactical concepts which should underlie NATO's military plans.

The President reported on his discussions with Dr. Adenauer in which they reaffirmed their agreement to use their best efforts to bring into being a

---

[1] *D.S.B.*, 22 July 1963, pp. 132–3.   [2] Texts in *Documents, 1962*, pp. 753–61.
[3] See pp. 322–42 below.   [4] See pp. 31–3 above.
[5] For text, see *Documents, 1962*, pp. 482–4.

multilateral sea-borne MRBM force and to pursue with other interested govern-ments the principal questions involved in the establishment of such a force.[1]

The President and the Prime Minister agreed that a basic problem facing the NATO Alliance was the closer association of its members with the nuclear deterrent of the Alliance. They also agreed that various possible ways of meeting this problem should be further discussed with their allies. Such discussions would include the proposals for a multilateral sea-borne force, without prejudice to the question of British participation in such a force.

The President and the Prime Minister also reviewed the state of East-West relations and considered in particular the possibility of concluding in the near future a treaty to ban nuclear tests. They agreed that the achievement of such a treaty would be a major advance in East-West relations and might lead on to progress in other directions. They agreed the general line which their repre-sentatives, Mr. Averell Harriman and Lord Hailsham, should take during their visit to Moscow in July. The President and the Prime Minister reaffirmed their belief that the conclusion of a test ban treaty at this time is most urgent and pledged themselves to do all they could to bring this about.

Statement issued by the Office of the Prime Minister of Great Britain, 1 October 1963[2]

At their meeting in Nassau last December, the President of the United States and the Prime Minister of the United Kingdom agreed to use their best en-deavours to develop a Nato multilateral nuclear force, to which both the United States and the United Kingdom Governments would contribute national forces.[3]

The United Kingdom Government have assigned the V-bomber force to Nato[4] and are pledged to make their Polaris submarines, when completed, available for inclusion in a Nato nuclear force for the purposes of international defence of the western alliance in all circumstances, except where they may decide that supreme national interests are at stake. In so doing they have ful-filled the specific obligation which they assumed at Nassau.

On the same occasion the President explained to the Prime Minister that he also intended to pursue the formation of a mixed-manned nuclear force to be assigned to Nato and to which nonnuclear powers could contribute.

The United Kingdom Government have, from the outset, recognized the importance of this further proposal. They have agreed that the conception is one which deserves examination, together with other possible means of develop-ing the concept of a Nato multilateral nuclear force; but they have never given any undertaking to participate in the mixed-manned component although they have agreed to consider providing it, if it is formed, with operational facilities.

It was in this spirit that, at their meeting at Birch Grove in July,[5] the Presi-dent of the United States and the Prime Minister of the United Kingdom agreed that various possible ways of promoting a closer association of the members of the Nato alliance with its nuclear deterrent should be further discussed with

---

[1] See pp. 28–32 above.   [2] *The Times*, 2 October 1962.
[3] See *Documents, 1962*, pp. 482–4.
[4] See Communiqué of the N.A.T.O. Council, pp. 31–3 above.
[5] See pp. 41–2 above.

their allies, on the basis that such discussions should include proposals for a mixed-manned force without prejudice to the question of United Kingdom participation in it.

The terms of reference for the discussion now proposed, although specifically reserving national decisions on participation in the mixed-manned force to individual governments, state that those taking part, will be prepared 'to enter into detailed discussions with that end in view'.

In the light of the attitude which they have consistently adopted towards this project, as indicated above, the United Kingdom Government do not feel that they could in good faith enter these discussions on terms of reference which imply this degree of commitment in principle to participation in a mixed-manned force of surface ships, especially since the value of a force of this kind in relation to the expenditure of resources which it would entail has been publicly questioned and this issue is now under examination in the context of the Nato strategic review.

Therefore, if they are to take part in the discussions it must be on the clear understanding that it does not commit them to participate in such a force.

Subject to this reservation, the United Kingdom Government are prepared to join in an objective examination of the project in all its aspects and possible variations.

Communiqué of the N.A.T.O. Council, Paris, 17 December 1963[1]

The North Atlantic Council met in Ministerial Session in Paris on the 16th and 17th of December, 1963.

The Ministers expressed their profound grief at the heavy loss sustained by the Alliance and the whole of mankind in the tragic death of President Kennedy.[2] They welcomed a message from President Johnson renewing United States pledges to support the Alliance with all its strength and to maintain its forces in Europe.[3]

The Ministers, reaffirming their faith in the North Atlantic Alliance, emphasized that the continuing strength of the Alliance, the solidarity of its member states, and their determination to defend freedom and to resist aggression, remain essential prerequisites for the maintenance of world peace.

The Ministers stressed the peaceful and defensive purposes of the North Atlantic Alliance. In subscribing to the North Atlantic Treaty the members of NATO, whether members of the United Nations or not, had affirmed their faith in the principles of the United Nations Charter and had pledged themselves to refrain in their international relations from the threat or use of force in any manner inconsistent with the purposes of the United Nations. In the pursuit of peace, the achievement of general and complete disarmament, under effective international control, remains an essential objective.

In reviewing the international situation, the Ministers noted that there had been no major crisis since the confrontation over Cuba. They emphasized that the unity and military strength of the Alliance had largely contributed to this result and to the international atmosphere now prevailing. At the same time the

---

[1] *D.S.B.*, 6 January 1964, pp. 30–1.

[2] President Kennedy was assassinated on 22 November 1963.

[3] For text, see *D.S.B.*, 6 January 1964, pp. 24–30.

Ministers emphasized the importance not only of seeking agreement on limited measures which would help to reduce tension, but of achieving a genuine and fundamental improvement in East-West relations. They expressed the hope that Soviet policy would not limit the possibilities of making progress in this direction and of reaching solutions for the problems which are the real causes of tension in the world, in particular those of Berlin and Germany. Despite recent incidents, freedom of access to Berlin had been upheld; in this connection the Ministers reiterated their determination, as expressed in the declaration of 16th of December, 1958, to defend and maintain the freedom of West Berlin and its people.[1]

The Ministers also reviewed the situation in various areas of the world threatened by internal conflict and external force. They noted developments which continued to be a cause of concern in Southeast Asia, in the Caribbean area and elsewhere.

The Ministers reaffirmed their determination to improve and intensify their political consultation on subjects of common concern. They also agreed on the necessity of maintaining and strengthening the defensive capability of the Alliance, having regard to the constant advances in science and technology. They reviewed the implementation of decisions reached at Ottawa[2] regarding fuller information on nuclear questions for national authorities and broader participation by member countries in the organization and operational planning functions of SACEUR's nuclear forces. Finally, they took note of the progress achieved to give effect to the decisions made at Ottawa to pursue the study of the inter-related questions of strategy, force requirements, and the resources available to meet them. This study is under way.

The Ministers reviewed the progress made during the year in improving cooperation in research, development and production of military equipment. They also noted with satisfaction the recent decisions in regard to the establishment of a NATO air defence ground environment system.

In the economic field, the Ministers noted that the economies of the NATO countries have been steadily expanding and, in contrast to what has been happening in the Communist world, the economic systems of the West have shown themselves capable of flexible adaptation to circumstances. This has permitted not only an increase in the standards of living of their own peoples but has also enabled large-scale assistance to be extended to the developing countries.

The Council, having noted progress made in the implementation of earlier resolutions concerning the defence problems of Greece, reaffirmed its interest in the further effective application of these resolutions.

The Ministers agreed to give urgent priority to a study of the military and economic problems of the defence of Greece and Turkey, and, if possible, a report is to be made to the spring Ministerial meeting of the Council.

The Ministers examined a report on civil defence and civil emergency planning, which are an essential complement to the defence effort.

The next meeting of the North Atlantic Council at the Ministerial level will be held, on the invitation of the Netherlands Government, at The Hague from the 12th to the 14th of May, 1964.

[1] *Documents, 1958*, pp. 373–4.
[2] See pp. 31–3 above.

Communiqué issued by President Johnson and the Federal German Chancellor, Dr. Erhard, Johnson City, Texas, 29 December 1963.[1]

President Johnson and Chancellor Erhard have held a series of frank and far-ranging talks at the President's ranch in Texas in the last two days. A number of their discussions were private; in other talks they were joined by Secretary Rusk, Foreign Minister Schroeder, and other advisers.

The Chancellor told the President of the deep sorrow and sense of personal loss which the German people have felt over the death of President Kennedy. The President expressed deep appreciation for himself and for the American people for this expression of sympathy. He paid a tribute to the late President Heuss, the distinguished first President of the Federal Republic.

The President and the Chancellor both emphasized the importance which they attach to this opportunity to meet early in their Administrations. Their extensive discussions serve to confirm the close understanding and high measure of agreement between the two governments on major international issues. These conversations have made it emphatically clear that there will be continuity in the policies of the United States and the Federal Republic of Germany as they work toward common objectives.

The President and the Chancellor had an extended discussion of the current state of East-West relations. They were determined that the basic rights and interests of the free nations must be defended, and in particular they agreed that there should be no arrangement that would serve to perpetuate the status quo of a divided Germany, one part of which is deprived of elementary rights and liberties. On this basis, the President and the Chancellor agreed that it is highly important to continue to explore all opportunities for the improvement of East-West relations, the easing of tensions, and the enlargement of the prospects of a peace that can be stable because it is just. They continue to hope that this effort of the Western powers will meet a constructive response from the Soviet Union.

The President and the Chancellor agreed that the central requirement in the policy of the West must be to increase the strength and effectiveness of the emerging Atlantic partnership. They reaffirmed their conviction that an increasingly unified Europe is vital to this effort.

The Chancellor stated, and the President agreed, that efforts to achieve such unity must always respect the traditionally open trading relationship Europe has enjoyed with the United States and the rest of the Free World. The President and the Chancellor agreed that the forthcoming trade negotiations should be guided by the double objective of enlarged international trade and increasing economic integration in Europe. They agreed that agricultural as well as industrial products must be included and that the negotiations should proceed without delay.

The President reviewed the measures being taken to stabilize the United States' international payments position, and the Chancellor reaffirmed his cooperative support for this program.

---

[1] *D.S.B.*, 20 January 1964, pp. 74–5. Dr. Erhard was elected Chancellor on 16 October 1963.

The President and the Chancellor emphasized the importance of extending effective aid to the developing nations. The Chancellor described the progress being made in the work of the German Development Aid Service, and the President responded by describing the expansion of the American Peace Corps and the wide public support which it has won. The President and the Chancellor agreed that these two undertakings would gain from close cooperation, and as a part of this process of cooperation, the President has requested Mr. Sargent Shriver to make an early visit to Bonn to take part with German colleagues in discussions of the work of the two programs.

The President and the Chancellor reaffirmed their shared commitment to the peaceful reunification of the German people in freedom, by self-determination. The Chancellor stressed the desire of the Federal Republic to examine all paths that might lead to this goal. The Chancellor also stated that the Federal Republic of Germany would continue its efforts to improve its relations with the nations of Eastern Europe.

The President renewed the commitment of the Government and people of the United States to maintain the present six-division level of combat forces in Germany, as long as they are needed. The Chancellor welcomed the President's further assurance that the United States would continue to meet its commitments in Berlin. The President expressed appreciation for the cooperative arrangement whereby United States dollar expenditures for American military forces in Germany are offset by German purchases of military equipment in the United States. It was agreed that this arrangement should continue.

The President and the Chancellor agreed on the need for all members of NATO to cooperate closely in strengthening the ability of the Alliance to meet all challenges. In particular, they expressed their conviction that the proposal for a multilateral nuclear force now being discussed by several NATO partners[1] would provide a new means of strengthening Western defense.

The President and the Chancellor agreed that in all these matters there will be great value to both their governments in the maintenance of ever closer and more intimate exchanges of views and of information. Where common interest is so great, both sides can only gain from the closest cooperation and from the prompt and continuous exchange of views by whatever means are most appropriate in each case. In addition, the President and the Chancellor agreed that they themselves would establish and maintain the closest personal communication.

Finally, the President and the Chancellor reaffirmed their commitment not simply to close German-American cooperation, but to the wider interest of both countries in the growing partnership of free nations—of the Atlantic and of the world.

(c) Statements of French Policy

President de Gaulle's press conference, 29 July 1963[2] (extract)

... *Question.* — Pourriez-vous nous dire quelle est, à votre avis, l'incidence des récents accords internationaux qui viennent d'être signés à Moscou[3] sur l'évolution des rapports franco-américains?

---

[1] See pp. 28–31 above. [2] *La Documentation française*, No. 0.1419, 3 August 1963.
[3] See pp. 170–2 below.

Réponse. — On a été très agité, en particulier dans les journaux américains, depuis quelques mois. Je vous dirai que la pratique que je peux avoir personnellement depuis tantôt vingt-cinq années des réactions publiques aux Etats-Unis fait que je m'étonne assez peu des saccades de ce qu'on est convenu d'y appeler l'opinion. Cependant j'avoue que voici quelque temps le ton et la chanson en ce qui concerne la France m'ont paru assez excessifs.

Sans doute, pour en juger, convient-il de faire la part d'une certaine tension qui existe là-bas, naturellement causée par des soucis intérieurs et extérieurs pressants ainsi que par une conjoncture électorale sans cesse renouvelée. Sans doute avais-je moi-même à maintes reprises constaté combien ce pilonnage était aussi vain qu'exagéré.

Un certain nombre d'entre vous s'en souviennent: ce fut le cas par exemple dans les temps héroïques, quand je fus amené à faire occuper les Iles Saint-Pierre et Miquelon ou lors de la formation en Afrique du Nord du gouvernement de la Libération, ou bien quand il m'arriva de désapprouver Yalta et de décliner de me rendre à Alger pour y rencontrer Roosevelt qui revenait de cette déplorable conférence, ou bien après la victoire, à l'occasion du maintien de nos troupes à Stuttgart jusqu'à ce qu'une zone d'occupation en Allemagne eut été reconnue à la France. Ce fut le cas plus tard à propos du fameux projet de 'Communauté Européenne de Défense' qui consistait à priver notre pays non pas certes de ses dépenses militaires, mais bel et bien de son Armée, et auquel du fond de ma retraite je m'opposai catégoriquement. C'est le cas aujourd'hui sur des sujets d'ailleurs fort importants comme l'organisation de l'Europe, la création d'une force atomique française, le traité franco-allemand, etc....

Mais il me paraît utile de souligner tout de suite que ces agitations de presse, de milieux politiques, d'organismes plus ou moins officieux qui sévissent outre-atlantique, et qui naturellement rencontrent ici l'écho empressé de diverses sortes d'opposants inconditionnels, toutes ces agitations, dis-je, ne sauraient altérer en France ce qui est fondamental à l'égard de l'Amérique. Pour nous les données fondamentales des relations franco-américaines, ce sont l'amitié et l'alliance.

L'amitié! Voilà tantôt deux cents ans qu'elle existe comme une éminente réalité psychologique répondant à la nature des deux pays, développée par toutes sortes de penchants, d'influences, de rapports, de liens particuliers et réciproques maintenue par le fait que, de toutes les puissances du monde, la France est la seule — en dehors je dois le dire de la Russie — avec laquelle jamais les Etats-Unis n'ont échangé un coup de canon, tandis qu'elle est entre toutes sans exception la seule qui ait combattu à leurs côtés pendant trois guerres: la guerre de l'Indépendance, la Première et la Deuxième Guerres mondiales dans des conditions à jamais inoubliables.

Pour qu'un pareil capital moral puisse être entamé, il faudrait des dissensions infiniment graves et infiniment longues. Il peut y avoir, il y a des divergences politiques entre Paris et Washington, il y a des malveillances journalistiques, mais ce ne sont pas ces divergences et ce ne sont pas ces malveillances journalistiques du moment qui peuvent donner à croire à la France que l'Amérique cherche à lui faire du tort. Inversement, pour les Etats-Unis s'imaginer que la France cherche à leur nuire, ce serait d'une dérisoire absurdité.

Quant à l'alliance franco-américaine si depuis le temps de Washington et de

Franklin, de La Fayette, de de Grass, de Rochambeau, elle ne s'était nouée que pendant la Première guerre mondiale, en 1917 et 1918 et au cours de la Seconde à partir de décembre 1941, c'est un fait qu'elle existe actuellement et que tout impose aux deux pays de la maintenir. Aussi longtemps en effet que, devant le monde libre, se dressera le bloc soviétique capable de submerger tout à coup tel ou tel territoire et qui est animé par une idéologie dominatrice et détestable, il faudra que, de part et d'autre de l'Océan, les peuples qui veulent se défendre soient liés entre eux pour le faire.

L'alliance atlantique est une élémentaire nécessité et il va de soi qu'à ce point de vue, les Etats-Unis et la France ont une responsabilité capitale; les Etats-Unis parce qu'ils disposent d'un armement nucléaire sans lequel le sort du monde serait rapidement réglé, et la France parce que, quelle que soit l'infériorité actuelle de ses moyens, elle est politiquement, géographiquement, moralement, militairement essentielle à la coalition.

Si, donc, encore une fois, sur le fonctionnement, sur l'organisation de l'alliance il y a des divergences entre Washington et Paris, l'alliance elle-même — c'est-à-dire le fait qu'en cas de guerre générale la France, avec les moyens qu'elle a serait aux côtés des Etats-Unis, cela étant, je le crois, réciproque — est hors de la question, excepté dans les élucubrations de ceux qui font profession d'alarmer les bonnes gens en dépeignant chaque écorchure comme une inguérissable plaie. Ainsi donc, ni l'amitié, ni l'alliance franco-américaines ne sauraient être et ne sont en cause. Mais il est vrai que, devant les problèmes qui se posent actuellement aux deux pays, leur politique ne concorde pas toujours. Il n'y a d'ailleurs là rien d'essentiel ni de foncièrement inquiétant, ni même d'étonnant. Mais il faut nous adapter de part et d'autre à cette situation nouvelle.

A mon sens les différences d'aujourd'hui proviennent tout bonnement des changements intrinsèques qui se sont produits depuis quelques années et qui se poursuivent en ce qui concerne la situation absolue et relative de l'Amérique et de la France.

La France avait été, matériellement et moralement, démolie par l'effondrement de 1940 et la capitulation des gens de Vichy. Sans doute, le redressement réalisé par la Résistance, aux côtés des Alliées, lui avait-il rendu, comme par miracle, son intégrité, sa souveraineté et sa dignité. Mais elle sortait de l'épreuve très affaiblie à tous les égards.

D'autre part, l'inconsistance du régime où elle était retombée, l'empêchait de prendre son essor à l'intérieur et son rang à l'extérieur. En outre faute d'adopter et d'appliquer les décisions nécessaires au sujet de la décolonisation, elle était entravée dans son développement national et son action internationale par des luttes lointaines sans issue.

C'est pourquoi, vis-à-vis des Etats-Unis, riches, actifs et puissants, elle se trouvait en situation de dépendance. Il lui fallait constamment leur concours pour éviter une débâcle monétaire. Les armes de ses troupes, c'est de l'Amérique qu'elle les recevait. Sa sécurité ne tenait qu'à leur protection. Quant aux entreprises internationales auxquelles prenaient part ses dirigeants d'alors, c'était souvent en vue de l'y dissoudre, comme si le renoncement à elle-même était désormais sa seule possibilité, voire son unique ambition, tandis que ces entreprises, sous le couvert de l'intégration, postulaient automatiquement l'autorité américaine. Il en était ainsi de l'O.T.A.N. où la responsabilité de la défense de notre pays était attribuée en propre au commandement militaire américain. Il en était ainsi du projet d'une Europe dite 'supra-nationale' où la France, en tant que telle, aurait disparu, sauf pour payer et pour discourir, d'une Europe régie en apparence par des comités anonymes, technocratiques et apatrides, c'est-à-dire d'une Europe sans réalité politique, sans ressort économique, sans capacité de défense, et vouée par conséquent, face au bloc soviétique, à n'être qu'une dépendance de cette grande puissance occidentale qui avait, elle, une politique, une économie, une défense: les Etats-Unis d'Amérique.

Mais il se trouve que, depuis lors, la situation de la France a profondément changé. Ses institutions nouvelles la mettent en mesure de vouloir et d'agir. Son développement intérieur lui procure la prospérité et la fait accéder aux moyens de la puissance. Elle a rétabli sa monnaie, ses finances, l'équilibre de ses échanges. Si bien qu'à ce point de vue, elle n'a plus besoin de personne, tandis qu'elle se voit, au contraire, sollicitée de beaucoup de côtés. Aussi, loin d'emprunter à d'autres, notamment aux Américains, elle leur rembourse ses dettes et, même, leur assure, à l'occasion, quelques facilités. Elle a transformé en coopération entre Etats le régime de colonisation qu'elle appliquait naguère à ses Territoires d'Afrique, et, pour la première fois depuis un quart de siècle, elle vit dans une paix complète. Elle modernise son armée, l'équipe elle-même en matériel et entreprend de se doter d'une force atomique propre. Elle a dissipé les nuées qui enveloppaient et paralysaient la construction de l'Europe et entamé cette grande œuvre sur la base des réalités, en commençant par la mise sur pied de la Communauté Economique, en donnant avec l'Allemagne l'exemple de début de coopération politique et en marquant qu'elle veut être la France dans une Europe qui doit être Européenne. Encore une fois la condition nationale et internationale de notre pays ressemble de moins en moins à ce qu'elle était naguère. Comment les modalités de ses relations avec les Etats-Unis n'en seraient-elles pas modifiées? D'autant plus que, de leur côté les Etats-Unis voient se produire, quant à leurs problèmes, de grands changements qui modifient le caractère de solidarité hégémonique dont étaient, depuis la guerre mondiale, marqués leurs rapports avec la France.

Au point de vue politique, il est vrai que le bloc soviétique s'en tient à une idéologie totalitaire et menaçante et que, récemment encore le mur de Berlin, le scandale du mur de Berlin, ou l'installation d'un armement nucléaire à Cuba ont montré que, de son fait, la paix demeurait précaire. D'autre part, l'évolution humaine en Russie et chez les satellites, d'importantes difficultés économiques et sociales dans la vie de ces pays-là et surtout le commencement d'opposition qui se manifeste entre un empire européen détenteur d'immenses territoires asiatiques, qui font de lui la plus grande puissance coloniale de notre temps et l'empire de Chine son voisin sur 10·000 kms, peuplé de 700 millions d'hommes, empire indestructible, ambitieux et dénué de tout, tout cela peut, en effet, introduire quelques conjonctures nouvelles dans les soucis du Kremlin et l'amener à mettre une note de sincérité dans les couplets qu'il consacre à la coexistence pacifique. Du coup, les Etats-Unis qui, depuis Yalta et Potsdam, n'ont en somme rien à réclamer aux Soviets, les Etats-Unis voient s'offrir à eux des perspectives tentantes. De là, par exemple, toutes les négociations séparées entre les Anglo-Saxons et les Soviétiques qui, à partir de l'accord limité sur les expériences nucléaires, paraissent devoir s'étendre à d'autres questions, notamment européennes, jusqu'à présent en l'absence des Européens, ce qui, évidemment, contrevient aux vues de la France.

La France, en effet, croit depuis longtemps qu'il peut venir un jour où une détente réelle et même une entente sincère permettront de changer complètement les rapports entre l'Est et l'Ouest en Europe, et elle compte, si ce jour vient, je l'ai dit en d'autres occasions, faire des propositions constructives pour ce qui concerne la paix, l'équilibre et le destin de l'Europe. Mais, pour le moment, elle ne souscrirait pas à quelque combinaison qui serait réalisée par-dessus sa tête et qui concernerait l'Europe et notamment l'Allemagne. Quant à un projet de pacte de non-agression, dont on a, nous dit-on, parlé à Moscou entre les Etats qui font partie de l'O.T.A.N. et les dirigeants des pays soumis au joug du Kremlin,[1] je dois dire tout de suite que la France n'apprécie pas cette assimilation entre l'alliance atlantique et la servitude communiste. Et puis d'ailleurs, il n'y a besoin d'aucun pacte pour que la France déclare qu'elle n'attaquera jamais la première, étant entendu qu'elle se défendrait avec les moyens qu'elle peut avoir contre quiconque attaquerait, ou bien elle-même, ou bien ses alliés. Mais aujourd'hui, solennellement, elle déclare, par la bouche du Président de la République, qu'il n'y aura jamais d'agression française. Alors, du même coup, notre éventuelle participation à un pacte de non-agression n'a plus aucune espèce d'objet.

Mais il reste que ce qui s'est passé à Moscou montre que la voie suivie par la politique des Etats-Unis ne se confond pas avec la nôtre.

Pour ce qui est de la défense, jusqu'à ces derniers temps les Américains, grâce à leurs armes nucléaires, étaient en mesure d'assurer au monde libre une protection quasi absolue. Mais ils ont perdu ce monopole, tout en continuant à grands frais de renforcer leur puissance. Du fait que les Russes ont, eux aussi, maintenant, de quoi détruire l'univers et notamment le nouveau continent, il est tout naturel que l'Amérique voit dans sa propre survie, l'objectif principal d'un conflit éventuel et n'envisage le moment, le degré, les modalités de son intervention nucléaire pour la défense d'autres régions, en particulier de l'Europe, qu'en fonction de cette nécessité naturelle et primordiale. C'est d'ailleurs une des raisons pour lesquelles la France se dote d'un armement atomique propre. Il en résulte que pour le Gouvernement français des modifications importantes s'imposent pour ce qui est des conditions, des modalités de notre participation à l'alliance, puisque cette organisation a été fondée sur l'intégration, laquelle, aujourd'hui n'est plus valable pour nous.

Enfin, dans l'ordre économique, le moment est venu où les Etats-Unis, dont l'énorme capacité de production, d'échanges, n'est pas du tout entamée, voient s'élever celle des pays européens, en particulier de la France, au point d'en faire des concurrents assez incommodes. En outre, les charges que représentent pour les Etats-Unis le soutien financier qu'ils apportent à beaucoup d'Etats et les forces militaires qu'ils entretiennent à l'extérieur, ne laissent pas de leur peser très lourd, tandis qu'une part considérable de leurs capitaux vont s'investir au dehors. Pour ces raisons, la balance des paiements et le problème du dollar des Etats-Unis deviennent des soucis essentiels. On comprend donc parfaitement bien que leurs intentions ne soient plus celles qu'ils avaient naguère au sujet de l'organisation d'une Europe européenne et du rôle que peut y jouer la France.

[1] See pp. 157–8 below.

Mais on comprend aussi que la France, qui est industrielle et agricole, ne puisse pas et ne veuille pas voir se dissoudre ni l'économie naissante de l'Europe, ni la sienne dans un système du genre «Communauté atlantique» qui ne serait qu'une forme nouvelle de la fameuse intégration. Au total, pour la France et, je le crois, pour les Etats-Unis, l'amitié qui les unit et l'alliance qui les lie, sont au-dessus de toute atteinte. Mais il est vrai qu'il y a des différences entre les deux pays, face à certains problèmes internationaux. L'évolution de l'un et de l'autre pays a créé cet état de choses qui, encore une fois, n'a rien d'étonnant, pour incommode qu'il puisse, peut-être, paraître aux Américains. En tous cas, dans les rapports entre les deux peuples, nous pensons qu'il faut qu'on prenne son parti de cette situation nouvelle. Cela fait, il conviendra sans doute de concerter pour chaque cas, et, dans toute la mesure du possible, les politiques respectives. La France, pour sa part, y est cordialement, très cordialement disposée.

Question. — Que pensez-vous de l'accord sur l'interdiction des expériences nucléaires entre les trois puissances qui se sont réunies à Moscou et de la rupture qui a eu lieu entre la Chine et l'Union Soviétique dans un domaine qui est, semble-t-il, idéologique, mais qui est effectivement politique?

Réponse. — Je vais vous parler d'abord de la rupture idéologique, puis des réalités, c'est-à-dire de l'accord de Moscou.

La rupture? sur quelle idéologie? Depuis que je vis, l'idéologie communiste a été personnifiée par beaucoup de gens. Il y a l'époque de Lénine, de Trotsky, de Staline, que j'ai connu personnellement, de Beria, de Malinkov, de Khroutchtchev, et de Tito, et de Nagy, et de Mao-tsé-Toung. Je connais autant de détenteurs de l'idéologie communiste qu'il y a de pères de l'Europe, et cela en fait un certain nombre. Chacun de ces détenteurs, à son tour, condamne, excommunie, écrase et quelquefois tue les autres. En tout cas, il combat fermement le culte de la personnalité des autres.

Je me refuse à entrer dans une discussion valable sur le sujet de la querelle idéologique entre Pékin et Moscou. Ce que je veux considérer, ce sont les réalités profondes qui sont humaines, nationales et par conséquent internationales.

L'étendard de l'idéologie ne couvre en réalité que des ambitions. Et, je crois bien qu'il en est ainsi depuis que le monde est né.

Passons à l'accord de Moscou.

Que les Soviétiques et les Anglo-Saxons décident directement de cesser leurs expériences nucléaires dans l'espace, dans l'air et dans la mer est — en soi — satisfaisant et nous sympathisons à la joie que le Président Kennedy a si éloquemment exprimée avant-hier au sujet de cet événement.[1]

Il faut dire que ce n'est pas la première fois que les essais nucléaires seraient interrompus. Il y a déjà eu, à diverses reprises, de longues périodes où aucun des deux côtés n'exécutait d'essais importants. Mais, cette fois, le fait de s'engager réciproquement à l'abstention rend celle-ci beaucoup plus probable. D'ailleurs, après avoir effectué chacun des expériences qui se comptent par

---

[1] President Kennedy's address on American radio and television, 26 July 1963; for text, see *Current Documents, 1963*, pp. 978–84.

plusieurs centaines, dont les dernières sont toutes récentes, on voit mal, à quoi de nouveaux essais, pourraient à présent leur servir. Pourtant, le domaine des expériences souterraines reste en dehors de l'accord et chacun des partenaires se réserve la possibilité de dénoncer l'accord dans les trois mois, si cela lui convient.

Cependant, sans méconnaître que cet accord de Moscou n'a certes — et bien au contraire — rien qui puisse désobliger personne, et en tout cas pas nous, il faut constater qu'il ne change rien à la terrible menace que les armements nucléaires des deux rivaux font peser sur le monde et, avant tout, sur les peuples qui en sont dépourvus.

C'est un fait, qu'ils ont tous les deux de quoi anéantir l'univers et c'est un fait qu'il n'est pas question qu'ils s'apprêtent à y renoncer.

Dans ces conditions, la situation du monde par rapport à cette menace n'étant changée en quoi que ce soit, il est tout à fait naturel qu'un pays comme la France qui commence à avoir les moyens de s'affranchir, dans une certaine mesure, de cette terreur permanente, poursuive dans cette voie. D'autant plus que rien n'empêche les deux rivaux, leurs expériences ayant cessé, de continuer à fabriquer des projectiles de plus en plus nombreux, de plus en plus puissants et de se doter de véhicules de lancement, fusées, avions, sous-marins, satellites de plus en plus perfectionnés. Les économies que pourra, peut-être, leur procurer la cessation des expériences, leur permettra d'ailleurs de renforcer encore leurs moyens de destruction. C'est pourquoi, l'accord de Moscou, je le dis franchement, n'a qu'une importance pratique réduite, à moins naturellement, qu'il ne soit le point de départ d'autre chose qui s'étendrait à d'autres domaines très différents et c'est la raison pour laquelle, l'accord, tout en ayant l'approbation de la France, éveille pourtant sa vigilance.

Alors, me demandez-vous, que va faire la France après l'accord de Moscou?

Je vous répèterai, une fois de plus, que si un jour les Américains et les Soviétiques en venaient au désarmement, c'est-à-dire à la destruction et à l'interdiction contrôlées de leurs moyens nucléaires, c'est de grand cœur que nous-mêmes nous renoncerions à nous en procurer. Rien n'annonce malheureusement qu'on soit sur le point d'en venir là. Et la triste conférence de Genève aura, comme c'était à prévoir, interminablement siégé pour rien.

Cependant, je puis dire que de toute façon et à tout hasard, la France n'attendait que la fin de cette vaine figuration, je parle de la Conférence de Genève, pour proposer aux trois autres puissances atomiques certaines premières mesures de désarmement effectif portant, en particulier, sur les véhicules cosmiques, aériens et maritimes qui sont susceptibles de lancer des projectiles nucléaires.[1] Ce qui s'est passé à Moscou ne fait que la confirmer dans cette intention et elle compte, avant la fin de cette année, inviter les Etats intéressés à étudier avec elle ce problème essentiel alors qu'il n'est-peut-être pas encore devenu insoluable à son tour.[1] Mais nous répétons également qu'un simple accord sur les essais entre Soviétiques et Anglo-Saxons, déjà investis d'une puissance incommensurable qui ne cessent de la renforcer et qui par là confirment de jour en jour leurs hégémonies respectives, ne détournera pas la France de se doter, elle aussi, des moyens de la même sorte, faute de quoi, puisque d'autres en ont, sa propre sécurité et sa propre indépendance ne lui appartiendraient jamais plus.

[1] This proposal was not tabled during 1963.

Question. — Si par hasard les Etats-Unis et l'Angleterre venaient proposer à la France de lui fournir tout ce dont elle a besoin pour son armement nucléaire, après des expériences de vérification faites dans le Pacifique, accepteriez-vous de poser votre signature au bas de cet accord, consacrant ainsi la France comme la quatrième puissance nucléaire?

Réponse. — Vous savez, on ne donne pas la signature de la France sur une série d'hypothèses dont aucune jusqu'à présent n'a reçu le moindre commencement d'exécution.

Question. — La France est-elle d'accord pour favoriser un développement qui, sur le plan militaire, politique et scientifique, éviterait que, dans l'Europe de demain, les petits pays soient aussi dépendants envers la France que l'Europe l'est à présent, pour les mêmes raisons, envers l'Amérique?

Réponse. — C'est encore une série d'hypothèses sur lesquelles je vous demande de ne pas entrer. Nous parlons de réalités, de choses effectives, et j'en reviens à l'Europe qui commence à être quelque chose d'effectif.

Question. — Depuis votre dernière conférence, le traité franco-allemand a été mis à l'épreuve, en beaucoup de domaines.[1] En ce qui concerne la coordination des politiques franco-allemande dans le Marché commun ou vis-à-vis de l'adhésion éventuelle de l'Angleterre, dans l'organisation atlantique ou dans les rapports de l'Europe vis-à-vis de l'Amérique ou, sur des plans plus modestes, dans les achats de produits agricoles français par l'Allemagne; dans la fabrication d'un char européen, etc...., est-ce que les faits ont dépassé, satisfait ou déçu vos espérances?

Réponse. L'organisation économique de l'Europe continue de faire des progrès et le traité franco-allemand y contribue directement. La première réunion des deux gouvernements qui, conformément au traité, s'est tenue à Bonn au début de ce mois a eu d'abord l'avantage de ménager et d'élargir les contacts pour l'examen des problèmes d'intérêt commun. C'est ainsi que moi-même, par exemple, indépendamment de mes entretiens avec le Chancelier Adenauer, ai eu l'occasion de converser d'une manière approfondie avec le Vice-Chancelier Erhard, ce dont je me félicite. D'autre part, la réunion de Bonn a renforcé dans l'esprit de ses participants le sentiment que la coopération franco-allemande devait, au cours de cette année même, s'affirmer dans un domaine essentiel: l'organisation économique de l'Europe, la mise sur pied complète et effective du Marché commun. Il est bien clair que c'est là, si l'on peut dire, le banc d'essai du traité.

Si, en pareille matière, celui-ci fait la preuve de son efficacité, on peut croire qu'il ira ensuite se développant et s'affermissant sur d'autres sujets tels que ceux que vous avez évoqués et où il n'y a encore que des ébauches.

Pour ce qui est du Marché commun, au développement duquel nous espérons que le Traité franco-allemand contribuera d'une manière effective, c'est bien entendu, le problème agricole que les Six ont encore à régler. Que signifieraient les mots mêmes «Communauté économique européenne» si l'Europe n'assurait pas, pour l'essentiel, son alimentation grâce à ses propres produits agricoles,

---

[1] See pp. 54–5 below.

lesquels peuvent y suffire largement? Et qu'irait faire la France dans un système à l'intérieur duquel il n'y aurait bientôt plus de douane excepté pour son blé, sa viande, son lait, son vin et ses fruits? Sans doute, le Traité de Rome, assez complètement agencé pour ce qui concerne l'industrie, se bornait-il à évoquer sans la résoudre la question de l'agriculture. Mais depuis le mois de janvier de l'année dernière où la France a obtenu de ses partenaires l'engagement formel d'aboutir dans ce domaine, faute de quoi le développement de l'ensemble serait arrêté, d'importants progrès ont été faits. Il reste à en accomplir de plus importants encore et cela doit avoir lieu avant la fin de cette année.

En effet, le terme adopté pour l'achèvement des règlements qui demeurent en suspens est le 31 décembre; d'abord, parce que le déséquilibre entre les conditions des échanges industriels et celle des échanges agricoles ne saurait durer plus longtemps; ensuite, parce que c'est sous cette condition, que les Six ayant pris acte du fait que la Grande-Bretagne ne peut entrer actuellement dans l'organisation d'une Europe européenne, se sont mis d'accord pour utiliser l'U.E.C., déjà existante, afin d'échanger leurs vues avec celles des Britanniques sur les problèmes économiques mondiaux. Enfin, c'est pour cette raison que les négociations tarifaires entre les Etats-Unis et l'Europe vont s'ouvrir au printemps prochain et que devant les grands vents qui ne manqueront pas de se lever à cette occasion, il faudra alors que le Marché Commun soit debout, complet et assuré, ou bien qu'il disparaisse.

Ainsi, l'année 1963 est-elle décisive pour l'avenir d'une Europe unie. Si, au cœur de l'univers, une communauté réelle s'établit entre les Six dans le domaine économique, on peut penser, en effet, qu'ils seront plus portés qu'ils ne le sont à s'organiser pour mener en commun une politique qui soit européenne. A ce point de vue aussi, le traité franco-allemand offre un exemple qui peut être suivi et un cadre qui peut s'élargir. D'autant mieux que les événements dont nous avons parlé tout à l'heure et notamment les contacts directs qui s'établissent de nouveau entre les Anglo-Saxons et les Soviétiques et qui, une fois de plus, peuvent engager son propre sort devraient convaincre l'Europe que c'est le temps d'être elle-même ou qu'elle risque de ne l'être jamais...

(d) *Franco-German Relations*

Preamble to the Act of the Federal German Government ratifying the Franco-German Treaty of Cooperation, approved by the Bundestag, 16 May 1963[1]

CONVINCED that the treaty concluded on 22 January 1963 between the Federal Republic of Germany and the French Republic will intensify and develop the reconciliation and friendship between the German and the French peoples,

STATING that this treaty does not affect the rights and obligations resulting from multilateral treaties concluded by the Federal Republic of Germany,

RESOLVED to serve by the application of this treaty the great aims to which the Federal Republic of Germany, in concert with the other States allied to her, has aspired for years, and which determine her policy,

[1] Germany, Federal Republic, Press and Information Office, *The Bulletin*, 21 May 1963; for the text of the treaty, see *Documents, 1962*, pp. 435–8.

TO WIT, the preservation and consolidation of the unity of the free nations and in particular of a close partnership between Europe and the United States of America, the realisation of the right of self-determination for the German people, and the restoration of German unity,

collective defence within the framework of the North Atlantic Alliance, and the integration of the armed forces of the States bound together in that Alliance,

the unification of Europe by following the course adopted by the establishment of the European Communities, with the inclusion of Great Britain and other States wishing to accede, and the further strengthening of those Communities,

the elimination of trade barriers by negotiations between the European Economic Community, Great Britain, and the United States of America as well as other States within the framework of the General Agreement on Tariffs and Trade,

CONSCIOUS that a Franco-German co-operation inspired by such aims will benefit all nations and serve the peace of the world and will thereby also promote the welfare of the German and French peoples,

the Bundestag enacts the following Law:

Communiqué issued following President de Gaulle's visit to the Federal German Republic, 5 July 1963[1]

A la suite de l'entrée en vigueur du traité du 22 janvier 1963 sur la coopération franco-allemande,[2] le président de la République française et le chancelier de la République fédérale ont eu, à Bonn, les 4 et 5 juillet 1963, la première des consultations régulières prévues audit accord. Le général de Gaulle a eu, d'autre part, un entretien, le 5 juillet, avec M. Luebke, président de la République fédérale d'Allemagne.

Le président de la République française était accompagné de M. Pompidou, Premier Ministre, de M. Couve de Murville, ministre des Affaires étrangères, de M. Messmer, ministre des Armées, de M. Giscard d'Estaing, ministre des Finances, de M. Pisani, ministre de l'Agriculture, de M. Fouchet, ministre de l'Education nationale, et de M. Herzog, secrétaire d'Etat à la Jeunese et aux Sports.

Du côté allemand, ont pris part aux entretiens, M. Shroeder, ministre fédéral des Affaires étrangères, le professeur Erhard, vice-chancelier et ministre fédéral de l'Economic, M. Dahlgruen, ministre fédéral des Finances, M. Schwarz, ministre fédéral de l'Alimentation, de l'Agriculture et des Forêts, M. Von Hassel, ministre fédéral de la Défense, M. Heck ministre fédéral de la Famille et de la Jeunesse, et M. Kiesinger, Premier Ministre de Bade-Wurtemberg, commissaire de la République fédérale pour la coopération culturelle dans le cadre du traité franco-allemand.

Dans une première réunion, le général de Gaulle et chancelier Adenauer ont procédé à l'examen de la situation politique générale. Au cours de trois réunions ultérieures, ils ont examiné, avec la participation de leurs ministres, les diverses questions qui se posent actuellement dans le domaine de la coopération.

---

[1] *La Documentation française*, 13 July 1963.   [2] Text in *Documents, 1962*, pp. 435–8.

Les questions économiques, abordées sous l'angle du Marché Commun, ont donné lieu à des échanges de vues approfondis. Ceux-ci portent avant tout sur l'agriculture et sur la négociation qui doit s'engager dans le cadre de l'accord général sur les tarifs douaniers et le commerce au mois de mai 1964.

Les deux gouvernements ont constaté que les décisions arrêtées le 9 mai dernier à Bruxelles, fixant un programme de travail de la Communauté Economique Européenne pour les mois à venir, doivent permettre d'accomplir, à brève échéance, des progrès considérables dans les divers domaines d'activité prévus.

Ainsi en ce qui concerne l'élaboration de la politique agricole commune, la mise en vigueur, pendant le premier trimestre 1964, des règlements visant la viande de bœuf, les produits laitiers, et le riz est apparue aux deux gouvernements comme un objectif essentiel.

Quant aux difficiles problèmes soulevés par la définition d'une politique européenne des prix agricoles, et notamment des céréales, leur complexité a conduit les deux gouvernements à s'entendre pour proposer, dans le cadre de la C.E.E., une méthode de travail comportant des recherches et études destinées à isoler les difficultés et à dégager des solutions adéquates.

La négociation commerciale menée dans le cadre de l'accord général sur les tarifs douaniers et le commerce est apparue comme fournissant une occasion propice de libérer davantage les échanges internationaux et de faciliter les rapports entre les groupements économiques régionaux. Aussi les deux gouvernements ont-ils marqué leur intention de continuer à orienter leur action au sein de la C.E.E. en vue d'assurer le succès de la négociation. La participation de tous les gouvernements intéressés, une juste réciprocité des avantages consentis de part et d'autre, la réduction des tarifs en même temps que celle des disparités existantes et le maintien, aux frontières de la C.E.E., d'un tarif commun extérieur abaissé mais cohérent constituent des objectifs communs aux deux gouvernements.

Dans le domaine militaire, les questions stratégiques et d'armement en cours ont été passées en revue et des décisions ont été prises afin de faire progresser un certain nombre de projets. L'échange d'unités entières des forces des deux Etats commencera dans un proche avenir. Le ministre fédéral de la Défense et le ministre des Armées ont signé un accord sur l'étude en commun d'un avion à décollage vertical.

Pour ce qui concerne l'éducation, les recommandations faites récemment à Hambourg par la commission culturelle mixte franco-allemande ont été examinées par MM. Kiesinger et Fouchet et approuvées ensuite en séance plénière. Ces recommandations ont trait à l'extension de l'enseignement des langues des deux pays dans les établissements secondaires ainsi que dans les universités ou écoles supérieures. Elles portent aussi sur les équivalences de scolarité et de diplômes universitaires ainsi que sur la coopération dans le domaine de la recherche scientifique. Il a été réaffirmé, de part et d'autre, la volonté commune de favoriser le développement de l'enseignement du français en Allemagne et de l'allemand en France, condition nécessaire d'une meilleure connaissance réciproque.

Les ministres des Affaires étrangères des deux pays ont, d'autre part, procédé à la signature d'un accord portant création d'un office franco-allemand de la

Jeunesse. Cet accord a pour but d'encourager des échanges entre jeunes Allemands et jeunes Français. A cet effet, l'office prévu sera administré par un conseil mixte franco-allemand. Des crédits importants versés à parts égales par les deux gouvernements en permettront le bon fonctionnement.

Les pourparlers ont fait ressortir la communauté de vues qui existe du côté français comme du côté allemand sur les méthodes à observer pour donner au traité du 22 janvier sa pleine signification. Ils se sont déroulés dans l'esprit prévu dans cet accord en ce qui concerne notamment la recherche de l'unité européenne.

Communiqué issued following the visit of Chancellor Erhard to Paris, 22 November 1963[1]

Le Professeur Ludwig Erhard, Chancelier de la République fédérale d'Allemagne, s'est rendu à Paris les 21 et 22 novembre pour rendre visite au général de Gaulle, Président de la République Française. Le Chancelier Erhard était accompagné de M. Shroeder, ministre fédéral des Affaires Etrangères.

Le général de Gaulle et le Chancelier Erhard, ainsi que le Premier Ministre français, M. Pompidou, et les deux ministres des Affaires Etrangères, M. Schroeder et M. Couve de Murville, ont eu des conversations approfondies.

Au cours de ces entretiens, qui se sont déroulés dans l'atmosphère de cordialité, d'amitié et de confiance qui est de règle dans les rapports entre les deux pays, les principaux problèmes concernant la situation politique mondiale ont été passés en revue.

Il a été noté que le Traité du 22 janvier 1963[2] avait pris un bon départ: les mécanismes communs prévus par le Traité ont été mis en place et vont pouvoir contribuer efficacement au développement des relations franco-allemandes dans tous les domaines. A cette occasion, il a été souligné que la coopération franco-allemande n'a pas de caractère exclusif mais est ouverte aux autres partenaires des Communautés Européennes.

Lors de l'examen de la situation internationale, une attention spéciale a été apportée au problème de l'Allemagne et à la question berlinoise. Le général de Gaulle et le Chancelier Erhard ont constaté l'accord de leurs gouvernements sur la politique à suivre à cet égard et sur la nécessité de faire bénéficier le peuple allemand du droit à l'autodétermination.

Une discussion approfondie des problèmes européens a eu lieu. Ceux-ci ont été évoqués essentiellement sous leur aspect économique, compte tenu du programme de travail adopté le 9 mai dernier, à l'exécution duquel les deux gouvernements sont également attachés.

Le général de Gaulle et M. Erhard ont reconnu l'importance que présentait, pour la France et pour la Republique Fédérale aussi bien que pour la Communauté Economique elle-même, l'adoption dans les délais convenus des réglements agricoles et financiers encore en suspens, et se sont mis d'accord pour que soient déployés tous les efforts nécessaires en vue d'assurer le succès des travaux de Bruxelles.

---

[1] *La Documentation française*, No. 0.1464, 30 November 1963.
[2] Text in *Documents, 1962*, pp. 435–8.

L'aboutissement heureux des négociations de Genève est également un objectif commun des deux gouvernements désireux l'un et l'autre de réduire les obstacles au commerce international et de faciliter les rapports entre la C.E.E. et les pays tiers, en particulier les Etats-Unis et les pays membres de l'A.E.L.E.

Le Président de la République et le Chancilier fédéral ont également procédé à un échange de vues sur les propositions de grande portée que la Commission du Marché Commun vient de déposer en vue de l'établissement d'un niveau commun des prix des céréales dans la Communauté Economique Européenne.

La mise en œuvre du programme susvisé du 9 mai permettra, c'est l'espoir des deux gouvernements, de poursuivre l'œuvre entreprise, non seulement sur le terrain économique, mais sur le terrain politique et de promouvoir ainsi la construction d'une Europe unie.

(e) *The European Community*

Statement by Mr. Macmillan to the House of Commons, 11 February 1963[1] (extracts)

... I will not disguise from the House, as I have not attempted to disguise from the country, the deep disappointment of the Government and, I think, of the whole nation, at the turn of events. As I have already made clear, I do not believe that there is a simple alternative, in the sense of a sort of ready-made plan, which is better than the one we have been pursuing. There are, indeed, measures which we can and will adopt, and action which we can and will take. Meanwhile, it would be right for me, first, to give some account of the effects of the breakdown in the negotiations upon the Commonwealth economy, on that of our E.F.T.A. partners, and on our own. There were clearly some very substantial gains for some of the Commonwealth countries in the terms negotiated by the Lord Privy Seal.

First, to take an important example in Asia, both India and Ceylon depend for their earnings of foreign exchange very largely upon the export of tea. The sale of tea represents £91 million, or 47 per cent., of the total of Indian exports to Britain. In Ceylon, the figures are £84 million and 90 per cent. of total exports to Britain. It had been agreed that instead of the tariffs now operating in the Common Market countries, which will shortly be at a uniform 10·8 per cent., there would be free entry to all Europe—that is, the Six—from the date of Britain's acceptance.

This would not only have safeguarded exports of tea to the British market, but would have opened up the markets of the Community as a whole, and when we realise what a high proportion tea represents of these countries' exports and, consequently, of their earnings of foreign exchange, we realise the full measure of these lost opportunities.

In the case of those manufactured goods which are of special importance to India, Pakistan and Hong Kong, we had hoped, by the negotiation of comprehensive trade agreements, to inaugurate in Europe as a whole a move towards

[1] *H.C. deb.*, vol. 671, cc. 943–61.

those advantages which we in Britain have given to these Commonwealth countries, often at very great sacrifice to ourselves.

Let us turn to Africa and the Caribbean. The Lord Privy Seal negotiated an agreement for association should they wish to take it, under which almost all of their raw materials and tropical foodstuffs would have entered freely to this great European market. Most of the new African countries were unwilling, for political reasons, to accept association. But I feel sure that as the years had gone on this process would have developed. Already, some of the West Indian countries have seen the advantages of association and some, undoubtedly, would have accepted it from the beginning.

As regards the old Commonwealth countries, perhaps the most important question facing Canada, Australia and New Zealand in the field of temperate foodstuffs is the hope of being able to negotiate world commodity agreements. It is clear that our absence from the Community will weaken the forces working for reasonable prices and limiting artificial stimulation of production, and this will make commodity agreements correspondingly more difficult. On other items, too, while there was to have been, of course, a gradual disappearance of the preferences and some products which now enter this country free of duty would gradually have become dutiable, it should not be thought that all free entry would have been eliminated.

Many of the most important commodities of Commonwealth producers, such as wool and jute, would still have been duty free. Where items become subject to duty, the loss of the duty-free entry into Britain would have been compensated —perhaps more than compensated—by the reduction of duty in the whole European market. These were the direct benefits. Moreover, all the Commonwealth countries recognised, and made clear at our conference that they recognised, the necessarily limited character of the British market. They accepted the advantage of strengthening the wealth and resilience of that market over the years as well as seeking new outlets elsewhere.

Considerable difficulties must follow for some of the E.F.T.A. countries. The case of Denmark is a particular one because of the character of her food exports, divided between Britain and Germany. The case of Austria also presents a special problem. Yet, broadly speaking, in spite of the difficulty of taking care of every single individual interest, the E.F.T.A. countries were looking forward to entering into the Community with us. I think it right to underline these advantages, not merely for Britain but for the Commonwealth and the E.F.T.A. countries, which would have followed a successful negotiation.

Having said that, let us now turn to the future. First the Commonwealth. In our discussions over the last eighteen months I think that we have all studied with greater precision than ever before the character of Commonwealth trade. It is sometimes argued that some form of free trade or common market could be developed among the Commonwealth countries. Even sixty years ago, when these ideas were first put forward, when the independent Commonwealth countries were confined to very few, and Britain was solely responsible for all the Colonial Empire, such a plan was found to be impracticable and unacceptable. Far more so today.

The Commonwealth cannot be a single economic unit in the sense of any other trading community like, let us say, the United States or the Common Market.

It is not only the mere separation by distance; this could be overcome. It is quite a different sort of obstacle. The different stages of industrial development, and the different sorts of trade which meet the needs of individual Commonwealth countries, make it impossible for them all to be unified with us in a free trade area.

Some have very high tariffs, some very low. Some are at the beginning of their industrialisation, some are far advanced. Some are determined to protect—as they have the perfect right to do—their nascent industries with high protective tariffs, and would not for a moment accept what they would call being flooded by cheaper products from Britain. This is true of Australia, Canada and, to some extent of New Zealand.

That is not to say that trade between Britain and the Commonwealth countries cannot be extended. It must be. It is only to say that a uniform system cannot be applied between the Commonwealth countries because of those variations which, on the political and moral side, represent the strength of the Commonwealth. This is an attitude which is shared by all the Commonwealth countries. It means, therefore, that neither an immediate Commonwealth Prime Ministers' conference, nor any other conference, could devise, either in their interests or in ours, a substitute for what we had hoped to obtain, for us and for them, from Europe. It is for this reason that it does not seem right at this stage to suggest a Commonwealth Prime Ministers' conference.

This view is shared by Mr. Menzies and Mr. Holyoake, and I think that it would be accepted by most of the Commonwealth Prime Ministers. What we must do in the Commonwealth falls into two categories: first, individual consultation where special arrangements are under review, or there are trade agreements to be made or renewed; secondly, general consultation for any problem in which we can play a joint part. With regard to the first, I shall have an opportunity to see the Prime Minister of Canada at the end of this month and I hope that Mr. Menzies, and Mr. Holyoake will be able to come over soon.

As regards the second, that is where we could have a co-operative approach, there is a special field in which we could work together and that is the approach to some of the problems presented by the various world agreements. The main hope which we now have in this field is in making effective the so-called Kennedy Round. We hope that this can soon begin. We have, therefore, proposed a meeting of Commonwealth Trade Ministers shortly before the time of the coming ministerial session of G.A.T.T. It is hoped that the G.A.T.T. session will take place in the early summer.

We have suggested that this Commonwealth meeting should be held in London and it will provide an opportunity not only for discussing questions in relation to the Kennedy Round, where we can all, I hope, get together, but other economic matters of common interest. I have sent those messages and so far as I have seen the replies there seems to be general hope that such a conference may meet. In addition, this conference will enable us to carry on discussions and negotiations on an individual or bilateral basis. I hope that we shall be able to arrange this conference. It is, of course, in line with the recent statement of Mr. Diefenbaker in the Canadian Parliament and, I think, with the thinking of all the Commonwealth Prime Ministers.

We in Britain are prepared to play our part fully in reducing our own tariffs if we can get comparable benefits for our export markets. As exporters our main interests are in the field of industrial products. The Kennedy Round will be concerned not only with the duties of industrial products, but also, we hope, with trade and agricultural products of no less interest to the Commonwealth.

International trade in temperate agricultural products is at present affected not only by tariffs, but also by a variety of protective devices which are themselves the reflection of various policies of protecting or subsidising domestic producers in both exporting and importing countries. These policies, combined with technical advances in all the producing countries, have aggravated the problems of the trade in temperate agricultural foodstuffs.

In our new situation we have, of course, to be particularly careful from the balance of payments point of view and conscious of the economic disadvantages of uncompensated price increases. This turns upon the degree of compensation in the negotiations. Also important are the obstacles to trade of less-developed countries, and, here again, it is not merely a question of tariffs but also a question of quantitative restrictions and revenue duties which inhibit the growth of trade not only in primary tropical products, but also in manufactured goods.

Commodity agreements to avoid excessive price fluctuations are, as we all know, a great hope which we had, and still have, for benefiting the economies of these countries. Since the war we have worked for international agreements on particular commodities—wheat, sugar, coffee, tin and now, we hope, the cocoa agreement will be completed. The Kennedy Round will be of crucial importance. We must work with enthusiasm to make it succeed. This means good will, as well as skilful negotiation. The United States, the Community and, indeed, all countries will have to accept, in spite of all internal pressures, the reduction of tariffs on a wide basis, if we are to succeed.

Turning to E.F.T.A., there is to be a Council meeting on 18th February,[1] and the House will not expect me to go into detail. As the House knows, E.F.T.A. has two broad purposes. It already offers a wide area of reduced tariffs among an important grouping of trading nations. Beyond this, we have always seen it as a step towards a fully integrated European market. These objects are not inconsistent. In practice, the E.F.T.A. countries have pursued them simultaneously.

Let us look first at the broader objective. A fully integrated European market could be attained in one of two ways, either by the establishment of a free trade area embracing the countries of E.E.C. and E.F.T.A., or by the negotiation by the individual member countries of E.F.T.A. of arrangements for membership of the Community or association with it.

So far, these efforts have proved abortive, in 1957 and 1958, as the House knows, because of the exclusion of agriculture, and now because of the breakdown of the Brussels conference. Nevertheless, the E.F.T.A. countries will seek to extend their trade and develop their association together on the lines provided in the Stockholm Convention. At the same time, they will no doubt seek to increase their exports to the countries of the Community as well as to other countries. We must, by all practical means within our power, preserve and strengthen the fabric of European trade until such a time as the obstacles preventing the establishment of a market, fully integrated, are removed and in this task the support of our E.F.T.A. partners will be of the greatest value.

[1] See p. 74 below.

I should like to say something, if the House will bear with me, about another of the problems which we have been discussing so much in recent months—that of home agriculture. Everyone will realise that this part of the Treaty of Rome presented great difficulties, both as regards our problems here at home and, of course, those of the old Commonwealth countries. It is no good discussing now the details of various approaches which either had been agreed or might have been agreed to resolve them. Nevertheless, the problem remains as regards our own country.

I think that the whole agricultural community recognises that whatever may be the different views about the so-called managed market, towards which we could have worked had we joined the Six, the present system of open-ended subsidy on a number of items, combined with free entry often at far lower prices, has serious drawbacks.

We must try to cure these defects without losing sight of our main purpose—a fair standard of living for the agricultural community, a strong and prosperous agricultural industry, and also, may I add, one which is all the time improving its methods both as to production and as to distribution. The record of the industry since the war is, indeed, remarkable. Improved agricultural techniques and the considerable inflow of capital into agriculture have, of course, benefited the industry and they have also been the foundation of one of the best of all our exports—the agricultural machinery industry.

However, it is the object that matters, and the methods must be looked at, of course, from time to time. The mere fact that the Common Market negotiations have failed does not relieve us of this responsibility or the need to fit our agricultural policy into overseas trading arrangements. We have been saying for some time now—my right hon. Friend the Minister of Agriculture has said it on many occasions—that, whether we join the Common Market or not, some changes in our support system are inevitable. The amount of agricultural support, particularly the Exchequer's open-ended commitment, must be brought under greater control.

My right hon. Friend the Minister will be ready, beginning at this year's Price Review and continuing thereafter, to discuss with agricultural representatives what can be done, in the full spirit of our pledges, to work out new and constructive ideas. Many of these steps will, of course, involve special consultation and special agreements with our overseas suppliers, including the Commonwealth countries. . . .

Turning to the general effect of the Brussels breakdown upon our British economy, I know that some economists have differed as to the value which we should obtain or would have obtained by entering the Common Market. Nevertheless, I think that most economists, and certainly the mass of business opinion in this country, had no doubt about the balance of advantage. Some feared certain pressures upon the balance of payments which might develop from an increase in the cost of food imports. Others feared a corresponding increase in the cost of British industrial products. But, broadly speaking, the great majority were looking forward eagerly and enthusiastically to this new adventure.

We shall not now obtain automatically the larger market for which we had hoped. At least, we shall not obtain it on the favourable terms for which we had hoped. But that certainly does not mean that we cannot win it by our own efforts. Our sales to Europe have shown very remarkable increases, and that in spite of the tariff. We have already leapt over the wall and if, as we hope, the collective decision of the Six keeps the tariff reasonably low, then it should not be more insurmountable than in the past. But it will be there, and we must, therefore, face that fact and try to reduce our internal costs by all possible means.

We must enlarge our own home market by all the measures of expansion which can increase consumer demand without undue pressure upon imports. I will not embark today on the great economic problem of how to expand without inflation—[HON. MEMBERS: 'Oh.']—but, whatever may be the views of hon. Members, there is, undoubtedly accepted by all serious students, one vital condition for a lasting solution. That is to adopt in principle and make effective in practice a reasonable incomes policy. At any rate, we must now try to increase consumer demand as the basis for the export demand.

We shall have to do it in conditions where we shall not have the competitive stimulus of European exports into this country which the open, free competition would have provided, and we must, therefore, provide the stimulus ourselves. This can be done partly by modernising the structure of industry and partly by encouraging a general climate of competition at home. In addition, it is becoming more and more recognised that the old concept of every man starting in one industry and spending his whole life in the same industry may have to be changed as industries and techniques change——

Mr. E. Shinwell (Easington): It is changing.

The Prime Minister: It has changed and is changing and this brings the need for plans based on a wide scale to deal with the need for workers to move from one industry to another. My right hon. Friend the Minister of Labour has already made certain proposals for industrial retraining. This is only a start and I believe that we shall be able to develop wider schemes especially in those areas where some radical changes must be faced in the character of industry.

But success or failure will depend more than ever on the future of British exports. On the whole, at present British prices compare not unfavourably with the general European level. If we can expand at home without destroying this equilibrium, our exports should have a fine chance of going across the tariff barriers, wherever they may be, in the Six, or the United States, or in the Commonwealth, or indeed, in any other country in the world. Since we now have to carry rather more burdens than we expected, at least in Europe more than we had hoped for, we must not handicap ourselves unduly in the future.

It is natural that in the present situation we should look again at the whole question of export incentives. I must warn the House that this is a very difficult and complicated matter. So far as direct subsidies are concerned, we have spent a long time trying to get agreements between the main trading nations against export subsidies in any form and in this we have been remarkably successful. Since we depend so much more heavily on exports than do others, it is clearly in our interests to maintain and strengthen this policy.

The same is broadly true of tax relief. Nevertheless, it may be possible to find methods of helping exporters which do not conflict with the undertakings into which we have entered and done so much to persuade other countries to accept. Meanwhile, we have made a tremendous improvement, even during the last eighteen months or so, in the flexibility of our export credits system. What has been done is shown by the volume of orders obtained by British firms with the support of the export credits system. By 1959, they were running at over £600 million. By 1962, they had risen to nearly £900 million.

Of course, our export drive must be made from a sound internal base. Tremendous changes have been brought about by technical development. This has involved a shrinking of some industries and an overall expansion of new industry. Nevertheless, it would be a mistake to suppose that the older industries have no prospects before them. Apart from other measures which may be taken, great improvements have been made by the best-organised shipbuilding firms and there are signs of much better co-operation between employers and trade unions and, what is equally important, between the trade unions themselves.

There are also quite new techniques just ahead of us. The House has taken much interest in the prospect of a nuclear merchant ship. We have always been anxious, not merely to build a nuclear engine which could propel a ship—that, of course, can easily be done—but the Atomic Energy Authority and its experts have been concentrating on how to get a nuclear reactor which is economically attractive. We are now getting very near to this point. My right hon. Friend the Minister of Transport will very soon be discussing with all those concerned the arrangements for the construction, ownership and operation of such a vessel.

To sum up on the economic side. First, we have proposed a conference of Commonwealth Trade Ministers. Secondly, we shall work for close co-operation with the Commonwealth, the United States, E.F.T.A. and we hope the Six, for the Kennedy Round. Next we shall maintain our E.F.T.A. association. We shall work for world commodity agreements. At home we shall work for an expanding economy, without inflation, based upon an incomes policy.

Finally, we will accept and encourage changes in the technique and structure of industry while paying particular attention to areas of temporary unemployment. If the breakdown of this long negotiation is a serious set-back, it is one which, as so often before in our history, we are confident we shall be able to overcome.

Mr. Harold Davies (Leek): I am grateful to the Prime Minister for giving way. From this plan for the expansion of trade, on which hon. Members on both side of the House will agree, I have noticed one omission. That is a reference to the economies of Africa, Asia, China, Eastern Europe and the rest of the Communist world, which are expanding whether we like it or not. What plans have the Government for a new and dynamic approach to these new countries, which have awakening expectations? We have heard not a word about that.

The Prime Minister: The discussions which I have called the Kennedy Round are among the members of the G.A.T.T. We have tried to do, and have also done, a great deal to expand our trade with various Communist countries which do not trade in our way but trade by barter agreement—Poland, Russia and, to some extent, China—and that, where possible, we shall continue.

I now turn to a consideration of some of the political conclusions which one might draw from what has happened. We do not need, in my view, at any rate, to reproach ourselves about the manner in which the present phase closed. It is the end of a chapter, though not, in my view, necessarily the end of the whole volume. The negotiations did not break down, as they might have done, on a long-drawn-out series of detailed bargains.

If the European vision has been obscured, it has not been by a minor obstruction on one side or the other. It was brought to an end by a dramatic, if somewhat brutal, stroke of policy. As I said in my broadcast the next day, the end did not come because the discussions were menaced with failure. On the contrary, it was because they threatened to succeed. That the French Government, in their hearts, had long feared success I do not now doubt, but I had always hoped that they might be animated by two considerations: first, by the underlying good will that undoubtedly links France and Britain. This friendship is very deep between our peoples, and the links have been forged in the purging fire of war, twice in my lifetime, during terrible years when Britain and France suffered side by side.

Secondly, I had hoped that the French Government would be unwilling to place themselves in the public position of opposing the will of all their colleagues in the Community and, indeed, of disappointing the hopes of every country in the free world. Of course, they may have hoped that the responsibility for this decision would not have to be placed upon their shoulders. They may have felt that the British Government would not be able to carry their policy forward, either through their party or through the assent of the Commonwealth, or through the House of Commons. But when these expectations began to fail the head of the French Government decided to act.

Even so, there was some confusion in the method. So many different reasons were given for Britain's exclusion—that she is an island; that our people were not sufficiently European-minded; that we do not accept the Treaty of Rome— a statement wholly incorrect: that the Nassau Agreement on Polaris was a sudden and unexpected blow—equally incorrect. It was clear that none of these reasons was the real one.

It was common knowledge that the whole French Government had every expectation that the negotiations would be carried through successfully. M. Pompidou, the French Prime Minister, was reported in the French Press as having told a group of journalists as late as 11th January—that is, three days before the matter was brought to a sudden close that France desired to see Great Britain join the Six and accede to the Common Market. Other French Ministers had given us similar assurances in private discussions at much the same time.

The French Government have taken their decision and it would be wrong to ignore the division of purpose which has grown up between us—for a time, at any rate. Of course we wish to continue close relations with France, but it is right that it should be clearly understood that we will do all we can to secure that the Community develops liberal and outward-looking policies and that we shall sustain the efforts and determination of our friends in the Community to work to this end. We have, therefore, to bear in mind the loyalty that we owe to the other nations of Europe which have stood so firmly by us and on whose continued strength of purpose the hope of Europe must now largely depend.

I ought perhaps to refer to the decision to advise Her Royal Highness Princess Margaret to cancel her forthcoming visit to Paris. We here at home are so used to our Head of State and the Royal Family standing scrupulously aloof from day-to-day political affairs that we tend to forget that abroad other considerations obtain. There is no doubt that foreign countries regard royal visits as having a political significance, and, indeed, it is natural that they should. Although this particular visit was, in the main, of an unofficial nature, it was bound, in the circumstances, to assume a semi-official character. [HON. MEMBERS: 'Oh.'] So soon after recent events a Royal visit and entertainment at the Elysée seemed hardly timely just at this moment. . . .

Apart from any question of possible embarrassment, such an occasion must have been given a significance which would have been misunderstood, both in France and in the countries of Europe. Now that the entry of Britain into Europe has been barred by a decision of principle, a decision which, I think, in all common fairness, might have been taken long ago, not after fourteen months of negotiation——

Mr. Harold Wilson (Huyton): We shall deal later with the petty and peevish decision to cancel the Royal visit. Will the Prime Minister, now that he has said that the reason was the political effects of such a visit, kindly tell the House why the Government put out the statement last week that it had nothing to do with that and was a question of maintaining an adequate number of Counsellors of State in this country?

The Prime Minister: I think that it was in full accordance with diplomatic courtesies and usages to use that form of words.

We have now been barred by a decision which I think in fairness might have been taken fourteen months ago. We cannot hide from ourselves, therefore, that a situation has arisen more serious and with deeper implications than the mere breakdown of an economic plan. It would be wrong not to express frankly to the House and to the country some of the apprehensions which we feel. There have always been two ways of looking at European unity.

There are those who felt that the continental countries, which were so battered by the war, should get together primarily with a view to their reconstruction, and that was natural. It is true that, had it not been for the generous American aid under the Marshall Plan, all these ambitions would have come to nothing or been much delayed; but by the help of the allies in their policies towards the defeated countries—for instance, in the constitution of Federal Germany and, as I have said, by generous outside aid—the first emphasis was, naturally, upon internal reconstruction.

On the Continent, the founders of the European movement were, among many other distinguished men, Dr. Adenauer, Signor de Gasperi, M. Schuman, M. Spaak, M. Monnet, and many others. Nor did Britain stand apart. The British Foreign Secretary of the day, Mr. Bevin, gave every help, including the signature of the Brussels Treaty. My right hon. Friend the Member for Woodford (Sir W. Churchill) took himself a leading rôle in the movement and played a dramatic part.

At the beginning, Europeans were, naturally, in a sense obsessed by their own problems. For many years France depended upon outside aid and her adverse balance of payments had to be supported by monetary arrangements with her partners in the European Payments Union. Her technical and industrial recovery and reconstruction were largely due to the work of M. Monnet and his team.

As Europe's revival began to succeed, the European outlook began to widen. There were some—there are some—who have kept the narrow view, who still seem to regard a united Europe as a restricted or autarchic community on a protectionist basis; in other words, they would like a community which would retain all the errors of high protectionism which had often been the policy of some of the constituent nations. That is not the vision of the European movement as a whole. It is not, happily, the view of the five countries which have stood so loyally by our side. It is certainly not our view. It is not the view of our E.F.T.A. partners. It is not the view of the older Commonwealth countries. And it is certainly wholly contrary to the interests of the younger Commonwealth countries. In spite of the long tradition of protectionism in the United States, it is not the view of the American Administration and the forward-looking people of the United States. This narrower concept is, therefore, in a true sense a reactionary view.

One of the main reasons why there was such universal support for our entry was the belief of our friends, as well as many of our critics, that Britain, added to this company, would give as well as take, that she would contribute to the tradition of outward-looking development. If the French Government object to us as an island, it is also as an island that we bring this rich heritage to the world.

So much for what I would call the economic philosophy. I am convinced that in spite of the disappointments, which none of us can conceal, what we have done in the last years is not and will not be in vain. There is, as a result of these negotiations, a far greater understanding between European countries, certainly between the Five and ourselves. There is, as a result of the day-to-day contact with the Commonwealth countries, a more accurate and a more balanced view of the economic possibilities, both the difficulties and the prospects. The same is true of the E.F.T.A. countries. All this is good and, at least, some compensation.

Here, I think, it would be right to pay a tribute to the German, Italian, Dutch, Belgian and Luxembourg Ministers, who worked so hard and so persistently and were frustrated by the veto and by nothing else. As a result of this experience, there is, I believe, a greater degree of understanding and sympathy than ever before. I found it so in Rome when I was there the other day. I believe that German opinion has never been so universally on our side in this matter as it is today, and here, perhaps, I may be allowed to make a plea for the future.

It is natural that there should be lingering in our country a certain reserve—the memories of two wars are not lightly wiped out—but the German people are also sensitive over this, and in my view great harm can be done by ungenerous attitudes, whether in the Press or among any of us. Curiously enough, I have observed that this feeling is often strongest amongst people who have taken the least active part in these great struggles.

I remember very well the doubt expressed when a German regiment was coming over for training in Wales. In fact, it was received, as might have been foreseen, by ordinary people with good will and friendship. The truth is that just as good Anglo-French relations and a close co-operation between us and the people of France are fervently desired here, we also recognise that the fruitful development of Anglo-German relations should be one of the props on which the unity of Europe must depend.

With the peoples of the Benelux countries we have long and historic links, and the memory of troubles shared is poignant and strong. They were particularly anxious for Britain to join, and to join in time. This was not merely because of our mutual friendship, but because it corresponds to what throughout history has been their deepest interest.

Why have the Five Powers shown such anxiety and such emotion? Partly, perhaps, because of their genuine sympathy and wish to work in with Britain; partly because they share our economic and political point of view about the future of Europe, and, therefore, thought that the Community would be strengthened by our adhesion. But there are other anxieties, and deeper anxieties, in the political field that also trouble them. First, there is the suspicion that one of their partners wants to unite Europe on a sham basis. They and we have had enough of this idea that Europe could be united by a single nation or a single man, not on a basis of agreement, partnership or co-operation, but on a basis of power.

At present, European institutions—and, indeed, all the institutions we have created—depend in their early stages on unanimity, although later on, in many respects, a different system of voting is developed. At present, the strength of the French Government's position depends on the veto—the principle that one black ball excludes. So, in negotiations undertaken by the Community, whether at G.A.T.T. or elsewhere, there is a danger that the position of stalemate may be repeated.

Another aspect of French policy has equally alarmed the old world and the new—the tendency to treat the N.A.T.O. Alliance with a certain selectiveness, to say the least. Of course, during the great difficulties of France and Algeria, which are happily dealt with, everyone understood that, but now there have been very many other cases. France's refusal to let her navy play any part in N.A.T.O. plans and, still more important, in a way, her refusal to join in N.A.T.O.'s air defence arrangements, has left a serious gap in that system.

As I say, some of these aspects of French policy we can understand, but they are continuing, and they may develop. It is, therefore, inevitable that people are beginning to wonder whether these are not indications of a policy which, if it were pursued, would bring the whole Western Alliance into great jeopardy, if not collapse.

In the great balance of actual power today we all know that the nuclear strength of America is and must remain essential, but a common alliance must be based on mutual respect. Naturally, the great countries of the old world which, at different periods of their history, have held unique or commanding positions, sometimes suffer from a certain nostalgia. As regards our own country, it is a sentiment certainly inapplicable today as, indeed, it was in most of the most inspiring periods of our history. But this feeling represents what is really a weakness and not a strength of human nature. It is curiously similar, this jealousy— for it is only that—to that emotion which makes many people more able to forget an injury than to forgive a benefit.

I do not want to exaggerate these tendencies, but it is because of them that we in this country must do all we can to range ourselves and the influence we have on the right side. We have, partly as the result of the outcome of Brussels, partly because of the growing anxiety in Europe, the great majority of the countries of Europe in one way or another ranged on our side in this matter. These anxieties do not merely affect this island, or Europe, or even the whole of the N.A.T.O. Alliance.

For the European nations, whether in or out of N.A.T.O., and those on the periphery—above all, the Scandinavians—anything that threatens the Western Alliance, and particularly its organisation in N.A.T.O., must be a source of deep alarm. No countries have more reason to fear than these should there be an agonising reappraisal of the American position. No countries have more to lose should America, under any Administration, be almost forced into isolation by the slighting attitude of Europe and European statesmen.

With regard to the old Commonwealth countries, Canada has a leading and powerful rôle in N.A.T.O. Australia and New Zealand, however great the contribution they are able to make to their defence, must, in fact, depend for their safety on the co-operation between Britain and America—and indeed, these two countries have entered into their own alliance with the United States.

These assets are fundamental and we shall try by all means to keep them alive and thus to rally European opinion for the future. I do not mean that we look forward to an early resumption of these particular negotiations for Britain's entry into the Community. That is impossible. This is not a kind of business deal that, if it fails one week, can be taken up the next. It is, for good or ill, a great historic event. It cannot be disregarded, but its importance and, perhaps, its permanence, must not be exaggerated. While it would be absurd not to recognise with our heads that Britain's entry is not now capable of early realisation, we should surely strive to keep the vision in our hearts.

These, then, are the major lessons to be learned from what has happened in the political field, but until the day comes—and we pray that it may come some day—when the great gulf between East and West can be bridged, the fundamental principle of our policy must be summed up in a single phrase, 'On the strength and unity of the Western Alliance depends the peace of the world'.

Statement by the Lord Privy Seal, Mr. Heath, to the House of Commons, 12 February 1963[1] (extract)

... I now turn to the present position. We recognise that the way to full membership is at present barred. It is a great loss to the Community countries as well. The Five countries recognise that, but it is also a loss to France, and they recognise that their farmers will not be able now to obtain a share of the British market. They recognise, too, that the likelihood of getting world commodity agreements at good prices in cereals is much less. This was fully recognised throughout the negotiations.

The question asked was whether there could be some other relationship short of full membership. No alternative arrangements have been offered to us by the Community and it does not lie in the hands of one country to offer that. In particular, the French Government have never discussed this question with us, either privately or in the negotiations. They have never explained what President de Gaulle meant by 'association',[2] but they mentioned it to many other people

[1] *H.C. deb.*, vol. 671, cc. 1155–62.

[2] See President de Gaulle's press conference of 14 January 1963; *Documents, 1962*, esp. p. 494.

as long ago as last spring. We recognised it then as a kite being flown to see whether we were prepared to accept just the economic arrangements, so that it could be said that we had no genuine interest in the political union of Europe. I have often explained our reasons, both the political and the economic ones. Those criteria were always before us during the negotiations and any alternative must be judged against those criteria; political and economic.

Some hon. Members have talked of association; broadly speaking, the position is this. Full membership gives one all one's rights in all the activities of the Community. As an associate one does not have such rights. One tries to use one's influence and these facts must be weighed in the balance if or when any alternative arrangement is put forward. I do not wish to go further into the details of this, but I think that we agree on three things.

First, if there is to be any alternative arrangement, whatever it may be, it must come from the whole Community. Secondly, it cannot involve another long set of negotiations; and that point was made by the Opposition Front Bench yesterday. Thirdly, the good faith of all those in the negotiations must be demonstrated from the beginning. The will to succeed must be there, as apparently it was not there in our negotiations for full membership. If any alternative is put forward in this way then, of course, it is bound to receive consideration.

What of future developments of another kind? The right hon. Gentleman the Leader—[*Laughter.*]—the right hon. Gentleman the Member for Huyton castigated my right hon. Friend yesterday for, as he said, not putting forward any alternative proposals. But what happened when he himself came to that point? He did not propose any alternatives. What he said was:

'What we are really discussing today is not a packaged alternative to the Common Market, but a plan for the future of Britain. . . .'—[OFFICIAL REPORT, 11th February, 1963; Vol. 671, c. 967.]

The right hon. Gentleman put forward a list of countries with which we could trade—incidentally, the list was already known to us—and various other minor proposals.

Surely the important point is that we continue to develop trade on a multilateral basis. Everything that the hon. Member for Cardiff, South-East said confirms that the basis for our trade should be multilateral agreements. I know that some of my hon. Friends do not agree with this and would like to see increased development of a preferential area, but that is not the basis on which our trade has been developing since the war. It is interesting to note that whereas, in 1938, our exports and re-exports covered less than 60 per cent. of the cost of our imports, in 1955, under multilateral trading arrangements, they covered 75 per cent., and by 1962 88 per cent. That is in the multilateral trading world.

We have been asked to play our full part in the Kennedy Round. Of course, we shall do that. I did not quite understand the right hon. Gentleman's point about everyone sitting on one side of the table with the Community on the other. Surely the confrontation is bound to be between the United States and the Community, because they are the two major economic forces, and we play our part in addition—and the Commonwealth, of course. It would have been a better balance if we and the E.F.T.A. countries had become members of the Community—Norway and Denmark; but that has not come about.

I want to say one word about the effect of the Kennedy Round. It has never been our intention, although this has been said in European capitals, that Europe should be swamped by American goods or American goods dumped in Europe as a result of action taken under the Kennedy Round. There must be a fair balance. I do not wish to deal with trade in other parts of the world and the Commonwealth, because that was dealt with by my right hon. Friend the Prime Minister and my right hon. Friend the Secretary of State for Commonwealth Relations yesterday, but I want now to deal with E.F.T.A. and with the E.E.C. in particular.

Mr. Philip Noel-Baker (Derby, South): Before the right hon. Gentleman leaves the subject of the Kennedy Round, he should not imply that we shall not take our full part in all these negotiations. Is it not a fact that as an exporting and importing nation we are much more important than the United States?

Mr. Heath: I am afraid that the right hon. Gentleman has missed my remarks. Of course we will play our full part in the Kennedy Round, but the two main groups are bound to be the United States and the Community.

Mr. P. Noel-Baker: Why?

Mr. Heath: Because of their size and their tariff structures. But that does not alter the fact that we shall play our full part.

I turn now to E.F.T.A. The right hon. Member for Huyton said that we should strengthen the links in E.F.T.A., but he did not explain what that meant.

Mr. H. Wilson: The right hon. Gentleman knows perfectly well.

Mr. Heath: I do not. It was a metaphorical description which seemed to bear no relation to reality.

I will tell the right hon. Gentleman what we should do in E.F.T.A. It is to expand the trade among E.F.T.A. countries and to build it up on the basis of the Stockholm Convention. British industrialists have never taken full advantage of the E.F.T.A. markets because of the lure of the Common Market itself, and it is now time that they did.

Mr. H. Wilson: What about the Commonwealth?

Mr. Heath: I had said that as my right hon. Friend has already dealt with the Commonwealth, I propose to deal with E.F.T.A. and the E.E.C.

At the E.F.T.A. meeting, we can discuss this development of trade. I hope that at least we shall continue to keep pace with the Community in tariff changes. I recognise, too, that Denmark and Norway will want to discuss agriculture and fisheries at these meetings and we have an understanding of the difficulties of these two countries. I believe, too, that there should be a greater appreciation in the E.F.T.A. countries themselves and not only in the United States, where it exists, of the opportunities available for trade there.

We must also recognise that, as a result of the break-up of the Brussels negotiations, businessmen will not gain the advantages of an immense home market, nor—and this was the point which was overlooked by the right hon. Gentleman—the advantages of certainty in that very large market. Therefore, the effort required will be all the greater.

I come to the question of our future relations with Europe. The European Economic Community will remain the largest and strongest grouping in Europe. It has sustained a severe blow to its confidence, but it will continue to develop according to its plan. Our desire has always been to join wholeheartedly in the building of a wider Europe and to do nothing to obstruct it, and this attitude will continue to govern our policy. We start with all the important assets which we gained in the negotiations. We have to keep open and enlarge the channels of communication and consultation and we shall seek to co-ordinate our policies with the Community as far as possible.

In the economic field, we shall expand and strengthen the permanent mission to the European Communities, not only with the Foreign Office element, but also with representatives from other Whitehall Departments. We shall maintain close contact with them, enabling both the Community and ourselves to take account of each other's interests. Secondly, we shall make more intensive use of bilateral machinery. Already, Anglo-German, Anglo-Italian and Anglo-French machinery exists. Thirdly, I hope that firms and trade associations in this country will strengthen and develop their contacts with the Commission and with their opposite numbers in Europe. Not only will that help exports, but it will help to safeguard our interests in the developing Community.

On the political side, since the breakup we have discussed political co-operation with the majority of members in the Community and they agree that it is urgent that there should be closer political arrangements between us. I described the Europe we would like to see in my speech to Western European Union in April last year[1]—strong and stable, a more equal partnership in N.A.T.O. with the United States, outward looking, associated with all its former friends and territories. We wanted to strengthen Europe, not to make it lose its distinctive European characteristics, but to enable it to play its part in the West as a whole.

The right hon. Gentleman asked how this should be done. He proposed a conference of the heads of all the European countries, and he brought in Yugoslavia, but missed out Spain. I am not arguing, but perhaps the right hon. Gentleman will not describe it as 'all' the European countries. What are they to do when they meet? For many of them it would be embarrassing, for neutral countries who never wish to take part in general political co-operation.

However, where I do agree with him is that we can use O.E.C.D., not, as he seemed to suggest, on the political side, but on the economic side. This is not an original suggestion, of course.

We have begun to examine with our friends the question of the machinery to be used for political co-operation and I agree with the right hon. Gentleman that the first forum must be N.A.T.O. However, consultation in N.A.T.O. does not exclude a full measure of agreement between those in Europe who think alike on these questions.

At the W.E.U. meeting I said that a general view of European defence might emerge in a wider Europe. That is still our view. During the last few weeks the Nassau Agreement[2] and the work which is now in train to give effect to that agreement have strengthened the Atlantic Alliance by giving it a nuclear capacity for the first time. They have also strengthened the European voice in the Alliance since N.A.T.O. forces are to be targetted in accordance with N.A.T.O. requirements.

[1] 10 April 1962; see *Documents, 1962*, pp. 460–4.
[2] Joint statement by President Kennedy and Mr. Macmillan, Nassau, 21 December 1962; see *Documents, 1962*, pp. 482–7.

Whatever is said elsewhere, the policy of Nassau is certainly not in contradiction with our European policy. Indeed, the Nassau Agreement has been warmly welcomed by the majority of our allies in Europe.

Side by side with N.A.T.O., we have other European organisations, exclusively European, of which we are members. Western European Union is the only formal point of political consultation between all seven Powers recently engaged in the Brussels talks.

There is much to be said for maintaining our relations with our friends through an existing organisation. I see that Dr. Schroeder, in the Bundestag last week, took the view that if there were to be a meeting in Western European Union it should be to seek more progress than could be achieved by bilateral talks.[1] With that I agree. I believe that W.E.U. can contribute positively to the present situation. But we should also make use of all the opportunities available, including the Council of Europe for cultural matters. Our attitude is widely reciprocated in Europe. We are encouraged by this, and we shall do everything possible to move closer to the European countries and to work with them to create the sort of Europe that we want to see.

To sum up. The work on which we have been engaged, and in which we have been trying to get a wider unity in Europe between the Community and E.F.T.A. countries, with far-reaching connections with the Commonwealth and the associated States, has had an immense appeal for our people. Why should that have been so? It is because it seemed to them, in some way—with all its imperfections—to be looking towards a better society in Europe as a whole, because it seemed to be working for something which was bigger than themselves and, above all, because it gave them a sense of purpose.

Of course there have been divisions in the country. There have been many honourable opponents, and there have been others who, alas, have played upon the people's natural fears of change. They have played upon these fears and upon old national hatreds. But it has been the great debate of modern times, and the debate will continue, because the relationships between ourselves and Europe are bound to be of the greatest concern both to ourselves and to the Continent.

What the House has been discussing is what our sense of purpose is today. Many have spoken of the need for this, but few have ventured to define it. The hon. Member for Pembroke (Mr. Donnelly), however, in a speech which I admired, did endeavour to do so. Our purpose must be to develop the potentialities we have along the lines that we have been discussing in this debate and to do so with determination, with clear thinking and with far-sightedness—to strip away pretence, and to live up to the standards of our own integrity. That must be our purpose in the phase which is now opening before us.

Right hon. Gentlemen opposite say that after the breakdown in Brussels Her Majesty's Government cannot tackle this task. In fact, the reverse is the case. We can do it the better, knowing that we did everything possible to achieve success in the venture on which we embarked in Brussels. We have nothing with which to reproach ourselves. It was through no fault of ours that the venture was brought to nought. Thus we can go forward, with a clear heart and mind, and with determination and ability, to deal with the tasks which lie ahead.

[1] The remarks of the Federal German Foreign Minister were made on 7 February 1963, during the Federal Government's foreign policy debate.

Communiqué of the E.F.T.A. Council of Ministers, Geneva, 19 February 1963[1]

The EFTA Ministerial Council met in Geneva on 18th and 19th February under the Chairmanship of Mr. Correia de Oliveira, Portuguese Minister of State.

The Lord Privy Seal informed the Ministers of the circumstances in which the members of the European Economic Community had been prevented from continuing the negotiation with the United Kingdom. Ministers took note of this and regretted the setback which this meant in achieving the economic integration of Europe. They reaffirmed their aim, as declared in the Preamble of the Stockholm Convention, of working together to promote the creation of a large unified European market which would be outward-looking towards the rest of the world.

For the present, however, the Association's task must be to provide a further stimulus to trade by pursuing the dismantlement of barriers between the members. This was important not only in the interest of creating a wide and flourishing market among themselves but also in order to provide a strong base from which to play their full part in the development of multilateral trade throughout the world.

Accordingly, the Ministers agreed on the broad lines of EFTA's future development. They instructed the permanent representatives to prepare a programme of action to be put into effect after consideration and decision by a further Ministerial meeting. This mandate extends to all the fields of action covered by the Stockholm Convention, and includes in particular the revision of the remainder of the time-table for tariff reductions providing for the more rapid dismantlement of tariffs with their final elimination during 1966. Similarly the mandate covers the arrangements relating to trade in agricultural goods and fishery products, and co-operation between member States on economic and technical matters.

Desiring to contribute to the liberalisation of international trade, the EFTA countries will support all practical proposals designed to increase world trade. They will participate actively in the tariff negotiations which are due to take place within the framework of GATT.

The EFTA Council will meet again at Ministerial level on 9th and 10th May in Lisbon.

Statement by the Federal German Foreign Minister, Dr. Schroeder, to the Council of Ministers of the European Economic Community, 2 April 1963[2]

Colleagues, we have just commemorated the fact that today is the 100th session of the Council of Ministers. It is probably just a happy coincidence that today we meet to discuss the general situation in the Community. We have just exchanged many kind words of congratulation on the occasion of the commemoration, as is customary on anniversaries, and I hope that what I am going to say, although it is not an anniversary speech, is nevertheless, as far as feelings are concerned, inspired by as constructive a spirit as that in which the introductory speeches were made.

[1] W.E.U., Assembly, General Affairs Committee, *The British application for membership of the European Communities, 1963–1968* (Paris, May 1968), p. 20.   [2] Ibid., pp. 22–7.

I think that we cannot ignore the fact that the European Communities are going through a crisis. There are two sides to this crisis or rather the crisis is two-fold; on the one hand, in the external sphere, on the other hand, internally.

I should like first of all to speak about the crisis abroad. Developments during the period which has elapsed have been fruitful beyond all hopes and made it possible to hope for further success in the future. Internal integration has been speeded up at many points and geographical extension was envisaged. In this field we have for the time being reached a dead end. The hopes of the Community, the hopes expressed in the rest of free Europe and in the whole of the free world, have been dashed to the ground. The fear shown in the eastern bloc over the progress towards building up Europe has now been lessened, and the shadow of uncertainty about the future hangs over the Community. This uncertainty about the future is not only a subject for anxiety for us in our closed circle, it is clearly a matter for anxiety to the whole of the western world. It is now a little over two months since the greatest failure that the Community has known in negotiations over the years and we are certainly all aware that this failure will bring other consequences in its wake.

The internal crisis in our opinion resulted from the following factors: the sequence of events in question up to 29th January ended up by causing a serious deterioration in mutual feelings, and I do not think I am exaggerating when I speak of a crisis of confidence. We all know that the most necessary condition for progress towards economic integration is the constant affirmation of the political will to advance.

Our experience up till the present shows that this is a fact. The constantly reavowed political will, which was the driving force behind everything, was hard hit by this upset in our relations. We are now facing the danger that national interests will take precedence over Community interests. This is a completely natural consequence of such a setback. But if this attitude gets the upper hand it will mean stagnation. And stagnation during the present period of transition— during the period of development of the Common Market—would be tantamount to regression.

This is the situation with which we are faced. But I think that we are all agreed that this crisis must be overcome and in our opinion there are three reasons for this:

First, it is in the interests of the six member States to overcome the crisis. In all essential sectors the Community has expanded at a rate much higher than the world average. This is the case for the increase in production, trade, employment and other sectors of activity. The six Community countries have all derived benefit from this expansion, although it must be said that they have derived benefit in varying degrees. Everything points to the fact that the vigorous pursuit of integration will have, or to be more cautious, should have equally favourable consequences,

The Commission's memorandum on the programme for the second stage[1] gives an excellent idea of the work which has to be done in many fields. I say this in spite of the criticism which has been levelled against parts of the memorandum, for I think that this memorandum could be a basis for our future policy.

[1] European Economic Community, Commission, *Memorandum of the Commission on the Action Programme for the Second Stage*, Com(62)300, Brussels, 24 October 1962.

A second point of view is this. I believe in as fair a distribution as possible of the advantages and disadvantages in Community measures between the different members. We cannot get tied up with a system of prior conditions, notably with regard to countries who have already made large concessions. To take an example: Germany's contribution to the common agricultural policy was made in the expectation of future progress. We relinquished the rights guaranteed by the Treaty such as quotas and minimum prices. We took upon ourselves weighty financial burdens. We gave producing countries large openings for selling their goods on the German market. But what did not take place—and it was this which for us was the essential counterpart of our contribution—was the widening of the boundaries of the European Economic Community.

To take another example: relations with the African countries have been encouraged. Various Community countries have made great sacrifices for the non-European countries in which the Community countries have special interests of very varying importance. This fact should not be overlooked when further developments take place. In the negotiations with important European countries, Turkey for example, there has been delay. Germany does not demand any 'préalables', to use the French word, but we recommend that the work be synchronised so that the expectations of the different member countries are met in as even a way as possible.

The third principle is this. We consider, as regards procedural matters, that it is of capital importance to concentrate the process of integration. Centrifugal interests should be contained. The separation between specialised Councils of Ministers and the general Council of Ministers is, in our opinion, one of these centrifugal tendencies, and this is seen clearly in the agricultural field. The Rome Treaty only speaks of the one general Council of Ministers. All the specialised sectors are tied up with one another—agricultural policy is intimately linked with commercial policy, price policy, social policy, and general economic cycle policy. Harmonious development along the lines indicated above can only take place by means of concentration. We must therefore conclude that decisions binding on the governments of member States or on member States themselves can only be taken by the general Council of Ministers except in cases where the latter explicitly delegates the power to other bodies. Naturally one welcomes meetings of the specialised Ministers, insofar as these are to prepare the decisions to be taken by the general Council of Ministers; but we can only recognise as binding those decisions taken in accordance with the principles we have just outlined.

And a fourth principle: the need for a definite programme of work. In our opinion, there is a need for a programme which covers a period of about one year. The contents of the programme should be problems considered as essential by a majority of the member States. Above all we wish to avoid a kind of war of 'priorities' which would be likely to block any work at all. Nevertheless we consider it is a sound and practical aim to wish to solve all these problems satisfactorily and in a synchronised manner.

I now propose to make some remarks about the major problems: I shall speak first of all of foreign affairs, beginning with the Kennedy round. This is a point which is going to present the Community with a serious problem in the near future. The Community must not turn away from the outside world, for this is not in either its own interests or in the interests of the West. We shall speak of this at a later stage, when my esteemed colleague Dr. Erhard will deal with the subject.

The second problem is connected with Great Britain. In our opinion nothing should take place in the Community which would unduly hinder the future possibility of Great Britain becoming a member. This does not mean that we want to give Great Britain a kind of right of veto: neither do we want to make the internal events of the Community subordinate to the idea of joining the Community, but we wish developments to be in harmony with this objective. We therefore think that it would be a good thing to consider our moves in the light of the future presence of a seventh, eighth, ninth or tenth member and to take our decisions accordingly. In practice this means that we must maintain the contacts made in the course of negotiations for membership, which have besides only been interrupted, that we must encourage these contacts, by consultations— and in this connection we consider that multilateral consultations are far better than bilateral contacts, for the latter take place anyway and there is nothing to stop them. It must be considered whether the European Economic Community ought to establish advisory association relations like the ones existing between the ECSC and Great Britain; and those between Euratom and Great Britain. If Great Britain is prepared to do so, the Community countries should consent to such relations.

I shall now say a few words on the technical feasibility of these contacts: they should take place either—and this would probably be the best way—within the framework of periodical meetings of the six Permanent Representatives and the British Representative in Brussels, or within the framework of a sub-committee of Western European Union. The aim of these contacts should be to prevent new obstacles to eventual accession being created, and, as far as possible, to prepare for accession by harmonising 'Community' measures and British measures in the appropriate fields. It should also be studied whether it would be possible to take preparatory steps in matters of commercial policy: the German Federal Government consider this is essential.

What has been said about Great Britain applies also to Denmark, Norway, and Ireland, although to a lesser degree. But in our opinion Denmark is worthy of particular attention because its fate depends very closely on its relations with the European Economic Community.

One word about Austria. Austria obviously wishes the negotiations for association to be continued. In our opinion, given the position that it holds between the East and the West, Austria deserves the special attention of the countries of Western Europe. It is sufficient to point out that over 50% of its foreign trade is with the EEC and that, for this reason alone, it is necessary to settle this problem in the near future. The talks Austria has had with EFTA and with the Soviet Union are a purely Austrian affair and I feel that Austria coped with the difficulties of the matter very skilfully, particularly in its dealings with the Soviet Union. The Community has every interest in continuing the process of geographical expansion everywhere possible, so as not to be wrongly accused of wishing to cut itself off, or of adopting a restrictive attitude, or of lacking understanding of the world around it.

Turkey is an important associate: it is one of the geographical pillars of the western alliance and makes large sacrifices itself in the military sphere.

Turkey's attitude has proved to be worthy of confidence. Moreover it has great need of assistance. In our opinion the negotiations for the association with Turkey have been neglected in a way which is difficult to justify, and we consider that it is necessary to make substantial financial aid and show a spirit of conciliation in the sphere of commercial policy. The duty of the European Communities is to think first of Europe.

Now we come to Africa. In our opinion—and we have already outlined our position above—the association agreement should be signed as soon as possible.[1] It would be wrong to try to settle an inter-European dispute at the expense of the African countries. Germany is prepared to adopt temporary measures in financial and commercial policy. We consider that we are making a particular sacrifice in doing this, for, together with France, we are the ones who pay the highest contributions, and we do not receive advantages in return which can be compared even with those received by France. Moreover, we will not give our signature without any objections; preferential areas, for instance, are beneficial to some but harmful to others, and it will take time before being able to find an overall solution to the problems of the countries in the process of development. The Convention—and this is one of the unfavourable points—draws boundaries which should be considered outdated. The Convention puts in the hand of the Community—although in a gradually lessening extent—measures which date from a former epoch. Despite these objections which I wished to list once again, we consider that the Agreement should be signed as soon as possible; in spite of our objections we have always been in favour of association with these countries because of Europe's political responsibility towards Africa. I should like to commend the move made by the Netherlands the object of which is to make it quite clear that in principle the Community is also prepared to enter into association with other African States, notably those of the Commonwealth.

The first thing to be considered, in connection with the internal development of the Community, is the problem of merging the Executives. This problem has existed since 1961 and we all know that the Assembly and numerous political figures in Europe have repeatedly come out in favour of it. At the present time it would be highly desirable to merge the Executives as a sign of the desire to overcome the crisis by strengthening the Community. And, besides this consequence which would be more a matter of European policy, the merger would have the advantage of greatly simplifying the work on the energy policy. Preparations for the merger are already at an advanced stage, and all that is necessary is the political decision. We in Germany also attach particular importance to this matter.

The second question arising in this context is the strengthening of the position of the Assembly. There are reasons for this similar to the reasons outlined in connection with merging the Executives. The Assembly could be granted the power to take decisions concerning the Community budgets; it could be given the power to take decisions on agreements signed by the Community; and one might then, in the near future, envisage further measures such as elections by direct suffrage.

The third problem is that of the tariff reductions which are to take place on 1st July of this year. Care must be taken that the decisions taken earlier are put

---

[1] The Convention was finally signed on 20 July 1963; see pp. 404–34 below.

into effect according to the proper time schedule, i.e. bringing forward both the tariff reductions and the moves towards a common external tariff, at the same time bearing in mind that the basis has to be a reduced external tariff. Dr. Erhard will give a more detailed account of this point too, later on.

Finally, a fourth point would consist in putting the Commission's programme of action into effect.

The second reason which makes it essential to overcome the crisis is tied up with the idea of the geographical expansion of the European Economic Community. It is essential, if Great Britain and the other countries of free Europe are to continue in their policy of rapprochement with the European Communities, for the latter to preserve their attractiveness. Whichever countries in the Communities are in favour of their geographical expansion—and in the last analysis the Six are probably all agreed on this point—whichever countries wish for expansion are bound to favour the overall development in the Community and to work for integration.

The third reason why it is essential for the crisis to be overcome is the interests of the free world. The European Communities represent one of the greatest hopes of the free world. The good results obtained by the Communities up till now represent, seen in the overall political context, one of the greatest successes of the western world during the past few years.

This European grouping means a strengthening of the position of the West. And in the light of the East-West tension which will continue to exist for some time yet, a unified Europe is a partner of equal rights with the United States in the Atlantic Alliance and an essential element in the struggle to overcome the rivalry between East and West.

However, friends and colleagues, it will not be possible to overcome the crisis unless due note is taken of the causes. In this connection I should like to stress one point. First, concerning the foreign crisis—i.e. the breakdown of the negotiations for membership and association—I think that in the Community's future work, the fact cannot be ignored that there is a crucial problem still to be solved. To use an English expression, it is undoubtedly no longer possible to take up 'business as usual' and to behave as if the negotiations with the United Kingdom had never taken place. It is my opinion, on the contrary, that we should never lose sight of this problem. The German Government, for important political and economic reasons, will continue to ask for Great Britain's membership and for close relations with the other European countries wishing them. In this respect the Federal Government expresses the wish not only of German public opinion, but of public opinion in the majority of its five partner countries. I should like to recall once again the resolution passed in the European Parliament on 27th March. All these wishes must not remain mere rhetoric, they should crystallise into action on the part of the Community. Even if it is not unfortunately possible for the negotiations to be resumed in the near future, we must nevertheless maintain close contact, which, later on, will develop into more concrete forms. Our aim should be to create a Europe grouping all the European countries who are so inclined and who consent to subscribe to the provisions of the Treaty of Rome.

I shall confine myself to a few words on the internal crisis of confidence. I believe that this crisis of confidence can only be overcome provided the

Community spirit is put first, that the principle of equal rights among the member countries is respected, and lastly, that each country is prepared, now and in the future, to make concessions.

I am now going to outline some of the principles which, in our opinion, should be the basis for the future work of the Community. First, I put the harmonious development of integration, i.e. putting into effect at as harmonious a rhythm as possible the provisions of the Treaty of Rome in all the fields covered by the Treaty. Up till now, and I think there is no doubt about this, the development has been irregular. In some fields there has been great progress, but we have to note that in others there has been much delay. We must make up for lost time in these fields. One field, for instance, in which there has been much time lost, is that of external relations. In this connection I must mention once again the breakdown in the European negotiations for membership and association. There is still no common commercial policy and in the agricultural sector too foreign relations have been neglected. Other fields are fiscal policy, transport policy, and energy policy.

The fifth problem is that of agricultural policy. The German Federal Government considers it important to go ahead with the common agricultural policy, but nevertheless it considers the very high speed at which work has up till now been rushed through as harmful, because it could well distort the general movement towards integration. Moreover there are some serious shortcomings in some parts of the common agricultural policy. We recommend that a more moderate rhythm be adopted, for the following three reasons:

First, we must harmonise and synchronise the progress towards integration. Secondly, we must be able to revise steps already taken in order to remedy the shortcomings, and consolidate experience so that it can be used as a basis for future work. As examples of the shortcomings which have arisen, I would mention the steep decline in imports from third countries, which was far more marked than had been expected. We shall perhaps provide some figures about this later.

Thirdly, the breakdown in the negotiations for accession and association gave rise to a new and very different situation. For example, let us take the regulation for beef. In this field the situation is very different according to whether the main source of supply in Europe—i.e. Denmark—will be a member of the Community, as we thought up till now, or not.

All that I have said, Mr. Chairman and colleagues, leads me to suggest that the Permanent Representatives be given the job of working out, on the basis of the statements which have just been made, a programme for 1963, which should if possible be submitted for decision at the next session of the Council of Ministers.

I do not think that I have painted too pessimistic a picture of the situation nor too bright a picture. I think that we do ourselves and the Community a great service by being realistic. We should, in accordance with the objectives of the Rome Treaty and with decisions already taken by the Council, work towards our goal, not losing sight of the fact that we can be successful only by showing a spirit of co-operation and by ensuring that this co-operation takes the form of synchronised progress.

Speech by President de Gaulle on French radio and television, 19 April 1963[1] (extracts)

In order to be prosperous, to be masters of ourselves and to be powerful, we French have done a great deal. Much remains for us to do. For progress demands effort. Independence is not free. Security is costly. That is of course why the State, whose role and raison d'être is to serve the general interest, has no right to let things go. . . .

. . . After the last world war, our country saw, in fact, its power and its influence terribly diminished in relation to those of the two world colossi. And again, until last year, it was divided and paralyzed by the after effects of a colonization that had its merits and its glories but that, in our time, was nothing more than vain and outdated. Thus, imbued once more with the spirit of renovation, in the full flush of invention, production and demographic growth, provided with solid institutions, released from colonial bonds, France finds itself, for the first time in half a century, with a free spirit and free hands. And thus it can and must play throughout the world the role that belongs to it.

This policy is not an easy one. The world abounds with sirens that sing to us the sweetness of renunciation, unless, annoyed at seeing us indifferent to their seduction, they raise toward us a noisy chorus of invectives. But without our being cocksure, in the interest of everyone as much as in our own, our ship is pursuing its course. There is absolutely no chance that, giving in to facility, we would allow France to be pushed into the background.

That is why, if the union of Western Europe—Germany, Italy, the Netherlands, Belgium, Luxembourg, France—is a capital aim in our action outside, we have no desire to be dissolved within it. Any system that would consist of handing over our sovereignty to august international assemblies would be incompatible with the rights and the duties of the French Republic. But also, such a system would undoubtedly find itself powerless to sweep along and lead the peoples and, to begin with, our own people, in the domains where their souls and their flesh are in question. This abdication of the European States, of France in particular, would inevitably lead to subjection from without. It is, moreover, in order to avoid such an inconsistency and, as its consequence, such a dependence that we are bent on seeing the union of Europe constituted by nations which can and really wish to belong to it. While retaining the hope that one day, perhaps, the great British people, freeing themselves from that which keeps them out of our community, will come to join it in accordance with the conditions which are those of the institution, we consider that our community must develop as it is and without delay. In short, it appears essential to us that Europe be Europe and that France be France.

In addition, within the Atlantic Alliance—indispensable so long as the ambitions and the threats of the Soviets are raised—our country, while combining its defense with that of its allies, intends to remain the master and, if necessary, contribute to the common effort something quite different from the soulless and powerless assistance of a people that would no longer be responsible for themselves. This leads us to provide ourselves with the modern means of ensuring our security, in other words, with the means for deterring any country whatsoever

[1] French Embassy, Press and Information Service, *French Affairs, No. 154*, 19 April 1963.

from attacking ours, at the risk of subjecting itself to frightful destruction. I mean, of course, atomic weapons. It is true that our American allies possess in this respect a colossal power, capable of throwing into chaos all or part of the Soviet empire, that they are resolved, as we know, to fight if necessary to prevent Europe from falling, dead or alive, into the other camp, that they are our good allies as we are theirs. But that is not the entire question.

Indeed, the possible adversary is himself equipped with enormous means of the same kind. This being the case, no one, nowhere, can know in advance whether, in the event of a conflict, the atomic bombs would or would not be used at the start by the two principal champions; whether, if they did use them, they would use them in Central and Western Europe only, without striking each other directly and immediately; or whether, on the contrary, they would be led right away to hurl death at each other's vitals. Anyhow, and in light of this enormous and inevitable uncertainty, France must itself have the means of directly reaching any State that would be its aggressor, that is, the means of deterring it from being so and, according to the circumstances, the means of assisting in the defense of its allies, including—who knows—America.

In sum, our country, perpetually threatened, finds itself once again faced with the necessity of possessing the most powerful weapons of the era unless, of course, the others cease to possess them. However, to dissuade us, the voices of immobility and demagogy are as always simultaneously raised. 'It is useless,' say some. 'It is too costly,' say others. These voices France listened to, sometimes and to its misfortune, notably on the eve of the two world wars. 'No heavy artillery,' they exclaimed in concert, until 1914. 'No armored corps, no fighter aircraft,' the same backward and brainless groups cried in unison before 1939. But this time we shall not allow routine and illusion to invite invasion of our country. Moreover, in the midst of the strained and dangerous world in which we live, our chief duty is to be strong and to be ourselves.

Women and men of France, after many trials, we had to decide in favor of progress or decline. The choice has been made. We are going forward. But there must be order and effort. Let us leave facility to others.

Long live the Republic! Long live France!

Speech by Dr. Schroeder, Düsseldorf, 28 June 1963[1] (extracts)

. . . It may be that the success of the Common Market during its first five years raised our expectations too high; the temporary suspension of the negotiations on the entry of Great Britain plunged the Community into a crisis. The progress which we have made since the new German initiative last April in Brussels[2] is only a beginning; great and outstanding efforts will be needed to advance further. I am, however, convinced that we shall overcome the difficulties in the end, since the individual economies have already so far adjusted themselves to the process of integration that this trend can no longer be reversed. For this reason both economic factors as well as political necessity will compel the governments to take new joint action. Our aim of including Great Britain in the Community remains unchanged. This was not just a passing political notion

[1] *The British application for membership in the European Communities, 1963–1968*, pp. 28–9.
[2] See pp. 74–80 above.

but was the imperative conclusion to be drawn from the mighty changes which have taken place in Europe and the world during the last thirty years. . . .

To take first the question of Britain's entry, it is our opinion that the Common Market should pursue a policy which gives consideration to Great Britain as the welcome member of tomorrow. For this it is necessary that a permanent exchange of ideas, opinions and information should take place between the EEC and Britain, and the best form for this must be found as quickly as possible. . . .

It is not only in our own interest that we demand an increase of trade between the Common Market and outside countries. The EEC holds first place in world trade today. Its trade policy therefore has a very marked effect on the whole of international trade, and this fact imposes the duty upon us in the EEC to behave with exemplary responsibility. Only if customs barriers are removed can great economic areas such as the Common Market or the United States be of benefit in world trade. We therefore welcome the negotiations which were begun recently in GATT.[1] . . .

My impression of the situation today makes it appear to me advisable first of all to emerge from the present crisis in the economic sphere of the Community of the Six, before we once again turn to the political statute.

We hope that the Treaty of Franco-German Co-operation[2] which has meanwhile been ratified by both sides will cause European development to progress both in the economic and in the political sphere. The fact of Franco-German reconciliation is in itself a proof that bold ideas may sometimes materialise more rapidly than might be expected. When Sir Winston Churchill, in his famous speech in Zürich in 1946, appealed for reconciliation between France and Germany, it was thought that he was far in advance of his time and of the possibilities. The memories of the war, the occupation and dismantling, and finally the Saar problem, all appeared as insurmountable hindrances. Today reconciliation has become a fact which we welcome with joy and which we shall continue to foster with care. There has been some talk recently of differences of opinion between Germany and France in the sphere of European and Atlantic politics. But the widespread satisfaction with which the Franco-German Treaty was greeted in both countries shows that the will to co-operate—and moreover the realisation of the need for co-operation—goes very deep. This guarantees that differences of opinion between friends can be dealt with openly and overcome.

We clearly realise that the political union of Europe is necessary, not least in order to establish a genuine and balanced relation of partnership with the United States of America, and to make this relation a sound and lasting one. This is also in accordance with the opinion of the United States, which as a matter of principle actively supports efforts towards European unification.

Decision of the E.C.C. Council of Ministers on contacts with Great Britain, Brussels, 11 July 1963[3]

The Council propose to the British Government to organise quarterly contacts in the framework of WEU designed to permit the seven countries, in the

---

[1] See pp. 129–32 below.   [2] *Documents, 1962*, pp. 935–8.
[3] *The British application for membership of the European Communities, 1963–1968*, p. 29.

course of discussions, to take stock of the political and economic situation in Europe. It proposes to inscribe on the agenda of the ministerial meetings every three months, in addition to political questions, an item headed as follows: 'Exchange of views on the European economic situation'.

Discussions will take place in principle at ministerial level.

When economic problems are to be discussed the Commission of the EEC will be invited by the Ministers of the Six to participate in the meeting.

(f) *Economic Relations of the Western Powers*

(a) *Financial Diplomacy*

Statement by the British Chancellor of the Exchequer, Mr. Maudling, to the House of Commons, 3 April 1963[1] (extract)

. . . At this stage, I must say something about the external position and the future of sterling. We can reasonably hope for some continued improvement in our current balance this year. On the other hand, we must expect that our long-term capital outflow will also tend to increase. The needs of other countries for economic aid are rising. In the last two years we have experienced a substantial inflow of capital in conditions which are not likely to be repeated this year. The change on the capital side might, therefore, well offset any improvement on current payments. But, as shown by the figures for 1962 which were published last Thursday, the underlying position from which we start is much sounder than has sometimes been realised.

I absolutely reject the proposition that a vigorous economy and a strong position for sterling are incompatible. A healthy expansion based on increasing efficiency and control of costs is the key to the strength of sterling. Of course, if expansion leads to inflation and to rising costs, then it cannot be sustained, both for external and for internal reasons. So long, however, as we can keep our costs steady and competitive, I am convinced that our basic strength is such that we shall have no need to be deflected by external factors from a policy of modernising and expanding our economy.

It is, of course, possible that in the early stages of a programme of more vigorous expansion, imports may rise faster than exports. But the pace at which imports are likely to rise with expansion is frequently over-estimated because there is normally a lag in the building up of stocks to correspond to higher levels of output. Moreover, in so far as there is a stocking up movement related to expansion, in effect the building up of working capital, then I think that it is perfectly reasonable and sensible to finance such a movement out of our reserves or out of our borrowing facilities in the International Monetary Fund and elsewhere.

This is surely what these various facilities exist for. It is wrong to use reserves or borrowing facilities to boost up an internal position which is unsound because costs, prices and incomes have got out of hand. But it is equally unsound to refuse to use reserves and borrowing facilities for the purposes for which they

[1] *H.C. deb.*, vol. 675, cc. 470–2; this statement was made by Mr. Maudling in the presentation of his Budget.

exist, namely, to deal with temporary situations and prevent temporary difficulties obstructing the proper long-term development of the economy.

Sterling is subject to many influences. As an international currency it is to some extent open to the shifting currents of world trade and payments, and to political developments. But we must always distinguish between the intrinsic strength of sterling, which is what is most important, and temporary movements of confidence. So long as our economy is sound and our position competitive, the intrinsic strength of sterling must be great. We may face short-term fluctuations of one kind or another, but we have substantial resources available to meet them.

In addition to our first-line gold and dollar reserves, we have a stand-by arrangement with the I.M.F. which permits us quick access to 1 billion dollars of external finance—and this is only part of our Fund drawing rights, which total nearly $2\frac{1}{2}$ billion dollars. And in saying this I have taken no credit for the dollar securities we own, which naturally fluctuate in value, but average around 1 billion dollars.

These are all large, tangible assets which we have available. In addition, there is the intangible asset of the developing co-operation between countries of the free world in tackling monetary problems, not least in dealing with speculative attacks against particular currencies. The Committee will, of course, be aware that at times during the past two months or so sterling has been subject to speculative pressure of this kind.

We have, therefore, called upon the support available to us from other central banks, which has been willingly given. In all, 250 million dollars have been advanced to us during the months of February and March, and these borrowings have, of course, been reflected in the published figures of the change in our gold and convertible currency reserves for the two months. I have no doubt that what we have done is wise. Short-term capital movements one way or the other do not add to or detract from the economic strength of the country. The effect of recent movements has been that we have temporarily exchanged obligations to central banks for obligations to a wide variety of other holders of sterling.

Special message of President Kennedy to the United States Congress, 18 July 1963[1]

To the Congress of the United States:

Soon after my inauguration, I reported to the Congress on the problems presented to this Nation by 3 successive years, beginning in the late 1950's, of mounting balance of payments deficits accompanied by large gold outflows; and I announced a program designed to restore both confidence in the dollar and eventual equilibrium in our international accounts.[2] The challenge posed by those pressures was heightened at that time by the need to halt and reverse the spread of unemployment and revive our faltering economy. Rejecting a choice between two equally unpalatable alternatives—improved employment at home at the cost of a weaker dollar abroad or a stronger dollar at the cost of a weaker economy and Nation—we sought a new course that would simultaneously increase our growth at home, reduce unemployment, and strengthen the dollar by eliminating the deficit in our international payments. It is appropriate now—

---

[1] *D.S.B.*, 12 August 1963, pp. 250–9.   [2] *Documents, 1961*, pp. 521–34.

nearly $2\frac{1}{2}$ years later—to look back on the problems faced, to review the progress made and to chart the course ahead.

There is much from which to take heart. Our economy has resumed its growth and unemployment has been reduced. The dollar remains strong, bulwarked by nearly 40 percent of the free world's monetary gold stock as well as by a newly constructed network of bilateral and multilateral financial arrangements. Our gold outflow has been halved. There are signs of longer run improvement in our world competitive position, as our prices and costs hold steady while others are rising. The deficit in our balance of payments has been reduced—from $3.9 billion in 1960 to $2.4 billion in 1961 and $2.2 billion in 1962.

Our basic strength, moreover, is vast, real, and enduring. Our payments deficits, measured in terms of our loss of gold and the increase in our short-term liquid liabilities to foreigners, have consistently been equaled or exceeded by the growth of our long-term, high-yielding foreign assets—assets which have been and will continue to be an increasing source of strength to our balance of payments. Today, Americans hold more than $60 billion of private investments abroad, and dollar loans repayable to the U.S. Government total over $11 billion. At the end of 1962, all of these assets exceeded our liabilities to foreigners by an estimated $27 billion. And they have shown an increasing strength over the years: our total income from these sources in 1959 was $3 billion; in 1962 it had risen to $4.3 billion; and we expect further substantial increases in the coming years.

These are all signs of progress. But unemployment is still too high; our growth rate is still too low; and it is now clear that, despite the favorable forces at work over the long run, more remains to be done today to eliminate the continuing payments deficit.

A significant portion of our progress so far has been due to special agreements with friendly foreign countries—for debt prepayments, advance payments for military equipment, and U.S. borrowings abroad. While similar arrangements may once again prove capable of covering a substantial amount of the gross deficit in 1963, such special transactions cannot be relied upon for the indefinite future. Moreover, while our commercial trade balance and Government expenditures overseas have shown modest improvement, capital outflows, both short term and long term, have increased.

Although there is urgent need for further effort I want to make it clear that, in solving its international payments problem, this Nation will continue to adhere to its historic advocacy of freer trade and capital movements, and that it will continue to honor its obligation to carry a fair share of the defense and development of the free world. At the same time, we shall continue policies designed to reduce unemployment and stimulate growth here at home—for the well-being of all free peoples is inextricably entwined with the progress achieved by our own people. I want to make it equally clear that this Nation will maintain the dollar as good as gold, freely interchangeable with gold at $35 an ounce, the foundation stone of the free world's trade and payments system.

But continued confidence at home and cooperation abroad require further administrative and legislative inroads into the hard core of our continuing payments deficit, augmenting our long-range efforts to improve our economic performance over a period of years in order to achieve both external balance and internal expansion, stepping up our shorter run efforts to reduce our balance of payments deficits while the long-range forces are at work and adding to our stockpile of arrangements designed to finance our deficits during our return to equilibrium in a way that assures the continued smooth functioning of the world's monetary and trade systems.

Before turning to the specific measures required in the latter two categories, I must emphasize once again the necessity of improving this Nation's overall long-range economic performance—including increased investment and modernization for greater productivity and profits, continued cost and price stability, and full employment and faster growth. This is the key to improving our international competitiveness, increasing our trade surpluses, and reducing our capital outflows.

That is why early enactment of the comprehensive *tax reduction and revision* program previously submitted[1] is the single most important step that can be taken to achieve balance abroad as well as growth here at home. The increased investment incentives and purchasing power these personal and corporate tax reductions would create, combined with last year's actions giving special credits for new investment and more favorable depreciation treatment, will promote more employment, production, sales, and investment, particularly when accompanied by the continued ample availability of credit and reasonable long-term rates of interest. A prosperous, high-investment economy brings with it the rapid gains in productivity and efficiency which are so essential to the improvement of our competitive position abroad.

To gain new markets abroad and retain the gains of new growth and efficiency here at home, we must continue the *price-cost stability* of recent years, limiting wage and profit increases to their fair share of our improving productivity. That is why we have, for 2 years, been urging business and labor to recognize and use reasonable wage-price guideposts for resolving the issues of collective bargaining. Our success in holding down our price level relative to that of our major competitors is a powerful force working to restore our payments balance over the longer run. This fact should not be obscured by current short-run developments.

While these long-range forces are taking effect, a series of more immediate and specialized efforts are needed to reduce the deficit in our international transactions and defend our gold reserves:

1. Export Expansion

Our commercial sales of goods and services to foreign countries in 1962 exceeded our purchases by $4.3 billion, and they are continuing at about the same rate this year. This is our greatest strength, but it is not enough. Our exports of goods have risen only moderately over the past 3 years, and have not kept pace with the rapid rise of imports which has accompanied our domestic expansion. As a result, rather than furnishing increased support for our other transactions, 1962 saw a decline in our commercial trade surplus.

[1] *Message from the President of the United States transmitting recommendations relative to the revision of our tax structure, 24 January 1963*, U.S. House of Representatives, 88th Congress, Doc. No. 43.

The primary long-term means for correcting this situation is implementation of the Trade Expansion Act of 1962.[1] The Special Representative for Trade Negotiations is preparing to use to the fullest extent the authority given to me by the act, in an across-the-board drive for lower tariffs and against other barriers to trade. This should open new markets and widen existing markets for American exports.

As mentioned above, our whole long-range domestic program—including increased investment, improved productivity, and wage-price stability—is designed to better the competitive position of our products both at home and abroad. Continued price stability at home, contrasted with the upward trend in prices abroad, will create an increasingly favorable climate for American exports; and this administration is concentrating on six immediate measures to help American businessmen take advantage of our export potential.

First, the Export-Import Bank has created a wholly new program of export financing which now provides U.S. business with credit facilities equal to any in the world. The major element in this new program is the guarantee of short- and medium-term export credits by the Foreign Credit Insurance Association, composed of more than 70 private insurance companies in conjunction with the Export-Import Bank. I urge the Congress to act promptly to restore the Bank to full operating efficiency by renewing its charter and authorizing adequate financing.

Second, the Departments of State and Commerce have strengthened and expanded efforts overseas to probe for new markets and promote the sale and distribution of American products.

Third, the Department of Commerce has developed a broad program of education and assistance to present and potential American exporters. I have requested a relatively small amount of additional funds to strengthen the Department's efforts to stimulate our exports. These funds, amounting to $6 million, were not approved by the House of Representatives. It is essential, if we are to increase our trade surplus, that they be included in the final appropriation bill. This modest sum would pay for itself many times over in increased exports, lower payments deficits, and protection for our gold reserves.

Fourth, the Department of Agriculture announced last March a new auction program for direct sales of cotton abroad. It is expected that this new technique will insure competitive pricing for our cotton in export markets and will increase exports by as much as $100 million over last year's levels.

Fifth, present ocean freight rates discourage our exports as compared to imports. The freight charges on Atlantic crossings are far higher for eastbound freight than for comparable items bound for our shores. A similar situation prevails on other trade routes. While these substantial differentials may have been acceptable in the immediate postwar period of the dollar shortage when Europe was struggling to get on its feet, their magnitude is clearly unjustified today. Accordingly, I have directed the Secretary of Commerce to take corrective action through the Maritime Administration; and I am urging the Federal Maritime Commission in its role as an independent regulatory agency to question those specific export rates which appear unduly high. Should legislation prove necessary, it will be sought.

[1] For text, see *Current Documents, 1962*, pp. 1383–96.

Sixth, in order to give further momentum to the expansion of our export performance, I will convene a White House Conference on Export Expansion on September 17 and 18, to alert American firms, whether or not they are now exporting, to the opportunities and rewards of initiating or expanding export efforts. We shall use this opportunity to emphasize to American businessmen that vigorous action to increase their exports would serve their own private interests as well as the national interest.

2. Tourism

Another element that requires attention in our commercial transactions is the increase in our unfavorable net tourist balance. With increasing prosperity encouraging American travel abroad, total tourist spending in foreign countries rose another 10 percent last year, to nearly $2\frac{1}{2}$ billion. This was partially offset by increased foreign tourist expenditures in the United States, but the net result was an outflow of $1.4 billion, or two-thirds of last year's over-all balance of payments deficit. This year the cost is estimated to be still greater. That is why we have had to limit the duty-free exemption for returning tourists to $100 per person. Last year this measure achieved a saving of more than $100 million, and I am gratified that Congress has extended the limitation for another 2 years. We have also sought, through establishment of the U.S. Travel Service, to increase our income from visitors coming to our country. To further that effort, I strongly recommend that Congress approve the full amount of the appropriation requested for the U.S. Travel Service.

In addition, in cooperation with the appropriate Government agencies, I am asking the domestic travel and tourism industry to launch a more unified drive to encourage Americans to learn more about their own country and the glory of their heritage. A 'See America Now' program, to be in full operation by the spring of 1964, will make the most of our magnificent resources and make travel at home a more appealing alternative to travel abroad.

3. Federal Expenditure Abroad

Federal expenditures abroad go largely for defense and aid. These represent the obligations which flow from our position of world leadership and unrivaled economic strength. With the recovery of other economically advanced nations, particularly our allies in Western Europe, we have made vigorous and increasingly successful efforts to work out with them a better sharing of our common responsibilities. These efforts—combined with rigorous scrutiny of offshore expenditures—have enabled us, in spite of mounting worldwide requirements and costs, to reduce the overall total of our own oversea expenditures while we increase the security of the free world and maintain a high level of assistance to developing countries.

A continual process of modernizing our Armed Forces and increasing efficiency, resulting in heightened defense effectiveness, is reducing the requirements for oversea dollar expenditures. At the same time, by tying our aid more effectively to domestic procurement and cutting civilian expenditures sharply, we should be able to achieve further savings. In fact, by January 1965, these processes should result in a reduction of the rate of our Federal oversea dollar expenditures by approximately $1 billion from that of 1962.

(A) Military expenditures

The Defense Department has, since the beginning of this administration, been making vigorous efforts to restrain oversea expenditures, without reducing military effectiveness.

Thus, despite the Berlin buildup of 1961 and rising costs overseas, gross expenditures abroad by the Defense Department have been held below 1960 levels. As a result of the desire of our allies to acquire from us modern military equipment, which they need to strengthen free world defenses, at lower cost than they could produce the equipment themselves, substantial offsets to these expenditures have also been achieved, so that our net outlays abroad for defense have declined from $2.7 billion in 1960 to $1.9 billion in 1962.

In line with these continuing efforts, the Secretary of Defense has informed me that the annual rate of expenditures abroad by the Department of Defense will be reduced—by measures to be put into effect before the end of calendar year 1964—by more than $300 million from the 1962 level. At the same time the Department of Defense will continue to seek arrangements with major allied countries to increase their military procurement from the United States so as to reduce the net outflow still further. The Secretary has further assured me that this reduction will be accomplished without any reduction in the effectiveness of our military posture and with no impairment in our ability to meet our commitments to our allies in all parts of the world.

In addition to direct expenditures by the Defense Department, our defense expenditures abroad have for many years been increased by the cost of programs for the acquisition of strategic materials from foreign sources. The cost of these programs is now steadily declining since they have largely fulfilled their purpose and are no longer needed. Within 2 years they will be reduced by over $200 million as compared to 1962, insuring a total reduction in defense dollar expenditures well in excess of $500 million.

(B) Agency for International Development

During 1960 only about one-third of AID program expenditures were in the form of U.S. goods and services. Last year that proportion had risen to about 50 percent. But during the fiscal year which ended last month, fully 80 percent of AID's commitments were 'tied' to the export of U.S. goods and services. The balance was virtually all committed for purchases in the less-developed countries rather than in the developed nations where the payments surpluses exist which give rise to our deficit. During fiscal year 1964, for which funds are now being considered by the Congress, AID commitments tied to U.S. exports will rise beyond 80 percent of the total. I have directed the Administrator of AID to continue and intensify this policy so that AID expenditures entering our balance of payments in fiscal year 1965 may be further reduced by about $500 million as compared to fiscal year 1961, from about $1 billion to not over $500 million, the lowest practicable minimum.

(C) Other departments and agencies

The oversea disbursements of all other departments of government have also been brought under special review and control by the Director of the Bureau of the Budget. Total Federal expenditures abroad (excluding Defense, AID, Treasury payments on foreign-held debt, and Federal pension payments) coming within the scope of this review now amount to approximately $600 million per year. The Director of the Budget has assured me that vigorous screening of expenditures abroad by these other Federal departments and agencies will achieve further substantial balance of payments savings. These savings, together with those which may be expected from revisions of programs under the Agricultural Trade Development and Assistance Act, should amount to some $100 million a year. This includes my request to the Congress to enact legislation permitting freer use of our present holdings of the currencies of a number of other countries.

4. Short-Term Capital Flows

By skillful use of the tools of debt management and monetary policy, the Treasury Department and the Federal Reserve System have substantially reduced the outflow of short-term capital through a series of carefully managed increases in short-term money rates, while maintaining ample credit availability and keeping both long-term rates and bank loan rates low and, in many cases, declining. Experience in the recovery underway over the past $2\frac{1}{2}$ years provides a solid basis for expecting that a determined effort can succeed in keeping long-term investment and mortgage money plentiful and cheap while boosting short-term interest rates. From February 1961 through July 12, 1963, the rate on newly issued 3-month Treasury bills rose 76 basis points, while the rise in long-term Treasury bond yields was held to only 22 basis points and the yields on high-grade corporate bonds and mortgages actually declined.

However, the recorded outflows of short-term funds, together with unrecorded net outflows, a large portion of which undoubtedly represent short-term capital movements, still amounted to approximately $1.6 billion in 1962 and have continued on a substantial scale so far this year. A sizable reduction in this drain would do much to strengthen our overall balance of payments. It is for this reason that the Federal Reserve has decided to increase the rediscount rate from 3 to $3\frac{1}{2}$ percent. At the same time, the Board of Governors of the Federal Reserve System and the Federal Deposit Insurance Corporation have raised the interest-rate ceilings on time deposits payable in 90 days to 1 year, in order to enable our banks to compete more effectively with those abroad and thus attract funds that might otherwise leave the country.

While none of us welcomes higher interest rates at a time when our economy is operating below capacity, an increase in short-term rates—at a time when liquid savings are growing rapidly, and when there are no accompanying restrictions on credit availability nor parallel increases in the interest rates on bank loans, home mortgages or other long-term obligations—should have little, if any, adverse effect on our economy. The unprecedented flow of liquid savings should largely insulate the longer term markets from the effect of higher short-term rates. I have been assured by both Treasury and Federal Reserve officials that they intend to do everything possible through debt management policy and open-market operations to avoid any reduction in domestic credit availability and any upward pressure on long-term interest rates while the economy operates below capacity without inflation. Other agencies of the Federal Government will work to maintain continued ready availability of private mortgage loans at stable interest rates. Nevertheless, the situation lends increased urgency to the fiscal stimulus that would be provided by the prompt enactment of the substantial tax reductions I have recommended.

5. Long-Term Capital Outflows

Long-term capital outflows consisting of direct investment in productive plants abroad appear to have leveled off in recent years, whereas portfolio investments in the form of long-term loans or securities purchases have been rising rapidly. While our long-range program should increase the attractiveness of domestic investment and further reduce the outflow of direct investment, the rising outflow of long-term capital for portfolio investment abroad shows no sign of abating. It is up from $850 million in 1960 to $1.2 billion in 1962, and so far this year is running at an annual rate of well over $1.5 billion.

In view of the continued existence of direct controls and inadequate capital market mechanisms in many foreign countries, and the wide differential between the long-term rates of interest in the larger industrial countries and the United States, there appear to be only three possible solutions to this problem, two of which are unacceptable under present circumstances:

A substantial increase in our whole long-term interest rate structure would throw our economy into reverse, increase unemployment, and substantially reduce our import requirements, thereby damaging the economy of every free nation.

The initiation of direct capital controls, which are in use in most countries, is inappropriate to our circumstances. It is contrary to our basic precept of free markets. We cannot take this route.

A third alternative—the one which I recommend—would stem the flood of foreign security sales in our markets and still be fully consistent with both economic growth and free capital movements. I urge the enactment by the Congress of an interest equalization tax, which would, in effect, increase by approximately 1 percent the interest cost to foreigners of obtaining capital in this country, and thus help equalize interest rate patterns for longer term financing in the United States and abroad. The rate of tax should be graduated from 2.75 percent to 15 percent of the value of debt obligations, according to the remaining maturity of the obligation, and should be 15 percent in the case of equity securities. This tax should remain in effect through 1965 when improvements in both our balance of payments and in the operation of foreign capital markets are expected to permit its abandonment.

Under this alternative, the allocation of savings for investment in securities will continue to be the result of decisions based on market prices. There will be no limitations on the marketing of foreign issues and no governmental screening of borrowers. Reliance will be placed on price alone to effect an overall reduction in the outflow of American funds for stocks, bonds, and long-term loans—both new or outstanding, whether publicly marketed or privately placed.

The tax would not apply to direct investment. It would not apply to securities or loans that mature in less than 3 years. Nor would it apply to the loans of commercial banks. These exemptions will assure that export credit will remain fully available. Furthermore, purchases of the securities of less developed countries or of companies operating primarily in such countries will not be taxed.

Nor will the tax apply to transactions in foreign securities already owned by Americans, or to the purchase of securities by foreigners. Underwriters and dealers would be exempted from the tax on stock or securities resold to foreigners as part of the distribution of a new issue. But all Americans who purchase new or outstanding foreign securities from foreign issuers or owners would be subject to this tax. In order to avoid unfair burdens on transactions which are nearly complete, the tax should not apply to offerings of securities for which active registration statements are now on file with the Securities and Exchange Commission. Purchase commitments which have already been made should also not be affected.

The Secretary of the Treasury is submitting the details of this proposal to the Congress; and I have been assured that the House Ways and Means Committee will be prepared to give high priority to this proposal after action has been taken with respect to the overall program of tax reduction and reform now before it. Since the effectiveness of this tax requires its immediate application, I am asking Congress to make the legislation effective from the date of this message. The Internal Revenue Service will promptly make available all instructions necessary for interim fulfillment of the provisions of this recommendation, pending the enactment of legislation by the Congress.[1]

6. Investment by Foreign Savers in the Securities of U.S. Private Companies

Investment by foreign savers in the securities of U.S. private companies has fallen rapidly to less than $150 million in 1962. The better climate for investment that will flow from enactment of the program for tax reduction and reform now before the Congress will do much to improve this situation but a direct action program is also needed to promote oversea sales of securities of U.S. companies. Such a program should also be designed to increase foreign participation in the financing of new or expanded operations on the part of U.S. companies operating abroad.

To meet these two facets of a single problem, a new and positive program should be directed to the following areas of effort:

(a) The identification and critical appraisal of the legal, administrative and institutional restrictions remaining in the capital markets of other industrial nations of the free world which prevent the purchase of American securities and hamper U.S. companies in financing their operations abroad from non-U.S. sources;

(b) A review of U.S. Government and private activities which adversely affect foreign purchase of the securities of U.S. private companies; and

[1] See pp. 108–14 below.

(*c*) A broad and intensive effort by the U.S. financial community to market securities of U.S. private companies to foreign investors, and to increase the availability of foreign financing for U.S. business operating abroad.

Such a program will necessarily involve a pooling of the know-how and efforts of the Government and the financial community. I have asked the Treasury Department, in consultation with the State Department, to develop an organization plan and program.

The increased freedom of capital movement and increased participation by foreign citizens and financial institutions in the ownership and financing of American business, toward which these efforts are directed, will serve to strengthen the economic and political ties of the free world as well as its monetary system. Securities of U.S. private firms could be and should be one of our best selling exports. An increasing foreign investment in these securities will encourage a more balanced two-way capital traffic between the United States and other capital markets and minimize the impact of net long-term capital outflows from the United States on our balance of payments.

7. Special Government Transactions

Special Government transactions covered $1.4 billion of our deficit in 1962. These included prepayment of debt by foreign countries, advance payments on military purchases here, and the issuance by the Treasury of medium-term securities to foreign official holders of dollars. Further debt prepayment is expected in 1963—France has just announced a prepayment of $160 million—but it is clear that these are temporary gains which cannot be repeated for very long. Nor is it likely that advance payments on military purchases will again be large, as the pace of deliveries against purchases is now rising.

Therefore, as our continuing balance of payments deficit leads to accruals of dollars by foreign central banks, exceeding the size of the dollar balances which they normally carry, it has been particularly helpful that a number of foreign governments and central banks have begun purchasing a new type of non-marketable, medium-term Treasury security, denominated either in dollars or in their own currencies, as a convenient alternative to the purchase of gold. Some $610 million of such securities have been newly issued thus far in 1963.

Further debt prepayments and further sales of these securities during the remainder of this year will reflect the unprecedented degree of cooperation now prevailing in international finance and the growing recognition that correction of payments imbalances is a responsibility of the surplus as well as the deficit countries. In this spirit we shall also continue to press for a fuller and fairer sharing of the burdens of defense and aid and for the reduction or elimination of the trade barriers which impede our exports.

8. Gold Sales and Increased Dollar Holdings

Gold sales and increased dollar holdings serve to finance what remains of our deficit after special governmental transactions. In 1962, this deficit amounted to approximately $2.2 billion. It was financed by the sale of $890 million in gold and $17 million of our holdings of foreign exchange as well as by an increase in foreign holdings of dollars and U.S. Government securities amounting to $653 million, and an increase of $626 million in the holdings of dollars by the International Monetary Fund.

The total outflow of gold for the 2 years 1961 and 1962 combined only slightly exceeded the outflow in the single year 1960; and the outflow in 1963 is running at a rate well below last year. Since the rise in short-term interest resulting from the recent action of the Federal Reserve will make it considerably more attractive for foreigners to hold their assets in dollars, including short-term U.S. Government securities, prospects are improved that increased foreign holdings of these assets instead of gold will finance a still larger share of our deficit.

9. The International Monetary Fund

The International Monetary Fund, however, presents a different situation. Last year the Fund's dollar holdings increased as other countries paid off their debts in dollars and concentrated new borrowings in other convertible currencies to the extent practicable. But the Fund's rules provide that, except in the case of a drawing—that is, a borrowing—it cannot hold more of any currency than was paid in at the time of original subscription (in effect, 75 percent); and the Fund's holdings of dollars have now nearly reached that level.

To meet this situation, the United States has requested, and the Executive Board of the IMF has approved, a $500 million standby arrangement which authorizes us to draw on the Fund from time to time during the coming year. It is our intention to utilize this authority for the purpose of facilitating repayments which are expected to total about $500 million during the course of the next 12 months. When a country desires to repay the Fund, we will draw convertible foreign currencies from the Fund, paying for them with dollars. The country making the repayment will use its own dollars to buy these foreign currencies from us in order to repay the Fund. All transfers will take place at par. Thus the Fund will continue to finance a portion of our deficit by increasing its holdings of dollars and its various debtors will continue to have a simple and costless method by which they can redeem their obligations to the Fund. The alternative under present circumstances, now that they cannot pay off directly in dollars, would have been either to buy gold from the United States with which to repay the Fund, or to purchase other convertible currencies in the market with their dollars at extra cost and inconvenience.

Drawings by the United States under this new arrangement will be repayable in 3 years, with a 2-year extension available if needed. No interest will be payable, but the drawings will be subject to a one-time service charge of one-half of 1 percent.

10. Evolution of International Monetary System

During the past 2 years great progress has been made in strengthening the basic fabric of the international monetary system upon which the whole free world depends. Far closer cooperation among the central banks of the leading industrial countries has been achieved. Reciprocal credit arrangements have been established to meet instantly any disruptive disturbance to international payments—arrangements which successfully contained the monetary repercussions of the Berlin crisis in 1961, the heavy pressure on the Canadian dollar in the spring of 1962, the Cuban crisis last autumn, the reaction that followed the exclusion of the United Kingdom from the Common Market, and a number of less striking events that might, in other years, have set off dangerous rounds of currency speculation. An informal but highly effective operating relationship has grown up among a number of the same countries with respect to the London gold market, ruling out for the future any repetition of the alarming rise in the price of gold which created such uncertainty in October 1960. Finally, 10 of the leading industrial countries have established a $6 billion facility for providing supplemental resources to the International Monetary Fund, which will be available in the event of any threat to the stability of the international monetary system.[1]

The net result has been to provide strong defenses against successful raids on a major currency. Our efforts to strengthen these defenses will continue. While this process is taking place, the United States will continue to study and discuss with other countries measures which might be taken for a further strengthening of the international monetary system over the longer run. The U.S. interest in the continuing evolution of the system inaugurated at the time of Bretton Woods is not a result of our current payments deficit—rather it reflects our concern that adequate provision be made for the growth of international liquidity to finance expanding world trade over the years ahead. Indeed, one of the reasons that new sources of liquidity may well be needed is that, as we close our payments gap, we will cut down our provision of dollars to the rest of the world.

As yet, this Government is not prepared to recommend any specific prescription for long-term improvement of the international monetary system. But we are studying the matter closely; we shall be discussing possible improvements with our friends abroad; and our minds will be open to their initiatives. We share their view that the problem of improving the payments mechanism is one that demands careful joint deliberation. At the same time, we do not pretend that talk of long-range reform of the system is any substitute for the actions that we ourselves must take now.

The Promise of the Future

Full implementation of the program of action I have outlined today should lead to substantial improvement in our international payments. The rate of Government expenditures abroad will drop by $900 million over the next 18 months, and the combined effect of the increase in short-term interest rates and the interest equalization tax should equal, and more probably exceed, this figure. Gains of this magnitude—approximately $2 billion—will give us the time our basic long-term program needs to improve our international competitive position, and increase the attraction for investment in the United States.

These two objectives must be the basis of any permanent closing of the

[1] *Documents, 1962*, pp. 529–36.

payments gap, and this program will achieve them without threatening our growth at home. It will also do so without compromising our adherence to the principles of freer trade and free movements of capital. It will, in fact, help prevent pressures for more restrictive measures. In short, while we must intensify our efforts, we can do so with full confidence in the future.

Joint statement by the Governments of Canada and the United States, Washington, 21 July 1963[1]

Representatives of Canada and the United States met in Washington during the weekend to appraise the impact on the Canadian financial markets of the proposed United States 'interest equalization tax.'

The two Governments recognize the need for effective action to improve the balance-of-payments positions of both countries and both are equally determined that such action shall not impair the intimate economic relationships between the two countries, nor impede the growth essential for both economies.

For many years the capital markets of the two countries have been closely interconnected, and U.S. exports of capital to Canada have financed a substantial portion of the Canadian current account deficit with the U.S. This need continues. A portion of these flows must be supplied through the sale of new issues of Canadian securities in American markets. U.S. officials had considered that ample flows for these needs would continue under the proposed 'interest equalization tax.' However, Canadian representatives stated that this would require a very substantial rise in the entire Canadian interest rate structure. It was recognized by both Governments that such a development would be undesirable in the present economic circumstances.

In the light of this situation U.S. officials agreed that the draft legislation to be submitted to the Congress would include a provision authorizing a procedure under which the President could modify the application of the tax by the establishment from time to time of exemptions, which he could make either unlimited or limited in amount. The President would thus have the flexibility to permit tax-free purchases of new issues needed to maintain the unimpeded flow of trade and payments between the two countries, and to take care of exceptional situations that might arise in the case of other countries. U.S. officials made clear that this did not modify their proposals regarding the taxation of transactions in outstanding securities; over the past year such transactions between Canada and the U.S. have not been a major factor.

The Canadian authorities stated that it would not be the desire or intention of Canada to increase her foreign exchange reserves through the proceeds of borrowings in the U.S., and it is the hope and expectation of both Governments that by maintaining close consultation it will prove possible in practice to have an unlimited exemption for Canada without adverse effects on the United States.

It was agreed that active consultations would continue to strengthen the close economic relations between the two countries and at the same time facilitate measures for making the maximum practicable contribution to economic expansion and the strength and stability of both currencies.

[1] *D.S.B.*, 12 August 1963, p. 256. The text was released simultaneously in Ottawa and Washington on 21 July 1963.

C 9261 E

Eighteenth Annual Meeting of the Board of Governors of the International Monetary Fund, Washington, 30 September–4 October 1963

(i) *Statement by M. Pierre-Paul Schweitzer, Chairman of the Executive Board and Managing Director of the Fund, in presentation of the Annual Report*[1]

I feel very deeply honored to be addressing you today and to be presenting for the first time the Annual Report of the Fund to the Board of Governors. But the joy it should give me to be in my present position is overshadowed by the great sorrow and sense of loss I feel at Per Jacobsson's tragic and untimely departure.[2] We have already heard moving tributes to him from President Kennedy and Governor Carli.[3] I think the highest tribute we in the Fund can try to pay to Per Jacobsson's memory is to strive to maintain the stature and the effectiveness of this organization which he did so much to promote, and to be worthy of the ideals and the inspiration which he imparted to it. May I be allowed to add my personal expression of sympathy to Mrs. Jacobsson and to her daughters, who played so important a role in his life and added so much to the charm of the relations we had with him.

Before I proceed to discuss the more general developments reviewed in the Annual Report which you have before you, I would like to welcome the Governors of the 20 member countries who have joined the Fund since the last Annual Meeting. They are Algeria, Burundi, Cameroon, Central African Republic, Chad, Congo (Brazzaville), Congo (Leopoldville), Dahomey, Gabon, Guinea, Ivory Coast, Jamaica, Malagasy Republic, Mali, Mauritania, Niger, Rwanda, Trinidad and Tobago, Uganda and Upper Volta. In addition, we have received an application for membership from one more—Kenya. We extend a warm welcome to the Governors and the representatives of all these countries. The total membership of the Fund is now 102—almost three times as many as had joined the Fund when the Articles took effect at the end of 1945.

In the fiscal year ended last April, as mentioned in the Annual Report, 18 countries purchased the equivalent of $580 million from the Fund and the equivalent of $807 million was received in repurchases. Both purchases and repurchases were less than in the previous fiscal year, when the very large United Kingdom drawing took place; they represented, nevertheless, a substantial volume of financial support extended by the Fund to a good many of its members. In addition, the Fund has at present stand-by arrangements in effect with 20 countries under which $1.8 billion is available, including the recently renewed stand-by of $1.0 billion with the United Kingdom and the $500 million stand-by arrangement with the United States, concluded only two months ago.

The United States stand-by was clearly one of the most important events in the Fund since the conclusion of the period covered by the Annual Report. The United States had not previously resorted to the Fund, although the financing of its balance of payments deficit has been assisted by the Fund's operations. This stand-by is evidence of the readiness and the ability of the Fund to assist all its members, be their quotas large or small. In addition, I should like in a

---

[1] International Monetary Fund, *Summary Proceedings of the Eighteenth Annual Meeting of the Board of Governors* (Washington, D.C., 1963), pp. 15–30; delivered 1 October.

[2] Dr. Jacobsson died on 5 May 1963.

[3] *Summary Proceedings, 1963*, pp. 1–6 and pp. 7–14.

few words, to place the stand-by in the context of the policies we have been pursuing with respect to the currencies to be used in drawings from, and in repayments to, the Fund. The criteria appropriate to these operations have been gradually worked out in recent years and given concrete form in a Decision of the Executive Directors in July 1962. In conformity with these criteria, the Fund, having regard to the continuing balance of payments deficits of the United States, encouraged countries to make repurchases to the Fund in U.S. dollars and to draw in other currencies. As a result, in the course of the last financial year, the Fund increased its holdings of U.S. dollars by $340 million, and assisted to this extent in the financing of the United States' balance of payments deficit.

For some time, Fund holdings of U.S. dollars have been in the vicinity of 75 per cent of quota, beyond which they cannot, under the Articles of Agreement, be accepted in repurchase. This threatened to cause inconvenience to the many countries which prefer to make their repurchases in dollars since they accumulate them in their reserves. In July of this year, however, the difficulty was resolved when the Fund entered into a stand-by arrangement authorizing the United States to draw other member currencies to the equivalent of $500 million during the next 12 months. The United States intends to use this facility to sell such currencies for dollars at par to other members to be used by them to make repurchases to the Fund. In this way not only will repurchases be facilitated but the United States will continue to receive balance of payments assistance similar to that formerly provided by repurchases in dollars.

*   *   *

Another important development with respect to members' access to Fund resources was the Decision of the Executive Directors in February of this year regarding the Compensatory Financing of Export Fluctuations.[1] By this Decision, the Fund created a new drawing facility which, we hope, will greatly benefit primary producing countries adversely affected by temporary declines in their export earnings.

It has always been one of the recognized functions of the Fund to provide financial assistance in case of balance of payments difficulties arising from export shortfalls, and there have been many instances of countries drawing on the Fund under such circumstances. Yet it was felt that this problem had become sufficiently pressing to deserve special consideration. The Executive Directors and the staff spent many months in studying and discussing it. Indeed, this was the last major task to which Mr. Jacobsson devoted his efforts. The Decision which finally emerged and which is published in the Annual Report is, in my opinion, a useful further development of the basic principles and aims of Fund policy.

In essence, it establishes a new facility to provide assistance to members experiencing balance of payments difficulties arising from export shortfalls. This facility will become available in cases where the shortfall is temporary and largely caused by circumstances beyond the member's control, and where the member is willing to cooperate with the Fund in an effort to find appropriate solutions for its balance of payments difficulties, where such solutions are needed.

Given these conditions, a country is assured that its request for a compensatory drawing will be met in amounts not normally exceeding 25 per cent

[1] For text see International Monetary Fund, *Annual Report, 1963* (Washington, D.C.), pp. 196–9.

of the member's quota. Besides facilities available under these liberal terms, members may, of course, draw under the Fund's ordinary drawing policies for the purpose of meeting difficulties arising from export fluctuations.

Furthermore, in order to enable members to have the full benefit of the facility, the Fund will be willing to exercise its authority to waive the limits which are prescribed in the Articles, firstly, on the amount that a member may purchase within any 12 months and secondly, on the Fund's holdings of a member's currency, which should not exceed 200 per cent of its quota. The latter is a new development in the Fund's policy; hitherto, there has been no waiver of the 200 per cent limit.

I have been glad to note that the Fund's new policy on compensatory financing has been well received both by Fund members and by international organizations. In particular, the United Nations Commission on International Commodity Trade has concluded that the new facility can make a substantial contribution toward solving the problems arising from export fluctuations in primary exporting countries.

So far only one country—Brazil—has made a compensatory drawing under the new facility. But the Fund stands ready, in accordance with the Decision, to extend compensatory drawings to other countries whenever the need arises. The fact that no further requests have been made so far is, I believe, largely attributable to the rather favorable developments in primary product markets over the last 12 months, which have tended to raise export earnings of primary exporting countries; I shall briefly revert to this encouraging development a little later.

The Decision on Compensatory Financing also referred to the question of members' quotas in the Fund. These serve both to define the amounts that members may draw from the Fund and to determine to a considerable degree the size of the Fund's resources. The thorough review of quotas in 1958 and 1959, arising from a Resolution adopted by the Board of Governors at their New Delhi Meeting in 1958,[1] resulted in a general increase in quotas of 50 per cent, although there were a number of increases of more than 50 per cent. As the years pass, however, changes inevitably occur in the relative importance of different countries in the world economy, in their relative need for temporary balance of payments assistance, and in their relative ability to provide the resources for such temporary assistance to others through the medium of the Fund.

Under the Articles of Agreement, the quotas of all members are reviewed every five years, and on this occasion a review is also made of their general structure. At any time, however, a member may request the adjustment of its quota. Moreover, the Executive Directors, in their Compensatory Financing Decision, have declared that '. . . where adjustment of the quotas of certain primary exporting countries, and in particular of countries with relatively small quotas, would be appropriate to make them more adequate in the light of fluctuations in export proceeds and other relevant criteria, the Fund is willing to give sympathetic consideration to requests for such adjustment.' In pursuance of this paragraph of the Decision, the Directors, on the requests of El Salvador,

---

[1] *Summary Proceedings of the Thirteenth Annual Meeting of the Board of Governors, October 1958.* (Washington, D.C., 1959). Resolution No. 13–10, p. 178. See also *Summary Proceedings, September 1959.* Resolution No. 14–1, pp. 158–60.

Honduras, and the Syrian Arab Republic, have recommended to the Board of Governors increases in the quotas of these members. The Executive Directors have also adopted a Decision under which members that require assistance to facilitate the payment of the gold portion of these quota increases can obtain such assistance from the Fund.

*   *   *

The Fund's relations with individual countries extend far beyond its financial transactions. The annual consultations under Article XIV of the Fund Agreement, and those which since 1961 have been conducted with Article VIII countries, provide for continuing contact between the Fund and its members and account for a substantial part of our work. These consultations have provided the means for a periodic exchange of views between the members concerned and the Fund on monetary and financial developments. By giving the Fund a deeper understanding of the problems and policies, particularly of the larger industrial countries, they have assisted the Fund in its role of maintaining and defending the international monetary system, as well as helping individual members to deal with their balance of payments difficulties. In addition, in the Article XIV consultations, the Fund's reviews of members' restrictive systems and the advice which it has given through the consultation procedure have, over the years, played an important role in the substantial reduction of exchange restrictions and discriminations. In this process we have seen, for example, the considerable reduction in the application of bilateral payments arrangements among Fund members. These consultations, as well as others undertaken when particular needs arose, have also been important in enabling the Fund to assist members to simplify multiple currency systems and to move toward realistic unitary rates of exchange.

Another important form of Fund cooperation with members consists in the provision of technical advice and assistance. In a number of instances, Fund staff members have been assigned upon request to provide such assistance to the national authorities of countries adopting programs designed to establish the conditions of internal and external stability necessary for sound economic development. Technical aid has also been given to help the authorities of newly independent countries, including some not yet members of the Fund, to deal with the many problems facing them.

In recent years the Fund has found a growing demand among less developed countries for technical assistance in strengthening their fiscal systems and in establishing central banking arrangements along sound lines. We are taking new steps to meet these demands. We are establishing a technical staff specialized in fiscal matters, especially taxation, budget, and financial controls. This Fiscal Affairs Group will be available to participate in Fund technical missions and to work with officials in member countries in efforts to improve the effectiveness and scope of their fiscal systems, thus contributing to their financial stability and to their economic development. In addition, the Fund is setting up a panel of outside experts, mainly from established central banks, whose services the Fund could provide from time to time for technical assignments on various aspects of central banking, such as the setting up of new central banks or improving existing organizations and filling executive or advisory positions.

*   *   *

I turn now from what has been happening inside the Fund to what has been happening in the world at large. As outlined in the Annual Report, the structure of international payments, in recent years, has been dominated by the external deficit of the United States, with the corresponding surpluses appearing now in one group of countries and now in another. The main characteristics of the United States' international transactions are a large surplus on ordinary commercial transactions in goods and services, more than offset by deficits arising from U.S. Government expenditures abroad, from a substantial investment of U.S. private long-term capital, and from an outflow of short-term capital. This underlying pattern continued in the first half of 1963 and, in fact, the deficit worsened. A rise in the surplus on goods and services account was more than offset by a considerable increase in the capital outflow, including larger direct investment in Western Europe, and by a rapid expansion, starting late in 1962, of new Canadian security flotations on U.S. markets.

During 1962, the extreme surplus position of most continental European countries, which in earlier years had been the counterpart of the U.S. deficit, were largely eliminated. Only France continued to show a major surplus by the end of the year. On the other hand, there were marked improvements in the balance of payments positions of Japan and the United Kingdom, while a number of primary producing countries also achieved better results. In the current year the surplus in France has persisted, although it is now attributable to a greater extent to capital inflow. Apart from an inflow of capital into Germany, the position of other countries in continental Europe has, on balance, not changed much. In the United Kingdom, despite a continued improvement on trade account, other factors (including a rise in overseas private investment and withdrawal of foreign funds in the first quarter) have led to a slight deficit. On the other hand, many of the primary producers have continued to acquire reserves at a substantial rate.

The present international payments situation has many favorable aspects. The improvement in the payments balances of the less developed countries is desirable in itself, and is unlikely to constitute any enduring drain on reserves elsewhere. Even before the recent measures in the United States aimed at tempering the outflow of capital, policies in Canada and Japan were such as to reduce their increase of reserves to small proportions. The United Kingdom's balance of payments, though probably in smaller surplus than in 1962, appears reasonably stable. The fairly expansionary fiscal program may be expected to lead to some rise in imports. But if exports continue to expand as they have in the past year there should be a sufficient surplus on goods and services account to provide resources for the continuation of capital exports and aid on a reasonable scale. The stand-by arrangement of $1 billion which the United Kingdom has entered into with the Fund should help the Government achieve its objectives of more rapid economic expansion without giving rise to inflation.

There is some cause for concern in the continued U.S. deficit, the accelerated flow of capital to Western Europe, and signs of renewed growth in the exchange reserves of certain continental countries. But, notwithstanding these developments, there are encouraging features. It is probable that private capital outflows from the United States in the last year or two have been greater, and those from Europe smaller, than correspond to the true saving and investing potential of the respective areas. Quite apart from the proposed Interest Equalization Tax, the other fiscal measures currently being proposed by the Government of the United States to raise the level of domestic activity and the attractiveness of home investment, while they may have adverse effects on the balance of trade, may also, for a time at least, have an even greater favorable impact by making the domestic capital market more attractive to both foreign and domestic lenders. The recent tendency to a convergence of short-term interest rates in most countries and the downward movements in the long-term interest rates of the United Kingdom and some other European countries should work in the same direction, subject to the possible effects of anti-inflation measures which may be taken by some other countries. Any improvements that might be made in the structure of European capital markets, along the lines recommended by the Lorain Committee in France, and the De Voghel Commission in Belgium, should make these markets relatively more accessible to borrowers. With the foreign exchange reserves of most European countries in a comfortable position, the existing restrictions on foreign borrowing in European markets might well be re-examined, though in some European countries the high level of interest rates still presents a formidable obstacle to the export of capital. Finally, a number of industrial countries whose wealth is rapidly increasing should be in a position to expand substantially their assistance to less developed countries.

Exclusive emphasis should not be laid, however, on the rectification of capital flows. The balance of payments of the United States cannot be said to have attained a satisfactory equilibrium until there is a surplus on goods and services sufficient to provide a flow of capital exports and aid, especially to the less developed countries, on a scale consistent with the capacity of the huge American capital market. The tendency, in recent years, for wages and domestic prices to rise faster in Europe than in the United States promotes the attainment of such an equilibrium. As yet, however, these changes in relative domestic price levels seem to have had little effect on relative export price levels, or on the competitive strength of the different industrial countries in export markets. Moreover, domestic demand in Europe may be slackening and it is unlikely, and indeed undesirable, that the rise in labor costs and prices in Europe will be allowed to continue at anything like its recent pace.

I should, however, not wish it to be inferred that we should underestimate the great underlying strength of the United States' payments situation. I might particularly emphasize that in the last decade new U.S. private investment abroad exceeded the balance of payments deficit by $7 billion, and this increase in the level of U.S. assets abroad has led to a steadily rising stream of income from foreign investment. But, as has been stressed by President Kennedy, the restoration of a sound and lasting equilibrium in the U.S. balance of payments will call for determined and patient efforts over a number of years, with strong emphasis on keeping costs stable or falling. Other countries in a surplus position can help if they maintain the impetus of their growth. It is not realistic to expect quick removal of imbalances in the structure of international payments but, fortunately, the United States has ample reserves and other sources of international liquidity to finance an orderly adjustment, compatible with the objectives of a high level of employment and a satisfactory rate of growth.

* * *

The payments position of the less developed countries in 1962 was somewhat more favorable than in the previous year, and this improvement was not due to aid or to capital inflow. In fact, the inflow of private capital was quite a bit smaller than in 1961 and the rise in government loans and grants was insufficient to make up for this. The most encouraging development, and the one mainly responsible for the net improvement, was the increase in export earnings. In contrast to developments in 1961, when a moderate rise in the export volume of the less developed countries had been almost entirely offset by the decline in the prices for their products, export earnings in 1962 increased at nearly the same rate as the export volume. The downward movement in the prices of basic commodities, which had persisted for some time, was reversed late in 1962 and recovery has continued into 1963. There has been a further gain in exports in the early part of this year and, with price developments more favorable, it may be hoped that the payments position of the less developed countries will show a further improvement.

However, as uncertainties still exist in the payments picture, I welcome the fact that, in general, these countries are taking the opportunity provided by this improvement to strengthen further their reserve positions. For though recent developments have improved the payments positions of the less developed countries, this should not obscure the fact that over the last decade the growth in their export earnings has been sluggish. Imports of primary products have not kept pace with the growth of national income or of manufacturing production in the industrial countries; moreover, export receipts of the less developed countries have been adversely affected by a worsening of their terms of trade. This reflects to a certain extent displacement of primary products by the rapidly rising use of synthetic materials. Moreover, there are other obstacles which the less developed countries encounter in most of their foreign markets. Even some tropical products, grown exclusively in those countries, are subject to import duties or high consumption taxes imposed by industrialized countries. For the most part, however, the trade barriers which the industrial countries impose against imports from the less developed countries are maintained for the protection of domestic output of temperate climate foodstuffs, raw materials, and manufactured goods. The importance of this last item should not be underestimated. Many of the developing countries are becoming increasingly equipped for the production of manufactures, and access to export markets is important for the diversification of their economies.

More generally, it is vital that ways be found to improve the exchange earnings of the less developed countries, on which they depend to finance both their growing import demands and the service of their growing foreign debt. A two-pronged attack is now being made on this important problem. On the one hand, many of the industrial countries are considering what they can do to allow freer access to their markets, for both primary and manufactured products of the less developed countries, even though this may involve some domestic economic adjustments. On the other hand, consideration is being given to international arrangements, in which the importing countries would cooperate, aimed at maintaining at a tolerable level the prices paid for primary products. I very much hope that ways may be found to deal successfully with these problems, notably through the GATT and at the forthcoming United Nations Conference on Trade and Development.

The growth in exports, and indeed the growth in the real income of the less developed countries, has also been adversely affected by the persistence of inflationary tendencies within those countries. For the most part these tendencies are closely linked with efforts to accelerate economic development and to raise the living standards of their rapidly growing populations. There are also, however, sharply rising expenditures in some countries for nondevelopment purposes which add to the problem. Domestic resources from savings and taxation in these countries are meager and inadequately mobilized and the available foreign funds are not sufficient to bridge the gap. This tempts many countries to turn to inflationary finance, mostly through government borrowing from the banks.

Experience over many years has shown that the inflationary process in the end hampers rather than promotes real growth, and the Annual Report this year has emphasized again the close and organic relation between financial stability and economic growth. We in the Fund draw much encouragement from the growing awareness of this fact in the less developed countries, very many of which have taken steps, frequently in close cooperation with the Fund, designed to achieve and preserve a sound and stable currency and financial structure which will contribute effectively to economic growth. It is indeed one of the most important functions of the Fund in its relations with the less developed member countries to assist them in every way possible—through technical advice and by providing financial support—to realize the objective of sustained economic growth.

The Fund cannot itself provide long-term loans for development. However, success in the fight against inflation helps to restore an environment attractive to foreign investors and favorable to the repatriation of domestic capital, and one in which governments and international institutions can feel more confident that assistance in the form of loans and grants will be put to effective productive use.

* * *

I turn now to the subject of international reserves and liquidity which has attracted increasing interest over the past year and to which, as you will have seen, the Executive Directors have devoted a chapter in their Annual Report.

The provision of an appropriate level and distribution of international liquidity is an essential aspect of any effective international monetary system and is important to the pursuit of the main economic objectives of the community of nations, such as high employment, satisfactory growth without inflation, exchange stability, and an expansion of international trade. At the same time, we should bear in mind that these desirable objectives cannot be achieved through liquidity measures alone. Other forms of international cooperation are equally of importance. I have in mind efforts to push ahead with the removal of obstacles to trade and payments, and to achieve a measure of international coordination of interest rate and other financial policies, and also, where practicable, to encourage the coordination of other economic policies.

People often speak of international liquidity as if it were a sort of money used in the financing of international trade. Trade financing, however, is ordinarily carried on by means of private trade credit or private bank credit. International liquidity, on the other hand, consists of international reserves and other resources which are at the disposal of monetary authorities and which serve to

finance balance of payments deficits, and thus provide time to make any adjustments that may be required to eliminate those deficits without resort to measures
that would be damaging to the prosperity of the countries concerned or to the
rest of the world.

Reserves constitute the most definite and easily measurable form of international liquidity. By 'reserves' we mean official holdings of gold, foreign
exchange, and positive, or 'gold tranche' positions in the Fund, which indicate
the amount which a member can draw from the Fund without increasing the
Fund's holdings of its currency beyond 100 per cent of its quota. One of the
factors which gives rise to pessimistic views of the future adequacy of international liquidity is the tendency for the rate of growth of world reserves to
slow down. Fears are sometimes expressed that, as the United States succeeds
in its efforts to eliminate its payments deficit, the effect may be to slow down the
growth of foreign exchange holdings and therefore of total reserves. But it is
not always realized that reserves are not the only means of financing payments
deficits. Other forms of international liquidity, though perhaps less readily
available than reserves, are nonetheless of great importance. A country's borrowing potential should be recognized as an alternative form of liquidity. Facilities
that countries may have to draw upon the Fund or to draw upon each other,
their access to other international financial institutions, and their general ability
to borrow abroad—all provide them with a greater or lesser degree of assurance
of being able to finance payments deficits. These facilities are not, in my view,
made less valuable by the fact that their utilization depends in some cases on
the condition that timely action should be taken to rectify the balance of payments deficits which they serve to finance.

Much of the progress that has been made over recent years in providing the
means of financing deficits and preserving the stability of exchange rates relates
to these types of liquidity other than reserves. For example, there are the inter-
central-bank credits, which helped to defend sterling in 1961, and the more
extensive and formalized network of swap arrangements established over the
last two years by the United States with as many as ten industrial countries and
with the Bank for International Settlements, to an aggregate value of $1,550
million. The very fact that such arrangements were in existence helped to keep
the exchange markets calm despite several events that occurred during the year
which threatened confidence. Last year also saw the United States begin borrowing from abroad in foreign currency as a further instrument for the defense
of the balance of payments. As for the Fund, the formal entry into force of the
General Arrangements to Borrow in October 1962[1] provides the fund with the
means of extending massive support to members whenever this is necessary to
forestall or cope with an impairment of the international monetary system. The
establishment by the Fund of its new compensatory financing facility may also be
regarded as an additional element of liquidity, provided more especially for the
less developed countries of the world.

The network of credit arrangements between individual countries that has
been worked out over the past two years provides a valuable additional bulwark
for the international monetary system. We in the Fund welcome this striking
illustration of the progress made in cooperation between monetary authorities in

[1] See *Documents, 1962*, pp. 529–36.

recent years. It is likely to be particularly useful in calming apprehensions that might otherwise disturb the foreign exchange markets at times of crisis and in deterring or offsetting spasmodic movements of short-term capital.

Such arrangements are necessarily of a short-term nature, and give rise to claims of a bilateral character. Other suggestions have been put forward for multilateral arrangements under which lending countries would acquire claims on an international institution rather than directly on the debtor country. The International Monetary Fund, of course, already provides a means whereby a creditor country gives assistance indirectly to a debtor country to meet the latter's need and thereby acquires a generalized international claim which can be used to meet its own external financial needs on a later occasion.

Perhaps I may be excused for expressing my belief that insofar as it is found necessary from time to time to expand the level of world liquidity by international action, the Fund will be found to be the instrument through which the bulk of the required expansion can most suitably be carried out. The provision of supplementary international liquidity is, after all, one of the principal reasons for which the Fund was set up and is a matter with which it is concerned from day to day. The Fund's policies and practices are not static. They have been modified and adapted to meet changing world conditions over the years. They can be further modified to enable the Fund to continue to play an effective role both in the provision of liquidity and in the implementation of its other principal function, namely, that of guardian of a code of international good behaviour in the currency sphere. In time to come, it may be found that to enable the Fund more fully to achieve its purposes, changes may be needed in the legal provisions governing its operations. Even if a case for the amendment of the Articles were made out, and this has not yet been demonstrated, we may expect that in the evolving international monetary system of the future, primary reliance will be placed on an ever-improving Fund.

In my view the members of the Fund, taken as a whole, are not at present being prevented from adopting or carrying out desirable policies by any shortage of international liquidity. But it is wise and prudent to look into the future to consider what difficulties might arise and to devise ways of meeting them. This has been the habit of the Fund. All the main developments in the policies and practices of the Fund, whether it be quota increases, drawing policies, the General Arrangements to Borrow, or Compensatory Financing, have been preceded by long periods of study which have laid the foundation for positive action. In the coming year the Fund will develop and intensify its studies regarding international liquidity, the functioning of the international monetary system, and the effective role of the Fund in this field. At the same time there is a wholly understandable interest in this important range of problems which extends beyond the Fund, and I have no doubt that other bodies, groups of countries, and individual members will be engaged on similar inquiries. We welcome all forms of international cooperation in this field, and I am sure the efforts of the Fund will be helpful to all members who are engaged in the important task of subjecting to critical examination the international monetary system. It is a system which is serving us well, but which can without doubt over the years be even better equipped to meet the needs and stresses which may develop in the future.

(ii) *Statement by the Governor for the United States, Mr. Dillon*[1]

At the outset of my remarks, I ask you to join with me in paying tribute to our late great colleague and good friend, Per Jacobsson. Firmly dedicated throughout this long and distinguished career to the cause of financial stability, he guided the International Monetary Fund with a deep understanding of the needs and realities of his times. The responsibilities of Managing Director have now passed into the capable hands of Pierre-Paul Schweitzer. His willingness to assume these duties provides us with fresh assurance that the Fund, building on its current strength and influence at the center of the international monetary system, will successfully meet the fresh challenges that lie ahead.

It is also a pleasure to welcome to the Fund family an unusually large number of new members, bringing our group to more than 100. The election of a nineteenth Executive Director, who will cast the votes of a group of the many new African members, is symbolic of the increasing usefulness of the Fund to the emerging nations.

I am sure that each of these new members will profit from the important assistance the Fund can render to their further development, through its expanding program of technical assistance in the areas of central banking and fiscal practices and policies, through its regular consultations, and by providing timely financial support for well-conceived stabilization programs. In addition, the new compensatory financing facilities[2] announced last March mark an important and constructive advance in the services available to members heavily dependent upon exports of primary commodities.

These activities in support of balanced, dynamic growth are, of course, complemented by those of the Fund's companion Bretton Woods institution, the World Bank and its affiliates, now under the able direction of George Woods. I should mention particularly at this year's Meeting the work of the International Development Association, whose activities in so short a span of time offer so much promise for the future. Action by the Part I[3] countries on the proposals for increasing its resources will mark another milestone in the work to which it is dedicated and in which we are all joined together.

The successive Annual Reports of the International Monetary Fund have expertly traced the evolution of our international monetary system since World War II. They have also made clear that new problems have a way of emerging as older ones are solved. The Report for 1963 is no exception. In particular, it deals at some length with the adequacy of existing arrangements for providing international liquidity during the coming years. The authors point out that liquidity is not simply a matter of the aggregate of official holdings of gold or foreign exchange, and they review the progress made in recent years—in considerable part under the auspices of the Fund itself—in supplementing these resources with international credit. But the Report also recognizes that the needs of nations for assured means of financing balance of payments deficits—either

---

[1] *Summary Proceedings, 1963*, pp. 42–53; delivered on 1 October.

[2] I.M.F., *Annual Report, 1963*, pp. 196–9.

[3] Cf. International Bank for Reconstruction and Development, *Articles of Agreement of the International Development Association*, 1 February 1960. Schedule A. Part I countries are those 'developed' member states, ninety per cent of whose initial subscription was payable in gold or freely convertible currency.

by drawing upon a stock of liquid assets or by means of borrowing—can be expected to increase over time. At the same time, as the deficit in the balance of payments of the United States is narrowed and closed, that deficit will no longer contribute to the liquidity of other nations in the manner and magnitude of the last few years.

The Fund's Report has now been supplemented by the thoughtful and important statement of its new Managing Director.[1] Mr. Schweitzer indicated that the Fund expects to study the problem of international liquidity and has expressed the Fund's readiness to cooperate with others in such a study. He points out that studies of this problem are timely even though there is at present no sign of any shortage in international liquidity. He has also given us his view that the Fund should be at the center of whatever strengthening of the international monetary system may prove to be desirable. The United States finds itself in general agreement with all of these thoughts.

But in discussing this matter, I would like to make one point crystal clear: The United States does not view possible improvements in the methods of supplying international liquidity as relieving it of the compelling and immediate task of reducing its own payments deficit. Indeed, it is largely the prospect of the elimination of the United States payments deficit that makes it necessary and advisable to undertake these studies.

Nor can the provision of appropriate facilities for international liquidity relieve nations of their joint responsibilities for effective and timely action to eliminate such imbalances in trade and payments as may arise in the future. In a world of fixed exchange rates and convertible currencies, deficits and surpluses emerge from a wide variety of causes, both domestic and international. The necessity to make cash outlays for defense and aid, shifts in the basic pattern of demand for internationally traded goods, the developments of new products, resources, and production techniques (and developments in capital markets) can be just as important as changes in average price levels and aggregate demand within countries.

The adjustments necessary to correct these deficits and surpluses take time if they are to proceed in an orderly fashion, without damaging consequences for either domestic growth and stability or the free flow of trade among nations. That is why, as part of the adjustment process, a country experiencing deficits needs reserves to draw upon, or credit that it can rely upon. That is also why a country receiving the counterpart in surpluses needs assets of assured value, in amounts and forms that will not disrupt its own economy. But in the last analysis, without effective adjustments by both deficit and surplus countries, no amount of liquidity will enable us to achieve the mutual benefits of a closely integrated world economy within a framework of steady growth accompanied by monetary stability.

The challenge implicit in this situation is clear. Side by side with our studies of possible liquidity needs, we must consciously seek out means of improving the process of international adjustment itself, while preserving our separate abilities to meet our respective domestic needs.

This is a large order, but one that is well within our capacities. Much has been learned from the experience of recent years. We have come to recognize that

[1] See pp. 98–107 above.

in shaping domestic policies and choosing from the various tools available for use, their varying impact upon our external accounts, and upon those of our trading partners, must be taken fully into account. There is greater awareness of the need to identify and eliminate those market rigidities that inhibit the process of adjustment. And we are learning that new techniques can be developed for assisting the process of adjustment that are consistent with domestic goals and competitive markets.

Much of this can be illustrated by analysis of the position of the United States, faced as we are with the twin tasks of achieving more rapid growth at home while simultaneously closing the troublesome gap in our balance of payments. And many of the lessons of this experience, I believe, will prove sooner or later to be more generally applicable to the problems of international adjustment.

Business activity in the United States has continued to expand over the past year at a fairly steady pace. Total output has now reached a rate of over $585 billion a year—in real terms more than 13 per cent above the level of early 1961.

Measured against other peacetime expansions of the past 40 years, this performance has been encouraging. All but one of these recovery periods have now been equaled or exceeded in terms of percentage increase in output, and that single exception took place only after the steep declines in production during the early 1930's. Prices of manufactured goods have remained virtually unchanged during the current expansion, extending the period of stability that has existed since 1958. However, unemployment is still excessive. And we are not fully utilizing our available savings or our existing productive plant capacity. True, investment activity has risen in response to increases in demand and to measures introduced a year ago to liberalize the tax treatment of depreciation and provide an investment tax credit. But new investment still remains below the levels required to support a full employment economy and to assure the position of our industry among the leaders in technological progress.

At the same time, our over-all balance of payments has responded slowly to the series of measures we have undertaken since 1961. The over-all deficit was reduced to $2.2 billion in 1962, from $3.9 billion in 1960 and $2.4 billion in 1961. But the deficit grew markedly larger during the first half of 1963.

When this situation first became apparent, we made a thorough-going review of our entire balance of payments program, which culminated in a series of decisions announced by the President on July 18.[1] Resulting programs now under way will, by the end of next year, bring a reduction of $1 billion in the annual rate of dollar expenditures abroad for defense, aid and other government programs. Savings of similar magnitude are also expected on capital account as a result of the proposed Interest Equalization Tax and the firmer structure of short-term interest rates accompanying the recent one-half per cent increase in the Federal Reserve discount rate. We can already see indications that the deterioration in our accounts during the first half of the year is being arrested.

These new actions will complement and reinforce the longer-run measures we have been taking to achieve both external balance and more rapid domestic growth. Basic to our strategy for achieving these twin goals is a broad program of individual and corporate tax reduction totaling $11 billion, which, after passage by our House of Representatives last week, is now before our Senate.

[1] See pp. 85–97 above.

It will provide an impetus to the domestic economy in a manner consistent with our international position. It will give increased flexibility to our monetary authorities in meeting balance of payments requirements. The added incentives for use of capital in the United States will enhance the relative attractiveness of investment here for Americans and foreigners alike. At the same time, the increased productivity associated with rising investment, together with greater incentives to develop and market new products and to apply more rapidly the fruits of our vast research capabilities, will reinforce the efforts we are making to increase our exports.

Our ability to expand production—which is implicit in our current unemployment, in our rapidly growing labor force, and in our margin of underutilized industrial capacity—provides protection against upward price pressures as the stimulus from the tax program takes hold. Meanwhile, we are continuing successfully to finance our budgetary deficit outside the banking system. For instance, in the year that ended August 31, the latest date for which figures are available, the combined holdings of government debt in the hands of our Federal Reserve and commercial banks declined by more than $1½ billion. We have also made further progress in improving the maturity structure of our marketable debt. As a result of our latest advance refunding, the average life of that debt exceeded 5¼ years for the first time since 1956. We are not faced, therefore, with the kind of excessive liquidity that could fuel inflationary developments as our economy moves toward fuller employment.

Perhaps most significant of all in terms of the outlook for prices, our manufacturing labor costs per unit of output have declined over the past 3 years—the first time since World War II that this basic measure of our competitive strength has improved for so long a period, or during a time of substantial recovery. And the rate of wage increases in our manufacturing industry is holding within the range of past and anticipated productivity increases.

In this way we are encouraging basic corrective forces in terms of costs and prices that should provide a firm base for improving our trading position, thus contributing to the orderly adjustment of our entire balance of payments. Highly tentative, but nonetheless encouraging, signs of an improvement in our international competitive position are developing. But it is clear that the contribution that exports can make to over-all balance will be heavily dependent upon the adjustment policies of other nations as well. By this I do not, of course, mean to suggest that surplus nations have a responsibility to inflate, any more than it would be consistent with our internal needs to force deflation. Nor, in our particular situation, would it be reasonable to look only—or primarily—to increases in our commercial trade balance as the solution for our payments problem.

But opportunities do exist for surplus nations, in instances where inflationary pressures are evident, to serve the interests both of their own domestic stability and of external balance by reducing or eliminating barriers to imports, including those from the United States. In the search for effective adjustment mechanisms within the context of a convertible currency system, this kind of action, it seems to me, can become, for surplus countries, a modern substitute for the inflationary price adjustments that we must all do everything we can to avoid.

A basic factor in our own deficit position has been the heavy burden we carry for the defense of the free world and for assisting the development of less favored nations. This burden, in a wider context, is an inescapable part of the kind of world we live in. But we are also learning that methods of handling these government outpayments, and more appropriate distribution of their balance of payments impact, can also contribute to the adjustment process without subverting their essential purpose.

Important savings have already been made in this area, reducing net outflows under our defense and aid programs from $3.8 billion in 1960 to $3.0 billion in 1962. A large portion of this improvement can be traced to the recognition by some European countries of their growing capacity to assume a greater share of the foreign exchange costs of the common defense. As a result, the drain on our payments from maintaining our troops in Germany and Italy is now virtually fully offset by their purchase of military equipment and supplies from the United States—equipment which, because of the size and flexibility of our defense industry, can be produced more rapidly and more economically in the United States than in their own countries. Thus these arrangements have simultaneously strengthened the free world's military and economic defenses.

In addition, we have adopted a policy of providing the great bulk of our economic aid to developing countries in the form of goods and services, so that it can be brought within the limits of our capacity without impairing its effectiveness. When current commitments are fully reflected in actual disbursements, only some 10 per cent of the aid from our various foreign assistance programs will be provided in the form of dollars. At the same time, I believe that we must guard against any tendency to make the 'tying' of aid into a subtle new form of protection for home industries. Rather, the logic of our efforts to expand multilateral trade and promote international efficiency through competition among the producers of all nations demands that it be used as a temporary device, reserved for periods of balance of payments strains.

With forces of adjustment under way in both our government and our commercial trade accounts, the most pressing problem in terms of our balance of payments has been the recent acceleration in the outflow of long-term capital. The net outflow of such capital during the first half of this year reached an annual rate of $3.8 billion. This was fully $1.3 billion higher than the already substantial figure for 1962 and nearly double the rate maintained over the years 1959–61. While some of this recent increase stemmed from direct investment, a flood of new foreign borrowings totaling nearly $1 billion in only six months was the major factor. This is considerably more than three times the volume we have been accustomed to.

It is entirely consistent with restoration of full equilibrium in international payments that the United States, with its capacity to generate large savings, continue to supply reasonable amounts of capital to aid the development of other nations. But it is perfectly clear that maintenance of outflows at the recent pace, far from being a constructive force in world payments, would soon put intolerable strains on the international monetary system as a whole.

As our program of tax reduction takes hold and there are stronger incentives to employ a larger portion of our savings at home, normal market forces will work strongly in the direction of reducing this outflow of long-term capital to more tolerable levels. But the experience of the past year makes clear that we cannot rely on these longer-term forces of adjustment to meet our immediate problems. Nor is it feasible to speed the process of adjustment by artificial attempts to force our entire structure of long-term interest rates sharply and suddenly higher. If possible at all in the face of the huge supply of savings flowing into our markets, this course of action would require so drastic a tightening of credit as to seriously jeopardize the prospects for domestic expansion.

In this situation, we have recommended enactment of a temporary Interest Equalization Tax which will have the effect of raising the costs of portfolio capital in our market by 1 per cent for borrowers in the developed countries abroad. This will bring these costs into a rough alignment with those in most other industrialized countries. The purpose is quite simple—to speed the essential redirection of capital flows in a manner comparable to an equivalent, but presently impracticable, rise in our entire structure of interest rates.

We view this tax solely as a necessary—but temporary—expedient to meet a specific situation that has arisen in large part out of a structural imbalance in the capital markets of the free world. Borrowers from deficit and surplus countries alike converge upon the New York market, not only because of our lower structure of long-term interest rates—since equivalent or lower rates can be found in at least two other countries—but because it is still the only source for international capital in whatever size and form desired, freely available to any borrower able to meet the normal market test of creditworthiness, and offering highly efficient distribution facilities with low issuing costs. In contrast, potential alternative markets are in most cases subject to official controls or have difficulty in supplying the needed funds in the volume required. And, with few exceptions, they are characterized by high and rigid rate structures. In the face of this situation, we must temporarily help to redirect the demands pressing on our market through a tax that will increase the costs of long-term borrowing here by foreigners.

The impediments to the development of more adequate European capital markets are currently under close and continuing study within the Organization for Economic Cooperation and Development, and progress is beginning to be visible. As efforts to improve European capital markets come to fruition and the remaining controls and restrictions are eliminated—and as our own domestic demands for capital put increased pressures upon our supply of savings—there is every reason to believe that the need for extraordinary action of the kind we are now taking will be eliminated.

When the Fund was established, there was great apprehension that sudden and massive short-term capital movements might again become a disruptive influence as they had in the disturbed climate of the 1930's. Gratifying progress has been made in developing sturdy defenses against such threats to our convertible currency system through the concerted cooperative efforts of the industrialized countries. A chain of new facilities for coping with such pressures is now in place and tested, and there are grounds for confidence that the processes of adjustment can be shielded from perverse speculative flows in the future.

With the restoration of convertibility, however, it has become apparent that a sizable volume of capital is ready to move from country to country in response to relatively small shifts in interest rates. Thus, the stability of exchange rates and freedom of markets toward which we have all worked in the postwar period carries with it the implication that short-term interest rates in the major trading countries must inevitably be kept reasonably well in line with each other.

Both problems and opportunities are implicit in these circumstances. Domestic objectives will sometimes limit the practicable range of fluctuation in interest rates that can be undertaken for facilitating balance of payments adjustment. But, since the margin between rate relationships that attract or repel short-term funds is likely to be relatively narrow, it will usually be feasible to encourage small changes in short-term rates in the interest of speeding restoration of international equilibrium without disturbing the domestic economy.

Most promising of all in terms of facilitating the adjustment process is the increasingly close and continuous consultation on these matters that has developed in the forums provided by this institution, by the Organization for Economic Cooperation and Development, and by the Bank for International Settlements. This has been particularly evident in the area of short-term capital flows and interest rates. But we are also coming to understand that this same kind of consultation and cooperation is essential in other areas as well. We know that any adjustment demands offsetting changes in the position of deficit and surplus nations. We also know, in the last analysis, that these adjustments must take place, for no workable international monetary system will allow a nation to continue to run a deficit—or for that matter a surplus—for an indefinite period.

The critical question is how the adjustments are to be made. Balance can be —and too often in the past has been—forced by measures that endanger domestic stability or the prospects for growing trade. Those alternatives are not open to us today if the bright promise of all that has been accomplished since Bretton Woods is to be fulfilled. Nor can the industrialized countries afford to undermine the defenses of freedom or to withdraw their support of the developing nations.

The only realistic solution is to find effective ways for reconciling the requirements of a convertible currency system based on fixed exchange rates with the freedom of each nation to pursue domestic growth and stability. No methods will work instantaneously, and one prerequisite to their proper functioning is the availability of adequate liquidity—in the form of international reserves or ready access to credit. The studies now being launched provide fresh assurance that these liquidity needs will be met effectively in the more distant future, just as they are being met effectively today.

But adequate liquidity will not make our machinery of adjustment work automatically, nor can its development be safely put off until emergencies arise. Instead, its effective use will require governments of all nations with a stake in a liberal trading order to work together continuously in many areas: in developing a mix of domestic policies appropriate to external circumstances, in adjusting trade policies, in sharing the burdens of aid and defense, in providing long-term capital, and in eliminating rigidities and inefficiencies in their economies that impede and distort the adjustment process. That willingness, I believe, is now being demonstrated more fully than at any time in the past. This is the real source of my confidence, not only that the United States will restore balance in its own accounts—for we intend to carry out that responsibility in any event— but also that a true equilibrium can be restored within a framework of expanding trade, flourishing growth, and monetary stability.

(iii) *Statement by the Governor for France, M. Giscard d'Estaing*[1]

International cooperation in the monetary and financial fields, to which our meetings are dedicated, a few months ago lost one of its most eminent promoters, Mr. Jacobsson, whose passing was deeply mourned by all of us. He devoted his intelligence, his insight and his human qualities to that cause. I should like, personally and on behalf of the French Government, to join in the tribute rightly paid to him. My country does not forget that a few years ago he brought competence and understanding in considering its monetary and financial difficulties.

The problems which we must solve are becoming ever more complex; they require that the men heading our institutions should have a high sense of their international responsibilities. It is indeed gratifying that Mr. Woods, who is taking part in our deliberations for the first time, is now the President of the International Bank. This is also why I am pleased to greet here my friend, Mr. Schweitzer; his intellectual ability and talent will, I know, be devoted unstintingly to the achievement of the aims of the Monetary Fund.

Our Meeting this year is attended by a larger number of representatives from friendly countries which recently attained independence; this is gratifying, and I wish to emphasize the great importance that France attaches to the strengthening of the links between the countries here represented.

Looking backward on the past twenty years one takes stock of the progress achieved through international solidarity. Sizable obstacles to economic development and to safeguarding the international monetary equilibrium nevertheless still remain. Further steps will be necessary in the years ahead.

My Government has already played a large part in the efforts to find new solutions to international economic problems; it will go on in that direction. It also wishes that approaches toward improving our methods of cooperation be made in a lucid manner. The decisions to be taken must involve a fair share of boldness and generosity as well as of wisdom and realism, without which there can be no lasting progress in international relations.

Mr. Chairman, in accordance with your invitation, I shall not refer to the policies that deal with the International Bank. I should like, however, these particular messages to be included in the proceedings.

In this spirit, I shall touch briefly on matters concerning the policies of the International Bank and its affiliated institutions. I shall then review the questions relative to the International Monetary Fund.

The International Bank has for the past fifteen years proved to be a fruitful institution. It has brought into being new agencies designed to supplement its task. It has collected each year increasing resources for the benefit of the developing countries. But this very vitality has given rise to the problems of growth which Mr. Woods has so clearly analyzed.

The increase of the funds available to the Bank is in itself gratifying, since it reflects the strength of its credit. France, by the way, has contributed to this liquidity through the recent redemption of the last maturities outstanding of the 1947 loan, which were to be repaid by 1977. The recent slowing down of the rate of loan commitments therefore does not arise from a shortage of funds. Nor

[1] *Summary Proceedings, 1963*, pp. 55–63; delivered 1 October.

should it be attributed to the strict standards of selection applied by the Bank to the projects submitted to it; the Bank must remain attached to the basic principle of financing only profitable projects, and one cannot say that there is any lack of such projects in the developing countries. The conventional terms of its loans should not be blamed either; were the Bank to stop using periods of repayment adapted to the rate of economic depreciation of the projects and were it to decide to depart from conventional interest rates, the very elements of its success would be threatened. There could, however, be various ways of enabling the Bank to carry on activities commensurate with its means.

The Bank might broaden the range of projects that it will agree to finance, as, for example, in the field of manufacturing industries and agriculture, without going so far as to finance undertakings outside the economic field and for which other forms of assistance would be appropriate. It might also intensify the efforts already made in the field of preinvestment or technical assistance. Lastly, there must above all be close coordination between the Bank and the International Development Association. The continuation of the large and excessively uniform discrepancy between the lending terms of the two institutions might indeed tend to cause a relative coolness toward Bank loans and an excess of applications for assistance addressed to the Association.

At the last Annual Meeting we discussed the difficulties arising out of the premature exhaustion of the Association's initial capital. The present situation is obviously better, since the total amount of new contributions pledged by the industrialized countries will enable increasing the granting of loans on special conditions to a satisfactory level. In its future policy, however, the Association will have to heed the lessons learned from the crisis that threatened it. That crisis was due to the fact that the rate of commitments to borrowing countries had since the previous year exceeded the rate of actual payment of the member countries' contributions. So unorthodox a practice would necessarily expose the Association to the risk of curtailing its activity. Now, while sufficient additional funds have finally been gathered, it has been done only thanks to a large increase in the contributions of the industrialized countries.

As a counterpart to this effort it would be advisable for the credits granted henceforth to remain within the limits of the available resources. This limitation does not mean that the annual volume of IDA's commitments should be limited strictly to the total of the national contributions; it would, in fact, be possible to increase the available funds by building a sort of 'bridge' between the resources of the Association and some of the Bank's assets. But the main effort required of the Association will be to adapt its activity to the means at its disposal; it will have to choose carefully those cases in which it will be most generous.

In a more general way, the action of the Bank and the Association should fit harmoniously into the coordination of assistance of various forms and sources that has been successfully developed for some years. We should be satisfied with the work done in this direction within the Bank itself. The efforts in which the Bank has participated along with the main capital exporting countries in the Development Assistance Committee of the OECD have also contributed to strengthening the effectiveness of the aid granted to other countries.

I think, in fact, that financial development assistance can reach its goal only if all those who participate in it, work in ever closer unity. Only then can the application of financial techniques take on its true significance in view of the economic and human purposes that they are expected to serve.

In the last 15 years the scope of coordinated development policies has become progressively wider; in turn, attaining equilibrium in the international payments now raises more than mere problems of financial technique.

For this reason I should like this year to devote the remaining part of my statement to the functioning of the international monetary system.

A brief summing up shows that this is the 459th speech devoted to this question in this forum; one hesitates therefore to touch again upon a matter that has been dealt with at such length already. I venture, however, to overcome this hesitation, and shall do so for the following reasons:

1. The evolution of the basic data of the world monetary problem has been such, in the course of this year, as to give rise to a clearer awareness of its importance and of the interests at stake.

2. Since this problem has been widely debated throughout the world, we would fail to give due respect to the international institutions, if we were to satisfy ourselves with an academic approach. It should always be our rule to make these institutions the place where the problem should be stated in clear, and, if possible, constructive terms.

Awareness of the international monetary problem has centered around the question of the volume of liquidity. As recently pointed out in an excellent study, this approach to the problem reflects a certain amount of confusion. I shall merely concur with the two following conclusions:

The first one, in line with the conclusions of the Report of the International Monetary Fund, is that there is at the present time no over-all shortage of world liquidity.[1]

The second one, in agreement with the views recently and courageously expressed by authorized American sources, is that a possible increase in liquidity will not discharge the major deficit countries from the obligation to re-establish, as soon as possible, the balance of their external accounts.

Therefore, concern over the monetary problem seems to me, today, to be related less to the volume of liquidity than to the various questions raised by the functioning of the international monetary system.

Why are these questions being raised more and more often? Probably because of the criticism to which recent developments have given rise. But before spelling out these objections, I think we should first recall their merits. One must indeed stress the fact that the present world monetary system has made it possible to restore convertibility of the main currencies, a result which, between 1945 and 1950, appeared unattainable. This system then provided credit mechanisms to cope with the crises, both severe and temporary, which affected certain currencies.

I wish to emphasize that these results have been secured while maintaining a relatively high level of employment in the world, an outstanding contrast to the situation that prevailed in years when the world monetary system was based on different principles.

I stress these facts because I do not want us to give in to this kind of intellectual nomadism by virtue of which one tries to escape from an existing system as

[1] I.M.F., *Annual Report, 1963*, pp. 49–52.

soon as weaknesses become apparent in it, while forgetting the substantial benefits that it has brought, and the perils which it has helped avoid.

In any case, however, the manner in which the world monetary system has been operating for the past few years seems to me to call for criticism on three main points: the lack of corrective mechanisms—the lack of reciprocity in the granting of the assistance—the uneven sharing of risks between lenders, depending on the various types of assistance which they grant.

1. The present situation, whereby central banks accumulate holdings of the currencies of other countries, does not include any automatic machinery for a prompt return to equilibrium. The creditor country which accumulates foreign exchange congratulates itself on the increase in its holdings, while overlooking some of the unsound aspects of these gains. The deficit country tends to attach insufficient importance to the increase in foreign holdings of its currency, all the more so since, at the outset, losses of gold represent only a small part of its deficit. Owing to the very form they take, the credits extended remain invisible for too long, and corrective measures may be taken too late.

The inflationary effect resulting in the creditor country from a lasting surplus in the balance of payments is matched in the debtor country by that which comes from the use that foreign central banks make of their holdings in its currency. For, in their legitimate desire to earn interest on these holdings, they normally invest them on the markets. Without overrating the size of this phenomenon in relation to the evolution of the money supply, one must admit that it tends to offset one of the automatic corrective mechanisms.

2. The holding of reserve currencies by the foreign central banks brings benefits which might not be reciprocated, to the extent that—should the balance of payments be reversed—the reserve currency countries might not accumulate so readily the currencies of their new debtor. To say the least, full reciprocity is not achieved.

3. Within the monetary system itself, certain countries maintain a policy of keeping their reserves in gold, and of holding foreign currency only to the minimum extent required by current transactions. Other countries, the list of which varies, hold large amounts of foreign currencies, at times as much as half their total reserves. This situation certainly does not reflect an equitable distribution of the burdens of international monetary cooperation.

How far some of these imperfections derive from basic deficiencies in the system, and to what extent they arise from distortions that developed in practice, is a question that ought not to be evaded. I do not intend to decide it now. Yet, it seems clear to me that in financing deficits that have proved to be of a lasting nature, there has been too much recourse to short-term lending facilities provided by the system, instead of reliance on means of assistance more appropriate in nature and in duration.

This concern would become still more serious if the volume of liquidity were to increase, either because lasting deficits of some debtor countries were met in the same manner, or because, should an increase in international liquidity be deemed advisable, such an increase were expected from existing mechanisms.

I believe, therefore, that our discussions should lead us to two conclusions, one of which is outside, but the other one clearly inside, our competence.

The first conclusion is to take note of the firm intention expressed by both our colleague, Mr. Douglas Dillon, in his statement,[1] and by President Kennedy, in his opening address,[2] regarding the restoration of the balance of payments of the United States by way of measures taken in this country. Even if, as President Kennedy mentioned, some of those measures might give rise to problems for some of our countries, this, I believe, should not prevent our organization from supporting such steps. The attainment, within an appropriate period, of the balance in the external payments of the United States is indeed the precondition for our reaching decisions which do fall within our competence.

These decisions would result in making a thorough examination of the problems raised by the functioning of the international monetary system, particularly on the assumption that the development of world trade might require increasing liquidity. If such should be the case, we should also make our judgment on the nature of this liquidity and on the methods used for providing it. Thus an answer could be brought to the question which I took the liberty to raise, and to any others that may arise in the course of our studies.

I think that these studies should be undertaken as soon as possible, and that they should lead to positive conclusions on three essential points: the existence of an automatic adjustment machinery, reciprocity of the benefits granted, and the equality of the risks assumed.

These studies will no doubt lead us to clarify our policies as regards the three means of international settlement that may supplement payments in gold: transactions between central banks; credits granted on a more durable basis within international monetary organizations; and last, what might, in the final analysis, take the form of long-term loans.

I have taken the liberty frankly to state my remarks about the functioning of the international monetary system because, in my view, the most tangible proof of our spirit of cooperation is for us to set forth as openly as possible the thoughts which come to our minds after 18 years of useful and creative work by the monetary institutions so wisely set up at Bretton Woods.

To the success and development of these institutions in a world in which stability constantly requires renewed imagination and effort, the French Government is ready to lend its support.

(iv) *Statement by the Governor for Great Britain, Mr. Maudling*[3]

None of us assembled here today can approach our work, at this Eighteenth Meeting of the Fund, without a deep sense of loss at the death of Per Jacobsson. Indeed, it scarcely seems possible that we should be present at a Fund Annual Meeting without him, so much had these meetings come to center round his wise and genial personality. Many men, many nations, and many talents must go to the making and moulding of a great international institution such as the IMF, but Per Jacobsson's contribution was unique. We shall miss him as a fine administrator, as a distinguished economist, and as an outstanding architect of international cooperation; but above all, we shall miss him as a great and kindly man, and as a friend.

[1] See pp. 108–14 above. [2] *Summary Proceedings, 1963*, pp. 1–6.
[3] Ibid., pp. 63–9; delivered 1 October.

We can, however, take consolation in the fact that his responsibilities have now passed into the hands of a truly worthy successor. Mr. Schweitzer's brilliant attainments and distinguished career make him eminantly suited to the great task which he has undertaken, and we know that in his capable hands the Fund can be sure of a continuation of its high prestige and of its traditions of wise and distinguished leadership. We wish him, wholeheartedly, a long and happy and successful stay with the Fund, and in welcoming him amongst us, I want to assure him, on behalf of my Government, of our fullest and most sincere cooperation.

Turning for a moment to our own position, I am glad to be able to say that recently economic conditions in the United Kingdom have been buoyant. And the indications are that the balance of payments will continue in a healthy state. But even so, the level of reserves against liabilities is still relatively low, and our external position could be affected by confidence movements, or by temporary trade imbalance while expansion builds up. I would therefore like to take this opportunity of expressing the gratitude of my Government to the Board of the Fund for its understanding and cooperative attitude toward the United Kingdom's request for the renewal of its stand-by agreement. The ready availability of a drawing under this stand-by will provide a safeguard against temporary disturbances; and the existence of the agreement will in itself act as a factor making for confidence in sterling, and so for stability in international payments.

At last year's meeting I referred to the problems of international liquidity, and I should like to do so again this year. I do not think any apology is necessary for this, as it is the function of the IMF to contribute to world economic expansion. We have all of us, through our membership of the Fund and the GATT, chosen the course of freedom in trade and payments. Our task is to ensure that the financial basis for this system is adequate. In the words of the Fund Annual Report:

> International liquidity should be sufficient to allow these countries [that is, the industrial countries] to take the expansionary steps needed for the benefits of their own economies, as well as to assure continued expansion of the world economy.[1]

I mean by liquidity, stocks of gold and other internationally accepted means of payment, including particularly the dollar, the pound sterling, and readily available credit either obtained through the Fund or arranged bilaterally. In considering whether existing liquidity is adequate for its task we must, of course, consider not only the total quantity but also its distribution and the policies adopted by member countries in using their individual resources.

Turning to the practical problems, I would like first to eliminate two matters that are sometimes confused with them. First, we are not discussing the actual means of financing international trade. As has often been pointed out, this is done through commercial channels. We are dealing with the problems arising for governments when the operations of the market threaten the strength of their reserves and the position of their currency. Secondly, the problems of the provision of development capital and of long-term trends in international growth are essentially ones for the Bank and its affiliated institutions rather than for the Fund, which is concerned more with short-term movements.

[1] I.M.F., *Annual Report, 1963*, pp. 50–1.

The primary purpose of international liquidity is to give time for individual countries to make adjustments in their balance of payments without sharp changes in the volume of imports or in the growth of domestic demand. But at the same time the availability of liquid resources should not be such as to promote, or encourage countries to tolerate, the continuance of basically unsound domestic or international positions in the guise of temporary fluctuations. The basic dilemma is clear. If adequate resources are not available automatically or nearly automatically, their usefulness in times of trouble may be problematic; but to the extent to which they are automatically available, they may present a temptation to refrain from the necessary corrections of policy. This, I believe, lies at the core of our problems.

There are basically three types of situations in which a country may need access to substantial liquid assets. They are

(i) short-term speculation against the currency;
(ii) serious fluctuations in short-term balance of payments experience— whether on current or capital account—arising from external influences, such as abrupt changes in the terms of trade or substantial capital movements; and
(iii) the initial phase of a domestic expansion accompanied by substantial restocking of materials.

Such a clear distinction is, of course, to some extent unnatural. The various situations can coexist or merge into one another; but they are distinct elements and to some extent should be met from different sources.

Short-term speculation may best be met by such schemes as the Basle arrangements, the gold pool, and by swap arrangements, with the Fund resources also available.

Fluctuations in the balance of payments resulting from temporary deterioration in the terms of trade are particularly suitable for recourse to the Fund. I therefore welcome the introduction by the Fund of the Compensatory Financing Scheme[1] which should be of help to certain primary producers. But it is important here to emphasize once again that for many producers the main problem may often be one of long-term relative price levels, which cannot be tackled by the Compensatory Financing Scheme.

I would like to stress the need for adequate liquidity to allow the financing of a high and rising level of world trade, on which the future prosperity of developing countries depends. I had the advantage of discussing these matters with my Commonwealth colleagues in London last week. At our Conference we reviewed the preparations being made for the Kennedy Round, and other steps which are being taken in the GATT, to reduce or eliminate barriers to international trade in primary products, agricultural commodities, and manufactures. In the words of the communiqué we issued, we 'emphasized the importance of these negotiations for the trade of developing countries, and recognized that special efforts must be made to reduce barriers to their exports of manufactures as well as of primary products and to foster their capacity to contribute to the growth of world trade.'[2]

[1] See ibid., pp. 196–9.
[2] See The Times; Dawn, 26 September 1962.

Returning now to the third and last of my three situations, the initial cost of restocking for expansion is also a suitable candidate on the analogy of the use of bank finance for expanding stock in trade.

But none of these forms of support should be used to finance an unsound domestic situation. The test of what is sound or unsound is of course very difficult. To what extent does a current deficit stem from excessive pressure of demand and rising costs and prices in a given country? To what extent does an outflow of capital reflect short-term speculation or long-term influences? It is important to be clear on the tests that should be applied in either case.

It is clear that in the present situation we are concerned with two simultaneous problems, which are separate but are interlinked: the sufficiency of world liquidity and the United States deficit. I ventured to say at last year's meeting that there is a fundamental difficulty about the present system, namely, that the reserve currencies are short-term liabilities of the United States and the United Kingdom —one nation's reserves is another nation's debt. I said:

> If the amounts of such currencies held as reserve assets increase too much there will inevitably be some doubt as to whether any further extension of these holdings would be prudent and practicable.[1]

The current availability of liquid reserves has been for several years sustained by the outflow of U.S. dollars. We can see more clearly now that this creates problems not only for the United States but also, in some cases, for surplus countries, who feel that their current accruals are such as to cause problems for internal monetary management. While this leads us to give what help we can to the United States in dealing with the problem of their deficit, we must recognize the truth of President Kennedy's statement when he said in July:

> One of the reasons that new resources of liquidity may well be needed is that, as we close our payments gap, we will cut down our provision of dollars to the rest of the world.[2]

It has been said that if the United States got back into balance and subsequently started to earn a surplus, they could avoid creating problems for the rest of the world by purchasing and holding other currencies. This is true as a short-term expedient; but the real question is what alternative sources of liquidity will be available as the need for them is felt, and as the United States progressively reduces the scale on which it is adding to the world's reserves.

In considering world liquidity needs, we must, as I have said, be concerned with the total, with its distribution, and with the use of available reserves. I would agree with the Fund Report that the total at present available is large, but I would certainly echo also their cautionary words: 'But if a substantial proportion of it is, for one reason or another, considered to be available "for emergency use only," then the risk is correspondingly increased, not only of slowing down the world economy but also of being unable smoothly to deal with emergencies.' This, I suggest, applies not only to national holdings of gold and foreign exchange, but also with equal strength to national drawing rights in the Fund.

It is rather an irony of the present distribution of liquid reserves that while there are some countries who could do with more, there are others who feel that

[1] *Documents*, 1962, p. 569.   [2] See p. 96, above.

they have or are likely to have too much, not only from the external point of view but also from its effect on their domestic economies. I must say that I cannot help feeling that this is a dilemma that should be capable of solution. Speaking as an individual I see no difficulty in disposing of excessive cash, either by spending it or lending it. There are inhibitions affecting both these processes where nations are concerned. But I would suggest that we should bend a good deal of effort to getting these overcome and, in particular, to seeing whether by stimulation of capital markets and growth of long-term lending, a more economical use could not be made through better distribution of the available total of world liquidity.

I turn finally to the future. First the United States deficit. I should like for my part to say that I warmly support the general means whereby the United States Government is tackling this problem. It must be recognized, however, that whatever method it adopts may easily have painful results for someone. I am sure the United States administration will lend an attentive ear to individual countries that are seriously affected by its measures. But if a country, like an individual, has a deficit, the only way to solve it is to earn more, spend less, or lend less.

The United States has been making great progress in the expansion of its export trade and it is well to remember that its current balance still shows a very healthy surplus. I am sure we must all continue to adhere to the GATT declaration not to stimulate our exports by artificial means such as subsidies. Equally, we welcome the attitude of the United States in attempting to solve the balance of payments problem by an expansion of the domestic economy rather than by restraint on its imports. Direct restrictions on United States imports would have a serious effect on world trade, as indeed would policies designed to solve the problem by holding back the expansion of the United States domestic economy.

The remaining moves open to the United States, therefore, can only be reducing overseas government spending or reducing overseas lending. I think we would all regret seeing a sharp cutback in United States aid to developing countries, whether by grant or loan. It is therefore in the realm of private capital movements, long-term and short-term, that it seems most necessary to find a solution; and this, as I understand it, is how the United States is going about things.

The more successful it is, the sooner will come the time when the world will be faced with the problem of how to find alternative sources of expanding liquidity.

I strongly support, therefore, the suggestion that this problem should be studied; and I consider that it should be studied as a matter of urgency. There are many possibilities: I mentioned one last year—a Mutual Currency Account. Others would be increases of Fund quotas and more flexibility in the use of Fund resources. These possibilities are not exhaustive or mutually exclusive. All should be considered.

What matters more than methods is the results, and it is important to ensure that we do not spend so long looking for the ideal solution that we fail to make progress on improvements that can be achieved in the meantime. I should like to propose that we make it clear that, in our view, the studies of the problem should proceed at a pace which will enable definite practical decisions to be taken at our meeting in Tokyo a year from now.

(v) *Statement by the Alternative Governor for the Federal Republic of Germany, Herr Westrick*[1]

I want to join all those that have expressed their deep sadness and regret at the fact that Per Jacobsson, due to his tragic and premature passing away, cannot be among us. Thus, we can pay him only posthumously the well-deserved praise and tribute for his outstanding work for the Fund and for the international monetary order. His sudden death was a great shock and grief to me personally, as to all his friends, of whom he had so many in this gathering.

We must, of course, be grateful for the fact that we have found so quickly a successor to Mr. Jacobsson in the person of Mr. Pierre-Paul Schweitzer, and I have no doubt that he will successfully take over the reins at the Fund, which Per Jacobsson so suddenly and unexpectedly had to lay down. We wish Mr. Schweitzer the very best success in his difficult job.

*   *   *

You may remember that Per Jacobsson, in his speech at the last annual meeting, laid great stress on the 'much better balance' that had been attained in the international payments situation, and on certain basic developments which seemed to point to the restoration of a more enduring international equilibrium.[2] In looking at the present situation in the foreign payments field, it might seem at first glance that since the autumn of 1962 we have made very little further progress towards that goal.

Now it has already been pointed out by some of the previous speakers that the trouble has resided mainly in the field of international capital movements, which have, in some instances, developed in a way which—to say the least—was not conducive to a better international equilibrium. We fully understand that the United States Government has, under the pressure of some of these developments, felt compelled to undertake and to propose some measures in order to bring about more appropriate interest rate relationships in the international sphere, and we wish these measures a quick success.

In my own country, we also have recently seen some developments in the international capital field which have not contributed to a better external equilibrium, but have rather led us away from it. In the year 1962, Germany had a moderate external deficit on current account and a near-balance in long-term capital movements, so that its basic over-all balance was in deficit; this contributed, under the circumstances, toward a better international equilibrium and towards a redistribution of international reserves. In the course of 1963 up to now, German foreign trade has further expanded on the export and import side, and in the last few months there has been a particularly strong upturn in our exports; but, nevertheless, Germany has had also in 1963 a small deficit on current account. At the same time, however, we have had a rather sizable net inflow of capital since the beginning of 1963, so that in contrast to last year, our over-all basic balance is at present in surplus again.

---

[1] *Summary Proceedings, 1963*, pp. 87–91; delivered 1 October.
[2] *Documents, 1962*, pp. 550–61.

This change in our external capital balance cannot easily be explained by changes in interest rate relationships, as these were not much different from the year before, and as our monetary authorities have, out of consideration for the international payments equilibrium, deliberately refrained from letting occasional pressure on our resources be reflected in higher interest rates. If we try to appraise the experiences of the last few years in the field of international capital movements, we cannot avoid the conclusion that there are still structural discrepancies and maladjustments between many countries, and that it may take some time until they can be reduced to such an extent as to allow the free flow of capital to play its full beneficial role in the world economy.

*   *   *

In worrying over the still existing imbalances in the capital field, we should, however, not overlook the fact that international cost and price relationships and international transactions on current account have in fact made some further progress towards a better international equilibrium. It is particularly noteworthy that the six countries of the European Common Market, whose combined surplus on current account had already in 1962 declined by over a billion dollars from its former high in 1961, have experienced a further deterioration in their trade transactions with third countries in the course of this year, and thus have come nearer to an equilibrium in their current account vis-à-vis the outside world. It is, of course, very regrettable that in some instances this development was due to, or at least accompanied by, inflationary pressures in European countries. But on the other hand, and in a more general way, it is noteworthy that the strong upward movement in imports in a number of continental European countries has proved to be one of the main supports for an enlarged world trade both in the last and in the current year, and we welcome it, especially since this has also been to the benefit of less developed countries. Thus the process of adjustment toward a better international equilibrium has, up to now, been achieved not through contraction, but, on the contrary, through ever higher levels of world trade. This experience, and in addition, the general movement of prices in a number of countries, certainly do not point to a general lack of international liquidity at the present moment.

*   *   *

Let me add here a few words on the adequacy of our international monetary system. In looking at the past, I would say that, considering the difficult adjustment problems posed by a number of important structural shifts and distortions in the international economy over the last ten years, the present international monetary system comes out relatively well, and certainly better than some of its critics would have it; it has, after all, permitted a liberalization of trade and payments and, at the same time, an expansion in world trade which is without precedent in history. I would also stress that the support and defenses which have been built into the monetary system over the last few years have strengthened it greatly, so that we may expect it to deal successfully with future problems as well.

On the other hand, I would not deny the possibility that at some future time our system may get under pressure and may experience some difficulties, for instance because of its present dependence on some key currencies to supply an important part of the growth of national currency reserves. I think it therefore wise to study this and related problems, as a precautionary measure. Let me, however, add some provisos here. *First*, I should like to emphasize that we cannot afford to let such studies of the international monetary system drift apart in separate directions; if we want to achieve convincing results, such a study will have to be made in a well-coordinated way by a joining of forces of the best brains we can get both from the staff of the Fund and from experts in our own countries.

Second, I should like to warn against the illusion that, as if by some purely technical reform, one could solve in an automatic or painless way the adjustment problems which are due either to structural distortions or to policy discrepancies between the member countries of our international system. We should not waste our time by chasing such a will-o'-the-wisp. As long as there are dynamic shifts between the member countries of our system, and as long as we are not able to achieve a complete coordination of national policies, there will always arise balance of payments problems; and these balance of payments problems will usually not disappear by themselves, but only through deliberate, often unpalatable, policy measures on the part of the countries concerned.

Third, I want to stress that any improvements that might be thought out for our international monetary system—and there is always room for improvements —should not be concentrated only on the question how best *to finance* balance of payments deficits, but also on the even more important question of how to provide sufficient incentives for *curing* them. The main problem, it seems to me, will be to strike the right balance between providing, on the one hand, the international liquidity needed for an expanding world economy and, on the other hand, safeguarding an adequate degree of balance of payments discipline. Only in this way can we hope to maintain not only expansion but also stability in our international economic system; and to preserve expansion together with stability is certainly the foremost goal of our great institution.

(vi) *Statement by the Governor for South Africa, Mr. Dönges*[1]

May I first join my voice with those who have paid tribute to the late Per Jacobsson. To me his most outstanding quality was his generosity of spirit. A man of many talents, he gave of them all unsparingly to the organizations which he served and to the world. In this it could truly be said of him:

> '. . . For his bounty,
> There was no winter in 't; an autumn 'twas
> That grew the more by reaping.'

May I also join in the welcome to our new Managing Director, Mr. Schweitzer. We hope his association with the Fund and its member countries will be a very happy and successful one. I would assure him that, as in the past, my country will gladly cooperate with him and with the Fund to promote economic stability and progress.

The Annual Report of the Executive Directors contains this year, as in other years, a penetrating analysis of international monetary conditions. It is therefore

---

[1] *Summary Proceedings, 1963*, pp. 140–3; delivered 3 October.

significant that the opening chapter in this section of the Report should bear the title 'International Reserves and Liquidity.' I am glad to see that this subject has been placed in the forefront—where it rightly belongs.

There are two sentences in this portion of the Report on which I wish to comment. The first is the statement that 'International liquidity should be sufficient to allow these countries [i.e., the industrial countries] to take the expansionary steps needed for the benefits of their own economies, as well as to assure continued expansion of the world economy.' It is not quite clear whether this is intended as a statement of what is desirable, i.e., of what should be, or as a statement of fact, i.e., of what is. But in any case, I wish to make two points. The first is the familiar one that, as the United States succeeds in correcting its balance of payments deficit, so the major source of additional international liquidity in recent years will tend to dry up, unless special measures are taken to counteract this tendency. Secondly, in international liquidity, just as in the internal liquidity of a national banking system, we require not merely a bare sufficiency; we need at least a reasonable margin so as to cover unforeseen contingencies and still maintain confidence.

The second sentence on which I wish to comment is the following: 'The quantitative and qualitative adequacy of the international liquidity structure requires continued close attention.' I wish to draw especial attention to the word 'qualitative.' The major part of the increase in international reserves in recent years has taken the form of an increase in foreign currency holdings: in other words, the gold component of international reserves has not increased proportionately. This, I believe, is a process which can be continued only at grave risk to confidence in our international monetary mechanism.

At previous meetings and elsewhere, I have argued that a simultaneous, uniform, and substantial change in the par values of all currencies in terms of gold would be of great benefit to the key currency countries, the industrial countries and the developing countries, and would provide the essential firm base for the international monetary system or for any new monetary mechanism which may be evolved. I do not intend to repeat these arguments today.

What I do wish to emphasize very briefly, however, is that such a revaluation of currencies in terms of gold is not, as has been said, a 'radical' proposal. On the contrary, it is essentially a conservative proposal, specifically envisaged by the Fund's Articles of Agreement, and designed to give greater weight to the traditional role of gold in international payments rather than to experiment with new, untried, and perhaps over-ambitious mechanisms.

There are three main forms in which international liquidity may be increased. The first is through an increase, actual or potential, in the supply of foreign exchange, i.e., dollars, sterling, and perhaps certain other currencies. The second is the creation of a new international currency, i.e., claims against some international monetary organization or 'world central bank.' The third is an increase in gold reserves, through an upward revaluation of gold in terms of all currencies. I would suggest that only in the case of this third method can we be really sure that the delicate structure of international financial confidence will not be impaired.

The important role of gold in the international payments mechanism is given expression throughout the Fund's Articles of Agreement. Moreover, as I have often pointed out before, the Articles make specific provision for a uniform change in par values. This provision (i.e., Article IV, Section 7) was not included by accident; the South African delegate at Bretton Woods made a comprehensive statement on this section, pointing out that this approach was 'the only one which offered a hope for an orderly change of the relationship between gold and currencies in the future.' No delegation expressed disagreement with this statement. The United States representative did indeed say—quite rightly—that such a change should not be lightly made, but this in itself shows that the Bretton Woods Conference did contemplate such a change at the appropriate time.

We welcome the intention of the Fund to intensify its studies regarding international liquidity, the functioning of the international monetary system and the effective role of the Fund in this field. We propose to avail ourselves of the general invitation of the Managing Director to cooperate in this field by placing at the disposal of the Fund a more comprehensive exposition of our views regarding the place of gold in the international financial system, with special regard to the provisions of Article IV, Section 7.

Statement by the United States Secretary of the Treasury, Mr. Dillon, on behalf of the 'Group of Ten' members of the International Monetary Fund, Washington, 30 October 1963[1]

1. In the course of the annual meeting of the International Monetary Fund, the Ministers and Central Bank Governors of the 10 countries (Belgium, Canada, France, Germany, Italy, Japan, the Netherlands, Sweden, the United Kingdom and the United States) participating in the agreement of December, 1961, to supplement the resources of the International Monetary Fund[2] met in Washington, together with Mr. Pierre-Paul Schweitzer, Managing Director of the Fund. In this meeting, they discussed the international payments situation and reviewed the functioning of the international monetary system now and in the future in the light of their common aims as reflected in the Fund's charter.

2. They agreed that the removal of the imbalances still existing in the external accounts of some major countries was the most important objective to be pursued over the near future. For this reason they welcomed the recent efforts of certain deficit countries to improve their balances of payments, as well as actions by a number of countries designed to reduce or remove surpluses, as evidence of progress toward a better basic international equilibrium. The Ministers and Governors reaffirmed the objective of reaching such balance at high levels of economic activity with a sustainable rate of economic growth and in the climate of price stability.

3. In examining the functioning of the international monetary system, the Ministers and Governors noted that the present national reserves of member

---

[1] U.S.I.S., *Press Release*, 3 October 1963.

[2] The agreement originated in a series of meetings between the Finance Ministers of the ten countries in Paris. Details of the procedures to be followed were set out in a letter from the French Finance Minister, M. Baumgartner to the U.S. Secretary of the Treasury, Mr. Dillon, on 15 December 1961. For text, see J. Keith Horsefield (ed.), *The International Monetary Fund, 1945–1965, Volume III: Documents* (I.M.F., Washington, 1969), pp. 252–4. For the text of the subsequent decision of the Executive Directors of the I.M.F. on General Agreements to Borrow, 5 January 1962, see *Documents, 1962*, pp. 529–36.

countries, supplemented as they are by the resources of the IMF, as well as by a network of bilateral facilities, seemed fully adequate in present circumstances to cope with possible threats to the stability of the international payments system. In this connection, the Ministers reviewed the 'general arrangements to borrow'[1] in the International Monetary Fund and reiterated their determination that these resources would be available for decisive and prompt action.

4. In reviewing the longer-run prospects, the Ministers and Governors agreed that the underlying structure of the present monetary system—based on fixed exchange rates and the established price of gold—has proven its value as the foundation for present and future arrangements. It appeared to them, however, to be useful to undertake a thorough examination of the outlook for the functioning of the international system and of its probable future needs for liquidity. This examination should be made with particular emphasis on the possible magnitude and nature of the future needs for reserves and for supplementary credit facilities which may arise within the framework of national economic policies effectively aiming at the objectives mentioned in Paragraph 2. The studies should also appraise and evaluate various possibilities for covering such needs.

5. The Ministers and Governors have noted with approval the statement by the Managing Director that the International Monetary Fund will develop and intensify its studies of these long-run questions.[2] They, for their part, have now instructed their deputies to examine these questions, and to report to them on the progress of their studies and discussions over the course of the coming year. They requested the deputies in carrying out these studies to maintain close working relations with the International Monetary Fund and with other international bodies concerned with monetary matters. Any specific suggestions resulting from the studies by the deputies will be submitted to the Ministers and Governors for consideration.

6. The Ministers and Governors believe that such an examination of the international monetary system will further strengthen international financial co-operation, which is the essential basis for the continued successful functioning of the system.

(b) Tariff Negotiations

Resolution adopted by the Ministerial Meeting of the Contracting Parties to the General Agreement on Tariffs and Trade, Geneva, 21 May 1963[3]

The Ministers agreed—

A. Principles

1. That a significant liberalization of world trade is desirable, and that, for this purpose, comprehensive trade negotiations, to be conducted on a most-favoured-nation basis and on the principle of reciprocity, shall begin at Geneva on 4 May 1964, with the widest possible participation.

2. That the trade negotiations shall cover all classes of products, industrial and non-industrial, including agricultural and primary products.

---

[1] Ibid.
[2] See pp. 98–108 above.
[3] D.S.B., 24 June 1963, pp. 995–6.

3. That the trade negotiations shall deal not only with tariffs but also with non-tariff barriers.

4. That, in view of the limited results obtained in recent years from item-by-item negotiations, the tariff negotiations, subject to the provisions of paragraph B 3, shall be based upon a plan of substantial linear tariff reductions with a bare minimum of exceptions which shall be subject to confrontation and justification. The linear reductions shall be equal. In those cases where there are significant disparities in tariff levels, the tariff reductions will be based upon special rules of general and automatic application.

[NOTE: The Chairman offered paragraphs A 4 and B 3(b) as amendments[1] to paragraphs A 4 and B 3(b), respectively, in the U.S. proposal.[2] In presenting this amendment, the Chairman established the following two interpretations for the record:[3]

'In paragraphs A 4 and B 3(b) "significant" means "meaningful in trade terms" and this is accepted by the Conference.'

'The purpose of the special rules mentioned in paragraphs A 4 and B 3(b) is, among other things, to reduce such disparities, and this is accepted by the Conference.'][4]

5. That in the trade negotiations it shall be open to each country to request additional trade concessions or to modify its own offers where this is necessary to obtain a balance of advantages between it and the other participating countries. It shall be a matter of joint endeavor by all participating countries to negotiate for a sufficient basis of reciprocity to maintain the fullest measure of trade concessions.

6. That during the trade negotiations a problem of reciprocity could arise in the case of countries the general incidence of whose tariffs is unquestionably lower than that of other participating countries.

7. That, in view of the importance of agriculture in world trade, the trade negotiations shall provide for acceptable conditions of access to world markets for agricultural products.

8. That in the trade negotiations every effort shall be made to reduce barriers to exports of the less-developed countries, but that the developed countries cannot expect to receive reciprocity from the less-developed countries.

B. *Procedures*

1. That a Trade Negotiations Committee, composed of representatives of participating countries, shall be set up, and that it shall be the function of the Trade Negotiations Committee, directly or through committees (including the Special Groups referred to in paragraph 3(d) below):

(a) To elaborate a trade negotiating plan in the light of the principles in paragraphs A 1–8 above, with a view to reaching agreement on the details of

---

[1] G.A.T.T. doc. MIN(63)6, dated 21 May 1962, restricted.

[2] G.A.T.T. doc. MIN(63)4, dated 21 May 1962, restricted.

[3] Reference to the statement of 21 May of Mr. Schaffner (Switzerland); see G.A.T.T. doc. MIN(63)SR, dated 21 May of Mr. Schaffner (Switzerland); see G.A.A.T. doc. MIN(63)SR, dated 30 May 1963, p. 4.   [4] Bracketed note in the source text.

the plan of tariff reductions referred to in paragraph A 4 above by 1 August 1963, and to completing the remainder of the task by the date of the beginning of the twenty-first session of the Contracting Parties.

(b) To supervise the conduct of the trade negotiations.

2. That the trade negotiating plan will have to take into account the issues raised by the Ministers, and that the acceptability of the trade negotiating plan, from the point of view of individual countries, will depend upon the degree to which it succeeds in dealing with such issues.

3. That the Trade Negotiations Committee, in elaborating the trade negotiating plan, shall deal *inter alia* with the following issues and special situations:

(a) The depth of the tariff reductions, and the rules for exceptions.

(b) The criteria for determining significant disparities in tariff levels and the special rules applicable for tariff reductions in these cases.

(c) The problem for certain countries with a very low average level of tariffs or with a special economic or trade structure such that equal linear tariff reductions may not provide an adequate balance of advantages.

[NOTE: The Chairman offered paragraph B 3(c) as an amendment to paragraph B 3(c) in the U.S. proposal. In presenting this amendment, the Chairman established the following interpretation for the record:[1]

'Under this language, the Trade Negotiations Committee will consider the case of certain countries where it is established that their very low average level of tariffs or their economic or trade structure is such that the general application of equal linear tariff reductions would not be appropriate to achieve an adequate balance of advantages. For such countries the objective shall be the negotiation of a balance of advantages based on trade concessions by them of equivalent value, not excluding equal linear reductions where appropriate.'

In response to a question by the Australian Delegation, the Chairman established the following additional interpretation for the record:[2]

'The reference to "special trade structure" includes countries whose exports consist predominantly of agricultural or other primary products, and this is accepted by the Conference.']³

(d) The rules to govern, and the methods to be employed in, the creation of acceptable conditions of access to world markets for agricultural products in furtherance of a significant development and expansion of world trade in such products. Since cereals and meats are amongst the commodities for which general arrangements may be required, the Special Groups on Cereals and Meats shall convene at early dates to negotiate appropriate arrangements. For similar reasons a special group on dairy products shall also be established.

(e) The rules to govern and the methods to be employed in the treatment of non-tariff barriers, including *inter alia* discriminatory treatment applied to products of certain countries and the means of assuring that the value of tariff

---

¹ Reference to the statement of 21 May of Mr. Schaffner (Switzerland); see G.A.T.T. doc. MIN(63)SR, dated 30 May 1963, pp. 7–8.

² See ibid., p. 8.   ³ Bracketed note in the source text.

reductions will not be impaired or nullified by non-tariff barriers. Consideration shall be given to the possible need to review the application of certain provisions of the General Agreement, in particular Articles XIX and XXVIII,[1] or the procedures thereunder, with a view to maintaining, to the largest extent possible, trade liberalization and the stability of tariff concessions.

B. EAST–WEST RELATIONS

(a) *Statements of Soviet Policy*

Speech by Mr. Khrushchev at the Sixth Congress of the Socialist Unity Party of the German Democratic Republic, Berlin, 16 January 1963[2] (extracts)

. . . Dear comrades, I am taking this opportunity of speaking in Berlin, at the Congress of the Socialist Unity Party of Germany, to voice my ideas concerning one of the most important and acute international problems—the German problem.

What is the present state of affairs in this connection?

In place of the former Hitler empire, there are two states—a peace-abiding socialist Germany and a militarist, revenge-seeking, imperialist Germany. In addition, standing apart, West Berlin is a capitalist island in the territory of the German Democratic Republic. Such is the existing picture of modern Germany. It is a task of worldwide importance to secure, with due regard for the existing situation, the peaceful coexistence of the two German states.

It may appear at first glance that nothing has changed since the time when we raised the question of a German peace treaty with the two German states and the normalisation, on this basis, of the situation in West Berlin.[3] Four years have gone by, but there is no peace treaty.

The occupation régime, which has long since outlived its day, is still being maintained in West Berlin. Revenge-seeking and militarist sentiments are in full bloom in Western Germany under the wing of the aggressive elements of the western powers. Some people may be inclined to say that the time has been wasted, that the socialist countries have gained nothing by putting the question of a German peace treaty so sharply.

But those who think so fail to see, or do not in the least understand, the changes that have occurred. If we give this matter thought and analyse the course of events in those four years, we shall be sure to see that much water has flowed under the bridge and that far-reaching changes have occurred since the question was raised.

---

[1] Article XIX deals with Emergency Action on Imports of Particular Products and Article XXVIII with Modification of Schedules. For text see General Agreement on Tariffs and Trade, *Basic Instruments and Selected Documents. Volume IV* (Geneva, 1969), pp. 36–7 and 46–8. Also General Agreement on Tariffs and Trade, *Analytical Index, Third Revision, March 1970, Notes on the drafting, interpretation and application of the Articles of the General Agreement* (Geneva, 1970), pp. 106–15 and 157–60.

[2] *Soviet Booklet, No. 106* (London, January 1963), also in *Soviet News*, 17 and 18 January 1963.

[3] See *Documents, 1959*, pp. 40–53.

The positions of the German Democratic Republic have grown stronger. For a long time your republic did not have all the due resources to protect its sovereignty effectively.

Its border with West Berlin was like an open gate which subversive forces used without restriction and with impunity, not only to suck the lifeblood out of you in the full sense of the word, to rob the working people of the republic of many thousands of millions of marks every year, but also to undermine the very foundations of socialism.

On August 13, 1961, an end was put to these outrages. August 13, 1961, was a historic day in the development of the German Democratic Republic.

The West Berlin border was put under your control. This was an all-important step in consolidating the sovereignty of the German Democratic Republic. It has become the really fully fledged master and guardian of its own frontiers and has been enabled to safeguard its socialist gains and the peaceful labour of its citizens reliably from any external encroachments.

Before the defensive measures were taken on the West Berlin border, the reactionary forces were able to infiltrate freely into your republic for subversive purposes and to smuggle imperialist agents into other socialist countries. A socialist state had emerged, but a breach was left in its frontier, as it were, which was brazenly abused by the enemies of socialism. The situation was intolerable. The interests of the German Democratic Republic, and those of the socialist community as a whole, had to be safeguarded. And this was done by your government with the full support of the Warsaw Treaty countries.

The statement of the socialist Warsaw Treaty countries said that the defensive measures on the West Berlin border involved certain discomforts for the city's population.[1]

But the blame for this fell upon those who had made of West Berlin a centre of criminal subversive activities against your republic, upon those who had abused the good will of the government of the German Democratic Republic.

The significance of the changes could be illustrated by, say, the following example. An American journalist asked a Soviet journalist:

'Well, did you obtain on August 13 everything you wanted to obtain through the German peace treaty?'

The Soviet journalist replied:

'No, the peace treaty has not been signed and, consequently, that is not the case.'

Then the American said:

'True, the peace treaty has not been signed yet, but the goal you were pursuing when you insisted on its conclusion, has been almost completely achieved by you. You have closed the border; you have cut off access for the West to the German Democratic Republic.

'Thus, although the peace treaty is still unsigned, you have got what you were after and what you wanted to obtain through the conclusion of the treaty.

'Having achieved what you wanted,' the American journalist continued, 'you have in addition gained the chance of stepping on the pet corns of the West. The lanes of access to West Berlin running across the German Democratic

---

[1] Joint declaration of the Governments of the Warsaw Treaty States, 13 August 1961; in *Documents, 1961,* pp. 343–5.

Republic are precisely pet corns of that sort. There are no conclusive international commitments to speak of for regulating access. It depends largely on the G.D.R. government, and it can always intensify or weaken pressure whenever it wishes.'

He is not entirely accurate. But, to some extent, he is close to the truth.

The German Democratic Republic, our ally and friend, has gained the essentials for every sovereign state—the right to control its frontiers and to act against those who try to weaken the socialist system in the German Democratic Republic. That is a big common gain for all the socialist countries that are parties to the Warsaw Treaty. And now, if we view the matter from the standpoint of the immediate interests of the socialist countries, the problem of the German peace treaty is not really what it was before the defensive measures were taken on the German Democratic Republic's border with West Berlin.

This does not mean to say, of course, that the socialist countries, the countries that fought against Hitler Germany, have lost interest in concluding the peace treaty. No, they have not lost interest in it.

On the contrary, the question is still of most vital importance, not only for the peoples of the socialist countries, but also for the peoples of all countries, who wish to see an end to the cold war and to make world peace secure.

The German peace treaty will not yield profit to one side and loss to the other. Neither now, nor ever before, have we raised the question of revising the existing frontiers in Europe in our favour, or of any other acquisitions. The Soviet Union proposes that a treaty be concluded in order to write *finis* to the Second World War and to put on record the changes that transpired following the crushing defeat of Hitler Germany. That sort of settlement, which would put an end to the ranting claims of the revenge-seekers and would serve as a legal basis for post-war peace in Europe, is of great importance.

The Soviet Union, the German Democratic Republic and the other socialist countries are equally interested in this, and so are the neutralist countries, and members of the imperialist camp, that is to say, the capitalist countries that were at war with fascist Germany, provided they favour coexistence and do not want a new world war to break out. . . .

The peace treaty is the way to improve the atmosphere in Europe, to clear away the survivals of the Second World War and to create a more reliable basis for the peaceful coexistence of states.

It will serve to remove or cut the knot which obstructs the solution of other issues. That is why everybody who cherishes peace and greater international security will work together with us for a peace settlement with Germany.

Take the vital question of disarmament. So long as there is no German peace treaty, it will probably be difficult to expect any telling progress towards a disarmament agreement. Those two questions are not juridically connected. They are independent questions. Yet disarmament is not possible until the international atmosphere has cleared, that is to say, until confidence is built up between states and conditions are created that will not prompt ever new allocations for armaments and bigger armies. Yet it is precisely the unsolved German problem that is prompting the arms build-up and increased military expenditures. . . .

Therefore, if certain powers want to maintain the existing tension, the arms race and, consequently, the state of uncertainty, of painful maladjustment, which may at any moment end in an armed conflict, they will, of course, continue to resist the conclusion of a peace treaty and the ending of the occupation régime in West Berlin. If those are really their intentions, it is scarcely to be expected that they will deal objectively and soberly with the proposals of the Warsaw Treaty countries on the German question, though we are doing all we can to find a mutually acceptable solution.

The socialist countries agree to the peace treaty being signed with the two German states, or with one of them. They propose that through the peace settlement West Berlin be granted the status of a free city. They are willing to provide this free city with the most reliable of guarantees of non-interference in its affairs, guarantees of freedom for the population of West Berlin to choose whichever social and political system they prefer. The United Nations organisation should be the guarantor. It may be recalled that the German Democratic Republic, the Soviet Union and their socialist allies have even consented to foreign troops staying in West Berlin for a fixed period under the United Nations flag. . . .

The military organisation of the socialist countries was established, not for the purpose of attacking other countries, not for aggression, but to prevent the threat of war. It was a measure we were compelled to take. It is appropriate to recall that as soon as the Warsaw Treaty Organisation was founded, the socialist countries declared that, as in the past, they continued to favour the dissolution of all military blocs and were prepared to abolish the Warsaw Treaty at once, provided the imperialist countries agreed to dissolve their own military groupings. We repeated this time and time again, and we adhere to the same point of view today.

That is how things stand with regard to the substance and nature of the imperialist military blocs and the Warsaw Treaty Organisation. Such is the fundamental difference between them.

Now about the other side of this question. Some statesmen of countries freed from colonial oppression show an incorrect understanding, whether consciously or not, of where the dividing line passes in the contemporary world. They divide the world into two military blocs, referring the imperialist countries and their military alliances—NATO, CENTO and SEATO—to one bloc, and the countries of the socialist community to the other.

But does the dividing line in the world pass only between the military alignments in our day? Of course not. Look at it from the purely military point of view and you will easily see that not all countries of the capitalist world are aligned with the military pacts. The Warsaw Treaty Organisation, too, represents only the European socialist countries.

There are two opposed social systems in the world—the socialist and the capitalist systems.

Yet the military blocs cannot be identified with the systems. The division does not follow the principle of military organisations, military blocs, and the identification of countries with these blocs.

To obtain an accurate picture of the contemporary world, it is essential to see the dividing line that follows the political, economic and social principle. On the one hand, there are the capitalist, imperialist countries that preserved, and so far still preserve, the old social system of exploitation and oppression. These countries are headed by monopolists who want to save and perpetuate the exploiting system. On the other hand, countries are growing stronger and developing where the working people have overthrown capitalism, destroyed its oppression and exploitation, established people's rule, and follow the path of socialist and communist construction. The number of these countries will increase, while the capitalist world will shrink.

Thus, it is not a question of military blocs, but of two different social systems. Military alliances, blocs and pacts arise out of the practical policies of the imperialist countries, which see them as a means of safeguarding their exploiter interests, suppressing the struggles of the working people, and paving the way for, and starting, military conflicts. Military alliances, blocs and pacts are brought into being through international treaties and agreements. The rise of a new social system is in no way a result of the arbitrary activity of particular individuals or the product of an international agreement. It is an objective law of social development, a result of the internal contradictions of society, the contradictions between the productive forces and the relations of production.

Many countries which have recently freed themselves from colonial oppression want to take the socialist path. On the other hand, statesmen of some of those countries say they intend to manoeuvre between the two military blocs, thereby mixing up 'blocs' and 'systems'. This mixing up does no good to the working class and the peoples who have won their freedom from colonial oppression. It confuses the newly free peoples and makes it easier for the colonialists to maintain their position in the young independent states.

Most of the former colonies have gained their freedom and independence. But the independence of many of them is still nominal. There is no ignoring the fact that the colonialists still keep their administration, their people and their capital in many of those countries.

They are not resigned to the liberation of those peoples and are doing their utmost to retain the opportunity of further exploiting the former colonies by taking advantage of their backwardness.

As regards the Soviet Union and the other socialist countries, they have rendered, and will continue to render, all-round assistance to the peoples of the former colonies in consolidating their political and economic independence, to the nations engaged in a just struggle to abolish the shameful colonial system. This assistance will grow as the might of the countries of the socialist community increases.

It is not only we who say that the balance of world forces has changed in favour of socialism. This change is in effect admitted by our enemies, who speak of the 'balance of fear'.

We do not adhere to the doctrine of the 'balance of fear', but we cannot help taking note of conclusions of this kind reached by our enemies. These conclusions are nothing but an acknowledgement of the growing might of the world socialist system by the ruling circles of the imperialist powers. Their talk about 'balance' is something different from 'flinging back communism' and so on. We not only declare, but we know full well that the forces of socialism and peace are superior to those of imperialism. The increased influence of the forces of peace and socialism, and the effectiveness of our foreign policy of peace proved their worth all the more conclusively during the Caribbean crisis. . . .

From the standpoint of those who maintain that we installed our rockets in

Cuba in order to mount a nuclear attack on the United States and thereby begin a nuclear world war, and then renounced this objective and withdrew the rockets from Cuba, it might seem that we abandoned our objective. But the point is that the Soviet Union had no such objective. The only reason why we installed our rockets in Cuba was to stop the United States imperialists' aggression against Cuba.

It may be argued that the U.S. imperialists, being under the influence of the most rabid elements, will not keep their pledge and will again turn their arms against Cuba. But then the forces which defended Cuba have not ceased to exist and are growing mightier day by day.

The point is not whether the rockets will be in Cuba or elsewhere. In all circumstances, they can be used just as effectively against any aggression.

I repeat that when we installed our rockets in Cuba, we did not at all intend to precipitate a war between the socialist countries and imperialism. We had a different aim in view—we wanted to prevent an imperialist invasion of Cuba, a new world war. If the events are assessed from this standpoint, we are the winners. It is a gain for the peace forces, for the forces of socialism, the forces building communism.

Some people who consider themselves Marxists say that the struggle against imperialism does not imply that we must above all else build up the economic power of the socialist countries—a real factor with which our enemies reckon; they have invented a new method for waging this struggle, a method that is supposedly the cheapest.

This method, you see, does not depend on the economic level of a country or on the quality and quantity of armaments; it is nothing but abuse. Those people imagine that to fling interminable curses at imperialism means precisely doing what will help the socialist countries more than anything else.

This sort of thing was done by medicine men and quacks.

If only this were required in order to combat imperialism, the Russian people, as you know, are very good at swearing, too. Germans also have their strong expressions, but I think the Russians would have the upper hand in such a competition with you.

But cursing is not the strongest means of fighting your enemies. It runs off like water from a duck's back. That is why we must not fight imperialism by cursing. We must compete with imperialism, with capitalism, on an economic basis. And to have a firm foundation for competition, we must develop the economic potential of the socialist countries and have actual strength, nuclear rocket forces, which would be a warning to the imperialists: If you poke your nose in here, you will lose your head! This is the language the imperialists understand. . . .

Of course, one must expose imperialist intrigues, for this mobilises the masses to fight the exploiters, and helps them to see the bestial nature of imperialism.

But one must remember that the imperialists reckon only with real strength. This is why communists at the helm are in duty bound to do everything possible to increase our strength. And this means vigorously promoting the economy and improving the living standards of the peoples on the basis of the continuously growing economic might of socialism. This will serve as the best example for all working people and all the nations fighting for their freedom. As economic strength grows, the defensive power of the socialist countries is increasing, too.

Comrades, allow me to deal with some important and pressing issues of the world communist movement. To begin with, I would like to stress the interconnection of the struggle for peace, for peaceful coexistence, and the revolutionary struggle of the working class and all working people for the triumph of socialism on earth.

As things are in our day, the struggle for peace has become a most important factor in the struggle for socialism. No problem of the revolutionary movement of the working class or the national liberation movement can now be considered in isolation from the struggle to preserve peace and avert a nuclear world war. This is the important lesson in tactics for the world communist movement to learn from the recent events in the Caribbean area.

The history of the working-class movement has recorded instances of the struggle for peace becoming the prime factor in the struggle for socialism. That was how matters stood during the October Socialist Revolution. Lenin said:

> 'Nothing could be more indisputable and obvious than the following truth: A government which gave Soviet power, land, workers' control and *peace* to a people worn out by three years of predatory war would be invincible. Peace is the important thing.' (*Collected Works, Russian edition, vol. 27, p. 17.*)

The Bolsheviks won peace for the peoples of Russia; they found a way out of the imperialist war and rallied the broadest masses of the working people to Soviet power in the struggle for socialism.

It is typical of our time that the struggle for peace has become, more than ever before, a paramount historic task, not only for the working class, but for all the other sections of the population. It is a knot in which the interests of all mankind intertwine. In face of the threat of a nuclear war, a single torrent of the most diverse mass movements is arising, movements which can be united by the common desire to deliver mankind from the disaster of war. The international working class and the socialist countries are the leading and organising force of this torrent.

Nor is this because the socialist countries have simply taken up the slogan of the struggle for peace, which enjoys popularity among the peoples. No, the fact is that the objective interests of the socialist countries, of the international working-class movement and the national liberation movement are inseparable from the struggle to ward off a nuclear war. . . .

Today some people who call themselves Marxist-Leninists allege that the defence of peace and the struggle against the war danger are contrary to the spirit of Marxism-Leninism and hamper the progress of the revolutionary movement.

According to what these people say, Lenin, Karl Liebknecht, Rosa Luxemburg and the Russian Bolsheviks were not Marxists, since they were opposed to war. Only people who do not understand the essence of the Marxist doctrine of revolutionary struggle can affirm such a thing.

The theory of scientific socialism created by Marx and Engels maintains that capitalism inevitably meets its doom in the course of its development, as a result of the antagonistic contradictions arising and growing in society.

Concentration and centralisation of capital lead to monopolies and to the increasing decay of capitalism, which provides conditions for the transition to a higher social system—socialism. Marx said that as capitalism develops, it creates its own grave-digger—the working class.

Life has proved the Marxist-Leninist doctrine to be perfectly correct. According to this doctrine, the working class defeats capitalism by its class struggle against the exploiters and not by starting wars between countries.

History willed that the Russian proletariat should achieve victory for the revolution during the First World War. After the Second World War there arose a number of socialist countries.

When a war breaks out between imperialist countries, all the internal and external contradictions of imperialism become aggravated, the machinery of the bourgeois state is shaken and a favourable situation is created for the victory of the working class, particularly in those countries defeated in the war.

Marxist-Leninists have always devoted a great deal of attention to the problems of war and peace, and have always considered them in their specific historical context. One cannot solve problems of war and peace without taking the actual situation into account. It is necessary to have the courage to face up soberly to the facts as they are and to weigh with scientific precision the eventual results of a modern war, should attempts to prevent it fail. Foreign scientists and military experts estimate that the United States now has roughly 40,000 hydrogen bombs and warheads. Everyone knows that the Soviet Union, too, has more than enough of this stuff.

What would happen if all these nuclear weapons were brought down on people? Scientists estimate that the first blow alone would take a toll of 700 to 800 million human lives. All the big cities would be wiped out or destroyed—not only in the two leading nuclear countries, the United States and the U.S.S.R., but in France, Britain, Germany, Italy, China, Japan and many other countries of the world. The effects of a nuclear war would continue to tell throughout the lifetime of many generations, causing disease and death and the worst deformities in the development of people.

I am not saying these things to frighten anyone. I am simply citing data at the disposal of science. These data cannot but be reckoned with.

There can be no doubt that a world nuclear war, if started by the imperialist maniacs, would inevitably result in the downfall of the capitalist system, a system breeding wars. But would the socialist countries and the cause of socialism all over the world benefit from a world nuclear disaster? Only people who deliberately shut their eyes to the facts can think so. As for Marxist-Leninists, they cannot propose to establish a communist civilisation on the ruins of centres of world culture, on land laid waste and contaminated by nuclear fall-out. We need hardly add that in the case of many peoples, the question of socialism would be eliminated altogether, because they would have disappeared bodily from our planet.

I shall let you into a secret: Our scientists have developed a 100-megaton bomb. But a 100-megaton bomb, our military men hold, cannot be dropped on Europe, if our probable adversary unleashes a war. Where can we drop it here —on Western Germany or France? But the explosion of such a bomb on this territory would also destroy you and certain other countries. That is why this weapon can be used by us, apparently, only outside Western Europe. I say this only to give you a clearer idea of the terrible means of destruction that now exist.

A 100-megaton bomb is still not the limit. This, if I may say so, is the limit from the point of view of probable military expediency, because more powerful means of destruction might constitute a huge threat to those who dared to use them as well.

In other words, comrades, as I have already said in the report to the session of the U.S.S.R. Supreme Soviet, it is not advisable to hasten to heaven: no one has returned from there to say that life is better there than here. What we want is not a heavenly kingdom, but a kingdom on earth, a kingdom of labour. This is the kingdom we are fighting for without sparing our efforts, and we shall fight for it and win.

The Soviet Union, which has rockets and nuclear arms, is well aware of the potentialities of these weapons. We have made them to defend our country and the other socialist countries.

We therefore take a responsible attitude to the problems of war and peace. We do not want war, but neither are we afraid of it. Should a war be imposed on us, we will know how to administer the most resolute rebuff to the aggressors, and the aggressors know that.

To use a familiar phrase: 'Blessed is he who talks about war without knowing what he is talking about.' The Albanian leaders talk a lot about rocket and nuclear war but nobody is worried by their talk. Everyone knows that they have nothing to their name but idle talk, and that they have no real possibilities. As you see, our positions on these questions and our responsibilities are different.

We have always considered and still consider the principle of the peaceful coexistence of countries with different social systems—a principle proclaimed by Lenin—to be the only correct one. Its significance has always been confirmed by the entire practice of international relations.

The policy of peaceful coexistence has acquired special significance in present conditions. When there was only one socialist country in the world, one surrounded by imperialist countries, the policy of peaceful coexistence was aimed at gaining time, at winning a respite to strengthen the proletarian state and build socialism in our country. Now that the nature of war has changed and the balance of world forces is favourable to peace and socialism, the policy of peaceful coexistence has far more important tasks to accomplish and goals to attain; it is acquiring what is, in effect, a new content. Its ultimate objective is to provide the most favourable conditions for the victory of socialism over capitalism through peaceful economic competition.

Some people misrepresent our Marxist-Leninist attitude, alleging that by proclaiming the policy of peaceful coexistence, we are calling on the revolutionary forces, on the Communist Parties of the capitalist countries, to renounce the class struggle, the struggle to establish the rule of the working class, of the working people, to abandon the national liberation struggle of the peoples. That invention and slander is not clever.

It is not only through its declarations and statements that the Soviet Union supports the just wars of peoples; its support has more than once taken the form of concrete assistance. Many peoples have used our armaments in their liberation struggles and have been victorious, have freed themselves from colonial oppression. The colonial peoples' wars for their liberation are holy wars, and it is for this reason that we have been, are, and always shall be, on the side of the peoples fighting for their independence.

The advocates of the so-called theory of the victory of socialism through war also deny that socialism can win by peaceful means, saying that this is a departure from Marxism. We must say for the edification of these admirers of the cult of Stalin that it was none other than Stalin who, in an interview with British communists after the Second World War, spoke of using the peaceful, parliamentary way to bring about the victory of socialism, and this is recorded in the programme of the Communist Party of Great Britain. The leaders of the British Communist Party know that this wording was proposed by Stalin.

The Albanian leaders persist in the allegation that the Communist Party of the Soviet Union advocates only the peaceful road and rules out the method of armed struggle. One may well ask them: Can they cite an example of a Communist Party maintaining that there was a revolutionary situation in its country and wanting to begin a revolt, when the C.P.S.U. was opposed to using the method of armed struggle? Can the Albanians cite such an example by any chance? No, they cannot, because no such example exists.

The Albanian leaders believe that it is possible to call forth a revolution artificially when they wish, and that no objective or subjective conditions are required to accomplish a revolution. According to their 'theory', everything works out very simply: there emerge heroes who come and organise a revolt. But there have been no such facts in history, nor will there be. This 'theory', if one may call it that, has nothing in common with Marxism. . . .

Comrades, firm unity of the world communist movement is a most important condition for our success in the struggle for peace and socialism throughout the world.

Every communist should be fully aware of the great importance of the unity of the revolutionary forces on an international scale and of the solidarity of all the contingents of our movement.

Our unity is based on a common ideology—Marxism-Leninism, the principles of proletarian internationalism. The main thing which unites us is the common class interests of the proletariat in all countries, of all working people, the proper Marxist-Leninist understanding of the international tasks of the working class, and deep faith in the justice of our great cause and the inevitable victory of socialism on a world scale.

Our duty is to unite all revolutionary forces, to steel and ideologically equip the communist movement. The Communist Party of the Soviet Union abides by the common, agreed line of the world communist movement.

It has adhered, and will adhere, to the platform elaborated by the representatives of the Marxist-Leninist parties at their meetings in 1957 and 1960.[1]

It is true that there may arise a difference of opinion on certain problems, including vital ones, between communists of different countries. The Marxist-Leninist doctrine has become the practice for the peoples of one-third of the globe. Over 1,000 million people are building a new life, achieving splendid results in socialist construction.

[1] See *Documents, 1957*, pp. 527–39, and *1960*, pp. 222–38.

The countries of the world socialist system are at different stages of the construction of a new society, and their experience in developing relations with the outside world is not identical in every respect.

These circumstances give rise to different approaches to certain problems. While this is not exactly a pleasant fact, it has to be taken into account because it is a reality.

Differences may and do arise in life, but we must not forget that the differences arising between Communist and Workers' parties are no more than fleeting episodes, whereas the relations between the peoples of the socialist countries are even now being shaped for centuries to come. This is why the relations between fraternal parties, especially between socialist countries—relations based on a common social and economic system and aimed at building communism—can and should be determined by the main thing which unites us. Everything else is, in the final analysis, of secondary importance by comparison.

That is the reason why we must not give vent to feelings when differences arise. We must be patient, must look at the root of the matter, so to speak, and must see the main thing. As far as the fraternal parties are concerned, especially the parties of the socialist countries, the main thing is the common cause for which they are fighting, that is, the construction of socialism and communism. . . .

Even if we diverge over certain ideological questions, possibly including rather important ones, we must try to ensure that these questions are properly understood. In so doing we must not go to extremes, must not take a subjective stand in appraising the general situation in a particular country. We must not, for example, assess the political system of this or that socialist country only by the erroneous views of leaders, views which have prevailed for a while. It is objective and not subjective factors that should be taken as the principal indications.

And this implies, first of all, the question of who owns the means of production, who holds the power and on what lines the state is developing.

If we disagreed on certain questions and quarrelled, and then said at once that the socialist country whose leaders differed with us on fraternal parties, they must recant their erroneous views and revert to the path of unity and close co-operation in the fraternal family that is the socialist commonwealth, to the path of unity with the entire world communist movement.

The Communist Party of the Soviet Union follows Lenin's behests. While taking an uncompromising stand on the fundamental issues of the theory and tactics of the communist movement, we have done, and will do, all we can to persuade the erring or those who have lost their bearings and do not see clearly enough the tasks facing us in our struggle under present conditions.

The unity of world communism on the basis of Marxism-Leninism is the most sacred principle of our party, and we will spare no effort to strengthen it. . . .

In discussions, particular discretion should be shown by the parties of those countries whose peoples are already building socialism and are building communism. It is our common duty not to scatter our forces in the face of the imperialist camp but, on the contrary, vigorously to strengthen them all along the line—economically, militarily, ideologically and politically.

Practice has shown that occasionally we have different opinions on questions bearing on the internal development of a country. In this respect, our relations have been shaping more or less correctly in recent years, and there has been tolerance and moderation, so to speak, as regards lecturing, to say nothing of interfering in the internal affairs of other countries.

In foreign policy matters, and in matters concerning the international working-class and communist movement, we occasionally also approach events and understand them differently. Here, of course, there may be a certain difference of opinion, as well as discussions intended to elaborate a correct, agreed policy. But it is particularly essential to show restraint and patience.

The central committee of our party would consider it useful now to call a halt to polemics between Communist Parties, to stop criticising other parties inside one's own party, and allow some time for the passions to subside.

Some comrades suggest calling a meeting of all the fraternal parties to discuss the questions that are ripe for it. Our party has always favoured such meetings. We believe, however, that if we convene that meeting immediately there will probably be little hope of successfully eliminating the existing differences.

Such a meeting would lead, not to a calm and judicious removal of differences, but to their aggravation and to the danger of a split. We must not forget that there is a logic to every struggle and that political passions run high.

The Soviet communists are true and resolute adherents of the unity of all the Communist and Workers' parties, and of the consolidation of our common forces on the basis of Marxism-Leninism. This is why we consider that it would be more reasonable, in the interests of the working class and our future, to stop now the polemics in the press on the disputed questions. Let us give time a chance to work for us. It will help us understand who is right and who is wrong. Moreover, during this time we should get rid of all that is extraneous and accidental.

We will be able, then, to come to agreement all the more effectively, to sum up the results achieved and to elaborate general conclusions expressing a common point of view on the fundamental issues of the development of the world communist and working-class movement.

The Communist and Workers' parties of the world are conscious of their immense responsibility for the fortunes of world socialism, of mankind, and they still stint no effort to sweep out of their way all that hinders the promotion of the unity and solidarity of our ranks on the basis of Marxism-Leninism.

Dear comrades, we are particularly happy to point out today that there is complete unity of views on all questions of principle between our two parties, the Communist Party of the Soviet Union and the Socialist Unity Party of Germany.

We can also say with great satisfaction that friendly, truly fraternal relations exist between the leaders of the Soviet Union and of the German Democratic Republic, and personally between the Soviet leaders and comrades Walter Ulbricht, Otto Grotewohl and other G.D.R. leaders. There has always been as there is now, complete mutual understanding on all questions arising in the relations between our countries, and also on problems of the international situation.

Fraternal relations between the Communist Party of the Soviet Union and the Socialist Unity Party of Germany have played the decisive role in establishing indestructible friendship between the peoples of the Soviet Union and the German Democratic Republic.

We consider it our supreme duty to continue doing everything to strengthen our friendship still further—the friendship of our parties and our peoples, the friendship of the peoples of all the socialist countries. . . .

Speech by Mr. Khrushchev, Berlin, 2 July 1963[1] (extract)

. . . Dear Comrades, every time I speak here in Berlin I speak about questions the solution of which is directly connected with the normalisation of the situation in Europe. And I hope that you understand why I do this. For Germany and West Berlin are a complex knot of international problems. The political climate in the whole of Europe and in the entire world greatly depends on the settlement of these problems. Many years have elapsed since the last shots were fired in the second world war. But, as hitherto, the sinister shadow of soldiers' steel helmets and bayonets falls on the soil of Europe, the war sword of Damocles hangs over it as before. A more sinister shadow has now been added—the shadow of nuclear rocket weapons. The peoples live in constant lack of confidence and fear for the future, for the future of their children. They want to put an end to this state of affairs as soon as possible. This is a legitimate and understandable desire.

The Soviet Union, the GDR, all socialist countries, are vitally interested in the complete liquidation of tensions, in the establishment of stable good-neighbourly relations between all European countries. We want all nations of Europe, just as of the whole world, to be able to look calmly into the future and devote themselves to peaceful labour. We uphold the policy of peaceful coexistence between States with a differing social system both on a world-wide scale and as applicable to various regions of the world. One cannot speak of the establishment of an enduring peace throughout the world, if hotbeds of tension are constantly maintained in various parts of it. This refers to all regions of the world, including such an important region as Europe. It is difficult to overestimate the importance and part to be played by the policies of the European States in strengthening peace not only in Europe but throughout the world. It is precisely here that serious conflicts have arisen, which twice in the last half century plunged all mankind into bloody world wars. It is difficult for the mind of man to perceive what an unimaginable calamity would be the outcome of a third world war for Europe. The conscience of the peoples cannot even tolerate such a prospect. The Soviet Union, the GDR, like the other socialist States, regard the question of the establishment of an enduring peace in Europe as an important matter. . . .

After the war the peoples hoped that lasting peace would be established and problems of a peaceful settlement reasonably solved. These hopes of the peoples have not been justified, however. A militaristic, revanchist State, the Federal Republic of Germany, was created in the Western part of Germany with the assistance of the aggressive circles of international imperialism. No matter how much verbiage the West uses to justify the present policy of the imperialist Powers, there is no getting away from the fact that the preservation of a hotbed of tension in the centre of Europe kindles the cold war, brings to red heat the relations between the peoples, primarily between Western Germany and the socialist countries. The peoples expect the German problem to be solved and

---

[1] *S.W.B.*, EE/1891, 4 July 1963, c1/1–c1/14.

thus more favourable conditions created for a peaceful development of friendship and co-operation between the peoples.

What must be done to consolidate peace in Europe and therefore throughout the world? It is essential to eliminate the remnants of the second world war, to sign a peace treaty with Germany. I have had more than one opportunity to speak on this problem. But let us return once more to the question of what the German people, the peoples of all Europe, would get from the signing of a peace treaty. Not only the peoples of the Soviet Union and the other countries which stand for a policy of peace would gain from the signing of a peace treaty with Germany. It is also essential to other European States, to the peoples of the whole world. It would be especially in accord with the interests and hopes of the population of Western Germany. May the Germans residing in Western Germany ponder, may German workers, peasants, intellectuals, businessmen and statesmen reflect on this—let them with German thoroughness weigh in the balance: in whose interests is it to preserve now the remnants of the world war and the tension in Europe? And if they reflect on this without prejudice, realistically, soberly, if they strike a balance of all the pluses and minuses, they will see clearly that the interests of the German people demand the elimination of the remnants of the war and the hotbeds of tension, that they demand the normalisation of the situation in Central Europe. Such a road would open up wide prospects for fruitful economic co-operation between the Federal Republic of Germany and the GDR and other socialist countries. More and more thinking Germans in Western Germany are beginning to reflect on these problems. They are beginning to realise more deeply and clearly that it is necessary to put an end irrevocably to the policy of militarism and revanchism.

This policy weighs especially heavily on the life of the population of West Berlin which, first and foremost, needs the normalisation of the situation. And this can be achieved only on the basis of a peace treaty. Only then will stability appear in the life of West Berlin, as well as favourable prospects for its economic development.

What does the Soviet Union propose in insisting on the earliest elimination of the remnants of the second world war? We do not propose anything that would change the conditions and the situation in Europe existing at the present time which have come about as a result of the smashing of Hitler Germany. We only want to formalise the present situation legally and thus make it difficult for the revenge-seekers to prepare for touching off a new war.

In Western countries they are still maintaining the outcry over the so-called Berlin wall. But what the West calls a wall is the legitimate border of the German Democratic Republic. It enables the working peoples of the GDR to curb provocative activities against their country and the other socialist States. And this means that the so-called Berlin wall helps the cause of normalising relations between States, helps the cause of peace. It is high time, at last, to take a sober look at things. It is necessary to understand that the GDR is not a myth but an actual State which has its own Government and its own laws, its own system and its own borders. Every sovereign State has the right to safeguard and control its borders. There are many who cry that the border in Berlin interferes with communications between the population of the West Berlin and the residents of the GDR capital. But this is untrue. Such contentions can come only from people who would like to use entry into the GDR for unlawful, anti-popular activity. We know that the working people of socialist Germany give a warm and hospitable welcome to those who really want to establish friendly exchanges and to communicate with the working people of the GDR, who come here with a pure heart and an open soul. If there do exist difficulties in communication between the West Berlin population and the residents of the GDR capital, the blame is on the occupation authorities and on the West Berlin authorities.

The second world war has changed the political map of Europe and this must be reckoned with. In vain certain short-sighted people think that by fanning the cold war, that by reviving the policy of brinkmanship it will be possible to compel the working people of the GDR to surrender their socialist State voluntarily. The working people of the GDR are aware of the great honour of being the first to raise the red banner over German soil. They will never agree to reimposing on themselves the yoke of capitalism; they will never allow landlords and capitalists to set foot on their soil. I mean that the working people will never agree to this voluntarily; if the enemies want to do this by force, they have no such force!

Revenge-seeking circles turn a deaf ear to any mention of a peace treaty. Their aim is to liquidate the GDR, to swallow it up. But they realise quite clearly that on their own they would not achieve this. Their stomach is too weak and will not digest it—and, incidently, such a piece would stick in their throat. This is why they so stubbornly sought to join NATO—the aggressive military bloc of the Western Powers. Hitlerite survivors saw in NATO an opportunity to realise their dream of taking revenge for defeat in the second world war. In their turn, the aggressive Western circles wanted to use Western Germany as the main shock force against the socialist countries. It is here, on the ground of these plans of brigandage that their interests coincided. What did the West German revenge-seekers bank upon? They pinned their hopes on the USA which, far from suffering during the war, grew rich on war profits. The West German militarists were especially attracted by American atomic weapons which at that time were the monopoly of the USA.

You remember how heavily the reactionary forces of imperialism banked on atomic weapons in their striving to crush the countries of socialism. These aims were most outspokenly formulated by the late Dulles, whom Adenauer regarded as the spiritual leader of the aggressive NATO bloc. You will remember his policy of 'rolling back communism', the 'on the brink of war' policy, the gist of which was to abolish socialism in the East European countries by armed force. These designs of the imperialists were aimed in the first place against the GDR. This was exactly the aim pursued by the so-called reunification programme which all reactionary circles of the Western Powers were clinging to. In the language of the imperialists reunification meant the swallowing up of the GDR. Is it not a fact that division of Germany is not so much a national, as a socio-political question? One part of Germany is building socialism while the other goes along the capitalist way. This is why the word reunification conceals the striving of the imperialist Powers to liquidate the first German State of workers and peasants, the GDR. Nothing will come out of this now, as nothing did before, Messrs. revenge-seekers!

We understand the aspirations of Germans who want to see their country united, who want to have a unified peace-loving and democratic German State. This is a natural and legitimate desire. The policy of peace and co-operation brings this future nearer, the policy of war and revenge makes it more remote. I will not conceal my sympathies and I think it will be no news to anyone if I say that the best way to solve the question of reunification of the two German States is to abolish capitalism in Western Germany and create a single German State on a socialist foundation. Such a way would be the most progressive and in accord with the spirit of our time, with the interests of the German people, of the working people of the whole world. But, naturally, when and how this will happen is a matter of the future; it is the business of the German people themselves, and of no one else except the German people.

One cannot fail to see that the imperialist forces are trying to play on these natural aspirations of the Germans in their own interests, striving to liquidate the GDR. But such a way of solving the German problem is impossible in our time. It is the way of civil war, the way of a world war. And what does war mean in present-day conditions with the existence of nuclear-missile weapons? Even Chancellor Adenauer, a man who is more than others afflicted by the disease of revanchism, understands that if a war breaks out, it is Western Germany that would perish in its flames quicker than anyone else. Even the maddest representatives of capitalism are beginning to realise that in present-day conditions war would be suicide for any aggressor. Equally vain and hopeless are the attempts of the revenge-seekers and reactionaries to subvert the GDR from within by means of instigation and provocations. Recently a great hullabaloo was raised in Western Germany over the tenth anniversary of the fascist putsch in Berlin which failed disgracefully. On this occasion the leaders of the Federal Republic made speeches imbued with the spirit of bellicose revanchism. What can one say about that?

I believe one can somehow understand the outgoing Chancellor when he makes palpably absurd and inconsistent statements, trying to vindicate the policy he conducted persistently for many years. But how can one understand the incoming Chancellor when he takes over this entire burden, this heap of absurdities and futile hopes? Is it not a fact that he will have to clear away this heap and sooner or later seek new ways, new approaches? Why then does he right from the start make his own task more difficult, taking onto his shoulders the crushing burden of the past? This is hardly a reasonable policy.

Statesmen of the Federal Republic of Germany speak about good relations with the Soviet Union, advancing as a condition a change in the policy and the social system of the GDR. It is fitting to ask them: gentlemen, are you serious people? Can you seriously and soberly assess the situation that has arisen in the world, your own situation and our situation? And if you mean to celebrate this date you ought to be told how your hopes, your efforts to do away with the GDR, were smashed to smithereens ten years ago.

Messrs. revenge-seekers would do well to remember that that was in 1953 and today we have 1963. If they failed then to turn back the development of the GDR, now it is all the more out of question. Great changes have occurred in the world in that time and these changes were not in their favour. Whereas then they relied on American atomic bomb blackmail and nevertheless failed to achieve their purposes, how can they frighten us now? It is a fact that they realise full well that if they unleash a war, they themselves will perish in its flames in the very first hours. To what end did a gang of Hitlerites who escaped from us alive in the last war, gather in West Berlin? Why did they turn up in West Berlin? They know perfectly well, after all, that West Berlin is a city which under the Potsdam Agreement has a special status, that it did not, does not and will not form part of Western Germany.

Revenge-seekers needed this to whip up passions, not to improve relations, not for reconciliation, but to keep up war psychosis. They would like to educate the German people in the spirit of revenge, constantly remind them about the shrinking German territory. But if they want to restore the German Reich in its former borders why be hypocrites? Let them make Hitler's crazy ideas a part of their arsenal, let them draw maps of Germany including the Ukraine, let them draw her right up to the Urals! Indeed, Hitler wanted to achieve these aims but perished ingloriously. This must be remembered, remember how the war ended. If the revenge-seekers will live by Hitler's ideas the same fate will befall them. Therefore the best thing would be to adopt realistic and sober positions as soon as possible. If the outgoing Chancellor is incapable of reasonably assessing the world situation and ingloriously terminates his activities, the same fate is in store for the new Chancellor, unless he finds in himself the strength and sanity to choose the road of realism.

Quite recently Chancellor Adenauer and his hanger-on Brandt, who calls himself a socialist, and other reactionaries of Western Germany and West Berlin invited the American President to visit West Berlin. There is nothing wrong in the fact of Mr. Kennedy's coming to West Berlin. Such a visit might have been welcomed if it had been a visit with good intentions. But those who invited the President were of course not guided by good motives. They wanted to boost their unreasonable revenge-seeking aspirations.

That is precisely why the President was accompanied by the outgoing Chancellor and other West German politicians who in fact have nothing to do with West Berlin since, as has been repeatedly stated by us and our allies, West Berlin is not a part of Western Germany. Judging by press reports, the American President did not immediately agree to travel to West Berlin in the company of the outgoing Chancellor. Apparently he realised that such a company could not fail to cast a shadow on his trip. The fact that Mr. Kennedy bowed to the aspirations of the West German revanchists cannot but disappoint those who would like to see a confirmation of the President's recent speech in the American University in Washington,[1] that was notable for its sober appraisal of the international situation. In his speech he spoke about the need of revising and improving relations with the Soviet Union, of easing international tensions and liquidating the state of cold war.

But, low and behold, only 13 days have elapsed since the day this speech was made; the President of the USA came to Western Germany and then to West Berlin and began to make utterly different speeches there. If one reads what he said in Western Germany and especially in West Berlin[2] and compares it with the speech in the American University, one might think that the speeches were made by two different Presidents. It is difficult to imagine how one and the same

[1] See pp. 14–20 above.
[2] For texts, see pp. 34–41 above and pp. 200–1 below.

man can in such a brief period when no essential changes occurred in the international situation, make speeches containing mutually exclusive statements.

What is the reason for this? The reason is a very dangerous symptom. The President of the USA is competing with the President of France in courting the old West German widow. Both try to win her heart that has already grown cold and which often prompts its possessor to utterly unconstructive thoughts. And if this widow is wooed in such a way by these two suitors, each seeking to draw her to his heart, the widow can become conceited and think that the solution of world problems really depends on her. In fact little now depends on her, while such courting leads to tension, to a very dangerously tense situation in the world.

This is, for instance, borne out by the nuclear policy of the USA. It thrusts these nuclear weapons upon its allies under the signboard of the so-called NATO multilateral force. And this is done despite the refusal of some of these allies to take part in the setting up of such a nuclear force. Why is all this being done? Above all, to satisfy the desire of the West German revenge-seekers, blinded as they are by their hatred of communism, to receive nuclear weapons. Such a policy can lead to disastrous consequences.

By his speeches in West Berlin the President of the USA hardly convinced anyone of the correctness of his position, nor did he scare anyone by his support of the revanchist leaders of Western Germany and West Berlin, he only added poison to the international atmosphere, already poisoned by the imperialists.

To make such anti-communist speeches as the American President made in Western Germany and West Berlin, he apparently thoroughly studied the speeches of the late Secretary of State Dulles; moreover, not the Dulles as he became in the last months of his life, but, so to speak, the early Dulles who imposed his will in the White House. Does the US President plan to return now to the bankrupt policy that was proclaimed by Dulles when he was in power? Such a policy bodes nothing good for the USA.

As for us we can say: gentlemen, take the corners more slowly. Just as the dreams of all reactionary politicians, who tried to destroy the Soviet State, were shattered, just as history buried all the plans of Churchill, Dulles and their like, so the revanchist plans of the West German politicians and all who are behind them, support them and egg them on to rash actions against the Soviet Union, the GDR and the mighty community of socialist countries, will be buried just as ingloriously.

We believe that the West German people will be realistic in understanding the situation, will realise what tremendous danger lies in the policy of revenge, will take their destinies into their own hands and will press for a policy in line with their own vital interests. And the vital interests of the German working people point to the necessity of improving relations with the Soviet Union, with all the socialist countries, which want to safeguard peace.

If Western Germany follows another course it will mean that she will move towards war. And in our time apparently only madmen can hope to solve outstanding issues between States by means of war. The US President also repeatedly spoke about this.

For example, in his speech in the American University, that I have already mentioned, President Kennedy said: Total war has no sense in an age when the great Powers can keep large and comparatively invulnerable forces and refuse to surrender without resorting to the use of these forces. President Kennedy called for the building of relations with the Soviet Union on a new basis, so as to preserve peace and not burn to death in the flames of a nuclear-rocket war. If the US President really strives for an improvement in the international situation, why does he make such speeches as those he delivered in Western Germany and West Berlin, speeches designed to aggravate the international situation?

I should like to reaffirm that the Soviet Union and other socialist countries, as true friends and allies in the common struggle for the victory of communism, have always been and continue to be with the GDR.

The hopes of the West German revanchists to settle by military means the question of liquidating the GDR are a foolish and dangerous idea. And if, as the saying goes, God deprives the revanchists of their senses [animation in the hall] and war is unleashed, this would be the end of Western Germany. But I think even half-wits who have preserved as much as a shred of common sense will hardly risk suicide. Had Hitler foreseen his end he would hardly have risked such a venture. He unleashed war because he anticipated victory. Hitler never thought he would be forced to commit suicide so as to escape the just retribution of the peoples, to escape standing trial as an enemy of mankind.

It is precisely a sober realisation of the outcome of a modern war that induces such a politician as the President of France, de Gaulle, to state soberly that the eastern frontiers of Germany are unalterable. The same thing is said by some statesmen in America, Britain, and other NATO countries. Some of them state this publicly, others admit it in conversation at meetings with statesmen from socialist countries.

I think that the leading statesmen of capitalism understand well what the outcome would be of a world war with the use of modern arms. Why then do the Western Powers not agree to the signing of a German peace treaty? If one is to reply to this question in general terms one could say that the Western imperialist Powers do not want to meet in any way the cardinal interests of the German people because these interests run counter to the plans and aims of imperialist quarters.

Look at the essence of the policy promoted by the present Government of Western Germany and you will see that this policy proceeds not from the interests of the West German people but from the interests of West German revanchists who are closely linked with the US imperialists. It is profitable for the US imperialists to keep their allies in constant fear of the Soviet Union and the other socialist countries. The bogy of 'communist menace' is used to swell military budgets and increase the contributions to the so-called defence within the framework of NATO.

But it is clear to anyone that the more funds this or that country spends on defence, the less resources it will have for the development of peaceful branches of the economy. And this is precisely what the American monopolists press their allies into doing so as to ensure for themselves more favourable conditions in the competitive struggle with the West German and other monopolist quarters.

We were frankly told about these aims of the American monopolies by the former US President Eisenhower. When we pointed out to him the danger of the arming of the German Federal Republic and asked him why the USA supported it, Eisenhower replied: Do understand our position; if Western Germany had not definite commitments in the field of defence she would have great advantages over other countries in the field of economic competition. He thus admitted that the USA is afraid of the development of Western Germany as its rival in the world market. From the point of view of the American ruling circles she is successfully waging this competitive struggle because she does not spend big funds on armaments and uses them for the development of the economy. If this continues the USA will find itself in an even less favourable situation, and therefore it forces Western Germany to arm, to spend.

Indeed if a large part of the product created by the hands of the working class is spent on military aims, this means that the national wealth, the labour of workers and peasants is thrown to the winds.

One must also take into account another selfish calculation of the American imperialists in this policy. Pushing Western Germany along the road of the arms race, they think that in the event of a military conflict, Western Germany would be the first to receive a nuclear blow, while the United States would for some time remain aside. It follows that it is not without ulterior motives that the Western Powers are supporting the present unrealistic policy of the German Federal Republic and want to keep it on this position.

Does this meet the aspirations of the population of Western Germany? Of course not! The interests of the people of the German Federal Republic lie on quite a different plane—on the plane of peaceful development of Germany and the all-round normalisation and development of relations with socialist countries. Do the objective conditions for this exist? We are confident that they do.

First of all there are no insurmountable barriers between the Soviet Union and the German Federal Republic that would preclude the possibility of co-operation between our countries. Of course, we are on different ideological poles. There are different social systems in our countries. But this divides not only the Soviet Union and the socialist countries on the one hand and the German Federal Republic on the other. The social and political division is between two different systems—the socialist and the capitalist—and not only Western Germany, but also the United States, France, Britain, Italy and many other countries belong to the capitalist system.

In these conditions, there is only one reasonable road of relations between States with different social systems—the road of peaceful coexistence and peaceful economic competition. But if differences in the social and political system do not prevent other capitalist countries from developing co-operation with the Soviet Union and other socialist countries, why cannot Western Germany take to this road? Questions of the social and political system are an internal matter for each State and for each people. We have said more than once, and we repeat, that we stand on positions of non-interference in the internal affairs of other peoples—that we do not wish to impose, and shall never consider imposing, our system on any country.

Secondly, the Germans in Western Germany have political and economic interests which coincide with those of the peoples of the socialist countries. This refers above all to the question of peace. One does not have to be particularly clever to understand the simple truth that the people of Western Germany are vitally interested in a stable and lasting peace. I think that no thoughtful West German will doubt that the Soviet people, the working people of the other socialist countries, are enthusiastically coming out for an end to international tension—that they want a peaceful life on earth.

If we look at the sphere of the economy, here we find much that can provide a dependable basis for the development of relations between our countries. Without doubt, West German business circles want to develop their economy, to raise still higher the industry of Western Germany. The Soviet people have great plans for developing their economy and are successfully carrying them out. Indeed, to ensure the growth of her industry and of her entire economy, Western Germany must have a reliable and stable foreign market. And this is a field where she is already clashing with her Western partners—the United States, Britain, France, Italy and other countries. The law of competition inevitably comes into force here.

For our country, Western Germany is not a competitor. If Western Germany produces more steel and machinery, that does not damage us. Machines will become cheaper, and we shall be able to buy them in greater quantity. This is of mutual advantage. Historically, and as a result of the structure of the economy of our two countries, we can be good trade partners with tremendous potentialities. Of course, when a trading partner ostentatiously refuses to fulfil orders agreed upon earlier this is a far cry from conscientiousness in commercial matters. Characteristic in this respect is the recent pipes affair. The oil monopolies of the USA forced the German Federal Republic to refuse to deliver large-bore tube to the Soviet Union. This action, of course, did not create insurmountable problems for us. Soviet enterprises increased their output of tube. Who gained from the violation by the Government of the German Federal Republic of a trade deal with the Soviet Union? The gainers were the monopolies of the USA: West German industrialists suffered a loss. Moreover trust in the German Federal Republic as a trade partner has been undermined.

The businessmen of Western Germany realise well and clearly all the benefits to be gained from the establishment of enduring and stable economic ties with the Soviet Union, the GDR and other socialist countries, but clearly they are strongly influenced by political considerations which do not permit them to take the road of sound economic co-operation with us. It is like the swan in the fable which tried to fly up to the clouds while the pike tugged it down into the water. The political leaders of Western Germany follow an unreasonable policy, disregarding the economic damage suffered by the West German economy as a result. West German leaders, if they really want to be sober-minded politicians, should not forget either the substantial circumstance that the economic upsurge observed in Europe and the USA after world war II is long past its climax. It is not only we Marxists but bourgeois economists who are saying this. The business circles of certain capitalist countries are already beginning to take definite measures to put off the impending upheavals. In these conditions it is hardly reasonable or far-sighted to disdain economic ties with socialist countries and even to set out to disrupt them. The fact is that this rebounds on the West German economy.

When one turns to the past and analyses historical experience, which has demonstrated the full possibility of mutually beneficial economic relations between the Soviet Union and Germany, one involuntarily thinks: Why not give some thought to the idea of reviving and utilising the good experience of the past? If it were possible to surmount the difficulties that remained as a legacy from Hitler even broader and stronger economic ties could be established between the Soviet Union and the Federal Republic of Germany. They would have promoted the successful development of both the Soviet and the West German economies. The economy of Western Germany has now been restored and has surpassed the pre-war level. The socialist economy of the GDR is developing successfully. The Soviet Union is evincing miracles of economic growth. In regard to the level of its economy our country ranks second in the world, and in some fields it has already outstripped the most highly developed capitalist Power—the USA. Life affords ample evidence of the exceptional dependability of trade and economic relations with the Soviet Union and the other socialist countries. Our socialist economy is developing on a planned basis, without crises or recessions. It is steadily on the up grade. Thanks to the socialist nature of our economy we can plan our economic and trade relations for many years ahead. We can ensure a stable and reliable market that any capitalist State can only envy. It is well known that Western Germany needs a number of products exported by our country. The Soviet Union could place substantial orders in Western Germany and also in West Berlin, which needs a stabilisation of the political situation and dependable orders for normal economic development. For their part Western Germany and West Berlin could buy from us those manufactured goods it is more profitable for them to obtain from external sources rather than to make for themselves. Such in our view are the possibilities of establishing normal economic relations between the Soviet Union and the German Federal Republic and the clear mutual advantages that could accrue to the peoples of our countries. It must also be stressed that the development of trade between the Federal German Republic and the Soviet Union and the GDR would definitely benefit the peoples. The most important gain from this would be the strengthening of trust and friendly relations, without which it is impossible to consolidate peace in Europe.

The conclusion of a German peace treaty is a radical means to normalise relations not only between the Soviet Union and Western Germany but also between all the States of Europe—and not of Europe alone. A German peace settlement would strengthen the peoples' faith in the possibility of preserving and strengthening peace. The burden of military expenditure would be reduced and the living standards of the population rise as a result. Many already understand that our proposal for a peace treaty with Germany is prompted not by the interests of one side only. Western Germany and West Berlin have no less interest in the conclusion of a peace treaty. All peace-loving countries and people have an interest in the realisation of this step. Formerly, when the frontier between the GDR and West Berlin was not controlled, it was to the advantage of the imperialists to preserve the remnants of the second world war in order to conduct subversive activities against the GDR and other socialist countries. Now that a firm, controlled and guarded frontier has been established the imperialists have lost this advantage. Now it might be said perhaps that the West too should have no less interest in the signing of a peace treaty, but the aggressive circles of the Western Powers do not want it. They are doing everything in their power to prevent the signing of a German peace treaty. The enemies of a peace settlement with Germany fear—as the Devil fears incense—that in the event of a peace treaty being signed the West German population would realise the entire sense-lessness of the continuation of the cold war against the GDR and other socialist countries. The reactionary circles oppose a peace treaty because they fear the disintegration of the aggressive NATO bloc. If we add to this that the socialist countries have repeatedly expressed their readiness not only to sign a peace treaty but also to conclude a non-aggression pact between the two principal groups—the Warsaw Treaty countries and the NATO countries—it becomes quite obvious who is really for a peace settlement and who is hatching plans for military adventures and fostering the 'cold war'.

We believe that it is impossible to freeze for ever the minds of the peoples of Western Germany and other West European countries. One cannot assume that the people will never grasp these cunning zigzags of imperialist policy. The ice has already been broken. More and more people begin correctly to understand for what purposes the aggressive NATO bloc was set up and what aims its founders pursue, and the West Germans will become aware of the secret meaning of the policy of the Western Powers, which is designed to deprive Western Germany of the possibility of pursuing an independent policy in the interests of the West German people. All working men and women in Western Germany will soon understand this. The time will come, sooner or later—the time will come when all German working men and women realise the necessity of firmly taking the road of struggle for the maintenance of peace, for the resolute liquida-tion of the remnants of world war II and for the signing of a German peace treaty. We believe that the time will come when Western Germany will have a Government which will take the road of co-operation with the Soviet Union, the GDR and other socialist countries and will pursue a policy of peace and friend-ship with all peoples.

Comrades, I should like to speak on the question of ending nuclear tests. It will be recalled that the resumption of talks on this question has been planned for mid-July in Moscow. The thought, of course arises everywhere—will a test ban agreement be concluded now at last? This is a legitimate interest, and I should like to set out our views on this score.

The Soviet Government has expressed more than once its readiness without any delay to sign a treaty banning all nuclear tests for all time—I repeat: all nuclear tests no matter where they are staged. Many years ago we raised the question of banning nuclear weapons and banning their tests. However, the Western Powers, above all the United States, do not accept such an agreement. They are endlessly stalling the discussions, advancing various artificial pretexts in order to evade the discontinuance of all nuclear tests. They are insisting most obstinately on international inspections.

It has been proved by science and fully confirmed by practice that there is no need whatever of any inspections to check the discontinuance of tests, including underground tests. The national facilities for detecting nuclear explosions at the disposal of States, all the more so if combined with automatic seismic stations, whose installation we accept, guarantee reliable control over the discontinuance of all tests. Notwithstanding all this, the Western Powers stubbornly link a solution of the problem of ending nuclear tests with so-called international inspections. This means that the demands of the Western Powers on inspection have another explanation. What is this? We have long realized that the Western

Powers need international inspection not to control the discontinuance of tests, but to penetrate by any means various regions of the Soviet Union for intelligence purposes. Thus, it is not an issue of control over the discontinuance of tests, but essentially, the legalisation of espionage.

If anyone could have had any doubts before about the real purposes of the Western Powers when they called for inspection, there are now no longer any foundations for this. It is common knowledge that the Soviet Government late last year made a big concession to the Western Powers accepting two or three inspections annually. What was the Western Powers' reply to this manifestation of good will? Far from properly appreciating this step of ours, they tried to force us to bargain over the number of inspections and the conditions of holding them. After this it has become still clearer that our Western partners are not interested in concluding an equitable agreement but want to obtain the opportunity of flying over Soviet territory, engaging in aerial surveys and other things which are not at all linked with the discontinuance of tests but answer to the requirements of NATO military headquarters.

However, it is time the imperialist gentlemen knew that the Soviet Government will never abandon the interests of the security of its country, of all the socialist countries, and will not open their doors to NATO intelligence agents. This is no subject for bargaining. Our stand in this respect is clear and unshaken.

The Soviet Government is convinced that the early conclusion of an agreement banning all nuclear tests—in the atmosphere, in outer space, under water and under ground—is in the interests of the peoples. However, this is now obviously impossible in view of the position of the Western Powers.

Carefully analysing the obtaining situation, the Soviet Government, prompted by a sense of high responsibility for the destinies of the peoples, declares that since the Western Powers obstruct the conclusion of an agreement banning all nuclear tests, the Soviet Government expresses its willingness to conclude an agreement banning nuclear tests in the atmosphere, in outer space and under water. We have made this proposal before, but the Western Powers frustrated an agreement by advancing supplementary conditions which envisaged large-scale inspection of our territory.

If the Western Powers now agree to this proposal, the question of inspection no longer arises. For the Western Powers declare that no inspections whatever are needed to check the fulfilment by the States of their commitments to stop nuclear tests in the atmosphere, in outer space and under water. Hence, the road to a solution of the problem is open. The Soviet Government expresses the hope that the Western Powers, heeding the aspirations of the peoples, will take a positive attitude on this Soviet Government proposal.

The conclusion of a test ban agreement will eliminate the hazards of radioactive contamination of the atmosphere, will remove the threat to the health of present and future generations. The conclusion of such an agreement, undoubtedly, will also help to improve the international climate, ease tension and, hence, may facilitate mutually acceptable solutions of other international problems as well.

Of course, an agreement on the ending of nuclear tests, notwithstanding all the importance of this major act, cannot stop the arms race, cannot avert or even substantially weaken the danger of thermonuclear war. That is why the Soviet

Government believes that already now, at the conclusion of a test ban agreement, it is necessary to take also another big step towards easing international tension and strengthening of confidence between States—to sign a non-aggression pact between the two main military groups of States—the NATO countries and the Warsaw Treaty States. The Soviet Union and other socialist countries have been proposing such a pact for a number of years.[1] We note with satisfaction that this proposal is enlisting increasing international support, including in some NATO countries. The time has now come to implement this proposal.

A test ban agreement combined with the simultaneous signing of a non-aggression pact between the two groups of States will create a fresh international climate more favourable for a solution of major problems of our time, including disarmament. These problems affect the interests of the broadest masses of the people. That is precisely why the Communists urge all peoples, all sections of the population, irrespective of their political views and convictions, to rally in the common struggle to avert another world war, to maintain an enduring peace between States. . . .

(b) *Negotiations on a Nuclear Test Ban and on Disarmament*

Draft declaration on the Renunciation of the Use of Foreign Territory for Stationing Strategic Means of the Delivery of Nuclear Weapons, submitted by the Soviet Union to the Eighteen Nation Disarmament Committee, Geneva, 12 February 1963[2]

The Governments of . . . .
(States—signatories of the present Declaration
to be listed)

Desiring to contribute in every possible way to the easing of international tension, the consolidation of peace and the creation of the most favourable conditions for general and complete disarmament,

attaching particularly great importance to the adoption of measures aimed at reducing the danger of a military conflict between the nuclear Powers,

solemnly undertake, within the period of . . . . from the date of signature of this Declaration, to carry out the following measures which they regard as a step towards more extensive disarmament measures:

1. To dismantle bases located in foreign territory for submarines carrying nuclear and rocket weapons and to renounce the use of foreign ports as bases for such submarines.

2. To withdraw from foreign ports aircraft carriers having on board aircraft armed with nuclear weapons.

3. To dismantle strategical rocket installations located in foreign territory and to transfer to their own national territory rockets of 1,500 km range and over and the corresponding nuclear warheads.

---

[1] See pp. 157–8 below.

[2] U.N. doc. ENDC/75, 12 February 1963. Text as reprinted in *Documents on Disarmament, 1963*, p. 49.

4. To withdraw strategical aircraft designed for delivering nuclear bombs to their targets as well as these nuclear bombs, from bases located in foreign territory to within their own national boundaries.

The Governments of States parties to this Declaration undertake not to station in future in foreign territories and ports the means of delivery of nuclear weapons, nuclear warheads and bombs referred to in paragraphs 1, 2, 3, 4 above.

Draft Nonagression Pact between the Warsaw Treaty and N.A.T.O. member countries, submitted by the Soviet Union to the Disarmament Committee, Geneva, 20 February 1963[1]

The States parties to the Warsaw Treaty of Friendship, Co-operation and Mutual Assistance of May 14, 1955,[2] on the one hand, and the States parties to the North Atlantic Treaty of April 4, 1949,[3] on the other hand,

Being firmly resolved to take measures to eliminate international tension and to create an atmosphere of confidence in relations between States in order to help forward the consolidation of universal peace and the speediest possible achievement of agreements on the most vital problems of today and particularly on general and complete disarmament,

Confirming their intention to comply strictly with the purposes and principles of the United Nations Charter in their relations with one another,

Have agreed on the following:

Article 1

The States parties to the Warsaw Treaty and the States parties to the North Atlantic Treaty solemnly undertake to refrain from attack, the threat or use of force, in any manner inconsistent with the purposes and principles of the United Nations Charter, against one another or in their international relations in general.

Article 2

All disputes that may arise between one or more States parties to the Warsaw Treaty, on the one hand, and one or more States parties to the North Atlantic Treaty, on the other hand, shall be resolved by peaceful means only, through negotiations between the parties concerned or by using other means for the pacific settlement of international disputes as provided for by the United Nations Charter.

Article 3

Should situations affecting the interests of both sides arise which are likely to endanger the maintenance of peace and security, the States parties to the Pact shall consult together, with a view to taking and implementing such joint measures as may, in conformity with the United Nations Charter, be considered appropriate for the peaceful settlement of such situations.

[1] U.N. doc. ENDC/77, 20 February 1963. Text as printed in *Documents on Disarmament, 1963*, pp. 57–8.

[2] *Documents, 1955*, pp. 193–5.   [3] *Documents, 1949*, pp. 257–60.

Article 4

This Pact shall remain in force so long as the Warsaw Treaty of Friendship, Co-operation and Mutual Assistance of May 14, 1955 and the North Atlantic Treaty of April 4, 1949, are valid.

Article 5

This Pact shall be ratified by the signatory States in accordance with their respective constitutional processes. The ratifications shall be deposited with the United Nations Secretary-General, who shall notify all the States signatories to the Pact as well as all the other States members of the United Nations, of each deposit.

This Pact shall come into force on the day of the deposit of the last ratification.

Article 6

This pact, of which the Russian, English and French texts are authentic, shall be registered and remain deposited with the UN Secretariat. Duly certified copies thereof shall be communicated by the United Nations Secretary-General to the Governments of the States signatories to this Pact.

In faith whereof the undersigned representatives of the States parties to the Warsaw Treaty and the States parties to the North Atlantic Treaty have subscribed to this Pact and thereto have affixed their seals.

Done at .... 1963.

Anglo-American memorandum concerning the cessation of nuclear weapon tests, submitted to the Disarmament Committee, Geneva, 1 April 1963[1]

During the course of the present session of the Conference of the Eighteen Nation Committee on Disarmament the United Kingdom and the United States have presented their new position for the purpose of arriving at agreement on a treaty ending all nuclear weapon tests. This position is outlined in this memorandum. They emphasize in particular the importance of the arrangements concerning the conduct of on-site inspections. This memorandum deals with arrangements for inspections only on territory under the jurisdiction or control of the Soviet Union, the United Kingdom and the United States. The treaty would, of course, have to deal with inspections on the territories of other parties.

I. *General Principles*

1. There now exists a new basis for agreement on a nuclear weapon test ban arising from the exchange of letters between Chairman Khrushchev and President Kennedy.[2] Under this basis for agreement each nuclear side would place primary reliance on its national detection stations for the collection of seismic data, supplemented by the use of automatic seismic stations. Each nuclear side would use a small number of on-site inspections to check the nature of potentially

---

[1] U.N. doc. ENDC/78, 1 April 1963. Text as printed in *Documents on Disarmament, 1963*, pp. 141–5.

[2] *Documents, 1962*, pp. 142–4, 144–6, and 146–9.

suspicious unidentified events. It is a system which differs from the kinds of systems under discussion by this Conference before the last recess.

2. The United Kingdom and the United States have also indicated that, under certain conditions related to the conduct of inspections, they would accept an annual quota of seven on-site inspections in the territory of each nuclear power. This reduction in the number of inspections emphasizes the need to maximize the deterrent effect of each on-site inspection. This, in turn, will enhance the feeling of confidence each nuclear side will have in the verification system, and consequently, in the fact that treaty obligations are being observed.

3. With this end in view, the present position of the United Kingdom and the United States is strongly influenced by the concept of reciprocal inspection, in accordance with which each nuclear side plays a primary role in the arrangements concerning on-site inspection in the territory of the other. Members of the international staff of the commission would also participate in the inspection.

II. *On-Site Inspection Arrangements*

1. A state would have up to sixty days from the time a seismic event took place to designate that event as one which it may later wish to inspect. Under the designation process the designating state would send a statement to the international commission for transmission to the country in which the event occurred. The statement submitted by the designating state would indicate the location of the event and the time of its occurrence. Accompanying data would include four clearly measurable and mutually consistent arrival times. These would have to include P-wave arrival times at three different stations. The data would have to meet certain location criteria listed in the treaty. The statement would also have to indicate that the event could not be identified, from the data submitted by the designating state, as an earthquake by the use of agreed criteria. These agreed criteria would also be listed in the treaty.

2. For the purposes of the preceding paragraph, location criteria such as those contained in Article VIII of the UK/US draft comprehensive treaty of August 27, 1962 (ENDC/58)[1] would be used.

3. The state on whose territory the event took place would have one week to provide any data which it might wish to make available concerning the designated event. Such data would be made available to the international commission for transmission to the designating state.

4. During the one-week period the designating state would have the right, if it so desired, to send its personnel, accompanied by members of the international staff, to retrieve and examine the data collected by the recording instruments in the sealed vaults of the automatic seismic stations in the territory of the receiving state.

5. The designating state would then be given an additional week to analyze the information which might be received concerning the event, including that from the automatic seismic stations. If the designating state wished to initiate an on-site inspection of the event it would have to submit a further statement to the international commission for transmission to the receiving state. If this one-week period passed without the event being selected for inspection, it would no longer be eligible for inspection.

[1] Ibid., pp. 116–25.

6. A state selecting an event for on-site inspection would have to indicate in its further statement the location and boundaries of the area selected for inspection. The area may be an ellipse with a semi-major axis of no more than fifteen kilometers, with a maximum area of 500 square kilometers.

7. The statement selecting an event for inspection would also include information on the proposed time and place of arrival of the inspection team at a point of entry in the receiving state. The receiving state would then have a period of five days to reply, setting forth the arrangements it would make for the reception of the inspection team.

8. In its reply, the receiving state would also have the right to indicate the presence in the inspection area of a sensitive defense installation, consisting of buildings or similar facilities. The designating state would then decide whether to continue with the inspection, excluding the defense installation from the area to be inspected, or to cancel the inspection without charging the inspection to the annual quota. If, in its judgment, a party felt this procedure was being abused, it could invoke the withdrawal procedures of the treaty.

9. The receiving state would be responsible for transporting the team and its equipment to the site of the inspection. It would be permitted to institute all safeguards it considered necessary to assure the security of military and other sensitive defense installations, subject only to the condition that the inspection team arrive promptly at the inspection area. These safeguards could include the use of its own aircraft and pilots to transport the inspection team, measures to prevent the inspection team from being able to view the territory of the receiving state en route to the inspection area, and the use of flight routes to avoid passing over certain portions of the receiving state.

10. The inspection team would consist partly of persons from the inspecting nuclear side and partly of persons from the international staff. The leader of the team would be one of the team members from that nuclear side. To ensure that certain functions of the team are carried out by highly trained technical personnel so that the maximum deterrent and confidence-building effect of each on-site inspection would be achieved, at least fourteen technical experts from the designating nuclear side would be necessary for a typical inspection in the Soviet Union, the United Kingdom or the United States.

11. Personnel of the inspection team could be accompanied by official personnel, including observers, designated by the receiving state to assure itself that the on-site inspection and the activities of the team members were carried out in accordance with the terms of the treaty.

12. The inspection process would include low-level aerial flights to examine the area both visually and photographically for any evidence of a nuclear weapon test. Members of the team would have access throughout the area for the purpose of surface inspection and would be permitted entrance to any sub-surface cavities, such as mines, to look for evidence of a nuclear weapon test.

13. Inspection teams would have, unless drilling were required, a maximum of six weeks to complete the inspection, a period which could be extended by mutual agreement.

14. If it were determined that drilling was necessary, the team leader would be obliged to notify the receiving state. This notification would state what persons and equipment would be required and their length of stay.

15. The team leader would be responsible for submitting a report to the commission on the findings of the inspection no later than thirty days after completion of the inspection.

III. *Automatic Seismic Stations*

1. Automatic seismic stations, with the exception of certain instrumentation, would be built by the Soviet Union and the United States, each in its own territory, in accordance with agreed specifications. The other nuclear side would then supply recorders and other necessary instruments, some of which would be sealed in the vaults of these stations. The United Kingdom and the United States propose that there be seven such stations in the territory of the Soviet Union and seven such stations in the territory of the United States.

2. At each automatic station data would be produced and recorded in both a sealed vault and a separate structure. The information recorded in the unsealed structure would be forwarded by host country nationals to the international commission and the other nuclear states at frequent intervals.

3. Personnel from the other nuclear side accompanied by personnel from the international staff would have the right to visit each station a maximum of eight times per year. These visits might be used in order to obtain the data from the instruments in the sealed vault in one or more stations in connection with the clarification of a particular event. Automatic stations could also be visited within the annual limit for routine recovery of data, maintenance, calibration of instruments, installation of improved instrumentation or checking of seismic noise levels.

Declaration on the denuclearization of Latin America, issued by the Presidents of the Republics of Bolivia, Brazil, Chile, Ecuador, and Mexico, 29 April 1963[1]

The Presidents of the Republics of Bolivia, Brazil, Chile, Ecuador and Mexico,

Deeply concerned about the present turn of events in the international situation, which is conducive to the spread of nuclear weapons,

Considering that, in virtue of their unchanging peace-loving tradition, the Latin American States should unite their efforts in order to turn Latin America into a denuclearized zone, thus helping to reduce the dangers that threaten world peace,

Wishing to preserve their countries from the tragic consequences attendant upon a nuclear war, and

Spurred by the hope that the conclusion of a Latin American regional agreement will contribute to the adoption of a contractual instrument of world-wide application,

In the name of their peoples and Governments have agreed as follows:

1. To announce forthwith that their Governments are prepared to sign a multilateral Latin American agreement whereby their countries would undertake not to manufacture, receive, store or test nuclear weapons or nuclear launching devices;

2. To bring this Declaration to the attention of the Heads of State of the

[1] *G.A.O.R.*, Eighteenth Session, Agenda item 74, Annexes, p. 1, Doc. A/5415/REV. 1, 14 November 1963.

other Latin American Republics, expressing the hope that their Governments will accede to it through such procedure as they consider appropriate;

3. To co-operate with one another and with such other Latin American Republics as accede to this Declaration, in order that Latin America may be recognized as a denuclearized zone as soon as possible.

Note from the Soviet Embassy in Washington to the United States Department of State, 20 May 1963[1] (extracts)

The Government of the Soviet Union deems it necessary to state to the Government of the United States the following:

Quite recently the Soviet Government was compelled to utter a warning against the plans for the creation of a NATO nuclear force which would give the West German *Bundeswehr* access to atomic weapons and unleash a nuclear armaments race knowing neither State nor geographical bounds.[2] Today the peoples are witnessing the fact that the Governments of the United States and certain other NATO members are taking further steps in the same direction.

The point in question is the already started implementation of plans for the deployment of United States nuclear submarines equipped with Polaris nuclear missiles in the Mediterranean area. As possible bases for these submarines, ports in Spain and British military bases in Cyprus and Malta have been mentioned. There are reports that submarines equipped with Polaris missiles will also use ports in Turkey, Greece and Italy. Two such nuclear submarines have already entered the Mediterranean and are settling down in the coastal waters of Greece and Turkey.

Thus the United States and some of its allies are demonstrating once again that concern for the prevention of a thermonuclear war or at least for the reduction of the danger of its outbreak is alien to their policy. Instead of joining in the efforts of those States which, in anticipation of the implementation of a programme of general and complete disarmament, are already striving to narrow the field of preparations for a nuclear war, the Powers in the lead in NATO are bringing within the orbit of these preparations yet another extensive area with a population of approximately 300 millions.

What will be the result of turning the Mediterranean Sea into a gigantic reservoir filled with scores of missiles having megatons of nuclear load? What does it mean to turn the Mediterranean basin into a kind of missiledrome where every mile of the sea's surface can be used by an aggressor as a launching site for nuclear weapons?

In the first place, it increases immeasurably the danger that the Mediterranean and the adjacent countries may become the theatre of devastating military operations. Even States which neither have nor wish to have anything to do with the aggressive preparations of NATO—and these are the overwhelming majority in the Mediterranean—in fact find themselves in a situation where the right to control their future is appropriated by those who command the nuclear submarines cruising in the vicinity of their coasts. Under their security and

---

[1] *Current Documents, 1963*, pp. 1041-3. Similar notes were sent to Great Britain and to all Mediterranean countries with the exception of Albania and Yugoslavia.
[2] See pp. 190-7 below.

sovereignty are being spread the trammels of the same dangerous policy in which the countries which have made their territories available for the location of NATO military bases have been caught. . . .

The introduction into the Mediterranean Sea of NATO military vessels with nuclear weapons on board makes it necessary for the States whose security is being threatened by the North Atlantic bloc to carry out effective defensive counter-measures in order to be in a position to repulse any encroachment upon the peaceful life of their peoples and not to leave the NATO Powers a free hand to use the Mediterranean as a spring-board for possible aggression. The peace-loving States will have no other choice than to keep their means of neutralization trained on the routes along which the nuclear submarines move, as well as on the coasts of NATO members and those countries which make their territories available to this bloc as permanent or periodic bases for nuclear missile weapons.

It should be clear to everyone that the NATO military staffs are leading matters to the point where the Mediterranean, instead of being the shortest commercial sea route linking West and East and a traditional place of rest and international tourism, would become the lair of the carriers of nuclear death and yet another area of dangerous rivalry and conflict. . . .

The Governments of the Western Powers try to justify their plans to station Polaris submarines in the Mediterranean Sea on the grounds that it is an open sea and that whether or not to make ports available for missile-carrying vessels is a domestic affair of the individual States. But by what right are four or five States, which have linked themselves with the policy of NATO, without considering the interests of the other Mediterranean countries, prepared to throw open the gates of Gibraltar to a stream of nuclear weapons? If, for example, the Governments of Turkey, Greece, Italy or Spain allow submarines or surface vessels with nuclear weapons on board to shelter in their waters, they will not only be trifling with the fate of their own countries but will also endanger the security of neighbouring countries.

The Governments of the United States and the other NATO countries have not been lacking in assurances that the United States Polaris submarines are being sent to the Mediterranean Sea for 'defensive purposes' and even for the 'protection' of the countries of this area. It would be no exaggeration, however, to say that of all the existing means of waging war the United States weapon now being stationed in the Mediterranean Sea is the least fitted to serve defensive purposes but, on the other hand, it is the most suitable for any kind of provocation. The distinctive feature of the use of nuclear submarines as mobile missile bases is that they are designed to conceal preparations for, and to ensure the sudden delivery of, a nuclear attack.

Furthermore, in the Soviet Union, and no doubt in other countries as well, one remembers the recent statements of highly placed persons in the United States to the effect that under certain circumstances the United States might take the initiative in a nuclear conflict with the USSR. The Soviet Government could not fail to pay attention also to the statements of leading military personalities in the United States to the effect that the United States submarines which have been sent to the Mediterranean Sea have been previously assigned certain targets in the Soviet Union. . . .

What are the United States Navy ships seeking in the Mediterranean Sea, thousands of miles away from the national boundaries of the United States? What are the real aims that are being pursued when, in addition to surface vessels, nuclear submarines with nuclear weapons are now being sent there? The NATO measures for spreading nuclear weapons to new areas speak for themselves. And further light on the intentions of the United States is shed by the statements of United States military leaders who recently justified the need to station United States nuclear weapons in Canada[1] by saying that in the event of war this would make it possible to draw part of a nuclear counter-blow away from the United States and divert it to Canada. This was said, it is true, in respect to Canada and not the Mediterranean Sea. But what is concerned in both cases is preparation for a nuclear war, which is being carried out within the framework of one and the same policy, and one and the same strategy.

Some people may consider it almost the summit of military thinking to hide their nuclear missile bases as far away as possible from their own vital centres and closer to the borders of other countries. But can the millions of people living in the Mediterranean area be content with the position of hostages in which the leading Powers of NATO are trying to place them? Everything shows that the military plans of these Powers—today more than ever—include the intention, in the event of a conflict, to divert to States wholly innocent in such a conflict, part of the nuclear counter-blow which would be duly delivered to the aggressor.

In the interests of ensuring international security, the Soviet Government proposes that the whole area of the Mediterranean Sea should be declared a zone free from nuclear missile weapons. It is prepared to assume an obligation not to deploy any nuclear weapons or their means of delivery in the waters of this area provided that similar obligations are assumed by the other Powers. If this area is declared a zone free from nuclear missile weapons, then, jointly with the United States and the other countries of the West, the Soviet Union is prepared to give reliable guarantees that in the event of any military complications the area of the Mediterranean Sea will be considered as outside the sphere of use of nuclear weapons.

Implementation of these proposals would contribute to mutual understanding and friendship in the relations between the countries of the Mediterranean area; it would enable the States of the Mediterranean basin to devote more of their forces and resources to the solution of their economic and social problems. It would at the same time be a substantial contribution towards lessening the general international tension and towards ensuring peace in Europe, Africa and throughout the world.

The Soviet Government expresses the hope that the Government of the United States will consider with due attention the considerations set forth in this note.

Memorandum of Understanding between the United States and the Soviet Union regarding the Establishment of a Direct Communications Link, 20 June 1963, with Annex[2]

For use in time of emergency, the Government of the United States of America and the Government of the Union of Soviet Socialist Republics have agreed to establish as soon as technically feasible a direct communications link between the two governments.

---

[1] See pp. 480–1 below.   [2] *D.S.B.*, 8 July 1963, pp. 50–1.

Each government shall be responsible for the arrangements for the link on its own territory. Each government shall take the necessary steps to ensure continuous functioning of the link and prompt delivery to its head of government of any communications received by means of the link from the head of government of the other party.

Arrangements for establishing and operating the link are set forth in the Annex which is attached hereto and forms an integral part hereof.

Done in duplicate in the English and Russian languages at Geneva, Switzerland, this 20th day of June, 1963.

Annex

The direct communications link between Washington and Moscow established in accordance with the memorandum, and the operation of such link, shall be governed by the following provisions:

1. The direct communications link shall consist of:

A. Two terminal points with telegraph-teleprinter equipment between which communications shall be directly exchanged;

B. One full-time duplex wire telegraph circuit, routed Washington-London-Copenhagen-Stockholm-Helsinki-Moscow, which shall be used for the transmission of messages;

C. One full-time duplex radio telegraph circuit, routed Washington-Tangier-Moscow, which shall be used for service communications and for coordination of operations between the two terminal points.

If experience in operating the direct communications link should demonstrate that the establishment of an additional wire telegraph circuit is advisable, such circuit may be established by mutual agreement between authorized representatives of both governments.

2. In case of interruption of the wire circuit, transmission of messages shall be effected via the radio circuit, and for this purpose provision shall be made at the terminal points for the capability of prompt switching of all necessary equipment from one circuit to another.

3. The terminal points of the link shall be so equipped as to provide for the transmission and reception of messages from Moscow to Washington in the Russian language and from Washington to Moscow in the English language. In this connection, the USSR shall furnish the United States four sets of telegraph terminal equipment, including page printers, transmitters, and reperforators, with one year's supply of spare parts and all necessary special tools, test equipment, operating instructions and other technical literature, to provide for transmission and reception of messages in the Russian language. The United States shall furnish the Soviet Union four sets of telegraph terminal equipment, including page printers, transmitters, and reperforators, with one year's supply of spare parts and all necessary special tools, test equipment, operating instructions and other technical literature, to provide for transmission and reception of messages in the English language. The equipment described in this paragraph shall be exchanged directly between the parties without any payment being required therefor.

4. The terminal points of the direct communications link shall be provided

with encoding equipment. For the terminal point in the USSR, four sets of such equipment (each capable of simplex operation), with one year's supply of spare parts, with all necessary special tools, test equipment, operating instructions and other technical literature, and with all necessary blank tape, shall be furnished by the United States to the USSR against payment of the cost thereof by the USSR.

The USSR shall provide for preparation and delivery of keying tapes to the terminal point of the link in the United States for reception of messages from the USSR. The United States shall provide for preparation and delivery of keying tapes to the terminal point of the link in the USSR for reception of messages from the United States. Delivery of prepared keying tapes to the terminal points of the link shall be effected through the Embassy of the USSR in Washington (for the terminal of the link in the USSR) and through the Embassy of the United States in Moscow (for the terminal of the link in the United States).

5. The United States and the USSR shall designate the agencies responsible for the arrangements regarding the direct communications link, for its technical maintenance, continuity and reliability, and for the timely transmission of messages.

Such agencies may, by mutual agreement, decide matters and develop instructions relating to the technical maintenance and operation of the direct communications link and effect arrangements to improve the operation of the link.

6. The technical parameters of the telegraph circuits of the link and of the terminal equipment, as well as the maintenance of such circuits and equipment, shall be in accordance with CCITT [Comité consultatif international télégraphique et téléphonique] and CCIR [Comité consultatif international des radio communications] recommendations.

Transmission and reception of messages over the direct communications link shall be effected in accordance with applicable recommendations of international telegraph and radio communications regulations, as well as with mutually agreed instructions.

7. The costs of the direct communications link shall be borne as follows:

A. The USSR shall pay the full cost of leasing the portion of the telegraph circuit from Moscow to Helsinki and 50 percent of the cost of leasing the portion of the telegraph circuit from Helsinki to London. The United States shall pay the full cost of leasing the portion of the telegraph circuit from Washington to London and 50 percent of the cost of leasing the portion of the telegraph circuit from London to Helsinki.

B. Payment of the cost of leasing the radio telegraph circuit between Moscow and Washington shall be effected without any transfer of payments between the parties. The USSR shall bear the expenses relating to the transmission of messages from Moscow to Washington. The United States shall bear the expenses relating to the transmission of messages from Washington to Moscow.

Note from the United States Embassy in Moscow to the Soviet Ministry of Foreign Affairs, 24 June 1963[1]

The Embassy of the United States of America presents its compliments to the Ministry of Foreign Affairs of the U.S.S.R. and, with reference to the note of

[1] *D.S.B.*, 15 July 1963, pp. 83–4.

May 20, 1963, of the Embassy of the U.S.S.R. in Washington,[1] has the honor to transmit to the Ministry the views of the Government of the United States of America on the proposal that the area of the Mediterranean Sea be declared a nuclear-free zone.

The Soviet Government's note appears to be devoted primarily to a propagandistic attack against the presence of United States missile-launching submarines in the Mediterranean and contains a large number of gross misrepresentations of both the position of the United States and the recent history of the Mediterranean area. In its note of May 18, 1963,[2] the Government of the United States replied to a similar set of groundless charges contained in the Soviet Government's note of April 8, 1963,[3] and drew the attention of the Soviet Government to the defensive nature of the North Atlantic Treaty Organization and to the reasons for its development. The remarks made in the note of May 18 apply to the Mediterranean area, as well as to all other areas covered by the North Atlantic Treaty.

In this connection the Government of the United States wishes to emphasize that it was compelled to strengthen the security of its Allies in the Mediterranean only after their security had been directly threatened by the Soviet Union's deployment of an extensive array of missiles aimed at countries in the area. Consequently the United States and the threatened Mediterranean countries were forced in their own defense to counteract the striking power of these Soviet nuclear missiles and Soviet nuclear-equipped aircraft which were poised for attack on the region. If it had done otherwise, the United States would have failed in its duty to help its Allies to defend themselves against a form of nuclear blackmail under which the Soviet Union could have attempted to force the Mediterranean countries to succumb to Soviet dictation or Soviet domination.

This is not an imaginary danger, as may be seen from a number of provocative statements by senior members of the Soviet Government threatening devastating attacks on countries of the Mediterranean region, including threats to attack the Acropolis and the orange groves of Italy.[4] If, as stated in its note, the Government of the Soviet Union is in fact 'engaged in peaceful labor and wishes only peace and prosperity to other peoples', it has nothing to fear from the presence of Polaris submarines in the Mediterranean, which are stationed there solely to defend the integrity of the countries in that region.

With respect to the proposal in the Soviet Government's note to declare the Mediterranean area a nuclear-free zone, the Government of the United States wishes to recall that, being thoroughly aware of the catastrophically destructive nature of thermonuclear weapons, it has continuously sought and advanced proposals designed to eliminate or if this were not possible at least to reduce the danger that such weapons might be used. Despite a discouraging lack of progress it continues to pursue this path unflaggingly and with increased effort. In doing so, it welcomes the proposals of others. At the risk of stating the obvious, however, it must be noted that for a measure in the field of disarmament and arms control to have a beneficial rather than an unsettling and therefore dangerous effect, it must be balanced so that no state or group of states gain military

---

[1] See pp. 162–4 above.   [2] See pp. 197–200 below.   [3] See pp. 190–7 below.
[4] The reference is to a speech by Mr. Khrushchev at a Soviet-Rumanian friendship meeting, 11 August 1961; text in *Documents on Disarmament, 1961*, pp. 278–9.

advantage. To disrupt this balance can only create a condition of insecurity that would increase tension and lead to the danger the measure was designed to obviate. This principle of balance was in fact recognized in the Joint Statement of Agreed Principles of September 20, 1961.[1]

The Note of May 20 of the Soviet Government seems to be designed precisely and solely to change the existing military balance at the expense of the United States and its Allies. The fact that the Government of the United States is constantly seeking ways of decelerating and halting the arms race does not mean that it is prepared to strip itself of its means of defense, or to withhold the protection of those means from its Allies, when the countries from which it and its Allies may be threatened maintain their armaments at full scale.

Speech by Mr. Khrushchev on the occasion of the visit of the First Secretary of the Hungarian Communist Party, Mr. Kadar, Moscow, 20 July 1963[2] (extract)

. . . Comrades, a few words should be said about the exchange of opinion which is taking place in Moscow between representatives of the Soviet Union, the USA and Britain on the question of banning nuclear tests and other questions of mutual interest. We have the impression that there is now hope of achieving an agreement on the banning of tests in the atmosphere, in space and under water if, of course, there is no subsequent alteration in the positions of the American and British representatives. The Soviet Government would like to reach an agreement that would envisage a banning of all tests, including those below ground. Science and practice has proved that the banning of all tests, including underground ones, can be controlled with the aid of technical means of detection available to these States. The Governments of the USA and Britain, however, continue to insist on the necessity for international inspections. They do not want to renounce efforts which in actual fact bear no relation to the banning of tests. Why, and for what aims, is this being done? In order of course to get the opportunity to spy.

We thus get a fairly clear picture: it appears that at present it will not be possible to reach an agreement on the banning of underground nuclear tests. Nevertheless, the Soviet Government considers that an agreement on the banning of tests in the atmosphere, space and under water—if reached—would be an important and useful step forward. This agreement will put an end to the contamination of the air with radiation, and hence will prevent the dangerous consequences of further nuclear tests to the health of the present and of future generations. We Communists, who are defending the vital interests of the nations and of all mankind, consider that the conclusion of an agreement on banning the testing of nuclear weapons is in keeping with the noble principles of socialist humanism.

We hope that the reaching of an agreement on a nuclear test ban will also be useful from the point of view of a general improvement in the international atmosphere. It will show the readiness of States belonging to opposite social systems to seek out paths towards reaching mutually acceptable agreements on the basis of peaceful coexistence.

Documents, 1961, pp. 375–7.   [2] *S.W.B.*, su/1306, 22 July 1963, c1/12–c1/13.

The Soviet Government is convinced that, if the representatives of the Soviet Union, the USA and Britain now reach agreement not only on banning nuclear tests, but also, at the same time, on the question of a non-aggression pact between the NATO countries and the member-States of the Warsaw Treaty,[1] then such an agreement would assist towards a significant improvement in the whole international situation. The signing of such a pact would be met with great satisfaction by the world public. Sometimes one hears that certain people in the West are embarrassed by the form of a non-aggression pact. We think that the question of how to draw up a non-aggression pact could be solved, without particular effort, to the mutual satisfaction of both sides. The main thing is not the form but the content: the main thing is that the other side too should display a desire to reduce tension and to end the state of cold war. We should like to hope that, at the exchange of opinions taking place in Moscow, agreement on a non-aggression pact may also be reached.

It would also be very useful to solve such questions as the freezing of the military budgets of the States concerned, and, better still, their reduction. This would unquestionably be approved by millions and millions of people in all countries.

We also think that it would be useful to return as well to our proposals, tabled as far back as 1958, on carrying out certain measures for preventing a surprise attack.[2] What is required for this? In the first place, to make it impossible for an aggressor secretly to concentrate large masses of troops, without which a surprise attack is impossible. For this we consider it expedient to establish in certain areas of the Soviet Union, as well of other countries, land control posts on airfields, railway junctions, motor roads and big ports. Naturally, all this must be done on a reciprocal basis. Such a measure does not in itself guarantee the maintenance of peace, but it would be a step forward towards the prevention of a surprise attack.

We are ready to carry on talks with the Western Powers on reaching an agreement whereby the Western Powers could have representatives with the Soviet armed forces stationed in the GDR and we in our turn could have representatives with the forces of the Western Powers stationed in Western Germany. We also agree to holding talks on the reduction of foreign armed forces stationed in the GDR as well as on the territory of Western Germany. If an agreement were reached on all these questions it would be a big step towards the reduction of international tension and the liquidation of the cold war, and an important prerequisite in reaching an agreement on the fundamental question, general and complete disarmament. Naturally, one must finally solve the main question on which depends the liquidation of international tension—the German question. One can only solve this question by way of the conclusion of a German peace treaty and the recognition of the conditions established as a result of the rout of the Hitler Reich. I repeat, the solution of the German question can be solved only on the basis of the signing of a peace treaty.

As for the imperialists reckoning on the liquidation of the German Democratic Republic—they will never see this any more than they will see their own ears, for this is a path that leads to war. Only madmen would risk unleashing a world thermonuclear war. Imperialists must understand that such an adventure would

[1] See pp. 157–8 above.　　　[2] See *Documents, 1958*, pp. 94–7.

end with their own doom. The interests of all peoples, and in the first place, of the German people, demand the conclusion of a German peace treaty and the solution on this basis of the question of West Berlin, in order to obtain a radical improvement of the situation in Europe and throughout the world. . . .

Communiqué issued by the Governments of the United States, Great Britain and the Soviet Union, Moscow, 25 July 1963[1]

The special representatives of the President of the U.S.A. and of the Prime Minister of the U.K., W. A. Harriman, Under Secretary of State for Political Affairs of the United States, and Lord Hailsham, Lord President of the Council and Minister for Science for the United Kingdom, visited Moscow together with their advisers on July 14. Mr. Harriman and Lord Hailsham were received by the Chairman of the Council of Ministers of the U.S.S.R., N. S. Khrushchev, who presided on July 15 at the first of a series of meetings to discuss questions relating to the discontinuance of nuclear tests, and other questions of mutual interest. The discussions were continued from July 16 to July 25 with A. A. Gromyko, Minister of Foreign Affairs of the U.S.S.R. During these discussions each principal was assisted by his advisers.

The discussions took place in a businesslike, cordial atmosphere. Agreement was reached on the text of a treaty banning nuclear weapons tests in the atmosphere, in outer space and under water. This text is being published separately and simultaneously with this communique. It was initialed on July 25 by A. A. Gromyko, Mr. Harriman and Lord Hailsham. Mr. Harriman and Lord Hailsham together with their advisers will leave Moscow shortly to report and bring back the initialed texts to their respective Governments. Signature of the Treaty is expected to take place in the near future in Moscow.

The heads of the three delegations agreed that the test ban treaty constituted an important first step toward the reduction of international tension and the strengthening of peace, and they look forward to further progress in this direction.

The heads of the three delegations discussed the Soviet proposal relating to a pact of non-aggression between the participants in the North Atlantic Treaty Organisation and the participants in the Warsaw Treaty.[2] The three Governments have agreed fully to inform their respective allies in the two organisations concerning these talks and to consult with them about continuing discussion on this question with the purpose of achieving agreement satisfactory to all participants. A brief exchange of views also took place with regard to other measures, directed at a relaxation of tension.

Treaty Banning Nuclear Weapon Tests in the Atmosphere, in Outer Space and Under Water, signed by the Governments of the United States, Great Britain and the Soviet Union, Moscow, 5 August 1963[3]

The Governments of the United States of America, the United Kingdom of Great Britain and Northern Ireland, and the Union of Soviet Socialist Republics, hereinafter referred to as the 'Original Parties',

[1] *D.S.B.*, 12 August 1963, p. 239.   [2] See pp. 157–8 above.   [3] Cmnd. 2245.

Proclaiming as their principal aim the speediest possible achievement of an agreement on general and complete disarmament under strict international control in accordance with the objectives of the United Nations which would put an end to the armaments race and eliminate the incentive to the production and testing of all kinds of weapons, including nuclear weapons,

Seeking to achieve the discontinuance of all test explosions of nuclear weapons for all time, determined to continue negotiations to this end, and desiring to put an end to the contamination of man's environment by radioactive substances,

Have agreed as follows:

Article I

1. Each of the Parties to this Treaty undertakes to prohibit, to prevent, and not to carry out any nuclear weapon test explosion, or any other nuclear explosion, at any place under its jurisdiction or control:

(a) in the atmosphere; beyond its limits, including outer space; or underwater, including territorial waters or high seas; or

(b) in any other environment if such explosion causes radioactive debris to be present outside the territorial limits of the State under whose jurisdiction or control such explosion is conducted. It is understood in this connection that the provisions of this subparagraph are without prejudice to the conclusion of a treaty resulting in the permanent banning of all nuclear test explosions, including all such explosions underground, the conclusion of which, as the Parties have stated in the Preamble to this Treaty, they seek to achieve.

2. Each of the Parties to this Treaty undertakes furthermore to refrain from causing, encouraging, or in any way participating in, the carrying out of any nuclear weapon test explosion, or any other nuclear explosion, anywhere which would take place in any of the environments described, or have the effect referred to, in paragraph 1 of this Article.

Article II

1. Any Party may propose amendments to this Treaty. The text of any proposed amendment shall be submitted to the Depositary Governments which shall circulate it to all Parties to this Treaty. Thereafter, if requested to do so by one-third or more of the Parties, the Depositary Governments shall convene a conference, to which they shall invite all the Parties, to consider such amendment.

2. Any amendment to this Treaty must be approved by a majority of the votes of all the Parties to this Treaty, including the votes of all of the Original Parties. The amendment shall enter into force for all Parties upon the deposit of instruments of ratification by a majority of all the Parties, including the instruments of ratification of all of the Original Parties.

Article III

1. This Treaty shall be open to all States for signature. Any State which does not sign this Treaty before its entry into force in accordance with paragraph 3 of this Article may accede to it at any time.

2. This Treaty shall be subject to ratification by signatory States. Instruments

of ratification and instruments of accession shall be deposited with the Governments of the Original Parties—the United States of America, the United Kingdom of Great Britain and Northern Ireland, and the Union of Soviet Socialist Republics—which are hereby designated the Depositary Governments.

3. This Treaty shall enter into force after its ratification by all the Original Parties and the deposit of their instruments of ratification.

4. For States whose instruments of ratification or accession are deposited subsequent to the entry into force of this Treaty, it shall enter into force on the date of the deposit of their instruments of ratification or accession.

5. The Depositary Governments shall promptly inform all signatory and acceding States of the date of each signature, the date of deposit of each instrument of ratification of and accession to this Treaty, the date of its entry into force, and the date of receipt of any requests for conferences or other notices.

6. This Treaty shall be registered by the Depositary Governments pursuant to Article 102 of the Charter of the United Nations.

Article IV

This Treaty shall be of unlimited duration.

Each Party shall in exercising its national sovereignty have the right to withdraw from the Treaty if it decides that extraordinary events, related to the subject matter of this Treaty, have jeopardized the supreme interests of its country. It shall give notice of such withdrawal to all other Parties to the Treaty three months in advance.

Article V

This Treaty, of which the English and Russian texts are equally authentic, shall be deposited in the archives of the Depositary Governments. Duly certified copies of this Treaty shall be transmitted by the Depositary Governments to the Governments of the signatory and acceding States.

IN WITNESS WHEREOF the undersigned, duly authorized, have signed this Treaty.

DONE in triplicate at the city of Moscow the fifth day of August, one thousand nine hundred and sixty-three.

Amendment to the United States Outline of a Treaty on General and Complete Disarmament in a Peaceful World, submitted by the United States to the Disarmament Committee, Geneva, 14 August 1963[1]

Stage I. Section C. Nuclear Weapons

1. Replace the present text of subparagraph 2a. Transfer of Fissionable Materials to Purposes Other Than Use in Nuclear Weapons, by the following:

'a. Upon the cessation of production of fissionable materials for use in nuclear weapons, the United States of America and the Union of Soviet

[1] U.N. doc. ENDC/30/Add. 3, 14 August 1963. Text as printed in *Documents on Disarmament, 1963*, p. 327. For text of the U.S. outline treaty, see *Documents, 1962*, pp. 71–97; for texts of previous amendments, see *Documents on Disarmament, 1962*, vol. II, pp. 718, 728–30.

Socialist Republics would each transfer to purposes other than use in nuclear weapons agreed quantities of weapons grade U-235 from past production. The United States of America would transfer ——— kilograms, and the Union of Soviet Socialist Republics would transfer ——— kilograms of such weapons grade U-235. For this purpose, "weapons grade U-235" means the U-235 contained in metal of which at least 90 per cent of the weight is U-235.'

Draft Articles VI to XII of the United States Draft Treaty on General and Complete Disarmament in a Peaceful World, submitted by the United States to the Disarmament Committee, Geneva, 14 August 1963[1]

ARTICLE VI

Production and Use of Fissionable Material for Nuclear Weapons

1. Each Party to this Treaty shall:

a. Halt, prohibit and prevent the production, at facilities under its jurisdiction and control, of fissionable material for use in nuclear weapons;

b. Halt, prohibit and prevent the use in nuclear weapons of all fissionable material produced after the beginning of Stage I; and

c. Refrain from causing, encouraging, or in any way assisting or participating in, the production anywhere of fissionable material for use in nuclear weapons.

2. Each Party shall limit the production, at facilities under its jurisdiction or control, of fissionable material for purposes other than use in nuclear weapons in accordance with the Table of Allowances set forth in the Annex on Stage I Nuclear Disarmament.

3. Each Party shall submit to the International Disarmament Organization declarations, within ——— days after the beginning of Stage I and thereafter every ———, which shall list (a) the name, location, and production capacity of each facility under its jurisdiction or control capable of producing or processing fissionable material and (b) the amounts and types of fissionable material being produced at each such facility. The form of such declarations shall be in accordance with the requirements set forth in the Annex on Stage I Nuclear Disarmament.

ARTICLE VII

Transfer of Fissionable Material to Purposes Other than Use in
Nuclear Weapons

1. The United States of America and the Union of Soviet Socialist Republics agree that each of them shall, during Stage I, transfer to depots, as stated in Paragraph 2 of this Article, specified amounts of weapons grade U-235 from its stock of such U-235 in existence at the beginning of Stage I, in order to transfer such amounts to use other than in nuclear weapons. The United States of America shall transfer not less than ——— kilograms, and the Union of Soviet Socialist

---

[1] U.N. doc. ENDC/109, 14 August 1963. Text as printed in ibid., pp. 327–30.

Republics shall transfer not less than ———— kilograms of such weapons grade U-235. For the purposes of this Article 'weapons grade U-235' means the U-235 contained in metal of which at least 90 per-cent of the weight is U-235.

2. Transfers pursuant to this Article shall take place at depots under the supervision of the International Disarmament Organization. The schedule of transfers, the location, establishment and operation of depots, and the safeguard procedures to be observed in making the transfers, in withdrawing transferred material from depots, and in transporting, handling and utilizing such material after withdrawal shall be as provided in the Annex on Stage I Nuclear Disarmament and in rules adopted by the Control Council of the International Disarmament Organization in accordance with Article ————.

3. The Party owning any transferred material prior to transfer shall continue to own it after transfer, subject to the limitations contained in this Article, and may withdraw such material for any purpose other than use in nuclear weapons, providing it submits to the International Disarmament Organization prior to withdrawal a statement setting forth the purpose of the withdrawal, the amount of material needed for such purpose, and the time and place at which such material will be used.

Article VIII

Transfer of Fissionable Material for Peaceful Uses of Nuclear Energy

1. No Party to this Treaty shall transfer, or permit any individual or association under its jurisdiction or control to transfer, to any other state, or to any individual or association under the jurisdiction or control of such other state, fissionable material for use in nuclear weapons.

2. Any transfer of fissionable material not prohibited by this Article, and the transportation, handling, and utilization of such material after such transfer, shall be subject to the safeguard procedures provided in the Annex on Stage I Nuclear Disarmament and in rules adopted by the Control Council of the International Disarmament Organization in accordance with Article ————.

Article IX

Non-Transfer of Nuclear Weapons

The Parties to the Treaty agree to seek to prevent the creation of further national nuclear forces. To this end the Parties agree that:

1. Any Party to the Treaty which has manufactured, or which at any time manufactures, a nuclear weapon shall:

    a. Not transfer control over any nuclear weapons to a state which has not manufactured a nuclear weapon before (an agreed date);

    b. Not assist any such state in manufacturing any nuclear weapons.

2. Any Party to the Treaty which has not manufactured a nuclear weapon before the (agreed date) shall:

    a. Not acquire, or attempt to acquire, control over any nuclear weapons;

    b. Not manufacture, or attempt to manufacture, any nuclear weapons.

ARTICLE X

Nuclear Weapon Test Explosions

The Parties to this Treaty agree to be bound by the provisions of 'The Treaty Banning Nuclear Weapon Tests in all Environments', which is set forth in the Annex on Stage I Nuclear Disarmament.

ARTICLE XI

Preparation for Stages II and III

The Parties to this Treaty agree to examine unresolved questions related to the means of accomplishing in Stages II and III the reduction and eventual elimination of nuclear weapons stockpiles and, in the light of this examination, shall agree upon arrangements for the accomplishment of such reduction and elimination.

ARTICLE XII

Verification

The obligations set forth in this part of this Treaty shall be verified by the International Disarmament Organization in accordance with the provisions of this Treaty, the Annex on Stage I Nuclear Disarmament, and the Annex on Verification.

General Assembly resolution on 'stationing weapons of mass destruction in outer space', 17 October 1963[1]

The General Assembly,

Recalling its resolution 1721 A (XVI) of 20 December 1961, in which it expressed its belief that the exploration and use of outer space should only be for the betterment of mankind,[2]

Determined to take steps to prevent the spread of the arms race to outer space,

1. *Welcomes* the expressions by the Union of Soviet Socialist Republics and the United States of America of their intention not to station in outer space any objects carrying nuclear weapons or other kinds of weapons of mass destruction,[3]

2. *Solemnly calls upon* all States:

(*a*) To refrain from placing in orbit around the earth any objects carrying nuclear weapons or any other kinds of weapons of mass destruction, installing such weapons on celestial bodies, or stationing such weapons in outer space in any other manner;

(*b*) To refrain from causing, encouraging or in any way participating in the conduct of the foregoing activities.

[1] *G.A.O.R.*, Eighteenth Session, Supplement No. 15, p. 13, A/RES/1884 (XVIII).

[2] Ibid., Sixteenth Session, Supplement No. 17, p. 6.

[3] Made in speeches to the United Nations General Assembly by the Soviet Foreign Minister, Mr. Gromyko, 19 September 1963, and President Kennedy, 20 September 1963; see *Documents on Disarmament, 1963*, p. 523 and p. 528.

General Assembly resolution on the 'effects of atomic radiation', 11 November 1963[1]

The General Assembly,

Reaffirming the objectives of its resolutions 1629 (XVI) of 27 October 1961[2] and 1764 (XVII) of 20 November 1962,[3]

Recalling the important part which the study of the effects of atomic radiation has played in alerting world opinion to their dangers,

Emphasizing the importance, from the point of view of harmful atomic radiation, of the cessation of nuclear tests in the atmosphere, in outer space and under water,

Noting with satisfaction the progress achieved towards implementing the scheme for monitoring and reporting levels of atmospheric radio-activity,

Convinced that international co-operation in this field continues to be necessary to gain knowledge of the levels of radio-activity from all sources,

1. *Takes note* of the report of the United Nations Scientific Committee on the Effects of Atomic Radiation on the work of its twelfth session;[4]

2. *Invites* the International Atomic Energy Authority, the specialized agencies, international and national nongovernmental scientific organizations and individual scientists to continue to extend to the Scientific Committee the co-operation which it requires;

3. *Recommends* the Governments of Member States, the International Atomic Energy Authority, the specialized agencies, and international and national non-governmental scientific organizations to take appropriate action to carry out, with the means at their command, information programmes on the effects of atomic radiation;

4. *Urges* the World Meteorological Organization to proceed with the implementation of the scheme for monitoring and reporting levels of atmospheric radio-activity, taking into account the recommendations made by the Scientific Committee at its twelfth session;

5. *Requests* the Scientific Committee to continue its programme and its co-ordinating activities to increase the knowledge of the levels and effects of atomic radiation from all sources;

6. *Notes* the intention of the Scientific Committee to submit to the General Assembly at its nineteenth session a further report on the results of its work.

General Assembly resolution on the 'question of general and complete disarmament', 25 November 1963[5]

The General Assembly,

Conscious of its responsibility under the Charter of the United Nations for disarmament and the consolidation of peace,

[1] *G.A.O.R.*, Eighteenth Session, Supplement No. 15, pp. 19–20, A/RES/1896 (XVIII).
[2] Ibid., Sixteenth Session, Supplement No. 17, pp. 9–10.
[3] Ibid., Seventeenth Session, Supplement No. 17, pp. 10–11.
[4] U.N. doc. A/5406.
[5] *G.A.O.R.*, Eighteenth Session, Supplement No. 15, pp. 13–14, A/RES/1908 (XVIII).

Convinced that the goal of general and complete disarmament under effective international control is the surest safeguard for world peace and national security.

Recognizing that mankind demands with increasing urgency that decisive measures be taken towards the realization of that goal,

Recalling its resolution 1378 (XIV) of 20 November 1959,[1]

Reaffirming its resolutions 1722 (XVI) of 20 December 1961[2] and 1767 (XVII) of 21 November 1962,[3]

Having considered the report of the Conference of the Eighteen-Nation Committee on Disarmament of 29 August 1963,[4]

Expressing its satisfaction that agreement has been reached on a partial test ban treaty[5] and on the establishment of a direct communications link between Moscow and Washington,[6] and its satisfaction over the expressions of intention recorded in its resolution 1884 (XVIII) of 17 October 1963[7] not to station in outer space or place in orbit any objects carrying nuclear weapons or other kinds of weapons of mass destruction,

Noting that all signatories to the partial test ban treaty have proclaimed in its preamble, as their principal aim, the speediest possible achievement of an agreement on general and complete disarmament under strict international control, and that they have emphasized the advisability that the partial test ban should be followed by other initial steps,

Noting further that the Eighteen-Nation Committee, in fulfilment of paragraph 3 of General Assembly resolution 1767 (XVII), has under consideration various proposals for other collateral measures,

I

1. *Calls upon* the Conference of the Eighteen-Nation Committee on Disarmament to resume, with energy and determination, its negotiations on general and complete disarmament under effective international control, in accordance with the joint statement of agreed principles for disarmament negotiations[8] and in a spirit of goodwill and mutual accommodation;

2. *Recommends* the Eighteen-Nation Committee to continue to encourage the widening of the areas of basic agreement or similarity in the principal parties' approaches to the fundamental issues of general and complete disarmament.

II

Urges the Eighteen-Nation Committee to make efforts to seek agreement on measures which could serve to reduce international tension, lessen the possibility of war and facilitate agreement on general and complete disarmament;

III

1. *Requests* the Eighteen-Nation Committee to submit to the General Assembly an interim report on the progress of its work at an early appropriate date, and a comprehensive report not later than 1 September 1964;

[1] *Documents, 1959*, p. 115.   [2] *Documents, 1961*, pp. 401–2.
[3] *G.A.O.R.*, Seventeenth Session, Supplement No. 17, pp. 4–5.
[4] U.N. doc. A/5488–DC/208.   [5] See pp. 170–2 above.
[6] See pp. 164–6 above.   [7] See p. 175 above.
[8] Text in *Documents, 1961*, pp. 375–7.

2. *Commends* the Secretariat of the United Nations for its services to the Eighteen-Nation Committee and requests the Secretary-General to continue to make available to the Committee the necessary assistance and services.

General Assembly resolution on the 'question of convening a conference for the purpose of signing a convention on the prohibition of the use of nuclear and thermonuclear weapons, 27 November 1963[1]

The General Assembly,

Recalling the declaration on the prohibition of the use of nuclear and thermonuclear weapons, contained in its resolution 1653 (XVI) of 24 November 1961,[2]

Cognizant that the subject can be speedily and effectively studied by the Conference of the Eighteen-Nation Committee on Disarmament in Geneva,

1. *Requests* the Conference of the Eighteen-Nation Committee on Disarmament to study urgently the question of convening a conference for the purpose of signing a convention on the prohibition of the use of nuclear and thermonuclear weapons, and to report to the General Assembly at its nineteenth session;

2. *Requests* the Secretary-General to transmit the text of the present resolution and all other relevant documents to the Eighteen-Nation Committee.

General Assembly resolution on the 'urgent need for suspension of nuclear and thermonuclear tests', 27 November 1963[3]

The General Assembly,

Fully aware of its responsibility with regard to the question of nuclear weapon testing and of the views of world public opinion on this matter,

Noting with approval the Treaty banning nuclear weapon tests in the atmosphere, in outer space and under water, signed on 5 August 1963 by the Union of Soviet Socialist Republics, the United Kingdom of Great Britain and Northern Ireland and the United States of America, and subsequently by a great number of other countries,[4]

Noting further with satisfaction that in the preamble of the Treaty the parties state that they are seeking to achieve the discontinuance of all test explosions of nuclear weapons for all time and are determined to continue negotiations to this end,

1. *Calls upon* all States to become parties to the Treaty banning nuclear weapon tests in the atmosphere, in outer space and under water, and to abide by its spirit and provisions;

2. *Requests* the Conference of the Eighteen-Nation Committee on Disarmament to continue with a sense of urgency its negotiations to achieve the objectives set forth in the preamble of the Treaty;

3. *Requests* the Eighteen-Nation Committee to report to the General Assembly at the earliest possible date and, in any event, not later than at the nineteenth session;

[1] *G.A.O.R.*, Eighteenth Session, Supplement No. 15, p. 14, A/RES/1909 (XVIII).
[2] Ibid., Sixteenth Session, Supplement No. 17, pp. 4–6.
[3] Ibid., Eighteenth Session, Supplement No. 15, p. 14, A/RES/1910 (XVIII).
[4] See pp. 170–2 above.

4. *Requests* the Secretary-General to make available to the Eighteen-Nation Committee the documents and records of the plenary meetings of the General Assembly and the meetings of the First Committee at which the item relating to nuclear testing was discussed.

General Assembly resolution on the 'denuclearization of Latin America', 27 November 1963[1]

The General Assembly,

Bearing in mind the vital necessity of sparing present and future generations the scourge of a nuclear war,

Recalling its resolutions 1380 (XIV) of 20 November 1959,[2] 1576 (XV) of 20 December 1960[3] and 1665 (XVI) of 4 December 1961,[4] in which it recognized the danger that an increase in the number of States possessing nuclear weapons would involve, since such an increase would necessarily result in an intensification of the arms race and an aggravation of the difficulty of maintaining world peace, thus rendering more difficult the attainment of a general disarmament agreement,

Observing that in its resolution 1664 (XVI) of 4 December 1961[5] it stated explicitly that the countries not possessing nuclear weapons had a grave interest and an important part to fulfil in the preparation and implementation of measures that could halt further nuclear weapon tests and prevent the further spread of nuclear weapons,

Considering that the recent conclusion of the Treaty banning nuclear weapon tests in the atmosphere, in outer space and under water, signed on 5 August 1963,[6] has created a favourable atmosphere for parallel progress towards the prevention of the further spread of nuclear weapons, a problem which, as indicated in General Assembly resolutions 1649 (XVI) of 8 November 1961[7] and 1762 (XVII) of 6 November 1962,[8] is closely connected with that of the banning of nuclear weapon tests,

Considering that the Heads of State of five Latin American Republics issued, on 29 April 1963, a declaration on the denuclearization of Latin America,[9] in which, in the name of their peoples and Governments, they announced that they are prepared to sign a multilateral Latin American agreement whereby their countries would undertake not to manufacture, receive, store or test nuclear weapons or nuclear launching devices,

Recognizing the need to preserve, in Latin America, conditions which will prevent the countries of the region from becoming involved in a dangerous and ruinous arms race,

1. *Notes with satisfaction* the initiative for the denuclearization of Latin America taken in the joint declaration of 29 April 1963;

---

[1] *G.A.O.R.*, Eighteenth Session, Supplement No. 15, pp. 14–15, A/RES/1911 (XVIII).
[2] *Documents, 1959*, p. 138.   [3] *Documents, 1960*, pp. 107–8.
[4] *G.A.O.R.*, Sixteenth Session, Supplement No. 17, pp. 5–6.
[5] *Ibid.*, p. 5.   [6] See pp. 170–2 above.
[7] *G.A.O.R.*, Sixteenth Session, Supplement No. 17, p. 4.
[8] *Documents, 1962*, pp. 131–3.   [9] See pp. 161–2 above.

2. *Expresses the hope* that the States of Latin America will initiate studies as they deem appropriate, in the light of the principles of the Charter of the United Nations and of regional agreements and by the means and through the channels which they deem suitable, concerning the measures that should be agreed upon with a view to achieving the aims of the said declaration;

3. *Trusts* that at the appropriate moment, after a satisfactory agreement has been reached, all States, particularly the nuclear Powers, will lend their full co-operation for the effective realization of the peaceful aims inspiring the present resolution;

4. *Requests* the Secretary-General to extend to the States of Latin America, at their request, such technical facilities as they may require in order to achieve the aims set forth in the present resolution.

General Assembly resolution on the 'conversion to peaceful uses of the resources released by disarmament', 11 December 1963[1]

The General Assembly,

Recalling its resolution 1837 (XVII) of 18 December 1962 entitled 'Declaration on the conversion to peaceful needs of the resources released by disarmament'[2] and Economic and Social Council resolution 982 (XXXVI) of 2 August 1963 entitled 'Economic and social consequences of disarmament'[3] concerning, *inter alia*, the advantages which disarmament could have for economic and social programmes throughout the world,

Encouraged by the conclusion of the Treaty banning nuclear weapon tests in the atmosphere, in outer space and under water,[4]

Hopeful that further agreements will be reached which will lessen world tensions and lead ultimately to general and complete disarmament under effective international control,

Noting the report submitted by the Secretary-General to the Economic and Social Council[5] and made available to the General Assembly pursuant to paragraph 7 of Assembly resolution 1837 (XVII) with regard to the activities of Member States, the various United Nations bodies, the specialized agencies and the International Atomic Energy Agency in studying the economic and social consequences of disarmament, and pursuant to Council resolution 982 (XXXVI),

Noting further the report submitted by the Secretary-General to the General Assembly[6] pursuant to paragraph 8 of Assembly resolution 1837 (XVII) with regard to development plans and projects for an economic programme for disarmament,

Noting with satisfaction that a number of Governments as well as some specialized agencies and regional economic commissions have already initiated, or expressed their readiness to start, in co-operation with the Secretary-General, the study of the economic and social consequences of disarmament,

---

[1] *G.A.O.R.*, Eighteenth Session, Supplement No. 15, pp. 25–6, A/RES/1931 (XVIII).
[2] Ibid., Seventeenth Session, Supplement No. 17, pp. 24–5.
[3] *Economic and Social Council, Official Records*, Thirty-sixth Session, 2 July–2 August 1963, Supplement No. 1, pp. 4–5.
[4] See pp. 170–2 above.   [5] U.N. docs. E/3736 and Addenda 1–9.
[6] U.N. doc. A/5538.

1. *Endorses* Economic and Social Council resolution 982 (XXXVI) and urges that Member States do everything possible to facilitate the carrying out of General Assembly resolution 1837 (XVII) and Council resolution 982 (XXXVI);

2. *Invites* the specialized agencies concerned, the International Atomic Energy Agency and the regional economic commissions to co-operate with the Secretary-General in advancing studies, within their fields of competence, of various problems concerning international economic and trade relations relevant to the economic and social aspects of disarmament, as requested in Economic and Social Council resolution 982 (XXXVI) and General Assembly resolution 1837 (XVII), and in particular, as requested in paragraph 5 of Council resolution 982 (XXXVI), in making an adequate survey of the possibilities of undertaking studies of the problems that might arise in relation to primary commodities;

3. *Expresses the hope* that the Governments of all States will intensify their efforts to achieve an agreement on general and complete disarmament under effective international control, with the desire to realize the benefits for mankind to which the Declaration on the conversion to peaceful needs of the resources released by disarmament is addressed;

4. *Hopes also* that Member States, particularly those significantly involved, will continue, in the light of developments bearing on disarmament, to pursue studies and activities relating to the economic and social consequences of disarmament, to the problems which it will entail for them and to means of dealing with those problems, and invites Member States to co-operate with the Secretary-General;

5. *Requests* the Economic and Social Council at its thirty-seventh session to consider all pertinent aspects of the question of conversion of resources released by general disarmament to peaceful uses, including, *inter alia*, the possibility of the establishment of an *ad hoc* group, having due regard to equitable geographical distribution, for the purpose of accelerating activities in this field of study, and to report thereon to the General Assembly at its nineteenth session;

6. *Endorses* the intentions and plans of the Secretary-General to proceed in carrying out a work programme pursuant to General Assembly resolution 1837 (XVII) as described in his report, and requests the Secretary-General to present to the Assembly at its nineteenth session a further report on this matter.

Declaration of Legal Principles Governing the Activities of States in the Exploration and Use of Outer Space, adopted by the General Assembly, 13 December 1963[1]

The General Assembly,

Inspired by the great prospects opening up before mankind as a result of man's entry into outer space,

Recognizing the common interest of all mankind in the progress of the exploration and use of outer space for peaceful purposes,

Believing that the exploration and use of outer space should be carried on for the betterment of mankind and for the benefit of States irrespective of their degree of economic or scientific development,

---

[1] *G.A.O.R.*, Eighteenth Session, Supplement No. 15, pp. 15–16.

Desiring to contribute to broad international cooperation in the scientific as well as in the legal aspects of exploration and use of outer space for peaceful purposes,

Believing that such cooperation will contribute to the development of mutual understanding and to the strengthening of friendly relations between nations and peoples,

Recalling its resolution 110 (II) of 3 November 1947,[1] which condemned propaganda designed or likely to provoke or encourage any threat to the peace, breach of the peace, or act of aggression, and considering that the aforementioned resolution is applicable to outer space,

Taking into consideration its resolution 1721 (XVI) of 20 December 1961[2] and 1802 (XVII) of 14 December 1962,[3] adopted unanimously by the States Members of the United Nations,

Solemnly declares that in the exploration and use of outer space States should be guided by the following principles:

1. The exploration and use of outer space shall be carried on for the benefit and in the interests of all mankind.

2. Outer space and celestial bodies are free for exploration and use by all States on a basis of equality and in accordance with international law.

3. Outer space and celestial bodies are not subject to national appropriation by claim of sovereignty, by means of use or occupation, or by any other means.

4. The activities of States in the exploration and use of outer space shall be carried on in accordance with international law, including the Charter of the United Nations, in the interest of maintaining international peace and security and promoting international cooperation and understanding.

5. States bear international responsibility for national activities in outer space, whether carried on by governmental agencies or by non-governmental entities, and for assuring that national activities are carried on in conformity with the principles set forth in the present Declaration. The activities of non-governmental entities in outer space shall require authorization and continuing supervision by the State concerned. When activities are carried on in outer space by an international organization, responsibility for compliance with the principles set forth in this Declaration shall be borne by the international organization and by the States participating in it.

6. In the exploration and use of outer space, States shall be guided by the principle of cooperation and mutual assistance and shall conduct all their activities in outer space with due regard for the corresponding interests of other States. If a State has reason to believe that an outer space activity or experiment planned by it or its nationals would cause potentially harmful interference with activities of other States in the peaceful exploration and use of outer space, it shall undertake appropriate international consultations before proceeding with any such activity or experiment. A State which has reason to believe that an outer space activity or experiment planned by another State would cause potentially harmful interference with activities in the peaceful exploration and use of outer space may request consultation concerning the activity or experiment.

[1] *G.A.O.R.*, Second Session, Resolutions, 16 September–29 November 1947, p. 14.
[2] Ibid., Sixteenth Session, Supplement No. 17, pp. 6–7.
[3] Ibid., Seventeenth Session, Supplement No. 17, pp. 5–7.

7. The State on whose registry an object launched into outer space is carried shall retain jurisdiction and control over such object, and any personnel thereon, while in outer space. Ownership of objects launched into outer space, and of their component parts, is not affected by their passage through outer space or by their return to the earth. Such objects or component parts found beyond the limits of the State of registry shall be returned to that State, which shall furnish identifying data upon request prior to return.

8. Each State which launches or procures the launching of an object into outer space, and each State from whose territory or facility an object is launched, is internationally liable for damage to a foreign State or to its natural or juridical persons by such object or its component parts on the earth, in air space, or in outer space.

9. States shall regard astronauts as envoys of mankind in outer space, and shall render to them all possible assistance in the event of accident, distress, or emergency landing on the territory of a foreign State or on the high seas. Astronauts who make such a landing shall be safely and promptly returned to the State of registry of their space vehicle.

(c) *Germany and Berlin*

Report by the President of the German Democratic Republic, Herr Ulbricht, to the Sixth Congress of the Socialist Unity Party, Berlin, 14 January 1963[1] (extracts)

. . . In view of the objective conditions of development not only do we consider the continuation of the negotiations between the Soviet Union and the USA concerning the German peace settlement and the West Berlin question necessary, but we hold that an understanding is possible. It would help to ease tension in Germany if negotiations were conducted between the Government of the two German States on the establishment of at least a modicum of normal relations. We are ready to take into consideration that certain prestige factors play a part for the Western Powers in connection with West Berlin. We are therefore ready to consider a step-by-step settlement in the transformation of West Berlin into a peaceful, neutral city. We are also ready, in the interest of a peaceful settlement of the problem, to give consideration to the proposal that the flag of NATO should in West Berlin first be replaced by the UN flag, and that the UN undertake there certain international obligations and functions. Such a settlement would of course be acceptable to us only if it included respect on the part of all parties concerned for the sovereignty of the GDR, above all, also with regard to the use of the GDR communications leading to West Berlin by land, on sea and in the air.

We are of the opinion that anybody who has no war provocations in mind, who is not out to misuse West Berlin for diversionary activities against the GDR, can negotiate about such a compromise and put his signature under such a promise.

Government organs in Bonn have given information in the Western press that contacts have been established between the Government of the Federal Republic

[1] *S.W.B.*, EE/1150, 16 January 1963, c/1–c/14, and EE/1151, 17 January 1963, c/1–c/4.

and the GDR Government—I expressly stress: between the two Governments—
for the preparation of political discussions. Both sides had agreed to nominate
representatives of their Governments for such talks. These talks were disturbed
in connection with the events in the Caribbean area. It would have been in the
interest of the matter concerned if these contacts had been nursed confidentially,
calmly and objectively. But there are evidently certain circles in Bonn which
would like to prevent normal negotiations, and for this reason, for months past,
have launched the most diverse stories into the press which are mostly contrary
to the facts.

Every sensible person ought to have realised that if negotiations are conducted
about the German peace settlement between the Soviet Union and the USA, such
negotiations should even more assuredly take place between representatives of
the two German Governments. This of course is possible only on the basis of
equality of rights. The development of normal commercial relations between the
two German States could not but have a favourable influence on such negotiations.

Some time ago, the representative of the Bonn Government offered the representative of the Ministry of Foreign and Intra-German trade a credit of DM.
1,000,000,000. To avoid all misunderstandings: this offer of the credit of one
milliard came from the Bonn Government. It was explicitly stated that there
should be no political strings to this offer of a credit. The GDR Government
agreed to this proposal, and talks on points of detail were initiated. Meanwhile,
the Bonn Government changed its mind. It has apparently withdrawn its offer
and has launched an international campaign against the 'impoverished' GDR
which was so badly off that it had to buy goods on credit from West German
businessmen. That really is a bit thick.

Now as you know, long-term credit agreements were not invented by the
GDR, or for that matter by the communists. Such agreements have been customary throughout the world for centuries past. All former German Governments
conducted credit talks; so that is really not our own discovery.

The Bonn Government has now made the proposal through its official representatives to increase the swing in the trade between the two German States by
400,000,000 units of account. But—and this was the big snag—the Bonn Government is demanding in return that the GDR should agree to the inclusion of West
Berlin in the Federal Republic. They have also informed us what the first step
should be: the thing should start with the conclusion of an agreement between
the GDR and Bonn Governments about the crossing of the GDR frontier by
the people of West Berlin. Of course, the GDR Government could not accept
such an immoral deal.

It is well known—to the three Western Powers, too—that the Bonn Government has no competence whatever as far as West Berlin is concerned. We are, of
course, prepared to arrange talks between the GDR Government and the West
Berlin Senate about establishing normal relations. To this end the GDR Foreign
Ministry a short while ago approached the Mayor of West Berlin and suggested
talks on questions of interest to both sides. Owing to pressure being brought to
bear by certain Bonn circles it proved impossible, after contacts had been established—as indeed they were established—to initiate negotiations. I think this
disposes of the entire Western Press propaganda concerning the visits of West

Berliners to the GDR capital. There can be no settlement without negotiations between the competent authorities, and those who decline negotiations obviously do not want a settlement. We want a settlement; therefore we favour negotiations.

There are, then, the following questions which need elucidation but which are not connected with each other:

First, the relations between West Berlin and the GDR can be settled only by representatives of the GDR and the West Berlin Senate. If the West Berlin Senate were ready to avail itself of the real situation it would act not only in the interest of the people of West Berlin—who naturally feel ill at ease in that confined space in West Berlin—but also in the interest of a German peace settlement. To the extent that it becomes a neutral, free city West Berlin can play a positive role in bringing about a lessening of tension between the two German States.

Secondly, improvement of trade relations between the two German States is also of great importance for lessening tension. But it is not realistic to tie up questions of trade with political considerations which, moreover, are contrary to international law.

Thirdly, it would be in the interest of the German people if the contacts between the Governments of the two German States were to lead to negotiations on normalising relations between them. This would be the first step to the gradual filling up of the ditch which has been dug right across Germany.

I turn now to the question of safeguarding peace and to the national question of the German people. Dear comrades! It is our great historic task to fight with all our strength, passion and perseverance to banish war once and for all from the life of the German people. The road we are pursuing leads to this goal. The SED, says the Programme, unshakably adheres to the aim of restoring the unity of Germany, of overcoming the division carried out by the imperialist Western Powers in conspiracy with West German monopoly capital. Without disarmament, without an assured peace, however, the division of Germany cannot be overcome. In this sense peace and national unity are inseparably linked in the policy of the SED. A peace-loving Germany needs neither atomic weapons nor other superlative arms. On the contrary, rearming—and especially arming with nuclear weapons—is absolutely incompatible with a peaceful solution of the German question and reunification.

It has already been made clear at the National Congress that the national question of the German people is the safeguarding of peace by overcoming militarism and imperialism. It was therefore of decisive national importance that solid foundations for a consistent peace policy were created in the GDR by the eradication of imperialism. The struggle for the solution of the national question is a question of social power, and the policy of revenge and atomic war is pursued by the representatives of a certain class, monopoly capital, which in Western Germany holds the power of the State in its hands. The Party Programme, in principle, sets out our point of view on the solution of the national question and explains why we fight to eliminate once and for all the source of war in Western Germany.

As a way to establishing normal relations between the two German States we want to achieve a confederation which will prevent the people from moving further apart and clear the road to reunification. This presupposes the curbing of the military by the struggle of the peace-loving forces in Western Germany.

The Programme says that it is the historic mission of the GDR to create—by the comprehensive achievement of socialism in the first German worker-peasant State—a firm foundation for the working class to take over leadership in the whole of Germany, the monopoly bourgeoisie being deprived of its power also in Western Germany, and the national question being solved in the sense of peace and national progress. . . .

It is well-known that Herr Adenauer never omits to shed crocodile tears in any of his speeches about the supposedly starving population of the GDR and to demand more humanity from the GDR Government. He means, of course, more humanity to revanchists and other agents infiltrated into the GDR from West Berlin.

However, I do not want to talk about this today. It is a matter for the State organs of the GDR. It is the desire for a lasting peace which inspires the population of both German States at the moment. Thus, if Herr Adenauer would like to do something for humanity, the simplest step would be an agreement between the two German States on the renunciation of atomic militarisation, a halt to armaments, and on a non-aggression pact. After all, this would be relatively simple. We suggest an agreement of reason and goodwill. We suggest that the prerequisites of objective and normal relations between the two German States should be created step by step. For this purpose we advocate an agreement of reason and goodwill which is based on the existence of two German States with different social systems and which could have roughly the following contents:

(1) Respect for the existence of the other German State and its political and social order. In other words—let us say so openly—reciprocal non-intervention. Solemn renunciation of the use of force in any form.

(2) Respect for the frontiers of the other German State. This should not be difficult since the frontiers cannot be changed in any case. Solemn renunciation of all attempts and endeavours to touch or alter these frontiers. Delimitation and consolidation of the existing German borders with other countries as well.

(3) Solemn renunciation of the testing, ownership, manufacture and acquisition of nuclear weapons and of control over them.

(4) Armaments stop in both German States, linked with the obligation not to increase expenditure for military purposes. Further agreements on disarmament in both German States.

(5) Reciprocal recognition of the passports and citizenship of the citizens of both German States as the prerequisite for the normalisation of travel. Renunciation of any discrimination against, and unequal treatment of, the citizens of either German State at home and abroad.

(6) Establishment of normal sports and cultural relations between the two German States. The Federal Republic, its representatives abroad, and its social organisations to renounce any discrimination against citizens of the GDR in cases of joint participation by representatives of both German States in international conferences, congresses and sports events. We for our part would undertake to do likewise in the case of citizens of the Federal Republic. Part of this is that the Government of the Federal Republic should give up the practice, which is undignified from any national point of view, of advocating within NATO discrimination against the citizens of the GDR through the Travel Bureau in West Berlin.

(7) Conclusion of a trade agreement between the Government of the two German States with the aim of expanding and developing trade between them.

These are our proposals. We are of course ready to negotiate on West German proposals which serve the same peaceful aims. We are of the opinion that after the conclusion of a German peace treaty, it will be possible gradually to develop co-operation between the two German States. . . .

Statement by the Mayor of West Berlin, Willy Brandt, to the Berlin House of Representatives, 18 March 1963[1] (extract)

. . . The Senate will continue to pursue unchanged the present principles of Berlin policy approved by the House of Representatives[2] which have repeatedly met with the express approval of the Federal Government and the Bundestag. The correctness of these principles has been confirmed by the experiences of the past years.

The starting-point of this policy is the realisation that there is no isolated Berlin problem. From the very beginning it has formed a part—even if an integral one—of the German problem, and it will remain inextricably tied up with the German problem. Even the Soviet Union must know that. The continued pressure it is exerting against Berlin is directed not only against the city itself but also against Free Germany as a whole, and therefore quite simply against the western community and the Free World, too. The Soviet side has deliberately played the Berlin problem up to become a world problem, being helped in this by its threats which were in the nature of an ultimatum. As a result of the pressure on Berlin the Soviet side wished to secure that political power in Germany switched in its favour.

The status of this city and the situation in it are not the cause, but only one of the effects, of the antagonisms and tensions between East and West. This status is not in the least a hindrance to the efforts being made to bring about a relaxation of international tensions. On the contrary, from the Soviet Union's policy vis-à-vis Berlin it is possible to infer how far it is really interested in a relaxation of tension internationally, above all in Europe.

The Senate sticks firmly to the opinion that there is no reason to change the status of Berlin prior to a peace settlement for Germany. There is, however, no way leading to a peace settlement for Germany as a whole which by-passes the right of the German people to self-determination. As long as the Soviet Union debars the German people from exercising the right to self-determination there is no genuine solution to the German problem.

Until that point is reached the Western Powers must keep up firmly their legal claim to the whole of Berlin. There originary rights in Berlin are valid until a peace settlement for Germany has been reached. The Soviet Union cannot dispose of these rights unilaterally.

All the same, the fundamental distinction between the superiority of the legal claims and the political reality in this city must not be overlooked.

[1] Deutsche Gesellschaft für Auswärtige Politik, *Documents on Berlin, 1943–1963*, eds. Wolfgang Heildelmeyer and Guenter Hendrichs (Munich, 1963), pp. 354–7.
[2] Cf. the statement by Willy Brandt to the Berlin Parliament on 13 August 1961; in ibid., pp. 276–9.

Berlin's four-Power status has been undermined to the extreme limits by the unilateral and unlawful measures taken by the Soviet Union.

The erection of the Wall represents the most grievous attack on the four-Power status. To all intents and purposes it signifies the de facto annexation of the Eastern Sector by the Zonal authorities that the Soviet Union desires and encourages.

At present the Western Powers are in a position to exercise their full rights and responsibilities only in and in respect of West Berlin and, unfortunately, not in respect of Berlin as a whole.

The guarantees holding good for West Berlin give expression to this special responsibility of the Three Powers for West Berlin. This special responsibility is the strongest support of our security and of our life in freedom. Its most visible expression lies in the presence of the Western troops. This responsibility must be upheld to the full.

That cannot and must not prevent the Federal Government from sharing to the full, politically and in practice, the responsibility for West Berlin. Its unreserved commitment does not weaken but strengthens the West's position in Berlin.

There cannot be, and must not be, a four-Power status restricted solely to West Berlin. The Soviet Union must not retain and exercise rights in West Berlin beyond those granted to the Western Powers in the Eastern Sector of the city.

The Western Powers have entered into the strongest commitment in regard to West Berlin it is possible to conceive. In stipulation and repeated confirmation of the three basic essentials they have given unmistakable expression to their readiness to face an extreme risk should it be a matter of safeguarding the presence of their troops in the city, the free access to Berlin, and the freedom and vitality of the population.

The steadfastness evidenced by the United States during the Cuban crisis holds good once and for all. Thus it naturally holds good for Berlin also, in that it precludes all future talk as to whether, and how often, the Americans and their President have yet again to reiterate their definite promises of protection. We can hope that the clarification of the situation following the Cuban crisis also benefits Berlin, without, however, forgetting that the German problem, and as a part of it the Berlin problem, still remains unsettled.

So far as world politics are concerned we are no longer living in the phase that was characterised by the Soviet ultimatum and the 13th of August. This means that, so far as the main issue of those days is concerned, the Berlin crisis as unleashed in November, 1958, has been largely surmounted. Today the world knows that West Berlin is no city that is fair game for all and sundry, that it is not a corpus separatum on German soil, that it is no city without Western troops. Nor will the future change anything of that as long as the German problem remains unsolved.

Four years after the opening of their general political offensive against Free Berlin the Soviet leaders have had to take due cognisance of two facts: in the first place, that Berlin is a city of the West. The Western troops remain in Berlin until the Wall comes down and until the settlement of the German problem in peace and freedom has been reached. Here they remain by virtue of treaty and conviction and because the Berliners wish it. And secondly, and interrelated to the first point, Berlin is a German Federal Land. Neither by frontal attack in the political field nor by the running fire of propaganda nor by undermining with tactical flanking and nuisance manoeuvres, subversive activity, allurements or threats, can the will of its people to preserve their own position and the viability of Free Berlin be broken.

Fresh exploratory talks between the United States and the Soviet Union are imminent. Such talks took place once before, in 1962. Then they resulted in no basis for negotiations on Berlin. One will have to wait and see whether or not, on the basis of the changed situation in the field of world politics and a new appreciation of the situation by the Soviet Union, the new exploratory talks finally develop into negotiations.

No negotiations on Berlin can overlook the fact of the indissoluble connection between the German and the Berlin problems. Unfortunately, however, it has to be added, if one wishes to be honest, that not one of us should indulge in the pipe-dream that a solution to the German problem is attainable in the near future. Thes ubject of negotiations between the Western Powers and the Soviet Union on Germany and Berlin—or on Berlin only—could, therefore, be at the most directed towards finding a tolerable interim solution, in which connection it would be a matter of whether or not to write down the deductions and inductions drawn during the course of the Berlin crisis.

The Senate of Berlin supports the aim of German policy to reach—as the Federal Foreign Minister puts it in the introduction to the Foreign Office's last annual report—a 'modus vivendi' agreement. By such an agreement we understand a tolerable interim solution keeping the German question open. Berlin would decline to accept a 'modus vivendi' agreement if it meant in practice closing the book on the German problem.

The Senate of Berlin is prepared to co-operate in an interim solution which leaves the foundation of the city's existence untouched and which helps to ease the life of its citizens.

It is the view of the Senate that, in any possible interim solution, the following conditions must be fulfilled:

1. The United States, Britain and France must keep their troops stationed in Berlin and bear full responsibility for the security of Berlin until the Wall comes down and the German problem is settled.

2. With the approval of the Three Powers, with the knowledge of the Soviet Union, and through the will of the population concerned, West Berlin in the last fifteen years has become interwoven economically, financially, juridically and politically with the remainder of the Federal Republic. These ties which have developed are vital. They should be strengthened so far as this is possible in international law and consonant with security.

3. Never must the right of the population concerned to settle their own affairs themselves and to be free to determine their own future be left out of account.

Now and again Berlin has been brought publicly into conjunction with the United Nations also. In regard to this, the view of the Senate is that it would not run counter to our interests were this great world organisation to take an active interests in the infringement of human rights, but that it would be pointless, unrealistic and dangerous to absolve France, Britain and the United States from their protective task.

Ladies and Gentlemen, tied up with the conditions just mentioned we see the following requirements which, even independently of any interim solution, are well founded:

4. The particularly brutal consequences of the Wall must be rendered less severe. In regard to access to East Berlin, in any event the West Berliners must be placed on an equal footing with all other people. In the interests of humanity and reason and to re-tie the bonds between families and friends in the two parts of the city that have been so arbitrarily torn asunder no one will be able to strike this item off the agenda.

5. Just as today by air, free access to Berlin on the surface must be realised and guaranteed. An international access authority, its actions based on the principle of free traffic, could signify a material improvement on the present situation.

6. As we have confidently represented to the allied Protective Powers, obsolete claims of Soviet Zone officials are to be replaced by arrangements doing justice to Berlin's needs. This applies particularly for the former German railway system and thus for the city railway too. The unilateral and unlawful changes in Greater Berlin have abrogated the competences the Soviet Zone's administrative officials originally had in West Berlin.

The Senate will resolutely reject any attempt made by the other side to utilise the affliction of our fellow-citizens in both parts of the city as a medium of political blackmail. There will be no negotiations between Berlin and the Soviet Zone officials as if between bodies independent in international law; nor will there be any negotiations which can be misconstrued as back-door recognition. Here Berlin carries a responsibility not only for its own destiny. The Senate is ever conscious of its responsibility for our countrymen and women on the other side of the Wall.

The Senate reaffirms its readiness to help in the settlement, on a reasonable basis, of technical problems within the whole of Berlin. For this purpose, above all the services of existing institutions, capable of being enlarged, are already available between the two German currency areas.

The Government of the Soviet Union to the Government of the United States, 8 April 1963[1]

The Government of the U.S.S.R. deems it necessary to state the following to the Government of the United States:

For some time now, members of the North Atlantic alliance—NATO—have been working out plans for the establishment of an integrated nuclear force of the bloc. As can be seen from the published official statements, it is proposed to gather into a single fist, known as a 'multilateral force', the nuclear formations of the United States and Britain, together with corresponding contingents of the German Federal Republic and, probably several other NATO members. It is further meant to establish special naval and rocket nuclear forces under multi-lateral possession and multilateral control. Special stress is being made on the establishment of naval forces equipped with atomic weapons, including surface vessels armed with Polaris missiles and disguised as merchant ships. Moreover, the Government of the United States has announced its intention to station

---

[1] *D.S.B.*, 3 June 1963, pp. 862–6.

American nuclear submarines with Polaris rockets in the Mediterranean and in other European and Asian waters even now, without waiting for the establishment of an integrated NATO nuclear force.

All these plans are being tied in with an accelerated buildup of conventional armaments, above all in West European NATO countries, including small ones. Thus, armament programs are being worked out by NATO for decades to come in which it is stipulated, down to the smallest details, who should supply NATO with nuclear, rocket, and other formations and in what numbers, what additional means each country should spend on preparations for war, and so forth.

Whatever the final form plans for the establishment of NATO nuclear forces may take—whether they will be 'multinational' or 'multilateral', or combined—the information already divulged makes one thing perfectly clear: The United States and other NATO powers are planning to give the Bundeswehr and the armed forces of other countries access to rocket-nuclear weapons, further broaden the preparations for thermonuclear war, and launch a race in rocket and nuclear armaments transcending all national and geographical boundaries.

In the age of rocket-nuclear weapons, concern for universal peace is the first commandment of mankind, and this puts a great responsibility on the governments in power. It is to them that the peoples address the universal demand: Prevent thermonuclear war; do not allow it to flare up.

For many years the Soviet Government has been pressing for the adoption of agreed decisions which would eliminate the threat of rocket-nuclear war and extinguish the sources of possible conflicts. The Soviet Union offers to all countries and peoples peace, good-neighborly cooperation, and economic competition. It is ready to advance consistently and unswervingly toward the establishment of relations of trust and mutual understanding.

How do the NATO powers reply to the peace-loving policy of the socialist countries? They counter it with a policy of the cold war, a policy aimed at undermining international cooperation and at extending both in depth and in breadth the rivalry between states in developing and stockpiling ever more lethal means of warfare. Suffice it to turn to the events of the past few weeks only to see what a dangerous path the NATO powers are pushing the world.

Ignoring the will of the peoples and the resolution of the U.N. General Assembly, the United States, later followed by France, resumed testing of nuclear weapons. The Government of France concluded an openly militaristic pact with the German Federal Republic.[1] The Federal Republic Government, for its part, has once more demonstrated that the interests of peace and security in Europe are deeply alien to its policy.

In recent weeks the world witnessed new and hostile acts on the part of the United States against the freedom-loving Republic of Cuba, new breaches of the principles of the U.N. Charter and of universally recognized principles of international law with regard to freedom of navigation. Dangerous provocations by German militarists follow one another in West Berlin.

It is true that the governments of the United States of America and other NATO countries, taking part in international negotiations on the settlement of problems at issue, infrequently vote in the United Nations for the adoption of

[1] The reference is to the Treaty on Franco-German Cooperation of 22 January 1963; for text, see *Documents, 1962*, pp. 435–8.

constructive decisions. Unfortunately, however, this does not determine by far the main direction of the policy of the Western powers.

Facts show that in their strategic calculations the governments of the Western powers rely not on a peaceful settlement of the main problems that sustain international tension, but on achieving some kind of a superiority in the arms race, and ultimately on the use of force. The plan for creating a multilateral NATO force is a modern expression of the 'from a position of strength' policy, a policy of pressure and diktat, with nuclear weapons being proclaimed the main factor and core thereof.

It is known that the former American government of Eisenhower, not long before it stepped down from the political scene, promoted vigorously the idea of turning NATO into some kind of a nuclear power. At that time, there was much talk about each of the 15 participants in this bloc being able to keep its finger at the pushbutton of a rocket-nuclear war.

The U.S. Government, in point of actual fact, was accepting the spread of nuclear weapons within NATO and was close to satisfying the demands of the German Federal Republic Government which was clamoring for 'equality' in nuclear armaments.

At one time there were grounds to think that the present U.S. Government was aware of the dangers involved into putting into effect the plans to make NATO a nuclear power. It had repeatedly assured that it attached exceptional significance to the achievements of an agreement on the nonspreading of nuclear weapons and that in conformity with its national policy the United States would not turn over nuclear weapons to any country. However, by every indication, neither its own assurances, nor warnings sounded by many states, including a number of NATO countries, concerning the dangerous consequences of the spreading of nuclear weapons, have deterred the U.S. Government.

At the Nassau meeting of the heads of government of the United States and Great Britain, it was decided to establish the NATO nuclear force on almost the same pattern as was advocated three or four years ago. One can only wonder that the Nassau decision,[1] which makes the states plunge deeper into the vortex of rocket-nuclear armaments, is described by those who have accepted it as all but a service to their peoples, and even to the world.

The governments of the United States and certain of its allies pretend that the plans for the establishment of a multilateral nuclear force do not contradict the principle of the nonspread of nuclear weapons. What is more, it may be heard from the most high-ranking representatives of NATO countries that the plans for the establishment of a multilateral nuclear force are in themselves the product of a desire to eliminate concern over the 'unlimited spread of nuclear weapons to all states'.

But only two sharply delimited approaches are possible here; either abide unswervingly by the principle of the nonspread of nuclear weapons, and consequently prevent any access to these weapons for other states, or take the way of supplying nuclear weapons to one's allies, and then the question of the form in which it is done—bilateral or multilateral—would not play any essential role. No 'intermediate' approach is possible without starting a chain reaction with

---

[1] For text, see *Documents, 1962*, pp. 482–4.

all attendant dangerous consequences. Western statesmen cannot be so naive as to fail to understand this.

It appears that those who see one of the reasons for the submission of plans for a multilateral NATO nuclear force in the striving of the U.S. Government to gear the economic resources of West European countries more fully to the arms race and make the West European allies ante up another 6 to 10 billion dollars are not far from the truth. But, however complicated the bookkeeping concerning the distribution among the NATO members of the expenditures involved in the arms race may be, the full 100 percent of these expenditures will, in the final analysis, fall on the peoples. It is they, too, who would have to pay for the consequences of this race—should matters come to the worst—by an incalculable toll of life, and by cities and villages reduced to ashes.

What other arguments are advanced to justify the plans for the establishment of a multilateral nuclear force? The first argument called upon to sanctify and legalize everything is that of security requirements. But apart from the fact that nobody threatens the NATO countries, the establishment of multilateral and multinational nuclear forces cannot change anything in the existing balance of power in the world. The sides have stockpiled so many nuclear weapons that, to use a comparison, they have enough to churn up the earth and make the oceans leave their shores.

The moving by the NATO powers of some nuclear weapons from one arsenal to another—which would be controlled, among others, by Bundeswehr generals and the warlords of some other countries—would merely greatly increase the danger of a thermonuclear conflict.

In addition to the existing ones, new drive belts would extend to the war machine, enabling it to be set into motion. And so, will the security of the member states of the North Atlantic alliance gain anything from the fact that some new corporal would be able to touch off the conflagration of a third world war? Will the peoples of West Europe feel more secure if submarines and chameleon ships carrying nuclear rockets lurk at the shores of their countries, if a multilateral NATO nuclear army should take up quarters on their territories, if they knew that NATO strategists intend to make the whole world the battlefield of a new war?

To every sane person, it is clear that with the realization of the plans of NATO leaders, nuclear weapons with their inevitable corollary, the war danger, would spread over our planet as oil spreads over water.

The extension of the area from which a nuclear attack could be undertaken would naturally extend the geographical sphere of the use of retaliatory measures inevitable in such cases. May no one seek a threat in this statement of the Soviet Government! All this is almost copybook truth, a simple acknowledgement of what can already be accurately assessed today. In this connection, the Soviet Government feels itself dutybound to raise a warning voice.

In the case of conflict, the laws of modern warfare would make it incumbent to apply all means to immediately subdue the aggressor, and, in particular to render harmless the stationary and mobile bases aimed at the vital centers of peace-loving states.

Ports used as anchorages for submarine and surface rocket carriers, be they in the North, Mediterranean, Baltic, or other seas, would not survive the very first minutes of the war. The consequences of this to the entire territory of such states are clear without any comments.

The countries against which the military preparations of the North Atlantic bloc are directed would be compelled to continually keep the sights of their means of retribution focused also on the busiest sea lanes, where ships carrying nuclear rockets might lurk disguised as peaceful mercantile vessels. Incidentally, The Hague Convention forbids, even in wartime, the secret arming of a mercantile ship which would thus convert it into a warship.

But NATO staffs want to practice such insidious methods even now in peacetime. Thus, in the plans for a multilateral NATO force, the morals of medieval pirates are interwoven with the latest achievements of nuclear missilery. Had NATO warships, using the mercantile flag as a cover, started poking about the seas, this would be practically tantamount to an undeclared state of war.

The opinion is broached in the West that the plans for creating a multilateral nuclear force are also designed to put pressure on the Government of France, whose position on a number of military and economic problems does not coincide with that of the powers which determine policy within NATO. The Soviet Government does not intend to go into the question of the principles on which the relations between the members of the North Atlantic bloc are based.

But it cannot overlook the fact that, within NATO, the Government of the United States, on the one hand, and the Government of France, on the other, are playing up to West German imperialism—although for motives which do not fully coincide—and, to make certain of its support, connive at the most aggressive aspirations of the ruling circles of the German Federal Republic. And these circles are only waiting to open either the French or American gates to nuclear arms, or both simultaneously.

It is to satisfy the ever-growing demands of the Federal Republic that the plans for the establishment of a multilateral NATO nuclear force have, in effect, been conceived. The Government of the United States is trying to resolve the differences within NATO by concessions to the militarist and revanchist circles of the German Federal Republic.

Whenever the Soviet Union calls attention to the dangers of encouraging militarism in the German Federal Republic, the Western powers as a rule hasten to throw up a smokescreen of talk about the Soviet warnings being dictated by excessive suspicion in regard to West Germans. It is hard to find anything further from the truth than these claims. It is by concrete facts, and only facts, that the Soviet Union is guided in its policy.

Revision of the results of World War II, revision of the existing German state, the German Democratic Republic—such are the officially proclaimed foundations of the foreign policy of the German Federal Republic. This is a policy of revenge, a policy of war. Hence the striving to be on a par with the other NATO powers in the field of armaments, and above all nuclear armaments.

Does the Government of the United States not know this? Or has it any other explanation of why it is precisely the Federal Republic of Germany that enthusiastically welcomes any plan for the spread of nuclear weapons within NATO?

The Government of the German Federal Republic voted with both hands for earlier plans of the rocket-nuclear equipping of the NATO forces. It also was the first to sing praises to the Nassau agreement and now encourages the governments of the United States and Britain to broaden the 'multilateral' atomic armaments in NATO and to station them not only on the seas, but also on land. The Government of the German Federal Republic has announced its readiness to provide German crews for ships armed with nuclear-tipped Polaris missiles and to include Bundeswehr air units capable of nuclear delivery into the nuclear force without delay.

Reports have appeared in the foreign press that the United States and the German Federal Republic are now considering the use of West German ports in the Baltic and in the North Sea as bases for American nuclear submarines.

The Government of the German Federal Republic has declared that it can assume a third of the expenditures involved in the establishment of a multilateral nuclear force. And it insists, according to published reports, that the say of each member country in questions concerning nuclear weapons be determined by its financial contribution to the multilateral NATO force. And this demand, it appears, is viewed favorably by influential circles in the United States and certain other NATO countries. Consequently, as in a joint stock company, decisions will be determined by the size of the capital of the shareholders.

Only this time methods of struggle with commercial rivals will not be put to the vote, but questions of war and peace, while the dividends will be expressed not in dollars, pounds, or marks, but in millions of human lives. The rivets have not yet been fitted into the hulls of the NATO missile-launching vessels, but the West German military has already reached out for the trigger of the NATO nuclear mechanism, crushing those who have a smaller purse and less adventuristic spirit.

The Western powers, meeting step by step the German Federal Republic's demands present the case every time as though this is the last concession. After the setting up of the German Federal Republic, the governments of the United States, Britain, and France tried to convince everybody that this creature of theirs would not have an army altogether and would be provided only with police units.

But a plan appeared only two years later to set up a 'European army' with the inclusion of a half-million West German contingent in it. Many words were then wasted in the West to prove that the purpose of this plan was to keep under control the arming of West Germany and to prevent the setting up of independent Federal Republic's armed forces.

The same motives were advanced also when the Paris agreements were signed in 1954, agreements which paved the way to the German Federal Republic's accession to NATO.[1] The Paris agreements were described in the parliaments and from rostrums of international conferences as a guarantee that the arming of West Germany would be limited strictly and that the Bundeswehr would not be provided with many types of conventional arms, let alone means of mass annihilation.

And what happened is that a 400,000-strong Bundeswehr is now under the command of former Hitlerite generals. Plans are being prepared to raise its numerical strength to 750,000. Relying on its growing military might, the Federal Republic is seizing one position after another in NATO. Restrictions on the building of warships, heavy arms, and several categories of missiles, were

---

[1] For texts, see *Documents, 1954*, pp. 28–36.

forgotten long ago. Now, advancing the plan for a multilateral NATO nuclear force, the Western powers are ready to permit the Federal Republic to obviate the last obstacle to the actual possession of nuclear arms.

Thus, having started with police formations 13 years ago, the Federal Republic's Government is now loudly knocking at the door of the atomic club. 'We want,' Chancellor Adenauer stated in the Bundestag on 6 February of this year, 'to bear full responsibility together with others for effective NATO nuclear deterrent forces.'

More than 100 U.N. members do not possess nuclear arms, and nevertheless they do not regard this as a hiatus in their sovereign rights. In the German Federal Republic, however, the possession of nuclear arms has been declared a criterion of its sovereignty.

Apparently a concession to militarist forces entails new concessions. And, of course, nobody will guarantee that the present plan for a NATO nuclear force will be the last 'yes' in reply to the demands of the most adventuristically minded quarters of West Germany. The case resembles very much the days preceding World War II, when those who made the policy of the Western powers sacrificed the security and freedom of one country after another for the sake of 'pacifying' Hitlerite Germany. The appetites of the Hitlerite militarists only grew from this, and the World War II catastrophe came closer and closer.

The expansion of the circle of nuclear powers planned in NATO and facilitation of the German Federal Republic's access to nuclear arms may greatly impair the prospects that reason in international affairs will triumph. A favorable outcome cannot be expected whenever new impulses to the arms race are provided and its forms are diversified endlessly. Such a course of events prods mankind to the fatal line.

The Western governments claim that they agree to the idea of general and complete disarmament, that they are ready to seek ways to an international agreement on disarmament. The Western powers protest when the peace-loving states accuse the NATO countries of using the disarmament talks as a screen to cover up the arms race.

But how else can the position of the Western powers be assessed if they put on the brake with one hand, preventing the 18-nation committee from making progress in Geneva, and draw up plans for NATO nuclear forces with the other, plans whose implementation would rule out disarmament talks for at least 10 years in advance? The purpose of this policy obviously is to win time and confront the peace-loving states with the implementation of NATO plans for the spread of nuclear arms.

If the United States, Britain, and France were to embark upon the road of spreading nuclear arms, the Soviet Government naturally would be compelled to draw a corresponding conclusion and take, with due account for the new situation, measures which would insure the maintenance at a proper level of the security of the Soviet Union, its friends and allies. The Soviet Government is confident that such defensive actions would meet understanding on the part of all states and peoples which cherish the cause of peace.

U.S. representatives present matters in such a way as if the alternative to multinational and multilateral NATO nuclear force is the creation by the German Federal Republic of its own nuclear potential. Well, the inference is that the

United States and its allies even now cannot control the course of the armament of the German Federal Republic and resist pressure and blackmail coming from that country. Therefore, the logical conclusion is that after gaining access to nuclear weapons the militaristic circles of the German Federal Republic would all the more heed no one within NATO.

The genuine alternative to the atomic armament of the German Federal Republic and to any spreading of nuclear weapons is quite different. It is general and complete disarmament under strict international control; the banning of nuclear weapons, including their removal from national armaments and destruction of their stockpiles; dismantling of foreign military bases; and discontinuation of nuclear test explosions of all kinds for all time.

It is elimination—by agreement between the sides—of the remnants of World War II, and the conclusion of a German peace treaty, with the normalization of the situation in West Berlin on this basis. It is the taking of measures to ease international tension and to increase trust among states, and, as the first measures among these, the signing of a nonaggression pact between the NATO and the Warsaw Pact countries. The realization of each of these proposals and, all the more, of all of them together would strengthen the foundations of peace on earth.

The Soviet Government urges the Government of the United States to contribute also to the settlement of the indicated problems and to stop by joint efforts the nuclear missile arms race. The Soviet Union is for the settlement at a conference table of questions put to the fore by the development of international relations.

The Soviet Government would like to hope that the U.S. Government will treat with due attention the considerations advanced in the present note.

The Government of the United States to the Government of the Soviet Union, 18 May 1963[1]

The Embassy of the United States of America presents its compliments to the Ministry of Foreign Affairs of the U.S.S.R. and has the honor to refer to the Ministry's Note of April 8, 1963,[2] which sets forth views of the Soviet Government in connection with plans now under discussion in the North Atlantic Treaty Organization relating to evolution in the organization of nuclear defense forces of NATO.

The Soviet Government, in the course of its observations, makes a series of groundless charges concerning the measures which the free countries of Europe and North America have been obliged to take to protect their security. It characterizes these actions as lacking in justification, as increasing the threat of outbreak of thermonuclear war, and as nullifying in advance any progress in the field of disarmament negotiations.

The United States rejects these charges. It is important to recall once again the need to judge the activities of NATO in the light of the circumstances which gave birth to the Western Alliance and of its purely defensive character, both in conception and in fact. The facts of postwar history show incontrovertibly that NATO came into being in 1949 as a free and spontaneous effort among the free

---

[1] *D.S.B.*, 3 June 1963, pp. 860–2.   [2] See pp. 190–7 above.

countries of Europe in association with the United States and Canada to organize jointly their self-defense. The motivation of these countries was to insure that they would avoid the fate of those nations which, in the period before NATO was organized, fell one by one under Soviet domination. Since that time, the countries of Western Europe and NATO have successfully preserved their freedom and national independence without changing the purely defensive and unaggressive character of the Alliance.

The United States believes that the NATO Alliance has both the right and the responsibility to insure the continued preservation of the freedom and independence of its members. This right and this responsibility includes the maintenance of the modern armaments required to counter any threat from a nation or nations possessing similar armaments. The United States rejects any implication that an alliance including countries of Europe which are within striking reach of hundreds of Soviet nuclear missiles and nuclear-equipped aircraft should be denied similar forces. It is preposterous to maintain that the Soviet Union should itself be privileged to deploy nuclear weapons in positions which threaten the cities of Western Europe and to hold that reciprocal defensive measures cannot properly be taken by NATO.

NATO's decisions in 1957 to arm itself with nuclear weapons were made only in response to repeated threats by the Soviet Union to use nuclear arms, and in the face of tremendous efforts of the Soviet Government to build up its armory of nuclear weapons and missiles. The Soviet Government has since not given any indication that it intends to slow down its buildup of nuclear strength and has continued its unwarranted and dangerous threats to use its nuclear potential and to destroy the NATO countries. To cite but one example, the United States draws the attention of the Soviet Government to the speech made by its Minister of Defense Marshal Malinovsky on the occasion of the 45th Anniversary of the Soviet Army on February 22, 1963.[1] His speech is one example of the justification for the efforts of the NATO countries to build up their defensive strength in order to safeguard peace and to protect their freedom. The Note of the Soviet Government seems to imply that only the Soviet Union has the right to build up its military and in particular its nuclear strength while corresponding efforts of the NATO countries to improve their defensive potential are a 'threat to world peace' and an expression of the 'policy of cold war'. It is obvious that the United States cannot accept such an argument, which is contrary to the professed desire of the Soviet Government to establish relations of trust and mutual confidence with the NATO countries.

The statements in the Soviet Note concerning the policy of the United States on the question of nuclear weapons are as baseless as the charges concerning Western defense measures in general. The United States has steadfastly opposed the spread of nuclear weapons to the ownership of individual nations and has taken numerous steps to prevent such a development in the context of disarmament negotiations, defense policy and international cooperation in the peaceful uses of atomic energy. Unfortunately, United States efforts to reduce the possibilities of war by accident or error pursued in disarmament negotiations have so far been for the most part rebuffed by the U.S.S.R., although the United States is encouraged by Soviet acceptance of the proposal for a direct communi-

[1] *S.W.B.*, SU/1184, 25 February 1963, c/1–c/10.

cations link.[1] Attempts to organize safeguards on atomic programs through the International Atomic Energy Agency have been rejected by the U.S.S.R. However, as regards steps for reducing the risks of war which can be taken unilaterally by the United States and its partners in defense, the most stringent safeguards have been instituted against the unauthorized or accidental use of nuclear weapons and ensure responsible control over atomic weapons at all times.

All defense programs with which the United States has been or will be associated, whether within NATO or any other free world alliance, are wholly consistent with these long-standing objectives. The Soviet Government has raised the question of the multilateral force which is now under discussion within NATO. Such a force would be fully consistent with the objective of preventing the development of new national nuclear weapons programs. Such a force would be multilaterally owned and manned and not at the disposal of any one government. The organization of such a force would tend to prevent, rather than encourage, the proliferation of independent nuclear capabilities. It would be subject to the same safeguards as other NATO nuclear forces to prevent its use in an unauthorized or accidental manner. In this connection it is necessary to clarify that, contrary to the Soviet charges, vessels would not be 'disguised' as merchant ships. They would be warships, in law and in fact, clearly identified as part of the Western defensive armory and no attempt would be made to camouflage these vessels as commercial ships.

The United States notes that the Soviet Union has once again made a series of unrestrained and unfounded accusations against the Federal Republic of Germany, whose democratic, freely elected government has joined with the other free nations in collective self defense. The defense framework of the Federal Republic has been conceived and executed within the framework of NATO and is designed for the sole purpose of contributing to the Atlantic Alliance's defensive requirements to meet any possible threat to members of the Alliance. All objective observers understand that tensions and dangers in Europe do not result from the policies of the Federal Republic but, rather, from the unnatural division of Germany which is manifested in its most grotesque and inhuman form by the wall through the center of Berlin; and from the refusal of the Soviet Government to agree to grant to the German people their inherent right of self-determination. It is to the correction of these injustices that the Soviet Government should devote itself, if it genuinely seeks a normalization of the situation in Central Europe.

The Soviet Government lists a number of problems in whose settlement it professes interest. The opportunities open to the Soviet Government to demonstrate a genuine willingness to achieve equitable solutions to international problems are manifold. To cite but one example: An agreement on a treaty to end the testing of nuclear weapons would have a profound effect on the international scene, would contribute materially to the slowing up of the arms race, and to the prevention of the further spread of nuclear weapons. Other fully practical steps to reduce the risk of war could be taken without delay along with the establishment of a direct communication link. The United States for its part will persevere in its efforts for progress in disarmament and a nuclear test ban.

The United States and its allies cannot and will not be diverted by threats from

[1] See pp. 164–6 above.

taking all steps necessary to safeguard their security. At the same time, the United States remains determined to pursue all paths which offer promise of reducing tension and of enlarging the prospects of peace.

Speech by President Kennedy in the Rudolph Wilde Platz, Berlin, 26 June 1963[1]

I am proud to come to this city as the guest of your distinguished Mayor, who has symbolized throughout the world the fighting spirit of West Berlin. And I am proud to visit the Federal Republic with your distinguished Chancellor who for so many years has committed Germany to democracy and freedom and progress, and to come here in the company of my fellow American, General Clay, who has been in this city during its great moments of crisis and will come again if ever needed.

Two thousand years ago the proudest boast was '*civis Romanus sum*.' Today, in the world of freedom, the proudest boast is '*Ich bin ein Berliner*.'

I appreciate my interpreter translating my German!

There are many people in the world who really don't understand, or say they don't, what is the great issue between the free world and the Communist world. Let them come to Berlin. There are some who say that communism is the wave of the future. Let them come to Berlin. And there are some who say in Europe and elsewhere we can work with the Communists. Let them come to Berlin. And there are even a few who say that it is true that communism is an evil system, but it permits us to make economic progress. *Lass' sie nach Berlin kommen*. Let them come to Berlin.

Freedom has many difficulties and democracy is not perfect, but we have never had to put a wall up to keep our people in, to prevent them from leaving us. I want to say, on behalf of my countrymen, who live many miles away on the other side of the Atlantic, who are far distant from you, that they take the greatest pride that they have been able to share with you, even from a distance, the story of the last 18 years. I know of no town, no city, that has been besieged for 18 years that still lives with the vitality and the force, and the hope and the determination of the city of West Berlin. While the wall is the most obvious and vivid demonstration of the failures of the Communist system, for all the world to see, we take no satisfaction in it, for it is, as your Mayor has said, an offense not only against history but an offense against humanity, separating families, dividing husbands and wives and brothers and sisters, and dividing a people who wish to be joined together.

What is true of this city is true of Germany—real, lasting peace in Europe can never be assured as long as one German out of four is denied the elementary right of free men, and that is to make a free choice. In 18 years of peace and good faith, this generation of Germans has earned the right to be free, including the right to unite their families and their nation in lasting peace, with good will to all people. You live in a defended island of freedom, but your life is part of the main. So let me ask you, as I close, to lift your eyes beyond the dangers of today, to the hopes of tomorrow, beyond the freedom merely of this city of Berlin, or your country of Germany, to the advance of freedom everywhere, beyond the wall to the day of peace with justice, beyond yourselves and ourselves to all mankind.

[1] *Public Papers, 1963*, pp. 524–5.

Freedom is indivisible, and when one man is enslaved, all are not free. When all are free, then we can look forward to that day when this city will be joined as one and this country and this great Continent of Europe in a peaceful and hopeful globe. When that day finally comes, as it will, the people of West Berlin can take sober satisfaction in the fact that they were in the front lines for almost two decades.

All free men, wherever they may live, are citizens of Berlin, and, therefore, as a free man, I take pride in the words '*Ich bin ein Berliner.*'

Statement by the First Vice Chairman on the Council of Ministers of the German Democratic Republic, Willi Stoph, to the People's Chamber, 14 November 1963[1] (extract)

. . . In conversations with parliamentarians and other influential people from NATO countries who in ever increasing numbers visit the GDR, the need for normalising the relations of their countries with our Republic has repeatedly been emphasised. The necessary first step towards this aim would have been the ending of the practice of restricting travel facilities for GDR citizens and of impeding international co-operation, especially in the cultural and scientific fields, by the arbitrary measures of the so-called Allied Travel Agency in West Berlin, an agency influenced by the Bonn Government and directed by occupation officers.

The Bonn Government is constantly clamouring for unrestricted travel while preventing it by its own actions. Is it not a fact that the world-renowned Berliner Ensemble was unable to perform in NATO countries? Is it not a fact that it was made impossible for GDR representatives to attend international conferences in NATO countries? Is it not a fact that Bonn quarters prevented big West German enterprises from exhibiting at the Leipzig Fair, and that West German businessmen who attended the Leipzig Fair are being discriminated against, which is clearly an infringement of the existing trade arrangements between the GDR and the West German Federal Republic? Anyone organising such obstructions is an enemy of peaceful co-operation and of unrestricted travel. Bonn's demands that the NATO partners should tighten up the policy of embargo towards the socialist countries and place obstacles in the way of normal trade show who is the trouble-maker in Europe. Our only comment on this is: although this policy interferes with peaceful international co-operation, the attempt thereby to impair economic development in the socialist States is doomed to failure.

Even though the Bonn Foreign Minister Schroeder is aware of this, he had the nerve at a press conference in Tokyo to couple the development of trade relations with socialist countries with the demand for political concessions;[2] in other words, he intends to make trade a means of political intervention in the domestic affairs of socialist countries. These attempts at blackmailing the socialist countries of Eastern and South-East Europe will fail, as did the attempts to blackmail the GDR. Bonn in one breath propagates embargo measures and speaks of the normalisation of trade relations between Western Germany and some socialist countries. We welcome all steps towards normalising relations

[1] *S.W.B.*, EE/1406, 16 November 1963, c/6–c/14.
[2] For an account see *Süddeutsche Zeitung*, 8 November 1963.

between Western Germany and socialist countries. We must point out, however, that West German authoritative quarters have said that they would like to use the establishment of trade missions in socialist States for purposes which have nothing in common with trade linking nations. They therefore continue to refuse to establish diplomatic relations with these countries.

In view of the efforts to establish international relations between Western Germany and East and South-East European socialist States, we ask what reasons exist for not establishing normal trade and economic relations between the GDR and European capitalist countries as well? Why cannot GDR trade missions be set up, for instance, in London, Paris and Rome, and vice versa— British, French and Italian trade missions in the GDR capital, Berlin. Would not these be highly practical steps, beneficial to all sides, towards an understanding and an international detente? We quite appreciate the views of British, French, Italian and other businessmen who regard the application of the notorious Hallstein doctrine to economic co-operation as an attempt by the Bonn Government to impair trade between their countries and the GDR. They should no longer tolerate this interference by the West German Government in their domestic affairs, and, in their own interest, they should press their governments to establish normal, economic, cultural and political relations between our States.

In the view of the Government, the time has come to admit the sovereign GDR as an equal member to the UN and, where this has not already been done, to other international organisations. It is all the more urgent to implement this demand since the GDR is the State of peace and justice on German soil. The GDR is the rightful German State because it has, in full accord with the Potsdam Agreement, exterminated militarism and fascism once and for all, because it has made peace the supreme principle of its policy and consistently works for peaceful coexistence, because it aims at friendly relations on a basis of equality with all States and stands for an anti-imperialist, anti-colonial policy.

I assure this House that the Government of the GDR will likewise in future use all its strength for a further normalisation of international relations on the basis of the principles of peaceful coexistence. We welcome the fact that the new peace initiative of the USSR and other socialist States has produced initial successes. The Government's appraisal of the results so far is a realistic and sober one. It is aware that the road to lasting peace in the world is a difficult one and that persistent efforts are needed to remove the still existing obstacles.

Our peace policy is reflected in the fact that the GDR was one of the first States to sign the Moscow treaty on the banning of nuclear tests in the atmosphere, in outer space and under water.[1] This treaty is of considerable importance not only for the life and health of the peoples; it is a first step towards an understanding about further international problems. The attempt made by the West German Government to discriminate against the GDR in connection with the signing of the Moscow treaty has failed. On the contrary, Bonn's intrigues against our policy of peace have further strengthened the word-wide awareness of the Bonn Government's hostile attitude to conciliation. The West German Government could not and cannot change the fact that the GDR is an equal party to the Moscow treaty, with all the rights and duties that flow from this circumstance.

[1] See pp. 170–2 above.

The GDR Government has also welcomed the resolution passed by the 18th session of the UN General Assembly about the banning of the dispatch of nuclear weapons into outer space, and has conveyed its statement of approval to the UN.

The GDR regards the renunciation, by both German States, of nuclear weapons, and the accession of the two States to a zone free of nuclear weapons in Central Europe as an important issue affecting peace in Europe and throughout the world. The proposals repeatedly submitted to the West German Government that both German States should renounce nuclear weapons remain fully valid. We suggest that both German States and West Berlin should undertake neither to produce nor acquire nuclear weapons of any kind, and not to strive for the control, or a share in the control, of nuclear weapons. Other States should pledge themselves to respect the two German States as well as West Berlin as zones free of nuclear weapons, and never to use nuclear weapons against them.

The Council of Ministers of our Republic has noted with interest that official circles in the USA and Britain have stated their agreement in principle to the establishment of zones free of nuclear weapons in Latin America and Africa.[1] This is gratifying. But we are asking the gentlemen in Washington and London: If you do not object in principle to zones free of nuclear weapons why, then, do you oppose the creation of such a zone in Central Europe, at the place where the two big military groupings meet directly, and where therefore a zone free of nuclear weapons would be of special importance for obviating the threat of nuclear war?

The GDR is emphatically in favour of the conclusion of the non-aggression pact between the NATO and Warsaw Treaty States,[2] and of measures to prevent surprise attacks. The Government once again declares its willingness to make an effective contribution towards the implementation of the German people's duty never again to threaten its neighbours or world peace. At the same time we remind the Governments of the USA, Britain and France of this solemn pledge they gave in the Potsdam Agreement. We are ready to take part in negotiations for the conclusion of agreements which would form further steps on the road to general, complete and controlled disarmament. Such steps could be: reduction in military expenditure and an armaments stop, reduction in the number of foreign troops both in West German and GDR territory; the dispatch of Soviet representatives to the troops of the Western Powers stationed in Western Germany, and of Western representatives to the USSR troops stationed in GDR territory; the setting up of ground control posts at airports, railway junctions, long-distance roads, and big harbours, for the purpose of preventing surprise attacks.

Esteemed deputies, in its policy towards Western Germany the GDR is guided by the national interests of our people. As Comrade Walter Ulbricht, First Secretary of the SED Central Committee and Chairman of the State Council, pointed out recently, the seven-point programme for an agreement of common sense and goodwill between the two German States, which he had made, and the proposals for the setting up of joint commissions of representatives of the two Governments continue to stand in full.

---

[1] See pp. 161–2 above and pp. 447–8 below.   [2] See pp. 157–8 above.

The proposals made by the GDR have met with a wide international echo. It is a sign of increasing good sense if ever more personages of public life, even in NATO countries, are freeing themselves from unrealistic ideas and are beginning to appraise the situation in Germany more soberly. This is borne out by the contents of the final declaration of the Brussels colloquium on the peaceful settlement of the German question.[1] Like our own proposals, these resolutions contain the fundamental idea of promoting the solution of the German question by negotiations and measures to ease tension.

In Western Germany, too, our proposals of common sense and goodwill have met with a positive response from wide sections of the people. The accommodating attitude of the GDR and its readiness for an understanding have been emphasised and the possibility of ending the cold war in this way and of beginning to normalise relations has been underlined.

The efforts of the peace forces have encountered the stubborn resistance of the most aggressive imperialist quarters, especially in Western Germany, in France and also in the USA. They want at all cost to continue and even intensify the cold war and the arms race. Just as the West German Government tried in vain, together with the French axis partner, to sabotage the Moscow treaty with its ban on most nuclear weapon tests, so it is now trying with the help of the EEC and NATO to block any further process of relaxing tension.

In the Government statement made in Bonn in connection with the change in the Chancellorship an effort was made to show, at least in words, respect for the wish of the peoples for a relaxation of tension and disarmament. But what is one to make of words which are not in harmony with the actions? The Erhard Government, like the Adenauer Government, has set itself the task of gaining control, by every means available, over nuclear weapons through the NATO multilateral nuclear force,[2] or of obtaining possession of weapons of mass destruction through the pact with de Gaulle.[3] The Bonn ultras are using the plan for a nuclear Europe to counter-balance America's nuclear monopoly in NATO so as to bring pressure to bear on the USA, and the proposed NATO nuclear force to exert pressure on France, the axis partner.

The plans for Western Germany's participation in a NATO multilateral nuclear force are directed against peace and against a relaxation of tension in Germany, they run counter to the Moscow treaty largely banning nuclear weapon tests. In signing this treaty, the West German Federal Republic, like all other signatories, undertook to work for general and total disarmament. Participation of the West German revanchists in control over nuclear weapons would at the same time be a blow to all efforts for an understanding between the two German States. The participation of Western Germany in a NATO joint nuclear force would be one of the gravest and most disastrous steps among the acts committed to date in violation of the Potsdam Agreement. Should the Western powers yield to the pressure of the West German militarists and grant them a share in the control of nuclear weapons, a dangerous and grave situation would arise.

This becomes particularly evident from the forward strategy proclaimed by the Bonn ultras regarding the socialist States. This strategy conceals nothing other than the old insidious concept of military attack, translated into practice

[1] For text, see *Neues Deutschland*, 15 May 1963.   [2] See pp. 28–31 above.
[3] *Documents, 1962*, pp. 435–8.

by the German imperialists in two world wars. How unscrupulously they act is clearly shown by the latest demarche of the Bundeswehr generals. To make quite certain that the planned war of revenge will be waged as nuclear war right from the beginning, the Bonn Hitlerite generals demand that nuclear weapons should be used at the very start of a warlike conflict. Nothing could underline more strongly our warning—that nuclear weapons in the hands of Hitlerite generals are intended to help unleash atomic war—than this new forward strategy.

The fact alone that the armed forces of the two greatest military alliances in the world are facing one another where the two world systems meet in the heart of Europe is fraught with many dangers for peace. Bonn's plan to station further contingents of NATO troops directly on the State frontier of the GDR and the Czechoslovak Socialist Republic can only be regarded as yet another provocation. It would serve the West German people well if the Federal Government showed more sense of the realities resulting from the international balance of power, and devoted itself at long last to the needed normalisation of the relations between the two German States.

The Bonn rulers should learn the lesson of the events of 13th August 1961 and the end of the Adenauer era. To carry on the dangerous policy of revenge and attempt to conquer the GDR by force is now more futile than ever. Mr. Erhard refers to the division of Germany as an intolerable reality, alleged to be a major cause of tension. Who created this intolerable reality? It was the West German big bourgeoisie, the aggressive forces of German imperialism and militarism who, together with the imperialist Western Powers, in violation of the Potsdam Agreement, against the will of the people and disregarding the national interests of the German people, separated the Western zones from the German body politic.

Mr. Erhard himself has, inasmuch as he was responsible for the introduction of a separate currency in Western Germany in 1948, and as a leading member of the Adenauer Government, actively helped to create the unreality which he, today, calls 'intolerable'. What is in fact intolerable? The West German policy which deepens Germany's division and blocks the road to reunification—that is what is intolerable. Western Germany's nuclear arming is intolerable. The abandonment of the national interests of the Paris Treaties, signed by the West German imperialists—that is intolerable. The foreign occupation of Western Germany and West Berlin—that is intolerable—an occupation which tramples the people's right to self-determination under foot. The dominant position of the militarists and the revanchists in the Bonn State is intolerable. These are the sources that feed international tension and hamper a rapprochement between the two German States.

In the vain endeavour to justify their adventurous foreign political aims, the West German ultras arrogate to themselves the right to place their views of right and wrong above all valid principles of international law. Disregarding realities and all international obligations, they cling to German imperialism's old practice of declaring everything to be wrong which interferes with the policy of revenge and rearmament. For German imperialism there were never any lawful frontiers or a lawful State order in those countries which the imperialists wanted to conquer. The consequences of these notions of law are well known. All peoples and States should pay attention to the fact that these views, which ignore all valid law, are still held in Western Germany. This is borne out by the fact that the fascist and militarist past has not been overcome in Western Germany.

Therefore, removal from the levers of the imperialist power-apparatus in Western Germany of Gestapo men, blood judges, hitlerite generals and others who took an active part in the fascist rule of violence is long overdue. In view of this, it is an insult to all the German victims of Hitler's rule that representatives of that State of wrong-doers should misuse, for purposes of their revanchist policy and outside their own territory, the ruins of the Reichstag building whose conflagration became a signal for terrorism and aggressive war. I wish to emphasise once again in this House that West Berlin is not part of Western Germany, that the Bonn Government possess no rights in or regarding West Berlin, and that it never will have any such rights.

The peaceful future of the German people makes it imperative that the influence of those West German forces which favour an understanding should grow so strong that militarism and revanchism will be pushed back. The people in Bonn like to play the role of champions of the right to self-determination. But is it self-determination when the West German Government, contrary to the declared wishes of the people, endeavours to obtain control over nuclear weapons? Are the demands of the arms kings, which have nothing in common with the self-determination of the working people?

Contrary to the wishes of the German workers, huge sums are being spent on armaments. According to the Bonn Budget estimates for 1964, the armaments budget is to exceed DM.20,000,000,000. This means that one third of total expenditure is to be frittered away on rearmament. Even prominent West German business experts admit that this policy is fraught with danger, and that their economy, however strong and prosperous it may appear, stands on feet of clay and on shaky ground. We understand very well that the West German workers are waxing more and more indignant at the growing arms burden. Rightly do they point out that the policy of military rearmament is tantamount to a policy of social disarmament. In view of this development, what is left of the people's self-determination? The West German rulers stand for the interests of the millionaires and trample under foot the interests of the millions of working people.

Is it not a fact that the West German working class—about 75 per cent of the population—has not one single representative in the Bonn Government. Anyway, what good is all the talk about the right of self-determination if, at the same time, the foreign occupation of Western Germany until the year 2005 is praised as a community of nations? Is it not tantamount to disregarding the West German people's right of self-determination if the Bonn ultras try to frustrate all measures aimed at peace and the relaxation of tension? In Bonn and in the West German papers any possible reduction in the number of occupation troops, even if it is intended on the smallest possible scale, is not welcomed. It is rejected with indignation and the demand is raised, for what is termed psychological reasons, to keep the occupation forces at full strength.

In view of these facts any discussion as to which of the two German States should be described as occupation zone and would like to remain one for a long time to come is superfluous. The West German Government should at least implement the requirement of its own Basic Law, Article 26 of which says that all acts interfering with the peaceful coexistence of nations and aiming at the preparation of an aggressive war are unconstitutional. Emergency legislation does not serve the vital interests of the people. It does not promote the peaceful coexistence of the nations. This requires a law for the protection of peace, similar to those long in existence in the GDR and other socialist States, a law for which the West German people are clamouring on an increasing scale.

While the threat of West German revanchism continues the GDR Government must devote the greatest attention to the strengthening and consolidation of the National People's Army and the constant enhancement of its readiness for defence in the interest of the safeguarding of the most elementary right of every citizen to a life in peace and security. It will provide the funds necessary to enable the National People's Army, in common with the fraternal armies of the Warsaw Treaty States, to discharge its duties in the defence of peace. Similar attention will be devoted to the armed organs of the Ministry of the Interior and the work of the Ministry of State Security for the protection of internal order and the security of the citizens of the GDR.

We are certain that all members of our armed organs will make great efforts to acquire great military and technical knowledge and that they will honourably discharge the national duty they owe to our worker-peasant State.

Esteemed Deputies, the Government has repeatedly stated its views on the anomalous situation in West Berlin. While everywhere in the world the national forces are making a stand against imperialist foreign rule and imperialist military bases, Herr Brandt, a zealous administrator of the NATO base of West Berlin, clings to the occupation regime and regards the presence of occupation forces and his subordination to their command as a special mark of freedom. Leaning on the occupiers, the West Berlin ruling circles are waging the cold war against the GDR. The maintenance of the imperialist foreign rule and the revanchist policy are the chief sources of the threat to peace emanating from West Berlin.

In recent weeks we have witnessed various attempts by Western quarters to disturb the beginning detente by provocative acts on GDR routes of communication. As regards these incidents it must be stated that West Berlin lies in GDR territory and that all routes of communication from and to West Berlin are part of GDR territory. These routes of communication therefore come exclusively under GDR jurisdiction which is not altered by the fact that our Government has temporarily transferred to the Soviet troops stationed in the GDR the control of the transit traffic of the Western Powers' troops still stationed in West Berlin. In accordance with the generally acknowledged rules of international law, transit traffic on GDR routes of communication proceeds according to our laws and regulations. The champions of the cold war and of revenge in Bonn should note that they have no business here.

Now that more than two years have passed since the anti-fascist protective wall was built it is more obvious than ever that that measure saved peace. Thanks to the resolute and level-headed conduct of the GDR Government and of the other Warsaw Treaty States the aggressive policy of the West Berlin and West German ruling circles was dealt a hard blow.

However, the West Berlin Senate has not as yet drawn the necessary conclusions from the failure of its policy that is hostile to an understanding with the GDR. It is in fact irresponsibly conducting a campaign of incitement against the

GDR State frontier. In so doing the West Berlin politicians do not shrink from the nonsensical argument that it was impossible to negotiate with the GDR Government on the ground that it had built the wall.

In fact, the West Berlin Senate did not seek an understanding with the GDR Government before 13th August either. The protective measures, necessary in the interest of peace and the security of the West Berliners, among others, created various personal problems for a number of citizens. Many of these problems could be resolved if the West Berlin Senate were to discontinue its cold-war policy against the GDR. Anyone trying to create the illusions that the GDR could be ignored and holes could be knocked into the wall is embarking on a dangerous road. To follow it amounts to making the violation of international law a principle of policy. Does the West Berlin Senate realise the danger of the road which it has chosen? The saying, He who lives on an island should not make the sea his enemy, still holds good.

I cannot help saying a few words in this context about the demagogy practised by West Berlin politicians in the matter of transit traffic through GDR territory from and to West Berlin. On the one hand, these people applaud, if, with the help of the illegal so-called Allied Travel Board in West Berlin, which is based on the long obsolete occupation regime, the free movement of GDR citizens to NATO countries is either hampered or prevented. On the other hand, they demand what is termed free access to West Berlin. In 1962, travellers passing through the GDR in transit from West Berlin to Western Germany and vice versa exceeded 8,500,000.

In September 1963 alone, nearly 700,000 transit travellers passed along on the railways and roads of the territory of the GDR. In 1962, the German Reich Railway, inland vessels and motor vehicles carried to and from West Berlin 9,925,000 tons of goods. In May 1963 alone, goods moved by these means totalled 1,021,000 tons.

These few facts speak a convincing language. The whole world ought to take note of them. Let people imagine what would happen if we behaved exactly like the West German Government, the West Berlin Senate and the illegally existing so-called Allied Travel Bureau in West Berlin. Everyone can see what effects this would have on travel to and from West Berlin.

It is therefore, first and foremost, in the interest of West Berliners that their Senate should respond to the repeatedly proclaimed willingness of the GDR and conclude normal treaties with the GDR Government about transit traffic by GDR road, rail, water and air routes from and to West Berlin. During the last few months members of the foreign occupation forces, especially of the USA, who drove into the GDR capital have infringed our laws. In conformity with the wholly justified indignation of our population, the GDR Government will no longer allow members of the occupation forces of the three Western Powers stationed in West Berlin, when driving in the GDR capital, to endanger the lives and safety of our citizens by illegal acts and like rowdies lay violent hands on socialist property and provocatively damage or steal flags of our Republic.

In the name of freedom, of the right of self-determination, and of the national dignity of the German nation we demand that an end be put to imperialist alien rule of NATO Powers in West Berlin. The transformation of West Berlin into a demilitarised, neutral, free city serves first and foremost the safeguarding of the peaceful life of the West Berlin population. The Council of Ministers will continue to advocate that the dangerous centre of tension, West Berlin, is further contained. We are in favour of the peaceful settlement of all questions and of the normalisation of relations by means of negotiation between competent representatives of the GDR Government and the Senate of West Berlin.

Our proposals are well known to Herr Brandt and to the members of the West Berlin Senate. We have named our commissioners for the negotiations. It is now for the West Berlin side to take at long last the requisite steps. . . .

Statement by the British Secretary of State for Foreign Affairs, Mr. Butler, to the House of Commons, 15 November 1963[1] (extract)

. . . I want to go at some length into the prospects of East–West relations. We find general support for our view that it would be valuable to probe for further progress in resolving, at any rate in the first place, the peripheral problems between the Soviet Union and ourselves. I must make clear that the discussions with the Soviet Union are subject to three conditions of the highest importance. The first is that the West can agree to nothing which would have the result of upsetting the military balance to our disadvantage. Our very survival may be at stake here.

Secondly, no agreements can be reached with the East and no negotiations conducted which are likely to impair the cohesion of the Western Alliance, for unless the Alliance remains clearly united it cannot fulfil its prime function of deterring aggression. And the unity of the Alliance could not survive the suspicion that the interests of its members were not being fully considered.

Thirdly, the Western position in West Berlin and the objective of self-determination for the East Germans are of vital interest to the free nations.

Negotiation does not imply one-sided concessions, nor could agreement be ever reached which was at the expense of the vital interest of any member of the Alliance. These three conditions impose the need for the fullest possible inter-allied consultation as a basis for all negotiations with the Soviet Union. The Soviet Union's fundamental aims remain unchanged, and we must recognise that.

In attempting to judge the future, it may be valuable if for a moment we get a clear idea of what the nuclear Test Ban Treaty[2] signifies and what it does not. It is an important and valuable measure in itself, and all credit goes to the ex-Prime Minister and the ex-Foreign Secretary and others who did so much in the international scene to make this possible. Its signatories can no longer pollute the atmosphere. It should make it more difficult for nuclear weapons to spread to countries which do not possess them at present. Although it is not a measure of disarmament I think that it prevents yet another spiral of costly competition.

We cannot be sure of Soviet motives in deciding to conclude the Treaty but, as the right hon. Gentleman for Smethwick said, it seems that during the Cuban crisis they were brought face to face with the full dangers of trying by sudden means to alter the strategic situation between East and West. In passing, in reply to the right hon. Gentleman the Member for Smethwick in relation to Cuba, I

---

[1] *H.C. deb.*, vol. 684, cc. 505–10.   [2] For the text of the treaty, see pp. 170–2 above.

should say that I was very close to my right hon. Friend the Member for Bromley (Mr. H. Macmillan) throughout these discussions, and I think that the right hon. Gentleman gravely underestimates our influence and contact during the course of the Cuba crisis. The strength of our voice, through the decision on policy and weapons which we had already adopted, was clear, in contra-distinction to the right hon. Gentleman and his friends.

The Soviets have come to see that high-risk policies only have the effect of strengthening Western will and defence capability. Besides this, there is a serious conflict of priorities on the use of Soviet resources. There are agricultural problems and increasingly powerful consumer and investment demands. Mr. Khrushchev himself has spoken about these problems.

It is also possible to speculate about other factors. Certainly the quarrel with China had gone so far that there was nothing to be lost by an agreement with the West. Indeed from the point of view of the other Communist parties there were advantages to be gained from having something to show for the policy of peaceful coexistence. Since the signature in Moscow and in subsequent discussions with the representatives of the Soviet Government, we have encountered a greater readiness to listen to the Western case even when they have disagreed.

Unfortunately the Soviet military on the Berlin Autobahn have not shown the same reasonable spirit. Since 10th October three American military convoys and one British military convoy have been held up for long periods because Soviet checkpoint officers tried to introduce new and more stringent procedures. Eventually the Russians dropped their demands and the convoys went through.

We trust and hope that there will be no more such incidents. I should like to make clear that there is no need for incidents, since the established procedures are well known to both sides and have not been changed by us. If the Soviet military do not make more difficulties we shall be forced to wonder whether the Soviet Government intend to cause renewed tension over Berlin despite the more hopeful signs elsewhere. I trust therefore that there will be no more incidents. In any case, we shall continue to work in close consultation and concert with our allies.

Mr. Arthur Henderson (Rowley Regis and Tipton): In view of the statements made from the Russian side, disputing the factual basis of established procedures, is there not something to be said for the Government publishing a short statement setting out exactly what was agreed upon in these established procedures?

Mr. Butler: We have already explained in a Note to the Soviet Government what are called the harmonised procedures of the allies in relation to convoys on the *Autobahn*.[1] Certainly every consideration will be given to everything said by the right hon. and learned Gentleman, but I cannot go further than that at this moment.

Against the background of the factors which I have described, it may be possible to discover other areas of agreement besides the Treaty. At least the question can now be raised, and that is already an important advance. There are two topics of particular interest as subjects for possible future agreements, such as the stationing of observer posts in the area of N.A.T.O. and the Warsaw

[1] For text see *D.S.B.*, 25 November 1963, p. 818. Identical notes were delivered by the British, French and United States Embassies in Moscow on 6 November 1963.

Pact, and a non-dissemination agreement. There has been already considerable discussion about these matters.

If observation posts under proper conditions could be set up over a wide area, stretching from the U.S.S.R. on one side to the United States on the other, there would be some gain to our security, but it is in the political and psychological aspects that the advantages would be greatest. An agreement would enable the nations in these two military alliances to have more confidence in the intentions of the other side, and it would help to diminish the fears which undoubtedly exist about the dangers of conventional attack in Europe.

I believe that such an agreement would be very useful. But, so far, the Soviet Government have insisted upon linking this subject with other measures, such as the thinning out of forces in Central Europe. They know this to be unacceptable and this illustrates some of the difficulty in concluding an agreement on observation posts, but I hope that the Russians will come to see its advantages.

Another possibility is a non-dissemination agreement by which the nuclear Powers would undertake not to allow control of nuclear weapons or nuclear knowledge to pass into the hands of third countries, and non-nuclear countries would undertake not to manufacture nuclear weapons or otherwise acquire control over them. This again would not alter the balance of power but would forestall the kind of development which might alter it in a most dangerous way. The United Nations Assembly unanimously adopted a Resolution in this sense as long ago as 1961,[1] and the time seems to us to have come to put it into formal effect.

There are therefore two possibilities. A suggestion of a different character which has been raised is a non-aggression agreement. This would not, of course, contain any new obligation which is not contained in the United Nations Charter. It would be important that any arrangement involving the members of N.A.T.O. and the signatories of the Warsaw Pact should not appear to enhance the position of the East German authorities or endanger the position of Germany and Europe.

It is not quite clear how far non-aggression should be related to the Berlin problem. I have in mind that the Western Powers must always be concerned with the possibility that the freedom and viability of Berlin could be undermined by acts on the Communist side which could not be classified as aggression. There may be some way round this difficulty and efforts to find one are continuing. If these difficulties are surmounted, then non-aggression arrangements might make their contribution towards the relaxation of tension which we are now seeking.

I have deliberately given the House some indication of some of the problems for negotiation. It would be wrong to raise false hopes. The Russians are stubborn negotiators and these are difficult matters, but I think we may draw encouragement from the fact that the United States of America and the Soviet Union have agreed not to place weapons of mass destruction in outer space, an agreement which has been welcomed and endorsed by the General Assembly of the United Nations.

In response to what the right hon. Gentleman said at the start of his speech, we intend to pursue the 18-Power Disarmament Conference in Geneva, and we shall

[1] U.N. doc. A/RES/1665, 4 December 1961; *G.A.O.R.*, Sixteenth Session, Supplement No. 17 (A/5100), pp. 5–6.

continue to urge forward an examination and further progress of what is called the American plan in relation to the Soviet plan. I have listened to what the right hon. Gentleman said about the importance of the Foreign Secretary himself taking an interest, but I should here like to pay tribute to the work which the Minister of State—who is sitting on my left—has already done, and to his recent speech in New York, in making progress in this matter.

Before I come to some of the military matters referred to by the right hon. Gentleman, I would sum up our attitude to East–West relations and negotiations as follows. Some people fear that this process of discussions with the Soviet Union is in some ways dangerous to the West. Of course it would be so if the West spoke with different voices, but flexibility, which I intend to see should prevail, is not synonymous with weakness. We are determined to uphold the vital interests which the overwhelming military power of the Western Alliance has been created to defend. I hope I shall have the support of the House therefore in further steps which we may take in these or other directions in the months which lie ahead. . . .

C. THE SINO-SOVIET DISPUTE

Speech by the First Secretary of the Central Committee of the Vietnam Workers' Party, Le Duan, on the Anniversary of the death of Karl Marx, 13 March 1963[1] (extracts)

. . . The ultimate aim of the world people's revolutionary struggle is to eradicate imperialism, abolish the capitalist system which is the source of oppression, exploitation and war, and to realize communism and lasting peace throughout the world. To achieve this the people of the world must now *wage a two-pronged anti-imperialist class struggle:* energetically to oppose warlike and aggressive imperialism and defend world peace, and at the same time to wage a determined revolutionary struggle to overthrow imperialism and strive for national liberation, democracy and socialism. The 1960 Moscow Statement[2] says:

> *This situation (of imperialist war-preparation) demands ever closer joint efforts and resolute actions on the part of the socialist countries, the international working class, the national anti-imperialist movement, all peace-loving countries and all peace champions to prevent war and assure a peaceful life for people. It demands the further consolidation of all revolutionary forces in the fight against imperialism, for national independence, and for socialism.*

The policies of war and aggression of imperialism, headed by U.S. imperialism, have confronted mankind with a grave danger of a new world war in which nuclear weapons will be used. Therefore, peace has become the urgent demand of millions. The *urgent task* of the people of all countries at present is to defend world peace. Moreover, since a practical possibility of preventing imperialism from launching a new world war has now appeared, people all over the world must energetically carry on the struggle and exert every effort to make this

---

[1] Le Duan, *On Some Present International Problems* (Hanoi, 1964), pp. 57–122.
[2] Text in *Documents, 1960*, pp. 222–38.

possibility a reality. The 1960 Moscow Statement points out, '*The communist parties regard the fight for peace as their prime task.*'

While we must perceive that there is a practical possibility of preventing a world war, we must also see that only through the persistent struggles of all peace forces against bellicose imperialism can this possibility be turned into a reality. On the other hand, while we must be fully aware of the grave danger resulting from imperialism's intensified preparations for a world war, we must also fully see that there are powerful forces for preventing war so that we may steadfastly develop and consolidate these forces and not weaken the fighting will of the masses. Only when we clearly and correctly realize both aspects and make the people of all countries realize them likewise, will we be able to arouse them to oppose all imperialist plots of war and aggression and defend and consolidate world peace with full confidence, determination and courage.

If the struggle against bellicose imperialism in the interest of world peace is an urgent task of the world's people, then the revolutionary struggle which aims at uprooting imperialism and striving for national liberation, democracy and socialism is also an *immediate, urgent task* of all peoples. These two struggles are closely related and strengthen each other. To conduct a revolution to overthrow imperialism is to weaken it step by step and to make it increasingly difficult for imperialism to carry out its plots for a world war. In this way the revolutionary movements in countries under the capitalist system, especially the sweeping national-liberation movements in Asia, Africa and Latin America, are making positive contributions to the defence of world peace. President Ho Chi Minh said:

> Peoples of colonial and semi-colonial countries are waging liberation wars and those who have just freed themselves from colonialist rule are taking action to safeguard their sovereignty and territorial integrity. They are people who are directly weakening imperialism and colonialism. This is a big force in the defence of world peace. Therefore, the peace movement must be closely bound to the movement for national independence.[1]

The revolutionary struggle to overthrow imperialism is tied up not only with the struggle to preserve and consolidate peace and democracy today but also with the fight for lasting peace. The source of war is imperialism. So long as imperialism exists, there exists the danger of war. And the danger of war can be finally removed and everlasting peace on earth realized only by carrying on revolution to destroy imperialism, at first piecemeal, then completely. Therefore whether from an immediate or long-term point of view, the revolutionary struggle, instead of being opposed to the fight in defence of world peace, strongly promotes it. In turn, the fight for world peace will augment the forces against imperialism and multiply its difficulties, thus creating favourable conditions for the triumph of the revolutionary struggle aiming at wiping out imperialism.

With the two systems of socialism and capitalism existing at the same time, *peaceful co-existence* between countries with different social systems is an objective necessity. Peaceful co-existence is a form of class struggle between socialism and capitalism and is part of the struggle against the imperialist warmongers and for the defence of world peace. Peaceful coexistence conforms

[1] Ho Chi Minh, *Selected Works* (FLPH, Hanoi, 1962), Vol. IV, p. 320.

to the fundamental interests of the socialist camp, all nations and the whole of progressive mankind. The conditions created by peaceful co-existence will enable the socialist system to demonstrate more and more clearly its superiority in the economic, political, cultural, scientific and technological fields, rapidly enhance its prestige and international influence and make it more and more attractive to working people throughout the world. The realization of peaceful co-existence between countries with different social systems will deepen the contradictions of imperialism, thus creating favourable conditions to spread the class struggle in the capitalist countries and speed up the struggle for national liberation in the colonies and dependent countries. In turn, victory in the revolutionary class struggle and national-liberation struggle will greatly contribute to the realization and consolidation of peaceful co-existence. The struggle for peaceful co-existence between countries of the two systems, the development of the revolutionary movements in capitalist countries and the development of the national-independence movements are closely interrelated and reinforce rather than conflict with one another.

Marxism points out that in the class struggle between the proletariat and the bourgeoisie, the proletariat must carry it out in the economic, political and ideological fields. At the same time, it points out, 'Every class struggle is a political struggle'. The object of the class struggle of the proletariat is to free itself and all other working people from bourgeois oppression and exploitation. To achieve this, the proletariat must first overthrow the rule of the bourgeoisie and establish its own political power. The political struggle, therefore, is essential and decisive. Economic and ideolgical struggle must serve the purpose of bringing about victory in the political struggle.

Today because of the emergence of a new factor—the existence of the socialist camp and nationalist states—*economic struggle* including economic competition between the two systems has become particularly important in the realm of the class struggle. Lenin pointed out that in any socialist revolution the proletariat must complete two tasks: first, to overthrow the bourgeois state power, take power into its own hands, smash the resistance of the exploiting classes and their plots for restoration of power, abolish the system of exploitation of man by man, safeguard the fruits of revolution and oppose external imperialist intervention; and second, to build a new economy as the foundation of a new society. It is the second task that distinguishes the socialist revolution from all previous revolutions in history. After basically fulfilling the first task, the most important work of the proletariat is to build a new economic relationship and perfect it, promote the development of productive forces and create a labour productivity higher than that of capitalism. Following Lenin's teachings, the communist and workers' parties in the socialist countries, having in the main abolished the exploiting classes, regard the task of leading the working people in building a new economy, socialism, and then communism as their primary domestic task. They regard it as the principal sphere of struggle to ensure the complete victory of socialism within the country.

At the same time, the communist and workers' parties of the socialist countries also regard economic struggle as an important realm to wage the class struggle on a world scale. The socialist countries carry out economic construction to ensure economic independence, strengthen national defence and oppose imperialist intervention. They struggle against the imperialists' hostile economic measures, such as the economic blockade and trade embargo. With their own economic achievements they exert influence on and help the revolutionary struggles of the countries in the capitalist world. The more advanced the economic construction of the socialist camp, the more effectively can the superiority of socialism and communism over capitalism be demonstrated. This will increasingly convince the people of the capitalist world and inspire them to carry out active struggles to overthrow monopoly capitalism and colonialism and build a new life on socialist principles. With its great economic power, the socialist camp also helps the under-developed countries build their own economy and shake off the imperialist yoke.

The people of the nationalist states also regard economic struggle, the building of their own economy and opposition to imperialist measures of economic oppression as an important field of struggle against imperialism.

We communists, however, maintain that economic struggle is only one aspect of the international class struggle at present, which remains primarily a political struggle. The reason is obvious. The struggle carried on by imperialism headed by the United States against the socialist camp and the people of all countries is primarily a political struggle. Imperialism concentrates its main efforts on all kinds of political means—preparations for world war, provoking local wars, waging 'special warfare', engaging in subversive activities, mass supression, and so on—with the political objective of eradicating the socialist countries, undermining national-liberation movements, stamping out the struggles in the capitalist countries and maintaining and strengthening capitalist rule. The imperialists make economic and ideological struggles serve this political struggle. In order to oppose the plots of imperialism and other reactionary forces, the socialist camp and the people of all countries must wage political, economic and ideological struggles, but the main struggle must be political. They must constantly rely on the strength of the people and must make both economic and ideological struggles serve the needs of the political struggle. The revolutionary struggle in the countries of the capitalist system for national liberation, democracy and socialism is a struggle of the broad masses, its chief aim being to solve the question of state power. The struggle to defend peace is in essence also a class struggle. War is not a natural calamity which strikes mankind like a bolt from the blue. Contrary to the Yugoslav revisionists' claim that the danger of war comes from imperialism and also from socialism, the source of war in fact lies in imperialism, in the policies of imperialism headed by the United States— the policies of war and aggression which aim at the maintenance of the system of exploitation and oppression. President Ho Chi Minh said, '. . . to maintain peace, it is necessary to oppose imperialism.'[1] He also said, 'To defend peace is to oppose war. Everyone knows that it is aggressive imperialism and colonialism with U.S. imperialism at the head that provokes war. Hence imperialism headed by the U.S. must be opposed if war is to be prevented and peace safeguarded.'[2] Consequently, the struggle for peace means to fully expose imperialism, first of all, the policies of war and aggression of U.S. imperialism. In other words, the people's forces throughout the world must be mobilized for a resolute struggle

[1] Ho Chi Minh, Vol. III, p. 225.
[2] Ibid., Vol. IV, p. 320.

against imperialism, particularly the U.S. imperialist policy of war. As the 1960 Moscow Statement points out, peace can be safeguarded and world war prevented only by the joint efforts of the world socialist camp, the international working class, the national-liberation movement, all the countries opposing war and all peace-loving forces.

. . . The 1957 Moscow Declaration[1] and the 1960 Moscow Statement clearly point out that the actual possibility of the one or the other way of transition to socialism in each individual country depends on concrete historical conditions. These documents also say that the working class and its vanguard—the Marxist-Leninist party—seek to achieve the revolution by peaceful means and that under present circumstances in a number of capitalist countries the working class has the opportunity to create the necessary conditions for peaceful realization of the socialist revolution. On the other hand, the Declaration and the Statement say that in the event the exploiting classes resort to violence against the people, the possibility of non-peaceful transition to socialism should be borne in mind.

An important characteristic of the situation today is that the socialist ideal is exerting an influence more far-reaching than ever. The working class and the peasant masses have a high level of political consciousness and high sense of discipline and militancy; the united front against monopoly capital and imperialism is expanding every day; the socialist camp is strong enough to check effectively any intervention by imperialist groups in regions where the working class has risen to seize state power. This has created new, favourable conditions for the working class to seize state power by various means. Another important characteristic of the present situation, however, is that imperialism is distinguished by a maximum and universal development of bureaucracy and militarism. Never before have the exploiting classes wielded such a gigantic apparatus of violence as they do today. In the capitalist countries, some nationalist countries included, there is a growing political tendency towards fascism, towards curbing and abolishing democratic freedoms, and towards military dictatorship. When one speaks of the possibility of the bourgeoisie using violence against the working class, one should always remember that never for a moment does the bourgeoisie fail to use violence in its most naked and brutal forms. Under such conditions, it would be impossible for the working class to seize state power without smashing the apparatus of violence of the bourgeoisie. The only way to destroy this apparatus is for the masses to use revolutionary violence. It should be easy to comprehend that the apparatus of violence of the ruling classes cannot be destroyed unless the revolutionary violence of the masses prevails over the counter-revolutionary violence. That is why the working class and the Marxist-Leninist parties, while seeking to make revolution by peaceful means which is the least painful course, must nevertheless make earnest preparation for *the seizure of power by violence*.

What is the form of revolutionary violence? It may be armed force or political force (in a narrow sense), or a combination of the two. As to what is the most suitable form of violence to be adopted for each country, this question has to be decided by the working class and its vanguard of that country. Whether political or armed force or a combination of the two is used, such forces can be created only when there is a dynamic, surging mass movement on the broadest

[1] *Documents, 1957*, pp. 527–39.

scale and when the vanguard itself is fully determined, and see to it that the masses—including the middle-of-the-roaders as well as the progressives—have full confidence in defeating the enemy, fear no sacrifices, and are always prepared to use whatever form of struggle is necessary to defeat the enemy.

The experience of the revolutionary struggle in the last two decades has proved that unarmed revolutionary masses can create a force greater than the enemy—imperialist and other reactionary cliques—and can destroy its counter-revolutionary violence. As to what will evolve in the forward process and what is the suitable form of struggle, the correct answer to every situation can be found only in actual struggles. The working class and its vanguard of every country can certainly find the answer if they have the full determination to defeat the enemy, if they take the initiative in creating the opportunity instead of passively waiting for it.

While making intensive preparation for violent revolution, it is necessary to actively strive, in the spirit of Lenin's teachings, for *the possibility of peaceful revolution* even when there is one chance in a hundred, regardless of whenever or wherever it may appear.

Which road to take—this is also a question confronting the people of the nationalist states at present. This question concerns not only the destinies of the people of these countries but also the common struggle of the people throughout the world against imperialism and for peace, national independence, democracy and socialism. . . .

Experience has proved that the primary internal condition for a nationalist country to advance along the non-capitalist path is a strong Marxist-Leninist party, and its ability to unite with and lead the broad masses of the peasantry, the largest revolutionary force, to form a solid worker-peasant alliance, and to unite with and lead other patriotic and democratic forces.

Experience has also proved that support and assistance from the socialist camp is an indispensable external condition for the advance of the nationalist countries along the non-capitalist road.

It is a lofty international duty of the socialist countries to support and assist the revolutionary movements of the people of the colonies, dependent countries and all nationalist states.

Socialist countries consistently and strictly adhere to the policy of peaceful co-existence in their relations with the nationalist countries. They resolutely refute the imperialist slanders about the 'export of revolution' and at the same time they expose and resolutely oppose imperialist intervention in the internal affairs of the nationalist states and expose all plots of the old and new colonialists.

The Yugoslav revisionists seek in every way to serve U.S. imperialism and to undermine the revolution of the peoples of the nationalist countries. Exploiting the urgent desire of these peoples to realize socialism, they are advocating a 'new' road, the 'Yugoslav road to socialism', that is a road of class compromise and the abolition of the dictatorship of the proletariat. It is clear to all that in order to seize state power and build socialism, the proletariat and the impoverished peasants must win over the intermediate strata, make them see the road of the class struggle and the proletarian dictatorship and isolate the lackeys of imperialism—the bourgeois reactionaries. However, both the theory and practice of world revolution have proved that the intermediate strata are by nature vacillating and tend to compromise. While they may dislike capitalism and favour socialism at present they dread class struggle and dictatorship of the proletariat. The vicious aims of the Yugoslav revisionists are to dangle as bait a so-called socialism without class struggle and proletarian dictatorship, to prevent the Marxist-Leninist parties from rallying their forces, to lead the intermediate strata away from the struggle for genuine socialism and to induce them to follow the bourgeois reactionaries. Herein lies the greatest danger which the Yugoslav revisionists are creating in the people's revolutionary movements in the nationalist countries. If it is the task of all communist and workers' parties to oppose the Yugoslav revisionists resolutely for the defence of the purity of Marxism-Leninism, for the defence of the 1957 Moscow Declaration and the 1960 Moscow Statement, for a vigorous struggle against imperialism, and for peace, national independence, democracy and socialism, then a thorough exposure of the Yugoslav revisionists is essential to the smooth progress of the people's revolutionary cause in the nationalist countries. . . .

Speech by Mr. Khrushchev on the occasion of the visit of the Cuban Prime Minister, Fidel Castro, Moscow, 23 May 1963[1] (extract)

. . . The Caribbean crisis was one of the most acute collisions between the forces of socialism and imperialism, between the forces of peace and war, in the entire post-war period. The American aggressive circles, preparing an armed invasion of Cuba, believed that the Soviet Union and the other socialist countries would be unable to render effective assistance to the Cuban republic.

The imperialists believed that Cuba's territorial remoteness from the socialist countries would enable them, using their overwhelming military superiority in that area, to attack the Cuban people and destroy its revolutionary gains.

As is known, the American imperialists have quite a good store of experience in suppressing the liberation struggle in Latin America and elsewhere in the world.

The plans of the imperialists to strangle the Cuban revolution were frustrated as a result of the firm position of the government of the Republic of Cuba with Comrade Fidel Castro at its head, the fighting unity of the Cuban people, the military assistance of the Soviet Union and also the mighty political and moral support of the socialist countries, and of all peaceloving peoples, who came forward in a united front in defence of the heroic Island of Freedom.

Because a real danger arose of an armed conflict between two nuclear powers —the Soviet Union and the United States—the crisis over Cuba turned from a local into a world crisis. In these conditions it was necessary to seek a way out of the situation on the basis of a sensible compromise.

Such a result of the Caribbean crisis amounts to the foiling of the plans of the American militarists. The unity and cohesion of the peoples, who united to rebuff the most aggressive and adventurous imperialist circles, tied the hands of those who, for their own selfish ends, were ready to doom millions of people to death and destruction.

It was a victory for the policy of peace, of peaceful co-existence, thanks to

[1] *Soviet News*, 24 May 1963.

which it has been possible to defend the revolutionary gains of the Cuban people, to raise still higher the prestige of the socialist countries, and to ward off the danger of a thermonuclear world war that would have brought incalculable suffering, loss of life and destruction to the peoples of all countries.

One can hear again the voices of 'madmen' in the United States calling for the blockade of, or even armed attack on Cuba. Some senators and some people in the Pentagon speak about the need for a tougher policy vis-à-vis Cuba. All this cannot but put one on one's guard. Can it be that these leaders are again thinking of building up a crisis like the one that took place in the Caribbean last October?

I must say, in all seriousness, that if the government of the United States does not show the necessary common sense and understanding of the situation, and permits itself to be drawn on to a dangerous path, a situation may arise in the world even more formidable than that of last October.

If such a situation is created by the aggressive forces of imperialism, clearly it will be much more difficult to emerge from the crisis than it was in 1962.

A breach of the obligations assumed by the United States could not be regarded otherwise but as perfidy. This would radically undermine trust and therefore make it more difficult to reach agreement. It is clear, therefore, that if the United States does not strictly observe the agreement which was reached, and aggravates the situation, the world may find itself in an even more dangerous situation than during last year's Caribbean crisis.

In that case we should have to discharge our international duty, our obligations to the fraternal Cuban people, and come to its assistance. We must say in all seriousness:

Do not play with fire, Gentlemen, and do not play with the destinies of the peoples!

We consider that the situation in the Caribbean could be normalised on the basis of the implementation of the well-known five points advanced by the Prime Minister of the Revolutionary Government of the Republic of Cuba, Fidel Castro.[1] The just demands of the Cuban people have the support of the Soviet Union, of all the socialist countries, and of all progressive humanity.

Comrades, the most important events that have occurred in the international arena in the post-war period show convincingly that mankind is steadily advancing towards the world-wide victory of communism.

Before our eyes the great forces of our time grow and gain in strength; the world socialist system becomes stronger; the national liberation movement scores ever new successes; the revolutionary struggle of the working class of the capitalist countries is on the upsurge; the movement of all the progressive forces for peace and democracy, for the vital rights of the people, is gaining new strength.

Our Land of the Soviets, the country of Lenin, the country of the great October Revolution, grows ever stronger and makes its contribution to the international cause of the working people of all countries.

We communists rejoice in the growth of all the progressive and all the liberation movements of our time. We wholeheartedly welcomed the wonderful victory of the Algerian people in the struggle against French imperialism, and

[1] See Documents, 1962, pp. 235–6.

the victory of the French miners in the struggle for higher living standards. We rejoice in the victory of the Italian communists in the parliamentary elections, won in a sharp struggle against the forces of reaction.

We rejoice in the achievements of the working people of the United Arab Republic in building the Aswan Dam; we hail the struggle of the people of Angola against the Portuguese colonialists, and the heroism of Portuguese and Spanish revolutionaries who do not spare their lives in the fight against fascism and the omnipotence of the monopolies.

No matter where the fighters for the revolution score a success, be it in Europe, Africa, Asia, or Latin America, all this, in the last analysis, serves the great cause of the liberation of all humanity.

Marxists-Leninists make no secret of the fact that they want to win all the people on the earth for socialism. This we regard as our most important aim on the world arena. But how are we advancing towards this goal?

We are advancing towards it not by unleashing war, not by imposing our system on other peoples. It is by creative labour, by the great constructive force of the liberated peoples, by the revolutionary energy of the working people, that we raise the authority of socialism and steadily change the balance of forces in the world.

We proceed from Lenin's proposition that, after the winning of power, the problems of economic construction come to the forefront for the Communist Party and for the people, that by our economic successes in the construction of socialism we shall decisively influence world development. The quicker the productive forces of the socialist countries develop, the higher their economic potential rises, the more confidently and successfully the struggle of the working people against capitalist oppression will develop.

Marxists-Leninists believe that the question of the victory of a new social system is decided in class struggle by the proletariat, by the toiling masses, by the people of each country.

This, however, does not mean that the socialist countries stand aloof from the class struggle of the working people of the capitalist countries for the establishment of a new system.

Far from that, the peoples of the socialist countries are exerting an enormous and increasing influence on the development of the entire liberation movement. By scoring victories in the course of economic competition, the socialist system demonstrates to the whole world the great advantages of the new system. The everyday facts of life convince more and more hundreds of millions of people of the great constructive possibilities of communism, and they resolutely take sides with it.

A radical change in the balance of class forces has already taken place on the world scene in the conditions of peaceful co-existence and economic competition with capitalism. Now it is no longer imperialism, but socialism, the revolutionary forces of our time, and all the peoples fighting for social and national liberation, that determine the main trend of world development.

The new balance of forces in the world arena, for the first time in history, make it possible to pose the task of preventing a world thermonuclear war as a quite realisable task. It is the great fortune of all working people and of all humanity that, at the crucial period of history when imperialism has accumulated lethal weapons of mass annihilation, there exist forces in the world capable of curbing the aggressors and barring the road to war.

Let us take the history of recent years as example. When thermonuclear weapons were developed, the imperialists more than once encroached on this or that country which had freed itself from the colonialists and tried to reimpose the yoke of colonialism on that country. However, the resistance of the newly liberated peoples, and the support of the socialist countries, beat back these aggressive forces.

The opportunities for struggle for peace and socialism are great, and are growing all the time. Even many western leaders today recognise our strength, and say that a certain balance of forces has been reached in the world. We shall not quarrel with these statements, though one should, in all fairness, admit that this balance is changing inexorably in favour of socialism.

Marxists-Leninists proceed from the assumption that the only reasonable principal of relations between countries with different social systems is peaceful co-existence. We have regarded, and continue to regard this policy, bequeathed to us by Lenin, as the general line of our foreign policy.

We followed this policy when we were much weaker than the joint forces of imperialism, and we follow this policy now, when the balance of forces is changing radically in our favour. We shall continue to fight steadfastly for the victory of the principles of peaceful co-existence.

Our party has always held that peaceful co-existence creates favourable conditions for the development of the class struggle by the working people of capitalist countries and for the steady development of the national liberation movement.

The record of the people's revolutionary struggle after the Second World War has shown convincingly that it is precisely in the conditions of peaceful co-existence, with the socialist countries and all the peace-loving peoples holding in check the aggressive aspirations of the imperialists, that the movement for liberation has developed with particular force throughout the world.

It is precisely in the conditions of peaceful co-existence of states with different social systems that the glorious Cuban revolution led by ardent champions of the cause of the people gained victory.

It is precisely in the conditions of peaceful co-existence that the strike struggles of the proletariat, its unity and organisation in the struggle for its vital rights against the omnipotence of the monopolies and the sway of reaction, are steadily growing.

The working class, led by Marxist-Leninist parties, is waging a broad offensive against the forces of imperialism, and it will win.

Communist influence in the working class movement is on the rise. Despite the brutal persecution to which they are subjected in the United States, West Germany, Spain, Portugal, Greece and other countries, the communists are extending their influence among the working people of the capitalist countries and are scoring fresh successes in rallying the forces of the people against the monopolies and reaction.

The Soviet communists, and all the Soviet people, who know what courage and heroism mean, admire the revolutionary staunchness and dedication of our class brothers in the countries of capital. We bow our heads before the glorious memory of such great sons of the working class as Comrades Salam Adil and Julian Grimau who have given their lives for the great cause of communism.

Comrades, the world bourgeoisie has committed many grave crimes against mankind, and one of the most heinous of them was enslavement of the peoples of Africa, Asia and Latin America. Like bandits, they arrogated to themselves the right to plunder whole continents and brutally exploit hundreds of millions of people. Who can measure the grief and suffering, the blood and tears that fell to the lot of the peoples enslaved by imperialism, peoples who accounted for a majority of the world's population?

This great historic injustice had to come to an end. The entire system of colonial oppression is now in its death throes. In our time, over 90 per cent. of the territory of Asia and about 80 per cent. of the territory of Africa belong to sovereign states. Over 50 independent states have emerged in place of former colonies. The giant colonial prison, which the imperialists erected in Asia and Africa, has collapsed, and the ground is trembling under the feet of the imperialists in Latin America.

The prophetic words of the great Lenin about the inevitable collapse of the colonial system, that the time would come when all the peoples would share in deciding the destinies of the world, are coming true.

By their victory in October 1917, the working people of the Soviet Union laid the foundations for a genuinely free life for the peoples. The victory of the great October Socialist Revolution, and the achievements of the Soviet country in building socialism, undermined the colonial system and the rule of capital throughout the world.

The road of October was followed by the People's Republic of China and the other socialist countries in Europe and Asia. Even better conditions were thereby provided for the complete collapse of the colonial system.

The working people of the Soviet Union wish the peoples of Asia, Africa and Latin America, who have freed themselves from colonial oppression, to rally themselves even closer in their struggle for a new life.

The colonialists, when they were still masters in the colonies, strenuously implanted the capitalist order of things there. When the colonial system collapsed, and the imperialists were thrown out, they left roots in many former colonies. This is why the only change in some cases was that the former exploiters were white, and when they left, the land and the capital remained in the hands of black owners, who exploit their fellow countrymen just as ruthlessly, even though both the exploiters and the exploited are black.

What matters in the class struggle is not the colour of one's skin, but one's ideological and class position. In the countries which have freed themselves from colonial oppression, the struggle will intensify, and it is only with victory of labour, with the elimination of the exploitation of man by man, that the genuine prosperity of the young states will be ensured.

The achievement of political independence does not yet mean the complete liberation of the peoples of the former colonies and semi-colonies from the yoke of foreign monopolies. The liberated countries are facing the task of achieving economic independence, of ensuring the more rapid development of their economy and social progress, and of improving the living conditions of the people. These countries have to do much to overcome the lag caused by the centuries long rule of the colonialists and imperialists.

Of course, it is above all on their own forces that the liberated countries have to rely in their struggle for economic independence and social progress. But these countries, impoverished and ruined by long colonial rule, find it extremely difficult, without outside assistance, to overcome their economic backwardness in a short time and to bridge the great gap between the former colonies and industrially developed countries.

The Soviet Union and all the socialist countries regard it as their international-ist duty to give every support and all-round assistance to the national liberation movement.

What does it mean in practice to help the national liberation movement? It means, firstly, to fight against interference by imperialism in the internal affairs of the peoples of the liberated countries, to give all-round assistance, including assistance in the form of armaments, to the peoples waging a just struggle against foreign oppression. Secondly, it means to come out against any forms of neo-colonialism, to help the peoples of the young states to develop the economy of their countries and to give these countries every support on the international scene.

It is by these principles that the Soviet Union is guided in its relations with the peoples of Asia, Africa and Latin America. The countries of socialism ex-tend a helping hand to the former colonies and semi-colonies. Our aid is not prompted by considerations of political expediency, but reflects the fundamental principles of the policy of the socialist countries.

How can it be otherwise, since our ideal is the equality and brotherhood of all peoples, the elimination of all exploitation, both class and national? The needs and interests of all working people are close and understandable to us, whether they live on the tropical island of Indonesia, in the Savannahs of Africa, or in the vast expanses of South America.

The peoples of the Soviet Union express their solidarity with the struggle of the Viet Namese people for the reunion of their country, for the liberation of South Viet Nam from the yoke of American imperialism and the venal Diem clique. The peoples of the Soviet Union express their solidarity with the struggle of the Korean people for the reunification of their motherland and for the liberation of South Korea. We sympathise with the progressive forces of Laos who are fighting to strengthen the independence and neutrality of their country.

We don't demand military bases or concessions in exchange for our aid; we don't impose enslaving agreements on anybody; we don't humiliate young states with 'charity'; we don't insult them with humiliating loan terms. Our principle is equality and mutual respect. Small wonder, therefore, that it is the socialist countries which the peoples of Asia, Africa and Latin America regard as their true friends.

In our relations with the young national states we are guided by the behests of our great teacher Lenin, who, even before the October Revolution, said that the victorious proletariat would be the firm stronghold for the national liberation of all the peoples oppressed by imperialism.

We are convinced that success in the struggle against imperialism is ensured by the interrelation and unity in action of the great revolutionary forces of our time: the countries of the world socialist system, which is becoming the decisive factor of world development; the international revolutionary working class movement; the national liberation movement of the oppressed peoples; and all the forces of peace, democracy and progress throughout the world. The cohesion of these forces is the guarantee of new successes in the anti-imperialist struggle.

The communists are fully aware of the historic responsibility they have assumed with regard to the peoples, and of the great tasks which history has set before us. To accomplish our mission we must march onward, shoulder to shoulder, and carry high the banner of proletarian internationalism.

In order that the socialist countries, the movement of the liberated peoples and the efforts of all progressive mankind have even greater force, the working class of all countries should rally even closer under the immortal call: 'Workers of all countries, unite!'

It is necessary to fight resolutely against any division, under any pretext, of the revolutionary forces.

Division, not by class but by continents, colour of skin or any other characteristic, means the division of the forces of the working class, the working people of all countries, and not their unity. This division weakens the revolutionary forces, and will help the enemies of the revolution to suppress the working people. Such a division is to the liking of the imperialists, because it benefits them, and helps them to carry out their bestial law of 'divide and rule.'

We all know very well that the imperialists dream of shaking the unity of the communist movement and the cohesion of the countries of the world socialist system.

The imperialists are becoming increasingly aware that they cannot overcome the socialist countries by military means. They are beginning to understand that they cannot defeat us in peaceful economic competition between the two systems, either. This is why they are now pinning their hopes on a split in the socialist community and in the whole world communist movement.

Lately, it has been possible to discern a new note in the angry chorus of anti-communists. Some western strategists are assuming that internal differences between the socialist countries will increase with the growth of their strength As you can see, the imperialists hope that with the growth of the economy and the power of the socialist countries, insuperable differences will arise between them. They obviously wish to measure the world of socialism by their own yard-stick.

In counting on the division of the socialist countries, the imperialists are especially hopeful of reviving the nationalist prejudices inherited from the old world. We must tell the enemies of socialism openly: This horse will not take you far, gentlemen!

To those schemes by the enemies of socialism, the communists oppose a consistent internationalist policy. In the relations between the countries of socialism they firmly abide by the principles of equality and respect for national sovereignty, and take full account of the national interests and features of each and every country.

At the same time, the Communist Parties of the socialist countries, true to the international solidarity of the proletarian movement, in their policy base themselves on the interests not only of their own country but also of the entire socialist system. They strengthen friendship, mutual assistance and co-operation.

Lenin taught us to understand profoundly, and consistently to implement, the noble principles of proletarian internationalism, and to wage implacable struggle against every manifestation of nationalism.

Life itself shows that nationalism can become a source of revisionist and dogmatic views. This is why communists consistently fight against any departure from Marxist-Leninist theory, both against right-wing opportunism and against 'leftist' opportunism, in order to strengthen the unity of the communist movement and to strengthen its influence on the entire course of world development.

It is our common task further to rally and strengthen in every way the unity of the world communist and working-class movement on the basis of Marxist-Leninist teaching.

The bourgeois press publishes more than a few ridiculous fabrications about relations between the Communist Parties of the Soviet Union and China.

As you know, a meeting will be held shortly between delegations of the C.P.S.U. and the Communist Party of China. We shall do everything to make this meeting lead to the rallying together of our forces and to eliminate differences in understanding on certain questions. We express the hope that this meeting will bring our parties, and the entire international communist and working class movement, even closer together. The great cause of communism will overcome all obstacles in its advance, and will triumph throughout the world.

By strengthening the unity of our ranks, we shall provide even more favourable conditions for the development of the world revolutionary process, for the strengthening of world peace, and for the building of socialism and communism in our countries.

I should like to assure our Cuban friends and all the champions of socialism and progress, that the Communist Party of the Soviet Union will spare no effort to strengthen the united anti-imperialist front, to develop co-operation and mutual assistance among the socialist countries, and to help the national liberation movement.

It is gratifying to us that Comrade Fidel Castro's visit to the Soviet Union has not only helped to strengthen unity between the Soviet and the Cuban peoples and our two parties, but has also added to the cohesion of the whole socialist community and the entire world communist movement.

Dear Comrade Fidel, Dear Cuban Friends, Comrades, the Soviet people rejoice in the successes scored in the development of the Soviet Union's economy and culture. The fulfilment and over-fulfilment of economic plans has become a law of the development of the Soviet Union. Year in and year out, industrial and agricultural production is growing. We are convinced that the Seven Year Plan for the development of our country will be fulfilled and over-fulfilled.

The workers of the Russian Federation have decided to give the country 30,000 million roubles worth of produce over and above the plan. To give our Cuban friends a clearer impression of the magnitude of this figure, I can tell them that this means 33,000 million pesos. This will be produced over and above the plan by the Russian federation alone, however. The workers of all other republics of our country, too, are working to produce in excess of the plan.

To get a clear picture of the scope of the Soviet Union's industrial progress, we should cast a glance back on the road travelled by the country.

Forty-five years ago, our country was one of the most economically backward in the world. Russia's incalculable wealth lay idle in the soil, and its gifted and hard-working people languished in poverty and ignorance. As for being equipped with the modern tools of production, the economy of tsarist Russia, Lenin pointed out, was at a quarter of the level of Britain, a fifth of the level of Germany and a tenth of the level of America. The peoples of Russia were literally robbed as regards education and culture.

When Lenin and the bolsheviks came to power in the country, there were only a few people in the world who believed in the feasibility of Lenin's plans. Now, when our successes are impossible to overlook or ignore, the west has begun to speak of a 'Russian miracle.' What this 'Russian miracle,' wrought in the years of Soviet power, means, is well shown in their documentary by our German friends, the film directors Annelie and Andrew Thorndike.

Working for oneself, for the society and the state one lives in, working for the sake of an even better future—this is the most miraculous force in the world, which is capable of bringing to life such manifestations of human genius as are unthinkable under capitalism.

In volume of production, the Soviet Union ranks first in Europe and second in the world. But, here, we make the reservation that we are second only 'for the time being.' We can at present put up with second place; but, in five to seven years, we shall say: 'Now for first place!' And we shall move unfailingly into first place. It is now a matter of the not-too-distant future.

In the rate of industrial development, we are confidently ahead of the United States of America. Last year we closely approached the U.S. level in steel production. The Soviet Union has already surpassed the Americans in the production of iron ore and coal, in the production of cement, metal-working lathes, in the power of tractors, and in the production of butter, sugar, woollen fabrics, and certain other products and goods.

A mere ten years ago, the Soviet Union's industrial production was 33 per cent. of the American; now it is already about 63 per cent. Figuratively speaking, in the rate of development, our country takes three steps for America's one. In twenty years' time, Soviet industry will produce twice as much as is now produced by the entire non-socialist world. But even that is not the limit; we shall move forward at an even faster rate.

Our country has twice as many doctors, and graduates three times as many engineers as the United States. It is significant that the Soviet people produced the world's first atomic power station, built the world's first atomic icebreaker, and were the first to send magnificent ships into space.

When peaceful economic competition with capitalism is spoken of, our progress is frequently judged only by the development of industry and agriculture; but the amount of oil, coal, steel and food produced by this or that country is not everything.

It is impossible not to see that in the United States and the other capitalist countries, the growth of industrial and agricultural production is accompanied by a further widening of the gap between the development of production and the rise in the living standards of the people; whereas, in our country, the living standards of the population steadily rise.

It is enough to say that such an acute social problem as housing is being solved in the Soviet Union at the fastest rate. The Soviet Union ranks first in the world for the scale of housing construction. In the first four years of the seven-year plan, 325 million square metres of housing were built in the cities alone. This is twice as much as the entire provision of housing in the cities of pre-revolutionary Russia, built over centuries. Six thousand new flats are occupied every day in our country. In the rural areas, during the same period, 2,350,000 houses have been built.

Communism is the only social-political force which solves social problems, consistently and fully, for the sake of man, for his benefit, and eliminates the alienation and distrust between people.

In the period between 1950 and 1961, industrial production in the Soviet Union and the other member-countries of the Council for Mutual Economic Assistance increased at the average rate of 11·7 per cent. a year, as compared with only a little over 5 per cent. in the capitalist countries.

These figures are borne out by data published a few days ago by the United Nations Department of Industrial Statistics. It can be seen from these figures that the economy of the socialist countries is developing twice as fast as that of the capitalist countries.

When correspondents asked a United Nations spokesman why production in the socialist countries was growing faster than in the capitalist ones, he refused to reply to this question. We can help them to get a truthful answer.

The faster growth of industrial production in the socialist countries in comparison with the capitalist ones is due primarily to the fact that our economy is built on socialist principles, on the social ownership of the means of production. It is in the hands of the people, and is a planned economy. Therein lies the 'secret' of our successes and therein lies the strength of the socialist system. The 'Russian miracle' is Marxism-Leninism in action.

Dear Cuban Friends! Comrades! We are advancing along with you, together with all the countries of socialism to the communist future under the banner of Marx, Engels and Lenin, under the militant banner of the Paris Commune and the October Revolution.

An ever-increasing number of the peoples of the world are gathering under this revolutionary banner, and the fine time is not far off when all the peoples will have discarded the shackles of the old world and have entered the age of their true history, the age of communism.

There is no greater happiness than to be a fighter for this future, to be a builder of a communist society!

The peoples of our countries are closely united in their common revolutionary upsurge, in their common advance forward towards a bright future. Brothers and comrades-in-arms in our common cause, we are marching in one and the same rank, towards one and the same cherished goal.

Our friendship is solid and unbreakable. It is pure like a mountainous spring, and strong as the handshake of the working people. The Soviet people, as a loyal friend, sincerely shares the successes and difficulties of their Cuban brothers.

There are no distances great enough, no oceans big enough to weaken or cool these warm feelings which come from the bottom of the heart.

Broad prospects are opening before us for political and economic co-operation, for cultural exchanges, and for the still greater spiritual closeness of our peoples. Our friendship will yield still more abundant fruit, will mutually enrich our peoples, and speed up our joint advance towards socialism and communism.

May the unbreakable fraternal friendship of the peoples of the Soviet Union and Cuba, therefore, flourish and develop!

Long live the militant vanguard of the Cuban people—the United Party of the Socialist Revolution!

Warmest greetings to the envoys of the Cuban people, their hero and leader, our great friend Fidel Castro Ruz!

Hurrah for revolutionary Cuba!

Joint statement by the Communist Parties of the People's Republic of China and New Zealand, Peking, 25 May 1963[1]

Comrade V. G. Wilcox, General Secretary of the Communist Party of New Zealand, visited China from May 19 to May 25 on the invitation of the Central Committee of the Communist Party of China.

During the visit, Comrade Mao Tse-tung, Chairman of the Central Committee of the Communist Party of China, met Comrade Wilcox, and they had warm and friendly discussions.

Comrade Wilcox, General Secretary of the Communist Party of New Zealand, and Comrade Teng Hsiao-ping, General Secretary of the Central Committee of the Communist Party of China, held talks. Those taking part for the Central Committee of the Communist Party of China also included Comrade Kang Sheng, Alternate Member of the Political Bureau and Member of the Secretariat of the Central Committee of the Communist Party of China, and Comrade Liu Ning-I, Member of the Central Committee of the Communist Party of China.

The results of the talks show that the Communist Party of China and the Communist Party of New Zealand completely agree in their stand and views on the important questions now confronting the international communist movement.

The Communist Party of China and the Communist Party of New Zealand reaffirm their loyalty to the Moscow Declaration of 1957[2] and the Moscow Statement of 1960[3] and hold that these two documents, unanimously agreed upon by the Communist Parties of various countries, are the common programme of the international communist movement.

Both Parties emphasize that in the present situation it is most important and urgent to uphold and strengthen the unity of the international communist movement on the basis of Marxism-Leninism and on the basis of the Declaration and the Statement.

Both Parties maintain that at the present time revisionism is the main danger in the international communist movement. In the last few years many events have

[1] *Peking Review*, 31 May 1963, pp. 15–17.   [2] *Documents, 1957*, pp. 527–39.
[3] ibid., *1960*, pp. 222–38.

further confirmed the conclusion of the Declaration of 1957 and the Statement of 1960 in this respect.

The modern revisionists emasculate the revolutionary soul of Marxism-Leninism, cast away the revolutionary principles of the Declaration and the Statement, paralyse the revolutionary will of the working class and working people and serve the needs of imperialism and the reactionaries of various countries. They do not want revolution themselves, and they do not allow others to make it; they do not support revolution themselves nor do they allow others to support it. The sharp struggle now being waged against the modern revisionists has a vital bearing on the future of the revolutionary cause of the world proletariat and working people and the fate of mankind. The task of all Marxist-Leninists is to unite more closely and defeat the onslaught of modern revisionism.

The Yugoslav revisionists are renegades from Marxism-Leninism and are representative of modern revisionism. They have been facilitating the restoration of capitalism in Yugoslavia and are providing imperialism with means to carry out its policy of 'peaceful evolution' which aims at restoring capitalism in the socialist countries. They serve as a special detachment of the U.S. imperialists, undermine the socialist camp, disrupt the international communist movement, wreck the revolutionary cause of the oppressed nations and peoples, and sabotage the struggle of the people of the world against imperialism. The Yugoslav revisionists cling to their revisionist programme which they counterpose to the common programme of the Communist Parties of all countries, and they are going further and further down the road of revisionism and have not in any way modified either their theory or their practice. It is the sacred duty of Communists in all countries to continue to wage an uncompromising struggle against Yugoslav revisionism in accordance with the 1960 Statement. To side with the Yugoslav revisionists is nothing but betrayal of Marxism-Leninism.

While fighting against revisionism, we must also combat dogmatism. Dogmatists have no understanding of how to integrate the universal truth of Marxism-Leninism with the concrete practice of the revolution in their own countries. They are divorced from reality, alienate themselves from the masses, disregard all facts and turn round and round to follow those who attack the basic principles of Marxism-Leninism as 'dogmatism' while claiming to be completely correct themselves. This can only bring harm to the revolutionary cause.

Both Parties hold that the present international balance of class forces is most favourable to the revolutionary cause of the people in all countries and most unfavourable to imperialism and reaction. The parties of the proletariat must correctly understand and make use of this favourable situation and vigorously promote the revolutionary struggles of the people of all countries. It is absolutely wrong to consider that because of the change in the international balance of class forces the nature of imperialism has changed, that the basic contradiction in the contemporary world can be reconciled or has disappeared and that Marxist-Leninist theories on class struggle, the national-liberation movement and the proletarian revolution and the dictatorship of the proletariat are already 'outmoded.'

Events in recent years have further proved that U.S. imperialism is the main bulwark of modern colonialism, the centre of world reaction, the main force of aggression and war and the common enemy of the people of the whole world. It is of the greatest importance to establish and expand the broadest united front against imperialism headed by the United States, and its lackeys. The destiny of mankind and the hope of world peace cannot be left to the 'wisdom' of U.S. imperialism or to the illusion of co-operation with U.S. imperialism.

It is possible to safeguard world peace and prevent a new world war and nuclear war by relying on the joint struggle of the people of all countries and by resolutely opposing the policies of aggression and war pursued by imperialism headed by the United States.

Confronted with the U.S. imperialists' policy of nuclear blackmail, we must organize the people to wage resolute struggles. On this matter, any act of adventurism or of capitulationism is extremely wrong and harmful.

Both Parties are concerned about peace and security in the Asian and Pacific region and resolutely oppose the efforts of U.S. imperialism to revive the forces of Japanese militarism and its use of the SEATO and ANZUS groupings to carry out activities of aggression and war.

Both Parties hold that the national-liberation movements are an important and organic part of the present-day world revolution and are an immense force for the defence of world peace. Both Parties warmly support the national democratic revolutionary struggles of the peoples of all the Asian, African and Latin American countries, their struggles against imperialism and old and new colonialism, and especially their struggles against the new colonialism of the United States.

Both Parties rejoice at the constant growth and development of the working-class movement in the capitalist countries of Western Europe, North America, Oceania and elsewhere. Both Parties maintain that in the working-class movement, the political parties of the proletariat should give active leadership to the struggle against monopoly capital, the struggle to defend democratic rights and the various other kinds of day-to-day political and economic struggles, and link these struggles with the general goal of proletarian revolution and the dictatorship of the proletariat.

In the struggle to realize this general goal, the party of the working class invariably wishes to achieve the transition to socialism peacefully, but it must at all times devote major attention to the arduous work of gathering revolutionary strength and must fully prepare itself for non-peaceful transition. Thus it will be able to hit back hard at the ruling classes if they refuse to accept the will of the people and resort to armed suppression of the revolution. If a political party of the proletariat pins all its hopes on a peaceful transition having the complete and willing approval of the reactionary ruling classes, this will inevitably dampen the revolutionary will of the people and bury the cause of the proletarian revolution. The illusory view that the reactionary ruling classes may hand over power voluntarily is, in fact, a modern version of social democracy.

Social democracy is a bourgeois ideological trend and an important pillar upholding the reactionary rule of imperialism and monopoly capital. Lenin pointed out long ago that social democratic parties are a variant of bourgeois political parties. In the day-to-day struggle of the working-class movement as well as in the struggle to safeguard world peace, Communists must in every possible way carry out extensive joint activities with the social democrats and the masses of the workers under the influence of the social democratic parties. At the same time, the Marxist-Leninist Parties must draw a strict and clear ideological line of demarcation between themselves and the social democratic parties and make efforts to win over the honest working-class elements in social democratic parties so as to enable these elements to free themselves from the ideological influence of social democracy, to understand Marxism-Leninism and to change to the stand of waging consistent class struggle against capitalism and for the victory of socialism.

The Communist Party of China and the Communist Party of New Zealand hold that the internationalist unity of the Communist and Workers' Parties of all countries should be built on the principles of independence, equality and the attainment of unanimity through consultation. In order to resolve the present ideological differences in the international communist movement, it is necessary to convene a meeting of representatives of all the Communist and Workers' Parties in the world. The Communist Party of New Zealand was an initiator of such a meeting. For more than a year now, the Communist Party of China has actively supported this proposal. Both Parties emphasize that the common desire of all Marxist-Leninists and all progressive people is to safeguard unity and oppose a split, have a genuine unity based on principle and oppose a sham unity which discards Marxism-Leninism and the Declaration and the Statement.

Both Parties hope that the forthcoming talks between the Communist Party of China and the Communist Party of the Soviet Union will contribute to the convening of a meeting of representatives of the Communist and Workers' Parties of all countries.

Both Parties also hope that the proposed talks between the Communist Party of New Zealand and the Communist Party of the Soviet Union will be helpful to the convening of a meeting of the fraternal Parties.

Both Parties point out with satisfaction that Comrade Wilcox's visit and the talks between the Communist Party of China and the Communist Party of New Zealand have strengthened the Marxist-Leninist unity of the two Parties and the friendship of the two peoples.

The Communist Party of China and the Communist Party of New Zealand firmly believe that Marxism-Leninism is invincible and that the international communist movement and the people's revolutionary cause throughout the world will ultimately overcome all obstacles along the road ahead and win complete victory.

Long live Marxism-Leninism!

Long live proletarian internationalism!

The Central Committee of the Communist Party of China to the Central Committee of the Communist Party of the Soviet Union, 14 June 1963[1] (extracts)

(1) . . . It is true that for several years there have been differences within the international communist movement in the understanding of, and the attitude

---

[1] *Peking Review*, 21 June 1963, pp. 6–22. This letter was published with the title 'A proposal concerning the general line of the international communist movement' and is commonly known as 'The Twenty-five Principles'. It was issued in response to a Soviet letter of 30 March 1963, suggesting that talks between the two parties be held in Moscow and requesting an end to polemics; for text, see *Pravda*, 30 March 1963.

towards, the Declaration of 1957 and the Statement of 1960. The central issue here is whether or not to accept the revolutionary principles of the Declaration and the Statement. In the last analysis, it is a question of whether or not to accept the universal truth of Marxism-Leninism, whether or not to recognize the universal significance of the road of the October Revolution, whether or not to accept the fact that the people still living under the imperialist and capitalist system, who comprise two-thirds of the world's population, need to make revolution, and whether or not to accept the fact that the people already on the socialist road, who comprise one-third of the world's population, need to carry their revolution forward to the end. . . .

(2) What are the revolutionary principles of the Declaration and the Statement? They may be summarized as follows:

Workers of all countries, unite; workers of the world, unite with the oppressed peoples and oppressed nations; oppose imperialism and reaction in all countries; strive for world peace, national liberation, people's democracy and socialism; consolidate and expand the socialist camp; bring the proletarian world revolution step by step to complete victory; and establish a new world without imperialism, without capitalism and without the exploitation of man by man. . . .

(3) If the general line of the international communist movement is one-siddly reduced to 'peaceful coexistence,' 'peaceful competition' and 'peaceful transition,' this is to violate the revolutionary principles of the 1957 Declaration and the 1960 Statement, to discard the historical mission of proletarian world revolution, and to depart from the revolutionary teachings of Marxism-Leninism. . . .

(4) What are the fundamental contradictions in the contemporary world? Marxist-Leninists consistently hold that they are:

the contradiction between the socialist camp and the imperialist camp;
the contradiction between the proletariat and the bourgeoisie in the capitalist countries;
the contradiction between the oppressed nations and imperialism; and
the contradictions among imperialist countries and among monopoly capitalist groups. . . .

(5) The following erroneous views should be repudiated on the question of the fundamental contradictions in the contemporary world:

(a) the view which blots out the class content of the contradiction between the socialist and the imperialist camps and fails to see this contradiction as one between states under the dictatorship of the proletariat and states under the dictatorship of the monopoly capitalists;

(b) the view which recognizes only the contradiction between the socialist and the imperialist camps, while neglecting or underestimating the contradictions between the proletariat and the bourgeoisie in the capitalist world, between the oppressed nations and imperialism, among the imperialist countries and among the monopoly capitalist groups, and the struggles to which these contradictions give rise;

(c) the view which maintains with regard to the capitalist world that the contradiction between the proletariat and the bourgeoisie can be resolved without a proletarian revolution in each country and that the contradiction between the oppressed nations and imperialism can be resolved without revolution by the oppressed nations;

(d) the view which denies that the development of the inherent contradictions in the contemporary capitalist world inevitably leads to a new situation in which the imperialist countries are locked in an intense struggle, and asserts that the contradictions among the imperialist countries can be reconciled, or even eliminated, by 'international agreements among the big monopolies'; and

(e) the view which maintains that the contradiction between the two world systems of socialism and capitalism will automatically disappear in the course of 'economic competition,' that the other fundamental world contradictions will automatically do so with the disappearance of the contradiction between the two systems, and that a 'world without wars,' a new world of 'all-round co-operation,' will appear. . . .

(6) The question of what is the correct attitude towards the socialist camp is a most important question of principle confronting all Communist and Workers' Parties.

It is under new historical conditions that the Communist and Workers' Parties are now carrying on the task of proletarian internationalist unity and struggle. When only one socialist country existed and when this country was faced with hostility and jeopardized by all the imperialists and reactionaries because it firmly pursued the correct Marxist-Leninist line and policies, the touchstone of proletarian internationalism for every Communist Party was whether or not it resolutely defended the only socialist country. Now there is a socialist camp consisting of thirteen countries, Albania, Bulgaria, China, Cuba, Czechoslovakia, the German Democratic Republic, Hungary, the Democratic People's Republic of Korea, Mongolia, Poland, Rumania, the Soviet Union and the Democratic Republic of Viet Nam. Under these circumstances, the touchstone of proletarian internationalism for every Communist Party is whether or not it resolutely defends the whole of the socialist camp, whether or not it defends the unity of all the countries in the camp on the basis of Marxism-Leninism and whether or not it defends the Marxist-Leninist line and policies which the socialist countries ought to pursue. . . .

(7) The 1960 Statement points out:

'U.S. imperialism has become the biggest international exploiter.'

'The United States is the mainstay of colonialism today.'

'U.S. imperialism is the main force of aggression and war.' . . .

To make no distinction between enemies, friends and ourselves and to entrust the fate of the people and of mankind to collaboration with U.S. imperialism is to lead people astray. The events of the last few years have exploded this illusion.

(8) The various types of contradictions in the contemporary world are concentrated in the vast areas of Asia, Africa and Latin America; these are the most vulnerable areas under imperialist rule and the storm-centres of world revolution dealing direct blows at imperialism. . . .

Certain persons now go so far as to deny the great international significance of the anti-imperialist revolutionary struggles of the Asian, African and Latin American peoples and, on the pretext of breaking down the barriers of nationality, colour and geographical location, are trying their best to efface the line of demarcation between oppressed and oppressor nations and between oppressed and oppressor countries and to hold down the revolutionary struggles of the peoples in these areas. In fact, they cater to the needs of imperialism and create a new 'theory' to justify the rule of imperialism in these areas and the promotion of its policies of old and new colonialism. Actually, this 'theory' seeks not to break down the barriers of nationality, colour and geographical location but to maintain the rule of the 'superior nations' over the oppressed nations. It is only natural that this fraudulent 'theory' is rejected by the people in these areas. . . .

The attitude taken towards the revolutionary struggles of the people in the Asian, African and Latin American countries is an important criterion for differentiating those who want revolution from those who do not and those who are truly defending world peace from those who are abetting the forces of aggression and war.

(9) In these areas, extremely broad sections of the population refuse to be slaves of imperialism. They include not only the workers, peasants, intellectuals and petty bourgeoisie, but also the patriotic national bourgeoisie and even certain kings, princes and aristocrats, who are patriotic. . . .

On the basis of the worker-peasant alliance the proletariat and its party must unite all the strata that can be united and organize a broad united front against imperialism and its lackeys. In order to consolidate and expand this united front it is necessary that the proletarian party should maintain its ideological, political and organizational independence and insist on the leadership of the revolution.

The proletarian party and the revolutionary people must learn to master all forms of struggle, including armed struggle. . . .

In some of these countries, the patriotic national bourgeoisie continue to stand with the masses in the struggle against imperialism and colonialism and introduce certain measures of social progress. This requires the proletarian party to make a full appraisal of the progressive role of the patriotic national bourgeoisie and strengthen unity with them. . . .

The policy should be to unite with the bourgeoisie, in so far as they tend to be progressive, anti-imperialist and anti-feudal, but to struggle against their reactionary tendencies to compromise and collaborate with imperialism and the forces of feudalism. . . .

(10) In the imperialist and the capitalist countries, the proletarian revolution and the dictatorship of the proletariat are essential for the thorough resolution of the contradictions of capitalist society. . . .

In order to lead the proletariat and working people in revolution, Marxist-Leninist parties must master all forms of struggle and be able to substitute one form for another quickly as the conditions of struggle change. The vanguard of the proletariat will remain unconquerable in all circumstances only if it masters all forms of struggle—peaceful and armed, open and secret, legal and illegal, parliamentary struggle and mass struggle, etc. It is wrong to refuse to use parliamentary and other legal forms of struggle when they can and should be used. However, if a Marxist-Leninist party falls into legalism or parliamentary cretinism, confining the struggle within the limits permitted by the bourgeoisie, this will inevitably lead to renouncing the proletarian revolution and the dictatorship of the proletariat. . . .

(11) In specific historical conditions, Marx and Lenin did raise the possibility that revolution may develop peacefully. But, as Lenin pointed out, the peaceful development of revolution is an opportunity 'very seldom to be met with in the history of revolution.'

As a matter of fact, there is no historical precedent for peaceful transition from capitalism to socialism. . . .

The proletarian party must never base its thinking, its policies for revolution and its entire work on the assumption that the imperialists and reactionaries will accept peaceful transformation. . . .

(12) If the leading group in any Party adopt a non-revolutionary line and convert it into a reformist party, then Marxist-Leninists inside and outside the Party will replace them and lead the people in making revolution. In another kind of situation, the bourgeois revolutionaries will come forward to lead the revolution and the party of the proletariat will forfeit its leadership of the revolution. When the reactionary bourgeoisie betray the revolution and suppress the people, an opportunist line will cause tragic and unnecessary losses to the Communists and the revolutionary masses.

If Communists slide down the path of opportunism, they will degenerate into bourgeois nationalists and become appendages of the imperialists and the reactionary bourgeoisie.

There are certain persons who assert that they have made the greatest creative contributions to revolutionary theory since Lenin and that they alone are correct. But it is very dubious whether they have ever really given consideration to the extensive experience of the entire world communist movement, whether they have ever really considered the interests, the goal and tasks of the international proletarian movement as a whole, and whether they really have a general line for the international communist movement which conforms with Marxism-Leninism.

In the last few years the international communist movement and the national-liberation movement have had many experiences and many lessons. There are experiences which people should praise and there are experiences which make people grieve. Communists and revolutionaries in all countries should ponder and seriously study these experiences of success and failure, so as to draw correct conclusions and useful lessons from them. . . .

(13) Certain persons have one-sidedly exaggerated the role of peaceful competition between socialist and imperialist countries in their attempt to substitute peaceful competition for the revolutionary struggles of the oppressed peoples and nations. According to their preaching, it would seem that imperialism will automatically collapse in the course of this peaceful competition and that the only thing the oppressed peoples and nations have to do is to wait quietly for the advent of this day. What does this have in common with Marxist-Leninist views?

Moreover, certain persons have concocted the strange tale that China and some other socialist countries want 'to unleash wars' and to spread socialism by 'wars between states.' As the Statement of 1960 points out, such tales are nothing but imperialist and reactionary slanders. To put it bluntly, the purpose of those who repeat these slanders is to hide the fact that they are opposed to revolutions by the oppressed peoples and nations of the world and opposed to others supporting such revolutions.

(14) In the last few years much—in fact a great deal—has been said on the question of war and peace. Our views and policies on this question are known to the world, and no one can distort them. . . .

There are different types of peace and different types of war. Marxist-Leninists must be clear about what type of peace or what type of war is in question. Lumping just wars and unjust wars together and opposing all of them undiscriminatingly is a bourgeois pacifist and not a Marxist-Leninist approach.

Certain persons say that revolutions are entirely possible without war. Now which type of war are they referring to—is it a war of national liberation or a revolutionary civil war, or is it a world war?

If they are referring to a war of national liberation or a revolutionary civil war, then this formulation is, in effect, opposed to revolutionary wars and to revolution.

If they are referring to a world war, then they are shooting at a non-existent target. Although Marxist-Leninists have pointed out, on the basis of the history of the two world wars, that world wars inevitably lead to revolution, no Marxist-Leninist ever has held or ever will hold that revolution must be made through world war.

Marxist-Leninists take the abolition of war as their ideal and believe that war can be abolished.

But how can war be abolished?

. . . Certain persons now actually hold that it is possible to bring about 'a world without weapons, without armed forces and without wars' through 'general and complete disarmament' while the system of imperialism and of the exploitation of man by man still exists. This is sheer illusion. . . .

The question then is, what is the way to secure world peace? According to the Leninist viewpoint, world peace can be won only by the struggles of the people in all countries and not by begging the imperialists for it. World peace can only be effectively defended by relying on the development of the forces of the socialist camp, on the revolutionary struggles of the proletariat and working people of all countries, on the liberation struggles of the oppressed nations and on the struggles of all peace-loving people and countries.

Such is the Leninist policy. Any policy to the contrary definitely will not lead to world peace but will only encourage the ambitions of the imperialists and increase the danger of world war.

In recent years, certain persons have been spreading the argument that a single spark from a war of national liberation or from a revolutionary people's war will lead to a world conflagration destroying the whole of mankind. What are the facts? Contrary to what these persons say, the wars of national liberation and the revolutionary people's wars that have occurred since World War II have not led to world war. The victory of these revolutionary wars has directly weakened the forces of imperialism and greatly strengthened the forces which prevent the imperialists from launching a world war and which defend world peace. Do not the facts demonstrate the absurdity of this argument?

(15) The complete banning and destruction of nuclear weapons is an important task in the struggle to defend world peace. We must do our utmost to this end.

Nuclear weapons are unprecedently destructive, which is why for more than a decade now the U.S. imperialists have been pursuing their policy of nuclear blackmail in order to realize their ambition of enslaving the people of all countries and dominating the world.

But when the imperialists threaten other countries with nuclear weapons, they subject the people in their own country to the same threat, thus arousing them against nuclear weapons and against the imperialist policies of aggression and war. At the same time, in their vain hope of destroying their opponents with nuclear weapons, the imperialists are in fact subjecting themselves to the danger of being destroyed.

The possibility of banning nuclear weapons does indeed exist. However, if the imperialists are forced to accept an agreement to ban nuclear weapons, it decidedly will not be because of their 'love for humanity' but because of the pressure of the people of all countries and for the sake of their own vital interests. . . .

In the view of Marxist-Leninists, the people are the makers of history. In the present, as in the past, man is the decisive factor. Marxist-Leninists attach importance to the role of technological change, but it is wrong to belittle the role of man and exaggerate the role of technology.

The emergence of nuclear weapons can neither arrest the progress of human history nor save the imperialist system from its doom, any more than the emergence of new techniques could save the old systems from their doom in the past.

The emergence of nuclear weapons does not and cannot resolve the fundamental contradictions in the contemporary world, does not and cannot alter the law of class struggle, and does not and cannot change the nature of imperialism and reaction.

It cannot, therefore, be said that with the emergence of nuclear weapons the possibility and the necessity of social and national revolutions have disappeared, or the basic principles of Marxism-Leninism, and especially the theories of proletarian revolution and the dictatorship of the proletariat and of war and peace, have become outmoded and changed into stale 'dogmas.'

(16) It was Lenin who advanced the thesis that it is possible for the socialist countries to practise peaceful coexistence with the capitalist countries. . . .

Since its founding, the People's Republic of China too has consistently pursued the policy of peaceful coexistence with countries having different social systems, and it is China which initiated the Five Principles of Peaceful Coexistence.[1]

However, a few years ago certain persons suddenly claimed Lenin's policy of peaceful coexistence as their own 'great discovery.' They maintain that they have a monopoly on the interpretation of this policy. They treat 'peaceful coexistence' as if it were an all-inclusive, mystical book from heaven and attribute

[1] See *Documents, 1955*, pp. 435–6.

to it every success the people of the world achieve by struggle. What is more, they label all who disagree with their distortions of Lenin's views as opponents of peaceful coexistence, as people completely ignorant of Lenin and Leninism, and as heretics deserving to be burnt at the stake.

How can the Chinese Communists agree with this view and practice? They cannot, it is impossible.

Lenin's principle of peaceful coexistence is very clear and readily comprehensible by ordinary people. Peaceful coexistence designates a relationship between countries with different social systems, and must not be interpreted as one pleases. It should never be extended to apply to the relations between oppressed and oppressor nations, between oppressed and oppressor countries or between oppressed and oppressor classes, and never be described as the main content of the transition from capitalism to socialism, still less should it be asserted that peaceful coexistence is mankind's road to socialism. The reason is that it is one thing to practise peaceful coexistence between countries with different social systems. It is absolutely impermissible and impossible for countries practising peaceful coexistence to touch even a hair of each other's social system. The class struggle, the struggle for national liberation and the transition from capitalism to socialism in various countries are quite another thing. They are all bitter, life-and-death revolutionary struggles which aim at changing the social system. . . .

In our view, the general line of the foreign policy of the socialist countries should have the following content: to develop relations of friendship, mutual assistance and co-operation among the countries in the socialist camp in accordance with the principle of proletarian internationalism; to strive for peaceful coexistence on the basis of the Five Principles with countries having different social systems and oppose the imperialist policies of aggression and war; and to support and assist the revolutionary struggles of all the oppressed peoples and nations. These three aspects are interrelated and indivisible, and not a single one can be omitted.

(17) For a very long historical period after the proletariat takes power, class struggle continues as an objective law independent of man's will, differing only in form from what it was before the taking of power. . . .

For decades or even longer periods after socialist industrialization and agricultural collectivization, it will be impossible to say that any socialist country will be free from those elements which Lenin repeatedly denounced, such as bourgeois hangers-on, parasites, speculators, swindlers, idlers, hooligans and embezzlers of state funds; or to say that a socialist country will no longer need to perform or be able to relinquish the task laid down by Lenin of conquering 'this contagion, this plague, this ulcer that socialism has inherited from capitalism.'. . .

To deny the existence of class struggle in the period of the dictatorship of the proletariat and the necessity of thoroughly completing the socialist revolution on the economic, political and ideological fronts is wrong, does not correspond to objective reality and violates Marxism-Leninism. . . .

(18) The fundamental thesis of Marx and Lenin is that the dictatorship of the proletariat will inevitably continue for the entire historical period of the

transition from capitalism to communism, that is, for the entire period up to the abolition of all class differences and the entry into a classless society, the higher stage of communist society.

What will happen if it is announced, halfway through, that the dictatorship of the proletariat is no longer necessary?

Does this not fundamentally conflict with the teachings of Marx and Lenin on the state of the dictatorship of the proletariat?

Does this not license the development of 'this contagion, this plague, this ulcer that socialism has inherited from capitalism'?

In other words, this would lead to extremely grave consequences and make any transition to communism out of the question.

Can there be a 'state of the whole people'? Is it possible to replace the state of the dictatorship of the proletariat by a 'state of the whole people'?

This is not a question about the internal affairs of any particular country but a fundamental problem involving the universal truth of Marxism-Leninism.

In the view of Marxist-Leninists, there is no such thing as a non-class or supra-class state. So long as the state remains a state, it must bear a class character; so long as the state exists, it cannot be a state of the 'whole people.' As soon as society becomes classless, there will no longer be a state.

Then what sort of thing would a 'state of the whole people' be?

Anyone with an elementary knowledge of Marxism-Leninism can understand that the so-called state of the whole people is nothing new. Representative bourgeois figures have always called the bourgeois state a 'state of all the people,' or a 'state in which power belongs to all the people.'

Certain persons may say that their society is already one without classes. We answer: No, there are classes and class struggles in all socialist countries without exception. . . .

In calling a socialist state the 'state of the whole people,' is one trying to replace the Marxist-Leninist theory of the state by the bourgeois theory of the state? Is one trying to replace the state of the dictatorship of the proletariat by a state of a different character?

If that is the case, it is nothing but a great historical retrogression. The degeneration of the social system in Yugoslavia is a grave lesson. . . .

(19) Can there be a 'party of the entire people'? Is it possible to replace the Party which is the vanguard of the proletariat by a 'party of the entire people'?

This, too, is not a question about the internal affairs of any particular Party, but a fundamental problem involving the universal truth of Marxism-Leninism.

In the view of Marxist-Leninists, there is no such thing as a non-class or supra-class political party. All political parties have a class character. Party spirit is the concentrated expression of class character. . . .

What will happen if it is announced halfway before entering the higher stage of communist society that the party of the proletariat has become a 'party of the entire people' and if its proletarian class character is repudiated?

Does this not fundamentally conflict with the teachings of Marx and Lenin on the party of the proletariat?

Does this not disarm the proletariat and all the working people, organizationally and ideologically, and is it not tantamount to helping restore capitalism? . . .

(20) The party of the proletariat is the headquarters of the proletariat in revolution and struggle. Every proletarian party must practise centralism based on democracy and establish a strong Marxist-Leninist leadership before it can become an organized and battle-worthy vanguard. To raise the question of 'combating the cult of the individual' is actually to counterpose the leaders to the masses, undermine the Party's unified leadership which is based on democratic centralism, dissipate its fighting strength and disintegrate its ranks. . . .

While loudly combating the so-called cult of the individual, certain persons are in reality doing their best to defame the proletarian party and the dictatorship of the proletariat. At the same time, they are enormously exaggerating the role of certain individuals, shifting all errors onto others and claiming all credit for themselves.

What is more serious is that, under the pretext of 'combating the cult of the individual,' certain persons are crudely interfering in the internal affairs of other fraternal Parties and fraternal countries and forcing other fraternal Parties to change their leadership in order to impose their own wrong line on these Parties. What is all this if not great-power chauvinism, sectarianism and splittism? What is all this if not subversion? . . .

(21) Relations between socialist countries are international relations of a new type. Relations between socialist countries, whether large or small, and whether more developed or less developed economically, must be based on the principles of complete equality, respect for territorial integrity, sovereignty and independence, and non-interference in each other's internal affairs, and must also be based on the principles of mutual support and mutual assistance in accordance with proletarian internationalism.

Every socialist country must rely mainly on itself for its construction. . . .

If, proceeding only from its own partial interests, any socialist country unilaterally demands that other fraternal countries submit to its needs, and uses the pretext of opposing what they call 'going it alone' and 'nationalism' to prevent other fraternal countries from applying the principle of relying mainly on their own efforts in their construction and from developing their economies on the basis of independence, or even goes to the length of putting economic pressure on other fraternal countries—then these are pure manifestations of national egoism.

It is absolutely necessary for socialist countries to practise mutual economic assistance and co-operation and exchange. Such economic co-operation must be based on the principles of complete equality, mutual benefit and comradely mutual assistance.

It would be great-power chauvinism to deny these basic principles and, in the name of 'international division of labour' or 'specialization', to impose one's own will on others, infringe on the independence and sovereignty of fraternal countries or harm the interests of their people.

In relations among socialist countries it would be preposterous to follow the practice of gaining profit for oneself at the expense of others, a practice characteristic of relations among capitalist countries, or go so far as to take the 'economic integration' and the 'common market,' which monopoly capitalist groups have instituted for the purpose of seizing markets and grabbing profits, as examples which socialist countries ought to follow in their economic co-operation and mutual assistance. . . .

(22) If the principle of independence and equality is accepted in relations among fraternal Parties, then it is impermissible for any Party to place itself above others, to interfere in their internal affairs, and to adopt patriarchal ways in relations with them.

If it is accepted that there are no 'superiors' and 'subordinates' in relations among fraternal Parties, then it is impermissible to impose the programme, resolutions and line of one's own Party on other fraternal Parties as the 'common programme' of the international communist movement.

If the principle of reaching unanimity through consultation is accepted in relations among fraternal Parties, then one should not emphasize 'who is in the majority' or 'who is in the minority' and bank on a so-called majority in order to force through one's own erroneous line and carry out sectarian and splitting policies.

If it is agreed that differences between fraternal Parties should be settled through inter-Party consultation, then other fraternal Parties should not be attacked publicly and by name at one's own congress or at other Party congresses, in speeches by Party leaders, resolutions, statements, etc.; and still less should the ideological differences among fraternal Parties be extended into the sphere of state relations.

We hold that in the present circumstances, when there are differences in the international communist movement, it is particularly important to stress strict adherence to the principles guiding relations among fraternal Parties as laid down in the Declaration and the Statement.

In the sphere of relations among fraternal Parties and countries, the question of Soviet-Albanian relations is an outstanding one at present. Here the question is what is the correct way to treat a fraternal Party and country and whether the principles guiding relations among fraternal Parties and countries stipulated in the Declaration and the Statement are to be adhered to. The correct solution of this question is an important matter of principle in safeguarding the unity of the socialist camp and the international communist movement.

How to treat the Marxist-Leninist fraternal Albanian Party of Labour is one question. How to treat the Yugoslav revisionist clique of traitors to Marxism-Leninism is quite another question. These two essentially different questions must on no account be placed on a par.

Your letter says that you 'do not relinquish the hope that the relations between the C.P.S.U. and the Albanian Party of Labour may be improved,' but at the same time you continue to attack the Albanian comrades for what you call 'splitting activities.' Clearly this is self-contradictory and in no way contributes to resolving the problem of Soviet-Albanian relations. . . .

We once again express our sincere hope that the leading comrades of the C.P.S.U. will observe the principles guiding relations among fraternal Parties and countries and take the initiative in seeking an effective way to improve Soviet-Albanian relations. . . .

(23) Certain persons are now attempting to introduce the Yugoslav revisionist clique into the socialist community and the international communist ranks.

This is openly to tear up the agreement unanimously reached at the 1960 meeting of the fraternal Parties and is absolutely impermissible.

Over the past few years, the revisionist trend flooding the international working-class movement and the many experiences and lessons of the international communist movement have fully confirmed the correctness of the conclusion in the Declaration and the Statement that revisionism is the main danger in the international communist movement at present.

However, certain persons are openly saying that dogmatism and not revisionism is the main danger, or that dogmatism is no less dangerous than revisionism, etc. What sort of principle underlies all this?

Firm Marxist-Leninists and genuine Marxist-Leninist parties must put principles first. They must not barter away principles, approving one thing today and another tomorrow, advocating one thing today and another tomorrow. . . .

On the one hand, it is necessary at all times to adhere to the universal truth of Marxism-Leninism. Failure to do so will lead to Right opportunist or revisionist errors.

On the other hand, it is always necessary to proceed from reality, maintain close contact with the masses, constantly sum up the experience of mass struggles, and independently work out and apply policies and tactics suited to the conditions of one's own country. Errors of dogmatism will be committed if one fails to do so, if one mechanically copies the policies and tactics of another Communist Party, submits blindly to the will of others or accepts without analysis the programme and resolutions of another Communist Party as one's own line.

Some people are now violating this basic principle, which was long ago affirmed in the Declaration. On the pretext of 'creatively developing Marxism-Leninism,' they cast aside the universal truth of Marxism-Leninism. Moreover, they describe as 'universal Marxist-Leninist truths' their own prescriptions which are based on nothing but subjective conjecture and are divorced from reality and from the masses, and they force others to accept these prescriptions unconditionally.

That is why many grave phenomena have come to pass in the international communist movement. . . .

(24) If a party is not a proletarian revolutionary party but a bourgeois reformist party;

If it is not a Marxist-Leninist party but a revisionist party;

If it is not a vanguard party of the proletariat but a party tailing after the bourgeoisie;

If it is not a party representing the interests of the proletariat and all the working people but a party representing the interests of the labour aristocracy;

If it is not an internationalist party but a nationalist party;

If it is not a party that can use its brains to think for itself and acquire an accurate knowledge of the trends of the different classes in its own country through serious investigation and study, and knows how to apply the universal truth of Marxism-Leninism and integrate it with the concrete practice of its own country, but instead is a party that parrots the words of others, copies foreign experience without analysis, runs hither and thither in response to the baton of certain persons abroad, and has become a hodgepodge of revisionism, dogmatism and everything but Marxist-Leninist principle;

Then such a party is absolutely incapable of leading the proletariat and the masses in revolutionary struggle, absolutely incapable of winning the revolution and absolutely incapable of fulfilling the great historical mission of the proletariat. . . .

(25) It is the duty of Marxist-Leninists to distinguish between truth and falsehood with respect to the differences that have arisen in the international communist movement. In the common interest of the unity for struggle against the enemy, we have always advocated solving problems through inter-Party consultations and opposed bringing differences into the open before the enemy.

As the comrades of the C.P.S.U. know, the public polemics in the international communist movement have been provoked by certain fraternal Party leaders and forced on us.

Since a public debate has been provoked, it ought to be conducted on the basis of equality among fraternal Parties and of democracy, and by presenting the facts and reasoning things out.

Since certain Party leaders have publicly attacked other fraternal Parties and provoked a public debate, it is our opinion that they have no reason or right to forbid the fraternal Parties attacked to make public replies.

Since certain Party leaders have published innumerable articles attacking other fraternal Parties, why do they not publish in their own press the articles those Parties have written in reply? . . .

Presumably, you are referring to these articles when towards the end of your letter of March 30[1] you accuse the Chinese press of making 'groundless attacks' on the C.P.S.U. It is turning things upside down to describe articles replying to our attackers as 'attacks.' . . .

The foregoing are our views regarding the general line of the international communist movement and some related questions of principle. We hope, as we indicated at the beginning of this letter, that the frank presentation of our views will be conducive to mutual understanding. Of course, comrades may agree or disagree with these views. But in our opinion, the questions we discuss here are the crucial questions calling for attention and solution by the international communist movement. We hope that all these questions and also those raised in your letter will be fully discussed in the talks between our two Parties and at the meeting of representatives of all the fraternal Parties.

In addition, there are other questions of common concern, such as the criticism of Stalin and some important matters of principle regarding the international communist movement which were raised at the 20th and 22nd Congresses of the C.P.S.U., and we hope that on these questions, too, there will be a frank exchange of opinion in the talks.

Interview given by Mr. Khrushchev to *Pravda* and *Isvestia*, 15 June 1963[2]

Question: In his speech[3] President Kennedy of the United States laid special emphasis on the problem of war and peace. In doing so he stated that in our age 'total war makes no sense,' and that 'peace need not be impracticable—and war need not be inevitable.' He also said that 'both the United States and its

---

[1] See footnote 1, p. 231 above. [2] *Soviet News*, 17 June 1963.
[3] Speech of 10 June at American University; see pp. 14–20 above.

allies, and the Soviet Union and its allies, have a mutually deep interest in a just and genuine peace and in halting the arms race.'

How do you assess these pronouncements of the United States President?

Answer: The statement made by President Kennedy of the United States has attracted attention both in the United States and other countries of the world, including the Soviet Union.

In his speech the President touched upon the most important question of our time: war and peace in conditions when nuclear weapons have assumed a colossal destructive force and their stockpiles are continuously increasing.

I think that the Soviet people have been interested to read the speech of the United States President since this speech was a step forward in a realistic appraisal of the international situation and stressed the need to find ways which would rid mankind of the arms race and the threat of a thermonuclear world war.

World opinion and the whole of the Soviet people know full well that the Soviet government in its foreign policy has always proceeded from the Leninist principle of peaceful coexistence between states with differing social systems. Our government has made specific proposals for ending the arms race, for general and complete disarmament, a nuclear test ban, the setting up of nuclear-free zones in various regions of the world, the withdrawal of foreign troops from foreign territories, the conclusion of a peace treaty with Germany and the solution on this basis of the problem of West Berlin, and the conclusion of a non-aggression pact between the members of the North Atlantic bloc (N.A.T.O.) and the parties to the Warsaw Treaty.

Many instances could be cited of the specific, purposeful activity of the Soviet government both within the framework of the United Nations and in various commissions, committees and sub-committees, where practical proposals have been made on the above-mentioned and many other controversial and outstanding issues.

President Kennedy in his speech emphasises the existence of a real threat to the world, including the United States of America, arising from the arms race and the stockpiling of a vast amount of nuclear weapons. He rightly says that in present conditions a world war makes no sense since it inevitably implies tremendous human losses and the destruction of the material values created by the labour of many generations. He also rightly remarks that the arms race, if it is not checked, can lead to a military catastrophe. Nuclear bombs are not cucumbers which can be stored and kept for a very long time when preserved.

The President's statement that a world war is not inevitable in present conditions is also noteworthy. It is common knowledge that we have drawn this conclusion long ago.

It follows from what I have said that the speech contains a number of positive factors reflecting a sober approach to the real state of affairs.

After reading the speech of the United States President, however, one cannot but draw attention to some contradictory theses it contains.

The President stresses the need to end the cold war. However, while declaring this, does the United States President seek to eliminate the sources of the cold war? This does not emerge from the speech.

Let us take, for instance, one of the major problems—the question of the conclusion of a German peace treaty.

President Kennedy declares: 'Our commitment to defend Western Europe and West Berlin, for example, stands undiminished because of the identity of our vital interests. The United States will make no deal with the Soviet Union at the expense of other nations and other peoples, not merely because they are our partners, but also because their interests and ours converge.'

This gives the impression that the United States government is not seeking to explore avenues for an agreed solution of the German problem but, on this question, remains in practice on the old positions which, in essentials, coincide with the positions of the most reactionary aggressive forces of Western Germany, headed by Adenauer, Brandt and other revenge-minded persons. One of the main sources of the cold war is thus not to be eliminated.

The Soviet government would like to sign a German peace treaty and, on this basis, solve the problem of West Berlin jointly with its former allies in the Second World War. It is well known from the Soviet government's repeated statements that a solution of this problem does not aim at creating advantages for one or disadvantages for the other side.

The signing of a German treaty would benefit the whole cause of peace and would benefit all peoples, including the American people. The Soviet proposals on the German question are specific and clear-cut. They rest on a recognition of the actual situation in Europe and Germany—the existence of two sovereign German states: the German Democratic Republic and the Federal Republic of Germany.

As regards West Berlin specifically, there is no more sensible and logical proposal than to set up a Free City of West Berlin, with the appropriate guarantees of its international status.

I reaffirm that the Soviet government is in favour of the strictest international guarantees of the Free City of West Berlin with United Nations participation. It is necessary to emphasise most emphatically that the conclusion of a German peace treaty cannot be evaded. This question must be settled, and will be settled. We would prefer to have it settled by agreement with the western powers.

Specific deeds and not mere wishes are necessary to eliminate the sources of the cold war, and not only of the cold war, but the dangerous sources which could unleash another world war.

Or let us take another very important issue. The President speaks of easing world tensions. But how can this be reconciled with the existence of American war bases on foreign territories? For it is a fact that the United States have ringed the Soviet Union and other socialist countries with their war bases. They have in effect occupied South Vietnam, South Korea, Japan and a number of other states. Moreover, as a result of United States aggression, the ancient Chinese territory of Taiwan [Formosa] is still occupied by American troops. In some countries United States forces are virtually discharging the functions of the world's policeman, waging military operations and suppressing the national liberation movement.

Or what about the flouting of the sovereign rights of other countries by the United States?

The most zealous politicians in the United States—and some of them hold rather high posts—bluntly call for open and even armed intervention in the domestic affairs of Cuba, and seek to impose upon the Cuban people a regime that would suit the imperialist monopolies of the United States.

If President Kennedy's statement on an end to the cold war and the consolidation of peace is to be taken to a logical conclusion, it is necessary to renounce interference in the domestic affairs of other states, to respect their sovereignty, to observe the rules of international law, and not merely to pay lip service to but to respect the United Nations Charter in practice, and to remove the war bases which are a springboard for aggression against other states.

Again, let us take such a quite clear-cut issue as the conclusion of a non-aggression pact between the N.A.T.O. and Warsaw Treaty countries. An agreement on this question would do more than improve the political atmosphere, since it is not an issue of territorial or other concessions, because the conclusion of such a pact would equally benefit all signatories.

Nevertheless it is said in the western countries that such a pact should not be signed. This is explained by saying that we are all members of the United Nations whose Charter provides for non-aggression by any country on another. But if the argument is based on the fact that the United Nations Charter provides for non-aggression, why, then, did the western powers build up aggressive blocs?

Statements that the N.A.T.O. bloc has been set up for defensive purposes is talk for naive people, for many responsible leaders of this military alliance do not conceal its aggressive nature, nor that it is spearheaded against the Soviet Union and other socialist countries.

It appears then that in order to create tension in the world even the establishment of military blocs is justified, but when a non-aggression pact is offered it is said that such a pact is unnecessary. Yet everyone can see that a non-aggression pact would be a positive factor making for better relations between countries.

Some leaders in the West cynically declare that a non-aggression pact should not be concluded because this would lead to a relaxation of tension, and better relations between states would not be advantageous for them. The purpose of such leaders is to support the revenge-seekers, and constantly to threaten the German Democratic Republic and other socialist countries, thus fostering the cold war and aggravating international tension.

What logic is there in the argument that a non-aggression pact is unnecessary?

The President of the United States speaks of an end to the cold war. We welcome such pronouncements. However, who says A must also say B, as the saying is. One must seal good statements and pronouncements with practical deeds.

Question: President Kennedy specially singled out the problem of banning nuclear tests and of disarmament. How do you assess the prospect for concluding a test-ban agreement, and, specifically, the forthcoming Moscow talks on this question?

Answer: As is well known, test-ban talks have been going on for several years, and many speeches are still being made in Geneva on this topic now.

On what does the question depend? The western countries put forward their conditions for a certain number of inspections for the conclusion of a test-ban agreement. What do they want? Basically, they want Soviet territory to be opened to spies from N.A.T.O. military headquarters.

The presentation of this demand shows that the governments of the western states make distrust the foundation of relations between nuclear powers.

If one adopts such an attitude, however, the result must be that it will be impossible to solve any controversial international problem. Something like the endless story of the white bull-calf follows: now we do not believe you, now you do not believe us.

The Soviet government has stated and states again that it will not agree to throw open the territory of our country for inspection which has the purpose of espionage.

Science has proved that it is possible to detect nuclear explosions by national means of control. We think that the President himself is well aware of this and so is also, one would think, the audience he was addressing. Moreover, we have agreed to accept the proposals of the British scientists—and we now repeat our agreement—for the installation of a limited number of automatic seismic stations for observation purposes.

The national means of detection, combined with automatic seismic stations, are a dependable guarantee for the detection of any possible attempts to violate a test-ban agreement.

It will be recalled that we agreed to two or three inspections to check the discontinuance of underground tests, and we did this for political considerations. This was, so to speak, a step to meet the wishes of the other side half-way. It is to be regretted that our proposal was not properly appreciated by our partners in the talks.

What is lacking today? It is the desire of the western powers to reach an agreement and to stop playing at negotiations.

As for the Soviet Union, we are ready to sign an agreement to end all nuclear tests even today. It is up to the West. We have agreed to a meeting between the representatives of the three powers in Moscow to try once again to reach an agreement on this question; but the success of this meeting will depend on the baggage the United States and British representatives bring with them to our country.

The President of the United States touches upon such an important problem of our time as general and complete disarmament. He is right when he says that this is not a simple or easy problem and that much effort and a certain time are needed for its solution.

The Soviet government does not stint any effort in the examination of the problems of disarmament, either. Statesmen must at last become aware of their great responsibility to mankind to find a solution to such an urgent task as ending the arms race.

President Kennedy said in effect that it would be good to direct the resources released from the arms race to better purposes. In the world there is, indeed, still much poverty, hunger and unemployment. It would be good if concrete actions by the United States government followed the good wishes for disarmament.

The Soviet government's proposals on this score are widely known.

Apart from the issues already mentioned, the expansion of economic contacts and the development of trade are of great importance for an improvement in the international situation and relations between states.

Unfortunately, the President of the United States says nothing on this score in his speech.

The government of the United States virtually bans trade with the Soviet Union. It is true, the embargo on the import of crabs from the Soviet Union to the United States has been lifted. Crabs indeed are tasty food. However, crabs do not carry you very far.

The Soviet Union is a large country. We have all the necessary resources for the development of our industry and agriculture. We can do without trade with the United States, and obviously we shall also be able to develop our economy successfully in the future without trading with it. I am speaking of the development of trade between the Soviet Union and the United States because trade is a pointer to good relations between states.

The United States not only does not trade with us, but also exerts pressure on its allies, and often bars them from trading with the Soviet Union. The most striking instance of such pressure is that the United States forced West German firms to violate contractual commitments and not to deliver steel pipes to the Soviet Union.

It is not we who have suffered from this; the losers were those who succumbed to the pressure. Another gust has been added to the winds of the cold war.

Just look how the American press reacts to the visit of a delegation of Soviet foreign trade officials to the United States! It almost charges this delegation with un-American activities because the Soviet delegation seeks to establish contacts with businessmen for the establishment of normal Soviet-American trade relations. If such activities are to be denounced in the United States as impermissible, what is there left of the words in favour of improving Soviet-American relations and of getting rid of the cold war?

Question: The President's speech implies that he recognises the inevitability and necessity of co-existence between states with different social systems. At the same time he repeats in his speech the conventional western propaganda allegations that the communists seek to impose their system upon other countries and that this is the main reason for international tension.

What can be said regarding such assertions by the United States President?

Answer: In this case the United States President, unfortunately, is using the language of Dulles, who often resorted to abusive language when speaking about communism. The capitalist system is tumbling down and cracking as a result of the objective laws of historic development. The President tries to explain this by 'the communist drive to impose their political and economic system on others.' The foundations of capitalism will not be brought down by abusive language, however, but as a result of the irreconcilable contradictions between labour and capital, and as a result of the people's struggle for their freedom.

It is common knowledge that in advocating peaceful co-existence between states with different social systems, we do not offer peaceful coexistence in the sphere of ideology, but neither are we exponents of a settlement of ideological disputes by war between states. Such are our views, such is our policy.

In conclusion, I would like to say that, on the whole, President Kennedy's speech makes a favourable impression. We have noted with satisfaction the call for better relations between the United States and the Soviet Union, and his statement that 'we must re-examine our own attitude' toward the Soviet Union. We agree with the President's statement that the peoples of our countries have a mutual interest in the maintenance of peace. The peoples of the Soviet Union respect the gifted and industrious people of the United States and want to have friendly relations with them.

We are profoundly convinced that President Kennedy's call for better relations between nations, for an end to the cold war, and for better relations between the peoples of the Soviet Union and the United States will have the support of the great majority of the American people; and the peoples of the Soviet Union have always stood and continue to stand on these positions.

We are striving to obtain the practical application of good relations between countries; but to achieve this it is necessary to spare no effort in the struggle against those forces that stand on the positions of the cold war and for settling disputes by engineering war.

Time will show whether specific deeds by the American government, its practical policy, will follow these statements. The words about peace must be sealed by practical deeds. In such concrete deeds the American government will meet with the understanding and support of the Soviet government.

For our part, we shall spare no effort to find a solution of outstanding problems and to establish good relations between our great powers.

Speech by the Chairman of the People's Republic of China, Liu Shao-chi, on the occasion of the visit of the President of the Democratic People's Republic of Korea, Choi Yong Kun, Peking, 15 June 1963[1] (extracts)

. . . We have had a full exchange of views on the further consolidation and development of the relations of friendship, unity, mutual assistance and mutual cooperation between our two parties and countries, and on major questions of the present international situation and the International Communist Movement. The result of these talks shows that our stands and points of view on all questions are completely identical. Both our parties and countries are determined to carry to the very end the cause of socialist revolution and socialist construction, the cause of opposing imperialism and supporting all the oppressed nations and people striving for liberation, and the cause of opposing modern revisionism and defending Marxism-Leninism.

. . . Comrade Choi Yong Kun highly appraised the achievements won by the Chinese people in their socialist construction under the leadership of the Chinese Communist Party and Comrade Mao Tse-Tung by holding aloft the three red banners, and gave vigorous support to the Chinese people in their struggle to oppose U.S. imperialism, defend world peace and promote human progress. This is a great inspiration to us.

. . . History has proved and will continue to prove that the aggressive nature of Imperialism will never change. U.S. Imperialism is the main force of aggression and war in the world. What calls for particular attention at the present time is the

[1] *Hsinhua News Agency*, 16 June 1963.

fact that the Kennedy administration is now carrying out with much fanfare its so-called 'strategy of peace'[1] in order to cover up its armament expansion and war preparation and its activities of aggression and expansion and to benumb the people of the socialist countries and the revolutionary people of the whole world. Therefore, now more than ever, it is urgently required that the peoples maintain sharp vigilance but never entertain any unrealistic illusions about Imperialism, that they further expose U.S. Imperialism but do not prettify it. As Comrade Choi Yong Kun has pointed out, we must continuously heighten the revolutionary vigilance of the masses so that they will rise in valiant struggles against Imperialism; we must oppose the opportunist line of talking volubly about peace while giving up the anti-Imperialist and Revolutionary struggles.

Together with the Korean people, the people of the other socialist countries and all the peace-loving people of the world, the Chinese people are ready to oppose the policies of aggression and war on the part of the Imperialist bloc headed by the United States, so as to prevent a new world war and defend world peace.

The Central Committee of the Communist Party of the Soviet Union to Party Organizations and All Communists of the Soviet Union, 14 July 1963[2]

Dear comrades,

The central committee of the C.P.S.U. considers it necessary to address this Open Letter to you in order to set out our position on the fundamental questions of the international communist movement in connection with the letter of the central committee of the Communist Party of China of June 14, 1963.[3]

The Soviet people are well aware that our party and government, expressing as they do the will of the whole Soviet people, spare no effort to strengthen fraternal friendship with the peoples of all socialist countries, with the Chinese people. We are united by a common struggle for the victory of communism; we have the same aim, the same aspirations and hopes.

For many years relations between our parties were good. But, some time ago, serious differences came to light between the C.P.C. on the one hand and the C.P.S.U. and other fraternal parties on the other. At the present time the central committee of the C.P.S.U. feels increasingly concerned over statements and actions by the leadership of the Communist Party of China which undermine the cohesion of our parties and the friendship of our peoples.

The C.P.S.U. central committee, for its part, did everything possible to overcome the differences which came to light and, during January this year, proposed that the open polemics in the Communist movement should stop in order that the disputed issues should be discussed calmly and in a businesslike manner and that they should be solved on a principled Marxist-Leninist basis. This proposal from the C.P.S.U. met with warm support on the part of all fraternal parties. Subsequently, agreement was reached to hold a meeting between representatives of the C.P.S.U. and the C.P.C., and this is taking place in Moscow at present.

The C.P.S.U. central committee hoped that the Chinese comrades, too, would display goodwill and would contribute to the success of the meeting in the

---

[1] See pp. 14–20 above.   [2] *Soviet News*, 16 July 1963.   [3] See pp. 231–43 above.

interest of our peoples and in the interest of strengthening the unity of the communist movement. To our regret, when agreement had already been reached on a meeting of representatives of the C.P.S.U. and the C.P.C. in Moscow, when the delegations had been appointed and the date of the meeting set, the Chinese comrades, instead of submitting the existing differences for discussion at the meeting, unexpectedly found it possible not only to set out the old differences openly, before the whole world, but also to make new charges against the C.P.S.U. and other Communist Parties.

This found expression in the publication of the letter from the C.P.C. central committee of June 14 of this year, which gave an arbitrary interpretation of the Declaration and Statement of the Moscow meetings of representatives of the Communist and Workers' Parties and distorted the principal propositions of these historic documents. The letter of the C.P.C. central committee contained groundless, slanderous attacks on our party and on other Communist Parties, on the decisions of the 20th, 21st, and 22nd Congresses and on the Programme of the C.P.S.U.

As you know from the statement by the C.P.S.U. central committee published in *Pravda* on June 19 of this year, the presidium of the C.P.S.U. central committee, having studied the letter of the C.P.C. central committee of June 14, arrived at the conclusion that its publication in the Soviet press at that time would have been inadvisable. Its publication would naturally have required a public reply on our part, which would have led to a further sharpening of the polemics and would have inflamed passions and thereby worsened relations between our parties. Publication of the letter of the C.P.C. central committee would have been the more untimely in that a meeting was to be held between representatives of the C.P.S.U. and the C.P.C. with the purpose, in our opinion, of contributing, through consideration of the existing differences in a comradely spirit, to better mutual understanding between our two parties on the principal questions of world development today and to the establishment of a favourable atmosphere for the preparation and holding of a meeting of representatives of all Communist and Workers' Parties.

At the same time, the presidium of the central committee of the C.P.S.U. found it necessary to acquaint the members of the C.P.S.U. central committee and all those taking part in the plenary meeting with the letter from the C.P.C. central committee, and it also informed them of the substance of the differences between the C.P.C. leadership and the C.P.S.U. and other Marxist-Leninist parties.

In its unanimously adopted decision, the plenary meeting of the central committee fully approved the political work of the presidium of the C.P.S.U. central committee and of Comrade Nikita Khrushchov, the first secretary of the C.P.S.U. central committee and Chairman of the U.S.S.R. Council of Ministers, in further rallying the forces of the world communist movement, and also all the specific actions and measures taken by the presidium of the C.P.S.U. central committee in its relations with the central committee of the Communist Party of China.

The plenary meeting of the C.P.S.U. central committee instructed the presidium of the central committee, at the meeting with the representatives of the C.P.C., to follow unswervingly the line of the 20th, 21st, and 22nd Congresses of our party, the line which was approved at the meetings of the representatives of the Communist Parties and set out in the Declaration and Statement, the line which was fully vindicated by life and by the course of international developments.

Emphatically rejecting as groundless and slanderous the attacks of the central committee of the Communist Party of China on our party and other Communist Parties, on the decisions of the 20th, 21st, and 22nd Congresses and on the Programme of the C.P.S.U., the plenary meeting of the central committee, expressing the will of the whole party, declared its readiness and determination consistently to pursue the course of rallying the fraternal parties and of overcoming the existing differences.

The plenary meeting declared that our party would continue to strive to strengthen unity on the basis of the principles of Marxism-Leninism and socialist internationalism and of fraternal friendship between the C.P.S.U. and the C.P.C. in the interest of the struggle for our common cause.

Unfortunately, the events of the past period have shown that the Chinese comrades interpret our restraint in their own way. They depict our sincere striving to avoid a sharpening of polemics in the communist movement as all but an intention to hide the views of the Chinese leaders from the communists and from the Soviet people.

Mistaking our restraint for weakness, the Chinese comrades, contrary to the standards of friendly relations between fraternal socialist countries, began, with increasing importunity and persistence, to spread illegally in Moscow and other Soviet cities the letter of the C.P.C. central committee of June 14, which was brought out in Russian in a mass printing. Not content with this, the Chinese comrades began sedulously to propagandise and spread this letter and other documents directed against our party throughout the world, not scrupling to use imperialist publishing houses and agencies for their distribution.

Matters were further aggravated by the fact that when the U.S.S.R. Ministry of Foreign Affairs called the attention of the Chinese Ambassador in the Soviet Union to the impermissibility of such actions, which crudely violate the sovereignty of our state, the Chinese representatives, far from halting them, declared in a demonstrative way that they considered it their right to continue to circulate the letter in the U.S.S.R.

On July 7, when the meeting in Moscow had already begun, a mass meeting was held in Peking at which officials gave a heroes' reception to the Chinese expelled from the Soviet Union for unlawfully distributing materials containing attacks on our party and on the Soviet government. Whipping up sentiments and feelings of hostility to the U.S.S.R. among the fraternal Chinese people, Chinese officials at the meeting sought again and again to prove their right to violate the sovereignty of our state and the standards of international relations. On July 10, the C.P.C. central committee issued another statement[1] in which it sought to justify these actions and, in effect, tried to arrogate to itself the right to interfere in the internal affairs of the Soviet Union, which the Soviet government, naturally, will never allow. Such actions, inevitably, only tend to aggravate relations, and can do nothing but harm.

In its leading article on July 13, the newspaper *People's Daily* again attacked our party and twisted the fact that the Soviet press had not published the letter of the C.P.C. central committee of June 14.

[1] *Hsinhua News Agency*, Supplement No. 15, 10 July 1963.

The frankly hostile actions of the C.P.C. leaders, their persistent striving to sharpen polemics in the international communist movement, the deliberate distortion of the position of our party and the incorrect interpretation of the motives for which we refrained temporarily from publishing the letter, impel us to publish the letter of the C.P.C. central committee of June 14, 1963, and to give our appraisal of this document.

All who read the letter of the C.P.C. central committee will see, behind the bombastic phrases about unity and cohesion, unfriendly and slanderous attacks on our party and the Soviet country and a striving to play down the historic significance of our people's struggle for the victory of communism in the U.S.S.R. and for the triumph of peace and socialism throughout the world. The document is crammed with charges—overt and covert—against the C.P.S.U. and the Soviet Union. The authors of the letter permit themselves unworthy fabrications—insulting to communists—about 'the betrayal of the interests of the whole international proletariat and all the peoples of the world,' about 'a departure from Marxism-Leninism and proletarian internationalism'; they hint at 'cowardice in face of the imperialists,' at 'a step back in the course of historic development,' and even at 'the organisational and moral disarming of the proletariat and all working people,' which is tantamount 'to helping to restore capitalism' in our country.

How can they say such things about the party of the great Lenin, about the motherland of socialism, about the people who first in the world carried out a socialist revolution, upheld its great gains in violent battles against international imperialism and domestic counter-revolution, and who are displaying miracles of heroism and dedication in the struggle for the building of communism, and are honestly fulfilling their internationalist duty to the working people of the world!

1

For nearly half a century the Soviet country, under the leadership of the Communist Party, has been leading the struggle for the triumph of the ideas of Marxism-Leninism, in the interest of the freedom and happiness of the working people of the whole world. From the very first days of the existence of the Soviet state, when the great Lenin stood at the helm of our country, to the present day, our people have rendered and are rendering an enormous and disinterested aid to all peoples fighting for their liberation from the yoke of imperialism and colonialism and for building a new life.

World history has known no example of one country rendering such extensive aid to other countries in developing their economy, science and technology.

The working people of China and the Chinese communists felt in full measure the fraternal solidarity of the Soviet people and of our party both in the period of their revolutionary struggle for the liberation of their homeland and in the years of the construction of socialism. Immediately after the forming of the Chinese People's Republic, the Soviet government signed with the government of People's China a Treaty of Friendship, Alliance and Mutual Assistance,[1] which

---

[1] *Documents, 1949–50*, pp. 541–7.

is a mighty means of rebuffing the encroachments of imperialism, and is a factor consolidating peace in the Far East and in the whole world.

The Soviet people generously shared with its Chinese brothers all its many years' long experience in socialist construction and its achievements in the field of science and technology. Our country has rendered and is rendering substantial aid to the development of the economy of People's China. With the active assistance of the Soviet Union, People's China built 198 industrial enterprises, shops and other projects equipped with the up-to-date machinery.

With the assistance of our country such new branches of industry as automobile, tractor, aircraft manufacturing, and others, were created in China. The Soviet Union handed over to the People's Republic of China over 21,000 sets of scientific-technical documentation, including more than 1,400 blueprints of big enterprises. We have unswervingly assisted China in consolidating the defence of the country and the creation of a modern defence industry. Thousands of Chinese specialists and workers were trained in Soviet establishments of higher education and at our enterprises. Now, too, the Soviet Union continues to render technical assistance to the Chinese People's Republic in the construction of 88 industrial enterprises and projects.

We speak about all this not to boast, but only because the leaders of the C.P.C. have recently sought to belittle the significance of Soviet aid, and we do not forget that the Soviet Union, in its turn, received the goods it needed from the People's Republic of China.

Only a short time ago, the Chinese leaders spoke much and justly about the friendship of the peoples of China and the Soviet Union, about the unity of the C.P.S.U. and the C.P.C., expressed great appreciation for Soviet aid, and urged the people to learn from the experience of the Soviet Union.

Comrade Mao Tse-tung said in 1957:

'In the course of struggle for national liberation, the Chinese people enjoyed the fraternal sympathy and support of the Soviet people. After the victory of the Chinese Revolution, the Soviet Union is also rendering tremendous all-round assistance to the cause of the construction of socialism in China. The Chinese people will never forget all this.'

One can only regret that the Chinese leaders have begun to forget it.

Our party and all Soviet people rejoiced at the successes of the great Chinese people in the building of a new life, and took pride in them. Speaking at a reception in Peking on the occasion of the tenth anniversary of the Chinese People's Republic, Nikita Khrushchov said:

'Under the leadership of its glorious Communist Party, the heroic and hard-working people of China have demonstrated what a people is capable of when it takes power into its own hands. . . .

'Now everybody admits the successes of the Chinese people and of the Communist Party of China. The peoples of Asia and Africa see how and under which system the talents and the creative forces of the peoples can be fully developed, and in which a people can demonstrate in both width and depth its mighty creative force.'

This was how matters stood until the Chinese leaders began to retreat from the general line of the world communist movement.

In April 1960 the Chinese comrades openly revealed their differences with the world communist movement by publishing a collection of articles called *Long Live Leninism*.[1] This collection, based on distortions, truncated and incorrectly interpreted theses from well-known works of Lenin, contained propositions in fact directed against the fundamentals of the Declaration of the Moscow Meeting of 1957,[2] which was signed on behalf of the C.P.C. by Comrade Mao Tse-tung, against the policy of peaceful co-existence between states with different social systems, against the possibility of preventing a world war in the present-day epoch and against the use both of the peaceful and non-peaceful road of the development of socialist revolutions.

The leaders of the C.P.C. began to impose their views on all the fraternal parties. In June 1960, during the session of the general council of the World Federation of Trade Unions, which took place in Peking, without the knowledge of the leaderships of fraternal parties, the Chinese leaders gathered a meeting of representatives of several parties, which were then in Peking, and started openly to criticise the positions of the C.P.S.U. and other Marxist-Leninist parties and the Declaration adopted by the Moscow meeting of 1957. Furthermore, the Chinese comrades made their differences with the C.P.S.U. and other fraternal parties a subject of open discussion in a non-party organisation.

These steps by the leadership of the C.P.C. aroused serious concern among the fraternal parties, and, in view of this, an attempt was made at the Bucharest meeting of Communist Parties in 1960 to discuss the differences which had arisen with the leaders of the C.P.C. Representatives of 50 Communist and Workers' Parties subjected the views and actions of the Chinese leaders to comradely criticism and urged them to return to the road of unity and co-operation with the international communist movement in conformity with the principles of the Moscow Declaration. Unfortunately, the C.P.C. leadership ignored this comradely assistance and continued to pursue its erroneous course and to deepen its differences with the fraternal parties.

Seeking to prevent such a development of events, the C.P.S.U. central committee came out with a proposal to hold talks with the central committee of the Communist Party of China. These negotiations took place in Moscow in September 1960. But, even then, it was impossible to overcome the differences that had arisen due to the stubborn unwillingness of the C.P.C. delegation to heed the opinion of the fraternal party. At the meeting of representatives of 81 Communist and Workers' Parties, which took place in November 1960, the absolute majority of the fraternal parties rejected the incorrect views and concepts of the C.P.C. leadership. The Chinese delegation at this meeting stubbornly upheld its own particular views, and signed the Statement only when the danger arose of its complete isolation.

Today it has become absolutely obvious that the C.P.C. leaders were only manoeuvering when they affixed their signatures to the Statement of 1960.[3] Shortly after the meeting they resumed propaganda for their cause, using the leadership of the Albanian Party of Labour as a mouthpiece. Behind the back of our party, they launched a campaign against the C.P.S.U. central committee and the Soviet government.

In October 1961, the C.P.S.U. central committee undertook new attempts to normalise relations with the C.P.C. Comrades Nikita Khrushchov, Frol

---

[1] *Documents, 1960*, pp. 198–209.   [2] Ibid., *1957*, pp. 527–39.   [3] Ibid., *1960*, pp. 222–38.

Kozlov and Anastas Mikoyan had talks with comrades Chou En-lai, Peng Chen and other leading officials, who arrived for the 22nd Congress of the C.P.S.U. Comrade Nikita Khrushchov set out in detail to the Chinese delegation the position of the C.P.S.U. central committee on the questions of principle, which were discussed at the 22nd Congress and declared our unswerving desire to strengthen friendship and co-operation with the Communist Party of China.

In its letters of February 22[1] and May 31, 1962,[2] the C.P.S.U. central committee drew the attention of the C.P.C. central committee to the dangerous consequences for our common cause which could be brought about by the weakening of the unity of the communist movement. We then offered to the Chinese comrades to take steps in order not to give the imperialists an opportunity to use in their interests the difficulties which had arisen in Soviet-Chinese mutual relations. The C.P.S.U. central committee also proposed that more effective measures should be taken on such questions as the exchange of internal political information and the co-ordination of the positions of fraternal parties in the international democratic organisations and in other spheres.

However, these letters and the other practical steps aimed at improving relations with the C.P.C. and the People's Republic of China in all directions, did not find a response in Peking.

In the autumn of last year, before the departure from Moscow of the former Chinese Ambassador in the Soviet Union, Comrade Liu Hsiao, the presidium of the C.P.S.U. central committee had a long discussion with him. In the course of this conversation the members of the presidium of the central committee once again displayed initiative in the matter of strengthening Chinese-Soviet friendship. Comrade Nikita Khrushchov asked Comrade Liu Hsiao to forward to Comrade Mao Tse-tung our proposal: 'to put aside all disputes and differences, not to try and establish who is right and who is wrong, not to rake up the past, but to start our relations with a clear page.' But we have not even received an answer to this sincere call.

Deepening their ideological differences with the fraternal parties, the leaders of the C.P.C. began to carry them over to international relations. The Chinese organs began to curtail the economic and trade relations of the People's Republic of China with the Soviet Union and other socialist countries. On the initiative of the government of the People's Republic of China the volume of China's trade with the Soviet Union has been cut almost 67 per cent. in the past three years, and deliveries of industrial plant have dropped to a fortieth. This reduction has taken place on the initiative of the Chinese leaders. We regret that the leadership of the People's Republic of China has embarked on such a course. We have always believed, and believe now, that it is necessary to go on developing Soviet-Chinese relations and to develop co-operation. This would have been mutually beneficial for both sides, and above all to People's China, which had received great assistance from the Soviet Union and other socialist countries. The Soviet Union developed extensive relations with China before, and, today, it also stands for their expansion and not their curtailment. It would seem that the C.P.C. leadership should have displayed primary concern for the development of economic relations with the socialist countries. However,

[1] *Documents, 1962*, pp. 696–700.   [2] This letter was apparently not published.

it began acting in the opposite direction, disregarding the damage caused by such actions to the economy of the People's Republic of China.

The Chinese leaders did not tell their people truthfully whose fault it was that these relations were curtailed. Extensive propaganda was started among the Chinese communists and even among the people aimed at discrediting the foreign and domestic policy of the C.P.S.U. and at stirring up anti-Soviet sentiments.

The C.P.S.U. central committee called the attention of the Chinese comrades to these incorrect actions. We told the Chinese comrades that the people should not be prompted to praise or anathematise this or that party on the basis of disputes or differences which arise. It is clear to every Communist that disagreements among fraternal parties are nothing more than temporary episodes, whereas relations between the peoples of the socialist countries are now being established for all time to come.

Every time, however, the Chinese leaders ignored the comradely warnings of the C.P.S.U. and further exacerbated Chinese-Soviet relations.

From the end of 1961 the Chinese representatives in international democratic organisations began openly to impose their erroneous views. In December 1961, at the Stockholm session of the World Peace Council, the Chinese delegation opposed the convocation of the World Congress for Peace and Disarmament. In the course of 1962, the activities of the World Federation of Trade Unions, the world peace movement, the Afro-Asian Solidarity Movement, the World Federation of Democratic Youth, the Women's International Democratic Federation and many other organisations were endangered as a result of the splitting activities of the Chinese representatives. They came out against the participation at the Third Solidarity Conference of the Peoples of Asian and African countries in Moshi of representatives of the Afro-Asian Solidarity Committees of the European socialist countries.

The leader of the Chinese delegation told the Soviet representatives that 'the Whites have nothing to do here.' At the journalists' conference in Jakarta the Chinese representatives took the line of preventing Soviet journalists from participating as full delegates on the plea that the Soviet Union . . . is not an Asian country!

It is strange and surprising that the Chinese comrades accused the overwhelming majority at the recent World Congress of Women of splitting activities and of a wrong political line, while at the adoption of the Appeal to the women of all continents the representatives of only two countries—China and Albania—out of the 110 countries represented at the congress, voted against it. So the whole multi-millioned army of freedom-loving women is marching out of step and only two are marching in step, keeping in line!

Such is in brief the history of the differences of the Chinese leadership with the C.P.S.U. and other fraternal parties. It shows that the C.P.C. leaders counterpose their own special line to the general course of the communist movement, and try to impose their own dictate and their deeply erroneous views on the key problems of our time on it.

2

What is the gist of the differences between the C.P.C. on the one hand and the C.P.S.U. and the international communist movement on the other? This question is no doubt asked by everyone who studies the letter from the C.P.C. central committee of June 14.

At a first glance many theses in the letter may seem puzzling: whom are the Chinese comrades actually arguing with? Are there communists who, for instance, object to socialist revolution or who do not regard it as their duty to fight against imperialism and to support the national-liberation movement? Why does the C.P.C. leadership set out these theses with such obsession?

The question may also arise why it is impossible to agree with the positions of the Chinese comrades set forth in their letter on many important problems? Take, for instance, such cardinal problems as war and peace. In its letter the C.P.C. central committee speaks of peace and peaceful co-existence.

The essence of the matter is that having started an offensive against the positions of the Marxist-Leninist parties on cardinal problems of today, the Chinese comrades first ascribe to the C.P.S.U. and other Marxist-Leninist parties views which they have never expressed and which are alien to them; secondly, by paying lip service to formulae and positions borrowed from the documents of the communist movement, they try to camouflage their erroneous views and incorrect positions. To come out openly against the peoples' struggle for peace and for peaceful co-existence between states with different social systems, against disarmament, etc., would mean to expose their positions in the eyes of the communists of the whole world and all peaceloving peoples and to repulse them. Therefore the further the polemics develop and the clearer the weakness of the positions of the C.P.C. leadership becomes, the more zealously it resorts to such camouflage.

If this method of the Chinese comrades is not taken into consideration, it may even seem from outside that the dispute has acquired a scholastic nature, that separate formulas far removed from vital problems are the points at issue.

In point of fact, however, the questions which bear on vital interests of the peoples are in the centre of the dispute.

> These are the questions of war and peace, the question of the role and development of the world socialist system, these are the questions of the struggle against the ideology and practice of the 'cult of the individual,' these are the questions of the strategy and tactics of the world labour movement and the national liberation struggle.

These questions have been brought forward by life itself, by the deep-going changes which have occurred in the socialist countries and throughout the world, the changes in the balance of forces in recent years between socialism and imperialism and the new possibilities for our movement.

The communist movement had to give and did give answers to these questions by outlining the general course applicable to the conditions and demands of the present stage of world development.

The unanimous opinion of the Communist Parties is that a tremendous role in this respect was played by the 20th Congress of the C.P.S.U. which ushered in a new stage in the development of the entire communist movement. This appraisal was recorded in the 1957 Declaration and in the 1960 Statement, the documents of the Communist Parties worked out collectively and formulating the general political course of the communist movement in our epoch.

The C.P.C. leaders, however, have now advanced a different course in opposition to it, and their positions diverge more and more from the joint line of the communist movement on basic issues.

This first of all refers to the question of war and peace.

In the appraisal of the problems of war and peace and in the approach to their solution, there can be no uncertainties or reservations, for this involves the destinies of peoples, the future of all mankind.

The C.P.S.U. central committee believes it to be its duty to tell the party and the people with all frankness that in questions of war and peace the C.P.C. leadership has cardinal differences, based on principle, with us and with the world communist movement. The essence of these differences lies in a diametrically opposite approach to such vital problems as the possibility of averting thermonuclear world war, peaceful co-existence between states with different social systems and the inter-connection between the struggle for peace and the development of the world revolutionary movement.

Our party, in the decisions of the 20th and 22nd Congresses, and the world communist movement, in the Declaration and Statement, set before communists as a task of extreme importance the task of struggling for peace and for averting a thermonuclear world catastrophe. We appraise the balance of forces in the world realistically, and from this draw the conclusion that, though the nature of imperialism has not changed, and the danger of the outbreak of war has not been averted, in modern conditions the forces of peace, of which the mighty community of socialist states is the main bulwark, can, by their joint efforts, avert a new world war.

We also soberly appraise the radical, qualitative change in the means of waging war and, consequently, its possible aftermaths. The nuclear rocket weapons which have been created in the middle of our century change the old notions about war. These weapons possess an unprecedented devastating force. Suffice it to say that the explosion of only one powerful thermonuclear bomb surpasses the explosive force of all the ammunition used during all previous wars, including the First and Second World Wars. And many thousands such bombs have been accumulated!

Do communists have the right to ignore this danger? Do we have to tell the people all the truth about the consequences of thermonuclear war? We believe that, without question, we must. This cannot have a 'paralysing' effect on the masses, as the Chinese comrades assert. On the contrary, the truth about modern war will mobilise the will and energy of the masses in the struggle for peace and against imperialism—the source of military danger.

The historic task of communists is to organise and lead the struggle of the peoples to avert a thermonuclear world war.

To prevent a new world war is a real and quite feasible task. The 20th Congress of our party came to the extremely important conclusion that in our times there is no fatal inevitability of war between states. This conclusion is not the fruit of good intentions, but the result of a realistic, strictly scientific analysis of the balance of class forces on the world arena; it is based on the gigantic might of world socialism. Our views on this question are shared by the entire world communist movement. 'World war can be averted'; 'A real possibility to exclude world war from the life of society will appear even before the complete victory of socialism on earth, while capitalism still remains in part of the world,' the Statement declares.

This statement also bears the signature of the Chinese comrades.

And what is the position of the C.P.C. leadership? What do the theses that they propagate mean: an end cannot be put to wars so long as imperialism exists; peaceful coexistence is an illusion; it is not the general principle of the foreign policy of socialist countries; the peace struggle hinders the revolutionary struggle?

These theses mean that the Chinese comrades are acting contrary to the general course of the world communist movement in questions of war and peace. They do not believe in the possibility of preventing a new world war; they underestimate the forces of peace and socialism and overestimate the forces of imperialism; in fact they ignore the mobilisation of the masses for the struggle with the war danger.

It emerges that the Chinese comrades do not believe in the ability of the peoples of the socialist countries, of the international working class, and of all democratic and peaceloving forces to frustrate the plans of the warmongers and to achieve peace for our and future generations. What stands behind the loud revolutionary phrases of the Chinese comrades? Lack of faith in the forces of the working class and its revolutionary capabilities, lack of faith both in the possibility of peaceful co-existence and in the victory of the proletariat in class struggle. All peaceloving forces unite in the struggle to avert war. They differ as to their class composition and their class interests. But they can be united by the struggle for peace and to avert war, because the nuclear bomb does not adhere to the class principle—it destroys everybody within the range of its devastating force.

To adopt the course proposed by the Chinese comrades means to alienate the masses of the people from the Communist Parties which have won the sympathies of the peoples by their insistent and courageous struggle for peace.

Socialism and peace are now inseparable in the minds of the broad masses!

The Chinese comrades obviously underestimate the whole danger of thermonuclear war. 'The atomic bomb is a paper tiger'; 'it is not terrible at all,' they contend.

The main thing, don't you see, is to put an end to imperialism as quickly as possible, but how, with what losses this will be achieved seems to be a secondary question. To whom, it is right to ask, is it secondary? To the hundreds of millions of people who are doomed to death in the event of the unleashing of a thermonuclear war? To the states that will be erased from the face of the earth in the very first hours of such a war?

No one, and this also includes big states, has the right to play with the destinies of millions of people. Those who do not want to make an effort to exclude world war from the life of the peoples, to avert a mass annihilation of people and the destruction of the values of human civilisation, deserve condemnation.

The letter of the C.P.C. central committee of June 14 says much about 'inevitable sacrifices,' allegedly in the name of the revolution. Some responsible Chinese leaders have also declared that it is possible to sacrifice hundreds of millions of people in war. 'On the ruins of destroyed imperialism the victorious peoples'—asserts the collection *Long live Leninism!* which was approved by the C.P.C. central committee—'will create with tremendous speed a civilisation a thousand times higher than under the capitalist system and will build their really bright future.'

It is permissible to ask the Chinese comrades if they realise what sort of 'ruins' a nuclear rocket world war would leave behind?

The C.P.S.U. central committee, and we are convinced that all our party and the whole Soviet people unanimously support us in this, cannot share the views of the Chinese leadership about the creation 'of a thousand times higher civilisation' on the corpses of hundreds of millions of people. Such views are in crying contradiction with the ideas of Marxism-Leninism.

It is permissible to ask the Chinese comrades: what means do they propose for the destruction of imperialism? We fully stand for the destruction of imperialism and capitalism. We not only believe in the inevitable destruction of capitalism but also are doing everything for this to be accomplished by way of class struggle and as soon as possible. Who must decide this historic question? First of all the working class led by its vanguard, the Marxist-Leninist party, the working people of each country.

The Chinese comrades propose another thing. They straightforwardly say: 'On the ruins of a destroyed imperialism'—in other words, as a result of the unleashing of war—'a bright future will be built.' If we agree to this, then, indeed, there is no need for the principle of peaceful co-existence and for the struggle for the strengthening of peace. We cannot agree to such an adventurist course: it contradicts the nature of Marxism-Leninism.

It is generally known that under present conditions a world war would be a thermonuclear war. The imperialists will never agree to withdraw from the scene voluntarily, to lie in the coffin of their own free will, without having used the extreme means they have at their disposal.

Apparently the people who refer to the thermonuclear weapon as a 'paper tiger' are not fully aware of the destructive force of this weapon.

We soberly consider this. We ourselves produce the thermonuclear weapon and have manufactured it in sufficient quantity. We know its destructive force full well. And if imperialism starts a war against us we shall not hesitate to use this formidable weapon against the aggressor; but if we are not attacked, we shall not be the first to use this weapon.

Marxist-Leninists strive to ensure an enduring peace not by begging for it from imperialism but by rallying the revolutionary Marxist-Leninist parties, by rallying the working class of all countries, by rallying the peoples fighting for their freedom and national independence, and by relying on the economic and defensive might of the socialist states.

We would like to ask the Chinese comrades who suggest building a bright future on the ruins of the old world destroyed by a thermonuclear war whether they have consulted the working class of the countries where imperialism dominates? The working class of the capitalist countries would certainly tell them: are we asking you to trigger off a war and destroy our countries while annihilating the imperialists? Is it not a fact that the monopolists, the imperialists, are only a comparatively small group, while the bulk of the population of the capitalist countries consists of the working class, working peasantry and working intelligentsia?

The nuclear bomb does not distinguish between the imperialists and working people, it hits great areas, and therefore millions of workers would be destroyed for one monopolist. The working class, the working people, will ask such 'revolutionaries': what right have you to decide for us the questions of our existence and our class struggle? We also are in favour of socialism; but we want to gain it through the class struggle and not by unleashing a thermo-nuclear world war.

The posing of the question in this way by the Chinese comrades may give rise to the well justified suspicion that this is no longer a class approach in the struggle for the abolition of capitalism, but has some entirely different aims. If both the exploiters and the exploited are buried under the ruins of the old world, who will build the 'bright future'?

In this connection it is impossible not to note the fact that instead of the internationalist class approach expressed in the call 'workers of all countries, unite!' the Chinese comrades stubbornly propagate the slogan which is devoid of any class meaning: 'The wind from the East prevails over the wind from the West.'

In the question of the Socialist revolution, our party firmly adheres to the Marxist-Leninist class positions believing that revolutions in every country are carried out by the working class and the working people, without military interference from outside.

There is no doubt, of course, that if the imperialist madmen do unleash a war, the peoples will wipe out and bury capitalism. But the communists, representing the peoples, the true advocates of socialist humanism, must do everything they can to prevent another world war in which hundreds of millions of people would perish.

No party which truly cherishes the interests of the people can fail to realise its responsibility in the struggle to avert another world war and to ensure peaceful co-existence between states with different social systems.

Expressing the line of our party, Comrade Nikita Khrushchev said:

> There will be wars of liberation as long as imperialism exists, as long as colonialism exists. These are revolutionary wars. Such wars are not only per-missible but even unavoidable, since the colonialists do not grant independence to people voluntarily. Therefore it is only through struggle, including armed struggle, that the peoples can win their freedom and independence.

The Soviet Union is rendering the broadest support to the national liberation movement. Everybody is familiar with the practical assistance our country rendered the peoples of Vietnam, Egypt, Iraq, Algeria, Yemen, Cuba and other peoples.

The Communist Party of the Soviet Union proclaimed the Leninist principles of peaceful co-existence as the general line of Soviet foreign policy and is follow-ing it unswervingly. Since 1953, and particularly after the 20th C.P.S.U. Con-gress, there was a sharp increase in the activity of our peace policy, and its influence on the whole course of international relations grew in the interests of masses of the people.

The Chinese comrades allege that we proceed from the premise that the con-cept of 'peaceful co-existence' covers all the principles of our relations, not only with the imperialist countries, but also with the socialist countries and the coun-tries that have recently got rid of the colonial yoke. They know very well that this is not so, that we were the first to proclaim the principle of friendship and comradely mutual assistance as the most important principle in the relations between the countries of socialism and we adhere to it firmly and consistently, that we render all-round and many sided assistance to the liberated peoples. And yet, for some motives, they find it advantageous for themselves to present all this is an entirely distorted light.

The Soviet Union's persistent struggle for peace and international security, for general and complete disarmament, for the elimination of the vestiges of the Second World War, for a negotiated settlement of all controversial international issues has yielded fruit. The prestige of our country throughout the world stands higher than ever, our international position is more solid than ever. We owe this to the steadily growing economic and military might of the Soviet Union and of other socialist countries, and to their peaceful foreign policy.

The C.P.S.U. central committee declares that we have been, are and will continue to pursue the Leninist policy of peaceful co-existence between states with different social systems. In this our party sees its duty both to the Soviet people and the peoples of all other countries. To ensure peace means to contribute most effectively to the consolidation of the socialist system, and, consequently, to the growth of its influence on the entire course of the liberation struggle and the world revolutionary process.

The deep difference between the views of the C.P.S.U. and other Marxist-Leninist parties on the one hand and the C.P.C. leaders on the other, on the questions of war, peace and peaceful co-existence was demonstrated with particular clarity during the 1962 crisis in the Caribbean Sea. It was a sharp international crisis: never before did mankind come so close to the brink of a thermonuclear war as it did in October last year.

The Chinese comrades allege that in the period of the Caribbean crisis we made an 'adventurist' mistake by introducing rockets into Cuba and then 'capitulated' to American imperialism when we removed the rockets from Cuba.[1]

Such assertions utterly contradict the facts.

What was the actual state of affairs? The C.P.S.U. central committee and the Soviet government possessed trustworthy information that an armed aggression by United States imperialism against Cuba was about to take place. We realised with sufficient clarity that the most resolute steps were needed to rebuff the aggression and to defend the Cuban revolution effectively. Curses and warnings —even if they are called 'serious warnings' and repeated two and a half hundred times over have no effect on the imperialists.

Proceeding from the need to defend the Cuban revolution, the Soviet government and the government of Cuba reached agreement on the delivery of missiles to Cuba, because this was the only effective way of preventing aggression on the part of American imperialism. The delivery of missiles to Cuba meant that an attack on her would meet with a resolute rebuff and the use of rocket weapons against the organisers of the aggression. Such a resolute step on the part of the Soviet Union and Cuba was a shock to the American imperialists, who felt for the first time in their history that if they were to undertake an armed invasion of Cuba, a shattering retaliatory blow would be dealt against their own territory.

[1] These allegations were made in the leading article in *People's Daily* on 8 March 1963, 'On the Statement of the Communist Party of the U.S.A.' [footnote in original].

Inasmuch as the point in question was not simply a conflict between the United States and Cuba, but a clash between the two major nuclear powers, the crisis in the Caribbean Sea area would have turned from a local into a world one. A real danger of thermonuclear world war arose.

There was one alternative in the prevailing situation: either to follow in the wake of the 'madmen' (this is how the most aggressive and reactionary representatives of American imperialism are dubbed) and embark upon a course of unleashing a world thermonuclear war or, profiting from the opportunities offered by the delivery of missiles, to take all steps to reach an agreement on a peaceful solution of the crisis and to prevent aggression against the Republic of Cuba.

As is known, we chose the second path and are convinced that we did the right thing. We are confident that all our people are unanimous on this score. The Soviet people have proved more than once that they know how to stand up for themselves, how to defend the cause of the revolution and the cause of socialism. And nobody knows better than they do how much sorrow and suffering a war brings, what difficulties and sacrifices it costs the peoples.

Agreement to remove the missile weapons in return for the United States government's commitment not to invade Cuba and to keep its allies from doing so, the heroic struggle of the Cuban people and the support rendered to them by the peaceloving nations, made it possible to frustrate the plans of the extreme adventurist circles of American imperialism, which were ready to go the whole hog. As a result it was possible to defend revolutionary Cuba and to save peace.

The Chinese comrades regard our statement that the Kennedy government also displayed a certain reasonableness and a realistic approach in the course of the crisis around Cuba as 'embellishing imperialism.' Do they really think that all bourgeois governments lack all reason in everything they do?

Thanks to the courageous and farsighted position of the U.S.S.R. and the staunchness and restraint of the heroic Cuban people and their government, the forces of socialism and peace have proved that they are able to curb the aggressive forces of imperialism and to impose peace on the advocates of war. This was a major victory for the policy of reason and for the forces of peace and socialism; this was a defeat for the forces of imperialism and for the policy of military ventures.

As a result of this, revolutionary Cuba is living in peace and building socialism under the guidance of its United Party of the Socialist Revolution and the leader of the Cuban people, Comrade Fidel Castro Ruz.

When agreement was reached with the President of the United States of America and a start was thereby made towards eliminating the crisis in the Caribbean Sea area, the Chinese comrades did their best in insulting and attacking the Soviet Union, trying to prove that the word of the imperialists cannot be trusted in anything.

We are living in an epoch when there are two worlds, two systems: socialism and imperialism. It would be absurd to think that all the questions which inevitably arise in relations between the countries of these two systems must be solved only by force of arms, ruling out all talks and agreements. Wars would never end then. We are against such an approach.

The Chinese comrades argue that the imperialists cannot be trusted in anything, that they are bound to cheat; but this is not a case of faith, but rather a case of sober calculation. Eight months have passed since the elimination of the crisis in the Caribbean Sea area, and the United States government is keeping its word—there is no invasion of Cuba. We also assumed a commitment to remove our missiles from Cuba, and we have fulfilled it.

It should not, however, be forgotten that we have also given a commitment to the Cuban people: if the United States imperialists do not keep their promise but invade Cuba, we shall come to the assistance of the Cuban people. Every reasonable person realises full well that, in the event of aggression by the American imperialists, we shall come to the assistance of the Cuban people from Soviet territory, just as we would have helped them from Cuban territory, too. True, in this case the rockets would be in flight slightly longer, but their precision will not be impaired.

Why then do the Chinese comrades stubbornly ignore the assessment which the leaders of the Cuban revolution themselves give to the policy of the government of the Soviet Union, which they call a policy of fraternal solidarity and genuine internationalism? What are the Chinese leaders dissatisfied with? Is it, perhaps, the fact that it was possible to prevent the invasion of Cuba and the unleashing of a world war?

And what was the line of behaviour of the C.P.C. leadership during the Caribbean crisis? At this critical moment the Chinese comrades opposed the realistic and firm stand of the Soviet government with their own particular position. Guided by some sort of peculiar concepts of their own, they concentrated the fire of their criticism not so much on the aggressive imperialism of the United States, but rather on the C.P.S.U. and the Soviet Union.

The C.P.C. leadership, which, prior to that, argued that imperialism might unleash a world war at any time, assumed the stand of a critic, not of a militant ally and comrade at the most responsible moment. Nobody heard any statements from the Chinese leaders during those days about their practical actions in defence of the Cuban Revolution. Instead of this, the Chinese leaders obviously tried to aggravate the situation in the Caribbean Sea area, which was tense even without this, and added fuel to the smouldering fire of the conflict.

The true position of the C.P.C. leadership is demonstrated very clearly in the questions of war and peace, in its complete underestimation, and what is more, deliberate ignoring, of the struggle for disarmament. The Chinese communists object even to the very raising of this question by communists, permitting themselves to make references to Marxism-Leninism and going out of their way to prove that disarmament is 'not feasible' on the one hand, and that there is no need for it, on the other. Juggling with quotations, they try to prove that general disarmament is possible only when socialism triumphs all over the world.

Must the Marxists sit on their hands, waiting for the victory of socialism all over the world, while mankind suffocates in the clutches of the arms race, while the imperialists, stockpiling nuclear arms, threaten to plunge mankind into the abyss of a world war?

No, this would be criminal inaction in face of the imperative call of the time.

This truth has long ago been understood by all true Marxists-Leninists, who realise their responsibility to the peoples and who have already been waging for a number of years—and will go on waging—a stubborn and persistent struggle for general and complete disarmament, for the ending of tests and the banning of nuclear weapons.

In fighting for peace and in advancing the slogan of universal disarmament, we proceed from the vital interests of the peoples, take the actual situation into account and do not shut our eyes to the difficulties. The imperialists are naturally doing everything to delay and wreck agreement on disarmament—they stand to gain by this. They use the arms race to enrich themselves and to hold the masses of the people in the capitalist countries in fear. But must we go with the current, must we follow in the wake of imperialism and refuse to mobilise all forces to struggle for peace and for disarmament?

No. To do this would be to capitulate to the aggressive forces, to the militarists and imperialists. We hold that the working class, the working people of all countries, can force the imperialist governments to consent to disarmament and can prevent war. For this, they must above all realise their strength and unite.

Against the forces of imperialism and war it is necessary to oppose the organised might of the world working class, which now has the advantage of being supported by the material power and the defensive might of the socialist countries opposed to imperialism. The time has gone when imperialism held undivided sway. The situation has also changed radically compared with the first decades after the October Revolution, when our country was alone and much weaker than today. In our time the balance of forces in the world has become entirely different. This is why to hold now that war is inevitable is to show lack of faith in the forces of socialism and to surrender to the mood of hopelessness and defeatism.

One can repeat *ad infinitum* that war is inevitable, claiming that such a viewpoint is evidence of one's 'revolutionary spirit.' In fact, this approach merely indicates lack of faith in one's strength and fear of imperialism.

There are still powerful forces opposed to disarmament in the imperialist camp; but it is precisely to compel these forces to retreat that we must arouse the anger of the people against them and force them to comply with the will of the peoples.

The peoples want disarmament and believe that it is the communists who are the vanguard and organisers of the peoples' struggle to achieve this aim.

Our struggle for disarmament is not a tactical expedient. We sincerely want disarmament. And here, too, we stand four-square on the positions of Marxism-Leninism. As early as the end of the last century Engels pointed out that disarmament was possible, and he called it a 'guarantee of peace.' In our time the slogan of disarmament was first advanced as a practical task by Lenin, and the first Soviet proposals for complete or partial disarmament were submitted as early as 1922, at the Genoa conference. This was in Lenin's lifetime, and the disarmament proposals were formulated by him.

The struggle for disarmament is a most important factor for averting war. It is an effective struggle against imperialism. In this struggle the socialist camp has on its side the absolute majority of mankind.

The Chinese comrades have advanced the slogan of 'spearpoint against spearpoint,' opposing it to the policy of the other socialist countries which aims at relaxing the international situation and ending the cold war. In actual fact, this slogan adds grist to the imperialist policy of brinkmanship, and helps the champions of the arms race. The impression is given that the leaders of the

C.P.C. regard as advantageous the preservation and intensification of international tension, especially in relations between the U.S.S.R. and the United States. They apparently hold that the Soviet Union should reply to provocations by provocations, fall into the traps set by the 'wild men' from the imperialist camp, and accept the challenge of the imperialists to a competition in adventurism and aggressiveness, that is competition not for ensuring peace but for unleashing war.

To take this path would be to jeopardise peace and the security of peoples. Communists, who cherish the interests of the peoples, will never follow this road.

The struggle for peace and to implement the principles of the peaceful co-existence between states with different social systems is one of the most important forms of the peoples' struggle against imperialism, against new wars prepared by it, against the aggressive actions of the imperialists in colonial countries, against the military bases of imperialists on foreign territories, against the arms race, etc. This struggle is in the interest of the working class and of all the working people, and in this sense it is class struggle.

Our party and all the fraternal parties remember, and are guided, in all their activities, by the conclusion in the Statement that struggle against the danger of a new world war should be developed without waiting for the first atom and hydrogen bombs to begin to fall; this struggle should be waged now and be intensified daily. The main thing is to curb the aggressors in time, to prevent war and not to allow it to flare up. To fight for peace today means to maintain the greatest vigilance, tirelessly to expose the policy of imperialism, vigilantly to follow the manoeuvrings and machinations of the war incendiaries, to arouse the holy anger of the peoples against those who aim at war, to enhance the organisation of all the forces of peace, continually to step up the actions of the masses in defence of peace, and to strengthen co-operation with all the states which are not interested in new wars.

The struggle for peace and peaceful co-existence weakens the front of imperialism, isolates its more aggressive circles from the masses of the people, and helps the working class in its revolutionary struggle and the peoples in the struggle for national liberation.

The struggle for peace and for peaceful co-existence is bound up organically with the revolutionary struggle against imperialism. The 81 Communist Parties wrote in their statement that: 'In conditions of peaceful co-existence, favourable opportunities are created for the development of the class struggle in the capitalist countries and of the national liberation movement of the peoples of the colonial and dependent countries. In turn, the successes of the revolutionary class and national liberation struggle help to strengthen peaceful co-existence.'

In conditions of peaceful co-existence, new and important victories have been scored in recent years in the class struggle of the proletariat and the struggle of the peoples for national freedom. The world revolutionary process is developing successfully.

This is why to separate the struggle for peaceful co-existence between states with different social systems from the revolutionary struggle against imperialism, against colonialism, for independence and socialism, to set one against the other, as the Chinese comrades are doing, is to reduce the principle of peaceful co-existence to an empty phrase, to emasculate it, to ignore in practice the need for a resolute struggle against imperialism and for peace and peaceful co-existence—which would only be to the benefit of the imperialists.

In its letter of June 14, the C.P.C. central committee accuses the Communist Parties of extending peaceful co-existence between states with different social systems to relations between the exploiters and the exploited, between the oppressed and the oppressing classes, between the working masses and the imperialists. This is a truly monstrous fabrication and a slander on the fraternal parties which lead the proletariat in its class battles against capital and which always support the revolutionary struggle and the just wars of liberation against imperialism.

The arguments of the C.P.C. leaders in the struggle against the C.P.S.U. and other fraternal parties are so weak that they have to resort to all sorts of ruses. They begin by ascribing to us views which are absolutely without foundation, of their own invention, and then they accuse us and fight us by exposing these views. This is precisely the case with their absurd allegations that the C.P.S.U. and other fraternal parties renounce revolution and substitute peaceful co-existence for the class struggle. In all political study groups in our country it is well known that when we speak of peaceful co-existence we mean the inter-state relations of the socialist countries with the countries of capitalism. The principle of peaceful co-existence, naturally, can in no way be applied to relations between the antagonistic classes inside the capitalist states; it is impermissible to apply it to the struggle of the working class for its class interests against the bourgeoisie and to the struggle of the oppressed peoples against the colonialists. The C.P.S.U. resolutely opposes peaceful co-existence in the ideological sphere. This is a simple truth which all who regard themselves as Marxist-Leninists should have mastered long ago.

3

There are serious differences between the C.P.C. and the C.P.S.U. and other Marxist-Leninist parties on the question of the struggle against the consequences of the Stalin personality cult.

The C.P.C. leaders have taken on themselves the role of defenders of the cult of the individual, propagators of Stalin's wrong ideas. They are trying to thrust upon other parties the practices, the ideology and ethics, and the forms and methods of leadership which flourished in the period of the cult of the individual. We must say outright that this is an unenviable role which will bring them neither honour nor glory. No one will succeed in luring Marxist-Leninists and progressive people on to the path of defending the cult of the individual!

The Soviet people and the world communist movement appreciated at their proper worth the courage and boldness, the truly Leninist firmness of principle, demonstrated in the struggle against the consequences of the cult of the individual by our party and by its central committee headed by Comrade Nikita Khrushchev.

Everybody knows that our party did so in order to remove the heavy burden which fettered the powerful forces of the working people and thus to speed up the development of Soviet society. Our party did so in order to free the ideals of socialism bequeathed to us by the great Lenin from the stigma of abuses of personal power and arbitrary rule. Our party did so in order to prevent recurrence of the tragic events which accompanied the cult of the individual and to make all the fighters for socialism draw the lessons from our experience.

The whole communist movement correctly understood and supported the struggle against the cult of the individual which was alien to Marxism-Leninism and against its harmful consequences. At one time it was approved by the Chinese leaders, too. They spoke about the tremendous international significance of the 20th Congress of the C.P.S.U.

Opening the Eighth Congress of the Communist Party of China in September of 1956, Comrade Mao Tse-tung said:

> The Soviet comrades and the Soviet people acted in accordance with Lenin's instructions. Within a short space of time they have achieved brilliant successes. The recent 20th Congress of the C.P.S.U. also worked out many correct political principles and denounced the shortcomings in the party. It can be said with confidence that in the future their work will result in exceptionally great developments.

In the political report of the C.P.C. central committee made at the congress by Comrade Liu Shao-chi this appraisal was developed further:

> The 20th Congress of the Communist Party of the Soviet Union, held in February this year, is a most important political event of world-wide significance. Not only did the Congress outline the magnificent sixth Five-Year Plan and a number of most important political propositions directed towards the further development of the cause of socialism, and condemned the cult of the individual which had led to serious consequences inside the party, but it also advanced proposals for further promoting peaceful co-existence and international co-operation and made an outstanding contribution to the cause of easing international tension.

Comrade Teng Ksiao-ping, in his report on the changes in the party rules at the same Eighth Congress of the Communist Party of China, said:

> Leninism demands that decisions on all important questions should be taken in the party by an appropriate collective, and not individually. The 20th Congress of the C.P.S.U. provided a convincing explanation of the most important significance of the unswerving observance of the principle of collective leadership and the struggle against the cult of the individual. This explanation had a tremendous influence, not only on the C.P.S.U. but also on other Communist Parties in all countries of the world.

In the well-known editorial in the newspaper *People's Daily*, 'Once more about the Historical Experience of the Dictatorship of the Proletariat' (December 1956) Chinese comrades wrote:

> The 20th Congress of the Communist Party of the Soviet Union showed tremendous determination and courage in eliminating the Stalin cult, in exposing Stalin's serious mistakes and in removing the consequences of Stalin's mistakes. Throughout the world the Marxist-Leninists and persons sympathising with the cause of communism support the efforts of the Communist Party of the Soviet Union directed towards correcting mistakes and wish the efforts of the Soviet comrades to be crowned with complete success.

And that is really so.

Any unbiased person who compares these pronouncements of the Chinese leaders with what is said in the letter of the C.P.C. central committee of June 14 will become convinced that they have made a 180° turn in evaluating the 20th Congress of our party.

But are any vacillations and waverings permissible on such questions of principle? Of course they are not permissible. Either the Chinese leaders then had no differences with the C.P.S.U. central committee on these questions of principle, or all these statements were false.

It is well known that practice is the best measure of truth.

It is precisely practice that convincingly proves the wonderful results in our country's life brought about by implementing the line of the 20th, 21st and 22nd Congresses of the C.P.S.U. In the course of the ten years that have gone by since the time when our party made a sharp turn towards the restoration of the Leninist principles and standards in party life, Soviet society has achieved truly magnificent results in developing the economy and promoting the advance of culture and science, in improving the people's wellbeing and strengthening the defence potential, and in the successes of foreign policy.

The atmosphere of fear, suspicion and uncertainty which poisoned the life of the people in the period of the cult of the individual has gone, never to return. It is impossible to deny the fact that the Soviet people now live better and enjoy the benefits of socialism. Ask the worker who has received a new flat (and there are millions of them!), ask the pensioner who is well provided for in his old age, the collective farmer who is now well-to-do, ask the thousands upon thousands of people who undeservedly suffered from reprisals in the period of the cult of the individual and to whom freedom and good repute have been restored, and you will realise what the victory of the Leninist cause of the 20th Congress of the C.P.S.U. means in practice for the Soviet people.

Ask the people whose fathers and mothers were victims of the reprisals in the period of the cult of the individual what it means for them to obtain recognition that their fathers, mothers and brothers were honest people and that they themselves are not outcasts in our society, but worthy, fully-fledged sons and daughters of the Soviet motherland.

Industry, agriculture, culture, science, art—no matter where we turn our eyes—everywhere we see rapid progress. Our spaceships are flying through the expanses of the universe, and this, too, provides brilliant confirmation of the correctness of the path along which our party is leading the Soviet people.

Of course, we do not consider that everything possible has already been done for Soviet men and women, to improve their lives. Soviet people realise that the implementation of this principle does not depend only on our wishes. We have to build a communist society and create an abundance of material benefits. That is why our people are stubbornly working in order to create material and spiritual values more rapidly and bring the victory of communism nearer. Everyone can see that we are following a correct course, that we clearly see the prospects of our development.

The C.P.S.U. programme maps out a concrete plan for building communism. The implementation of that plan will ensure for the Soviet people the highest living standards and will mean the beginning of a gradual transition to the cherished communist principle: 'From each according to his ability, to each according to his needs.'

Soviet people find it strange and outrageous that the Chinese comrades should be trying to smear the C.P.S.U. Programme—that magnificent plan for creating a communist society.

Alluding to the fact that our party proclaims as its task the struggle for a better life for the people, the C.P.C. leaders hint at some sort of 'bourgeoisification' and 'degeneration' of Soviet society. To follow their line of thinking, it transpires that if a people walks in rope sandals and eats watery soup out of a common bowl—that is communism, and if a working man lives well and wants to live even better tomorrow—that is almost tantamount to the restoration of capitalism!

And they want to present this philosophy to us as the latest revelation in Marxism-Leninism! This completely exposes the authors of such 'theories' as people who do not believe in the strength and capabilities of the working class, which has taken power into its own hands and created its own, socialist state.

If we turn to the history of our country, to the C.P.S.U. programme, we shall easily see from what we began, when under the leadership of Lenin we took power into our hands, and what summits the Soviet people have achieved. Our country has become a great socialist power. As regards the volume of industrial output the Soviet Union is first in Europe and second in the world, and will soon surpass the United States and move to first place. The Soviet working class, the Soviet collective-farm peasantry and the Soviet intelligentsia are the creators of all our victories.

We are convinced that not only the Soviet people, but also the peoples of other socialist countries, are capable of great feats of labour—it is only necessary that correct guidance of the working class and peasantry be ensured; it is necessary that the people giving this guidance should reason in a realistic way and take decisions that will make it possible to channel the strength and energy of the working people along the correct course.

In an attempt to justify the cult of the individual, the Chinese leaders have filled their letter with a lot of talk about class struggle in the U.S.S.R. and about the allegedly erroneous theses of the C.P.S.U. Programme on the state of the whole people and the party of the whole people—which are 'remote from Marxism.'

We do not intend in this letter to analyse all their arguments in detail. Anyone who reads the letter of the C.P.C. central committee of June 14, will undoubtedly pay attention to the utter inadequacy and the lack of knowledge about the life of the Soviet people shown in the outpourings contained in the letter of the C.P.C. central committee.

We are being taught that hostile classes still remain in Soviet society and therefore, you see, the need for the dictatorship of the proletariat remains. What then are these classes?

It can be seen from the letter of the C.P.C. central committee that these are 'bourgeois hangers-on, parasites, black-marketeers, swindlers, idlers, hooligans, embezzlers of public property.' It must be conceded that this is quite an original notion on the part of the Chinese comrades about classes and class struggle.

Since when have these parasitical elements been considered a class? And what class? A class of idlers, or a class of hooligans? A class of embezzlers of public property, or a class of parasites? In no society have criminals comprised a particular class. Every schoolboy knows this. Of course, in socialist society, too, these elements do not comprise a class. These are manifestations of the vestiges of capitalism.

The dictatorship of the proletariat is not necessary for the struggle against such people. The state of the whole people can cope, and is coping with this task. We know from our own experience that the higher the level of educational work in party, trade union and other public organisations, the greater the role of the public and the better the work of the Soviet militia, the more effective is the struggle against crime.

It is impossible to refute the fact that the present Soviet society is made up of two main classes—the workers and the peasants, as well as the intelligentsia—and that not a single class in Soviet society occupies a position permitting it to exploit other classes. Dictatorship is a class concept. Over whom do the Chinese comrades propose to effect a dictatorship of the proletariat in the Soviet Union? Over the collective-farm peasantry, or over the people's intelligentsia? One cannot ignore the fact that in socialist society the class of workers and the class of peasants have undergone considerable changes, and the differences and distinctions between them are disappearing more and more.

After the complete and final victory of socialism, the working class exercises its leading role, but no longer through the dictatorship of the proletariat. The working class remains the front-ranking class in society in the conditions of the full-scale construction of communism as well. Its front-ranking role is determined both by its economic position—it is directly connected with the highest form of socialist ownership—and the fact that it is the most tried and tempered class as a result of decades of class struggle and revolutionary experience.

The Chinese comrades refer to the pronouncement of Karl Marx that the content of the transitional period from capitalism to communism cannot be anything but a dictatorship of the proletariat. But in stating this, Marx was speaking of communism as a whole, as a single social and economic formation (of which socialism is the first stage), the transition to which would be impossible without a socialist revolution and the dictatorship of the proletariat. There are a number of pronouncements of Lenin which stress with absolute clarity that the dictatorship of the proletariat is needed precisely in order to overcome the resistance of the exploiting classes, to organise socialist construction, to ensure the victory of socialism—the first phase of communism. It is clear from this that the need for the dictatorship of the proletariat disappears after the victory of socialism, when only working people, friendly classes, the nature of which has entirely changed, remain in society, and there is no longer anyone to suppress.

If one is to extract the real content of all this mass of pseudo-theoretical talk contained in the letter of the C.P.C. central committee on these questions, it boils down to the following: The Chinese comrades come out against the line of the C.P.S.U. aimed at developing socialist democracy, which was proclaimed with such force in the decisions of the 20th, 21st and 22nd Congresses of our party and in the C.P.S.U. Programme. It is not by chance that nowhere in their long letter have they found room for even a mere mention of the development of democracy in the conditions of socialism, in the conditions of building communism.

It is difficult to pass judgment in full measure on the motives by which the Chinese comrades are guided when they uphold the cult of the individual. Actually, for the first time in the history of the international communist movement we encounter an open glorification of the cult of the individual. It must be said that even during the period when the cult of the individual was flourishing in our country, Stalin himself was forced, at least in words, to refuse to have anything to do with this petty bourgeois theory and said that it came from the Social Revolutionaries.

The attempts to use Marx and Lenin to defend the ideology of the cult of the individual arouses nothing but surprise. Can it really be true that the Chinese comrades do not know that Lenin, as long ago as the time when our party was being born, waged a gigantic struggle against the narodniks' theories about heroes and masses, that under Lenin genuinely collective methods of leadership were implemented in the central committee of our party and the Soviet state, that Lenin was extremely modest and lashed out mercilessly against the slightest manifestations of toadying and servility towards himself personally?

Of course, the struggle against the cult of the individual was never regarded by our party, or the other Marxist-Leninist parties, as the negation of the authority of party and government leaders. The C.P.S.U. has stressed time and time again —including the 20th and 22nd Congresses—that the party cherishes the authority of its leadership and that in dethroning the cult of the individual and fighting against its consequences, the party has a high estimation of leaders who really express the interests of the people and give all their strength to the struggle for the victory of communism, and for this reason enjoy well-deserved prestige.

4

The next important question on which we differ is that of the ways and methods of the revolutionary struggle of the working class in the capitalist countries, the struggle for national liberation, the paths of the transition of all mankind to socialism.

As depicted by the Chinese comrades, the differences on this question appear as follows: one side—they themselves—stands for the world revolution, while the other—the C.P.S.U., the Marxist-Leninist parties have forgotten the revolution and even 'fear' it, and, instead of revolutionary struggle, are concerned with things 'unworthy' of a real revolutionary, such as peace, the economic development of the socialist countries and the improvement of the living standards of their peoples, things such as the struggle for the democratic rights and vital interests of the working people of the capitalist countries.

In actual fact, the dividing line between the views of the C.P.C. and the views of the international communist movement lies on an entirely different plane: some—namely the leaders of the C.P.C.—talk about the world revolution in and out of place, throw about 'revolutionary' phrases on any and every occasion, and sometimes without any occasion, while others—precisely those whom the Chinese comrades are criticising—approach the question of the revolution with the utmost seriousness and, instead of indulging in phrase-mongering, work hard, seeking to find the best ways to the victory of socialism—the ways which are most in keeping with the present conditions—and fight hard for national independence, democracy and socialism.

Let us consider the main views of the Chinese comrades on questions concerning the revolutionary movement today.

Is the thesis of ceasing, in the name of the 'world revolution,' to fight for peace, renouncing the policy of peaceful co-existence and peaceful economic competition, and abandoning the struggle for the vital interests of the workers and for democratic reforms in the capitalist countries, conducive to the transition of countries and peoples to socialism? Is it true that in coming out for peace and pursuing the policy of peaceful co-existence, the communists of the socialist countries are thinking only of themselves and have forgotten about their class brothers in the capitalist countries?

Everyone who has pondered over the significance of the present struggle for peace and against thermonuclear war, realises that by their policy of peace the Soviet communists and the fraternal parties of the other socialist countries are giving inestimable aid to the working class, the working people of the capitalist countries. And this is not only because preventing nuclear war means saving the working class, the peoples of entire countries and even continents from death—although this alone is sufficient to justify our entire policy.

The other reason is that this policy is the best way to help the international revolutionary working-class movement to achieve its principal class aims. And is it not a tremendous contribution to the struggle of the working class, when the countries of socialism, in the conditions of peace which they themselves have won, achieve magnificent successes in developing the economy, win ever new victories in science and technology, constantly improve the living and working conditions of the people, and develop and improve socialist democracy?

Looking at these successes and victories, every worker in a capitalist country will say: 'Socialism is proving by deeds that it is superior to capitalism. This system is worth fighting for.' In the present conditions, socialism is winning the hearts and minds of the people, not only through books, but primarily by its deeds, by its living example.

The Statement of 1960 sees the main feature of our time in the fact that the world socialist system is becoming the decisive factor in the development of human society. All the Communist Parties which took part in the meeting arrived at the common conclusion that at the heart of our epoch there stands the international working class and its creation—the world system of socialism.

The carrying out of all the other tasks of the revolutionary movement depends to a tremendous extent on the consolidation of the world system of socialism. That is why the Communist and Workers' Parties have pledged themselves 'tirelessly to strengthen the great socialist community of peoples whose international role and influence on the course of world development is growing year by year.' Our party regards the fulfilment of this overriding task as its supreme international duty.

Lenin taught that 'We exert our main influence on the international revolution by our economic policy. . . . In this field the struggle has been transferred to a worldwide scale. If we accomplish this task, we shall win on the international scale, for certain and forever.' (*Collected works, vol. 32, page 413, Russian edition.*)

This behest of the great Lenin has been firmly learned by Soviet communists. It is followed by the communists of other socialist countries. But now it turns out that there are comrades who have decided that Lenin was wrong.

What is this—lack of faith in the ability of the socialist countries to defeat capitalism in economic competition? Or is it the attitude of persons who, on meeting with difficulties in building socialism, have become disappointed and do not see the possibility of exerting the main influence on the international revolutionary movement by their economic successes, by the example of the successful building of socialism in their countries? They want to achieve the revolution sooner, by other, and what seem to them to be shorter ways. But the victorious revolution can consolidate its successes and prove the superiority of socialism over capitalism by the work, and only by the work, of the people.

It is true that this is not easy, especially if the revolutions are accomplished in countries which have inherited an underdeveloped economy. But the example of the Soviet Union and many other socialist countries proves convincingly that in these conditions, too—if correct leadership is provided—it is possible to achieve great successes and demonstrate to the entire world the superiority of socialism over capitalism.

Moreover, what situation is more propitious to the revolutionary struggle of the working class in the capitalist countries—a situation of peace and peaceful co-existence, or a situation of permanent international tension and cold war?

There is no doubt as to the answer to this question. Who does not know that the ruling circles of the imperialist states exploit the situation of the cold war in order to whip up chauvinism, war hysteria and unbridled anti-communism, to put into power the most rabid reactionaries and pro-fascists, to suspend democracy and to do away with political parties, trade unions and other mass organisations of the working class?

The struggle of the communists for peace greatly strengthens their ties with the masses, their prestige and influence and, consequently, helps to build up what is called the political army of the revolution.

The struggle for peace and the peaceful co-existence of states with different social systems, far from hindering and delaying, makes it possible to develop in full measure the struggle to achieve the ultimate aims of the international working class.

It is hard to believe that the Chinese comrades, who are experienced men and who have themselves carried through a revolution, do not understand the main thing—that the world revolution today comes through the consolidation of the world system of socialism, through the revolutionary class struggle of the workers in the capitalist countries, through the struggle for national liberation, the strengthening of the political and economic independence of newly-liberated countries of Asia and Africa, and through the struggle for peace and against wars of aggression, through the struggle of the masses against the monopolies, and by many other ways which should not be set one against the other, but should be united and directed towards the same goal—the overthrow of the rule of imperialism.

The Chinese comrades, in a haughty and abusive way, accuse the Communist Parties of France, Italy, the United States and other countries of nothing less than opportunism and reformism, of 'parliamentary cretinism,' and even of slipping down to 'bourgeois socialism.' On what grounds do they do this? On the grounds that these Communist Parties do not put forward the slogan of an immediate proletarian revolution, although even the Chinese leaders must realise that this cannot be done without the existence of a revolutionary situation.

Every knowledgeable Marxist-Leninist realises that to put forward the slogan of an armed uprising, when there is no revolutionary situation in the country, means condemning the working class to defeat. It is common knowledge how exceedingly serious was Lenin's approach to this question, with what political perspicacity and knowledge of the concrete situation he approached the question of choosing the time for revolutionary action. On the very eve of the October Revolution, Lenin pointed out that it would be too early to start on October 24, too late on October 26—everything might be lost—and, consequently, power had to be taken, at whatever cost, on October 25. Who determines the intensity of class contradictions, the existence of a revolutionary situation, and chooses the moment for the uprising? This can be done only by the working class of each given country, by its vanguard—the Marxist-Leninist party.

The history of the international working-class movement shows that a party is bad, indeed, if, while calling itself a working-class party, it deals only with economic questions, does not bring up the working class in a revolutionary spirit, and does not prepare it for political struggle, for the seizure of power. In such a case it inevitably slips down to the positions of reformism. But equally bad is a party which sets the tasks of political struggle separately from efforts to improve the economic standards of the working class, the peasantry and all the working people. Such a party inevitably becomes divorced from the masses. Only given a correct use of all forms of class struggle, and given a skilful combination of those forms, can a party become a really revolutionary, Marxist-Leninist party, the leader of the masses, only in that case can it successfully lead the working class in storming capital, in winning power.

The Chinese leaders regard as a mortal sin of the Communist Parties of the developed capitalist states the fact that they see their direct tasks in the struggle for the economic and social interests of the working people, for democratic reforms, feasible even under capitalism and easing the living conditions of the working class, the peasantry and the petty bourgeois sections of the population, and contributing to the formation of a broad anti-monopoly front, which will serve as a basis for further struggle for the victory of the socialist revolution, that is to say, the fact that they are doing precisely what is recorded in the Moscow Statement of 1960.

Having come out against everything which the Communist Parties of the developed capitalist countries are doing, the Chinese comrades have not displayed either an elementary sense of solidarity with communists who are fighting against capital in the front line of the class struggle, or an understanding of the concrete conditions in those countries and the specific paths along which the revolutionary movement of the working class is proceeding there. In actual fact, 'for the sake of revolution,' they reject precisely the paths leading to revolution and try to impose a course which would place the Communist Parties in a position of isolation from the masses and would result in the working class losing its allies in the struggle against the domination of the monopolies, against capitalism.

The Chinese comrades have also disagreed with the world communist movement on the forms of the transition of different countries to socialism.

It is common knowledge that the C.P.S.U. and the other Marxist-Leninist parties, as is clearly pointed out in the documents of the Moscow meetings and in the Programme of the C.P.S.U., proceed on the basis of the possibility both of a peaceful and a non-peaceful transition to socialism. In spite of this, the Chinese comrades stubbornly ascribe to our party and the other fraternal parties recognition of the peaceful method alone.

In its letter of March 30, 1963,[1] the C.P.S.U. central committee has again outlined its position on this subject:

> The working class and its vanguard, the Marxist-Leninist parties, endeavour to carry out the socialist revolution in a peaceful way, without civil war. The realisation of such a possibility is in keeping with the interests of the working class and the entire people, and with the national interests of the country concerned. At the same time, the choice of the means by which the revolution is to be developed does not depend only on the working class. If the exploiting classes resort to violence against the people, the working class will be forced to use non-peaceful means of seizing power. Everything depends on the particular conditions and on the distribution of class forces within the country and in the world arena.
>
> Naturally, no matter what forms are used for the transition from capitalism to socialism, that transition is possible only by means of a socialist revolution and the dictatorship of the proletariat in its various forms. Greatly appreciating the selfless struggle of the working class, headed by the communists, in the capitalist countries, the Communist Party of the Soviet Union considers it its duty to render them every kind of aid and support.

We have repeatedly explained our point of view and there is no need to outline it in greater detail here.

And what is the position of the Chinese comrades on this question? It is the keynote of all their statements and of the letter of the C.P.C. central committee of June 14.

The Chinese comrades regard as the main criterion of revolutionary spirit recognition of the armed uprising always, in everything, everywhere. The Chinese comrades are thereby in fact denying the possibility of using peaceful forms of struggle for the victory of the socialist revolution, whereas Marxism-Leninism teaches that the communists must master all forms of revolutionary class struggle—both violent and non-violent.

Yet another important question is that of the relationship between the struggle of the international working class and the national liberation movement of the peoples of Asia, Africa and Latin America.

The international revolutionary working-class movement, represented today by the world system of socialism and the Communist Parties of the capitalist countries, and the national liberation movement of the peoples of Asia, Africa and Latin America—these are the great forces of our epoch. Correct co-ordination between them constitutes one of the main prerequisites for victory over imperialism.

[1] *Current Digest of the Soviet Press*, 1 May 1963.

How do the Chinese comrades solve this problem? This is seen from their new 'theory,' according to which the main contradiction of our time is, you see, the contradiction, not between socialism and imperialism, but between the national liberation movement and imperialism. The decisive force in the struggle against imperialism, the Chinese comrades maintain, is not the world system of socialism, not the struggle of the international working class, but again the national liberation movement.

In this way the Chinese comrades, apparently, want to win popularity among the peoples of Asia, Africa and Latin America by the easiest possible means. But let no one be deceived by this 'theory'. Whether the Chinese theoreticians want it or not, this theory in essence means isolating the national liberation movement from the international working class and its creation—the world system of socialism. Yet this would constitute a tremendous danger to the national liberation movement itself.

Indeed, could the many peoples of Asia have been victorious, in spite of all their heroism and selflessness, if the October Revolution, and then the formation of the world system of socialism, had not shaken imperialism to its very foundations, if they had not undermined the forces of the colonialists?

And now that the liberated peoples have entered a new stage in their struggle, concentrating their efforts on the consolidation of their political gains and economic independence, do they not see that it would be immeasurably more difficult, if not altogether impossible, to carry out these tasks without the assistance of the socialist states?

Marxist-Leninists always stress the epoch-making significance of the national liberation movement and its great future, but they regard as one of the main prerequisites for its further victories a firm alliance and co-operation with the countries of the world system of socialism as the main force in the struggle against imperialism, and a firm alliance with the working-class movement in the capitalist countries. This position was laid down in the Statement of 1960. It is based on Lenin's idea of working-class leadership (hegemony) as a prerequisite for victory in the anti-imperialist struggle. Only given such hegemony can this movement assume in the last analysis a truly socialist character, culminating in transition to the road of socialist revolution.

This idea of Lenin's has been tested by the experience of the October Revolution and by the experience of other countries, and it does not give rise to doubts in anyone's mind. However, the Chinese comrades, as has been seen, want to 'amend' Lenin and prove that it is not the working class, but the petty bourgeoisie or the national bourgeoisie, or even 'certain patriotically-minded kings, princes and aristocrats' who must be the leaders of the world struggle against imperialism. And after this the leadership of the Communist Party of China teaches the world communist movement that the proletarian, class approach must never, in any circumstances, be abandoned!

The guarantee of the future victories, both of the international working class and the national liberation movement, lies in their firm alliance and co-operation, in their joint struggle against imperialism, dictated by their common interests— a struggle in which the working class earns by its selflessness, by its devoted service in the interests of all peoples, recognition of its leading role and convinces its allies that its leadership is a reliable guarantee both of its own victory and of the victory of its allies, too.

Our Leninist party regards the national liberation movement as part and parcel of the world revolutionary process, as a mighty force coming out against imperialism. The great call of the founders of scientific communism, Marx and Engels: 'Workers of all countries, unite!' has become the battle standard of the international working class. Vladimir Ilyich Lenin, who carried forward the cause of Marx and Engels, noted particularly in the new historical conditions which emerged after the victory of the Great October Revolution, the inseparable bonds between the socialist revolution and the national liberation movement.

The slogan 'Workers of all countries, unite!' has been, and remains the main slogan in the struggle for the victory of the world revolution. In the new conditions this slogan has a broader connotation. It is common knowledge that Lenin approved of the slogan: 'Workers of all countries and oppressed peoples, unite!' This slogan stresses the leading role of the proletariat and the increased significance of the national liberation movement. In all its activities our party strictly abides by this Marxist-Leninist internationalist principle.

The question arises: What is the explanation for the incorrect propositions of the C.P.C. leadership on the basic problems of our time? It is either the complete divorcement of the Chinese comrades from actual reality, a dogmatic, bookish approach to problems of war, peace and the revolution, their lack of understanding of the concrete conditions of the present epoch, or the fact that behind the rumpus about the 'world revolution,' raised by the Chinese comrades, there are other goals, which have nothing in common with revolution.

All this shows the erroneous character, the disastrous nature of the course which the C.P.C. leadership is trying to impose on the world communist movement. What the Chinese leaders propose under the guise of a 'general line' is nothing but an enumeration of the most general tasks of the working class, made without due consideration for the time and the concrete correlation of class forces, without due consideration for the special features of the present stage of history. The Chinese comrades do not notice, or do not want to notice, how the tasks of our movement are changing in the conditions of the present epoch. By reducing the general line to general tasks which are valid for all stages of the transition from capitalism to socialism, they are depriving it of its concrete, purposeful and genuinely effective character.

In working out their present course, the fraternal parties have thoroughly analysed the alignment of class forces both in individual countries and on a worldwide scale, and the special features in the development of the two opposing systems and in the development of the national liberation movement at the present stage.

A thorough analysis of the changes taking place in the world situation has made it possible for the fraternal parties of the whole world to draw up a Marxist-Leninist description of the epoch:

> Our epoch, the essence of which consists in the transition from capitalism to socialism, started by the Great October Socialist Revolution, is the epoch of struggle between the two counterposed social systems, the epoch of socialist revolutions and national liberation revolutions, the epoch of the collapse of

imperialism, the abolition of the colonial system, the epoch of transition when ever new peoples embark upon the road of socialism, of the triumph of socialism and communism on a worldwide scale.

This definition of the present epoch served as the basis for a correct approach when drawing up the strategy and tactics of the world communist movement.

The Marxist-Leninist parties have determined their common line, the main provisions of which boil down to the following:

The nature and substance of the world revolutionary process in the present epoch is determined by the merging into one stream of the struggle against imperialism, waged by the peoples who are building socialism and communism, the revolutionary movement of the working class in the capitalist countries, the national liberation struggle of the oppressed peoples, and the democratic movements in general; in the alliance of the anti-imperialist revolutionary forces the decisive role belongs to the international working class and its main creation—the world system of socialism, which exerts the principal influence on the development of the world socialist revolution by the force of its example, by its economic construction;

Due to the prevailing objective historical conditions (the maximum growth of the aggressiveness of imperialism, the emergence of weapons of tremendous destructive power, etc.), a central place among all tasks facing the anti-imperialist forces in the present epoch is occupied by the struggle to prevent a thermonuclear war. The primary task of the Communist Parties is to rally all the peaceloving forces in defence of peace, to save mankind from a nuclear catastrophe;

The socialist revolution takes place as a result of the internal development of class struggle in every country, and its forms and ways are determined by the concrete conditions of each given country. The general regularity lies in the revolutionary overthrow of the power of capital and the establishment of a proletarian dictatorship in this or that form. It is the task of the working class and the Communist Parties to make the maximum use of the opportunities now available for the peaceful road of a socialist revolution, not involving civil war, and at the same time to be ready for the non-peaceful method, for armed suppression of the resistance of the bourgeoisie; the general democratic struggle is an indispensable part of the struggle for socialism;

The goals of the working class and the Communist Parties in the national liberation movement lie in carrying out to the end the tasks of the anti-imperialist democratic revolution, in developing and consolidating the national front, based on the alliance with the peasantry and the patriotically-minded national bourgeoisie, in preparing the conditions for setting up a national democratic state and the transition to the non-capitalist road of development;

Relations of co-operation and mutual assistance between the socialist countries, the cohesion and unity of the international communist and working-class movement, loyalty to positions and appraisals worked out jointly, to the Leninist principles of the life of the parties and the relations between them constitute the necessary conditions for the successful accomplishment of the historical tasks facing the communists.

Such, in our epoch, are the main ways of development of the world revolutionary process and such are the basic provisions of the general line of the international communist movement at the present stage. The struggle for peace, democracy, national independence and socialism—such is, in brief, the essence of this general line. The consistent implementation of this line in practice is the guarantee of the successes of the world communist movement.

All these most important principled theses of the international communist movement in present conditions, worked out collectively by the fraternal Communist and Workers' Parties in the Declaration and the Statement, have found expression in the new Programme of the C.P.S.U., which is based entirely on the Marxist-Leninist generalisation of revolutionary experience both in our country and on an international scale.

5

The erroneous views of the C.P.C. leaders on the paramount political and theoretical questions of our time are inseparably linked with their practical activities aimed at undermining the unity of the world socialist camp and the international communist movement.

In words Chinese comrades recognise that the unity of the U.S.S.R. and the People's Republic of China is a mainstay of the entire socialist community, but in actual fact they are undermining contacts with our party and with our country in all directions.

The C.P.C. leadership often speaks of its loyalty to the commonwealth of socialist countries, but the attitude of the Chinese comrades to this commonwealth refutes their high-sounding declarations.

The statistics show that in the course of the past three years the People's Republic of China cut the volume of its trade with the countries of the socialist community by more than 50 per cent. Some socialist countries felt the results of this line of the Chinese comrades particularly keenly.

The actions of the Chinese leadership stand in glaring contradiction, not only with the principles governing mutual relations between socialist countries, but in many cases even with the generally-recognised rules and standards which should be observed by all states.

The flouting of agreements signed earlier did serious harm to the national economies of some socialist states. It is quite understandable that China's own economy also suffers tangibly from the curtailment of her economic contacts.

In an effort to justify its actions in the eyes of the masses of the people, the leadership of the Communist Party of China recently put forward a theory of 'reliance on one's own forces.' Generally speaking, building socialism in each country, relying primarily on the efforts of its own people and making the best possible use of the internal resources of the country, is the correct way of creating the material and technical basis for socialism. The building of socialism in each country is primarily a matter of concern for the people of that country, for its working class and Communist Party.

The Soviet Union, which was the first country of socialism, had to build socialism relying only on its own forces and using its own internal resources. And although there is now a system of socialist countries, this in no way means that the people of some country can sit with their arms folded and rely exclusively on the assistance of other socialist countries. The Communist Party of each socialist country regards it as its duty to mobilise all the internal reserves for successful economic development. Therefore the statement of the C.P.C. central committee about building socialism mainly by its own forces, in its direct meaning, would give rise to no objections.

However, as is shown by the whole text of the letter of the C.P.C. central committee and numerous statements in the Chinese press, this thesis is actually given an interpretation with which it is impossible to agree.

The formula of 'building socialism mainly by our own forces' conceals the concept of creating self-sufficient national economies for which economic contacts with other countries are restricted to trade alone. The Chinese comrades are trying to impose this approach on other socialist countries, too.

The proclamation of the course of 'relying on our own forces,' was apparently needed by the leadership of the C.P.C. in order to weaken the bonds of close friendship between the socialist countries. This policy, of course, has nothing in common with the principles of socialist internationalism. It cannot be regarded otherwise than as an attempt to undermine the unity of the socialist commonwealth.

Parallel with the line directed towards curtailing economic contacts, the leadership of the C.P.C. took a number of measures aimed at worsening relations with the Soviet Union.

The Chinese leaders are undermining the unity, not only of the socialist camp, but also of the entire world communist movement, trampling underfoot the principles of proletarian internationalism and flagrantly violating the standards governing the relations between fraternal parties.

The leadership of the C.P.C. is organising and supporting various anti-party groups of renegades who are coming out against the Communist Parties in the United States, Brazil, Italy, Belgium, Australia and India. In Belgium, for instance, the C.P.C. is rendering support to the group of Gripp, which was expelled from the party at its last congress. In the United States support is being given to the subversive activities of the left opportunist 'Hammer and Steel' group, which has set itself the main task of fighting against the Communist Party of the United States. In Brazil Chinese comrades support factional groups expelled from the Communist Party (as for instance the Amazonas-Grabois group).

In Australia the C.P.C. central committee has tried to organise splitting activities against the Communist Party and its leadership, with the help of a former member of the leadership, E. Hill. Having visited the People's Republic of China at one time, Hill came out publicly against the Communist Party of Australia and tried to organise a group of persons of like mind. After the Communist Party of Australia had expelled Hill from the central committee of the party, he demonstratively went to Peking.

In Italy, Chinese representatives are encouraging the activity of a group of former officials of the Padua Federation of the Communist Party, who have issued leaflets with a provocative call for a 'revolutionary' uprising.

Comrades of the C.P.C. are making particular efforts to conduct subversive activities in the Communist and Workers' Parties in the countries of Asia, Africa, and Latin America.

Glorifying outcasts and renegades who have found themselves outside the ranks of the communist movement, the Chinese leaders reprint in their newspapers and magazines slanderous articles from the publications of these renegade groups directed against the policy of the C.P.S.U. and against the course of the entire world communist movement.

In Ceylon Chinese representatives are maintaining close contact with the grouping of E. Semarakkodi, which is a tool of the Trotskyist 'Fourth International.'

The Trotskyists of the 'Fourth International' are trying to use the position of the Chinese comrades for their own aims, and have even addressed an open letter to the C.P.C. central committee in which they have openly declared:

> The Fourth International, which from the very first day of its creation has been waging . . . a struggle with ideas against which you are coming out today, is standing by your side. . . . The international secretariat of the Fourth International welcomes this discussion which you have started in the entire communist movement. It urges you to develop it.

The Chinese leaders make sharp attacks on the fraternal Communist Parties and their leaders, who do not want to retreat from the general line of the international communist movement. They have published and circulated in many languages articles disparaging the activity of the Communist Party of the United States, and the French, Italian and Indian Communist Parties. To what kind of abusive phrases do the authors of these articles not resort when writing about prominent leaders of fraternal parties! Among them are 'double-dealing' and 'right-wing opportunism,' 'revisionism,' 'incompatibility with the standards of communist morality,' 'social democratic degeneration,' 'faint-heartedness,' 'irresponsibility,' 'parroting', and 'haughtiness and contempt for the revolutionary peoples of countries of Asia, Africa and Latin America.'

The Chinese leaders accuse the Communist Parties of the United States and Western Europe of acting 'at one with the most adventurist American imperialists.' The leadership of the Communist Party of India is not described otherwise than as a 'clique.' Against the leaders of the Communist Parties of France, Italy, India and the United States is hurled the monstrous accusation of 'solicitude for the fate of imperialism and all reactionaries.' And in its letter of June 14 the leadership of the C.P.C. sinks to insinuations that the C.P.S.U., too so it alleges—'comes out in the role of a helper of imperialism.' No one but Trotskyists has so far dared, in view of the obvious absurdity of this, to level such slanderous accusations against the great party of Lenin!

Should one be surprised that imperialist propaganda rejoices at such actions on the part of the Chinese comrades? It is not by chance that the bourgeois press often shouts about a 'crisis' in the international communist movement and urges the imperialist governments to utilise in their own interests the differences brought about by the position of the C.P.C. central committee.

Representatives of the C.P.C. left the editorial board of the magazine *World Marxist Review*—the collective theoretical and information organ of the Communist and Workers' Parties, and stopped the publication of this magazine in the Chinese language, striving in that way to deprive Chinese communists of an objective source of information about the activity of the international communist movement.

The splitting activity of the Chinese leadership in the ranks of the international communist movement arouses justified indignation and repudiation on the part of fraternal Marxist-Leninist parties.

The letter of the C.P.C. central committee says that in relations with fraternal Communist Parties it is 'impermissible for one party to place itself above the other fraternal parties; it is impermissible to interfere in the internal affairs of fraternal parties. . . .' This is quite a good statement. But it is precisely the Chinese comrades who are resorting to such impermissible actions.

Flouting the interests of the world communist movement, they are acting contrary to the standards and principles proclaimed in the Declaration and Statement and are trying to subordinate other fraternal parties to their influence and control.

One of the clear examples of the special line of the leadership of the C.P.C. in the socialist camp and the international communist movement is its position on the Albanian question. As is well known, in the second half of 1960 the Albanian leaders openly came out with a left opportunist platform on the main questions of our day and began to promote a hostile policy in relation to the C.P.S.U. and other fraternal parties. The Albanian leadership started an anti-Soviet campaign in the country, which led to a rupture of political, economic and cultural ties with the Soviet Union.

The overwhelming majority of Communist and Workers' Parties resolutely condemned this anti-Leninist activity of the Albanian leaders. The leaders of the C.P.C. took an absolutely different position and did everything in their power to use the Albanian leaders as their mouthpiece. It is now known that the Chinese comrades openly pushed them on to the road of open struggle against the Soviet Union and the other socialist countries and fraternal parties.

In their attacks on the C.P.S.U. and other Marxist-Leninist parties, the leaders of the C.P.C. assign a special place to the Yugoslav question. They try to present matters as if difficulties in the communist movement were being caused by an improvement in relations between the Soviet Union, other socialist countries and Yugoslavia. Contrary to the facts, they stubbornly allege that Yugoslavia is not a socialist country.

As is well known, in 1955 the C.P.S.U., together with other fraternal parties, took the initiative in normalising relations with Yugoslavia so as to end a protracted conflict, the main guilt for which rests with Stalin. At that time the leaders of the C.P.C. had no doubts as to the nature of the socialist system in Yugoslavia. Thus the newspaper *People's Daily* pointed out that 'Yugoslavia has already achieved notable successes in the construction of socialism.'

An objective analysis of the social and economic processes in Yugoslavia shows that the positions of socialism have been consolidated there in the years that have followed. Whereas in 1958 the socialist sector in industry amounted to 100 per cent., in agriculture to 6 per cent., and in trade to 97 per cent., now the socialist sector in industry amounts to 100 per cent., in agriculture to 15 per cent., and in trade to 100 per cent. A *rapprochement* between Yugoslavia's position and the position of the Soviet Union and other socialist states on questions of foreign policy has taken place in the period following the beginning of the normalisation of relations.

Why, then, have the Chinese leaders so drastically changed their attitude on the Yugoslav question? It is hard to find an explanation other than that they saw in this one of the pretexts advantageous, in their opinion, for discrediting the policy of the C.P.S.U. and other Marxist-Leninist parties.

Soviet communists know that differences on a number of ideological questions of principle continue to remain between the C.P.S.U. and the League of Communists of Yugoslavia. We have openly said, and continue to say this to the Yugoslav leaders. But it would be wrong to 'excommunicate' Yugoslavia from socialism on these grounds, to cut her off from socialist countries and to push her into the camp of imperialism, as the leaders of the C.P.C. are doing. That is precisely what the imperialists want.

At the present time there are 14 socialist countries in the world. We are profoundly convinced that in the near future their number will be considerably greater. The range of questions encountered by the fraternal parties which stand at the helm of state is increasing, and besides this, each of the fraternal parties is working in different conditions.

It is not surprising that in these circumstances the fraternal parties may develop different approaches to the solution of this or that problem. How should Marxist-Leninists act in this case? Should they declare that this or that socialist country, whose leaders do not agree with them, is no longer a socialist country? That would be really arbitrary behaviour. That method has nothing in common with Marxism-Leninism.

If we were to follow the example of the Chinese leaders, then, because of our serious differences with the leaders of the Albanian Party of Labour, we should long since have proclaimed Albania to be a non-socialist country. But that would be a wrong, subjective approach. In spite of our differences with the Albanian leaders, the Soviet communists regard Albania as a socialist country and, for their part, do everything in their power to prevent Albania from being split away from the socialist community.

We see with regret how the leaders of the C.P.C. are undermining the traditional Soviet-Chinese friendship and weakening the unity of the socialist countries.

The C.P.S.U. stands, and will continue to stand, for the unity and cohesion of the socialist community, of the entire world communist movement.

6

Let us draw some conclusions:

The period since the adoption of the Statement of 1960 has fully confirmed the correctness of the Marxist-Leninist programme of the world communist and working-class movement. The Soviet Union's successes in building communism, the successes of socialist construction in the other countries of socialism, are exerting an ever greater revolutionising influence on the minds of people throughout the world. Revolutionary Cuba has lit a beacon of socialism in the western hemisphere. Decisive blows have been struck against the colonial system, which is near to complete liquidation. New victories have been won by the working class of imperialist countries. The world revolutionary movement is developing inexorably.

All this shows that the Statement of 1960 correctly set the general line of the world communist movement. The task now is to act in accordance with this general line, to develop and specify it as applied to the conditions in which each particular Communist Party works. Therefore all attempts to impose some new general line on the world communist and working-class movement, as has been done in the letter of the C.P.C. central committee of June 14, are bankrupt and harmful. To accept such a 'general line' would be to depart from the Statement of 1960 and to agree to programmatic theses contrary to that Statement, which was adopted by 81 parties. Our party will not do this.

Throughout its history, our glorious Leninist party has waged an implacable struggle against right-wing and left-wing opportunism, Trotskyism and revisionism, dogmatism and sectarianism, nationalism and chauvinism, in all their manifestations, both within the country and in the international arena. Our party has been steeled and strengthened in this struggle for the purity of Marxism-Leninism, and fears no attacks by present-day splitters and opportunists from whatever quarter.

Life shows that the C.P.S.U., having become a political organisation of the whole people, has strengthened its ties with the masses, has become even stronger, and has an even higher discipline. With the victory of socialism the ideology of the working class—Marxism-Leninism—has become the ideology of the entire people, of its progressive section. The aim of the working class—the building of communism—has become the aim of the entire people. Marxist-Leninists can only rejoice, of course, in this growth of the influence of communist ideology. We can say that never since Lenin's death has our party been so strong, so capable of accomplishing the most daring tasks associated with building a new world.

Now, when socialism has won finally and completely in our country, when we are raising, stone by stone, the beautiful edifice of communism, our party, the whole Soviet people, are even more convinced that the great ideas of Marxism-Leninism will triumph throughout the world.

Our confidence is shared by the peoples of the socialist countries, by all the working people of the world. They highly appreciate the great contribution made by the Soviet Union to the common cause of the struggle for peace, democracy, national freedom, independence and socialism.

The Communist Party of the Soviet Union has stood, and continues to stand, for close friendship with the Communist Party of China. There are serious differences between us and the leaders of the C.P.C., but we consider that the relations between the two parties, between our two peoples, should be built, proceeding from the fact that we have the same aim—the building of a new communist society, from the fact that we have the same enemy—imperialism. United, the two great powers, the Soviet Union and the People's Republic of China, can do much for the triumph of communism. Our friends and enemies are well aware of that.

A meeting of the delegations of the C.P.S.U. and the C.P.C. is being held in Moscow at the present time. Unfortunately the C.P.C. representatives at the meeting are continuing to worsen the situation. In spite of this, the delegation of the C.P.S.U. are displaying the utmost patience and self-control, working for a successful outcome to the negotiations. The very near future will show whether the Chinese comrades agree to build our relations on the basis of what unites us and not what divides us, on the basis of the principles of Marxism-Leninism.

Our enemies build their calculations on deepening the contradictions between the C.P.C. and the C.P.S.U. They are now looking for something from which to profit. The American *Daily News* wrote recently: 'Let us set Red Russia and Red China against each other so that they tear each other to pieces.' We communists should never forget those insidious plans of the imperialists.

Aware of its responsibility to the international communist movement and to the peoples of the world, our party urges the Chinese comrades to take to the road of resolving the differences and strengthening the genuine unity of our parties on the basic principles of Marxism-Leninism and proletarian internationalism.

Together with all fraternal parties, our Leninist party has fought, and is fighting, to rally the working class, all the working people, in the struggle against imperialism, for peace, democracy, national independence and socialism.

The central committee of the C.P.S.U. declares with the utmost sense of responsibility before the party and the entire Soviet people that we have done and will continue to do everything in our power to strengthen unity with the Communist Party of China, to rally the world communist movement under the banner of Lenin, to rally the countries of the world system of socialism, to provide effective aid to all peoples fighting against colonialism, to strengthen the cause of peace, and to ensure the victory of the great ideas of communism throughout the world.

All the working people of the Soviet Union will rally even more closely round their own Communist Party and its Leninist central committee and will devote all their energy to carrying out the magnificent programme for building communism.

Statement by the Government of the People's Republic of China, 31 July 1963[1]

A treaty on the partial halting of nuclear tests was initialled by the representatives of the United States, Britain and the Soviet Union in Moscow on July 25.[2]

This is a treaty signed by three nuclear powers. By this treaty they attempt to consolidate their nuclear monopoly and bind the hands of all the peace-loving countries subjected to the nuclear threat.

This treaty signed in Moscow is a big fraud to fool the people of the world. It runs diametrically counter to the wishes of the peace-loving people of the world.

The people of the world demand a genuine peace; this treaty provides them with a fake peace.

The people of the world demand general disarmament and a complete ban on nuclear weapons; this treaty completely divorces the cessation of nuclear tests from the total prohibition of nuclear weapons, legalizes the continued manufacture, stockpiling and use of nuclear weapons by the three nuclear powers, and runs counter to disarmament.

The people of the world demand the complete cessation of nuclear tests; this treaty leaves out the prohibition of underground nuclear tests, an omission

[1] *Peking Review*, 2 August 1963, pp. 7–8.   [2] See pp. 170–2 above.

which is particularly advantageous for the further development of nuclear weapons by U.S. imperialism.

The people of the world demand the defence of world peace and the elimination of the threat of nuclear war; this treaty actually strengthens the position of nuclear powers for nuclear blackmail and increases the danger of imperialism launching a nuclear war and a world war.

If this big fraud is not exposed, it can do even greater harm. It is unthinkable for the Chinese Government to be a party to this dirty fraud. The Chinese Government regards it as its unshirkable and sacred duty to thoroughly expose this fraud.

The Chinese Government is firmly opposed to this treaty which harms the interests of the people of the whole world and the cause of world peace.

Clearly, this treaty has no restraining effect on the U.S. policies of nuclear war preparation and nuclear blackmail. It in no way hinders the United States from proliferating nuclear weapons, expanding nuclear armament or making nuclear threats. The central purpose of this treaty is, through a partial ban on nuclear tests, to prevent all the threatened peace-loving countries, including China, from increasing their defence capability, so that the United States may be more unbridled in threatening and blackmailing these countries.

U.S. President Kennedy, speaking on July 26, laid bare the substance of this treaty.[1] Kennedy pointed out that this treaty did not mean an end to the threat of nuclear war, it did not prevent but permitted continued underground nuclear tests, it would not halt the production of nuclear weapons, it would not reduce nuclear stockpiles and it would not restrict their use in time of war. He further pointed out that this treaty would not hinder the United States from proliferating nuclear weapons among its allies and countries under its control under the name of 'assistance,' whereas the United States could use it to prevent non-nuclear peace-loving countries from testing and manufacturing nuclear weapons. At the same time, Kennedy formally declared that the United States remains ready to withdraw from the treaty and resume all forms of nuclear testing. This fully shows that U.S. imperialism gains everything and loses nothing by this treaty.

The treaty just signed is a reproduction of the draft treaty on a partial nuclear test ban put forward by the United States and Britain at the meeting of the Disarmament Commission in Geneva on August 27, 1962.[2] On August 29, 1962, the Head of the Soviet Delegation Kuznetsov pointed out that the obvious aim of the United States and Britain in putting forward that draft was to provide the Western powers with one-sided military advantage to the detriment of the interests of the Soviet Union and other socialist countries. He pointed out that the United States had been using underground tests to improve its nuclear weapons for many years already, and that should underground nuclear tests be legalized with a simultaneous prohibition of such tests in the atmosphere, this would mean that the United States could continue improving its nuclear weapons and increase their yield and effectivity.[3] The Head of the Soviet Government Khrushchev also pointed out on September 9, 1961, that 'the programme of developing new types of nuclear weapons which has been drawn up in the United

---

[1] For the text of President Kennedy's remarks, see *Current Documents, 1963*, pp. 978–84.
[2] *Documents, 1962*, pp. 125–7.
[3] For text, see *Documents on Disarmament, 1963*, pp. 820–9.

States now requires precisely underground tests,' and that 'an agreement to cease only one type of testing, in the atmosphere, would be a poor service to peace; it would deceive the peoples.'[1]

But now the Soviet Government has made a 180 degree about-face, discarded the correct stand they once persisted in and accepted this reproduction of the U.S.-British draft treaty, willingly allowing U.S. imperialism to gain military superiority. Thus the interests of the Soviet people have been sold out, the interests of the people of the countries in the socialist camp, including the people of China, have been sold out, and the interests of all the peace-loving people of the world have been sold out.

The indisputable facts prove that the policy pursued by the Soviet Government is one of allying with the forces of war to oppose the forces of peace, allying with imperialism to oppose socialism, allying with the United States to oppose China, and allying with the reactionaries of all countries to oppose the people of the world.

Why should the Soviet leaders so anxiously need such a treaty? Is this a proof of what they call victory for the policy of peaceful coexistence? No! This is by no means a victory for the policy of peaceful coexistence. It is capitulation to U.S. imperialism.

The U.S. imperialists and their partners are with one voice advertising everywhere that the signing of a treaty on the partial halting of nuclear tests by them is the first step towards the complete prohibition of nuclear weapons. This is deceitful talk. The United States has already stockpiled large quantities of nuclear weapons, which are scattered in various parts of the world and seriously threaten the security of all peoples. If the United States really will take the first step towards the prohibition of nuclear weapons, why does it not remove its nuclear threat to other countries? Why does it not undertake to refrain from using nuclear weapons against non-nuclear countries and to respect the desire of the people of the world to establish nuclear weapon-free zones? And why does it not undertake in all circumstances to refrain from handing over to its allies its nuclear weapons and the data for their manufacture? On what grounds can the United States and its partners maintain that the United States may use nuclear threat and blackmail against others and pursue policies of aggression and war, while others may not take measures to resist such threat and blackmail and defend their own independence and freedom? To give the aggressors the right to kill while denying the victims of aggression the right to self-defence—is this not like the Chinese saying: 'The magistrate may burn down houses but the ordinary people cannot even light their lamps'?

The Chinese Government is firmly opposed to nuclear war and to a world war. It always stands for general disarmament and resolutely stands for the complete prohibition and thorough destruction of nuclear weapons. The Chinese Government and people have never spared their efforts in order to realize this aim step by step. As is known to the whole world, the Chinese Government long ago proposed, and has consistently stood for, the establishment of a zone free from nuclear weapons in the Asian and Pacific region, including the United States.

The Chinese Government holds that the prohibition of nuclear weapons and the prevention of nuclear war are major questions affecting the destiny of the

[1] Text in *Documents, 1961*, pp. 466–72.

world which should be discussed and decided on jointly by all the countries of the world, big and small. Manipulation of the destiny of more than one hundred non-nuclear countries by a few nuclear powers will not be tolerated.

The Chinese Government holds that on such important issues as the prohibition of nuclear weapons and the prevention of nuclear war, it is impermissible to adopt the method of deluding the people of the world. It should be affirmed unequivocally that nuclear weapons must be completely banned and thoroughly destroyed and that practical and effective measures must be taken so as to realize step by step the complete prohibition and thorough destruction of nuclear weapons, prevent nuclear war and safeguard world peace.

For these reasons, the Government of the People's Republic of China hereby proposes the following:[1]

(1) All countries in the world, both nuclear and non-nuclear, solemnly declare that they will prohibit and destroy nuclear weapons completely, thoroughly, totally and resolutely. Concretely speaking, they will not use nuclear weapons, nor export, nor import, nor manufacture, nor test, nor stockpile them; and they will destroy all the existing nuclear weapons and their means of delivery in the world, and disband all the existing establishments for the research, testing and manufacture of nuclear weapons in the world.

(2) In order to fulfil the above undertakings step by step, the following measures shall be adopted first:

a. Dismantle all military bases, including nuclear bases, on foreign soil, and withdraw from abroad all nuclear weapons and their means of delivery.

b. Establish a nuclear weapon-free zone of the Asian and Pacific region, including the United States, the Soviet Union, China and Japan; a nuclear weapon-free zone of Central Europe; a nuclear weapon-free zone of Africa; and a nuclear weapon-free zone of Latin America. The countries possessing nuclear weapons shall undertake due obligations with regard to each of the nuclear weapon-free zones.

c. Refrain from exporting and importing in any form nuclear weapons and technical data for their manufacture.

d. Cease all nuclear tests, including underground nuclear tests.

(3) A conference of the government heads of all the countries of the world shall be convened to discuss the question of the complete prohibition and thorough destruction of nuclear weapons and the question of taking the above-mentioned four measures in order to realize step by step the complete prohibition and thorough destruction of nuclear weapons.

The Chinese Government and people are deeply convinced that nuclear weapons can be prohibited, nuclear war can be prevented and world peace can be preserved. We call upon the countries in the socialist camp and all the peace-loving countries and people of the world to unite and fight unswervingly to the end for the complete, thorough, total and resolute prohibition and destruction of nuclear weapons and for the defence of world peace.

---

[1] These proposals, as printed here, were circulated in a letter from the Premier of the State Council, Chou En-lai, to all heads of government on 2 August 1963; see *Peking Review,* 9 August 1963, p. 7.

II. THE MIDDLE EAST

A. THE UNITED ARAB REPUBLIC, SYRIA AND IRAQ

Memorandum from the United Arab Republic to the Arab League, 10 March 1963[1]

God made the Syrian people and Army victorious. With their victory, He supported the over-all Arab struggle. The U.A.R. considers that the historic events of Damascus on the 8th of March are a complete and decisive answer to the poisonous attacks launched by the Syrian secessionist rulers which reached their climax at the meeting of the Arab League at Chtaura in August, 1962.[2]

In view of these events the U.A.R. has decided to resume fully its activities in the Arab League in this historic transitional period through which the Arab World is passing, and to participate positively in serving the goals of the Arab Nation.

Declaration of the Tripartite Union, issued by the Governments of the United Arab Republic, Syria, and Iraq, Cairo, 17 April 1963[3]

In the name of God, the Merciful, the Compassionate;
In the name of the Arab people;
Delegations representing the United Arab Republic, Syria and Iraq have met in Cairo. In response to the will of the Arab people in the three countries and in the greater Arab Nation, fraternal talks between the three delegations began on Saturday, 6th April and ended on Wednesday, 17th April 1963.

Throughout their talks, the delegations were inspired by their belief that Arab unity is an inevitable objective which derives from a common language which is the carrier of culture and thought, a common history which is the maker of sentiment and conscience, a common popular struggle which determines and shapes destiny, common spiritual and human values emanating from divine revelation, and common social and economic concepts based on freedom and socialism.

The delegations were guided by the popular will of the Arab people which demands unity, struggles to achieve it, and makes great sacrifices to protect and safeguard it, realizing that the nucleus of a strong unity consists in the unification of those parts of the homeland, which have achieved their liberty and independence, and in which there have been established nationalist progressive governments, determined to destroy the alliance between feudalism, capitalism, reaction and imperialism, and to liberate the active forces of the people to assert their solidarity and express their true will.

[1] American University of Beirut, Political Studies and Public Administration Department, *Arab Political Documents, 1963*, ed. Walidkhalidi and Yusuf Ibish (Beirut, 1964), p. 25.
[2] See *Survey, 1962*, pp. 479–81.　　　　　[3] *Arab Political Documents, 1963*, pp. 227–46.

The Revolution of July 23 was a historic turning point in which the Arab people of Egypt discovered themselves, recovered their will and thus pursued the road to Liberty, Arabism and Unity. The revolution of Ramadan 14 revealed the true Arab features of Iraq and lighted its way towards the horizons of unity which had been sought by such members of the Revolution of July 14 as were sincere. The Revolution of March 8 restored Syria to its place in the caravan of unity which had been destroyed by the reactionary secession, after this revolution had removed all the obstacles which the secessionists and imperialists had deployed on the road of unity.

The three revolutions converged on this point: the reaffirmation of the fact that unity is a revolutionary act which derives its concepts from the faith of the masses, its strength from their will and its aims from their aspirations to freedom and socialism.

Unity is a revolution—a revolution because it is popular and progressive and because it is a strong surge forward with the tide of civilization.

Unity is a revolution particularly because it is deeply connected with the cause of Palestine and the national duty to liberate it. It was the Palestine disaster which exposed the conspiracies of the reactionary classes and the treacheries of the subservient, anti-Arab parties and their betrayal of the people's aims and aspirations. It was this disaster which laid bare the weakness and backwardness of existing economic and social systems. It was this disaster which exploded the revolutionary energies of the masses of our people and sparked off the spirit of rebellion against imperialism, injustice, poverty and backwardness. It was this disaster which pointed the way to the road of salvation, the road of unity, freedom and socialism. The delegation had all this in mind during their talks. While unity is a sacred objective, it is also the instrument of the popular struggle and the means for the realization of its major aims which are: freedom, security, the liberation of all parts of the Arab Nation, the establishment of a society in which all enjoy an adequate standard of living, based on justice and socialism, the continued and undiverted flow of the revolutionary current with undiminished force and its extension to embrace the greater Arab Nation, and contribution to the progress of human civilization and the consolidation of world peace.

It has been agreed that unity between the three regions be established in accordance with the desires of the Arab people, on the basis of democracy and socialism, and that it be a real and solid unity which takes into consideration regional conditions and so strengthens the bonds of unity on a foundation of realistic understanding, rather than perpetuating factors conducive of division and separatism. Thus the strength of each region will be turned into a strength for the federal state and the Arab Nation as a whole, and the strength of the federal state as a whole into a strength for each state within it, and for the whole Arab Nation.

The three delegations declare in the name of the Arab people in Egypt, Syria and Iraq, the will of this people to establish federal unity on the following basis:

FIRST: IN THE FIELD OF NATIONAL ACTION

a) The drawing up of a charter for National Action in which all progressive, unionist, popular forces will meet in the definition of the principles, aims, and social philosophy of this National Action, so that the Charter may become the basis for their co-operation and unity.

b) Freedom to form popular organizations in member states so that the free popular will can find an organized means of self expression within the framework of a political front including these popular organizations.

c) The unification of political leaderships on the federal level to guarantee the coordination of the activities of popular organizations and their unification because the unity of political action and popular struggle guarantees the protection, strengthening and development of unity.

SECOND: THE BUILDING OF THE STATE

The federal organs must be consolidated so as to increase their capacity for planning, coordination and execution, and to guarantee their effectiveness to show that the union is genuine. This can be achieved by:

a) The unification of the international personality and foreign policy of the Federal State so that it becomes a single power to confront imperialism inside and outside the Arab Nation, and a united power supporting the freedom of the peoples of the world and consolidating world peace.

b) The achievement of military unity capable of liberating the Arab Nation from the perils of Zionism and imperialism, and of achieving its aims of security and stability, and mobilizing its forces for the establishment of truth, justice and peace.

c) The unification of the organs of planning to direct the potentialities of the federal nation towards economic and social development and to exploit all its powers and capacities to the best for the construction of a society in which all can attain an adequate standard of living and all have access to justice and a socialist society.

d) The devotion of maximum attention to the affairs of education, scientific research, culture and information, to develop revolutionary consciousness, to place science at the service of society, to inculcate progressive concepts, to propagate new values, and to spread this consciousness throughout the Arab Nation.

From its birth, the Federation is bound by certain fundamental rules which outline the course of its development and growth, lay down its revolutionary and progressive programme in all political, social and economic fields, and provide a true expression of the historic stage through which the Arab Nation is passing.

The delegations hereby declare their complete agreement that the Federation, with its political, social and economic constituents and with its constitution and constitutional organs, shall take the following general form which reveals the main lines of the Charter of National Action and the Constitution of the Federation.

POLITICAL CONSTITUENTS

Unity of aims and unity of values and principles require all unionist, socialist and democratic forces in each of the three states of the Federation to form a political front bound by a charter for democratic, socialist and unionist action with the purpose of unifying political action in the State and developing the revolutionary incentives of the masses in their quest for a better life in which their aspirations will be realised. These forces shall pool their efforts in a single political organization or front bound by the Charter of National Action. In so doing, they shall be bound by the majority decisions of this front in order that they may, at this level personify the unity of their will and be able to undertake their responsibilities and discharge their duties.

At Federal State level a unified political leadership is to be formed, which will lead and unify political action in the Federation within the framework of this Charter. Political fronts or unified organizations in the States shall be bound by the majority decisions of the federal leadership. This leadership shall gradually establish a unified political organization that will lead national political action inside and outside the Federation, and will work to mobilize popular forces so that they may enforce their will in life, and to lead them constantly towards new horizons. But this does not mean the dissolution of existing unionist parties.

Political action is not only the leadership of the masses but also the consolidation of the foundations of our society on a basis of socialism and democracy which emanate from the facts of our existence and have become an expression of our future.

Democracy is the assertion of the sovereignty of the people, the placing of full authority in their hands and its dedication to the realization of their aims.

It is only through socialism that unity can be transformed into progressive action. This consists in the establishment of a society in which all enjoy an adequate standard of living, based on justice, work, equal opportunity, production and services.

Democracy is political liberty and socialism is social liberty and they cannot be separated. They are the two wings of true liberty and deprived of either or both of them liberty cannot fly towards the horizons of the future towards which we aspire.

Political democracy cannot be achieved in the shadow of reaction and cannot be realized under the shadow of the dictatorship of a single class.

Therefore, the alliance between feudalism and capitalism must capitulate and be replaced by the democratic alliance of the working forces of the people: farmers, workers, intellectuals, soldiers, and national capitalism. It is this alliance which is the legitimate substitute for the former reactionary alliance, and capable of replacing reactionary democracy with true democracy.

Sovereignty in the United Arab Republic shall belong to the people, for freedom, all freedom belongs to the people though there can be no freedom for the enemies of the people.

The enemies of the people include the following elements:

a) Those disqualified from taking part in politics in accordance with the laws in force.

b) Anyone tried by the revolution and convicted of being a separatist, a conspirator or an exploiter.

c) Anyone who has collaborated in the past or who collaborates, in the future with foreign political organizations, thus becoming an agent of foreign powers.

d) All who have worked or work to establish the domination of classes that exploit society.

Political and popular organizations which are based on free and direct elections must rightfully and justly represent the forces comprising the majority. Thus we must guarantee to the workers and the farmers at least half of the seats in these organizations at all their levels, including the National Assembly. This, apart from being right and just in that it ensures proper representation of the majority, maintains the force of the revolutionary impulse. Thus the authority of elected popular assemblies is continuously confirmed in its superiority to that of the executive and administrative machinery of the State, and the people will always remain the leaders of national action. Also, local government must gradually but continuously transfer authority of the State as far as possible to the hands of the popular authorities as these are more capable of appreciating and solving the problems of the people.

The collective character of leadership of political and popular action at all levels must be guaranteed against the caprice of individuals, so as to strengthen democracy on the highest level and to ensure its continuity through constant renovation.

Popular organizations, particularly cooperatives, trade unions, youth and women's organizations, can play an influential and effective role in the consolidation of sound democracy. These organizations must be advance forces in the fields of democratic action. The growth of the cooperative and trade union movement provides an inexhaustible supply of enlightened leaders who have direct access to the masses and can feel their pulse. The pressure which used to stifle the freedom of these organizations and paralyze their activities must be removed.

The freedoms are guaranteed within the limits of the laws. The United Arab Republic shall guarantee all citizens, without discrimination, freedom of opinion and expression, freedom of criticism and self-criticism, the freedom of the press, freedom of assembly and the formation of associations, freedom of education, freedom of belief, worship and practice of religious rites, as well as other freedoms.

Citizens have equal rights and duties before the law. There shall be no discrimination between them because of race, origin, language, religion or belief. Women must be equal to men in the exercise of public rights; the remnants of the shackle which obstruct their freedom of movement must be removed so that they may play a real and effective part in the building of life.

Suffrage is a right enjoyed by all citizens in the manner specified by law. Their participation in public life is a national duty. The right of candidature and the right to vote are guaranteed to all citizens.

The principle of the sovereignty of the law is the ultimate guarantee of freedom. The right to litigate is guaranteed to citizens within the limits of the law. Judges are independent and are answerable only to the dictates of their conscience and to the law.

SOCIAL AND ECONOMIC CONSTITUENTS

Socialism is the road to social freedom and it can be realized only by the provision of all citizens with equal opportunities of enjoying a fair share of the national wealth. The bases of the national wealth must, therefore, be broadened to correspond with the legitimate rights of the working masses of the people.

The way of the revolution, which is the way of socialism, is a categorical imperative dictated by historical reality and by aspirations of the masses to cope with social and economic backwardness in the Arab Nation. It is also dictated by world conditions.

Capitalist experiments in progress have proceeded hand in hand with imperialism, and the countries of the capitalist world have been able to reach a stage of economic advancement by exploiting the wealth of colonized people. But gone are the days of imperialist piracy when the wealth of some peoples was plundered for the benefit of others without any legal or moral restraint.

There have also been other experiments in progress which attained their goals at the cost of misery for millions of working people, either for the benefit of capital, or in implementation of ideological theories which did not stop short of sacrificing whole generations of the living for the sake of those unborn.

Progress by plunder or by slavery is no longer acceptable to the new human values. These values have been able to defeat imperialism and slavery. Apart from defeating both systems, these human values have also used education to initiate other courses of action for progress.

In the countries which were forced to remain backward, capital is no longer capable of leading economic advancement at a time when major capitalistic monopolies have grown in advanced countries by their dependence on the exploitation of the resources of the peoples. Local capital is also no longer capable of competition unless it is protected by high customs barriers or unless it attaches itself to the world monopolistic movement, of which it then becomes the helpless client, drawing down with it the countries which finance it in its fatal plunge into the maelstrom.

Action to increase national wealth cannot be left to the haphazard caprices of private capital the only aims of which are exploitation and the selfish desire for profit. It is necessary, therefore, that economic advancement in the Arab Nation should be conditioned by three factors:

1 - The pooling of national savings.

2 - The full use of modern scientific experience in the investment of these savings.

3 - The drafting of an overall plan for production.

The aim of planning in the socialist community is:

1 - To achieve a balanced development of the economy in the various sectors.

2 - To meet the public and private requirements of the community and the individual.

3 - To effect a fair distribution of national wealth.

4 - To guarantee the workers a positive role in management, together with a genuine share in the profits of production and minimum wages ensuring a decent life for the working man.

It is necessary, therefore, that the people should control all means of production and direct the disposal of surplus production in accordance with a specific plan. This is at the same time the way of democracy in all its political and social forms. But this does not necessitate the nationalization of all means of production, the abolition of private ownership, or interference with legitimate rights of inheritance consequent thereupon. This aim can be achieved in two ways:

First: The creation of a competent public sector to lead the advance in all fields and shoulder the main responsibility for the development plan.

Second: The presence of a private sector participating in development within the framework of the overall plan without any exploitation.

Such planning ensures proper utilization of available, latent and potential resources. At the same time it guarantees a continuous distribution of basic services, the improvement of existing ones and their extension to areas which have been neglected as a result of long deprivation imposed by the selfishness of those classes which used to dominate and exploit the struggling people.

The machinery of production must realize that the aim of production is to widen the scope of the services and that these services constitute the driving force behind the wheels of production. This machinery must rely on centralized planning and decentralized execution to ensure that all programmes of the plan are in the hands of the masses of the people.

Private ownership and private capital must be so organized as to prevent the emergence of feudalism, monopoly, or exploitation. Private capital must also be subject to the direction of the popular authority, as is the case with the public sector. This authority shall promulgate legislative measures for it and shall direct it in the light of popular needs. It shall also put a stop to such activity of the private sector as is guilty of exploitation or deviation.

The Arab theory of socialism in the field of agriculture is primarily designed to liberate the farmers from exploitation and domination by the following means:

1 - Fixing a maximum limit for agricultural land ownership in order to eradicate feudalism and the exploitation of farmers and to prevent any resurgence thereof.

2 - Increasing the productivity of the land by using scientific and technical methods.

3 - Organizing individual and collective investment in such a way as to ensure a just distribution of agricultural produce.

Finally, the Arab people, living in an area which witnessed the rise of revealed religions, believe in the message of religion and find in the spiritual strength given by religions an incentive for their popular struggle to attain their objectives.

It is our firm conviction that religion is one of the fundamental elements on which Arab society must build its life and future, side by side with all material elements which religion upholds. With faith in God and confidence in themselves, the people will be able to impose their will on life and shape it anew in conformity with their principles and aspirations.

THE STRUCTURE OF THE FEDERAL STATE AND ITS PREROGATIVES

Agreement has been reached on the following principles:

1 - To create a Federal State called the United Arab Republic on the basis of free Federation between Egypt, Syria and Iraq. The names of the members of the Federation shall be: the Egyptian Region, the Syrian Region and the Iraqi Region.

2 - Any independent Arab Republic believing in the principles of liberty, socialism and unity, has the right to join this Federation by a free expression of

popular will and with the approval of the constitutional authority of the Federal State.

3 - The Federal State shall exercise full international sovereignty.

4 - Citizens of the Federal State shall belong to one nationality: the Arab nationality, which shall be held by all who hold the nationality of the member states. Arab nationality shall be defined by a federal law.

5 - Sovereignty in the Federal State belongs to the people and shall be exercised according to the Constitution.

6 - Islam is the religion of the Federation and Arabic is its official language.

7 - The flag of the Federation is the present flag of the United Arab Republic with three stars instead of two, and a further star shall be added each time a new state [accedes to the Federation]

8 - The capital of the Federal State is Cairo.

9 - The authority of the Federal State covers the following:

(a) Foreign policy in all its aspects including diplomatic representation and treaties with other countries and international organizations. Federal laws will give authority for certain cultural and trade agreements entered into by the member states to continue in force temporarily.

(b) Defence and national security, because the Armed Forces in the Federal State are a part of the people and owe their loyalty to the people, taking their orders only from the people through competent constitutional authorities at Federal level.

The province of defence and national security includes questions of war and peace, preparing the equipment, training and deployment of the land, sea and air forces, the Defence Council, the High Command of the Armed Forces, and the military commands in the member states, although these will be left under the authority of these states for a suitable time during the transitional period in accordance with an agreement. The province of defence also includes the questions of war industries, national security organizations, states of emergency, martial law, and special cases in which local state authorities are given the right to use their Armed Forces by the authorization of the federal authority.

(c) Finance and the Treasury: This covers the taxes of the Federal State and its budget, the issue of treasury bills, Federal State bonds for the financing of Federal projects; and foreign and domestic loans. It also covers tariff policy with the aim of establishing a customs union and an Arab common market to be developed into a united Arab market.

(d) Economy, Economic Planning and Development: This covers economic planning in industry, agriculture, trade and communications, the coordination of the economic plans of the regions, the drafting of economic policy, commercial exchanges, banking, the organization of relations with international economic organizations, currency, and organization of the exploitation of sources of natural wealth.

(e) Information, Culture and Education: This covers the establishment of a central federal agency to plan information affairs in the regions of the Federation. Implementation of information policy will be partly federal, partly regional. It also covers supreme councils charged with the planning and drafting of general policies for education, scientific research, culture and the arts, within the framework of the Federation, based on unity of thought, following unionist Arab nationalist trends, and with particular stress on the spiritual, scientific and moral preparation of the rising generation.

(f) Justice and Coordination of Laws: This covers the establishment of the principles of justice in the regions of the Federal State: the coordination of laws in force in these regions (penal, civil, commercial, procedural, labour and social insurance laws, etc.) with a view to their gradual unification, and the organization of the federal judicial system.

(g) Federal Communications: This covers the organization of Federal communications, including land, sea, air, radio, telephonic, and telegraphic communications, and meteorology, at a federal level.

(h) Other Affairs: This covers projects to be implemented jointly by the regions; exceptional powers during war or emergency; the composing of differences between the regions, and the formation of joint councils for various services within the framework of federal legislation. The regions will be obliged to implement all federal laws and decisions relevant to these matters.

10 - The regions shall exercise all powers not covered by the prerogatives of the Federal State. Through a federal law, the regions may be authorized to exercise certain of the prerogatives of the federal authorities for a specified period of time. In such a case, the federal authorities have the right to supervise the regional authorities' exercise of these prerogatives. It may also be agreed that these authorities be entrusted with the implementation of certain federal laws.

CONSTITUTIONAL ORGANIZATION OF THE FEDERAL STATE

It has also been agreed that the organs of the Federal State and relations between them will be as follows (and in accordance with Appendix II attached hereto):

First—*The National Assembly:*

1 - The National Assembly is the highest State authority in the United Arab Republic.

2 - It is the body which exercises legislative authority.

3 - It is formed of two Chambers: a) The Chamber of Deputies composed of a number of members in a ratio to the population of each state, to be elected through free and direct elections and by universal secret ballot. The term of membership is four years. b) The Federal Council, composed of an equal number of members from each state and elected according to the stipulations of the federal constitution. The term of membership is four years. Its members must number at least one-quarter of the number of members of the Chamber of Deputies and at most one-third of that number.

4 - The National Assembly elects the President of the Republic and the Vice-Presidents in accordance with the stipulations of the Constitution.

5 - Both the Chambers shall debate fundamental matters connected with the State's internal and external policies, and development plans, and make decisions concerning them.

6 - The President of the Republic and all members of the two Chambers have the right to propose laws. (The Constitution shall indicate the necessary procedure).

7 - No law may be issued unless ratified by both Chambers. In case of conflicting views of the two Chambers concerning a bill, it shall be submitted to a Conciliation Committee formed of an equal number of members of both Chambers.

8 - The President of the Republic shall promulgate the laws after their ratification by both Chambers. He shall have the right, during a period specified by the Constitution, to return the law to both Chambers and if both approve it by a three-quarters majority it shall become law and be promulgated.

9 - All members of both Chambers shall have the right to question and address an interpellation to the Prime Minister and the Ministers. (The Constitution and federal law shall determine the procedure).

10 - The responsibility of the Cabinet shall be based on the confidence of the National Assembly and confidence shall be granted and withdrawn by an absolute majority of all members of the National Assembly.

11 - The dissolution of either or both Chambers shall be by Presidential decree.

12 - The National Assembly shall consider applications by new states to join the Federation. Approval shall be by a three-quarters majority vote of each Chamber separately.

13 - The Federal Constitution shall be amended by a three-quarters majority vote of each Chamber.

14 - Regional constitutions must not conflict with the Federal Constitution and they must be agreed upon before the Federal Constitution is submitted to plebiscite.

15 - Amendment of a Regional Constitution shall be made by the legislature of the State concerned in accordance with the method stipulated by the Constitution. Such amendments shall not be operative unless ratified by the Federal Chambers with a three-quarters majority vote of each Chamber separately.

Second—*The President of the Republic:*

1 - The Head of State shall be the President of the Republic who shall be elected by the National Assembly to embody the authority of the State.

2 - Any citizen eligible for membership of the National Assembly may be elected President of the Republic, and a candidate is declared to be elected if he obtains a two-thirds majority vote of all members of the National Assembly. If he does not obtain the required number of votes another vote shall be taken and the candidate shall be considered to be elected if he obtains an absolute majority of the total number of members of the National Assembly. The Constitution shall define the other regulations connected with the election.

3 - The term of the Presidency shall be four years. If the term expires after the dissolution of the National Assembly and before a new one is elected, the President shall continue in office until re-election of the National Assembly is completed and a new President elected.

4 - The President shall be the Supreme Commander of the Armed Forces and shall head the National Defence Council.

5 - The Constitution shall define the prerogatives of the President of the Republic. In particular, the President of the Republic shall:

a) Represent the State
b) Issue laws

c) Propose laws
d) Contest laws
e) Appoint the Prime Minister and Ministers, who must enjoy the confidence of the National Assembly, and accept their resignation
f) Appoint and dismiss officers and promote commanders of the Armed Forces
g) Appoint judges of the Supreme Federal Court
h) Appoint high officials of the Federal State in such cases as the law provides for this.

II—Vice-Presidents:

1 - Three Vice-Presidents shall be elected, one for each region, in the same manner and at the same time as the President.

2 - The Vice-Presidents shall assist the President in his functions. The President shall have the right to appoint them as his deputies, to delegate to them certain of his prerogatives and seek their advice on matters entrusted to him.

3 - The Constitution shall define other regulations concerning the Vice-Presidents.

III—The Cabinet:

1 - The Council of Ministers shall be formed of the Prime Minister and the Ministers.

2 - The Council of Ministers and the Ministers shall be responsible for their actions to the National Assembly.

3 - The Prime Minister and the Ministers shall continue to occupy their posts as long as they enjoy the confidence of the President.

4 - The Federal Council of Ministers shall undertake the organization and execution of the duties of the Federal State and take the necessary decisions for this purpose (according to the Constitution and the federal laws).

5 - The Cabinet after its appointment shall present its programme to the National Assembly for approval.

6 - The Constitution and the federal laws shall define regulations relevant to the Council of Ministers and the Ministries and the various other government organizations.

7 - The Constitution and the federal laws shall define the regulations relevant to Ministers.

Third—The Judiciary:

1 - The Federation shall have a supreme court called the Supreme Federal Court, to be established by federal law in accordance with the provisions of the Constitution.

2 - The National Assembly shall choose the members of the Supreme Federal Court after their nomination by the President of the Republic from among members of the judiciary and the bar.

3 - The Constitution and the federal laws shall define the jurisdiction of the Supreme Federal Court, provide immunity for the members of the Court, decide their term of office and when they should be relieved of their duties.

GOVERNMENTAL MACHINERY IN THE REGIONS SHALL BE AS FOLLOWS

I—The President of the Region:

1 - The President of the Region shall be elected by the Legislative Council of the region for a term of four years and his election shall be approved by the President of the Republic.

2 - He shall exercise the prerogatives determined by the Federal Constitution and the Constitutions of the regions.

3 - He shall appoint the Cabinet of the region and accept its resignation.

II—The Regional Legislative Council:

1 - Each region shall have a Legislative Council, elected by free, direct secret ballot.

2 - The Constitution shall specify the functions of the Legislative Council.

3 - The Legislative Council shall enact legislation for its own region.

4 - The Regional Constitution shall be amended only in the manner specified by the Constitution. These amendments shall not be operative until ratified by majorities in the Chamber of Deputies and the Federal Council.

5 - Questioning of the Cabinet and Ministers, interpellation of the Ministers, and withdrawal of confidence from the Cabinet, shall be effected in the manner specified in the Constitution.

III—The Regional Cabinet:

1 - Each region shall have a Cabinet consisting of a Prime Minister and Ministers.

2 - The regional Cabinet shall be responsible to its regional Legislative Council whose confidence it must obtain.

3 - The Constitution shall specify cases in which confidence may be withdrawn from the Cabinet.

4 - The Constitution and the laws shall define the prerogatives of the Ministries, their operational procedure and the regulations relative to the Ministers.

IV—Courts of law in the Region:

The Constitution and laws of the region shall organize courts of law in the region and guarantee their independence and immunity.

THE TRANSITIONAL PERIOD

1 - The Constitution and President of the Federation shall be the subjects of a referendum within a maximum period of 5 months from the announcement of this communiqué.

2 - The constitutional establishment of the Federal State (the UAR) shall date from the announcement of the results of the referendum.

3 - The federal constitutional institutions shall complete the formation of all their constituent parts as stipulated by the Constitution within 20 months from the announcement of the referendum. This will mark the end of the transitional period.

4 - Each region has the right, during the transitional period, to choose its own constitutional institutions as a preliminary step to the full establishment of the federal institutions. Federal legislation shall determine the constitutional validity of such regional institutions as may be established within this period.

5 - The member states must agree on the programme for completing the unification of the Federal military, foreign, legislative, economic and cultural institutions, etc. etc... When this agreement is reached the programmes shall be embodied in a transitional article of the Constitution which shall give details of procedure during the transitional period.

6 - All legislative and executive powers in the Federal States during the transitional period shall be exercised by a Presidential Council, presided over by the President: the Vice-Presidents will be the members of this Council.

7 - The Presidential Council shall be formed of an equal number of members from each region.

8 - The members of the Presidential Council shall be selected by the legislative authorities in the member states at the time of the proclamation of the Federal State.

9 - The President of the Republic shall have the right to appoint and dismiss Ministers.

10 - The decisions of the Presidential Council shall be taken by a majority vote.

11 - The President of the Republic shall have the right to contest any decision or law issued by the Presidential Council.

12 - The Presidential Council shall be responsible for the following:

a) The appointment of the Vice-Presidents (a Vice-President for each region) through agreement with the legislative authorities in power in the region concerned during the transitional period.

b) The appointment of a President for each region, with the agreement of the legislative authorities in power in the region during the transitional period.

c) The appointment of members of the National Defence Council and supervision of its work.

d) The planning and drafting of the general policy of the State and the entrusting of the Ministers with the task of implementing it.

e) The coordination of public interests between the regions.

f) The appointment of members of the higher councils referred to in the section dealing with general principles.

13 - The Federal Cabinet shall consist of:

a) The Prime Minister.
b) The Ministry of Foreign Affairs.
c) The Ministry of Defence.
d) The Ministry of Information, National Guidance and Culture.
e) The Ministry of Education, Higher Education and Scientific Research.
f) The Ministry of Treasury and Finance.
g) The Ministry of Economy and Economic Planning, and Communications.
h) The Ministry of Justice.
i) The Ministry of State.

14 - Further ministries may be established by a federal law.

15 - The Federal Cabinet and the Presidential Council may hold joint meetings.

It has also been agreed to apply the following general rules:

1 - All legislation in force in any region shall continue in force until amended or repealed by the competent constitutional authority.

2 - Agreements and treaties, previously concluded by the government of any region, shall remain in force in that region.

3 - All existing government organizations and departments shall continue to perform their duties in accordance with various laws and regulations now in force until new rules and regulations are drawn up or until the old laws are amended.

4 - Until a plebiscite has been held on the Federal Constitution, the member states shall form the following committees and bodies, the formation and functioning of these bodies shall pave the way for the establishment of the federal institutions proper at the time of the establishment of the federation:

a) A Unified Military Command.
b) A Foreign Affairs Committee.
c) A Committee for Economic Coordination and an Arab Common Market.
d) Any other committees.

An appendix dealing with the various constitutional bodies has been attached to this declaration. This appendix, which also deals with the establishment of the Federal State and the relations among the three regions, is considered as being complementary to this declaration and is an indivisible part of it.

APPENDIX I

THE CONSTITUTIONAL AUTHORITIES OF THE FEDERAL STATE AND THE RELATIONS BETWEEN THEM

FIRST: THE NATIONAL ASSEMBLY

1 - The National Assembly is the highest body vested with the authority of the State in the United Arab Republic;

2 - The National Assembly is the organization which exercises legislative authority;

3 - The National Assembly consists of two houses:

A - The Chamber of Deputies, which shall consist of a number of members in proportion to the population of each region. It shall be elected by direct free elections and by universal secret ballot. The term of membership shall be four years.

B - The Federal Council, which shall consist of an equal number of members from each region, elected by direct free elections and by universal secret ballot. The term of membership shall be four years. The number of its members shall be at least one-quarter of the number of the members of the Chamber of Deputies, and at most one-third.

4 - Membership of these two houses, replacement of vacancies, cases of vacant seats in them and their internal regulations shall be laid down in the Federal Constitution and in federal laws.

5 - No one may be a member of either the Chamber of Deputies or the Federal Council, and of a Regional Legislative Council at the same time.

6 - Members of the National Assembly shall not be accountable for the opinions and views they advance in the exercise of their parliamentary duties. The Constitution shall provide for the immunity of members of the two Federal houses.

7 - The meetings of the Federal houses shall be held in the capital of the Federal State. The place of meeting may be fixed in any other region by a federal law. Both houses may also be convened, in case of emergency, in any other region by federal decree. Meetings of the two houses, held in any place other than that prescribed by law shall not be valid and any decisions taken by them shall be null and void.

8 - The sessions of both houses shall be as prescribed by the Constitution and shall be convened by the President of the Republic, in default of which the houses shall convene on the day fixed by the Constitution.

9 - Either house may hold extraordinary sessions at the request of the President of the Republic or of one-quarter of the total number of its members. The President of the Republic shall be informed of any such extraordinary session.

10 - The National Assembly shall be convened in the circumstances prescribed by the Constitution.

11 - Both houses shall debate the basic affairs pertaining to the State's internal and foreign policy, and its development plans, and shall adopt resolutions concerning them.

12 - The President and all members of the two houses shall have the right to propose laws and the Constitution shall prescribe the appropriate procedure.

13 - No law may be issued unless it is approved by the two houses. Should the two houses differ in opinion in respect of any law such a law shall be submitted to a Conciliation Committee consisting of an equal number of members of the two houses, on condition that the number chosen from the Chamber of Deputies shall have the same proportional formation as the Council. Should the Committee reach an opinion at variance with the law (or the law after being amended), it shall be referred to both houses. If the Committee does not reach an opinion or if either of the two houses does not approve it, reading of the law shall be postponed to the next session (or to a later meeting).

14 - The President of the Republic shall promulgate laws after their approval by the two houses. He shall have the right to return any law within a period to be specified in the Constitution. If such a law is approved by the two houses by a three-quarters majority vote of their members, it shall be promulgated.

15 - Neither house shall take any decision unless a majority of its members is present. In cases which do not require a special majority the resolutions shall be issued by an absolute majority of the members present.

16 - Every member of the two houses shall have the right to table questions or interpellations to the Prime Minister and the Ministers. The Constitution and the federal laws shall regulate the manner in which such questions and interpellations may be tabled.

17 - The Council of Ministers shall be responsible to the National Assembly. A vote of confidence or non-confidence may be passed by an absolute majority of all the members of the National Assembly.

18 - The Constitution and the federal laws shall define cases in which it is permissible to be a member of either of the two houses and at the same time assume public office.

19 - The dissolution of either or both houses shall be by a decision of the President of the Republic.

20 - The President of the Republic shall have the right to speak in the National Assembly or in the Chamber of Deputies or in the Federal Council, if he so requests. He shall also have the right to convey to them any messages or reports.

21 - The Prime Minister and the Ministers shall have the right to speak in either house and to take part in its debates. (The Constitution shall define the procedure).

22 - A member of the Cabinet may at the same time be a member of either of the two houses.

23 - The National Assembly shall elect the President and the Vice-President of the Republic (in the manner defined by the Constitution).

24 - The National Assembly shall have the right to accept a new member of the Federal State by a three-quarters majority vote of the members of each of the two houses.

25 - The Federal Constitution may be amended by a three-quarters majority vote of each house.

26 - The Constitutions of the regions must be compatible with the Federal Constitution. They must be approved before the Federal Constitution is made subject to a plebiscite.

27 - A Regional Constitution may be amended by the Legislative Council in the Region in a manner to be specified by the Constitution. These amendments shall not be considered effective until they are approved by the National Assembly by a three-quarters majority vote of each house.

28 - The two houses shall ratify treaties in a manner to be specified by the Constitution and the law.

29 - The National Assembly shall have the right to declare war (according to the Constitution).

30 - The Constitution shall define cases in which the President of the Republic may be impeached for high treason or disloyalty in a motion submitted by a specified proportion of the members of the National Assembly.

31 - The Constitution and the Federal laws shall regulate the trial of Ministers.

32 - During the recess of the National Assembly a presidential council of the National Assembly elected from among its members (in the manner specified by the Constitution) may issue laws provided that they are approved by the two houses on their convening.

SECOND: THE PRESIDENT OF THE REPUBLIC

1 - The Head of State is the President of the Republic elected by the National Assembly to embody the authority of the State.

2 - Any citizen of the State eligible for membership of the National Assembly may be elected President of the Republic. The election of a candidate shall be proclaimed if he obtains two-thirds of the votes of all the members of the Assembly. If this majority is not obtained, the election shall be repeated, and, in this case, if the candidate obtains an absolute majority of the votes of all the

members of the Assembly, his election shall be proclaimed. The Constitution shall define all other electoral laws.

3 - The term of the Presidency shall be four years. In case this term expires after the Assembly has been dissolved and before a new one is elected, the President shall continue to exercise his functions until the election of the Assembly is completed and a new President is elected.

4 - The President is the Supreme Commander of the Armed Forces and presides over the National Defence Council.

5 - The prerogatives of the President of the Republic are defined by the Constitution; however, he is empowered to deal with the following:

A - To represent the State in foreign relations, to approve the credentials of diplomatic representatives and to ratify international treaties.

B - To receive and approve the credentials of diplomatic representatives.

C - To convene and dissolve sessions of the Chamber of Deputies, and the Federal Council.

D - To appoint the Prime Minister and Ministers, who must enjoy the confidence of the National Assembly.

E - To accept the resignation of the Prime Minister and Ministers from their functions.

F - To promulgate laws ratified by the two federal houses.

G - To propose laws.

H - To contest laws.

I - To make declarations and transmit messages and reports to the National Assembly.

J - To appoint and retire officers, and to promote the commanders of the Armed Forces (in conformity with the Constitution and federal laws).

K - To attend and preside over meetings of the Cabinet, to ask for reports from it and from individual members of the cabinet and to discuss matters with the Cabinet and its members.

L - To proclaim a state of emergency (in conformity with the Constitution).

M - To declare war (in conformity with the Constitution).

N - To appoint the senior officials of the Federal State in the cases specified by law.

O - To lay down, in conjunction with the Cabinet, general policy for federal affairs.

P - To appoint the judges of the Supreme Federal Court (in conformity with the Constitution and the federal laws).

Q - To grant amnesty.

6 - The President of the Republic shall not occupy any post in the government of any region or be a member in any Legislative Council.

7 - Cases of vacancy of the post of President of the Republic shall be regulated by the Constitution.

VICE-PRESIDENTS

1 - Three Vice-Presidents shall be appointed (one for each region) by the same procedure as for, and simultaneously with, the election of the President of the Republic.

2 - The Vice-Presidents shall assist the President in the exercise of his functions, and he may appoint them as his deputies, delegate to them certain of his prerogatives, and consult them regarding matters entrusted to him.

3 - The Constitution shall regulate all other matters relating to the Vice-Presidents.

THE COUNCIL OF MINISTERS

1 - The Council of Ministers shall consist of the Prime Minister and the Ministers. Deputy Prime-Ministers and Deputy Ministers may also be appointed.

2 - The Council of Ministers and the Ministers shall be responsible to the National Assembly.

3 - The Prime Minister and the Ministers shall occupy their posts as long as they retain the confidence of the President.

4 - The Federal Council of Ministers shall be responsible for the organization and implementation of the affairs of the Federal State, and issue the necessary decisions, (in conformity with the Constitution and the federal laws).

5 - The Cabinet shall, after its formation, submit its programme to the National Assembly for approval.

6 - The Constitution and the federal laws shall lay down regulations relating to the Council of Ministers, the Ministers, and the various other governmental organizations.

7 - The Constitution and the federal laws shall lay down regulations relating to the Ministers.

Third: *The Judiciary:*

1 - A Supreme Court of the Federation shall be created with the title of 'The Supreme Federal Court'; it shall be constituted in conformity with the provisions of the Constitution, and by virtue of a federal law.

2 - The Federal State may create other Federal Courts, to be constituted by federal law.

3 - The competence of the Supreme Federal Court shall be defined by the Constitution and federal law.

4 - The members of the Supreme Federal Court shall be selected by the National Assembly on the nomination of the President of the Republic, and shall be chosen from amongst members of the judiciary and the bar, (in conformity with the Constitution and federal law).

5 - The Constitution and the federal laws shall define the immunities of the members of the Court, and their term of appointment, and the cases in which they may be relieved of their functions.

REGIONAL AUTHORITIES

I. *The Regional President:*

1 - The Regional President shall be elected by the Legislative Council of the Region, for a term of four years; the election shall be approved by the President of the Republic. (The procedure for candidature and election are laid down by the Constitution).

2 - The Regional President shall exercise the prerogatives specified by the federal and the regional Constitutions.

3 - The Regional President shall appoint the Cabinet of the region and accept its resignation.

II. *The Legislative Council:*

1 - Each region shall have a Legislative Council, freely and directly elected by secret ballot.

2 - The Constitution shall define the Legislative Council's powers.

3 - The Regional Legislative Council shall issue rules and laws relating to its own region.

4 - A Regional Constitution shall be amended only in the manner defined by the Constitution. Such amendments shall only come into force after approval by a three-quarters majority vote of the Chamber of Deputies and the Federal Council.

5 - The Legislative Council shall debate matters with the region's Cabinet and Ministers, shall question and interpellate the Ministers and shall withdraw confidence from the Government in the manner defined by the Constitution.

6 - A regional Legislative Council shall be dissolved as follows:

(a) In conformity with a decision issued by the Regional President.

(b) By a decision issued by the President of the Republic, in accordance with a decision taken by the Federal Council by a two-thirds majority.

III. *Regional Cabinets:*

1 - Each region shall have a Cabinet formed of a Prime Minister and Ministers.

2 - A Regional Cabinet shall be responsible to the Regional Legislative Council and must have its confidence.

3 - Cases of withdrawal of confidence from the Cabinet shall be regulated by the Constitution.

4 - The Constitution and the laws shall define the Ministries' powers, the manner in which they are to be exercised and the rules and regulations relating to the Ministers.

IV. *Regional Judiciaries:*

The Constitution and laws of each Region shall regulate its Judiciary and safeguard its immunity and independence.

LAWS FOR THE TRANSITIONAL PERIOD

I. *The Federal State:*

1 - A plebiscite on the Federal Constitution and the President of the Republic shall be held within a period not exceeding five months from the publication of this announcement.

2 - The Federal State (the United Arab Republic) shall be considered constitutionally existent as from the date of the announcement of the results of the plebiscite.

3 - Federal Constitutional authorities shall have established all machinery mentioned in the Constitution within a period of twenty months at the most from the publication of the results of the plebiscite. The transitional period will thus have come to an end.

4 - Each Region shall establish before this date the necessary constitutional machinery in preparation for the complete establishment of all the federal organizations during the transitional period.

Federal legislation shall decide the constitutional validity of regional organizations established during this period.

5 - Legislative and Executive Authority in the Federal State shall be exercised during the transitional period by a Presidential Council headed by the President of the Republic. The Vice-Presidents of the Republic shall be members.

6 - The Presidential Council shall be formed of an equal number of members from each of the Regions.

7 - The members of the Presidential Council shall be chosen by the Legislative Authorities in power in the States which are members of the Federation at the time of its establishment.

8 - The President of the Republic shall appoint the Prime Minister and Ministers, and shall relieve them of their functions.

9 - The Council's decisions shall be by the majority of its members.

10 - The President of the Republic has the right to contest any decision taken or law issued by the Presidential Council.

11 - The Presidential Council is responsible for the following:

a) The appointment of Vice-Presidents of the Republic (one Vice-President from each region), in agreement with the legislative authorities in power in the Regions during the transition period.

b) The appointment of a President for each Region, in agreement with the legislative authorities in power in the region during the transitional period.

c) The appointment of a National Defence Council and the supervision of its actions.

d) The planning and drafting of the State's general policy and the entrusting of the Cabinet with the task of its implementation.

e) The coordination of public services between the regions.

f) The appointment of the Higher Councils mentioned in the section on general principles.

12 - The Federal Cabinet: This shall include

a) The Prime Minister.
b) The Minister of Foreign Affairs.
c) The Minister of Defence.
d) The Minister of Information, National Guidance and Culture.
e) The Minister of Education, Higher Education and Scientific Research.
f) The Minister of the Treasury and Finance.
g) The Minister of Economy and Economic Planning, plus communications.
h) The Minister of Justice.
i) The Minister of State.

13 - Other Ministries may be established by the promulgation of a federal law.

14 - The Federal Cabinet may hold joint meetings with the Presidential Council.

II. *General Provisions:*

1 - All laws and regulations in any region shall continue to be in force in that region until their amendment or repeal by the competent constitutional authority.

2 - Agreements and treaties already concluded by the Government of any region shall remain in force as far as that region is concerned.

3 - All existing authorities and government departments shall continue to perform their duties in accordance with laws and regulations now in force until these have been amended or replaced by new laws and regulations.

4 - Member-States shall agree on a programme of completing the unification of the federal military, foreign affairs, legislative, economic, cultural, or other authorities, so that provision for a programme may be made in a transitional article of the Constitution.

5 - Until a plebiscite on the Federal Constitution has been held, Member States shall form the following committees and bodies, the formation and preliminary operations of which will pave the way for the ultimate establishment of the federal authorities when union is achieved:

    a) A unified Military Command.

    b) A Foreign Affairs Committee.

    c) An Economic Co-ordination and Arab Common Market Committee.

    d) Any other Committee or Committees.

APPENDIX II

THE ESTABLISHMENT OF THE FEDERAL STATE AND THE FEDERAL CONSTITUTION

The Federal State

First: *General Principles:*

1 - A Federal State called the UNITED ARAB REPUBLIC shall be established on the basis of free union between Egypt, Iraq and Syria. The names of the members of the Federal State shall be 'THE EGYPTIAN REGION' 'THE IRAQI REGION', and 'THE SYRIAN REGION'.

2 - Any independent Arab Republic which believes in the principles of freedom, socialism and unity may join this State by the free will of its people. Admission of new states shall be subject to the approval of the constitutional authority concerned in the Federal State.

3 - The Federal State alone shall have full international authority.

4 - The nationality of the Federal State shall be held by any one who holds the nationality of any of the member states at the time of the proclamation of the Federal State or on the date of its joining the Federation. The rules concerning the acquisition of the nationality of the Federal State or its loss or any matter related thereto, shall be defined by federal law.

5 - Sovereignty belongs to the people and they shall exercise it in accordance with the Constitution.

6 - Islam shall be the official religion of the State and Arabic shall be its official language.

7 - The Federal State's flag shall be that of the present United Arab Republic with three stars instead of two. A new star shall be added each time a new state joins the Federation.

8 - A Federal law shall decide on the insignia.

9 - A Federal law shall decide on the national anthem.

10 - There shall be one nationality (the Arab Nationality), which shall be defined by a Federal law.

11 - Cairo shall be the capital of the Federal State.

Second: *The Powers of the Federal State:*

The authority of the Federal State shall include:

1 - Foreign policy
2 - Defence
3 - National Security
4 - Finance and the Treasury (Budget, Customs, etc)
5 - Economy, Economic Planning and Development
6 - Information and National Guidance (at Federal level)
7 - Cultural Planning
8 - Coordination of General Education, Higher Education, and Scientific Research
9 - Justice and the Coordination of Laws
10 - Federal Communications
11 - Other Federal State powers may be added by the means specified by the Constitution.

1 - Foreign Policy: This shall include

A) All aspects of foreign representation (taking into consideration regional factors in certain fields, such as commerce and culture, which shall be gradually transferred from the field of regional to that of federal competence).

B) Affairs connected with the United Nations and other world organizations.

C) Treaties with foreign countries (the regions may conclude certain trade agreements with the approval of the Federal State).

D) Extradition of criminals and political asylum.

E) Issue of Arab passports and visas.

F) Entry of aliens into the territory of the Federal State, their residence and deportation according to federal laws.

G) Questions pertaining to nationality and all other foreign questions.

2 - Defence:

It is an established principle that the Armed Forces are part of the people and owe allegiance only to the people and take orders only from the people through the constitutional authority concerned at Federal level. The field of Defence shall include,

A) Matters of war and peace.

B) The equipment, arming, training and deployment of land, sea and air forces.

C) Military Command: A unified military command with local decentralization of the powers of local commands directly attached to the General Command. (But the regional authorities are to continue to be responsible for their local commands during the transitional period deemed suitable for each region).

D) The Defence Council and the General Command of the Armed Forces and the Regional Military Commands.

E) General Mobilization.

F) War Industries.

3 - National Security. This shall include:

A) National Security Organizations agreed upon in the Constitution or by federal laws.

B) Proclamation of martial law when the Federal State or any of the regions is exposed to danger.

C) States of emergency specified by federal law which would give the regional authorities the right to use the Armed Forces until the state of emergency ends.

4 - Finance and the Treasury. This shall include:

A) Federal taxes.

B) Federal budget (from Federal taxes or contributions from the regions in the way and for the aims agreed upon, or from loans or from other sources).

C) The issue of treasury bills and Federal State bonds to finance Federal projects.

D) Foreign or domestic loans, (and it is forbidden for regions to contract foreign loans except with the approval of the Federal State).

E) Customs regulations and policy (aimed at the gradual formation of a customs union and an Arab Common Market).

5 - Economy, Economic Planning and Development. This shall include:

A) A Higher Council for Planning.

B) Economic planning in industry, agriculture, trade and communications, and the coordination of the economic plans of the regions.

C) A Higher Economic Council to examine and coordinate joint economic questions, and study these questions in relation to other countries.

D) Economic policy.

E) Organization of foreign commerce (to include its regulation and commercial treaties and agreements).

F) Organization of trade between the regions of the Federal State.

G) Organization of payments between the regions of the Federation and foreign countries.

H) Currency.

I) Federal banking affairs.

J) Relations with international economic organizations.

K) Federal Industries.

L) Joint Projects.

M) Nuclear energy and the natural resources needed for its production.

6 - Information and National Guidance. This shall include:

A central Federal Agency for Federal planning of information. (The implementation of information policy shall be in part regional and in part Federal.)

7 - Cultural Planning. This shall include:

A) A Higher Council for Arts and Literature.

B) Arab culture and its relation to other cultures.

8 - Planning of Education, Higher Education and Scientific Research. This shall include:

A) A Higher Council or Councils for education and research.

B) General policy for education and research.

C) Curricula.

D) Guarantees for unity of thought and unionist Arab nationalist trends, and spiritual, scientific and moral preparation of the rising generation which will build complete unity and establish a free socialist Arab society.

E) The administration of Federal organizations concerned with educational and scientific affairs.

9 - Justice and Coordination of Laws. This shall include:

A) Unified bases for justice (the drafting of the basic principles of laws such as the penal code, the civil law, the commercial law, the law of procedure, the labour law, the social insurance law etc).

B) Coordination of laws with a view to their gradual unification.

C) Federal Judiciary.

10 - Federal Communications.

These include all means of land, sea and air transport and Federal communications such as railways, steamships, aircraft, posts, telegraphs, telephones, radio and meteorology at Federal level.

11 - Other problems to be dealt with in the manner prescribed by the constitution and to include:

A) All affairs and projects which jointly concern the three regions.

B) Exceptional powers during war or emergencies in the regions (in conformity with Federal law).

C) The obligation of the regions to implement Federal laws and decrees and respect any particular obligation and the giving of instructions to the regions to implement any decision taken by Federal authority.

D) Arbitration between the regions whenever differences arise.

E) Joint councils for various services in conformity with Federal legislation.

F) The right of the Federal State to grant total amnesty of criminals in conformity with Federal law.

G) Special pardon (a prerogative of the President).

Third: *Powers of the Regions:*

1 - The regions shall exercise all powers not included in the jurisdiction of the Federal State.

2 - By a Federal law, the regions may be authorized to exercise some of the powers of the Federal authorities for a specified period. In such a case, the Federal

authorities have the right to supervise the regional authorities, in their exercise of these powers.

3 - It is possible to entrust the regional authorities with the implementation of some Federal laws.

Military Charter, announced by the Governments of Syria and Iraq, Damascus, 8 October 1963[1]

The agreement hereby announced between Syria and Iraq has come about because Arab unity is one of the basic goals of the Revolutions of the 14th of Ramadan and March 8; because the common will and destiny of the two Revolutions made them in reality one single Popular Socialist Arab Nationalist Revolution which bears the responsibility for taking the first real steps towards laying the foundations of the Union desired by all; because imperialist and Zionist threats have increased with the collapse of Arab reaction and the victory of popular revolutionary forces in both Syria and Iraq; because the Revolutions of the 14th of Ramadan and March 8 are responsible not only for the protection of revolutionary achievements in the two states, but also—and this is enforced on them by their liberating unionist character—for the protection of all parts of the Arab homeland from the dangers by which it is surrounded; and because the unity of the army is a major step towards the achievement of comprehensive union. The following agreement was concluded in pursuance of the Iraqi-Syrian joint communiqué issued on September 8, 1963,[2] as a result of negotiations which have taken place between Damascus and Baghdad, and as a result of the visit made by the Iraqi Military Delegation, headed by the Minister of Defence, to Damascus on September 28, 1963.

The two parties have agreed on the following:

1 - To announce the Military Union between Syria and Iraq. This Union comprises all the armed forces in both states.

2 - To form a Supreme Defence Council consisting of the Commander-in-Chief of the Unified Army and three members from each state appointed by the National Revolutionary Council.

3 - To appoint Staff Brigadier and Minister of Defence, Saleh Mahdi Ammash of Iraq, as Commander-in-Chief of the Armed Forces.

4 - To make Damascus the seat of the General Headquarters.

In announcing the establishment of this Military Union between their two states, the Revolutionary Councils in Iraq and Syria call on the other Arab states to join them. They hereby declare their determination to achieve comprehensive Arab Unity, starting with the liberated Arab countries.

Speech by the President of the United Arab Republic Gamal Abdul Nasser, Port Said, 23 December 1963[3] (extracts)

. . . History cannot move backward. After the means of production are transferred to the people, we cannot put them back in the hands of the capitalists.

---

[1] *Arab Political Documents, 1963*, pp. 421–2.

[2] Ibid., pp. 370–1. This communiqué is, in fact, dated 2 September 1963.

[3] Ibid., pp. 501–6.

After the workers have obtained a share equal to 25% of the profits, we cannot say to them that they are hirelings in the service of the capitalist owners. This is impossible. There is no reverse movement in history. It was evident that the conjunction between the unity experiment and socialism had transformed Arab nationalism into a progressive movement with a social aim. But after all those intrigues, after all the attempts to strike down the Arab national movement, and the doctrine of Arab unity, has colonialism, for all its allies, and its machinations, been able to do away with it? No, because the currents of Arab nationalism and of Arab unity are still the driving current in the Arab world and in the whole Arab nation.

What happened to imperialism after 1956? The Baghdad Pact[1] collapsed. Nuri El-Said fell; Abdul-Ilah fell; the Imam of Yemen fell; Abdul-Karim fell. All the props they tried to lean on gave way. Saud—we have spoken about Saud before and we know his story from beginning to end. It is not right to beat a dead man.

We had many experiences with the Ba'thists. They began by calling for union. They gave us a bad time under the union but we thought that we could find a way of coming to terms with them. But their methods proved to be immoral and precluded any confidence in them. In spite of this, we opened our hearts to them when they said they wanted to discuss union and we started the Union Talks. You have all read the minutes of the Union Talks[2] in which we frankly said what we thought of them. But God hates arrogance. They were consumed by arrogance, probably with the encouragement of certain circles. And it turned out later that everything they did in connection with union was only a manœuvre to gain time. If the cause of union is going to be used as a manœuvre to gain time, then there can be no principles, no ideals, no morals. We agreed to sit and talk, and we could have resorted to manœuvres, but the cause of union is above manœuvres. It was known that the idea behind gaining time was to liquidate the situation in Syria and to put the unionists in prison or cashier them from the Army.

They were able to do so and said later that they would establish a union between Syria and Iraq under Ba'thist rule in both. Looking at the Ba'th Party today, we find that it is in its death throes. This is so because the opportunist Ba'th Party has not made good use of the opportunity which was presented to it. Nor did it make good use of the clean sheet that was offered to it for co-operation with all unionist and nationalist elements. It believed only in treachery and terror.

What happened in Iraq? One man in Iraq has carried out two revolutions; Abdul Salam Aref is this man. When a man carries out a revolution, he does not usually do it alone, but there are with him certain honourable, trustworthy individuals seeking to realize the objectives of this revolution. After Iraq had reached a pitiable state as was stated in the statement of November 18,[3] this fighter, this brave man, Abdul Salam Aref, in order to save the situation in Iraq, and in order to save the people of Iraq from this pitiable state and from these horrors, and in order to unify the people of Iraq in friendship and love, was, by the grace of God, victorious on November 18, and was able to save Iraq again from the domination of terrorists and the domination of the Ba'th Party. This is the result of the rule of the Ba'th Party in Iraq. Today, turning towards our

---

[1] See *Documents, 1955*, pp. 286–313.
[2] Published in *Arab Political Documents, 1963*, pp. 75–217.   [3] Ibid., p. 163.

brothers in Iraq and towards President Abdul Salam Aref, we can say to them, 'We have always been with you; in the Revolution of 1958, in the Revolution of Ramadan, and in the Revolution of November 18, this Revolution which was built on the Egyptian people; we are all here with you and we support you in the interests of Iraq, because the strength of Iraq is the strength of all the Arab people'.

As regards the Revolution in Yemen, we said at the start that the day before yesterday they were cheering and declaring that Lt. Gen. Anwar El Kadi, together with a thousand soldiers were completely annihilated. The Imam, while sitting chewing 'gat', had destroyed them all. Papers in Arabic and foreign languages came out joyfully with this piece of so-called news. Israel also broadcast these words day and night.

Our forces went to Yemen in order to support the right of the people of Yemen to revolt. The people of Yemen who lagged behind the procession of history by more than a thousand years, revolted, not for the first time, but for the tenth or the twentieth time, in order to live. But Saudi reaction does not want these people to live and therefore it opposed the Revolution in Yemen. When Yemen asked for our support, our sons and brothers hurried to it, and some of them sacrificed their lives and fell martyrs for a great cause and a high ideal, for our Arabism and nationalism, and in defence of the principles we believe in. Thanks to God, our forces were able to destroy all imperialist manœuvres. For some months past there have been no battles except for some minor skirmishes which took place to stop infiltration from Saudi Arabia. But the British are not happy—we are like a thorn in their flesh. The British want to occupy the world, they want to occupy the Arab world. They want to collaborate with the Saudi Arabians in order to remain in Yemen; this according to them should be no business of ours.

They go and occupy Aden, the Arab South, the Protectorates and the Gulf, and consider this their right. When the Yemeni Revolution asked for our support against the foe, the English were extremely angry and disappointed. We went to Yemen to help the Yemeni people to triumph and we resolved to confront any aggression; fighting is now ended. But there still remained British intrigues. They intrigue and proclaim that Yemen and Egypt are fomenting intrigues. The British work with Saud and furnish him with arms and despatch to him a military mission composed of 27 officers to organize their Army. After the relations between them had long been severed, they are in perfect agreement together, and relations between them now are very satisfactory. The British and Saud, or rather the British and the Saudis are allies today against Egypt and against Yemen. Then when we assist the Yemeni people against Saudi hostility, the British say that this is not permissible; but when Britain occupies territories in the Arab world, we must agree to it and remain silent about it. The British foment intrigues against us, and then accuse us of intriguing. Everybody knows that the British occupation of Aden and of the Arab South is against the will of their people. The United Nations instituted a commission of inquiry, and that commission recorded the methods of terrorization and the colonialist activities perpetrated by Britain in Aden and in the Occupied South. The United Nations adopted a resolution[1] calling for the independence of Aden and for terminating

[1] A/RES/1949 (XVIII), 11 December 1963; G.A.O.R., Eighteenth Session, Supplement No. 15, p. 6.

colonial rule in Aden and the occupied South, but Britain did not accept this resolution.

The United Nations decided to send a commission, but Britain did not accept. Thus there is colonialism and a terrorist British colonialism in Aden and in the Occupied South. Then when the nationalists threw a bomb at the British Governor, they were imprisoned. Men and women were put in prison. Then they alleged that this act was planned and carried out by Yemen with the encouragement of Cairo.

Yesterday, the British Government, in answer to a Member of Parliament, said: 'You want us to leave Aden in order that it may unite with Yemen and thus let Cairo rule'. Both Cairo and Yemen are Arab countries that will one day get together whether Britain wants it or not.

Had we wished for union with Yemen we could have carried it out. We rejected a union with Yemen as long as we have Egyptian forces there. We put off this question of union till our forces have fulfilled their duty in Yemen. When the Yemeni Army there assumes this duty, we can talk about union. Today you saw a brigade of the Yemeni Army marching in the parade. This brigade has been trained here in Egypt. At the same time, we support the liberals of Aden and those of the Occupied South with all our power. All the U.A.R. potentialities will be mobilized for the eradication of British imperialism from this zone, because Britain has no right to remain in Aden or in any of the protectorates or in any of the provinces which they allege are under their protection in accordance with treaties dating back to the last century.

People in these areas and in these protectorates are nationalists, even those in authority are nationalists, and the Egyptian plane that landed in one of these protectorates was given a brotherly welcome by the people and by the National Guard and by those in authority. They are our brothers. The British cannot become the brothers of the Arabs in Aden or in any other place in the pro-tectorates.

The Ministers who resigned in protest against terrorism, and the Ministers who resigned from the Aden Government in protest against the state of emergency, and the imprisonment of men and women, have set an able example, an example in honour, an example in nationalism. A people inspired by this spirit, the spirit of resistance, the spirit of determination, cannot possibly be defeated.

England has been defeated in many areas in the world and has given up all colonies. It is not tolerable under any circumstances that she should give up all her colonies, and still rule a part of the Arab nation, or a part of the Arab countries.

The Yemeni Revolution was a turning-point. Our forces in Yemen, with the Yemeni revolutionaries, played what we consider a vanguard role, and did their duty with sincerity and honour . . .

. . . Our international policy is straightforward. We do not say one thing and do something else. When I saw our brothers at the stadium returning from Yemen this morning, I was overjoyed to hear them cheering 'From Yemen to Palestine' just as they arrived from Yemen and even before taking leave to see their families, their fathers, their mothers, their sisters and brothers. They thought of Palestine before anything else. Naturally, the Palestinians are like our brothers, fathers and mothers, because we are one Arab people. It was not strange at all that our soldiers returning from Yemen should shout that slogan.

I would like to say something which we must all realize. The Palestine story of 1948 must never be repeated. The Palestine affair of 1948 was a political bargain. We were in Palestine at the time and we had weapons without ammunition. And while the Egyptian Army fought the Israeli army on the battlefield, the field of honour, King Abdullah was meeting Moshe Dayan and the Jordanian army was under the command of Glubb.

Everything we do today is for the strength of our country. Our heavy industries are steps on the road towards Palestine. We mention Palestine because we can never forget and abandon her and we cannot treat the problem of Palestine in the same way as it was treated in 1948 through bargaining and by isolating us from responsibility.

In 1960, during the union, I asked the Council of Ministers which included Syrian Ministers, to discuss what steps could be taken in the period between 1960 and 1964 as far as Israel and the project of diverting the River Jordan were concerned from the technical and political points of view, assuming that decisions on military action would be left until later. We reached certain decisions at that time—that the rivers which rise in Arab countries such as the Hasbani in Lebanon, the Banias in Syria and the Yarmuk in Jordan, have Arab waters and should be prevented from running into Israel. After that, we said that we would study the military aspects. But at that time, certain people also wanted to carry out political bargains and auctions and turn the problem into political manœuvres.

We show courage when the situation calls for courage. At the same time we work. If they take our water, why should we let it flow to them? The Arab people will unveil these bargaining operations. For example, the Da'thist newspapers come out saying that the U.A.R. is not participating in the River Jordan battle, and so on. We say that such words are familiar to the Arab people. The Arab people know who is fighting and who is calling for Arab nationalism consciously and with good faith. We called for Arab nationalism and when the need called in Yemen, we sent 40,000 soldiers there; at one time we had 40,000 soldiers in Yemen, we did not hesitate when the message came from Ben Bella asking for forces to help him stop the aggression against him, we answered him in 24 hours because this is the path of duty and it is our path. We do not put Arab nationalism into words and later put it into practice by manœuvres and worn-out political methods.

I naturally know all that took place in the Conference of the Chiefs-of-Staff of the Arab Armies. They all know this. I know, but I am not going to say anything to-day, so as not to let the Jews know. I know every word that was said in the Conference of the Chiefs-of-Staff. In my opinion, nothing can be decided in this manner by the Chiefs-of-Staff on this subject, because this is primarily a political matter before being a military one. Military action follows politics in these matters. What can the Chief-of-Staff of an army say? They are driving the people in a vicious circle. Then the newspapers come out and say: Abdul Nasser does not speak; he will not fight for the River Jordan; how can this be? The statements in the minutes of the meetings of the Chiefs-of-Staff of the armies, nobody says anything about them. Everyone says one thing at the meeting, and something else as soon as he leaves it. We shall not allow the kind of talk that went on in 1948 to occur another time; what we say at the meeting we shall say outside. If we cannot fight, we shall tell the people, that we cannot fight, and put off the battle to another time.

We do not use two languages. We use only one language. Our attitude here in the United Arab Republic is that we consider that a conference on the level of the Chiefs-of-Staff is of no avail. In order to confront Israel, which threw down a challenge to us last week, when its Chief-of-Staff stood up and said, 'We shall divert the water against the will of the Arabs and let the Arabs do what they can', a meeting between the Arab Kings and Heads of States must take place as soon as possible, regardless of the strifes and conflicts between them. Those with whom we are in conflict, we are prepared to meet; with those with whom we have a conflict, we are ready, for the sake of Palestine, to sit. In the situations which call for courage, Egypt has always shown courage. In 1948, when everybody collapsed, we stood and fought. I was besieged in Palestine, in the northern Negev, and we did not yield. We continued to fight, because that battle involved the honour of the Arabs, our own honour, the honour of our country and the honour of our army.

Egypt is ready to do its duty, to do its duty fully. Our brothers in Yemen are coming back. We need other forces. We manufacture weapons here, everything is available. We want to talk about the diversion of the River Jordan. I propose a meeting between the kings and the heads of Arab states and I will send to the Arab League this proposal to issue invitations to such a meeting, as soon as possible. We will sit and talk seriously at the meeting and it will be no shame if we come out and say that we cannot use force. We will tell you the truth and we will tell you every word which was said: that we cannot use force today because our circumstances do not allow us, that you must be patient with us, that the battle of Palestine can continue, and the battle of Jordan is part of the battle of Palestine. Or we may say that we shall be able, if they divert the waters of the River Jordan, to stop this diversion by force. But, we shall not say one thing behind closed doors and another thing outside. For myself what I say inside, I will repeat outside.

We can never bargain over this, for it is not a matter for bargaining. I mean that I would not be ashamed, if such were the case, to say to you that I cannot fight when I am really unable to fight. For I should be leading you to disaster if I proclaimed that I was ready to fight at the time when I was unable to do so. I will not lead my country to disaster and will not gamble with its destiny. I do not bargain in this matter. We are completely ready to undertake our duty to the full.

Let us try to forget all the stupidities and irritations which we have witnessed in the past few years. Also the disputes that have taken place and the words that have been spoken, and the treachery and so on. We say that we are ready, not only ready, but that we must discuss the problem of the River Jordan in a meeting attended by the highest authorities in every Arab country. This is not a small problem, this is a question of destiny. Chiefs-of-Staff cannot do anything, neither can the Defence Council. This is our attitude as far as the River Jordan question is concerned today. We hope that soon the time will come when we will tell you what is our attitude towards the Palestine question and the Israeli usurpation of Palestine.

Statement of the Council of the Kings and Heads of State of the Arab League member countries, Cairo, 17 January 1964[1]

The Council of the Kings and Heads of State of the Arab League, in its first session held at the Arab League Headquarters in Cairo, from January 13 to 17, 1964, upon the suggestion of President Gamal Abdul Nasser, President of the United Arab Republic;

— Having considered the threat and repeated use of force by Israel since it evicted the Palestine Arab population, and created in their territory a colonialist state which practices discrimination against the Arab minority, adopts a policy of aggression of which the fait accompli is the basic feature, flouts continuously the resolutions of the United Nations which affirm the right of the Palestine Arab people to repatriation, and insultingly ignores the many condemnations of it adopted by the United Nations authorities;

— Having discussed Israel's new and aggressive plan to divert the course of the River Jordan, thereby greviously endangering the riparian rights of the Arabs with the object of realizing Zionist designs for expansion through immigration, and Israel's plans to establish further centres of aggression against the security and progress of Arab countries, thus endangering world peace;

— In pursuance of the legitimate right of self-defense;

— Fully persuaded of the sacred right of the Palestine Arab people to self-determination and liberation from the Zionist colonization of their country, believing that Arab solidarity is the means to off-set imperialist designs, and convinced of the need for the realization of equitable common Arab interests to raise the living standard of the people and to implement programmes for reconstruction and rehabilitation,

— Has therefore adopted the practical resolutions essential to ward off the imminent Zionist menace, whether in the defensive or the technical domains or in the field of organizing the Palestinian people to enable them to play their part in the liberation of their country and attain self-determination.

The Council's meeting has brought the kings and heads of state to unanimous agreement to put an end to differences, clear the Arab atmosphere of all discord, suspend all campaigns by information media, consolidate relations among the Arab states, ensure collective cooperation and reconstruction, and frustrate aggressive expansionist designs menacing all Arab states.

The Council was also of the view that the convening of more of these meetings at the highest level is a matter necessitated by supreme Arab interests, and decided that the kings and heads of state should meet at least once a year and that the coming meeting be held during August, 1964, at Alexandria.

The Arab kings and heads of state declare that the Arab nation calls upon those nations and peoples of the world which cherish the right to self-determination, to extend to it the staunchest support in repelling the new Israeli aggression.

These leaders affirm that, in adopting this just and defensive stand, they will regulate their political and economic relations with other countries in accordance with the policy of these countries toward the legitimate Arab struggle against Zionist designs in the Arab world.

[1] *Arab Political Documents, 1964*, pp. 7–9.

The Arab kings and heads of state also hope that all those Afro-Asian countries which placed their faith in the Bandung principles[1] and committed themselves to the Addis-Ababa Charter[2] and which sacrificed a great deal in fighting imperialism, fought racial discrimination and have been and are still being subjected to the Zionist and imperialist dangers and designs—particularly in Africa—would extend their true support and assistance to the Arabs in their just struggle.

These leaders also hope for the support of all free nations which believe in peace based on justice.

The Arab kings and heads of state further affirm their belief in the justice of the Arab struggle and in the need for supporting this struggle against imperialism in Occupied South Yemen and in Oman, as well as their belief in the justice of the national struggle in Angola and South Africa and in every part of the world, that the cause of liberty and justice integral and indivisible.

The leaders confirm their faith in solving world problems through peaceful means in accordance with the United Nations Charter and affirm their belief in the principle of peaceful co-existence among nations and in the policy of non-alignment.

Inspired by this conviction, the Arab countries welcome the partial nuclear test-ban treaty of Moscow and have hastened to sign it.[3] They support the concerted efforts made towards achieving total and complete disarmament in ways that can safeguard world peace.

Inspired by their attachment to the principles of peace based on equity and justice, and their determination to participate in the economic development of the world through the elimination of economic and social under-development, the Arab countries played a major role in the Conference of Economic Development held in Cairo in the spring of 1963.[4] They pledge themselves to participate with the same spirit and determination in the World Conference of Development and Trade which will be held this year.

The kings and heads of state welcome the African Unity Charter in which they see a new hope for peace, freedom, and equality in Africa and the world.

Moreover, they affirm their determination to consolidate Afro-Asian cooperation, which began in earnest with the Bandung Conference of 1955.

The Arab kings and heads of state declare their devotion to their duty towards their Arab nation, towards the dignity of the human family, and in the service of peace and prosperity in the world.

B. THE YEMEN

Statement by the United States Department of State, 19 December 1962[5]

In view of the number of confusing and contradictory statements which have cast doubt upon the intentions of the new regime in Yemen,[6] the United States

[1] Documents, 1955, pp. 429–36. [2] See pp. 436–44 below. [3] See pp. 170–2 above.
[4] The Conference, which opened on 11 March 1963, was organized by the Egyptian National Institute of Planning in collaboration with the International Labour Organization.
[5] D.S.B., 7 January 1963, pp. 11–12.
[6] On 26 September 1962, a section of the army rose against the ruling Imam of Yemen and proclaimed a republic.

Government welcomes the reaffirmation by the Yemen Arab Republic Government of its intention to honor its international obligations, of its desire for normalization and establishment of friendly relations with its neighbors, and of its intention to concentrate on internal affairs to raise the living standards of the Yemeni people.

The United States Government also is gratified by the statesmanlike appeal of the Yemen Arab Republic to Yemenis in adjacent areas to be law-abiding citizens and notes its undertaking to honor all treaties concluded by previous Yemeni governments. This, of course, includes the Treaty of Sana'a concluded with the British Government in 1934,[1] which provides reciprocal guarantees that neither party should intervene in the affairs of the other across the existing international frontier dividing the Yemen from territory under British protection.

Further the United States Government welcomes the declaration of the United Arab Republic signifying its willingness to undertake a reciprocal disengagement and expeditious phased removal of troops from Yemen as external forces engaged in support of the Yemen royalists are removed from the frontier and as external support of the royalists is stopped.

In believing that these declarations provide a basis for terminating the conflict over Yemen and in expressing the hope that all of the parties involved in the conflict will cooperate to the end that the Yemeni peoples themselves be permitted to decide their own future, the United States has today [December 19] decided to recognize the Government of the Yemen Arab Republic and to extend to that Government its best wishes for success and prosperity. The United States has instructed its Chargé d'Affaires in Yemen to confirm this decision in writing to the Ministry of Foreign Affairs of the Yemen Arab Republic.

The President of the Yemen Arab Republic, Abdallah Al Sallal, to the President of the Security Council, 28 February 1963[2]

I should like to inform Your Excellency that we are sure of the arrival of British forces to Hareb area supported by tanks. British planes have also dropped circulars on the Yemeni forces warning them to withdraw from the surroundings of the Yemeni town of Hareb, otherwise they would be bombed by planes. This is aid from Britain to infiltrators coming from Saudi Arabia to help the dethroned Imam and those surrounded in Hareb. The planes have actually been aggressive at the Yemeni area of Hareb.

Considering that this flagrant aggression on the part of Britain against the territory of the Yemen Arab Republic constitutes a clear violation of the sovereignty of the Yemen Arab Republic and the inviolability of its territories as well as a threat to world peace and a clear violation of the United Nations Charter, the Yemen Arab Republic Government, while deeply regretting this glaring aggression on the part of the British forces, hastens to inform you of the contents of this message so that you would take immediate action to stop this aggression at once.

[1] Great Britain, *British and Foreign State Papers, 1934*, Vol. CXXXVII. (London, 1939), pp. 212–14.

[2] *S.C.O.R.*, Eighteenth Session, Supplement for January, February, and March 1963, S/5248.

We should also like to inform you that the Government of the Yemen Arab Republic reserves its full right in the defence of its sovereignty and the safety of its territories and citizens by all means.

In the sincere hope that this rash interference on the part of the British forces will not lead to a threat to peace in the area or in the world, we should like to assure you that we shall defend by all means every inch of our territory.

The Permanent Representative of Great Britain at the United Nations, Sir Patrick Dean, to the President of the Security Council, 4 March 1963[1]

I am instructed to bring to the attention of Your Excellency the sequence of events which have recently taken place inside the borders of the South Arabian Federation.

On 29 January 1963, a force from the Yemen about 120 strong and armed with mortars and machine-guns entered the Wadi Ablah in the territory of Beihan in the South Arabian Federation. A small patrol of the Federal National Guard which was sent to investigate was fired on by the Republican Force and withdrew. Fire continued intermittently until 31 January and was repeated on 5 February. One Federal guard was killed. In addition, on 30 January, an aircraft coming from the Yemen flew over part of the Wadi Ain more than three miles inside the South Arabian Federation frontier. On 8 February, before the closure of the Legation on 16 February at the request of the Republican authorities, Her Majesty's *Chargé d'Affaires* in Taizz delivered a protest against the violation of the land frontier and the attack by land forces from the Yemen and against the overflight of Federal territory. No reply was given and the forcee from the Yemen did not withdraw.

On 19 February the Under-Secretary of State for Colonial Affairs made a statement in the House of Commons, expressing concern at the presence of these forces on South Arabian Federal territory.[2] This statement was noted by the Republican authorities and on the following day they broadcast a denial that their forces had, as they put it, 'entered the territory of the so-called Federation'. On the same day Her Majesty's Government took steps to bring this matter formally to the attention of the Republican authorities in Sana'a through the good offices of the United States Government early on 25 February. This message said that Her Majesty's Government assumed that Republican Forces had entered this sector by error and that the Republican authorities as soon as their attention was drawn to the matter would issue instructions for the immediate withdrawal of the party, thus avoiding the need for other measures to preserve the integrity of Federal territory.

On 23 February, however, a party of reinforcements was sent by the Republican authorities to join the force already stationed on Federal territory, thus making the total size of the force approximately 300 men. The despatch of these reinforcements in the face of the statement made in the House of Commons four days previously could be regarded only as a deliberate challenge.

[1] *S.C.O.R.*, Eighteenth Session, Supplement for January, February, and March 1963, S/5240.
[2] *H.C. deb.*, Fol. 672, cc. 240–2.

It was becoming clear that the Republic authorities had no intention of withdrawing their force from Federal territory, and the High Commissioner in Aden was therefore authorized, some four weeks after the first violation of the frontier, to take action to evict them after suitable warning and using only the minimum force necessary. At 8.12 a.m., local time, on 26 February leaflets were dropped on the Republican force warning them to leave within three hours. A message to the same effect was also sent by runner to the forward commander of the forces from the Yemen. Three hours later, when there was no indication of any intention to withdraw, artillery fire was opened upon their positions. At 11.30 a.m., a message was received from the local Republican commander claiming that his force was within Yemeni territory. However, the Republican force thereafter withdrew. During the night of 26/27 February and again during the night of 27/28 February, mortar bombs were fired at Federal Regular Army positions from a point within the Wadi Ablah. On 27 February a Yak 11 aircraft coming from the Yemen machine-gunned a British medical post at the air strip in Al Ain about three miles inside the Federal border.

During the action which began on 26 February British aircraft patrolled the area on the South Arabian side of the frontier and dropped warning leaflets, but took no further part in the action.

It will be seen therefore that the account contained in the message addressed to the President of the Security Council on 28 February by the Republican authorities is incorrect.[1] No tanks were used and no bombs were dropped. The action taken by Her Majesty's Government was directed exclusively to the protection of the territory of the South Arabian Federation, to which Her Majesty's Government are committed by treaty.[2] Her Majesty's Government's policy is one of strict non-involvement in the internal dispute in the Yemen and it is clearly unacceptable that either party in the internal dispute should be allowed to use Federal territory as a springboard for action against the other party.

Her Majesty's Government regret that the Republican authorities should have committed these actions apparently designed to provoke an incident on the frontier. For their part Her Majesty's Government attempted for nearly one month to secure a settlement of this matter by peaceful means, and they note with regret that the action of the Republican authorities in requesting the withdrawal of the British Representative in Taizz has made it impossible to engage in direct discussions on this point.

Report by the Secretary General of the United Nations U Thant, to the Security Council, 29 April 1963[3]

1. Since the fall of 1962 I have been consulting regularly with the representatives to the United Nations of the Governments of the Arab Republic of Yemen, Saudi Arabia and the United Arab Republic, about certain aspects of the

---

[1] See pp. 323–4 above.

[2] Treaty of Friendship and Protection between the United Kingdom of Great Britain and Northern Ireland and the Federation of Arab Amirates of the South, 11 February 1959. For text, see Cmnd. 2451.

[3] *S.C.O.R.*, Eighteenth Session, Supplement for April, May, and June 1963, S/5298.

situation in Yemen of external origin, with a view to making my Office available to the parties for such assistance as might be desired toward ensuring against any developments in that situation which might threaten the peace of the area. I have encountered from the beginning a sympathetic and cooperative attitude on the part of all three representatives and their Governments.

2. It was in this context that, after clearance with the respective Governments, I asked Mr. Ralph J. Bunche to go to Yemen and the United Arab Republic in late February and early March on a fact-finding mission primarily devoted to talking with the Presidents of Yemen and the United Arab Republic, in that order, with the purpose of ascertaining their views on the situation and what steps might be taken to ease tension and restore conditions to normal. It was left open whether Mr. Bunche would eventually go also to Saudi Arabia, but developments made this unnecessary. Mr. Bunche carried out this mission and reported fully to me on his talks, which I found encouraging. Subsequently, I was informed that the United States Government, on its own initiative, sent Mr. Ellsworth Bunker to Saudi Arabia on a somewhat similar but unconnected mission. Mr. Bunker later visited Saudi Arabia on two other occasions and also had extensive talks in Cairo with President Nasser. Mr. Bunker kept me informed on the results of his missions. These talks in the end proved fruitful and from them emerged the agreed terms of disengagement. Mr. Bunker's efforts are much appreciated.

3. As a result of these activities, it is now possible for me to inform the Security Council that I have received from each of the three Governments concerned, in separate communications, formal confirmation of their acceptance of identical terms of disengagement in Yemen. The will of all three of the interested parties to ease the situation has been the decisive factor, of course, and they are to be commended for their constructive attitude.

4. In substance these terms are the following: the Government of Saudi Arabia, on its part, will terminate all support and aid to the Royalists of Yemen and will prohibit the use of Saudi Arabian territory by Royalist leaders for the purpose of carrying on the struggle in Yemen. Simultaneously, with the suspension of aid from Saudi Arabia to the Royalists, the United Arab Republic undertakes to begin withdrawal from Yemen of the troops sent on request of the new Government, this withdrawal to be phased and to take place as soon as possible, during which the forces would withdraw from field activities to their bases pending their departure. The United Arab Republic has also agreed not to take punitive action against the Royalists of Yemen for any resistance mounted by them prior to the beginning of their disengagement. There would likewise be an end to any actions on Saudi Arabian territory by United Arab Republic forces. A demilitarized zone to a distance of twenty kilometres on each side of the demarcated Saudi-Arabian-Yemen border is to be established from which military forces and equipment are to be excluded. In this zone, on both sides, impartial observers are to be stationed to check on the observance of the terms of disengagement and who would also have the responsibility of travelling beyond the demilitarized zone, as necessary, in order to certify the suspension of activities in support of the Royalists from Saudi Arabian territory and the outward movement of the United Arab Republic forces and equipment from the airports and seaports of Yemen. The United Arab Republic and Saudi Arabia

have further undertaken to co-operate with the representative of the United Nations Secretary-General or some other mutually acceptable intermediary in reaching agreement on the modalities and verification of disengagement.

5. In view of the provisions in these terms for a demilitarized zone and impartial observers, and with the consent of the parties, I have asked Major General Carl Carlson von Horn, Chief of Staff of the United Nations Truce Supervision Organization in Jerusalem, to proceed without delay to the three countries concerned for the purpose of consulting with the appropriate authorities on details relating to the nature and functioning of United Nations Observers in implementation of the terms of disengagement and to report to me with his recommendations as to the size of the set-up that might be required to discharge this responsibility. My preliminary view is that the requirements of men and equipment will be modest and will be needed for three or four months, at the most. I have been thinking in terms of not more than fifty observers, with suitable transportation, aerial and ground, for patrol purposes. A few helicopters, possibly three or four, and a similar number of small aircraft such as 'Otters', together with the required jeeps and lorries, should suffice.

6. As to the financing of any such activity by the United Nations, I have it in mind to proceed under the provisions of General Assembly resolution 1862 (XVII).[1]

7. I intend to make a further report to the Security Council[2] with particular reference to the question of United Nations Observers after General von Horn has reported to me on his discussions on this subject with the parties concerned.

Report by Secretary General U Thant to the Security Council, 27 May 1963[3]

1. In my report to the Security Council of 29 April 1963 concerning developments relating to Yemen,[4] I indicated in paragraph 7 my intention to present a further report to the Security Council on the specific subject of United Nations Observers, after I had received Major-General Carl Carlson von Horn's report on his exploratory talks on this matter with the parties concerned. General von Horn has now reported to me on his consultations.

2. The parties again confirmed to General von Horn their acceptance of the terms of disengagement in Yemen as set forth in paragraph 4 of my 29 April report, General von Horn's concern, of course, being primarily with the questions relating to the need for United Nations Observers and their functions in the proposed demilitarized zone and elsewhere, as provided in the terms of disengagement.

3. General von Horn held discussions with the appropriate authorities of the three parties in Cairo, Jeddah and San'a, obtaining the views of the parties on the role, functioning, scope and strength of the proposed United Nations observation operation. He also carried out ground and aerial reconnaissance on both sides of the Saudi Arabia-Yemen border, visiting Qizan, Najran, Sada and

[1] *G.A.O.R.*, Seventeenth Session, Supplement No. 17, p. 60, A/5217.
[2] See pp. 327-8 below.
[3] *S.C.O.R.*, Eighteenth Session, Supplement for April, May, and June 1963, S/5321.
[4] See pp. 325-7 above.

Hodeida, and covering the proposed demilitarized or buffer zone, totalling approximately 15,000 square kilometres.

4. On the basis of the information available to me, with particular reference to that provided by General von Horn, I have reached the following conclusions:

(*a*) United Nations Observers in the Saudi Arabia-Yemen area are vitally necessary and could well be the decisive factor in avoiding serious trouble in that area; their presence is desired by all parties concerned; moreover, as the need is urgent, they should be dispatched with the least possible delay;

(*b*) The terrain and climatic conditions in which the Observers will have to function in some sectors will be extremely difficult and even forbidding, and considerable danger may be encountered. Problems of movement and logistics will be great. But the provision and stationing of Observers is considered feasible and can be accomplished;

(*c*) The total personnel required for the observation mission would not exceed 200. This figure would include a small number of Officer-Observers; a ground patrol unit numbering about 100 men, in suitable vehicles, carrying arms for self-defence only; crews and ground crews for about eight small aircraft, fixed-wing and rotary, for reconnaissance and transport; and personnel for such essential supporting services as communications, logistics, medical aid, transportation and administration;

(*d*) It is estimated that the United Nations observation function would not be required for more than four months;

(*e*) It is expected that at least some of the personnel required for this short-term observation operation could be recruited from the United Nations Emergency Force (UNEF), the United Nations Truce Supervision Organization in Palestine (UNTSO), and possibly the United Nations Military Observers Group in India and Pakistan (UNMOGIP), subject to clearance with the Governments concerned. I plan to designate General von Horn as Chief of the Yemen Mission;

(*f*) The military personnel in the Yemen operation would be employed under conditions similar to those applying to other United Nations operations of this nature;

(*g*) It is estimated that the total cost of the Yemen Observation Mission will be less than $1,000,000. It has been my hope that the two parties principally involved, namely Saudi Arabia and the United Arab Republic, would undertake to bear the costs of the Mission and discussions toward this end are under way. These parties, I am sure, will agree to bear at least part of the costs, in money or in other forms of assistance. If necessary, to cover part of the cost of the operation, I would proceed, as previously indicated, under the provisions of General Assembly resolution 1862 (XVII).[1]

5. Because of the importance and urgency of the United Nations observation function to the peaceful resolution of the Yemen issues, I have it in mind to proceed with the establishment of the operation as soon as the necessary arrangements for the men and their requirements can be made. This should mean that a small advance party could be sent to the area within a few days.

[1] *G.A.O.R.*, Seventeenth Session, Supplement No. 17, p. 60, A/5217.

Report by Secretary General U Thant to the Security Council, 7 June 1963[1]

1. In paragraph 4 (g) of my report to the Security Council of 27 May 1963,[2] reference was made to the possibility that the two parties principally involved, namely Saudi Arabia and the United Arab Republic, would undertake to defray the costs of the Yemen operation. I am now able to report that Saudi Arabia has agreed orally to accept 'a proportionate share' of the costs of the operation, while the United Arab Republic agrees in principle to provide assistance in an amount equivalent to $200,000 for a period of two months, which would be roughly half of the cost of the operation over that period as indicated in my report on financial implications.[3] It is not precluded, of course, that an appeal to the United Arab Republic Government for additional assistance could be made at the end of the two months, should it be found necessary to extend the operation beyond that period. I have asked both Governments for written confirmation of these financial positions and I expect to have favourable replies shortly.

2. In the light of the foregoing circumstances, there are no financial implications for the United Nations in getting the Yemen observation mission established and the operation under way, or for its maintenance for an initial period of two months.

3. It is now my intention, therefore, to proceed with the organization and dispatch of the mission without further delay, and I am instructing General von Horn to go to the area with a small advance party within a day or two.

4. While it has been my assumption that the agreement has been in effect since the parties signified their acceptance of the terms of disengagement,[4] the arrival in the area of General Carl Carlson von Horn and an advance party of United Nations Observers will formally signify that all provisions of the terms of disengagement are in effect and that the agreement is being implemented in full.

Security Council resolution, 11 June 1963[5]

The Security Council,

Noting with satisfaction the initiative of the Secretary-General mentioned in his report of 29 April 1963[6] 'about certain aspects of the situation in Yemen of external origin', and aimed at achievement of a peaceful settlement and 'ensuring against any developments in that situation which might threaten the peace of the area',

Noting further the statement by the Secretary-General before the Security Council on 10 June 1963,[7]

Noting further with satisfaction that the parties directly concerned with the situation affecting Yemen have confirmed their acceptance of identical terms of disengagement in Yemen, and that the Governments of Saudi Arabia and the

[1] *S.C.O.R.*, Eighteenth Session, Supplement for April, May, and June 1963, S/5325.
[2] See pp. 327–8 above.
[3] *S.C.O.R.*, Eighteenth Session, Supplement for April, May, and June 1963, S/5323.
[4] See pp. 325–7 above.
[5] *S.C.O.R.*, Eighteenth Session, Supplement for April, May, and June 1963, S/5331.
[6] See pp. 325–7 above.
[7] *S.C.O.R.*, Eighteenth Session, 1037th meeting, pp. 2–3.

United Arab Republic have agreed to defray the expenses over a period of two months of the United Nations observation function called for in the terms of disengagement,

1. *Requests* the Secretary-General to establish the observation operation as defined by him;

2. *Urges* the parties concerned to observe fully the terms of disengagement set out in the report of 29 April and to refrain from any action which would increase tension in the area;

3. *Requests* the Secretary-General to report to the Security Council on the implementation of this decision.

The Deputy Permanent Representative of Saudi Arabia at the United Nations, Jamil M. Baroody, to the Secretary General, 14 June 1963[1]

Upon instructions from my Government it is my painful duty to report a summary record of the recent air-raids carried out by Egyptian military aircraft on Saudi Arabian territory,[2] thereby inflicting loss of life and causing injuries to peaceful inhabitants and destroying or damaging property including many dwellings, a mosque and a hospital.

In one of these raids on 8 June 1963 thirty lives were lost and twenty-two homes were demolished aside from wounding a good number of persons in the city of Qizan.

All these raids on Saudi Arabian territory by Egyptian planes constitute a violation of the rudiments of international law aside from ignoring all humanitarian principles. Indeed, such aggression might be considered an act of war.

Inasmuch as the Government of Saudi Arabia has exercised extreme self-restraint, having refrained from retaliatory action for no other reason than to avoid further bloodshed, my Government might be compelled in the future to take measures for self-defence which may lead to a regrettable situation in the Middle East and the possibility of world-wide repercussions.

Whilst the people of Saudi Arabia and their Government desire to live in peace and whereas my Government so far has consistently abided by the terms of the United Nations Charter which provide for the settlement of differences by peaceful means, the patience and self-restraint which my Government has manifested should not be misconstrued as a sign of weakness or helplessness. It is because of Saudi Arabia's deep desire for peace in order to carry out its extensive economic and social plans, instead of getting embroiled in a senseless bloody conflict, that my Government has put its confidence in the integrity of the Secretary-General in the hope that through his tact and wisdom, the recent agreement concluded with reference to the Yemen will be implemented in good faith by the parties concerned.

Since my Government wishes that the report of the recent Egyptian air-raids on Saudi Arabian territory be distributed, may I ask you to make it available to the members of the Security Council as well as to have it circulated among the States Members of the United Nations.

[1] *S.C.O.R.*, Eighteenth Session, Supplement for April, May, and June 1963, S/5333.
[2] Not published here; see ibid.

The Permanent Representative of the United Arab Republic at the United Nations, Mahmoud Riad, to the Secretary General, 20 June 1963[1]

I have the honour to bring to your attention that, when the Security Council met on 10 June 1963 to discuss 'the reports of the Secretary-General concerning developments relating to Yemen', the delegation of the United Arab Republic, considering that the position of its Government with regard to foreign intervention against Yemen had been amply explained, refrained from participating in the discussion in order to avoid a lengthy and involved debate which could have hindered the speedy dispatch of a United Nations Observation Mission to the Saudi-Yemeni border area and in the hope that the United Nations presence would end the aggression against the people of Yemen.

The letter addressed to Your Excellency on 14 June 1963[2] by the delegation of Saudi Arabia has, however, made it incumbent upon the delegation of the United Arab Republic to state the following facts.

1. In his letter addressed to Your Excellency on 18 January 1963,[3] the representative of the Yemen Arab Republic stated that on 26 September 1962 the Yemen people declared their determination to start a new era in their history and revolted against the corrupt medieval régime, which immediately collapsed. He stated further that the new Republic extended a hand of friendship to its Arab sister countries, as well as to other countries, provided naturally that the independence and integrity of Yemen would be respected and that no interference in its internal affairs would be tolerated. However, the representative of the Yemen Arab Republic concluded that the Government of Saudi Arabia took an openly hostile attitude. Continuous, premeditated armed attacks where launched against the people of Yemen. Consequently, the Yemen Arab Republic requested assistance from the United Arab Republic, in accordance with the provisions of the Mutual Defence Pact concluded between the two Governments, in repelling this aggression.[4]

2. Under such perilous circumstances facing the Yemeni people, the Government of the United Arab Republic, which gave its full support to the new Government of Yemen, could not but respond to its request. Military forces were dispatched and placed at the disposal of the Yemeni Supreme Command.

3. It is indeed most regrettable that Saudi Arabia was found to be actively engaged in playing a predominant role in the aggression against the people of Yemen. It is no secret that aggression against Yemeni territory emanated from inside Saudi Arabia, huge sums of money were tendered to incite mercenaries and provide them with arms to fight the people of Yemen, centres were established in Saudi Arabia to train those mercenaries in sabotage and laying mine fields. Furthermore, a flow of arms and ammunition were sent across the frontier to entice tribes to rise against their Government.

4. The armed forces of the Yemen Arab Republic and the United Arab Republic can undoubtedly deal with any military aggression against Yemen. Nevertheless, motivated by an earnest desire to avoid bloodshed and to restore

---

[1] *S.C.O.R.*, Eighteenth Session, Supplement for April, May, and June 1963, S/5336.

[2] See p. 330 above.

[3] This letter was apparently not published.

[4] The text was not published. For an account of the Pact see *La Bourse Egyptienne*, 11 November 1962 and 24 December 1962.

peace to the area, the two Governments have, in good faith, accepted the terms of disengagement which provided for the establishment of a United Nations observation mission whose main aim is the termination of outside military intervention against Yemen.

5. Obviously, therefore, the Government of Saudi Arabia should be the last to complain or protest. Offensive action against a peaceful people is a flagrant violation of the United Nations Charter and constitutes a threat to international peace and security.

6. The restoration of peace and security in this part of the world requires that those who are vainly trying to re-impose a feudal and reactionary régime on the people of Yemen should cease their futile attempts.

I should be grateful if you would arrange for the circulation of this letter to the President and members of the Security Council as well as to the Members of the United Nations.

The United States Assistant Secretary of State, Phillips Talbot, to Senator Hickenlooper, 30 July 1963[1]

The Secretary has asked me to reply to your letter of July 16 in which you discuss the political and military situation in Yemen and recommend certain lines of U.S. Government action.[2] I welcome your interest in a problem of considerable complexity and am most happy to comment on your reasoned and constructive letter.

You are correct in your understanding of the basis for U.S. Government recognition of the Yemen Arab Republic (YAR). This recognition was based essentially on (1) YAR control of the apparatus of government; (2) apparent popular support; (3) YAR control of most of the country; and (4) YAR willingness and capability to honor its international obligations. In addition, we realized that only by recognizing the regime could we play a useful role in preventing an escalation of the Yemen conflict causing even more foreign interference and placing in serious jeopardy major U.S. economic and security interests in the Arabian Peninsula. Furthermore, our presence in Yemen—including an AID mission—could not have been continued for long without recognition. The AID mission was originally established in Yemen for the purpose of maintaining a beachhead of U.S. influence in the face of a sustained Communist interest and a growing Soviet presence.

You are correct also in your understanding that Egyptian military forces are to be withdrawn from Yemen in accordance with the disengagement agreement negotiated by Special Presidential Emissary, Ambassador Ellsworth Bunker, and subsequently agreed to by the parties with the U.N. Secretary General.[3] It should be remembered that although the disengagement agreement was negotiated in early April, it did not go fully into effect until late June when United Nations observers began to arrive in Yemen to supervise the disengagement operation. In fact, the U.N. Secretary General has stated that he considers the operation to have officially begun only on July 4 when observers were placed in Jizan.

[1] U.S. Congressional Record—Senate, Vol. 109, Part 10, pp. 13668-9.

[2] ibid., p. 13668; Senator Hickenlooper recommended in particular the withdrawal of United States recognition of the Government of the Yemen Arab Republic.

[3] See pp. 325-7 above.

During the regrettable delay in putting the agreement into effect, there was no net reduction of Egyptian forces in Yemen nor did Saudi Arabia fully terminate its aid to the Royalists. However, we are satisfied that the Saudis have terminated their assistance since the date the disengagement went fully into effect and are hopeful the United Arab Republic will fulfill its part of the agreement.

Peace has not been established in the country, as you indicate. United Arab Republic troops are still tied down coping with guerrilla warfare mounted by the tribes—who are traditionally opposed to any central government—but it is our view that the intensity of the tribal resistance will abate once the drying up of the Saudi supply line takes full effect and a stabilizing of the situation permits reconciliation of tribal factions. We are not aware that the United Arab Republic troops have enlarged the area of attack in recent days. The United Arab Republic is not prohibited by the disengagement agreement from fighting tribes who continue to operate against the Central Government. However, the agreement does prohibit punitive attacks against tribes on the basis of resistance mounted before the agreement went fully into effect.

Regarding your suggestion that we give immediate consideration to withdrawing our recognition of the Yemen Arab Republic unless United Arab Republic troops are promptly removed from Yemen, I would like to make the following comments. In the first place, the original basis for our recognition of the Yemeni regime still applies. Whether or not the regime enjoys the same degree of popular support is a controversial question which it would be impossible to answer categorically without establishing a stable situation that would enable the populace to express its views freely. However, this does not mean that those disaffected with the leadership of the new Republican regime favor the restoration of the wholly discredited Imamate. Second, we do not believe that withdrawing our recognition would advance U.S. interests. Our essential concerns in Yemen are with: (1) keeping the Yemeni conflict and its repercussions from spreading and endangering vital U.S. and free world interests in the Near East outside of Yemen, particularly in Saudi Arabia and Jordan; (2) preventing the development by the Soviet bloc of a predominant position in Yemen; and (3) encouraging the prospects for a relatively stable and independent Yemen. Withdrawing recognition would not be in consonance with these objectives. On the contrary, U.S. Government effectiveness in containing and resolving the Yemeni conflict would thereby be seriously impaired; the Yemen Arab Republic could be expected to place greater reliance on the U.S.S.R.; and the viability of the Republican regime would be placed in jeopardy. The restoration of the notoriously despotic Imamate would not be supported by the Yemeni people at large and is generally acknowledged to be out of the question. In view of the sustained Communist interest and activity in Yemen, the most probable alternative to a Republican regime beset by tribal anarchy and without United Arab Republic help at least in the form of a military training mission would be one with a Communist coloration heavily dependent on Soviet support. It therefore behooves the free world to find ways and means of insuring the viability of the Republican regime while seeking to insure that it adequately represents all shades of Yemeni opinion.

I should like to add further that it is doubtful whether withdrawal of U.S. Government recognition of the Yemen Arab Republic would in fact achieve the desired result of inducing prompt UAR troop withdrawals. The UAR voluntarily entered into the disengagement agreement; it recently supported approval by the Security Council of the disengagement effort; it is paying one-half the costs of the United Nations operation; and UAR military forces currently are cooperating with the United Nations observation mission in Yemen as it gets established. In other words, the UAR wants to withdraw its troops from Yemen. Its delay in doing so appears to result, therefore, not from any lack of desire. Rather it seems to flow from the continuance of tribal guerrilla warfare in the Yemen highlands and perhaps also from the multiplicity of problems facing the new Government. I do not wish to imply that we feel these factors justify UAR foot-dragging; this is merely by way of explanation. Some observers believe that a broadening of the base of the Yemen Arab Republic leadership might strengthen the hand of the Government, reduce tribal disaffection and facilitate a more rapid UAR withdrawal. Withdrawal of U.S. Government recognition of the Yemen Arab Republic would only tend to weaken the Republican regime and put further pressure on the UAR to delay its withdrawal. This would not be in the interest of the United States, the Saudi Arabian Government, the UAR, nor the people of Yemen.

In the last paragraph of your letter you suggest the possibility that the United States review its program of economic assistance to the UAR in the light of the UAR performance in Yemen. I would like to note that we have witnessed a number of examples in recent years of the dangers and limitations of using foreign aid in a bludgeon fashion in forcing actions by foreign governments. This is particularly true in the highly sensitive and complex Middle East. Our experience shows that this type of action does not advance the objectives it is designed to promote, but instead has exactly the opposite result. It could ultimately have the effect of seriously damaging our security interests in the Near East by leading to greater UAR dependence as well as YAR dependence on the Soviets for aid. In our opinion such tactics would also be publicly disapproved by most of the Arab States on the nonalined countries.

In conclusion, I would like to assure you that we fully agree that the UAR should adhere to the terms of the disengagement agreement and should withdraw its troops from Yemen in a phased and expeditious fashion. You can rest confident that we are bringing to bear the full weight of U.S. influence in this connection. We consider it essential to have some flexibility in the measures we take to try to achieve the desired result and would find limitations that might be imposed by Congress an unnecessarily inhibiting factor.

I should be most happy to keep you informed periodically of further developments. If I can be of further assistance, please do not hesitate to let me know.

Report by Secretary General U Thant to the Security Council, 28 October 1963, with Addenda[1]

1. My last report on the functioning of the United Nations Yemen Observation Mission (UNYOM)[2] was submitted to the Security Council on 4 September

[1] *S.C.O.R.*, Eighteenth Session, Supplement for October, November, and December 1963, S/5447 and ADD. 1 and 2.

[2] Not printed here; for text see, *S.C.O.R.*, Eighteenth Session, Supplement for July, August and September 1963, S/5412.

1963, the date on which the period of two months originally envisaged for the operation had expired. In that report, I stated that since the task of the Mission, having to do with the disengagement agreement of the two parties, was obviously not completed, it would, at the wish and with the financial support of the Governments of Saudi Arabia and the United Arab Republic, be prolonged for a further two months, that is, until 4 November 1963. That two months' period is now drawing to an end.

2. In my previous report I was unable to say that encouraging progress had been registered towards effective implementation of the disengagement agreement, despite the co-operation of both parties with the United Nations Mission. There has been no decisive change in that situation in the subsequent two months.

Present situation in Yemen

3. Now it would seem useful to undertake a broad appraisal of the position in the Yemen and of the complexities there as a framework for an account of the operation of UNYOM.

4. South Yemen, that is the area south of San'a and the coastal strip, is more or less firmly in the hands of forces supporting the republican Government. Marib, Harib and the surrounding area on the eastern frontier are under the military control of United Arab Republic/Yemeni forces. San'a is firmly under republican control but there are two pockets close to it where some sections of the tribes have at times been unfriendly or even hostile to the Government. These are, respectively, to the west of San'a immediately north of the Hodeida/San'a road and north-east and east of San'a.

5. In the north, allegiance to the republican Government is loose and uncertain. This is due partly to conflicting loyalties, and partly to the traditional attitude of the tribes towards a central authority. It is here that the Imam and other royalist leaders have their main area of influence and the United Arab Republic/Yemeni forces are conducting military operations to retain administrative control. Military conflict of varying intensity, consisting of harassment, guerilla raids and attempts to cut the San'a–Sada road by the royalists, and reprisals from ground and air by the United Arab Republic/Yemeni forces, has continued in this area throughout the past year. In particular, the inaccessible and mountainous region running northward of Wash-Ha through the demilitarized zone to the border in which the Imam is said to have his headquarters, is not under the control of the Yemen Arab Republic and United Arab Republic forces. In the demilitarized zone the United Arab Republic still has forces in Harad to check on infiltration and assistance to the royalists across the passes south of El Kuba.

6. There is considerable traffic from Saudi Arabia into northern Yemen, and vehicles and animal convoys containing food, supplies and occasionally petrol are seen almost daily. It is said that this traffic is traditional since the people of northern Yemen have always relied on Saudi Arabian towns such as Jizan and Najran for their necessities. To reduce the possibilities of this trade covering traffic in arms and military supplies, a procedure has recently been developed by which United Nations military observers in co-operation with Saudi Arabian officials check this traffic. Nevertheless, it could be claimed that even peaceful

traffic could help those tribes which are resisting the republican Government.

7. The lack of allegiance of certain tribes, especially in the north, and the known presence and activity of the Imam and Prince Hassan among them, evidently with sizable stocks of ammunition (whatever their source may be) continues to be a serious problem for the Government of Yemen and, therefore, for the troops of the United Arab Republic. This problem is aggravated by the apparent fact that the Yemeni army has not yet reached that standard of training and competence which would enable it to cope with the situation without outside assistance, or, perhaps, even to defend republican controlled areas, should one or more of these areas be attacked by hostile tribes. This dependence on outside military aid, which in practice means aid from the United Arab Republic, which sees itself as committed to assist the Yemen Government in its time of need, inevitably impedes the improvement of relations, both between the United Arab Republic and Saudi Arabia and between Saudi Arabia and the Yemen. The problem is further complicated by both religious and political factors in Yemen itself.

Position of the two parties

8. In so far as the two parties to the disengagement agreement—Saudi Arabia and United Arab Republic—are concerned, the position may perhaps be briefly summed up as follows. The Saudi Arabian Government maintains that, while it is complying with the agreement, is no longer supplying war material to the royalists and has co-operated with UNYOM in verifying this contention, the other party has not withdrawn the main part of its military forces from Yemen and continues military activities, including bombing of royalist areas and over-flying of Saudi Arabian territory. In this situation, the warning is issued that it might be difficult for the Saudi Arabian Government to continue to carry on indefinitely what it considers to be a unilateral implementation of the agreement.

9. The Government of the United Arab Republic maintains that, whatever may be the present situation with regard to assistance to the royalists, the armaments and supplies sent previously or that would be again available to them subsequent to United Arab Republic withdrawal would permit and encourage them to continue operating in Yemen. Thus their resistance and active hostility constitute a most serious obstacle to the withdrawal of United Arab Republic forces. United Arab Republic authorities have given assurance that there will be no bombing of Saudi Arabian territory or extension by military action of the area at present under their control, and that the activities complained of, especially bombing, are exclusively for the safe-guarding of the security of troops of the United Arab Republic. Activities of this kind are being decreased as far as possible.

Functioning of the United Nations Yemen Observation Mission

10. The following paragraphs summarize the functioning and observations of UNYOM in this very complex situation. It perhaps bears repeating in this report that UNYOM's functions are limited, by the provisions of the disengagement agreement, to observing, certifying and reporting.

11. Mission personnel are deployed in the area as follows:

Yemen

San'a . . . . Headquarters and headquarters of the 134 ATU with 2 Caribou aircraft.

Hodeida . . . 1 United Nations military observer and a logistics detachment.

Sada . . . . 1 section of the Yugoslav Company.

Saudi Arabia

Jizan . . . . 2 United Nations military observers and 1 detachment of the 134 ATU with 2 Otter aircraft.

Demilitarized zone

Harad . . . 1 platoon of the Yugoslav Reconnaissance Company and 2 United Nations military observers.

Najran . . . 2 platoons less 1 section of the Yugoslav Reconnaissance Company, 4 United Nations military observers and 1 detachment of the 134 ATU with 2 Otter aircraft.

12. The main function of the detachments stationed in Sada and Harad is to observe and report on disengagement and withdrawal of United Arab Republic forces from field activities in these areas, while the main function of the post at Hodeida is to observe and report on the departure of United Arab Republic forces from Yemen. In the Harad and Sada areas there has been, so far, no withdrawal from field activities of United Arab Republic forces, although they are no longer in constant close contact with the royalists. In the Sada area, especially, fighting appears to have died down in recent weeks, apart from occasional ambushes and mine-laying by royalists, and shelling and occasional aerial bombing of hostile concentrations by the United Arab Republic forces. These activities also are on the decrease. The area east and north-east of Sada is also reliably reported to be quiet.

13. At Hodeida the embarkation of 4,000 United Arab Republic troops during the period 1 September to 12 October 1963 has been reported and observed by United Nations military observers. The arrival of 1,300 United Arab Republic troops was observed on 19 October. The Commander of the United Arab Republic forces in Yemen informed the Commander of UNYOM that between 4 July and 22 October, 12,000 officers and men of the United Arab Republic forces had left Yemen, of which half had been replaced by fresh troops. It was added that a further 2,000 officers and men would leave Yemen by 1 November. This information was confirmed to the Secretary-General by the Foreign Minister of the United Arab Republic. Since then, official word has been received to the effect that an additional 3,000 United Arab Republic troops will be withdrawn before the end of December 1963. That is to say, a total of 5,000 troops will leave between the end of October and the end of December. It is assumed that these would not be replaced, in whole or in part.

14. The main function of the detachments stationed at Jizan and Najran is to check on the reduction or cessation of assistance from Saudi Arabia to the

royalists. It has been found that vehicle and animal convoys, on account of terrain, water resources, population and communication centres, have been necessarily confined to certain routes. On this basis, a pattern of air and ground patrolling and check points has been established covering all main routes and tracks leading into north Yemen and the demilitarized zone. Air and ground patrols have been carried out daily on varied timings and routes, the patrol plan being planned and co-ordinated every evening by a senior observer.

15. Ground and air patrolling has proved, however, to have two main limitations, namely that traffic could be observed only by day while for climatic reasons travel during hours of darkness is customary in this area, and cargoes could not be checked. This problem has been met by periodically positioning United Nations military observers at various communications centres for forty-eight hours or more. Thus traffic could be observed by day and night and contents of cargoes could also be checked. Observers have also visited royalist areas more frequently in recent weeks.

16. In Saudi Arabian territory, including the demilitarized zone on the Saudi Arabian side of the frontier, most United Nations patrols and check points are accompanied by Saudi Arabian liaison officials, who check cargoes as requested by United Nations observers. Some check points are manned for three to four days at a time and some for shorter periods. Gaps in between manning periods do not exceed two days and in the intervening period the areas are covered by patrolling.

17. By these methods UNYOM has been able, since 10 September 1963, to make a more reliable assessment of the cessation of assistance to the royalists from Saudi Arabia. This assessment leads to the following conclusions:

(a) That the traffic across the frontier is now relatively sparse (some 28 vehicles and 48 animals per week) and contains normal consumer goods;

(b) That no military vehicles or materials have been seen nor military equipment or stores found in the cargoes checked by United Nations observers;

(c) That there were no signs of Saudi Arabian military assistance or heavy weapons in royalist areas visited by United Nations observers.

18. These conclusions indicate that in the period under review no military assistance of significance has been provided to the royalists from Saudi Arabia.

19. As regards aerial activity, two over-flights over Saudi Arabian territory from Yemen were observed by United Nations patrols and observers, one of an unidentified aircraft on 12 September and one of an aircraft reported as a United Arab Republic jet aircraft on 2 October. In addition, the Saudi Arabian authorities reported over-flights over Saudi Arabian territory by aircraft identified by them as of the United Arab Republic, on 10 September, 23 September and 20 October 1963. The Commander of United Arab Republic forces was informed of these complaints and stated in reply that the flights in question were not carried out by aircraft of the United Arab Republic.

20. United Nations observers verified as correct a report that the Nahuga area (in the demilitarized zone) had been bombed by United Arab Republic aircraft on 3 September. On 7 October a United Nations observer at El Kuba reported parachute flares in an easterly direction and, immediately afterward, the sound of a jet aircraft and two loud explosions from the same direction.

21. Royalist observers reported to United Nations observers attacks by United Arab Republic aircraft on the Wash-Ha area on 4 October, on the Al Hashiwz area on 5 October and on the Boyi area on 7 October 1963. These reports were delayed and could not be verified.

22. Thus, since my last report, air activity by the United Arab Republic has considerably decreased. Air attacks over Saudi Arabian territory and the demilitarized zone have ceased. The air attacks reported (mainly in the Sada area), are in a region where ground operations have also been reported.

23. In general, it may be said that in many areas, particularly in north and north-east Yemen, where there was active fighting in early July, the fighting has since almost entirely ceased. Military operations are at present confined to the Sada area and to the south-east of it. They too are of a sporadic nature—i.e. bursts of light automatic and artillery fire and isolated occasional air activity, although heavier activity by United Arab Republic forces in the Gof area in the period 18–21 October has been reported. These reports are now under investigation.

24. I pointed out in my last report that UNYOM, because of its limited size and function, can observe and certify only certain indications of the implementation of the disengagement agreement. I believe that in the period under review its capacity for this purpose has been increased and made more efficient, and that its observations show accurately certain trends and developments in the situation. Although these developments are far short of the disengagement and regularization of the situation which had been hoped for, they are in their limited way encouraging, in that the scale of fighting has been reduced and conditions of temporary truce apply in most areas.

25. I also said in my last report that UNYOM could, within limits, serve as an intermediary and as an endorser of good faith on behalf of the parties concerned. I believe that within its severe limitations it has fulfilled this role very well and that certain improvements in the situation have been the result. I do not, however, believe that the solution of the problem, or even the fundamental steps which must be taken to resolve it, can ever be within the potential of UNYOM alone—and most certainly not under its existing limited mandate.

Conclusions

26. The Security Council, by its resolution of 11 June 1963,[1] requested me to establish in Yemen a United Nations observation operation, on the basis of the fact 'that the parties directly concerned with the situation affecting Yemen have confirmed their acceptance of identical terms of disengagement in Yemen . . .', and the further fact that the Government of Saudi Arabia and the United Arab Republic had agreed to defray the expenses of this operation for two months. On the grounds that the disengagement agreement had not been fulfilled and United Nations observation was therefore still required, these two Governments undertook to meet the expenses of UNYOM for a further period as from 4 September 1963, until 4 November 1963.

27. In anticipation of this date, in order to be prepared either to withdraw the Mission personnel, vehicles and equipment, or to maintain it beyond that date

[1] See pp. 329–30 above.

should this be desired, I have been confering over the past fortnight with representatives of the Governments of Saudi Arabia, the United Arab Republic and Yemen. It emerges from these consultations that there is a general appreciation of the helpful assistance rendered by the United Nations Mission in Yemen and of the manner in which it has conducted itself. The view is also general among the parties that the continuation beyond 4 November of a United Nations presence in some form, although not necessarily including military components, would be desirable and useful. On the other hand, one of the two Governments concerned with financing UNYOM has indicated that it is not prepared, on the basis of the existing situation, to share the cost of UNYOM beyond the 4 November commitment. The position of the Government of Saudi Arabia on this question, as it has been communicated to me, is that any extension of UNYOM beyond 4 November would depend upon concrete evidence that the agreement on disengagement is to be implemented within a specified period of time, which in effect means a time schedule for the withdrawal of United Arab Republic troops. As of now, therefore, assuming no change in the situation as regards fulfilment of the disengagement agreement, the Government of Saudi Arabia has made it clear that it undertakes no commitment concerning an extension of UNYOM beyond 4 November.

28. In the light of this latter circumstance, it has been necessary for me to take the essential preparatory steps looking towards the complete withdrawal of UNYOM by 4 November, beyond which date there will be no financial support for it.

29. In the course of my consultations with the parties I have made clear my own dissatisfaction with the mandate of UNYOM as now defined. That mandate, set forth in the disengagement agreement, is so limiting and restrictive as to make it virtually impossible for UNYOM to play a really helpful and constructive role in Yemen. Indeed, given the nature of the situation and of the terrain, it is not possible for UNYOM with its present personnel, or for that matter, with a much expanded establishment, to observe fully, let alone to certify to the satisfaction of both parties, what specifically is being done in the way of disengagement. I frankly see little prospect that the disengagement agreement could be so amended as to correct this deficiency.

30. I have no doubt, however, that a continuing United Nations presence in Yemen, of some kind but not necessarily having military attributes, would be most helpful and might even be indispensable to an early settlement of the Yemen problem, which clearly is primarily political and will require a political solution.

31. It is my intention, therefore, to maintain a civilian United Nations presence in the area, given, of course, the necessary agreement of the parties directly concerned. The terms of reference of such a presence would need to be worked out in consultation with the States concerned. The cost of such a presence would be small and it could, in fact, be initially financed by the existing authorization to the Secretary-General to enter into commitments to meet unforeseen and extraordinary expenses relating to the maintenance of peace and security in the financial year 1963 [General Assembly resolution 1862 (XVII), para. 1a].[1]

[1] *G.A.O.R.*, Seventeenth Session, Supplement No. 17, p. 60, A/5217.

Addendum 1[1]

1. This report is supplemental to my report of 28 October 1963.

2. In the afternoon of 31 October, the Permanent Representative of the Government of Saudi Arabia communicated to me a new and urgent message from his Government on the subject of the extension of the United Nations Yemen Observation Mission (UNYOM) beyond 4 November. This message, in substance, stated that despite the fact that the other party to the disengagement agreement had not carried it out, the Government of Saudi Arabia, being desirous of helping the United Nations complete its mission of peace in the Yemen area, and desirous also of saving human lives, has decided to participate in the financing of UNYOM for a further period of two months as from 5 November.

3. In view of the fact that the Government of the United Arab Republic had previously expressed its view that UNYOM should be extended as well as its willingness to continue to share in the expenses of UNYOM for a further period of one or two months, the problem of financing a continuing mission is thus removed.

4. The Representative of the Government of Yemen had also indicated that it was the view of his Government that the continued presence of UNYOM beyond 4 November would be desirable and helpful.

5. In the light of these circumstances, and particularly of the new development incident to the latest message from the Government of Saudi Arabia, I have ordered the cancellation of the preparations that were under way for the withdrawal of UNYOM by 4 November. Therefore, UNYOM, in approximately its present form and size, will continue from that date for a further period of two months and its expenses will be borne in equal shares by the Governments of Saudi Arabia and the United Arab Republic.

Addendum 2[2]

1. This report is a further supplement to my previous reports, and is submitted for the purpose of information and clarification.

2. In document S/5447/Add.1, I informed the Security Council that the United Nations Yemen Observation Mission (UNYOM) would be continued from 4 November for a further period of two months, in pursuance of the wishes of the two parties to the disengagement agreement as indicated by their willingness to continue to share the cost of UNYOM for that additional period.

3. In my report to the Council on 27 May 1963[3] in which I communicated my intention to establish the mission in Yemen, I estimated that the observation function in Yemen would not be required for more than four months.

4. The continuation of UNYOM for another two months after 4 November, goes beyond that original estimate. Therefore, although believing that no meeting of the Council on the subject was required, I have consulted the Council members informally in order to ascertain that in the light of the circumstances as reported there would be no objection to the extension. There was none.

---

[1] Submitted by the Secretary General on 31 October 1963.
[2] Submitted by the Secretary General on 11 November 1963.
[3] See pp. 327–8 above.

C. OIL

Resolutions of the Fourth Arab Petroleum Congress, Beirut, 12 November 1963[1]

Believing in the importance of Arab petroleum as a national resource having a vital bearing on the development of the Arab economy and on raising the standard of living in the Arab homeland, and recognizing the heavy responsibilities of the Arab states in this regard, the Fourth Arab Petroleum Congress has issued the following resolutions:

Resolution No. 1

The Congress recommends and reaffirms the need for the companies to take positive steps to respond to Arab aspirations in such a way as to afford the Arab states a fair share of their national resources in order to enable them to develop their economies.

The Congress points out to the companies that their persistence in taking a negative attitude towards these just aspirations, will further complicate matters and eventually damage their own interests.

In particular, the Congress points to the need for the companies to respond to Arab demands in relation to the computation of royalties and the restoration of prices to their pre-August 1960 level. The Congress hopes that an announcement will be made in the near future to the effect that the companies have accepted the Arab point of view in respect to the above mentioned problems, thereby assuring the Arabs that they will attain a fair share of their own resources.

Moreover, such a step would no doubt safeguard foreign investments in the Arab countries, in view of the confidence and acceptance that such investments would enjoy among the Arab people.

Resolution No. 2

A. The Congress is of the opinion that the Arab States should endeavour to apply more strictly the previous recommendations of this Congress with regard to preventing the supply of crude oil and oil products to Israel by all countries and in particular those with whom the Arab States have common oil interests.

B. The Congress warns the member states of the European Common Market against allowing Israel to become associated with the Market in any way whatsoever.

Resolution No. 3

The Congress reaffirms the need to persist in its endeavours to create a generation of Arabs which is conversant with oil affairs, and to train Arab technicians and experts who can operate and develop the oil industry.

Accordingly the Congress recommends that the Arab States establish cooperative technical institutes and colleges which would coordinate their activities through the exchange of information, instructors, and technical aid so that this generation can be trained. The Congress also recommends that efforts should be made to establish an Arab Institute for Petroleum and petrochemical Research

[1] *Arab Political Documents, 1963*, pp. 469–70.

which would be financed by the Arab states and the companies operating in their territory, and which would promote the industry and contribute to resolving technical problems at all levels.

Resolution No. 4

The Congress reaffirms the need to grant the Arab worker priority of employment so that no foreigner is employed if there is an Arab capable of performing his work, and calls upon the companies to organize training courses which would prepare the Arab worker to replace the foreigner.

The Congress also reaffirms the need to establish complete equality between the Arab and foreign worker as regards basic pay so long as they perform the same work and as regards basic pay and other benefits if the foreign worker is a permanent and regular resident in the country.

The Congress recommends that the remuneration of Arab workers be increased with a view to raising their social, educational and technical standards, and that whenever possible this should be regulated by laws passed by the Arab governments.

Resolution No. 5

The Congress recommends that the Fifth Arab Petroleum Congress and Exhibition be held in Cairo in March, 1965.

III. THE FAR EAST

A. MALAYA, INDONESIA, AND THE PHILIPPINES

(a) *The Philippine claim to North Borneo*

Communiqué issued by the Governments of Great Britain and the Philippines, London, 1 February 1963[1]

A Philippine Delegation under the leadership of Mr. Emmanuel Polaez, Vice-President and Foreign Secretary, visited London from January 24 to February 1 for talks with a British Delegation under the leadership of the Earl of Home, Foreign Secretary. Mr. Pelaez was accompanied by Mr. Macario Peralta, Jr., Secretary of National Defense, Mr. Salvador P. Lopez, Under-Secretary of Foreign Affairs, Congressman Jovito R. Salonga, and Ambassador Eduardo Quintero. The British Delegation included Mr. Peter Thorneycroft, Minister of Defence, Mr. Peter Thomas, Parliamentary Under-Secretary of State for Foreign Affairs, Sir Robert Scott, Permanent Secretary of the Ministry of Defence, Lt.-General D. S. S. O'Connor, Deputy Chief of the Defence Staff. The Marquess of Lansdowne, Minister of State for Colonial Affairs, also took part in the meetings.

2. There was an extensive exchange of views on the problems of stability, security and defence in South East Asia and on the policies by which the two Governments pursue their common objectives in accordance with their obligation as members of the United Nations and as allies under the Manila Treaty (SEATO).[2]

3. The talks also dealt with matters affecting the Borneo territories of North Borneo, Sarawak and Brunei. It was agreed that the future political stability and progress of these territories was a matter of great importance to both Governments, although there were differences between them on the best means of securing these objectives. The British Delegation described the political advances already in progress in the territories and explained the reasons for the proposed establishment of the Federation of Malaysia. The Philippine Delegation expressed their view on the proposal and in particular their opposition to the inclusion of North Borneo in the Federation. The Philippine Delegation also explained the proposal of President Macapagal for a Confederation of Malay States.

4. The Philippine Delegation made a detailed statement of their Government's claim to parts of North Borneo and the British Delegation explained why this claim could not be accepted by Her Majesty's Government. For a clarification of issues the question was referred to the Legal Committee which reported back and on the Committee's recommendation it was agreed to exchange copies of certain documents for the purpose of further clarification.

[1] Foreign Office, *Press Release*, 1 February 1963.　　　　[2] *Documents, 1954*, pp. 153–6.

5. Without prejudice to the Philippine claim, a number of questions concerning local Philippine interests in North Borneo and Anglo-Philippine cooperation in that region were also discussed and agreement was reached for the improvement of cooperation between the two Governments in the prevention of piracy and armed raids and on the problems of smuggling and illegal immigration in the region.

6. The talks took place in a most frank and friendly atmosphere and both delegations agreed that they had achieved their purpose in promoting closer understanding between the two Governments. It was agreed that further discussions should be pursued through the diplomatic channel and that in due course another meeting between Ministers might be desirable.

(b) Regional Diplomacy

Communiqué issued by the President of the Republic of Indonesia, Dr. Sukarno, and the Prime Minister of the Federation of Malaya, Tunku Abdul Rahman, Tokyo, 1 June 1963[1]

President Sukarno of Indonesia and Prime Minister Tunku Abdul Rahman of Malaya, having agreed there was need for them to meet and clarify matters regarding the proposal for the formation of the Federation of Malaysia, held discussions on May 31 and June 1 in Tokyo.

The amicable and frank exchange of views over the two days has achieved this purpose.

President Sukarno and Prime Minister Rahman reaffirmed their faith in the treaty of friendship between Indonesia and Malaya concluded in 1959 and agreed that any outstanding differences on matters directly and exclusively affecting them, the two countries should seek to settle them in a spirit of neighborliness and goodwill through every available channel as envisaged in the treaty of friendship.

The two heads of Government, recognizing the desirability of restoring and maintaining friendly relations and historical ties that have bound the two countries, decided that their respective Governments would take every possible measure to refrain from making acrimonious attacks and disparaging references to each other.

The President and the Prime Minister have also cleared the way for a meeting of ministers to be held June 7 in Manila amongst Indonesia, the Philippines and Malaya, which they hope will lead to a meeting of heads of government of the three countries.[2] They would strive for the achievement of closer understanding between the three countries in matters of common concern and mutual interest.

The President and the Prime Minister wish to thank the Prime Minister and Government of Japan for their kind hospitality, and in particular the Foreign Minister of Japan, who so generously made available his home for the purpose of this historic occasion.

---

[1] *Japan Times*, 2 June 1963.   [2] See pp. 347–52 below.

Communiqué of the Conference of Foreign Ministers of Malaya, Indonesia, and the Philippines, Manila, 11 June 1963[1]

The Governments of the Federation of Malaya, the Republic of Indonesia and the Republic of the Philippines, prompted by their keen and common desire to have a general exchange of views on current problems concerning stability, security, economic development and social progress of the three countries and of the region, for the purpose of achieving common understanding and close cooperation, and upon the initiative of President Diosdado Macapagal, agreed that a Conference of Ministers of the three countries be held in Manila on 7th June, 1963. Accordingly, Tun Abdul Razak, Deputy Prime Minister of the Federation of Malaya; Dr. Subandrio, Deputy First Minister/Minister for Foreign Affairs of the Republic of Indonesia; and Hon. Emmanuel Pelaez, Vice President and concurrently Secretary of Foreign Affairs of the Republic of the Philippines, met in Manila from 7 to 11 June, 1963.

2. The deliberations were held in a frank manner and in a most cordial atmosphere in keeping with the spirit of the accord reached among President Sukarno of the Republic of Indonesia, Prime Minister Tunku Abdul Rahman Putra of the Federation of Malaya, and President Macapagal of the Republic of the Philippines. This Ministerial Conference was a manifestation of the determination of the nations in this region to achieve closer cooperation in their endeavor to chart a common future.

3. The three Ministers examined the Philippine proposal embodying President Macapagal's idea for the establishment of a confederation of nations of Malay origin and agreed on the acceptance of the idea as a means of bringing together their countries into the closest association.[2] Initial steps were agreed upon by the Ministers in order to implement the proposal. For this purpose, they agreed to recommend to the forthcoming Meeting of Heads of Government[3] the establishment of machinery for regular consultations among their governments at all levels on problems of common concern, such as security, stability, and economic, social and cultural development.

4. The Ministers were of one mind that the three countries share a primary responsibility for the maintenance of the stability and security of the area from subversion in any form or manifestation in order to preserve their respective national identities, and to ensure the peaceful development of their respective countries and of their region, in accordance with the ideals and aspirations of their peoples.

5. The three Ministers, in the context of their close and brotherly association, succeeded in reaching common understanding and complete agreement on how to resolve problems of common concern arising out of the proposal to establish a Federation of Malaysia.

6. In the same brotherly spirit the three Ministers discussed the Philippine claim to North Borneo and arrived at a common understanding and agreement on how this problem should be resolved justly and expeditiously.

[1] Malaysia, *Malaya/Philippine Relations, 31 August 1957–15 September 1963* (Kuala Lumpur, 1963), pp. 26–7.
[2] President Macapagal proposed the formation of a Confederation of Greater Malaya during a news conference in Manila on 27 July 1962. For an account of the Conference, see *Straits Times*; *N.Y. Times*, 28 July 1962.   [3] See pp. 347–52 below.

7. The three Ministers also exchanged views regarding current problems mutually affecting their respective countries in the field of economic, social and cultural cooperation.

8. The three Ministers have prepared a number of documents embodying their recommendations resulting from their deliberations which will be submitted to the meeting of the Heads of Government for their consideration and approval.

9. The Ministers recommended that a Meeting of their respective Heads of Government be held in Manila not later than the end of July 1963.

10. The Ministers expressed satisfaction over the atmosphere of brotherliness and cordiality which pervaded their Meeting and considered it as a confirmation of their close fraternal ties and as a happy augury for the success of future consultations among their leaders.

11. The Ministers of the Federation of Malaya and the Republic of Indonesia placed on record their profound appreciation and gratitude for the statesmanlike efforts of President Macapagal whose courage, vision and inspiration not only facilitated the holding of this historic Meeting but also contributed towards the achievement for the first time of a unity of purpose and common dedication among the people of Malaya, Indonesia and the Philippines. The Vice President of the Philippines and concurrently Secretary of Foreign Affairs placed on record the deep appreciation of President Macapagal and the Philippine Government for the ready response of the Heads of Government of Malaya and Indonesia and the unstinted and brotherly cooperation of their Ministers in bringing about the success of the Ministerial Conference.

The Tripartite Summit Meeting of the Presidents of Indonesia and the Philippines and the Prime Minister of Malaya, Manila, 30 July–5 August 1963[1]

(i) *Joint Statement*

The President of the Republic of Indonesia, the President of the Philippines, and the Minister of the Federation of Malaya met at a summit conference in Manila from July 30 to August 5, 1963.

1. Moved by a sincere desire to solve their common problems in an atmosphere of fraternal understanding, they considered, approved and accepted the report and recommendations of the Foreign Ministers of the three countries adopted in Manila on June 11, 1963 (hereafter to be known as the Manila Accord).[2]

2. In order to provide guiding principles for the implementation of the Manila Accord the Heads of Government have issued a declaration known as the Manila Declaration[3] embodying the common aspirations and objectives of the peoples and governments of the three countries.

3. As a result of the consultations amongst the three heads of Government in accordance with the principles enunciated in the Manila declaration, they have resolved various current problems of common concern.

---

[1] Malaysia, *Malaya/Indonesia Relations, 31 August 1957–15 September 1963* (Kuala Lumpur, 1963), pp. 45–55.

[2] See pp. 350–2 below.   [3] See pp. 349–50 below.

4. Pursuant to paragraphs 10 and 11 of the Manila accord the United Nations Secretary-General or his representative should ascertain prior to the establishment of the Federation of Malaysia the wishes of the people of Sabah (North Borneo) and Sarawak within the context of General Assembly Resolution 1541 (15), principle 9 of the annex,[1] by a fresh approach, which in the opinion of the Secretary-General is necessary to ensure complete compliance with the principle of self-determination within the requirements embodied in principle 9, taking into consideration:

(I) the recent elections in Sabah (North Borneo) and Sarawak but nevertheless further examining, verifying and satisfying himself as to whether

(a) Malaysia was a major issue, if not the main issue;
(b) Electoral registers were properly compiled;
(c) Elections were free and there was no coercion; and
(d) Votes were properly polled and properly counted; and

(II) the wishes of those who, being qualified to vote, would have exercised their right of self-determination in the recent elections had it not been for their detention for political activities, imprisonment for political offences or absence from Sabah (North Borneo) or Sarawak.

5. The Secretary-General will be requested to send working teams to carry out the task set out in paragraph 4.

6. The Federation of Malaya, having undertaken to consult the British Government and the Governments of Sabah (North Borneo) and Sarawak under paragraph 11 of the Manila accord on behalf of the three Heads of Government, further undertake to request them to cooperate with the Secretary-General and to extend to him the necessary facilities so as to enable him to carry out his task as set out in paragraph 4.

7. In the interest of the countries concerned, the three Heads of Government deem it desirable to send observers to witness the carrying out of the task to be undertaken by the working teams and the Federation of Malaya will use its best endeavors to obtain the cooperation of the British Government and the governments of Sabah (North Borneo) and Sarawak in furtherance of this purpose.

8. In accordance with paragraph 12 of the Manila accord, the three Heads of Government decided to request the British Government to agree to seek a just and expeditious solution to the dispute between the British Government and the Philippine Government concerning Sabah (North Borneo) by means of negotiation, conciliation and arbitration, judicial settlement, or other peaceful means of the parties' own choice in conformity with the Charter of the United Nations. The three Heads of Government take cognizance of the position regarding the Philippine claim to Sabah (North Borneo) after the establishment of the Federation of Malaysia as provided under paragraph 12 of the Manila accord, that is, that the inclusion of Sabah (North Borneo) in the Federation of Malaysia does not prejudice either the claim or any right thereunder.

9. Pursuant to paragraphs 6, 7, 8 and 9 of the Manila accord and the fifth principle of the Manila declaration, that is, that initial steps should be taken

---

[1] *G.A.O.R.*, Fifteenth Year, Supplement No. 16, pp. 29–30.

towards the establishment of Maphilindo by holding frequent and regular consultations at all levels to be known as Mushawarah Maphilindo, it is agreed that each country shall set up a national secretariat for Maphilindo affairs and as a first step the respective national secretariats will consult together with a view to coordinating and cooperating with each other in the study on the setting up of the necessary machinery for Maphilindo.

10. The three Heads of Government emphasized that the responsibility for the preservation of the national independence of the three countries and of the peace and security in their region lies primarily in the hands of the governments and the peoples of the countries concerned, and that the three governments undertake to have close consultations (MUSHAWARAH) among themselves on these matters.

11. The three Heads of Government further agreed that foreign bases— temporary in nature—should not be allowed to be used directly or indirectly to subvert the national independence of any of the three countries. In accordance with the principle enunciated in the Bandung Declaration,[1] the three countries will abstain from the use of arrangements of collective defence to serve the particular interests of any of the big powers.

12. President Sukarno and Prime Minister Tunku Abdul Rahman express their deep appreciation for the initiative taken by President Macapagal in calling the summit conference which, in addition to resolving their differences concerning the proposed Federation of Malaysia, resulted in paving the way for the establishment of Maphilindo. The three Heads of Government conclude this conference, which has greatly strengthened the fraternal ties which bind their three countries and extended the scope of their cooperation and understanding, with renewed confidence that their governments and peoples will together make a significant contribution to the attainment of a just and enduring peace, stability and prosperity in the region.

(ii) *Manila Declaration*

The President of the Republic of Indonesia, the President of the Philippines and the Prime Minister of the Federation of Malaya, assembled in a Summit Conference in Manila from July 30 to August 5, 1963, following the Meeting of their Foreign Ministers held in Manila from June 7 to 11, 1963:

Conscious of the historic significance of their coming together for the first time as leaders of sovereign States that have emerged after long struggles from colonial status to independence;

Desiring to achieve better understanding and closer cooperation in their endeavour to chart their common future;

Inspired also by the spirit of Asian-African solidarity forged in the Bandung Conference of 1955;[2]

Convinced that their countries, which are bound together by close historical ties of race and culture, share a primary responsibility for the maintenance of the stability and security of the area from subversion in any form or manifestation in order to preserve their respective national identities and to ensure the

---

[1] *Documents, 1955*, pp. 429–36.   [2] Ibid.

peaceful development of their respective countries and their region in accordance with the ideals and aspirations of their peoples; and

Determined to intensify the joint and individual efforts of their countries to secure lasting peace, progress and prosperity for themselves and their neighbors in a world dedicated to freedom and justice;

DO HEREBY DECLARE:

First, that they reaffirm their adherence to the principle of equal rights and self-determination of peoples as enunciated in the United Nations Charter and the Bandung Declaration;

Second, that they are determined, in the common interest of their countries, to maintain fraternal relations, to strengthen cooperation among their peoples in the economic, social and cultural fields in order to promote economic progress and social well-being in the region, and to put an end to the exploitation of man by man and of one nation by another;

Third, that the three nations shall combine their efforts in the common struggle against colonialism and imperialism in all their forms and manifestations and for the eradication of the vestiges thereof in the region in particular and the world in general;

Fourth, that the three nations, as new emerging forces in the region, shall cooperate in building a new and better world based on national freedom, social justice and lasting peace; and

Fifth, that in the context of the joint endeavors of the three nations to achieve the foregoing objectives, they have agreed to take initial steps towards the establishment of Maphilindo by holding frequent and regular consultations at all levels to be known as Mushawarah Maphilindo.

(iii) *Manila Accord*

The Governments of the Federation of Malaya, the Republic of Indonesia and the Republic of the Philippines, prompted by their keen and common desire to have a general exchange of views on current problems concerning stability, security, economic development and social progress of the three countries and of the region and upon the initiative of President Diosdado Macapagal, agreed that a Conference of Ministers of the three countries be held in Manila on 7th June, 1963 for the purpose of achieving common understanding and close fraternal cooperation among themselves. Accordingly, Tun Abdul Razak, Deputy Prime Minister of the Federation of Malaya; Dr. Subandrio, Deputy First Minister/Minister for Foreign Affairs of the Republic of Indonesia; and Honorable Emmanuel Pelaez, Vice President of the Philippines and concurrently Secretary of Foreign Affairs, met in Manila from 7 to 11 June, 1963.

2. The deliberations were held in a frank manner and in a most cordial atmosphere in keeping with the spirit of friendship prevailing in the various meetings held between President Soekarno of the Republic of Indonesia, and Prime Minister Tunku Abdul Rahman Putra of the Federation of Malaya, and President Diosdado Macapagal. This Ministerial Conference was a manifestation

of the determination of the nations in this region to achieve closer cooperation in the endeavor to chart their common future.

3. The Ministers were of one mind that the three countries share a primary responsibility for the maintenance of the stability and security of the area from subversion in any form or manifestation in order to preserve their respective national identities, and to ensure the peaceful development of their respective countries and of their region, in accordance with the ideals and aspirations of their peoples.

4. In the same spirit of common and constructive endeavor, they exchanged views on the proposed Confederation of nations of Malay origin, the proposed Federation of Malaysia, the Philippine claim to North Borneo and related problems.

5. Recognising that it is in the common interest of their countries to maintain fraternal relations and to strengthen cooperation among their peoples who are bound together by ties of race and culture, the three Ministers agreed to intensify the joint and individual efforts of their countries to secure lasting peace, progress and prosperity for themselves and for their neighbours.

6. In this context, the three Ministers supported President Macapagal's plan[1] envisaging the grouping of the three nations of Malay origin working together in closest harmony but without surrendering any portion of their sovereignty. This calls for the establishment of the necessary common organs.

7. The three Ministers agreed to take the initial steps towards this ultimate aim by establishing machinery for frequent and regular consultations. The details of such machinery will be further defined. This machinery will enable the three governments to hold regular consultations at all levels to deal with matters of mutual interest and concern consistent with the national, regional and international responsibilities or obligations of each country without prejudice to its sovereignty and independence. The Ministers agreed that their countries will endeavor to achieve close understanding and cooperation in dealing with common problems relating to security, stability, economic, social and cultural development.

8. In order to accelerate the process of growth towards the ultimate establishment of President Macapagal's plan, the Ministers agreed that each country shall set up its own National Secretariat. Pending the establishment of a Central Secretariat for the consultative machinery, the National Secretaries should coordinate and cooperate with each other in the fulfilment of their tasks.

9 The Ministers further agreed to recommend that Heads of Government and Foreign Ministers meet at least once a year for the purpose of consultations on matters of importance and common concern.

10. The Ministers reaffirmed their countries' adherence to the principle of self-determination for the peoples of non-self-governing territories. In this context, Indonesia and the Philippines stated that they would welcome the formation of Malaysia provided the support of the people of the Borneo territories is ascertained by an independent and impartial authority, the Secretary-General of the United Nations or his representative.

11. The Federation of Malaya expressed appreciation for this attitude of Indonesia and the Philippines and undertook to consult the British Government

[1] See footnote 2, p. 346 above.

and the Governments of the Borneo territories with a view to inviting the Secretary-General of the United Nations or his representative to take the necessary steps in order to ascertain the wishes of the people of those territories.

12. The Philippines made it clear that its position on the inclusion of North Borneo in the Federation of Malaysia is subject to the final outcome of the Philippine claim to North Borneo. The Ministers took note of the Philippine claim and the right of the Philippines to continue to pursue it in accordance with international law and the principle of the pacific settlement of disputes. They agreed that the inclusion of North Borneo in the Federation of Malaysia would not prejudice either the claim or any right thereunder. Moreover, in the context of their close association, the three countries agreed to exert their best endeavors to bring the claim to a just and expeditious solution by peaceful means, such as negotiation, conciliation, arbitration, or judicial settlement as well as other peaceful means of the parties' own choice, in conformity with the Charter of the United Nations and the Bandung Declaration.

13. In particular, considering the close historical ties between the peoples of the Philippines and North Borneo as well as their geographical propinquity, the Ministers agreed that in the event of North Borneo joining the proposed Federation of Malaysia the Government of the latter and the Government of the Philippines should maintain and promote the harmony and the friendly relations subsisting in their region to ensure the security and stability of the area.

14. The Ministers agreed to recommend that a Meeting of their respective Heads of Government be held in Manila not later than the end of July 1963.

15. The Ministers expressed satisfaction over the atmosphere of brotherliness and cordiality which pervaded their Meeting and considered it as a confirmation of their close fraternal ties and as a happy augury for the success of future consultations among their leaders.

16. The Ministers agreed to place on record their profound appreciation of and gratitude for the statesmanlike efforts of President Macapagal whose courage, vision and inspiration not only facilitated the holding of this historic Meeting but also contributed towards the achievement for the first time of a unity of purpose and a sense of common dedication among the peoples of Malaya, Indonesia and the Philippines.

(c) *The Establishment of Malaysia*

Agreement relating to Malaysia, concluded by Great Britain, the Federation of Malaya, North Borneo, Sarawak and Singapore, London, 9 July 1963[1]

The United Kingdom of Great Britain and Northern Ireland, the Federation of Malaya, North Borneo, Sarawak and Singapore;
Desiring to conclude an agreement relating to Malaysia;
Agree as follows:-

ARTICLE I

The Colonies of North Borneo and Sarawak and the State of Singapore shall be federated with the existing States of the Federation of Malaya as the States

[1] Cmnd. 2094, *Malaysia, Agreement concluded between the United Kingdom of Great Britain and Northern Ireland, the Federation of Malaya, North Borneo, Sarawak and Singapore* (London, 9 July 1963), pp. 1–3.

of Sabah, Sarawak and Singapore in accordance with the constitutional instruments annexed to this Agreement and the Federation shall thereafter be called 'Malaysia'.

ARTICLE II

The Government of the Federation of Malaya will take such steps as may be appropriate and available to them to secure the enactment by the Parliament of the Federation of Malaya of an Act in the form set out in Annex A to this Agreement and that it is brought into operation on 31st August, 1963 (and the date on which the said Act is brought into operation is hereinafter referred to as 'Malaysia Day').

ARTICLE III

The Government of the United Kingdom will submit to Her Britannic Majesty before Malaysia Day Orders in Council for the purpose of giving the force of law to the Constitutions of Sabah, Sarawak and Singapore as States of Malaysia which are set out in Annexes B, C and D to this Agreement.[1]

ARTICLE IV

The Government of the United Kingdom will take such steps as may be appropriate and available to them to secure the enactment by the Parliament of the United Kingdom of an Act providing for the relinquishment, as from Malaysia Day, of Her Britannic Majesty's sovereignty and jurisdiction in respect of North Borneo, Sarawak and Singapore so that the said sovereignty and jurisdiction shall on such relinquishment vest in accordance with this Agreement and the constitutional instruments annexed to this Agreement.

ARTICLE V

The Government of the Federation of Malaya will take such steps as may be appropriate and available to them to secure the enactment before Malaysia Day by the Parliament of the Federation of Malaya of an Act in the form set out in Annex E[1] to this Agreement for the purpose of extending and adapting the Immigration Ordinance, 1959, of the Federation of Malaya to Malaysia and of making additional provision with respect to entry into the States of Sabah and Sarawak; and the other provisions of this Agreement shall be conditional upon the enactment of the said Act.

ARTICLE VI

The Agreement on External Defence and Mutual Assistance between the Government of the United Kingdom and the Government of the Federation of Malaya of 12th October, 1957,[2] and its annexes shall apply to all territories of Malaysia, and any reference in that Agreement to the Federation of Malaya shall be deemed to apply to Malaysia, subject to the proviso that the Government of Malaysia will afford to the Government of the United Kingdom the

---

[1] Not reproduced here.   [2] Cmnd. 263.

right to continue to maintain the bases and other facilities at present occupied by their Service authorities within the State of Singapore and will permit the Government of the United Kingdom to make such use of these bases and facilities as that Government may consider necessary for the purpose of assisting in the defence of Malaysia, and for Commonwealth defence and for the preservation of peace in South-East Asia. The application of the said Agreement shall be subject to the provisions of Annex F to this Agreement (relating primarily to Service lands in Singapore).[1]

Article VII

(1) The Federation of Malaya agrees that Her Britannic Majesty may make before Malaysia Day Orders in Council in the form set out in Annex G[1] to this Agreement for the purpose of making provision for the payment of compensation and retirement benefits to certain overseas officers serving, immediately before Malaysia Day, in the public service of the Colony of North Borneo or the Colony of Sarawak.

(2) On or as soon as practicable after Malaysia Day, Public Officers' Agreements in the forms set out in Annexes H and I[1] of this Agreement shall be signed on behalf of the Government of the United Kingdom and the Government of Malaysia; and the Government of Malaysia shall obtain the concurrence of the Government of the State of Sabah, Sarawak or Singapore, as the case may require, to the signature of the Agreement by the Government of Malaysia so far as its terms may affect the responsibilities or interests of the Government of the State.

Article VIII

The Governments of the Federation of Malaya, North Borneo and Sarawak will take such legislative, executive or other action as may be required to implement the assurances, undertakings and recommendations contained in Chapter 3 of, and Annexes A and B to, the Report of the Inter-Governmental Committee signed on 27th February, 1963, in so far as they are not implemented by express provision of the Constitution of Malaysia.[2]

Article IX

The provisions of Annex J[3] to this Agreement relating to Common Market and financial arrangements shall constitute an Agreement between the Government of the Federation of Malaya and the Government of Singapore.

Article X

The Governments of the Federation of Malaya and of Singapore will take such legislative, executive or other action as may be required to implement the

[1] Not reproduced here.
[2] Cmnd. 1954. Chapter III and Annexes A and B of the Report deal with constitutional and administrative arrangements for the proposed Federation of Malaysia.
[3] See pp. 355–60 below.

arrangements with respect to broadcasting and television set out in Annex K[1] to this Agreement in so far as they are not implemented by express provision of the Constitution of Malaysia.

ARTICLE XI

This Agreement shall be signed in the English and Malay languages except that the Annexes shall be in the English language only. In case of doubt the English text of the Agreement shall prevail.

In witness whereof the undersigned, being duly authorised thereto, have signed this Agreement.

Done at London this Ninth day of July, 1963, in five copies of which one shall be deposited with each of the Parties.

Agreement between the Federation of Malaya and Singapore on Common Market and Financial Arrangements, London, 9 July 1963[2]

1. (1) The Federal Government, in order to facilitate the maximum practicable degree of economic integration of the territories of Malaysia, while taking account of the interests of the entrepôt trade of Singapore, Penang and Labuan and those of existing industries in Malaysia, and the need to ensure a balanced development of these territories, shall progressively establish a common market in Malaysia for all goods or products produced, manufactured or assembled in significant quantities in Malaysia, with the exception of goods and products of which the principal terminal markets lie outside Malaysia.

1. (2) Where the same protective duties or revenue duties are applicable throughout Malaysia in the case of any class of goods or products, then no tariff or trade barrier or trade restriction or discrimination shall be applied to such goods or products in regard to their circulation throughout Malaysia.

1. (3) The provisions of the preceding sub-paragraph shall not be construed to prevent the imposition of—

(a) any special production tax on producers in a low-tariff State which would offset the cost inequalities arising from the differential import duties; or

(b) any export duty or export restriction on primary products where the principal terminal markets lie outside Malaysia.

2. (1) The Malayan Government shall take steps to establish by law before Malaysia Day a Tariff Advisory Board to advise the Federal Government generally on the establishment of the common market as defined in paragraph 1 above, including the establishment and maintenance of a common external tariff for the protection (where required) of goods for which there is to be a common market.

2. (2) Appointments to the Board shall be made by the Federal Government but until five years from Malaysia Day the appointment of the Chairman shall require the concurrence of the Singapore Government; the first Chairman shall be appointed as soon as possible after the conclusion of this Agreement. During the first five years, there shall be three Deputy Chairmen, one of whom shall be

---

[1] Not reproduced here.   [2] Cmnd. 2094, Annex J.

nominated by the Singapore Government. In appointing members of the Board regard shall be had to the areas and interests involved.

2. (3) The Board shall sit in public to receive evidence except where the Board deems it necessary to receive evidence *in camera*. Within six months after their receipt the Federal Government shall publish the reports and recommendations of the Board other than those of which publication is not in the public interest.

3. (1) For the purposes of this Agreement a protective duty shall be defined as a duty which is levied in respect of a class of goods or products which are or are to be produced, manufactured, assembled or prepared and used or consumed in the Federation in significant quantities, or which are used or consumed in the production, manufacture, assembly or preparation in the Federation of goods or products of such a class or which are of a description providing a substitute for or alternative to goods or products of such a class. All other duties shall be defined as revenue duties. A duty shall be regarded as imposed in Singapore, if it is imposed on goods imported into Singapore for use or consumption there and not otherwise.

3. (2) Except in cases where it deems preventive action to be urgently necessary, the Federal Government shall not in Singapore make any class of goods or products subject to a protective duty or vary any protective duty before receiving the advice of the Tariff Advisory Board. In cases where a duty has been imposed or varied without prior reference to the Tariff Advisory Board, the Federal Government shall seek the advice of the Board thereon as soon as practicable thereafter.

3. (3) For a period of 5 years from Malaysia Day the Singapore Government shall have the right to require a delay not exceeding 12 months in the imposition in Singapore of any protective duty on the grounds that the duty would significantly prejudice the entrepôt trade. In any enquiry by the Tariff Advisory Board on a proposal to impose such a duty, the Singapore Government shall inform the Board of any item on which it may wish, in the interests of the entrepôt trade, to avail itself of this option. In regard to such items, the Tariff Advisory Board shall consider the possibility of anticipatory action in Singapore and shall, if necessary, include in its recommendations proposals to prevent such action. During the period of delay, the Singapore Government shall not grant any licence, concession or inducement to any industry which may be affected by the proposed protective duty without the concurrence of the Federal Government.

3. (4) The Tariff Advisory Board shall be required within six months after Malaysia Day to make its first report as to what protective duties should be imposed. For this purpose it shall consider any proposals made to it by the Federal Government or a State Government.

4. (1) In formulating its policy relating to the harmonisation of revenue duties, the Federal Government shall pay due regard to any representations made by the Singapore Government on the economic, financial and social implications of such harmonisation.

4. (2) Revenue duties in force in Singapore on 1st July, 1963, and the corresponding duties in force in the Federation of Malaya shall be harmonised as soon as practicable.

4. (3) Until 31st December, 1968, no revenue duty shall, except at the request or without the consent of the Singapore Government, be imposed in Singapore by the Federal Government in respect of any class of goods or products not chargeable with such a duty on 1st July, 1963. Such consent shall not be withheld except on the grounds that the duty would significantly prejudice the entrepôt trade of Singapore.

4. (4) Before 31st December, 1968, the Tariff Advisory Board shall review the revenue duties in force at that time in Singapore and in the remainder of Malaysia and shall make recommendations regarding the amendment of such duties or the imposition of additional duties. As from 1st January, 1969, the Singapore Government shall be entitled to withhold its consent to the imposition in Singapore of any revenue duty in respect of any goods or products referred to in subparagraph (3) for any period up to 31st December, 1975, on the grounds that it would significantly prejudice the entrepôt trade, and, in the absence of such consent, no such duty shall be imposed provided that the Singapore Government shall pay to the Federal Government annually compensation equal to the loss of revenue suffered by the Federal Government as a result of the withholding of such consent.

4. (5) For the purposes of this agreement, the entrepôt trade of Singapore means trade in goods and products imported into Singapore from outside Malaysia and primary products imported into Singapore from other parts of Malaysia, which goods or products, whether further processed or not, are subsequently re-exported from Singapore to destinations outside Malaysia.

5. Subject to the provisions of the Annex to this Agreement,[1] executive authority in respect of the collection in Singapore of customs duties and excise and income tax shall be delegated to the Singapore Government. The Federal Government may revoke this authority if the Singapore Government fails to comply with any direction properly given to it by the Federal Government for the collection or protection of these taxes or shows itself unwilling or unable to discharge these functions efficiently. This authority may extend to customs duties and other charges collected in Singapore on goods exported from or to be imported into Malaysia outside Singapore.

6. (1) All revenues collected in Singapore, with the exceptions specified below, shall be paid into a separate fund in a branch of the Central Bank to be established in Singapore and the fund shall be divided between the two Governments and paid to them at least once in every year, in the proportion of 60 per cent. to the Singapore Government and 40 per cent. to the Federal Government. The exceptions are—

(a) the revenues specified in Part III of the Tenth Schedule to the Federal Constitution, including property tax in lieu of rates (to be paid into the State Consolidated Fund);

(b) customs duties and other charges (including excise not in force at the date of this Agreement and any production tax imposed in respect of goods to which a protective duty is applicable) collected in Singapore on goods to be exported from or imported into Malaysia outside Singapore (to be paid into the Federal Consolidated Fund);

(c) income tax collected in Singapore and attributable to income derived from the States of Malaya (to be paid into the Federal Consolidated Fund).

[1] See pp. 359–60 below.

6. (2) 60 per cent. of income tax collected in the States of Malaya but attributable to income derived from Singapore shall be paid to the Singapore Government.

6. (3) Income tax attributable to income derived from Singapore and collected by an Agent outside Malaysia shall be paid into the separate fund referred to in paragraph 6(1) above.

6. (4) From the beginning of 1964 paragraphs 6(1)(c) and 6(2) shall apply as if references to the States of Malaya included references to the Borneo States.

6. (5) The provisions of Article 109 and Clauses (3), (3A) and (4) of Article 110 of the Federal Constitution shall not apply in relation to Singapore.

7. The Singapore Government shall pay to the Federal Government the cost of capital development of Federal projects in Singapore other than projects for defence and internal security. The two Governments shall agree together on projects to be covered by this paragraph which do not provide predominantly local services.

8. The arrangements specified in paragraphs 6 and 7 above shall remain in operation until 31st December, 1964. The two Governments shall then review these arrangements and shall decide upon any amendments to be made to them in respect of the two year period commencing 1st January, 1965. There shall be a similar review in respect of each subsequent period of two years. In default of agreement between the two Governments, any issue in dispute shall be referred to an independent assessor appointed jointly by the two Governments. In default of agreement between the two Governments on the choice of an assessor, the Lord President of the Federal Court, after considering the views of both governments, shall appoint an assessor from among persons recommended by the International Bank for Reconstruction and Development as being persons enjoying an international reputation in finance. The recommendations of the assessor shall be binding on both governments. Such reviews shall have regard to all relevant factors.

9. To assist development in the Borneo territories the Singapore Government shall make available to the Federal Government:

 (a) a 15-year loan of $100 million, bearing interest at current market rates in the Federation, subject to the proviso that the loan shall be free of interest during the first 5 years after drawing and that if, having regard to the economic growth in Singapore, it is so recommended in the financial review in respect of the period of two years commencing 1st January, 1969, under paragraph 8 above, the loan shall be free of interest for a further period of 5 years; and

 (b) a 15-year loan of $50 million bearing interest at current market rates in the Federation.

The above loans shall be drawn in equal annual instalments over a period of 5 years, commencing in 1964.

10. Any dispute between the Federal Government and the Singapore Government as to the interpretation or application of this Agreement may be referred by either Government to the Federal Court for determination by that Court in exercise of the jurisdiction conferred upon it by Article 128 of the Federal Constitution.[1]

[1] Malaysia, *The Federal Constitution* (Kuala Lumpur, 1964), p. 76.

ANNEX TO ANNEX J

PART I

CUSTOMS AND EXCISE

Subject to the provisions of Paragraphs 1–4 of this agreement the following powers under the Singapore Customs Ordinance are reserved to the Federal Government—

(1) The power to fix the rate of tax, duty or excise on any class of goods;

(2) The power to fix by order the value of goods for duty or excise purposes;

(3) The power to grant exemptions or refunds in respect of duties or excise other than in particular cases where the duty or excise is less than $2,000 in any one instance;

(4) The power to make regulations both in relation to Customs and Excise.

2. The Federal Government will also have the following powers:—

(1) The power to appoint Federal officers to inspect the Customs and Excise Department, Singapore. Reports would be submitted to the Federal Government direct with a copy to the Singapore Government and the inspecting officers would have the right of access to all documents and records of the Department.

(2) The right of the Federal Minister responsible for Customs to issue directions to the State Government which he considers necessary to ensure the effective collection or protection of Federal customs duties and/or excise.

PART II

INCOME TAX

Powers to be exercised by the Federal Government in relation to collection

(the references are to the *Singapore Income Tax Ordinance*)

Section 3A

The power of the Minister to give the Comptroller-General directions of a general character.

Section 13(2)

The power of the Minister to provide that interest on any loan charged on the public revenue of Singapore or the Federation shall be exempt from tax.

Section 106(1)

(1) The power to vary or revoke the whole or any part of any schedule to the Ordinance.

(2) The power to exempt any person or class of persons from all or any of the provisions of the Ordinance.

Section 7

The powers of the Malayan Board of Income Tax as at 4th June, 1963, to be retained with the deletion of subsection (3).

Section 19(2)

The Comptroller's powers to vary the rate of capital allowances prescribed for machinery and plant should be transferred to the Comptroller-General.

Pioneer Industries Ordinance

Certificates granted by Singapore to be subject to approval of the Federal Minister of Finance.

Industrial Expansion (*Relief from Income Tax Ordinance 1959*)

Section 5

Orders made by Singapore to be subject to approval of the Federal Minister of Finance.

Income Tax Bills

The powers conferred on the Minister or the Comptroller by any Income Tax Bills introduced between the 1st June, 1963, and the date of formal acceptance of the Heads of Terms of Agreement and enacted prior to Malaysia Day.

Between the date of formal acceptance of the Heads of Terms of Agreement and Malaysia Day the Singapore Government should not introduce any new legislation with respect to matters the subject of that Agreement.

Powers to be retained

Section 4(2)

The Income Tax Department of Singapore shall be subject to detailed inspection by the Comptroller-General in accordance with the existing provisions of Section 4(2) which require the Comptroller and his officers to be subject to the supervision and direction of the Comptroller-General.

Powers to be reserved

The right of the Federal Minister responsible for Income Tax to issue directions to the State Governments which he considers necessary to ensure the effective collection or protection of Income Tax shall be recognised.

The United Nations Secretary General, U Thant, to the Foreign Ministers of Indonesia, the Philippines and Malaya, 14 September 1963[1]

I have the honor to refer to the request that you addressed to me jointly with the Foreign Minister of the Federation of Malaya and the Foreign Minister of

[1] *N.Y. Times*, 15 September 1963.

the Philippines, on August 5, 1963, and to my reply of August 8, 1963,[1] concerning the ascertainment of the wishes of the people of Sabah (North Borneo) and Sarawak prior to the establishment of the Federation of Malaysia.

I attach herewith the conclusions which I have undertaken to communicate to your Government on the basis of the report of the United Nations Malaysian Mission.

I should like to take this opportunity to convey to your Government my deep appreciation for the confidence it has placed in me by requesting my assistance regarding the implementation of this part of the Manila Accord[2] and the Manila Joint Statement.[3]

My acceptance of this request was made in full awareness of the difficulties of the task, but I would like to assure you and, through you, your Government, that my sole desire in this matter has been to be able to contribute to the objectives of a better understanding and closer cooperation between the States of the region, as reaffirmed in the Manila declaration of August 3, 1963.[4]

Accept, Sir, the assurances of my highest consideration.

CONCLUSIONS

In response to the request made by the Governments of the Federation of Malaya, the Republic of Indonesia, and the Republic of the Philippines, on August 5, 1963, I agreed to ascertain, prior to the establishment of the Federation of Malaysia, the wishes of the people of Sabah (North Borneo) and Sarawak.

As foreseen in my communication of August 8, 1963, a mission was established, comprising two teams, one for Sarawak and the other for Sabah (North Borneo), working under the supervision of my personal representative. The mission has now completed the inquiry assigned to it, and has reported to me.

It was always understood that the ascertainment would be completed within a limited period of time, and my communication of August 8 noted that every effort would be made to complete the task as quickly as possible. I later informed the Governments concerned that I would endeavor to report my conclusions to them by September 14.

During the course of the inquiry, the date of September 16, 1963, was announced by the Government of the Federation of Malaya with the concurrence of the British Government, the Singapore Government and the Governments of Sabah and Sarawak, for the establishment of the Federation of Malaysia.[5] This has led to misunderstanding and confusion and even resentment among other parties to the Manila agreement, which could have been avoided if the date could have been fixed after my conclusions had been reached and made known.

There was no reference to a referendum or plebiscite in the request which was addressed to me. I was asked to ascertain the wishes of the people, taking into consideration certain questions relating to the recent elections. The mission

---

[1] See *Y.U.N., 1963*, p. 41.   [2] See pp. 350–2 above.
[3] See pp. 347–9 above.   [4] See pp. 349–50 above.
[5] See *N.Y. Times*, 24 August 1963; *Straits Times*, 25 August 1963.

accordingly arranged for consultations with the population through the elected representatives of the people, leaders of political parties and other groups and organizations, and with all persons who were willing to express their views, and every effort was made to ascertain the wishes of the special groups (political detainees and absentees) mentioned in the Manila Joint Statement. The mission gathered and studied all available documents, reports and other material on the governmental institutions, political organization, electoral processes in the two territories, and other matters relevant to its terms of reference.

The Governments of the Federation of Malaya ,the Republic of Indonesia and the Republic of the Philippines deemed it desirable to send observers to witness the carrying out of the task, and the Government of the United Kingdom decided that it also wished the same facility. I am pleased that an understanding was finally arrived at so that observers of all the Governments concerned could be present during at least part of the inquiry.

A more congenial atmosphere would have been achieved if the necessary facilities had been granted more promptly by the Administering Authority. The mission, however, made its records, including tape recordings of all its hearings, available for the use of the observer teams to enable them to inform themselves as fully as possible of what had occurred before their arrival.

The basic assessment which I was asked to make has broader implications than the specific questions enumerated in the request addressed to me by the three Governments.

I have given consideration to the circumstances in which the proposals for the Federation of Malaysia have been developed and discussed, and the possibility that people progressing through the stages of self-government may be less able to consider in an entirely free context the implications of such changes in their status, than a society which has already experienced full self-government and the determination of its own affairs. I have also been aware that the peoples of the territories are still striving for a more adequate level of educational development.

Having reflected fully on these considerations, and taking into account the framework within which the mission's task was performed, I have come to the conclusion that the majority of the peoples of Sabah (North Borneo) and of Sarawak have given serious and thoughtful consideration to their future, and to the implications for them of participation in a Federation of Malaysia.

I believe that the majority of them have concluded that they wish to bring their dependent status to an end and to realize their independence through freely chosen association with other peoples in their region with whom they feel ties of ethnic association, heritage, language, religion, culture, economic relationship, and ideals and objectives.

Not all of these considerations are present in equal weight in all minds, but it is my conclusion that the majority of the peoples of the two territories, having taken them into account, wish to engage, with the peoples of the Federation of Malaya and Singapore, in an enlarged Federation of Malaysia through which they can strive together to realize the fulfillment of their destiny.

With regard to the more specific questions referred to me, my conclusions concerning the recent elections in Sarawak and Sabah (North Borneo), and after the examination and verification reported by the mission, are:

(a) Malaysia has been the subject of widespread and intensive public debate, and was a major issue in the recent elections in the two territories.

(b) Electoral registers were properly compiled.

(c) The elections took place in an atmosphere free enough to enable the candidates and political parties to put their case before the electorate, and the people were able to express themselves freely by casting their votes in a polling system which provided the basic safeguards for secret balloting, and measures for the prevention and correction of abuses.

(d) The votes were properly polled and counted.

(e) Persons otherwise eligible to vote but who were unable to do so because of detention for political activities, or imprisonment for political offenses, numbered somewhat less than 100 in Sarawak, and even less in Sabah (North Borneo) at the time of the elections. Testimony given by this group, especially in Sarawak, indicated that they would have opposed the Federation of Malaysia if they had participated in the election. The actual votes of this group would not have been sufficient to have had a material effect on the result. The mission has given much attention to the possible effect which the absence of these persons, some of whom were officials of the anti-Malaysia party, might have had on the campaign. The mission considered the similar question concerning some 164 persons whose activity was restricted to some extent, but who retained the right to vote.

Noting that the anti-Malaysia party scored convincing electoral victories in many of the areas to which these persons belonged, I accept the mission's conclusion that a substantial limitation of the campaigning potential of the group opposed to the Federation of Malaysia has not occurred, so as seriously and significantly to have affected the result of the election.

(f) The mission made special efforts to obtain reliable information regarding persons who were absent from the territories at the time of the election, particularly as a result of possible political or other intimidation. The evidence available indicated that the number of such persons, otherwise qualified to vote, did not exceed a few hundred, and that their number could not have affected the results of the election. I note that the principal officials of the party in Sarawak opposed to the Federation of Malaysia, agree with this assessment, and I accept it.

Bearing in mind the fundamental agreement of the three participating Governments in the Manila meetings, and the statement by the Republic of Indonesia and the Republic of the Philippines that they would welcome the formation of Malaysia provided that the support of the people of the territories was ascertained by me and that, in my opinion, complete compliance with the principle of self-determination within the requirements of General Assembly resolution 1541 (XV), Principle IX of the Annex,[1] was ensured, my conclusions, based on

---

[1] Viz.: 'Principle IX: Integration should have come about in the following circumstances: (a) the integrating territory should have attained an advanced stage of self-government with free political institutions, so that its people would have the capacity to make a responsible choice through informed and democratic processes; (b) the integration should be the result of the freely expressed wishes of the territory's peoples acting with full knowledge of the change in their status, their wishes having been expressed through informed and democratic processes, impartially conducted and based on universal adult suffrage. The United Nations could, when it deems it necessary, supervise these processes.'

the findings of the mission, is that on both of these counts there is no doubt about the wishes of a sizable majority of the peoples of these territories to join in the Federation of Malaysia.

I am satisfied that the conclusions set forth above take cognizance of, and are in accordance with, the requirements set forth in the request addressed to me on August 5, 1963, by the Foreign Ministers of the Republic of Indonesia, the Federation of Malaya and the Republic of the Philippines.

In a sense, it was a pity that the work of the mission had to be accomplished within certain deadlines. But I do feel that, while more time might have enabled the mission to obtain more copious documentation and other evidence, it would not have affected the conclusions to any significant extent.

From the beginning of this year I have been observing the rising tension in South-east Asia on account of the differences of opinion among the countries most directly interested in the Malaysia issue. It was in the hope that some form of United Nations involvement might help to reduce tension that I agreed to respond positively to the request made by the three Manila Powers.

Whatever the origins of the proposal of Malaysia may have been, it seems to me in the light of actual events, including the present exercise, that we have witnessed in Sarawak and North Borneo the same process leading to self-government. I fervently hope that the people of these territories will achieve progress and prosperity, and find their fulfillment as component States of Malaysia.

B. VIETNAM

Speech by the United States Deputy Under Secretary of State, Mr. Johnson, to the Economic Club of Detroit, 8 April 1963[1] (extract)

... To be frank, the war was being lost fast in the fall of 1961, when General Taylor first led a mission there. Viet Cong attacks were accelerating both in numbers and size. In September they overran a provincial capital and held it overnight, long enough to behead publicly the Chief of Province. There was a real threat that they might be able to 'liberate' some remote area and hold it, possibly as the seat of a 'government' which the bloc could recognize and aid. Transportation was so disrupted that Saigon, normally a big rice-exporting port, was forced to import rice from the United States.

The situation has substantially changed since then. Viet Cong attacks declined steadily in 1962. They are now running at a rate considerably less than half the January 1962 average. No more provincial capitals have been attacked. Rice exports have resumed and are expected to be near normal this year. There are no Viet Cong areas immune to Government penetration. Perhaps even more significant is the fact that the Viet Cong have not escalated to larger units or to more conventional warfare.

There are other indicators of progress—increased voluntary intelligence from the people, increased Viet Cong weapons losses, the fact that Viet Cong strongholds are being systematically penetrated, their supplies and installations destroyed. But I think the most important reason for guarded optimism is the adoption by the Government of Viet-Nam of the 'strategic hamlet' program.[2]

[1] *D.S.B.*, 29 April 1963, pp. 635–41.   [2] See *Survey, 1962*, pp. 350–2.

The first step in setting up a strategic hamlet is largely military. A hamlet militia is trained and armed and a defensive perimeter constructed. The second step, however, is purely political. It is the election by a secret ballot of a hamlet council and the framing of a hamlet charter by the people's elected representatives.

The third step is more conventional but equally nonmilitary. This is the provision of Government services such as agricultural extension and low-interest agricultural loans, cheap fertilizer from Government-supported cooperatives, new schools, and hamlet-level medical aid. The aim is to give the farmer an economic stake which he will want to defend.

Communist guerrilla strategy is to erode Government support and isolate the Government from the people by attacks, assassinations, and threats. The guerrillas themselves are to live among the people like the fish in the sea, according to Mao Tse-tung's much-quoted statement. The strategic hamlet strategy is the opposite of this. It calls for tying the people to their Government by hamlet councils and Government services at the hamlet level, while at the same time isolating the Viet Cong from *their* sources of supplies and recruits among the people. The aim, in short, is to get the guerrilla fish out of the water.

To date about half the population—nearly 7 million people—live in about 5,000 strategic hamlets. Another 5,000 strategic hamlets must be organized before the program is complete even in the first, essentially military phase.

But already the program is beginning to pay off. One result is that an estimated half million people previously under Viet Cong control are now under Government control and protection. Morale in the countryside is up, and this is reflected by increased voluntary intelligence from peasants to the armed forces, a sign the people not only think the Government is winning but are willing to take risks to help it win. Perhaps the most important result is the intangible knitting together of Government and people.

Without in any way detracting from the vital heroic contribution of our advisers and logistic support personnel, of whom 20 were killed by Viet Cong action last year, we should in all of this be clear about one thing. The Vietnamese are fighting this war—and fighting it valiantly. About 5,000 of them were killed last year. While most of these were in the armed forces, this total also includes village officials and militia, schoolteachers and malaria workers. During the same period about 30,000 casualties of all kinds were inflicted on the Viet Cong.

I would thus say there is reason for some optimism. However, this is going to be a long, hard struggle. The Viet Cong remain very strong and very determined. There is no sign that the bloc is faltering in its support for the attack on South Viet-Nam. We are dealing with an enemy who is patient and counts on our impatience, who is willing to accept adversity and hopes we are not.

But we are satisfied that we have a sound strategy; progress is being made, and the Vietnamese have certainly demonstrated their capacity for sacrifice and the determination to survive as a free people. As President Kennedy said in his state of the Union message, 'The spearpoint of aggression has been blunted in South Viet-Nam.'[1]

The President's statement justifiably has an optimistic ring, and I think it well for me to close on that note.

[1] See pp. 1–6 above.

I close on that note not only for South Viet-Nam but for Southeast Asia as a whole. However, I would not want this to be interpreted as any cheap or careless optimism, for this would not be justified. Rather my optimism is based on the conviction that, working in free association with three peoples, we enjoy an advantage which the Communists can never hope to emulate. This we are doing in Southeast Asia. I have no doubt that our investment is a wise one and that to it the American people will continue to give that persevering support which freedom always demands of any people.

Speech by the United States Secretary of State, Mr. Rusk, to the Economic Club of New York, 22 April 1963[1] (extract)

. . . According to Communist propaganda, the war in South Viet-Nam is a civil war, a local uprising. The truth is that it is an aggression organized, directed, and partly supplied from North Viet-Nam. It is conducted by hardened Communist political organizers and guerrilla leaders trained in North Viet-Nam, who, upon their arrival in the South, recruit local assistance. This has been done in a variety of ways, including terror and assassination. Schoolteachers, health workers, malaria eradication teams, local officials to the Republic—these were the first targets of the assassins. But many ordinary villagers who refused to cooperate with the Communist guerrillas likewise have been ruthlessly killed.

This assault on South Viet-Nam was a major Communist enterprise, carefully and elaborately prepared, heavily staffed, and relentlessly pursued. It made headway. In 1961 President Diem appealed for further assistance and President Kennedy responded promptly and affirmatively.[2]

The strategic importance of South Viet-Nam is plain. It controls the mouth of the Mekong River, the main artery of Southeast Asia. The loss of South Viet-Nam would put the remaining states of Southeast Asia in mortal danger.

But there are larger reasons why the defense of South Viet-Nam is vital to us and to the whole free world. We cannot be indifferent to the fate of 14 million people who have fought hard against communism—including nearly 1 million who fled their former homes to avoid living under Communist tyranny. Since we went to the aid of Greece and Turkey 16 years ago, it has been the attitude of the United States to assist peoples who resist Communist aggression. We have seen this form of attack fail in Burma, Malaya, and the Philippines. The South Vietnamese are determined to win their battle, and they deserve our help.

Critics have complained that South Viet-Nam is not a full constitutional democracy and that our aid has been subject to waste and mismanagement. Let us be clear that these criticisms are not merely alibis for inaction. For in passing judgment, let us recall that we are talking about a nation which has been responsible for its own affairs for less than a decade, about a people who have had no peace since 1941 and little experience in direct participation in political affairs. Their four national elections, their thousands of elected hamlet councils, and their forthcoming village council elections show steady movement toward a constitutional system resting upon popular consent.

But let us also recall that Viet-Nam is fighting a war—a mean, frustrating,

---

[1] D.S.B., 13 May 1963, pp. 727–32.   [2] See Documents, 1961, pp. 593–5.

and nerve-racking struggle—and fighting it with courage and determination. The overriding unfinished business is to achieve public safety in order that the country can resume its march toward peace and prosperity. This in itself requires the utmost effort in good administration, in the effective use of available resources, as well as dedicated leadership of an aroused people. I do not defend mistakes or failures which can be put right; but I do wish to enlist your understanding for an effort which includes perseverance and gallantry and sacrifice. And I have no doubt about the ability of South Viet-Nam to take an honored place among modern nations as it rids itself of the enemies gnawing at its vitals.

Our role in South Viet-Nam is a limited and supporting role. We provide technical, logistical, training, and advisory assistance. We have no combat units as such in South Viet-Nam, although many of our military personnel—and some civilians—come under fire in combat situations and we have suffered some casualties. The some 12,000 men we have there are among our finest; their skill and courage and dedication make debtors of us all.

I would point out that we are not alone in assisting the Republic of Viet-Nam. Ten other nations are helping in one way or another in this struggle. We hope that they will do more and that many other non-Communists will contribute. For the whole free world has a vital interest in the defeat of this Communist aggression against South Viet-Nam.

Understandably there are occasional differences of view between the Government in Saigon or Vietnamese officers in the field and their American advisers. But they and we are all committed to success for the Republic of Viet-Nam. It is the Vietnamese who are waging the war. Some 4,000 Vietnamese soldiers were killed and some 6,000 wounded in action during the past year. And they exacted nearly 30,000 casualties in return.

Colonel Serong, the Commander of the Australian advisers in Viet-Nam, has said: 'The typical Vietnamese soldier is as good as you will find. He is brave and he is tough.'

We believe that the Vietnamese, with our help, have developed winning tactics.

With the assistance of helicopters, airplanes, and radios the Government forces are able to maintain the initiative and, increasingly, to achieve the advantage of surprise.

The 'strategic hamlet' program is producing excellent results. A strategic hamlet is a hamlet with a defensive perimeter and a trained and armed militia. Usually it also has a radio with which to call for help if it is under attack.

As the Communist attack is political and economic as well as military, so is the response. The Government of Viet-Nam—and we—attach the greatest importance to the civic action side of the strategic hamlet program. The hamlets are governed by councils elected by secret ballot. In addition—and not least important—the Government is supplying the hamlets with schools, medical aid, cheap fertilizer from Government-supported cooperatives, low-interest agricultural loans, and other agricultural extension services.

Already approximately 7 million Vietnamese live in well over 5,000 strategic hamlets. The program calls for the completion of another 3,000 by the end of this year. Morale in the countryside has begun to rise. An estimated half a million people formerly under Viet Cong control now have increasingly effective Government protection.

The strategic hamlet system provides strength against the Communists in the countryside. The Communists are no longer, in Mao's figure of speech, fish swimming in a sea of peasants. Every bush is no longer their ally. They are getting hungrier. To the Vietnamese peasant they look less and less like winners.

The villagers are fighting when attacked and are volunteering all-important information on their own initiative to the Government forces.

Thousands of the *montagnards*—the hardy mountain tribesmen—have been armed and trained to fight.

Rice production is up, and rice exports have been resumed. Defections from the Viet Cong have risen—though these are mostly locally recruited auxiliaries, not the hardened Communist cadres. The Viet Cong is losing more weapons than are the Government forces. Viet Cong attacks are running at less than half the rate of January 1962. Several Viet Cong strongholds have been penetrated and supplies and installations destroyed. The Viet Cong has been unable to carry out its plan to escalate to larger military units and to more conventional warfare.

The Communists have a lot at stake in this struggle and will not quit easily. But the men and women who were deceived, exploited, or enrolled by force by the Communists now have a chance to rally to the side of the national government. Last week, on the first anniversary of the initiation of the strategic hamlet program, President Diem proclaimed 'Campaign Open Arms.'[1] This is an offer of clemency and assistance and jobs to all who desert the Communists. And even those who have trespassed against the law, and have already been condemned, or who are subject to court trial, may redeem themselves by 'meritorious patriotic acts.'

We applaud this statesmanlike offer. It is similar to the one the late great Ramon Magsaysay used with such good effect in breaking the power of Huks in the Philippines a decade ago.

Communist aggression against South Viet-Nam is, of course, intimately related to the refusal of the Communists to give full support to the Geneva Accords on Laos.[2] Although it was not my intention to speak of Laos this evening—and anything I might say about that country might be disproved by the tickers which you will read on the way out of the hall—the most recent events in that unhappy land-locked country call for brief comment. The Pathet Lao, with strong backing from Hanoi and other Communist countries, have refused to give Prince Souvanna Phouma and his coalition the support and cooperation which were pledged at Geneva. The international machinery established by those accords has not been allowed to function with full effect. The writ of the Central Government has not run in Pathet Lao controlled areas. Viet Minh military personnel have not, we believe, been fully withdrawn.

We are making every effort to ascertain whether all signatories of the Geneva Accords are prepared to support those agreements or whether some are moving to destroy them. If those agreements collapse, most serious and dangerous issues will arise and once again we shall have to determine what steps can be taken to insure that the Laotian people are left alone in peace and not overrun and exploited by those who would commit aggression.

[1] *Current Documents, 1963*, p. 849.
[2] For the 1954 Geneva Accord on Laos, see *American Foreign Policy, 1950–1955, Basic Documents*, vol. I, pp. 775–85; for the 1962 Accord, see *Documents, 1962*, pp. 753–61.

Returning to Viet-Nam: We cannot promise, or expect, a quick victory there. The enemy is elusive and determined, and relatively small numbers can disrupt the normal processes of a going society. It took 8 years to wipe out the Communist terrorists in Malaya—and they were far from a major Communist base.

But there is a good basis for encouragement. The Vietnamese are on their way to success and need our help; not just our material help—they need that—but our sympathetic understanding and comradeship. I can understand the discontent which surrounds any important task still unfinished. I cannot understand anyone who would quit, withhold our resources, abandon a brave people to those who are out to bury us and every other free and independent nation. That we cannot and will not do.

Because this is a battle to the end between freedom and coercion. There are many signs that the other side is involved with difficulties and disappointments. This is no time for us to relax our effort. There are many ways to quit: by refusing us the defense budgets we need; by refusing us the foreign aid resources we need; by refusing to pursue energetically our own great private enterprises abroad; by withdrawing our full support from the United Nations and from our several alliances. There are many ways to quit.

But this is no time to quit, because it is being demonstrated right around the world that this great international community of independent states has seized the commitment of peoples in the most unsuspecting places and that those who have become independent are stubbornly resolved to remain so. And as we work with them toward that kind of a decent world community, of independent states cooperating across national frontiers, we shall find allies right around the world; in moments of great crisis there are not nearly so many neutralists as you might have supposed.

Communiqué issued by the President of South Vietnam, Ngo Dinh Diem, and the United States Ambassador, Mr. Nolting, Saigon, 17 May 1963[1]

The Government of Vietnam and the American Embassy announced on May 17 that agreement has been reached regarding funding for counter-insurgency and other economic development projects, particularly those supporting the Strategic Hamlet Program, during 1963. The agreement provides *inter alia* for the continuation of counter-insurgency projects supported under the piastre-purchase agreement announced in August, 1962.[2] As explained at that time, the latter was an extraordinary arrangement necessitated by the fact that full provision for the counter-insurgency operations in question was not made either in the Vietnamese budget for 1962 or in the United States AID Program. It was planned that the continuation of these operations would be budgeted and programmed in a manner calculated to be responsive to the requirements of the present situation.

Under the agreement just announced, the Government of Vietnam has undertaken to supplement U.S.-owned funds and counterpart, so as to make available up to $2.3 billion piastres during calendar year 1963. The United States is also

---

[1] *Current Documents, 1963*, pp. 854–5.
[2] This agreement was announced on 11 August 1962.

providing some $55 million in the form of agricultural products, barbed wire, weapons for hamlet militia, cement, fertilizer and other commodities for the program.

Counter-insurgency projects will continue to be initiated and developed by the Vietnamese authorities, and all of them will be fully coordinated between the Vietnamese and American central committees, as in the past. The execution of projects will also continue to be closely coordinated between the Vietnamese authorities and American experts in the provinces.

During the course of the discussions, it was also reaffirmed that the scale of the U.S. advisory and support effort in Vietnam is directly related to security requirements and to the need to bring about throughout the country the economic and social improvements envisaged in the strategic hamlet program. Although at this time the present level of the advisory and support effort is still necessary, as the security situation improves and as the strategic hamlet programme progresses, it is expected that the need for foreign assistance, both in terms of material and personnel, will be progressively lightened.

Proclamation by President Diem, 21 August 1963[1]

Recently, in the world, particularly in South East Asia, and more particularly still, in Laos, the Communists have provoked developments which have a direct bearing on the security of the borders of Viet Nam.

At the same time, at home, while among our people and our army, each and all are giving the best of themselves to fight Communist aggression, in the settlement of the problems raised by the General Association of Buddhism, the Government has adopted an attitude of extreme conciliation in the past three months—all our compatriots have seen this for themselves—but the Government's efforts have not met with a similar attitude on the part of a few who indulge in political speculation, exploit religion, and take advantage of the desire of extreme conciliation of the Government to multiply illegal acts with the aim of stirring up disturbances to sabotage that policy, prevent the application of the law, damage the prestige of Buddhism, thereby only benefiting Communism.

For those reasons,

Under article 44 of the Constitution of the Republic of Viet Nam,[2] I declare a state of siege throughout the national territory as from August 21, 1963, confer upon the Army of the Republic of Viet Nam the responsibility of taking all the necessary measures prescribed in the Decree[3] promulgating the state of siege to restore security and public order, so that the State may be protected, Communism defeated, freedom secured, and democracy achieved.

[1] *Current Documents, 1963*, p. 862.
[2] Which reads: 'The President of the Republic may sign a decree proclaiming a state of emergency, alert, or siege in one or many areas; this decree may temporarily suspend the application of one or many laws in these areas.'
[3] President Diem, on 20 August 1963, signed Decree 84–TTP declaring a state of siege throughout Vietnam beginning from the day of publication of the decree and continuing until further notice.

Declaration by the Government of South Vietnam, 21 August 1963[1]

I. Against a background of underdevelopment, dissension and Communist subversive war, our aim is to create the most favorable conditions for the implementation of the Constitution—with full respect for its spirit—and for the democratic and equal application of the law to all, without discrimination of classes, races or religions. Such is the national policy and the Government is absolutely determined to carry that policy fully into effect.

II. In the 'Buddhist affair', the Government's policy is essentially an endeavour to implement the national policy mentioned above. This endeavour is being pursued with the same patience and the same determination.

It is this very determination which has prompted the President of the Republic to decree martial law[2] first to break the systematic sabotage of this whole policy by a minority of bonzes of the General Association of Buddhists, and next, to restore the favourable conditions for the application of the policy of the Government. Everyone must admit that this policy is not only reasonable, but that it is also based on extreme patience.

III. The Government is therefore strongly determined not to tolerate: the exploitation of religion for political purposes; the turning of pagodas—high places for prayer, meditation and sanctification—into quarters for agitation and propaganda; terrorism and plotting against the security of the State; the intoxication of innocent people and the manipulation of minds in the process of which people are incited to commit suicide and their bodies exploited for 49 days for the purpose of organizing meetings, and manifestations against the security of the State.

In the higher interest of the State, and out of respect for Buddhism, the Government considers that all such acts are criminal, especially as the country is at war.

IV. All those who have been affected by the first measures of martial law are well treated, and freedom will be restored to them quickly in measure as they stop confusing the spiritual and the temporal and exploiting religion for political ends. On this condition, bonzes and nuns will all return to their own pagodas, excluding those who have actually plotted against the security of the state while the latter is at war.

V. All the civilian and military cadres must act in accordance with the directives defined above.

Statement by the United States Department of State, 21 August 1963[3]

On the basis of information from Saigon, it appears that the Government of the Republic of Viet-Nam has instituted serious repressive measures against Vietnamese Buddhist leaders. The action represents a direct violation by the Vietnamese Government of assurances that it was pursuing a policy of reconciliation with the Buddhists. The United States deplores repressive actions of this nature.

[1] *Current Documents, 1963*, p. 863.   [2] See p. 370 above.
[3] *D.S.B.*, 9 September 1963, p. 398.

The United States Department of State to the United States Ambassador in Saigon, Mr. Lodge, cablegram, 24 August 1963[1]

It is now clear that whether military proposed martial law or whether Nhu tricked them into it, Nhu took advantage of its imposition to smash pagodas with police and Tung's Special Forces loyal to him, thus placing onus on military in eyes of world and Vietnamese people. Also clear that Nhu has manœuvered himself into commanding position.

U.S. Government cannot tolerate situation in which power lies in Nhu's hands. Diem must be given chance to rid himself of Nhu and his coterie and replace them with best military and political personalities available.

If, in spite of all of your efforts, Diem remains obdurate and refuses, then we must face the possibility that Diem himself cannot be preserved.

We now believe immediate action must be taken to prevent Nhu from consolidating his position further. Therefore, unless you in consultation with Harkins perceive overriding objections you are authorized to proceed along following lines:

(1) First we must press on appropriate levels of GVN following line:

    (a) USG cannot accept actions against Buddhists taken by Nhu and his collaborators under cover martial law.

    (b) Prompt dramatic actions redress situation must be taken, including repeal of decree 10, release of arrested monks, nuns, etc.

(2) We must at same time also tell key military leaders that U.S. would find it impossible to continue support GVN militarily and economically unless above steps are taken immediately which we recognize requires removal of Nhus from the scene. We wish give Diem reasonable opportunity to remove Nhus, but if he remains obdurate, then we are prepared to accept the obvious implication that we can no longer support Diem. You may also tell appropriate military commanders we will give them direct support in any interim period of breakdown central government mechanism.

(3) We recognize the necessity of removing taint on military for pagoda raids and placing blame squarely on Nhu. You are authorized to have such statements made in Saigon as you consider desirable to achieve this objective. We are prepared to take same line here and to have Voice of America make statement along lines contained in next numbered telegram whenever you give the word, preferably as soon as possible.

Concurrently, with above, Ambassador and country team should urgently examine all possible alternative leadership and make detailed plans as to how we might bring about Diem's replacement if this should become necessary.

Assume you will consult with General Harkins re any precautions necessary protect American personnel during crisis period.

You will understand that we cannot from Washington give you detailed instructions as to how this operation should proceed, but you will also know we will back you to the hilt on actions you take to achieve our objectives.

Needless to say we have held knowledge of this telegram to minimum

---

[1] *New York Times* Staff, *The Pentagon Papers* (Chicago and New York, 1971), Doc. 35, pp. 194–5.

essential people and assume you will take similar precautions to prevent premature leaks.

The United States Central Intelligence Agency Station Chief in Saigon, Mr. Richardson, to the Director of the C.I.A. in Washington, Mr. McCone, cablegram, 28 August 1963[1]

Situation here has reached point of no return. Saigon is armed camp. Current indications are that Ngo family have dug in for last ditch battle. It is our considered estimate that General officers cannot retreat now. Conein's meeting with Gen. Khiem (Saigon 0346) reveals that overwhelming majority of general officers, excepting Dinh and Cao, are united, have conducted prior planning, realize that they must proceed quickly, and understand that they have no alternative but to go forward. Unless the generals are neutralized before being able to launch their operation, we believe they will act and that they have good chance to win. If General Dinh primarily and Tung secondly cannot be neutralized at outset, there may be widespread fighting in Saigon and serious loss of life.

We recognize the crucial stakes and involved and have no doubt that the generals do also. Situation has changed drastically since 21 August. If the Ngo family wins now, they and Vietnam will stagger on to final defeat at the hands of their own people and the VC. Should a generals' revolt occur and be put down, GVN will sharply reduce American presence in SVN. Even if they did not do so, it seems clear that American public opinion and Congress, as well as world opinion, would force withdrawal or reduction of American support for VN under the Ngo administration.

Bloodshed can be avoided if the Ngo family would step down before the coming armed action. . . . It is obviously preferable that the generals conduct this effort without apparent American assistance. Otherwise, for a long time in the future, they will be vulnerable to charges of being American puppets, which they are not in any sense. Nevertheless, we all understand that the effort must succeed and that whatever needs to be done on our part must be done. If this attempt by the generals does not take place or if it fails, we believe it no exaggeration to say that VN runs serious risk of being lost over the course of time.

Statement by President de Gaulle, 29 August 1963[2]

The French Government is following with attention and emotion the grave events occurring in Vietnam. The task accomplished in the past by France in Cochin China, Annam and Tonkin, the ties she has maintained in the country as a whole, and the interest she takes in its development explains why she understands so well and shares sincerely in the trials of the Vietnamese people. In addition, France's knowledge of the merits of this people makes her appreciate

[1] Ibid., Doc. 38, pp. 196–7.

[2] French Embassy Press and Information Division, New York, *Major Addresses, Statements and Press Conferences of General Charles de Gaulle: May 19, 1959–31 January, 1964* (New York, 1964), p. 241. This statement was made in the French Council of Ministers.

the role they would be capable of playing in the current situation in Asia for their own progress and to further international understanding, once they could go ahead with their activities independently of the outside, in internal peace and unity and in harmony with their neighbors. Today more than ever, this is what France wishes for Vietnam as a whole. Naturally it is up to this people, and to them alone, to choose the means of achieving it, but any national effort that would be carried out in Vietnam would find France ready, to the extent of her own possibilities, to establish cordial cooperation with this country.

United Nations Secretary General, U Thant, to President Diem, 31 August 1963[1]

I have the honour to inform Your Excellency that the Asian and African Member States of the United Nations, through their representatives to this Organization, have come to see me to express their grave concern at the situation that has arisen in the Republic of Viet-Nam, and have asked me to request Your Excellency's Government to take all necessary steps to normalize the situation by ensuring the exercise of fundamental human rights to all sections of the population in the Republic.

It is in the light of humanitarian considerations, to which we all, as members of the human family, are bound, that I have felt it my duty to transmit the above request, adding to it my own personal appeal to Your Excellency, as the head of the Government of Viet-Nam, to find a solution to the questions which are so deeply affecting the population of your country, in accordance with the principles laid down in the Universal Declaration of Human Rights.[2]

President Diem to Secretary General U Thant, 5 September 1963[3]

I have the honour to acknowledge the receipt of your message in which you were kind enough to inform me of the concern shown by the representatives of African and Asian States Members of the United Nations with regard to the situation in Viet-Nam.[4]

I thank you for the opportunity this gives me to clarify fully the Buddhist question, to which your message refers.

First of all, I can assure you that there has been no suppression of Buddhism in Viet-Nam since the establishment of the Republic. Any allegation to the contrary is nothing but an imperialist invention. The Buddhist question is not a question of suppression, but a phenomenon of the development of Buddhism, a growing-pain of Buddhism, which should be viewed in its historical context, that of an under-developed, newly independent country—a country, in other words, which is short of cadres and of financial resources but desirous of rapidly asserting itself. Like the other movements in process of expansion which are linked to the independence movement, the Buddhist movement began to develop all the more quickly because it was held in check during the colonial period. In this unduly rapid development, Buddhism, like other movements, both public and private,

---

[1] G.A.O.R., Eighteenth Session, Annexes, Agenda item 77, pp. 2–3.
[2] Documents, 1947–1948, pp. 855–61.
[3] G.A.O.R., Eighteenth Session, Annexes, Agenda item 77, p. 3.
[4] See immediately preceding document.

is suffering from a shortage of cadres both qualitatively and quantitatively, and this offers the East and the West an opportunity to infiltrate, if not to impose their own cadres who try to take over the leadership.

This results in ideological deviations, which in practice are reflected in techniques of political agitation and propaganda and in the organization of riots and *coups d'état* for the benefit of foreign interests. This is the tragedy of Buddhism in Viet-Nam; it will no doubt be the tragedy of Buddhism in the other countries of Asia.

We hope that, instead of allowing themselves to be poisoned by an international conspiracy of the East or the West against the Republic of Viet-Nam, the fraternal African and Asian countries will benefit from the experience in our country and forestall the crises which they will possibly have to face.

Every Government is in duty bound to uphold public order and also to ensure that alien cadres both from the East and the West, with their specific ideologies and policies, do not mar the original purity of Buddhism and the other movements. In other words, the action taken by the Government of the Republic of Viet-Nam in connexion with the Buddhist question has no other objective than to free the Buddhist hierarchy from all outside pressure and to shield the development of Buddhism from any external influence that works against the interests of the Buddhist religion and against the higher interests of the State.

I am also happy to be able to inform you that a solution has already been found to the Buddhist question which bears witness to the merits of the policy pursued by the Viet-Namese Government. Freed from the evil influence of foreign agitators and adventurers, the Buddhist hierarchy has resumed charge of the Buddhist community and of the pagodas throughout the territory of Viet-Nam.

I request you to be kind enough to communicate this message to the representatives of the African and Asian States Members of the United Nations.

White House Statement issued following the visit of the Secretary of Defence, Mr. McNamara, and the Chairman of the Joint Chiefs of Staff, General Taylor, to South Vietnam, 2 October 1965[1]

Secretary McNamara and General Taylor reported to the President this morning and to the National Security Council this afternoon. Their report included a number of classified findings and recommendations which will be the subject of further review and action. Their basic presentation was endorsed by all members of the Security Council and the following statement of United States policy was approved by the President on the basis of recommendations received from them and from Ambassador [Henry Cabot] Lodge.

1. The security of South Viet-Nam is a major interest of the United States as other free nations. We will adhere to our policy of working with the people and Government of South Viet-Nam to deny this country to communism and to suppress the externally stimulated and supported insurgency of the Viet Cong as promptly as possible. Effective performance in this undertaking is the central objective of our policy in South Viet-Nam.

[1] *D.S.B.*, 21 October 1963, p. 624. The Secretary of Defence and the Chairman of the Joint Chiefs of Staff visited South Vietnam from 24 September to 1 October 1963, on a special mission ordered by President Kennedy, 21 September 1963.

2. The military program in South Viet-Nam has made progress and is sound in principle, though improvements are being energetically sought.

3. Major U.S. assistance in support of this military effort is needed only until the insurgency has been suppressed or until the national security forces of the Government of South Viet-Nam are capable of suppressing it.

Secretary McNamara and General Taylor reported their judgment that the major part of the U.S. military task can be completed by the end of 1965, although there may be a continuing requirement for a limited number of U.S. training personnel. They reported that by the end of this year, the U.S. program for training Vietnamese should have progressed to the point where 1,000 U.S. military personnel assigned to South Viet-Nam can be withdrawn.

4. The political situation in South Viet-Nam remains deeply serious. The United States has made clear its continuing opposition to any repressive actions in South Viet-Nam.[1] While such actions have not yet significantly affected the military effort, they could do so in the future.

5. It remains the policy of the United States, in South Viet-Nam as in other parts of the world, to support the efforts of the people of that country to defeat aggression and to build a peaceful and free society.

Ambassador Lodge to the United States Department of State, cablegram, 5 October 1963[2]

1. Lt. Col. Conein met with Gen. Duong Van Minh at Gen. Minh's Headquarters on Le Van Duyet for one hour and ten minutes morning of 5 Oct. 63. This meeting was at the initiative of Gen. Minh and has been specifically cleared in advance by Ambassador Lodge. No other persons were present. The conversation was conducted in French.

2. Gen. Minh stated that he must know American Government's position with respect to a change in the Government of Vietnam within the very near future. Gen. Minh added the Generals were aware of the situation is deteriorating rapidly and that action to change the Government must be taken or the war will be lost to the Viet Cong because the Government no longer has the support of the people. Gen. Minh identified among the other Generals participating with him in this plan:
Maj. Gen. Tran Van Don
Brig. Gen. Tran Thien Khiem
Maj. Gen. Tran Van Kim

3. Gen. Minh made it clear that he did not expect any specific American support for an effort on the part of himself and his colleagues to change the Government but he states he does need American assurances that the USG will not rpt not attempt to thwart this plan.

4. Gen. Minh also stated that he himself has no political ambitions nor do any of the other General Officers except perhaps, he said laughingly, Gen. Ton That Dinh. Gen. Minh insisted that his only purpose is to win the war. He added

---

[1] On 14 September 1963 President Diem issued a decree ending martial law from 16 September 1963. See also, p. 371 above.
[2] *The Pentagon Papers*, Doc. 48, pp. 213–15.

emphatically that to do this continuation of American Military and Economic Aid at the present level (he said one and one half million dollars per day) is necessary.

5. Gen. Minh outlined three possible plans for the accomplishment of the change of Government:

a. Assassination of Ngo Dinh Nhu and Ngo Dinh Can keeping President Diem in Office. Gen. Minh said this was the easiest plan to accomplish.

b. The encirclement of Saigon by various military units particularly the unit at Ben Cat.

c. Direct confrontation between military units involved in the coup and loyalist military units in Saigon. In effect, dividing the city of Saigon into sectors and cleaning it out pocket by pocket. Gen. Minh claims under the circumstances Diem and Nhu could count on the loyalty of 5,500 troops within the city of Saigon.

6. Conein replied to Gen. Minh that he could not answer specific questions as to USG non-interference nor could he give any advice concerning the best of the three plans.

7. Gen. Minh went on to explain that the most dangerous men in South Viet-Nam are Ngo Dinh Nhu, Ngo Dinh Can and Ngo Trong Hieu. Minh stated that Hieu was formerly a Communist and still has Communist sympathies. When Col. Conein remarked that he had considered Col. Tung as one of the more dangerous individuals, Gen. Minh stated 'if I get rid of Nhu, Can and Hieu, Col. Tung will be on his knees before me.'

8. Gen. Minh also stated that he was worried as to the role of Gen. Tran Thien Khiem since Khiem may have played a double role in August. Gen. Minh asked that copies of the documents previously passed to Gen. Khiem (plan of Camp Long Thanh and munitions inventory at that camp) be passed to Gen. Minh personally for comparison with papers passed by Khiem to Minh purportedly from CAS.

9. Minh further stated that one of the reasons they are having to act quickly was the fact that many regimental, battalion and company commanders are working on coup plans of their own which could be abortive and a 'catastrophe.'

10. Minh appeared to understand Conein's position of being unable to comment at the present moment but asked that Conein again meet with Gen. Minh to discuss the specific plan of operations which Gen. Minh hopes to put into action. No specific date was given for this next meeting. Conein was again non-committal in his reply. Gen. Minh once again indicated his understanding and stated that he would arrange to contact Conein in the near future and hoped that Conein would be able to meet with him and give the assurance outlined above.

The White House to Ambassador Lodge, cablegram, 5 October 1963[1]

In conjunction with decisions and recommendations in separate EPTEL, President today approved recommendation that no initiative should now be taken to give any active covert encouragement to a coup. There should, however,

---

[1] Ibid., Doc. 50, pp. 215–16.

be urgent covert effort with closest security, under broad guidance of Ambassador to identify and build contacts with possible alternative leadership as and when it appears. Essential that this effort be totally secure and fully deniable and separated entirely from normal political analysis and reporting and other activities of country team. We repeat that this effort is not repeat not to be aimed at active promotion of coup but only at surveillance and readiness. In order to provide plausibility to denial suggest you and no one else in Embassy issue these instructions orally to Acting Station Chief and hold him responsible to you alone for making appropriate contacts and reporting to you alone.

All reports to Washington on this subject should be on this channel.[1]

Proclamation by the Military Revolutionary Council of South Vietnam, 1 November 1963[2] (extracts)

Soldiers in the army, security service, civil defense force, and people's forces:

During the last nine years countless numbers of us have sacrificed our blood and flesh to defend the country against the Communists. Innumerable soldiers have fallen on the battlefield in order to score glorious victories for the Fatherland. Meanwhile, the Ngo Dinh Diem Government, abusing power, has thought only of personal ambition and slighted the Fatherland's interests.

The people's lawful rights were trampled upon, thus creating great injustices in society. It maintained an incompetent system of cadres. If our sacrifices and victories won the people's confidence and love, the rottenness and corruption of the Ngo Dinh Diem clique destroyed the confidence of the people and of friendly nations in the free world.

Thus, let us ask whether all our merits achieved up to the present time had any chance of bringing about any result or security to the country at a time when the people are fed up with the family-rule regime, which places money and power above all.

Never has our soldiers' honor been damaged as it is now. Ngo Dinh Diem has utilized the army's name to carry out dark acts for personal aggrandizement and to consolidate his position. Countless genuine national elements have been arrested. It has abused the army's name to infringe on freedom of religion, arrested priests, and aroused immeasurable disgust and indignation among the people. . . .

Dear comrades in arms, will the tradition allow us to sit idly by and let the despots lead the nation to annihilation? Will it allow us to make sacrifices and bow our heads in obedience to a regime whose rottenness, injustice, and dictatorship are being condemned by all the people and the whole world?

No. We will never allow ourselves to remain silent. As you know, we have carried out a revolution to save the country and to rebuild a powerful army not controlled by incompetent cadres or an unjust rule.

We have no political ambitions; we act not for fame or benefit but to save our beloved Fatherland, which is in danger. Our acts have an urgent nature, because unless we act, we ourselves will be sacrificed, one by one and uselessly.

The army has swung into action. The task of you all is to unite. Obey discipline

---

[1] This cablegram was transmitted on the Central Intelligence Agency channel.

[2] *Current Documents, 1963*, p. 878.

and clearsightedly see the dangerous situation caused by the Communists and the Ngo Dinh Diem clique.

We officers call on you to continue the anti-Communist work that you have been valiantly carrying out on all battlefields and to unite and be single-minded in order to save our beloved Fatherland.

The revolution will certainly be successful. The army will certainly be victorious in building a sound country. You will be correctly and efficiently commanded. The people have confidence in you. We officers place all our expectations in you.

Salute of certain victory . . .

Message from President Johnson to the Chairman of the Military Revolutionary Council of South Vietnam, General Minh, 31 December 1963[1]

DEAR GENERAL MINH: As we enter the New Year of 1964, I want to wish you, your Revolutionary Government, and your people full success in the long and arduous war which you are waging so tenaciously and bravely against the Viet Cong forces directed and supported by the Communist regime in Hanoi. Ambassador [Henry Cabot] Lodge and Secretary [of Defense Robert S.] McNamara have told me about the serious situation which confronts you and of the plans which you are developing to enable your armed forces and your people to redress this situation.

This new year provides a fitting opportunity for me to pledge on behalf of the American Government and people a renewed partnership with your government and people in your brave struggle for freedom. The United States will continue to furnish you and your people with the fullest measure of support in this bitter fight. We shall maintain in Viet-Nam American personnel and material as needed to assist you in achieving victory.

Our aims are, I know, identical with yours: to enable your government to protect its people from the acts of terror perpetrated by Communist insurgents from the north. As the forces of your government become increasingly capable of dealing with this aggression, American military personnel in South Viet-Nam can be progressively withdrawn.

The United States Government shares the view of your government that 'neutralization' of South Viet-Nam is unacceptable. As long as the Communist regime in North Viet-Nam persists in its aggressive policy, neutralization of South Viet-Nam would only be another name for a Communist takeover. Peace will return to your country just as soon as the authorities in Hanoi cease and desist from their terrorist aggression.

Thus, your government and mine are in complete agreement on the political aspects of your war against the forces of enslavement, brutality, and material misery. Within this framework of political agreement we can confidently continue and improve our cooperation.

I am pleased to learn from Secretary McNamara about the vigorous operations which you are planning to bring security and an improved standard of living to your people.

[1] *D.S.B.*, 27 January 1964, pp. 121-2.

I wish to congratulate you particularly on your work for the unity of all your people, including the Hoa Hao[1] and Cao Dai[2] against the Viet Cong. I know from my own experience in Viet-Nam how warmly the Vietnamese people respond to a direct human approach and how they have hungered for this in their leaders. So again I pledge the energetic support of my country to your government and your people.

We will do our full part to ensure that under your leadership your people may win a victory—a victory for freedom and justice and human welfare in Viet-Nam.

C. JAPAN

Treaty of Commerce, Establishment and Navigation between Great Britain and Japan, London, 14 November 1962, with Protocols[3]

The United Kingdom of Great Britain and Northern Ireland and Japan;

Animated by the desire to maintain and strengthen the amicable relations existing between their respective countries;

Desiring to facilitate and extend still further their mutual relations of trade and commerce; and

Desiring to provide for the continued enjoyment of fair and equitable treatment by their respective nationals and companies;

Have resolved to conclude a Treaty of Commerce, Establishment and Navigation and have appointed as their Plenipotentiaries for this purpose:

The United Kingdom of Great Britain and Northern Ireland (hereinafter referred to as 'the United Kingdom'):

The Right Honourable the Earl of Home, K.T., Her Majestys' Principal Secretary of State for Foreign Affairs;

The Right Honourable Frederick James Erroll, M.P., President of the Board of Trade;

Japan:

His Excellency Mr. Katsumi Ohno, Ambassador Extraordinary and Plenipotentiary of Japan in London;

Who, having communicated their respective full powers, found in good and due form, have agreed as follows:

ARTICLE 1

The territories of the Contracting Parties to which the present Treaty applies are:—

(a) on the part of the United Kingdom, the United Kingdom of Great Britain and Northern Ireland, and any territory to which the present Treaty has been extended in accordance with the provisions of Article 32; and

(b) on the part of Japan, the territory of Japan.

[1] A political-religious sect in provinces southwest of Saigon.
[2] A political-religious sect in Tay Ninh and neighbouring provinces northwest of Saigon.
[3] Cmnd. 1874.

ARTICLE 2

In the present Treaty—

(1) the term 'territory' means, in relation to a Contracting Party any territory of that Contracting Party to which the present Treaty applies;

(2) the term 'nationals':—

(a) means physical persons;

(b) in relation to the United Kingdom means—
all citizens of the United Kingdom and Colonies, all citizens of any territory for the international relations of which the United Kingdom is responsible and all British protected persons; except in each case those who belong to any territory to which the present Treaty may be extended under the provisions of Article 32 but has not been so extended and

(c) in relation to Japan means—
all nationals of Japan;

(3) the term 'vessels':—

(a) in relation to the United Kingdom means all ships registered at a port in any territory of that Contracting Party to which the present Treaty applies; and

(b) in relation to Japan means all ships carrying the papers required by the law of Japan in proof of Japanese nationality;

(4) the term 'companies':—

(a) means all legal persons except physical persons;

(b) in relation to a Contracting Party means all companies which derive their status as such from the law in force in any territory of that Contracting Party to which the present Treaty applies; and

(c) in relation to a country means all companies which derive their status as such from the law in that country.

ARTICLE 3

(1) Nationals of one Contracting Party shall be accorded, with respect to entry into, residence in and departure from any territory of the other treatment not less favourable than that accorded to the nationals of any other foreign country.

(2) The nationals of one Contracting Party who are lawfully present within any territory of the other shall be free to travel anywhere within that territory and shall not be required, for this purpose, to obtain travel documents or permits. Nothing in this paragraph shall, however, be construed so as to prevent a Contracting Party from restricting entry into any place or area within the territory of that Contracting Party to authorised persons for reasons of national security, provided that in such cases the nationals of the other Contracting Party shall be accorded treatment not less favourable than that accorded to the nationals of the former Contracting Party or of any other foreign country.

(3) Any conditions as to the duration of his residence or as to his employment, profession, business or occupation which a national of one Contracting Party who is permitted to reside in any territory of the other is required to observe during the period of his residence in that territory shall be imposed at the time of the grant to him of permission to enter or to reside, shall be made known to him at the time when they are imposed and shall not thereafter be varied so as to make them more restrictive.

(4) Subject to any conditions imposed consistently with the provisions of paragraphs (1) and (3) of this Article, the nationals of one Contracting Party in any territory of the other shall be permitted to engage there in every lawful employment, profession, business or occupation on terms not less favourable than the nationals of any other foreign country.

ARTICLE 4

The nationals of one Contracting Party in any territory of the other shall be exempted from all compulsory service whatsoever in the armed forces, civil defence services or police forces; from all forms of compulsory labour; and from the compulsory performances of all judicial, administrative and municipal functions whatever, other than those imposed by the laws relating to juries. They shall also be exempted from all contributions, whether in money or in kind, imposed as an equivalent for such service or for the performance of such functions.

ARTICLE 5

(1) The nationals of one Contracting Party shall in any territory of the other be accorded liberty of conscience and freedom of worship. In the exercise of these rights they may conduct religious services provided that these services are not contrary to public morals or public order. They shall be at liberty to erect and to maintain buildings for religious purposes provided that such buildings conform to the law applicable generally to buildings of like nature. Such buildings shall be respected and shall not be entered or searched except by due process of law.

(2) The nationals of one Contracting Party shall in any territory of the other also be permitted to bury or cremate their dead according to their religious customs in suitable and convenient places established or maintained for the purpose, subject to the general law relating to the registration of deaths, to burials and cremations, and subject to any non-discriminatory sanitary or medical requirements laid down by the authorities of that territory.

ARTICLE 6

(1) The companies of one Contracting Party shall in any territory of the other be accorded treatment not less favourable than that accorded to the companies of any other foreign country in all matters relative to the carrying on of all kinds of business, including finance, commerce, industry, banking, insurance, shipping and transport, as well as in all matters relative to the establishment and

maintenance for such purpose of branches, agencies, offices, factories and other establishments appropriate to the conduct of their business.

(2) Neither Contracting Party shall in any territory enforce, as a condition for the operation of any company of the other, any requirements as to the nationality of the directors, administrative personnel, technicians, professional consultants, auditors or shareholders of that company more restrictive than requirements applied to the companies of any other foreign country.

ARTICLE 7

(1) The nationals and companies of one Contracting Party shall enjoy in any territory of the other constant and complete protection and security for their persons and property.

(2) Nationals of one Contracting Party taken into the custody of the authorities in any territory of the other, whether in connection with criminal proceedings or otherwise, shall be informed without undue delay of the grounds on which they are so taken. While they are detained in such custody they shall receive reasonable and humane treatment and their property shall not be disposed of except by due process of law.

(3) Nationals and companies of one Contracting Party accused in any territory of the other of crime shall enjoy, on the same conditions and to the same extent as nationals and companies of the latter Contracting Party or of any other foreign country, all rights and privileges in connection with their trials permissible under the law of that territory. They shall be entitled to a public trial without undue delay. This paragraph shall not, however, prohibit the exclusion of the public from all or any part of any trial in the interests of national security or of public safety, order or morals or for the protection of children and young persons.

(4) The nationals and companies of one Contracting Party shall have access to the courts of justice, tribunals and administrative authorities in any territory of the other for the declaration, prosecution or defence of their rights, on terms not less favourable than those enjoyed by the nationals and companies of the latter Contracting Party or of any other foreign country. In any event proceedings to which nationals or companies of one Contracting Party are parties in any territory of the other shall be heard and determined without undue delay.

(5) The nationals and companies of one Contracting Party shall in any proceedings in any territory of the other be at liberty to employ the services of legal advisers and representatives of their choice from among those competent to act in such proceedings. Without prejudice to the foregoing such nationals and companies shall enjoy treatment not less favourable than that accorded to the nationals and companies of the other Contracting Party or of any other foreign country.

(6) Nationals of one Contracting Party shall in all proceedings, other than criminal proceedings, before the courts of justice or tribunals in any territory of the other be at liberty to employ interpreters, who are acceptable to the courts of justice or tribunals, to translate the proceedings of the said courts or tribunals into a language which such nationals can understand, and to translate into the

language in which the proceedings are conducted statements, evidence or arguments put orally by them or on their behalf in any other language.

(7) Nationals of one Contracting Party against whom criminal proceedings are taken before the courts of justice in any territory of the other shall be entitled, if their acquaintance with the language in which the proceedings are conducted is insufficient for them to understand the proceedings and subject to the payment of any appropriate costs, to have the proceedings translated by interpreters into a language which such nationals can understand, unless the said courts consider that the interpretation of any part of the proceedings can without injustice be dispensed with and such nationals, or their representatives, do not object. In any event, any statements, evidence or arguments put orally in a language other than that in which the proceedings are conducted shall be translated into the latter language by interpreters, subject to the payment of any appropriate costs.

(8) In all matters dealt with in this Article, nationals and companies of one Contracting Party in any territory of the other shall not be required to make any payments which are other or more onerous than those imposed on nationals and companies of the latter Contracting Party or of any other foreign country. Moreover nationals of one Contracting Party shall in any territory of the other be admitted to the benefit of free legal assistance and exemption from court fees on the same conditions and to the same extent as the nationals of the latter Contracting Party or of any other foreign country.

ARTICLE 8

(1) The nationals and companies of one Contracting Party shall not be subjected in any territory of the other to any taxation or any requirement connected therewith except under the conditions and with the formalities prescribed by the law in force in that territory.

(2) The nationals and companies of one Contracting Party shall not be subjected in any territory of the other to any taxation or any requirement connected therewith which is other or more onerous than the taxation and connected requirements to which the nationals and companies of the latter Contracting Party in the same circumstances are or may be subjected.

(3) The nationals and companies of one Contracting Party not resident for tax purposes in any territory of the other shall not be subjected in respect of income attributable to their establishments in that territory in which their business activities are carried on to any taxation or any requirement connected therewith which is other or more onerous than the taxation and connected requirements to which the nationals and companies of the latter Contracting Party resident for tax purposes in that territory are subjected in respect of the like income.

(4) The provisions of paragraph (3) of this Article shall not be construed, in relation to any territory of a Contracting Party, as obliging that Contracting Party to grant to nationals of the other who are not resident for tax purposes in that territory the same personal allowances, reliefs and reductions for tax purposes as are granted to the nationals of the former Contracting Party resident for tax purposes in that territory.

(5) Subject to the provisions of paragraph (4) of this Article, the nationals and companies of one Contracting Party shall enjoy, at the hands of the fiscal authorities and tribunals of the other, treatment and protection not less favourable than that accorded to the nationals and companies of the latter Contracting Party.

(6) In all matters referred to in this Article, the treatment accorded by one Contracting Party to nationals and companies of the other shall not be less favourable than that accorded to the nationals and companies of any other foreign country.

(7) The provisions of paragraph (6) of this Article shall not apply to special tax advantages accorded in any territory of either Contracting Party solely by virtue of an agreement for the avoidance of double taxation and the prevention of fiscal evasion with any other foreign country.

(8) The term 'taxation' as used in this Article means taxes of every kind.

ARTICLE 9

The dwellings, offices, warehouses, factories, shops and all other premises owned, leased or occupied by nationals and companies of one Contracting Party in any territory of the other shall be respected. Except under the conditions and with the formalities prescribed by law and applicable to nationals and companies of the latter Contracting Party, such premises shall not be entered or searched, nor shall the contents thereof be seized, examined or inspected.

ARTICLE 10

(1) The nationals and companies of one Contracting Party shall be permitted in any territory of the other to acquire property, movable or immovable, or any interest therein on the same conditions as are applicable to the nationals and companies of any other foreign country.

(2) The nationals and companies of one Contracting Party shall be permitted in any territory of the other to own and to dispose of property, movable or immovable, or any interest therein on the same conditions as are applicable to the nationals and companies of the latter Contracting Party or of any other foreign country.

(3) The nationals and companies of one Contracting Party shall be permitted—

(a) to remove their movable property, and
(b) to transfer the proceeds of the sale of any property, movable or immovable, or of any interest therein, belonging to them

from any territory of the other subject to conditions or restrictions not other or more onerous than those applicable to the nationals and companies of the latter Contracting Party or of any other foreign country.

(4) The provisions of paragraph (2) of this Article relative to the grant of national treatment shall not be construed as extending to the conditions of registration of aircraft in the national register of any territory of either Contracting Party.

(5) Nothing in this Article shall be construed so as to prevent a Contracting Party from restricting in any territory the acquisition, ownership, or disposal of ships or of any interest in ships.

ARTICLE 11

In any case where nationals and companies of one Contracting Party are entitled, under the present Treaty, to carry on business in any territory of the other, they shall be entitled to exercise this right either in person or through agents of their own choice or in both such ways to no less an extent than nationals and companies of any other foreign country.

ARTICLE 12

(1) The nationals and companies of one Contracting Party shall enjoy in any territory of the other treatment not less favourable than that enjoyed by the nationals and companies of any other foreign country with regard to the formation under the law of that territory of new companies.

(2) The nationals and companies of one Contracting Party shall enjoy in any territory of the other treatment not less favourable than that enjoyed by the nationals and companies of the latter Contracting Party or of any other foreign country with regard to the formation and membership under the law of that territory of chambers of commerce or similar bodies.

(3) Neither Contracting Party shall in any territory enforce, in relation to the nationals and companies of the other, any requirements as to the nationality of directors, administrative personnel, technicians, professional consultants, auditors or shareholders of any company of the former Contracting Party more restrictive than requirements applied in relation to the nationals and companies of any other foreign country.

(4) The companies of one Contracting Party more than one half of the interests in which are owned or which are controlled, directly or indirectly, by the nationals or companies of the other shall in all the matters dealt with in the present Treaty be accorded treatment not less favourable than that accorded to the companies of the former Contracting Party more than one half of the interests in which are owned or which are controlled, directly or indirectly, by the nationals and companies of any other foreign country.

ARTICLE 13

The nationals and companies of one Contracting Party shall be accorded in any territory of the other treatment not less favourable than that accorded to the nationals and companies of any other foreign country with respect to the introduction of foreign capital or technology.

ARTICLE 14

The nationals and companies of one Contracting Party shall be accorded equitable treatment in any territory of the other in respect of any measure of

requisition, civil or military, of disposal, limitation, restriction or expropria-
tion, affecting their property, rights and interests, or affecting the property,
rights and interests of any company of the other Contracting Party in which they
own interests, and shall be accorded prompt, adequate and effective compensation for any such measures. Without prejudice to the foregoing, in all matters
dealt with in this Article they shall be accorded in any territory of the other
treatment not less favourable than that accorded to the nationals and companies
of the latter Contracting Party or of any other foreign country.

ARTICLE 15

With respect to customs duties and charges of any kind imposed on or in
connection with importation or exportation or imposed on the international
transfer of payments for imports or exports, and with respect to the method of
levying such duties and charges, and with respect to all rules and formalities in
connection with importation and exportation, the nationals and companies of
one Contracting Party shall be accorded in any territory of the other treatment
not less favourable than that accorded to the nationals and companies of the
latter Contracting Party or of any other foreign country.

ARTICLE 16

(1) With respect to customs duties and charges of any kind imposed on or in
connection with importation or exportation or imposed on the international
transfer of payments for imports or exports, and with respect to the method of
levying such duties and charges, and with respect to all rules and formalities in
connection with the foregoing, any advantage, favour, privilege or immunity
accorded in any territory by one Contracting Party to any product originating
in or destined for any other foreign country shall be accorded to the like product
originating in any territory of the other Contracting Party (from whatever place
arriving) or destined for any such territory.

(2) For the purposes of this Article and of Articles 17 and 18:

   (a) fish, whales and other natural produce of the sea taken by vessels of either
      Contracting Party, and

   (b) products produced or manufactured at sea in vessels of either Contracting
      Party from fish, whales and other natural produce of the sea

shall be deemed to be products originating in the territories of that Contracting
Party.

ARTICLE 17

(1) No prohibition, restriction, rule or formality shall be imposed or maintained on the importation into any territory of one Contracting Party of any
product originating in any territory of the other (from whatever place arriving)
which shall not equally extend to the importation of the like product originating
in any other foreign country.

(2) No prohibition, restriction, rule or formality shall be imposed or maintained on the exportation of any product from any territory of one Contracting

Party to any territory of the other which shall not equally extend to the exportation of the like product to any other foreign country.

(3) In so far as prohibitions or restrictions may be enforced in any of their territories on the importation or exportation of any products, the Contracting Parties undertake as regards import and export licences to do everything in their power to ensure—

(a) that the conditions to be fulfilled and formalities to be observed in order to obtain such licences should be published promptly in such a manner as to enable the public to become acquainted with such conditions and formalities;

(b) that the method of issue of the licences should be as simple and stable as possible;

(c) that the examination of applications and the issue of licences to the applicants should be carried out with the least possible delay;

(d) that the system of issuing licences should be such as to prevent traffic in licences. With this object, a licence issued to any person should state the name of the holder and should not be capable of being used by any other person.

(4) The conditions to be fulfilled or formalities to be observed before quotas are allotted or licences are given in any territory of one Contracting Party in respect of—

(a) the importation of products originating in any territory of the other, or

(b) the exportation of products to any territory of the latter Contracting Party

shall not be more onerous than the conditions to be fulfilled or formalities to be observed before quotas are allotted or licences are given in the case of any other foreign country.

(5) Subject to the requirement that such measures shall not be applied in any arbitrary manner, the general rules laid down in the preceding paragraphs of this Article shall not be construed so as to prevent the adoption by either Contracting Party of measures—

(a) necessary to protect human, animal or plant life or health;

(b) taken for the regulation of the trade in any narcotic substance which is within the scope of any international agreement which relates to the international control of narcotic substances and to which that Contracting Party is a party;

(c) taken in pursuance of obligations under any inter-governmental commodity agreement which conforms to criteria submitted to the CONTRACTING PARTIES to the General Agreement on Tariffs and Trade[1] and not disapproved by them or which is itself so submitted and not so disapproved.

(6) The provisions of paragraphs (1), (2) and (4) of this Article shall not prevent a Contracting Party, if a member of the International Monetary Fund, from taking measures in any territory to restrict imports from, or to direct exports elsewhere than to, the territories of the other Contracting Party in a

—————
[1] Cmd. 9413.

manner having equivalent effect to restrictions on payments and transfers for current international transactions which that Contracting Party may at that time apply under the Articles of Agreement of the International Monetary Fund,[1] provided that measures taken under the provisions of this paragraph shall not be applied in a manner which would cause unnecessary damage to the commercial or economic interests of the other Contracting Party or would constitute a means of arbitrary or unjustifiable discrimination against the other Contracting Party as compared with other foreign countries.

(7) Neither Contracting Party shall impose any measure of a discriminatory nature that hinders or prevents importers or exporters of products of either Contracting Party from obtaining marine insurance on such products from insurers of either Contracting Party.

ARTICLE 18

(1) The Contracting Parties recognise that internal taxes and other internal charges, and laws, regulations and requirements affecting the internal sale, offering for sale, purchase, transportation, distribution or use of products, and internal quantitative regulations requiring the mixture, processing or use of products in specified amounts or proportions, should not be applied to imported or national products so as to afford protection to national production.

(2) Products originating in any territory of one Contracting Party and imported into any territory of the other shall not be subject, directly or indirectly, to internal taxes or other internal charges of any kind in excess of those applied, directly or indirectly, to like products originating in any territory of the latter Contracting Party or in any other foreign country.

(3) Products originating in any territory of one Contracting Party and imported into any territory of the other shall in that territory be accorded treatment not less favourable than that accorded to like products originating in any territory of the latter Contracting Party or in any other foreign country in respect of all laws, regulations and requirements affecting their internal sale, offering for sale, purchase, transportation, distribution or use. The provisions of this paragraph shall not prevent the application of differential internal transportation charges which are based exclusively on the economic operation of the means of transport and not on the nationality of the product.

(4) Neither Contracting Party shall establish or maintain any internal quantitative regulation relating to the mixture, processing or use of products in specified amounts or proportions which requires, directly or indirectly, that any specified amount or proportion of any product which is the subject of the regulation shall originate in any territory of that Contracting Party or in any foreign country.

(5) The provisions of paragraphs (1), (2), (3) and (4) of this Article shall not apply to laws, regulations or requirements governing the procurement by governmental agencies of products purchased for governmental purposes and not with a view to commercial resale or with a view to use in the production of goods for commercial sale.

(6) The provisions of paragraphs (1), (2), (3) and (4) of this Article shall not

[1] Cmd. 6885.

prevent the payment by either Contracting Party of subsidies exclusively to producers in any territory of that Contracting Party, including payments to producers derived from the proceeds of internal taxes or charges applied consistently with the provisions of paragraphs (1), (2), (3) and (4) of this Article and subsidies effected through governmental purchases of national products.

(7) The provisions of paragraphs (1), (3) and (4) of this Article shall not apply to laws, regulations, or requirements relating to the exhibition of cinematograph films, provided that in this matter cinematograph films originating in any territory of one Contracting Party shall be accorded in any territory of the other treatment not less favourable than that accorded to like films originating in any other foreign country.

(8) Products destined for exportation from any territory of one Contracting Party to any territory of the other shall not be subject, directly or indirectly, to internal taxes or other internal charges of any kind in excess of those applied, directly or indirectly, to like products destined for exportation to any other foreign country.

ARTICLE 19

(1) Nothing in the present Treaty shall be construed so as to derogate from the obligations undertaken by either Contracting Party towards the other by virtue of the provisions of the Union Convention of Paris of 20th March, 1883,[1] for the Protection of Industrial Property, as revised at London on 2nd June, 1934,[2] or of any subsequent revision thereof, so long as such provisions are in force between the Contracting Parties.

(2) Without prejudice to the provisions of the foregoing paragraph, the nationals and companies of one Contracting Party shall be accorded in any territory of the other treatment not less favourable than that accorded to nationals and companies of the latter Contracting Party with regard to the protection of industrial property.

ARTICLE 20

(1) The vessels of one Contracting Party shall be entitled, *inter alia*—

(*a*) to have liberty of access to all ports, waters and places open to international commerce and navigation in any territory of the other;
(*b*) to compete for and carry passengers and cargoes, alike in any of the territories of the Contracting Parties and elsewhere.

(2) In all matters referred to in the foregoing paragraph of this Article and, in addition, in all other matters relative to commerce, navigation or the treatment of shipping, the vessels of one Contracting Party, their passengers and cargoes shall be accorded in any territory of the other treatment not less favourable than that accorded to the vessels, passengers and cargoes of the latter Contracting Party or of any other foreign country; the vessels of one Contracting Party, their passengers and cargoes shall be accorded all the rights, liberties, favours, privileges, immunities and exemptions accorded to the vessels, passengers and

---

[1] Commercial No. 28 (1884), C. 4043.   [2] Cmd. 5833.

cargoes of the other Contracting Party or of any other foreign country and shall not be subjected to any other or more onerous duties, charges, taxes or other impositions of whatsoever kind or denomination than would be levied in similar circumstances in relation to such vessels, passengers and cargoes.

(3) Neither Contracting Party shall apply exchange restrictions in such a manner as to hamper the participation of vessels of the other Contracting Party in the transportation of passengers or cargoes to or from any territory of either Contracting Party or elsewhere.

(4) The Contracting Parties shall ensure that all dues and charges levied for the use of maritime ports within any of their territories and all byelaws and regulations of such ports shall be duly published before coming into force and that in each maritime port the port authority shall keep open for inspection by all persons concerned a table of the said dues and charges and a copy of the said byelaws and regulations.

(5) The provisions of this Article shall not apply to inland navigation or coasting trade. However,

(a) the vessels of one Contracting Party, if engaged in trade to or from places not within the limits of the coasting trade or inland navigation in any territory of the other, may engage in the carriage between ports within those limits of passengers holding through tickets or cargoes consigned on through bills of lading to or from such places not within those limits, provided that such vessels obtain permits authorising such carriage in accordance with the law of that territory; and

(b) the vessels of one Contracting Party may proceed from one port to another in any territory of the other for the purpose of landing the whole or part of their passengers or cargoes brought from places not within those limits or taking on board the whole or part of their passengers or cargoes destined for such places not within those limits.

ARTICLE 21

(1) A vessel of one Contracting Party which is forced by stress of weather or any other cause to take refuge in any territory of the other shall be entitled to refit therein, to procure all necessary stores, and to put to sea again without paying any duty, charge, tax or other imposition of whatsoever kind or denomination exceeding that which would be levied in similar circumstances in relation to a vessel of the latter Contracting Party or of any other foreign country.

(2) If in the territory of one Contracting Party a vessel of the other Contracting Party is wrecked, runs aground, is under any distress, or requires services, it shall be entitled—

(a) to receive all such assistance and protection as would be given by the former Contracting Party to one of its own vessels or to a vessel of any other foreign country;

(b) to call upon any salvage or other vessels of whatever nationality to render such services as it may consider necessary; and

(c) to discharge or tranship its cargo, equipment or other contents in case of need; no payment of any duty, charge, tax or other imposition of whatsoever kind or denomination shall be levied in respect thereof unless such cargo, equipment or other contents is delivered for use or consumption in that territory; the authorities of the territory may, however, if they think fit, require security for the protection of the revenue in relation to such goods.

(3) Nothing in the foregoing provisions of this Article shall exempt any vessel of one Contracting Party from the operation of any law of the other Contracting Party which permits the removal or sale of any such vessel which is, or is likely to become, an obstruction or danger to navigation, or of any part thereof or property recovered therefrom, provided that the vessels of one Contracting Party shall be accorded in the territory of the other under any such law treatment not less favourable than that accorded to the vessels of the latter Contracting Party or of any other foreign country.

(4) Where a vessel of one Contracting Party, or any part thereof or its cargo, equipment or any other contents, is salved, such vessel or part thereof or such cargo, equipment or other contents, or the proceeds thereof, if sold, shall be delivered up to the owner or his agent when claimed, provided that the claim is made within the period fixed by the law of the other Contracting Party. The owner or his agent shall be liable for the payment of any expenses incurred in the preservation of the vessel and its contents and of the salvage fees and other expenses incurred, but such fees and expenses shall not exceed those which would have been payable in similar circumstances in respect of a vessel of the latter Contracting Party or of any other foreign country.

ARTICLE 22

(1) Nothing in the present Treaty shall be construed so as to derogate from the obligations undertaken by either Contracting Party towards the other by virtue of the provisions of the International Convention relating to the Simplification of Customs Formalities signed at Geneva on 3rd November, 1923,[1] or of the International Convention to facilitate the Importation of Commercial Samples and Advertising Material signed at Geneva on 7th November, 1952,[2] or of any subsequent revision thereof, so long as such provisions are in force between the Contracting Parties.

(2) Without prejudice to the provisions of the foregoing paragraph, all facilities or privileges in respect of commercial travellers, commercial samples and advertising material accorded in any territory by one Contracting Party to any other foreign country shall be accorded to the other Contracting Party.

ARTICLE 23

(1) Persons, baggage and goods and also vessels and other means of transport shall be deemed to be in transit across any territory of one Contracting Party when the passage across that territory, with or without trans-shipment, warehousing, breaking bulk, or change in the mode of transport, is only a portion of a complete journey beginning and terminating beyond the frontier of the

[1] Cmd. 2347.   [2] Cmd. 9644.

Contracting Party across whose territory the traffic passes. Traffic of this nature is termed in this Article 'traffic in transit'.

(2) There shall be freedom of transit through any territory of one Contracting Party, via the routes most convenient for international transit, for traffic in transit to or from any territory of the other. No distinction shall be made which is based on the nationality of persons, the flag of vessels, the place of origin, departure, entry, exit or destination, or on any circumstances relating to the ownership of goods, of vessels or of other means of transport.

(3) The Contracting Parties may require baggage and goods and also vessels and other means of transport in transit through any of their territories to be entered at the proper custom house.

(4) Traffic in transit through any territory of one Contracting Party to or from any territory of the other shall not, except in case of failure to comply with applicable customs laws and regulations, be subject to any delays or restrictions other than to the minimum extent that may be necessary to ensure compliance with the applicable customs laws and regulations, and shall be exempt from customs duties and from all transit duties or other charges imposed in respect of transit, except charges for transportation or those commensurate with administrative expenses entailed by transit or with the cost of services rendered.

(5) All charges and regulations imposed by one Contracting Party on traffic in transit to or from any territory of the other shall be reasonable, having regard to the conditions of the traffic.

(6) With respect to all charges, regulations and formalities in connection with transit, one Contracting Party shall accord to traffic in transit to or from any territory of the other treatment not less favourable than that accorded to traffic in transit to or from any other foreign country.

(7) One Contracting Party shall accord to baggage and goods which have been in transit through any territory of the other treatment not less favourable than that which would have been accorded to such baggage and goods had they been transported from their place of origin to their destination without going through that territory. Either Contracting Party shall, however, in relation to any territory, be free to maintain any requirements of direct consignment existing on the date of signature of the present Treaty, if such direct consignment is a condition of eligibility for preferential rates of duty.

(8) The provisions of this Article shall not oblige either Contracting Party to afford transit across any territory for persons whose admission into that territory is forbidden and, in relation to goods, shall not prevent either Contracting Party from taking non-discriminatory measures necessary to prevent abuse of transit facilities or to protect public morals or human, animal or plant life or health.

ARTICLE 24

Nothing in the present Treaty shall be construed so as to derogate from the obligations undertaken by either Contracting Party towards the other by virtue of the provisions of the Protocol on Arbitration Clauses signed at Geneva on 24th September, 1923,[1] or of the Convention on the Execution of Foreign

[1] Cmd. 2312.

Arbitral Awards signed at Geneva on 26th September, 1927,[1] or of any multi-lateral agreement amendatory or supplementary thereto, so long as such provisions are in force between the Contracting Parties.

ARTICLE 25

(1) Nothing in the present Treaty shall be construed so as to derogate from the obligations undertaken by either Contracting Party towards the other by virtue of the provisions of the Agreement of Madrid of 14th April, 1891, for the Prevention of False Indications of Origin on Goods,[2] as revised at London on 2nd June, 1934,[3] or of any subsequent revision thereof, so long as such provisions are in force between the Contracting Parties.

(2) Without prejudice to the provisions of the foregoing paragraph, either Contracting Party shall provide in any territory suitable civil remedies and, in cases of fraud, suitable penal sanctions in respect of the use of any indication that the goods in connection with which it is used have been produced or manufactured in any territory of the other, if such indication be false or misleading.

ARTICLE 26

Nothing in the present Treaty shall be construed so as to derogate from the rights and obligations that either Contracting Party has or may have as a contracting party to the General Agreement on Tariffs and Trade or any multilateral agreement amendatory or supplementary thereto.

ARTICLE 27

Nothing in the present Treaty shall affect the obligations of either Contracting Party under the Articles of Agreement of the International Monetary Fund nor preclude the imposition of particular exchange restrictions whenever the Fund specifically authorises or requests a Contracting Party to impose such particular restrictions.

ARTICLE 28

All the provisions of the present Treaty relative to the grant of treatment not less favourable than that accorded to any other foreign country shall be interpreted as meaning that such treatment shall be accorded immediately and unconditionally, without request or compensation.

ARTICLE 29

(1) Nothing in the present Treaty shall entitle the United Kingdom to claim the benefit of any treatment, preference or privilege which may at any time be accorded by Japan exclusively—

    (a) to persons who originated in the territories to which all right, title and claim were renounced by Japan in accordance with the provisions of

---

[1] Cmd. 3655.   [2] C. 6818.   [3] Cmd. 5832.

Article 2 of the Treaty of Peace with Japan signed at the city of San Francisco on 8th September, 1951[1] (hereinafter referred to as 'the Peace Treaty'); or

(b) to any area set forth in Article 3 of the Peace Treaty in so far as the situation provided for in the second sentence of the said Article continues with respect to the administration, legislation and jurisdiction over such area.

(2) Nothing in the present Treaty shall entitle Japan to claim the benefit of any treatment, preference or privilege which may at any time be accorded by any territory of the United Kingdom exclusively to any one or more of the other territories enumerated in the following list:

The United Kingdom of Great Britain and Northern Ireland,
Canada,
The Commonwealth of Australia,
New Zealand,
The Republic of South Africa,
India,
Pakistan,
Ceylon,
Ghana,
The Federation of Malaya,
The Federation of Nigeria,
The Republic of Cyprus,
Sierra Leone,
Tanganyika,
Jamaica,
Trinidad and Tobago,
Uganda,
Territories for the international relations of which the Governments of the United Kingdom, Australia, New Zealand and the Republic of South Africa are responsible at the date of signature of the present Treaty,
The Irish Republic, and
In relation to paragraph (1) of Article 16 only, Burma.

(3) The provisions of the present Treaty relative to the grant of treatment not less favourable than that accorded to any other foreign country shall not be construed so as to oblige one Contracting Party to extend to the other the benefit of any treatment, preference or privilege which may be extended by the former Contracting Party by virtue of—

(a) the formation of a customs union or a free trade area, or
(b) the adoption of an agreement designed to lead to the formation of such a union or area within a reasonable length of time.

(4) Without prejudice to the provisions of Article 4, nothing in the present Treaty shall be construed so as

(a) to prevent a Contracting Party from taking, either singly or with other

[1] Cmd. 8601.

countries, any action considered necessary by that Contracting Party for the protection of national security, where such action relates to

(i) special nuclear materials or to materials or equipment from which they are produced; or

(ii) the production of or traffic in arms, ammunition or implements of war, or to such production of or traffic in other goods or materials as is carried on directly or indirectly for the purpose of supplying a military establishment of the Contracting Party or of any other foreign country; or

(b) to prevent a Contracting Party from taking any action

(i) considered necessary by that Contracting Party to protect its essential security interests in time of war or other emergency in international relations or in time of public emergency threatening the life of the nation; or

(ii) in pursuance of its obligations under the United Nations Charter[1] for the maintenance or restoration of international peace and security;

provided that the Contracting Parties shall aim to restrict any such action to that involving the least possible deviation, both in extent and duration, from the provisions of the present Treaty.

(5) Nothing in the present Treaty shall be construed so as to grant any rights or impose any obligations in respect of—

(a) any matter concerning which provision is made in any treaty, convention or agreement relating to international civil aviation to which either or both of the Contracting Parties is a party; or

(b) copyright in literary or artistic works; or

(c) rights of performers, producers of phonograms and broadcasting organisations.

ARTICLE 30

Any representations which may be made by either Contracting Party with regard to any matter affecting the operation of the present Treaty shall be the subject of sympathetic consideration and, where appropriate, mutual consultation.

ARTICLE 31

Any dispute that may arise between the Contracting Parties as to the interpretation or application of any of the provisions of the present Treaty shall, upon the application of either Contracting Party, be referred to the International Court of Justice, unless in any particular case the Contracting Parties agree to submit the dispute to some other tribunal or to dispose of it by some other procedure.

ARTICLE 32

(1) The United Kingdom may, at the time of exchange of the instruments of ratification or at any time thereafter, give notice in writing through the

[1] Cmd. 7015.

diplomatic channel of its intention to extend the present Treaty to any territory for the international relations of which the United Kingdom is responsible.

(a) In a case where the intention of the United Kingdom is to extend the Treaty without modification or reservation, the Treaty shall be extended to the territory specified in such notice as from the thirtieth day after the date of such notice.

(b) In a case where the intention of the United Kingdom is to extend the Treaty with modification or reservation, both Contracting Parties shall consult as to the terms of modification or reservation to be made in connection with the extension of the Treaty to the territory specified in such notice. The Treaty shall be extended to such territory by an agreement setting out the terms of modification or reservation as well as necessary provision for the entry into force of such extension.

(2) After the expiry of a period of six years from the coming into force of the present Treaty either Contracting Party may, provided twelve months' prior notice to that effect has been given, terminate the application of the present Treaty to any territory to which it has been extended under the provisions of the foregoing paragraph.

ARTICLE 33

(1) The present Treaty shall be ratified and the instruments of ratification shall be exchanged at Tokyo as soon as possible. It shall come into force as from the thirtieth day after the exchange of the instruments of ratification, and shall thereafter remain in force during a period of six years.

(2) In case neither Contracting Party shall have given notice to the other twelve months before the expiry of the said period of six years of intention to terminate the Treaty, it shall remain in force until the expiry of twelve months from the date on which notice of such intention is given.

(3) A notice given under paragraph (2) of this Article shall apply to any territory to which the present Treaty has been extended under Article 32.

In witness whereof the above named Plenipotentiaries have signed the present Treaty and have affixed thereto their seals.

Done in duplicate at London this Fourteenth day of November, 1962, in the English and Japanese languages, both texts being equally authoritative.

Protocol of signature

At the time of signing the Treaty of Commerce, Establishment and Navigation between the United Kingdom of Great Britain and Northern Ireland and Japan (hereinafter referred to as 'the Treaty'), the undersigned Plenipotentiaries, duly authorised thereto, have further agreed as follows:

(1) The term 'territory of Japan' shall not be deemed to include, for the purposes of the Treaty, any area referred to in Article 3 of the Treaty of Peace with Japan signed at the city of San Francisco on 8th September, 1951, in so far as the situation provided for in the second sentence of the said Article continues with respect to the administration, legislation and jurisdiction over such

area. The term 'nationals' in relation to Japan includes inhabitants of such area who are nationals of Japan.

(2) The term 'nationals', in relation to the United Kingdom, shall also apply to all British subjects who have made a claim to retain the status of a British subject under Section 2 of the British Nationality Act, 1948, or who are British subjects without citizenship under Section 13 (1) of that Act, except in either case those who belong to any territory to which the Treaty may be extended under the provisions of Article 32 but has not been so extended. In this connection, any such person may be required by the Japanese authorities to produce a passport or other document in lieu thereof for the purpose of confirming that he falls under one or other of the said categories.

(3) With reference to paragraph (3) of Article 2, the term 'vessels' does not include warships.

(4) The provisions of paragraph (1) of Article 3 shall not apply to advantages relating to passports and visas accorded by a Contracting Party to the nationals of any other foreign country by virtue of a special agreement. However, the foregoing shall not be interpreted so as to nullify the provisions of paragraph (1) of Article 3.

(5) With reference to Article 3, the United Kingdom reserves the right to apply the provisions of the said Article in the United Kingdom as if Great Britain and Northern Ireland were each a separate territory.

(6) With respect to the profession of patent agent, the provisions of paragraph (4) of Article 3 shall not oblige Japan to accord to nationals of any territory of the United Kingdom treatment more favourable than that accorded by that territory to nationals of Japan.

(7) Without prejudice to the provisions of an agreement for the avoidance of double taxation and the prevention of fiscal evasion between any territory of the United Kingdom and Japan,

(a) the provisions of paragraph (2) of Article 8 shall not oblige the United Kingdom to grant, in respect of any territory of the United Kingdom, to nationals of Japan not resident for tax purposes in that territory the same personal allowances, reliefs and reductions for tax purposes as are granted to nationals of the United Kingdom not resident for tax purposes in that territory, and

(b) the provisions of paragraph (6) of Article 8 shall not oblige Japan to accord to nationals and companies of any territory of the United Kingdom treatment with respect to exemption from taxation in Japan more favourable than that accorded in that territory to nationals and companies of Japan.

(8) The provisions of Article 8 shall not be construed as affecting the provisions of the Japanese law under which distributed profits are, in the case of Japanese corporations, taxed at a lower rate than undistributed profits.

(9) With respect to the matter of enjoyment of rights pertaining to land in Japan, the provisions of Article 10 and of paragraph (4) of Article 12 shall not oblige Japan to accord to the nationals and companies of any territory of the United Kingdom, or to companies of Japan more than one half of the interests in which are owned or which are controlled, directly or indirectly, by such

nationals and companies, treatment more favourable than that accorded in that territory to nationals and companies of Japan.

(10) The provisions of paragraph (1) of Article 16 shall not preclude either Contracting Party from imposing a countervailing or anti-dumping duty in the circumstances and subject to the conditions laid down in the provisions of the General Agreement on Tariffs and Trade which govern the imposition of such duty in relation to the trade of contracting parties to that Agreement.

(11) The provisions of paragraph (2) of Article 16 shall not preclude Japan from treating fish, whales and other natural produce of the sea taken by vessels of the United Kingdom within the territory of any other foreign country, and products produced or manufactured at sea therefrom, as products originating in the territory of that foreign country.

(12) The provisions of Articles 17 and 23 shall not prevent the United Kingdom from requiring, as a condition of permitting

(a) the exportation of any product from any of its territories, or
(b) the transit through any of its territories of any product exported from the Sterling Area,

satisfactory evidence that payment for such product has been or will be made in accordance with any exchange control regulations in force in that territory.

(13) The permits referred to in paragraph (5) of Article 20 will be issued on a basis no more restrictive than that on which they were issued on the date of signature of the Treaty.

(14) With reference to paragraph (3) of Article 29, a Contracting Party shall, before entering into any customs union, free trade area or agreement designed to lead thereto, inform the other of its plans in so far as they are relevant to the Treaty and give adequate opportunity for consultation about the effect of the terms of entry on the benefits which the other Contracting Party might expect to gain from the Treaty. The former Contracting Party shall also, after its entry, keep the latter informed of developments relevant to the Treaty, in so far as this is compatible with the position of the former Contracting Party as a member of the customs union or free trade area or as a participant in the said agreement.

(15) Wherever the Treaty contains a provision according national treatment and also a provision according treatment not less favourable than that accorded in relation to any other foreign country in respect of any matter, the Contracting Party beneficiary in each particular case shall be entitled to claim the benefits of either provision.

(16) The present Protocol shall form an integral part of the Treaty.

In witness whereof the respective Plenipotentiaries have signed the present Protocol and have affixed thereto their seals.

Done in duplicate at London this Fourteenth day of November, 1962, in the English and Japanese languages, both texts being equally authoritative.

First Protocol concerning Trade Relations between the United Kingdom of Great Britain and Northern Ireland and Japan

At the time of signing the Treaty of Commerce, Establishment and Navigation between the United Kingdom of Great Britain and Northern Ireland and

Japan (hereinafter referred to as 'the Treaty'), the undersigned Plenipotentiaries, duly authorised thereto, have agreed as follows:

(1) If the Government of either Contracting Party find that any product of the territory of the other Contracting Party is being imported into the territory of the former Contracting Party in such increased quantities and under such conditions as to cause or threaten serious injury to producers in the territory of that former Contracting Party of like or directly competitive products, that Government, in case they wish to take action under the present Protocol to prevent or remedy such injury, shall give to the Government of the other Contracting Party notice to this effect with a full explanation of the circumstances, and the two Governments shall enter into consultation, not later than seven days after such notice is given, with a view to finding a mutually acceptable solution.

(2) If no mutually acceptable solution is found within thirty days after the consultation has begun, the Government of the importing Contracting Party may take action to prevent or remedy the injury referred to in paragraph (1) above, notwithstanding the provisions of Article 17 of the Treaty, provided that such action:

(a) shall not be taken lightly;

(b) shall be limited, so far as administratively practicable, to the specific products in respect of which it is necessary and shall not be more severe than is needed to remedy the injury caused or threatened; and

(c) shall be discontinued immediately either when a mutually acceptable solution is found or when the situation which gave rise to the action is rectified.

(3) In critical circumstances where delay would cause damage which it would be difficult to repair, action under paragraph (2) above may be taken provisionally within thirty days after the consultation has begun, on the condition that such consultation shall be continued in an endeavour to find a mutually acceptable solution.

(4) If the Government of either Contracting Party take action under the provisions of paragraph (2) or paragraph (3) above, the Government of the other Contracting Party may take counteraction substantially equivalent in scope and duration, notwithstanding the provisions of Article 17 of the Treaty, provided that such counteraction shall not be taken or shall be discontinued, as the case may be, if and to the extent that the Government of the former Contracting Party take measures having the effect of compensating for their initial action. If the Government of the former Contracting Party so request, the two Governments shall immediately enter into consultation in respect of any such counteraction.

(5) The term 'territory' in paragraph (1) above means, in relation to the United Kingdom, the United Kingdom of Great Britain and Northern Ireland, including The Channel Islands and the Isle of Man. The present Protocol may, however, be applied when it is necessary to protect the established interests in the United Kingdom market of any territory other than the United Kingdom for whose international relations the United Kingdom is responsible.

(6) The present Protocol shall be ratified and the instruments of ratification shall be exchanged at Tokyo as soon as possible. It shall thereafter come into force on the date of the coming into force of the Treaty. It shall terminate when the Treaty is terminated in accordance with the provisions of Article 33 thereof or at any time earlier by mutual consent of the two Governments. The two Governments shall consult together at any time at the request of either Government for the purpose of reviewing the necessity of the present Protocol.

In witness whereof the respective Plenipotentiaries have signed the present Protocol and have affixed thereto their seals.

Done in duplicate at London, this Fourteenth day of November, 1962, in the English and Japanese languages, both texts being equally authoritative.

Second Protocol concerning Trade Relations between the United Kingdom of Great Britain and Northern Ireland and Japan

At the time of signing the Treaty of Commerce, Establishment and Navigation between the United Kingdom of Great Britain and Northern Ireland and Japan (hereinafter referred to as 'the Treaty'), the undersigned Plenipotentiaries, duly authorised thereto, have agreed as follows:

(1) In case import restrictions have been continuously enforced by either Contracting Party with regard to any specific product and the sudden removal of import restrictions on such product of the other Contracting Party would result in serious injury to domestic producers of the former Contracting Party of like or directly competitive products, the importing Contracting Party may continue to apply import restrictions, notwithstanding the provisions of Article 17 of the Treaty, to any such products mentioned in agreements which are to be concluded in accordance with the present Protocol in such manner and under such conditions as may be specified in the said agreements.

(2) The Governments of the Contracting Parties shall review the operation of the agreements made in accordance with paragraph (1) above, with a view to ensuring orderly development of the trade between the Contracting Parties, at any time upon the request of the Government of either Contracting Party, and not less frequently than once a year unless otherwise mutually agreed.

(3) The present Protocol shall be ratified and the instruments of ratification shall be exchanged at Tokyo as soon as possible. It shall thereafter come into force on the date of the coming into force of the Treaty. It shall terminate when the Treaty is terminated in accordance with the provisions of Article 33 thereof or at any time earlier when there are no longer any import restrictions in force under the present Protocol.

In witness whereof the respective Plenipotentiaries have signed the present Protocol and have affixed thereto their seals.

Done in duplicate at London, this Fourteenth day of November, 1962, in the English and Japanese languages, both texts being equally authoritative.

Memorandum of Understanding between the Organisation for Economic Cooperation and Development and the Government of Japan, Paris, 26 July 1963[1]

THE ORGANISATION FOR ECONOMIC CO-OPERATION AND DEVELOPMENT (hereinafter called the 'Organisation'); and

THE GOVERNMENT OF JAPAN;

Considering that on 26th July, 1963, the Council of the Organisation has invited the Government of Japan to accede to the Convention on the Organisation for Economic Co-operation and Development of 14th December, 1960 (hereinafter called the 'Convention'), and to the Supplementary Protocols No. 1 and No. 2 to the Convention, signed on the same date (hereinafter called the 'Protocols');[2]

Having regard to Article 16 of the Convention, which provides that an invitation to accede to the Convention may be extended to Governments prepared to assume the obligations of membership of the Organisation;

Considering that the procedure of parliamentary approval of the accession of the Government of Japan to the Convention and Protocols has not been completed;

Having regard to the statement by the Government of Japan concerning the Acts of the Organisation, attached hereto as Annex A;[3]

Having regard to the statement by the Government of Japan concerning the Liberalisation of Current Invisible Operations and Capital Movements, attached hereto as Annex B;[4]

Having regard to the examination by the Committee for Invisible Transactions and the Maritime Transport Committee of the proposed accession of Japan to the Codes of Liberalisation of the Organisation;

HAVE AGREED as follows:

Article 1

The deposit by the Government of Japan of the Instrument of Accession to the Convention shall involve the assumption by Japan of the obligations of membership of the Organisation, including the views and aims resulting from the Report of the Preparatory Committee of the Organisation of December 1960, and the accession to the Acts of the Organisation which will be in force at that time, except as otherwise provided in the present Memorandum.

Article 2

a) The Council of the Organisation agrees that the Acts enumerated in paragraphs 2 and 3 of Annex A hereto shall not be applicable to Japan.

b) The Government of Japan may, within a period of six months after the date of signature of the present Memorandum, inform the Council of the Organisation that it wishes to accede to any of the Acts enumerated in paragraph 3 of Annex A hereto.

---

[1] The Council of Europe, *European Year book*, Vol. XII, Part I, 1964 (The Hague, 1966), pp. 157–9.
[2] See ibid., p. 179.   [3] Ibid., pp. 159–67.   [4] Ibid., pp. 167–79.

Article 3

The Council of the Organisation agrees to the reservations by the Government of Japan with regard to items covered by the Code of Liberalisation of Current Invisible Operations and by the Code of Liberalisation of Capital Movements, as enumerated in Part II of Annex B, taking into account the statements of intention of the Government of Japan set forth in the said Annex.

Article 4

In the event that the Government of Japan should wish to abstain from or to lodge a reservation to any Act of the Organisation or to any item of the Codes of Liberalisation which it failed by oversight to mention in paragraph 2 or 3 of Annex A, or in Part II of Annex B hereto, the Government of Japan may bring the matter to the Council of the Organisation for decision within a period of six months after the date of deposit of the Instrument of Accession.

Article 5

The Secretary-General of the Organisation shall inform the Government of Japan promptly of any Acts adopted by the Organisation between the date of signature of the present Memorandum and the date of deposit of the Instrument of Accession, and the Government of Japan shall notify the Organisation as soon as possible, within 30 days, whether or not it is willing to accede to the Act concerned. If the Government of Japan is unwilling to accede to a particular Act or if it proposes amendments or reservations thereto, the matter shall be submitted to the Council. However, the Government of Japan shall not be bound by any Act referred to in this Article unless it has signified its readiness to accede to such Act.

IN WITNESS WHEREOF, the undersigned Representatives, being duly authorised to that effect, have signed the present Memorandum.

DONE in Paris, this Twenty-Sixth day of July, Nineteen Hundred and Sixty Three, in two copies, in the English and French languages, both texts being equally authentic.

IV. AFRICA

A.

Revised Convention of Association between the European Economic Community and the associated African and Malagasy States, Yaoundé, 20 July 1963[1]

PRÉAMBULE

Sa Majesté le Roi des Belges,
Le Président de la république fédérale d'Allemagne,
Le Président de la République française,
Le Président de la République italienne,
Son Altesse Royale la Grande-Duchesse de Luxembourg,
Sa Majesté la Reine des Pays-Bas,
Parties contractantes au traité instituant la Communauté économique euro-
péenne signé à Rome le 25 mars 1957, ci-après dénommé le traité et dont les
États sont ci-après dénommés États membres,
et le Conseil de la Communauté économique européenne,
Sa Majesté le Mwami du Burundi,
Le Président de la république fédérale du Cameroun,
Le Président de la République centrafricaine,
Le Président de la république du Congo (Brazzaville),
Le Président de la république du Congo (Léopoldville),
Le Président de la république de Côte-d'Ivoire,
Le Président de la république du Dahomey,
Le Président de la République gabonaise,
Le Président de la République de Haute-Volta,
Le Président de la République malgache,
Le Chef de l'État, président du Conseil de gouvernement de la république du
  Mali,
Le Président de la république islamique de Mauritanie,
Le Président de la république du Niger,
Le Président de la République rwandaise,
Le Président de la république du Sénégal,
Le Président de la république de Somalie,
Le Président de la république du Tchad,
Le Président de la République togolaise,
dont les États sont ci-après dénommés États associés,

d'autre part,

vu le traité instituant la Communauté économique européenne,
réaffirmant en conséquence leur volonté de maintenir leur association,

[1] *Journal Officiel des Communautés Européennes*, 11 June 1964, pp. 1431–57/64.

désirant manifester leur volonté mutuelle de coopération sur la base d'une complète égalité et de relations amicales dans le respect des principes de la charte des Nations-Unies,

décidés à développer les relations économiques entre les États associés et la Communauté,

résolus à poursuivre en commun leurs efforts en vue du progrès économique, social et culturel de leurs pays,

soucieux de faciliter la diversification de l'économie et l'industrialisation des États associés en vue de leur permettre de renforcer leur équilibre et leur indépendance économiques,

conscients de l'importance que revêt le développement de la coopération et des échanges interafricains ainsi que des relations économiques internationales,

ont décidé de conclure une nouvelle convention d'association entre la Communauté et les États associés et ont désigné à cet effet comme plénipotentiaires:

[omitted here]

TITRE I

LES ÉCHANGES COMMERCIAUX

Article premier

En vue de promouvoir l'accroissement des échanges entre les États associés et les États membres, de renforcer leurs relations économiques et l'indépendance économique des États associés et de contribuer ainsi au développement du commerce international, les Hautes Parties contractantes sont convenues des dispositions suivantes régissant leurs relations commerciales mutuelles.

Chapitre 1

Droits de douane et restrictions quantitatives

Article 2

1. Les produits originaires des États associés bénéficient à l'importation dans les États membres de l'élimination progressive des droits de douane et taxes d'effet équivalant à de tels droits qui intervient entre les États membres conformément aux dispositions des articles 12, 13, 14, 15 et 17 du traité et aux décisions d'accélération du rythme de réalisation des objets du traité intervenues ou à intervenir.

2. Toutefois, dès l'entrée en vigueur de la convention, les États membres suppriment les droits de douane et taxes d'effet équivalant à de tels droits qu'ils appliquent aux produits originaires des États associés qui figurent à l'annexe à la présente convention.[1]

Simultanément, les droits du tarif douanier commun de la Communauté

---

[1] Omitted here: the list includes, in either their natural or processed form, bananas, coconut, coffee, tea, pepper, vanilla, cloves, nutmeg, and cocoa beans.

sont appliqués par les États membres aux importations de ces produits en provenance des pays tiers.

3. Les importations de café vert dans les pays du Benelux d'une part, et de bananes dans la république fédérale d'Allemagne d'autre part, en provenance des pays tiers, sont effectuées dans les conditions fixées respectivement, pour le cafe vert, au protocole conclu ce jour entre les États membres et, pour les bananes, au protocole conclu le 25 mars 1957 entre les États membres ainsi que dans la déclaration annexée à la présente convention.

4. L'application des dispositions du présent article ne préjuge pas le régime qui sera réservé à certains produits agricoles en vertu des dispositions de l'article 11 de la présente convention.

5. A la demande d'un État associé, des consultations ont lieu, au sein du Conseil d'association, sur les conditions d'application du présent article.

Article 3

1. Chaque État associé accorde le même traitement tarifaire aux produits originaires de tous les États membres; ceux des États associés qui n'appliquent pas déjà cette règle à l'entrée en vigueur de la convention, doivent y satisfaire dans les six mois qui suivent.

2. Les produits originaires des États membres bénéficient dans chaque État associé, dans les conditions fixées au protocole n° 1 annexé à la présente convention, de l'élimination progressive des droits de douane et taxes d'effet équivalant à de tels droits que chaque État associé applique à l'importation de ces produits dans son territoire.

Toutefois, chaque État associé peut maintenir ou établir des droits de douane et taxes d'effet équivalant à de tels droits qui répondent aux nécessités de son développement et aux besoins de son industrialisation ou qui ont pour but d'alimenter son budget.

Les droits de douane et taxes d'effet équivalant à de tels droits que les États associés perçoivent conformément à l'alinéa précédent, de même que les modifications qu'ils peuvent apporter à ces droits et taxes dans les conditions prévues au protocole n° 1 ne peuvent donner lieu, en droit ou en fait, à une discrimination directe ou indirecte entre les États membres.

3. A la demande de la Communauté et selon les modalités prévues au protocole n° 1, des consultations ont lieu au sein du Conseil d'association sur les conditions d'application du présent article.

Article 4

1. Dans la mesure où un État associé perçoit des droits à l'exportation sur ses produits à destination des États membres, ces droits ne peuvent donner lieu, en droit ou en fait, à une discrimination directe ou indirecte entre les États membres et ne peuvent être supérieurs à ceux appliqués aux produits destinés à l'État tiers le plus favorisé.

2. Sans préjudice de l'application de l'article 13 paragraphe 2 de la présente convention, les mesures appropriées sont prises par le Conseil d'association au cas où l'application de tels droits entraînerait de sérieuses perturbations dans les conditions de concurrence.

Article 5

1. En ce qui concerne l'élimination des restrictions quantitatives, les États membres appliquent aux importations des produits originaires des États associés les dispositions correspondantes du traité et des décisions d'accélération du rythme de réalisation des objets du traité intervenues ou à intervenir qui sont appliquées dans leurs relations mutuelles.

2. A la demande d'un État associé, des consultations ont lieu au sein du Conseil d'association sur les conditions d'application du présent article.

Article 6

1. Les États associés suppriment, au plus tard quatre ans après l'entrée en vigueur de la présente convention, toutes les restrictions quantitatives à l'importation des produits originaires des États membres ainsi que toutes mesures d'effet équivalent. Cette suppression s'effectue progressivement dans les conditions fixées au protocole n° 2 annexé à la présente convention.

2. Les États associés s'abstiennent d'introduire de nouvelles restrictions quantitatives ou mesures d'effet équivalent à l'importation des produits originaires des États membres.

3. Au cas où les mesures prévues à l'article 3 se révèlent insuffisantes pour faire face aux nécessités de leur développement et aux besoins de leur industrialisation ou en cas de difficultés dans leur balance des paiements ou, en ce qui concerne les produits agricoles, en raison des exigences découlant des organisations régionales de marché existantes, les États associés peuvent, par dérogation aux dispositions des deux paragraphes précédents et dans les conditions fixées au protocole n° 2, maintenir ou établir des restrictions quantitatives à l'égard de l'importation des produits originaires des États membres.

4. Les États associés dans lesquels les importations relèvent de la compétence d'un monopole national à caractère commercial ou d'un organisme par lequel les importations sont, en droit ou en fait, d'une manière directe ou indirecte, limitées, contrôlées, dirigées ou influencées, prennent toutes dispositions nécessaires pour atteindre les objectifs définis par le présent titre et pour l'élimination progressive de toute discrimination en ce qui concerne les conditions de l'approvisionnement et de l'écoulement des produits.

Sans préjudice de l'application de l'article 7 ci-dessous, les plans de commerce extérieur établis par les États associés ne peuvent comporter ou entraîner, en droit ou en fait, une discrimination directe ou indirecte entre États membres.

Les mesures prises en application des dispositions du présent paragraphe sont communiquées par les États associés intéressés au Conseil d'association.

5. A la demande de la Communauté, des consultations ont lieu au sein du Conseil d'association sur les conditions d'application du présent article.

Article 7

Sous réserve des dispositions particulières propres au commerce frontalier, le régime que les États associés appliquent en vertu du présent titre aux produits originaires des États membres ne peut en aucun cas être moins favorable que celui appliqué aux produits originaires de l'État tiers le plus favorisé.

Article 8

La présente convention ne fait pas obstacle au maintien et à l'établissement entre États associés d'unions douanières ou de zones de libre-échange.

Article 9

La présente convention ne fait pas obstacle au maintien ou à l'établissement d'unions douanières ou de zones de libre-échange entre un ou plusieurs États associés et un ou plusieurs pays tiers dans la mesure ou celles-ci ne sont pas ou ne se révèlent pas incompatibles avec les principes et les dispositions de ladite convention.

Article 10

Les dispositions des articles 3, 4 et 6 ci-dessus ne font pas obstacle aux interdictions ou restrictions d'importation, d'exportation ou de transit justifiées par des raisons de moralité publique, d'ordre public, de sécurité publique, de protection de la santé et de la vie des personnes et des animaux ou de préservation des végétaux, de protection des trésors nationaux ayant une valeur artistique, historique ou archéologique, ou de protection de la propriété industrielle et commerciale. Toutefois, ces interdictions ou restrictions ne doivent constituer ni un moyen de discrimination arbitraire, ni une restriction déguisée au commerce.

Chapitre 2

Dispositions relatives à certains produits agricoles

Article 11

Dans la détermination de sa politique agricole commune, la Communauté prend en considération les intérêts des États associés en ce qui concerne les produits homologues et concurrents des produits européens. Des consultations ont lieu à cet effet entre la Communauté et les États associés intéressés.

Le régime applicable à l'importation dans la Communauté de ces produits, lorsqu'ils sont originaires des États associés, est déterminé par celle-ci après consultation au sein du Conseil d'association, au fur et à mesure de la définition par la Communauté de sa politique agricole commune.

Chapitre 3

Dispositions relatives à la politique commerciale

Article 12

1. En ce qui concerne la politique commerciale, les Parties contractantes conviennent de s'informer mutuellement et, à la demande d'une d'entre elles, de se consulter aux fins de la bonne application de la présente convention.

2. Ces consultations portent sur les mesures relatives aux échanges commerciaux avec des pays tiers lorsque celles-ci sont susceptibles de porter atteinte aux intérêts d'une ou de plusieurs Parties contractantes et notamment en ce qui concerne:

a) La suspension, modification ou suppression des droits de douane;

b) L'octroi de contingents tarifaires à droit réduit ou nul, à l'exception des contingents visés par l'article 2 paragraphe 3 ci-dessus;

c) L'institution, la réduction ou la suppression de restrictions quantitatives, sans préjudice des obligations découlant pour certaines Parties contractantes de leur appartenance au G.A.T.T.

3. Dès l'entrée en vigueur de la présente convention, le Conseil d'association définit la procédure d'information et de consultation relative à l'application du présent article.

Chapitre 4

Clauses de sauvegarde

Article 13

1. Si des perturbations sérieuses se produisent dans un secteur de l'activité économique d'un État associé, ou compromettent sa stabilité financière extérieure, celui-ci peut, par dérogation aux dispositions de l'article 3 paragraphe 2 alinéa 1 et de l'article 6 paragraphes 1, 2 et 4, prendre les mesures de sauvegarde nécessaires.
Ces mesures ainsi que leurs modalités d'application sont notifiées, sans délai, au Conseil d'association.
2. Si des perturbations sérieuses se produisent dans un secteur de l'activité économique de la Communauté d'un ou de plusieurs États membres ou compromettent leur stabilité financière extérieure et si des difficultés surgissent pouvant se traduire par l'altération grave d'une situation économique régionale, la Communauté peut prendre ou autoriser le ou les États membres intéressés à prendre, par dérogation aux dispositions des articles 2 et 5, les mesures qui se révèleraient nécessaires dans leurs relations avec les États associés.
Ces mesures ainsi que leurs modalités d'application, sont notifiées, sans délai, au Conseil d'association.
3. Pour l'application des paragraphes 1 et 2 du présent article, doivent être choisies par priorité les mesures qui apportent le minimum de perturbations dans le fonctionnement de l'association. Ces mesures ne doivent pas excéder la portée strictement indispensable pour remédier aux difficultés qui se sont manifestées.
4. Des consultations ont lieu au sein du Conseil d'association sur les mesures prises en application des paragraphes 1 et 2 du présent article.
Elles ont lieu à la demande de la Communauté pour les mesures du paragraphe 1 et à la demande d'un ou de plusieurs États associés pour celles du paragraphe 2.

Chapitre 5

Dispositions générales

Article 14

Sans préjudice des dispositions particulières prévues par la présente convention et notamment de celles figurant à l'article 3 ci-dessus, chaque Partie contractante s'interdit toute mesure ou pratique de nature fiscale interne établissant directement ou indirectement une discrimination entre ses produits et les produits similaires originaires des autres Parties contractantes.

TITRE II

COOPÉRATION FINANCIÈRE ET TECHNIQUE

Article 15

La Communauté participe, dans les conditions indiquées ci-après, aux mesures propres à promouvoir le développement économique et social des États associés par un effort complémentaire de ceux accomplis par ces États.

Article 16

Aux fins précisées à l'article 15, et pour la durée de la présente convention, un montant global de 730 millions d'unités de compte est fourni:

a) Pour 666 millions d'unités de compte par les États membres; ce montant, versé au "Fonds européen de développement" ci-après dénommé le Fonds, est utilisé à concurrence de 620 millions d'unités de compte sous forme d'aides non remboursables et le solde sous forme de prêts à des conditions spéciales;

b) A concurrence de 64 millions d'unités de compte par la Banque européenne d'investissement, ci-après dénommée la Banque, sous forme de prêts accordés par celle-ci dans les conditions prévues au protocole n° 5 relatif à la gestion des aides financières annexé à la présente convention.

Article 17

Dans les conditions prévues par la présente convention et par le protocole n° 5, le montant fixé à l'article 16 ci-dessus est utilisé:

1. Dans le domaine des investissements économiques et sociaux:
— pour des projets d'infrastructure économique et sociale,
— pour des projets à caractère productif d'intérêt général,
— pour des projets à caractère productif et à rentabilité financière normale,
— pour l'assistance technique préparatoire, concomitante et postérieure aux investissements;

2. Dans le domaine de la coopération technique générale:
— pour des études sur les perspectives de développement des économies des États associés,

— pour des programmes de formation des cadres et de formation professionnelle;

3. Dans le domaine des aides à la diversification et à la production:

— pour des actions destinées essentiellement à permettre la commercialisation à des prix compétitifs sur l'ensemble des marchés de la Communauté, en encourageant notamment la rationalisation des cultures et des méthodes de vente et en facilitant aux producteurs les adaptations nécessaires;

4. Dans le domaine de la régularisation des cours:

— pour des avances en vue de contribuer à pallier les conséquences des fluctuations temporaires des prix mondiaux.

Article 18

Les aides non remboursables et les prêts sont affectés:

a) A concurrence de 500 millions d'unités de compte au financement des actions visées à l'article 17 paragraphes 1 et 2;

b) A concurrence de 230 millions d'unités de compte au financement des actions visées à l'article 17 paragraphe 3.

Article 19

Les prêts de la Banque visés à l'article 16 *b)* peuvent être assortis de bonifications d'intérêt. Le taux de ces bonifications peut atteindre 3% pour des prêts d'une durée maximum de 25 ans.

Les montants nécessaires au paiement des bonifications d'intérêt sont, pendant la durée de l'existence du Fonds, imputés sur le montant des aides non remboursables prévu à l'article 16 *a)*.

Article 20

1. La Communauté peut accorder sur les disponibilités de trésorerie du Fonds des avances dans la limite d'un plafond de 50 millions d'unités de compte pour les interventions prévues à l'article 17 paragraphe 4.

2. Ces avances sont accordées dans les conditions fixées au protocole n° 5.

Article 21

Pour le financement des actions visées à l'article 17, l'État associé ou le groupe d'États associés intéressé établit, dans les conditions fixées au protocole n° 5, un dossier pour chaque projet ou programme pour lequel il sollicite un concours financier. Il transmet ce dossier à la Communauté à l'adresse de la Commission.

Article 22

La Communauté instruit les demandes de financement qui lui sont présentées en vertu des dispositions de l'article précédent. Elle maintient avec les États associés intéressés les contacts nécessaires afin de statuer en pleine connaissance de cause sur les projets ou programmes qui lui sont soumis. L'État associé ou le groupe d'États associés intéressés est informé de la suite réservée à sa demande.

Article 23

Le concours apporté par la Communauté pour la réalisation de certains projets ou programmes peut prendre la forme d'une participation à des financements dans lesquels interviendraient notamment des États tiers, des organismes financiers internationaux ou des autorités et des instituts de crédit et de développement des États associés ou des États membres.

Article 24

1. Les bénéficiaires des aides du Fonds sont:

a) En ce qui concerne les aides non remboursables:

— pour les projets d'investissements économiques et sociaux, soit les États associés, soit des personnes morales qui ne poursuivent pas à titre principal un but lucratif, qui présentent un caractère d'intérêt général ou social et qui sont soumises dans ces États au contrôle de la puissance publique:

— pour les programmes de formation de cadres et de formation professionnelle ainsi que pour les études économiques, les gouvernements des États associés, les instituts ou organismes spécialisés ou, à titre exceptionnel, les boursiers et stagiaires;

— pour l'aide à la production, les producteurs;

— pour l'aide à la diversification, les États associés, les groupements de producteurs ou organismes similaires agréés par la Communauté ou, à défaut de ceux-ci, les producteurs eux-mêmes;

b) En ce qui concerne les prêts à conditions spéciales et les bonifications d'intérêt:

— pour les projets d'investissements économiques et sociaux, soit les États associés, soit des personnes morales qui ne poursuivent pas à titre principal un but lucratif, qui présentent un caractère d'intérêt général ou social et qui sont soumises dans ces États au contrôle de la puissance publique, soit éventuellement des entreprises privées sur décision spéciale de la Communauté;

— pour l'aide à la diversification, les États associés, les groupements de producteurs ou organismes similaires agréés par la Communauté ou, à défaut de ceux-ci, les producteurs eux-mêmes et éventuellement les entreprises privées sur décision spéciale de la Communauté.

2. Les aides financières ne peuvent être utilisées pour couvrir les dépenses courantes d'administration, d'entretien et de fonctionnement.

Article 25

Pour les interventions dont le financement est assuré par le Fonds ou par la Banque, la participation aux adjudications, appels d'offres, marchés et contrats est ouverte, à égalité de conditions, à toutes les personnes physiques et morales ressortissant des États membres et des États associés.

Article 26

L'utilisation des montants attribuées pour le financement des projets ou de programmes, en application des dispositions du présent titre, doit être conforme aux affectations décidées et se réaliser dans les meilleures conditions économiques.

Article 27

Le Conseil d'association définit l'orientation générale de la coopération financière et technique dans le cadre de l'association à la lumière notamment d'un rapport annuel qui lui est soumis par l'organe chargé de la gestion de l'aide financière et technique de la Communauté.

Article 28

La non ratification de la présente convention par un État associé dans les conditions prévues à l'article 57 ou la dénonciation de la convention conformément à l'article 62 entraîne pour les Parties contractantes l'obligation d'ajuster le montant de l'aide financière fixé aux articles 16 et 18.

TITRE III

DROIT D'ÉTABLISSEMENT, SERVICES, PAIEMENTS ET CAPITAUX

Article 29

Sans préjudice de l'exécution des mesures prises en application du traité, les ressortissants et sociétés de tous les États membres sont, dans chaque État associé, progressivement et au plus trois ans après l'entrée en vigueur de la présente convention, mis sur un pied d'égalité en matière de droit d'établissement et de prestation des services.

Le Conseil d'association peut autoriser un État associé sur sa demande à suspendre pour une période et une activité déterminées, l'application des dispositions de l'alinéa précédent.

Cependant les ressortissants et sociétés d'un État membre ne peuvent bénéficier, pour une activité déterminée, dans un État associé des dispositions du premier alinéa que dans la mesure où l'État dont ils relèvent accorde pour cette même activité des avantages de même nature aux ressortissants et sociétés de l'État associé en cause.

Article 30

Dans le cas où un État associé accorderait aux ressortissants ou sociétés d'un État qui n'est ni État membre de la Communauté ni État associé au sens de la présente convention, un traitement plus favorable que celui résultant, pour les ressortissants ou sociétés des États membres, de l'application des dispositions du présent titre, ce traitement est étendu aux ressortissants ou sociétés des États membres, sauf lorsqu'il résulte d'accords régionaux.

Article 31

Le droit d'établissement au sens de la présente convention comporte, sous réserve des dispositions relatives aux mouvements de capitaux, l'accès aux activités non salariées et leur exercice, la constitution et la gestion d'entreprises et notamment de sociétés, ainsi que la création d'agences, de succursales ou de filiales.

Article 32

Au sens de la présente convention, sont considérées comme services les prestations fournies normalement contre rémunération dans la mesure où elles ne sont pas régies par les dispositions relatives aux échanges commerciaux, au droit d'établissement et aux mouvements de capitaux. Les services comprennent notamment des activités de caractère industriel, des activités de caractère commercial, des activités artisanales et les activités des professions libérales, à l'exclusion des activités salariées.

Article 33

Par sociétés, on entend, au sens de la présente convention, les sociétés de droit civil ou commercial, y compris les sociétés coopératives et les autres personnes morales relevant du droit public ou privé, à l'exception des sociétés qui ne poursuivent pas de but lucratif.

Les sociétés d'un État membre ou d'un État associé sont les sociétés constituées en conformité de la législation d'un État membre ou d'un État associé et ayant leur siège statutaire, leur administration centrale ou leur établissement principal dans un État membre ou un État associé; toutefois, dans le cas où elles n'ont dans un État membre ou dans un État associé que leur siège statutaire, leur activité doit présenter un lien effectif et continu avec l'économie de cet État membre ou de cet État associé.

Article 34

Le Conseil d'association arrête toutes décisions nécessaires en vue de promouvoir l'exécution des articles 29 à 33 ci-dessus.

Article 35

Chaque État signataire s'engage, dans la limite de sa compétence en la matière, à autoriser les paiements afférents aux échanges de marchandises, de services et de capitaux et aux salaires, ainsi que le transfert de ces paiements vers l'État membre ou l'État associé dans lequel réside le créancier ou le bénéficiaire, dans la mesure où la circulation des marchandises, des services, des capitaux et des personnes est libérée en application de la présente convention.

Article 36

Pendant toute la durée des prêts et des avances visés aux chapitres III, IV et V du protocole n° 5, les États associés s'engagent à mettre à la disposition des débiteurs, les devises nécessaires au service de l'intérêt et de l'amortissement des prêts accordés pour les projets à réaliser sur leur territoire et au remboursement des avances consenties aux caisses de stabilisation.

Article 37

1. Les Étatsas sociés s'efforcent de n'introduire aucune nouvelle restriction de change affectant le régime des investissements et les paiements courants afférents aux mouvements de capitaux en résultant lorsqu'ils sont effectués par des personnes résidant dans les États membres ainsi que de ne pas rendre plus restrictives les réglementations existantes.

2. Dans la mesure nécessaire à la réalisation des objectifs de la présente convention, les États associés s'engagent à traiter sur un pied d'égalité au plus tard le 1er janvier 1965, les ressortissants et les sociétés des États membres en ce qui concerne les investissements réalisés par eux à compter de l'entrée en vigueur de la convention et les mouvements de capitaux en résultant.

Article 38

Le Conseil d'association formule toutes recommandations utiles aux Parties contractantes au sujet de l'application des articles 35, 36 et 37 ci-dessus.

TITRE IV

LES INSTITUTIONS DE L'ASSOCIATION

Article 39

Les institutions de l'association sont:

— le Conseil d'association assisté du Comité d'association,
— la Conférence parlementaire de l'association,
— la Cour arbitrale de l'association.

Article 40

Le Conseil d'association est composé, d'une part des membres du Conseil de la Communauté économique européenne et de membres de la Commission de la Communauté économique européenne, et, d'autre part, d'un membre du gouvernement de chaque État associé.

Tout membre du Conseil d'association empêché peut se faire représenter. Le représentant exerce tous les droits du membre titulaire.

Le Conseil d'association ne peut valablement délibérer qu'avec la participation de la moitié des membres du Conseil de la Communauté, d'un membre de la Commission et de la moitié des membres titulaires représentant les gouvernements des États associés.

Article 41

La présidence du Conseil d'association est exercée à tour de rôle par un membre du Conseil de la Communauté économique européenne et un membre du gouvernement d'un État associé.

Article 42

Le Conseil d'association se réunit une fois par an à l'initiative de son président.

Il se réunit en outre chaque fois que la nécessité le requiert, dans les conditions fixées par son règlement intérieur.

Article 43

Le Conseil d'association se prononce du commun accord de la Communauté d'une part, et des États associés d'autre part.

La Communauté, d'une part, et les États associés, d'autre part, déterminent, chacun par un protocole interne, le mode de formation de leurs positions respectives.

Article 44

Dans les cas prévus par la présente convention, le Conseil d'association dispose du pouvoir de prendre des décisions; ces décisions sont obligatoires pour les Parties contractantes qui sont tenues de prendre les mesures que comporte leur exécution.

Le Conseil d'association peut également formuler les résolutions, recommandations ou avis qu'il juge opportuns pour la réalisation des objectifs communs et le bon fonctionnement du régime d'association.

Le Conseil d'association procède périodiquement à l'examen des résultats du régime d'association, compte tenu des objectifs de celle-ci.

Le Conseil d'association arrête son règlement intérieur.

Article 45

Le Conseil d'association est assisté dans l'accomplissement de sa tâche par un Comité d'association composé, d'une part, d'un représentant de chaque État membre et d'un représentant de la Commission et, d'autre part, d'un représentant de chaque État associé.

Article 46

La présidence du Comité d'association est assurée par l'État assumant la présidence du Conseil d'association.

Le Comité d'association arrête son règlement intérieur qui est soumis au Conseil d'association pour approbation.

Article 47

1. Le Conseil d'association détermine dans son règlement intérieur la mission et la compétence du Comité d'association en vue notamment d'assurer la continuité de la coopération nécessaire au bon fonctionnement de l'association.

2. Le Conseil d'association peut, lorsque la nécessité le requiert, déléguer au Comité d'association, dans les conditions et les limites qu'il arrête, l'exercice des pouvoirs qui lui sont dévolus par la présente convention.

Dans ce cas, le Comité d'association se prononce dans les conditions prévues à l'article 43.

Article 48

Le Comité d'association rend compte au Conseil d'association de ses activités, notamment dans les domaines ayant fait l'objet d'une délégation de compétence.

Il présente également au Conseil d'association toute proposition utile.

Article 49

Le secrétariat du Conseil d'association et du Comité d'association est assuré sur une base paritaire dans les conditions prévues par le règlement intérieur du Conseil d'association.

Article 50

La Conférence parlementaire de l'association se réunit une fois par an. Elle est composée, sur une base paritaire, de membres de l'Assemblée et de membres des Parlements des États associés.

Le Conseil d'association présente chaque année un rapport d'activité à la Conférence parlementaire.

La Conférence parlementaire peut voter des résolutions dans les matières concernant l'association. Elle désigne son président et son bureau et arrête son règlement intérieur.

La Conférence parlementaire est préparée par une commission paritaire.

Article 51

1. Les différends relatifs à l'interprétation ou à l'application de la présente convention nés entre un État membre, plusieurs États membres ou la Communauté d'une part, et un ou plusieurs États associés d'autre part, sont soumis par l'une des parties au différend au Conseil d'association qui en recherche, au cours de sa plus proche session, le règlement amiable. S'il ne peut y parvenir et faute pour les parties d'être convenues d'un mode de règlement approprié, le différend est porté à la requête de la partie la plus diligente devant la Cour arbitrale de l'association.

2. La Cour arbitrale est composée de cinq membres: un président qui est nommé par le Conseil d'association et quatre juges choisis parmi des personnalités offrant toute garantie d'indépendance et de compétence. Les juges sont désignés dans les trois mois de l'entrée en vigueur de la convention et pour la durée de celle-ci par le Conseil d'association. Deux d'entre eux sont nommés sur présentation du Conseil de la Communauté économique européenne, les deux autres sur présentation des États associés. Le Conseil d'association nomme, suivant la même procédure, pour chaque juge un suppléant qui siège en cas d'empêchement du juge titulaire.

3. La Cour arbitrale statue à la majorité.

4. Les décisions de la Cour arbitrale sont obligatoires pour les parties aux différends qui sont tenues de prendre les mesures que comporte leur exécution.

5. Dans les trois mois de la nomination des juges, le statut de la Cour arbitrale est arrêté, sur proposition de celle-ci, par le Conseil d'association.

6. Dans le même délai, la Cour arbitrale arrête son règlement de procédure.

Article 52

Le Conseil d'association peut faire toute recommandation utile pour faciliter les contacts entre la Communauté et les représentants des intérêts professionnels des États associés.

Article 53

Les frais de fonctionnement des institutions de l'association sont pris en charge dans les conditions déterminées par le protocole n° 6 annexé à la présente convention.

TITRE V

DISPOSITIONS GÉNÉRALES ET FINALES

Article 54

Les traités, conventions, accords ou arrangements entre un ou plusieurs États membres et un ou plusieurs États associés, quelle qu'en soit la forme ou la nature, ne doivent pas faire obstacle à l'application des dispositions de la présente convention.

Article 55

La présente convention s'applique au territoire européen des États membres de la Communauté, d'une part, et au territoire des États associés, d'autre part.

Le titre premier de la présente convention s'applique également aux relations entre les départements français d'outre-mer et les États associés.

Article 56

La présente convention sera, en ce qui concerne la Communauté, valablement conclue par une décision du Conseil de la Communauté prise en conformité des dispositions du traité et notifiée aux Parties. Elle sera ratifiée par les États signataires en conformité de leurs règles constitutionnelles respectives.

Les instruments de ratification et l'acte de notification de la conclusion de la convention sont déposés au secrétariat des Conseils des Communautés européennes qui en informera les États signataires.

Article 57

1. La présente convention entre en vigueur le premier jour du mois suivant la date à laquelle ont été déposés les instruments de ratification des États membres et de quinze au moins des États associés, ainsi que l'acte de notification de la conclusion de la convention par la Communauté.

2. L'État associé qui n'a pas ratifié au jour de l'entrée en vigueur de la convention telle que prévue au paragraphe précédent, ne peut y procéder que dans les douze mois suivant cette entrée en vigueur sauf si, avant l'expiration de ce terme, il porte à la connaissance du Conseil d'association son intention de ratifier la convention au plus tard dans les six mois suivant ce terme et à condition qu'il dépose, dans ce même délai, ses instruments de ratification.

3. Pour les États n'ayant pas ratifié au jour de l'entrée en vigueur de la convention telle que prévue au paragraphe 1, les dispositions de la convention deviennent applicables le premier jour du mois suivant le dépôt de leurs instruments de ratification respectifs.

Les États signataires qui ratifient la convention dans les conditions énoncées au paragraphe 2 reconnaissent la validité de toute mesure d'application de la convention prise entre la date d'entrée en vigueur de la convention et la date où ses dispositions leur sont devenues applicables. Sans préjudice d'un délai qui pourrait leur être accordé par le Conseil d'association, ils exécutent six mois au plus tard après le dépôt de leurs instruments de ratification, toutes les obligations qui sont à leur charge au terme de la convention ou de décisions d'application prises par le Conseil d'association.

4. Le règlement intérieur des organes de l'association fixe si et dans quelles conditions les représentants des États signataires qui, à la date d'entrée en vigueur de la convention, ne l'ont pas encore ratifiée, siègent en qualité d'observateurs aux organes de l'association. Les dispositions ainsi arrêtées ne peuvent produire effet que jusqu'à la date à laquelle la convention devient applicable à l'égard de ces États; elles cessent en tout état de cause d'être applicables à la date à laquelle, selon les modalités du paragraphe 2 ci-dessus, l'État en cause ne pourra plus procéder à la ratification de la convention.

Article 58

1. Le Conseil d'association est informé de toute demande d'adhésion ou d'association d'un État à la Communauté.

2. Toute demande d'association à la Communauté d'un État dont la structure économique et la production sont comparables à celles des États associés qui, après examen par la Communauté, a été portée par celle-ci devant le Conseil d'association, y fait l'objet de consultations.

3. L'accord d'association entre la Communauté et un État visé au paragraphe précédent peut prévoir l'accession de cet État à la présente convention. Cet État jouit alors des mêmes droits et est soumis aux mêmes obligations que les États associés. Toutefois, l'accord qui l'associe à la Communauté peut fixer la date à laquelle certains de ces droits et obligations lui deviennent applicables.

Cette accession ne peut porter atteinte aux avantages résultant pour les États associés signataires de la présente convention des dispositions relatives à la coopération financière et technique.

Article 59

La présente convention est conclue pour une durée de cinq années à compter de son entrée en vigueur.

Article 60

Un an avant l'expiration de la présente convention, les Parties contractantes examinent les dispositions qui pourraient être prévues pour une nouvelle période.

Le Conseil d'association prend éventuellement les mesures transitoires nécessaires jusqu'à l'entrée en vigueur de la nouvelle convention.

Article 61

La Communauté et les États membres assument les engagements prévus aux articles 2, 5 et 11 de la convention à l'égard des États associés qui, sur la base d'obligations internationales applicables lors de l'entrée en vigueur du traité instituant la Communauté économique européenne et les soumettant à l'application d'un régime douanier particulier, estimeraient ne pouvoir dès à présent assurer au profit de la Communauté la réciprocité prévue par l'article 3 paragraphe 2 de la convention.

Les Parties contractantes intéressées réexaminent la situation au plus tard trois ans après l'entrée en vigueur de la convention.

Article 62

La présente convention peut être dénoncée par la Communauté à l'égard de chaque État associé et par chaque État associé à l'égard de la Communauté moyennant un préavis de six mois.

Article 63

Les protocoles qui sont annexés à la présente convention en font partie intégrante.

Article 64

La présente convention rédigée en un exemplaire unique en langues allemande, française, italienne et néerlandaise, chacun de ces textes faisant également foi, sera déposée dans les archives du secrétariat des Conseils des Communautés européennes qui en remettra une copie certifiée conforme au gouvernement de chacun des États signataires.

EN FOI DE QUOI, les plénipotentiaires soussignés ont apposé leurs signatures au bas de la présente convention.

Fait à Yaoundé, le vingt juillet mil neuf cent soixante-trois.

Sous réaserve que la Communauté ne sera définitivement engagée qu'après notification aux autres Parties contractantes de l'accomplissement des procédures requises par le traité instituant la Communauté économique européenne.

Protocol No. 1 regarding the application of Article 3 of the Convention of Association

LES HAUTES PARTIES CONTRACTANTES

SONT CONVENUES des dispositions suivantes, qui sont annexées à la convention :

Article premier

1. En vue de l'application de l'article 3 de la convention, chaque État associé communique au Conseil d'association dans un délai de deux mois à compter de l'entrée en vigueur de la convention son tarif douanier ou la liste complète des droits de douane et taxes d'effet équivalant à de tels droits perçus au 31 décembre 1962 sur les produits importés, en indiquant ceux de ces droits et taxes qui s'appliquent aux produits originaires des États membres et des autres États associés et ceux qui s'appliquent aux produits originaires des pays tiers ainsi que les droits perçus à l'exportation.

Dans cette communication, chaque État associé spécifie parmi les droits et taxes visés à l'alinéa précédent ceux qui répondent, à son avis, aux nécessités de son développement et aux besoins de son industrialisation ou qui sont destinés à alimenter son budget. Il indique les raisons de leur maintien ou établissement.

2. A la demande de la Communauté, des consultations sur les tarifs douaniers ou les listes visées au paragraphe 1 ci-dessus ont lieu au sein du Conseil d'association. Si dans un délai de trois mois aucune demande de consultation n'est formulé, le Conseil d'association est réputé avoir pris acte de ces tarifs ou listes.

Article 2

Sur la base des tarifs ou listes dont le Conseil d'association a pris acte, et sans préjudice des dispositions du paragraphe 1 de l'article 3 de la convention, chaque État associé réduit annuellement de 15%, à compter du premier jour du septième mois de l'entrée en vigueur de la convention, les droits de douane et taxes d'effet équivalant à de tels droits applicables aux importations des produits originaires des États membres, autres que ceux qui sont reconnus nécessaires au développement et à l'industrialisation de chaque État associé ou qui ont pour but d'alimenter son budget.

Article 3

Chaque État associé se déclare disposé à réduire les droits de douane et taxes d'effet équivalant à de tels droits à l'égard des États membres selon un rythme plus rapide que celui prévu à l'article ci-dessus si la situation de son économie le lui permet.

Article 4

Tout relèvement des droits de douane et taxes d'effet équivalant à de tels droits reconnus nécessaires au développement et à l'industrialisation d'un État associé ou qui ont pour but d'alimenter son budget, est communiqué par celui-ci au Conseil d'association préalablement à son entrée en vigueur et donne lieu à consultation à la demande de la Communauté.

Protocol No. 2 regarding the application of Article of the Convention of Association

LES HAUTES PARTIES CONTRACTANTES

SONT CONVENUES des dispositions suivantes, qui sont annexées à la convention :

Article premier

Pour tout produit originaire des États membres, qui fait l'objet, à l'importation sur le territoire d'un État associé, de restrictions quantitatives ou de mesures d'effet équivalent, cet État associé établit un contingent global qu'il ouvre sans discrimination aux États membres autres que celui qui bénéficie déjà de la liberté d'importation.

Lorsque le Conseil d'association constate que les importations d'un produit ont été, au cours de deux années consécutives, inférieures aux contingents ouverts en application de l'article 2 ci-dessous, l'État associé supprime le contingentement de ce produit.

Article 2

Le contingent global visé au premier alinéa de l'article premier ci-dessus est établi et élargi dans les conditions ci-après:

a) Dans chaque État associé où les importations sont limitées par des restrictions quantitatives, le montant du contingent de base est égal au montant du contingent de l'année 1959 calculé conformément à l'article 11 de la convention d'application relative à l'association des pays et territoires d'outre-mer à la Communauté signée le 25 mars 1957 et annexée au traité, augmenté de 75%. Ce contingent de base doit atteindre au moins 15% de l'importation totale dudit produit dans cet État associé, au cours de la dernière année pour laquelle des statistiques sont disponibles.

Lorsque pour un produit non libéré aucun contingent n'est ouvert à l'importation dans un État associé, celui-ci établit un contingent au moins égal à 15% de l'importation totale dudit produit dans cet État associé au cours de la dernière année pour laquelle des statistiques sont disponibles.

Pour les produits qui n'ont jamais été importés par un État associé, celui-ci établit un contingent d'un montant approprié.

Le contingent de base ainsi établi est augmenté de 20% pour la première année et ensuite annuellement par rapport à l'année précédente de 20% pour la deuxième année, de 30% pour la troisième année, de 40% pour la quatrième année.

b) Chaque État associé dans lequel l'importation est limitée autrement que par des restrictions quantitatives, établit pour chaque produit non libéré, à compter de l'entrée en vigueur de la convention, un contingent global, accessible sans discrimination aux États membres et égal au montant des importations de ce produit en provenance des États membres réalisées par cet État associé au cours de la dernière année pour laquelle des statistiques sont disponibles. Ce contingent ne peut pas être inférieur à 15% de l'importation totale du même pendant l'année de référence.

Le contingent de base ainsi établi est augmenté dans les conditions fixées à l'alinéa 4 du paragraphe *a*) ci-dessus.

Article 3

Chaque État associé ouvre à l'importation des produits originaires des États membres, au plus tard le 1er février de chaque année, les contingents établis conformément à l'article 2 du présent protocole. Ces mesures ainsi que celles visées à l'article 5 ci-dessus sont publiées dans le recueil des actes officiels de l'État intéressé et font, en outre, l'objet d'une communication au Conseil d'association.

Article 4

Chaque État associé se déclare disposé à éliminer les restrictions quantitatives à l'importation et les mesures d'effet équivalent selon un rythme plus rapide que celui qui est prévu au présent protocole, si la situation de son économie le lui permet.

Article 5

1. Dans les conditions prévues au paragraphe 3 de l'article 6 de la convention, un État associé peut maintenir ou établir des restrictions quantitatives à l'égard de l'importation des produits originaires des États membres, sous réserve d'une consultation préalable au sein du Conseil d'association et de l'établissement de contingents globaux accessibles sans discrimination aux produits originaires des États membres.

2. Le Conseil d'association doit procéder à la consultation prévue au paragraphe précédent dans un délai maximum de deux mois à compter de la date à laquelle l'État associé a demandé de pouvoir adopter les mesures visées au dit paragraphe.

Si la consultation n'a pas lieu dans ce délai, l'État associé peut adopter les mesures demandées.

Protocol No. 3 regarding the concept of 'goods of origin' for the application of the Convention of Association

LES HAUTES PARTIES CONTRACTANTES

SONT CONVENUES des dispositions suivantes, qui sont annexées à la convention:

1. Le Conseil d'association arrête, sur la base d'un projet de la Commission, au plus tard le premier jour du septième mois suivant celui de l'entrée en vigueur de la convention, la définition de la notion de «produits originaires» aux fins de l'application du titre I de la convention. Il détermine également les méthodes de coopération administrative.

2. Jusqu'à la mise en application des nouvelles dispositions, le régime en vigueur à la date du 31 décembre 1962 continue à être appliqué.

Protocol No. 4 regarding the action of the High Contracting Parties concerning their reciprocal interests especially with reference to tropical products

LES HAUTES PARTIES CONTRACTANTES

SONT CONVENUES des dispositions suivantes, qui sont annexées à la convention:

1. Les Parties contractantes conviennent de tenir compte de leurs intérêts réciproques sur le plan international, conformément aux principes qui sont à la base de la convention.

2. A cet effet, elles assurent la coopération nécessaire, notamment au moyen de consultations au sein du Conseil d'association, et se prêtent mutuellement toute l'assistance possible.

3. Ces consultations ont lieu notamment en vue d'entreprendre d'un commun accord sur le plan international les actions appropriées pour résoudre les problèmes posés par l'écoulement et la commercialisation des produits tropicaux.

Protocol No. 5 regarding the administration of financial aid

LES HAUTES PARTIES CONTRACTANTES

SONT CONVENUES des dispositions suivantes qui sont annexées à la convention:

Chapitre I

Investissements économiques et sociaux et assistance technique liée aux investissements

Article premier

1. Pour le financement des actions visées à l'article 17 paragraphe 1 de la convention, les gouvernements des États associés établissent, autant que possible dans le cadre d'un plan de développement, des projets d'infrastructure économique et sociale, des projets à caractère productif d'intérêt général, des projets à caractère productif et à rentabilité financière normale ainsi que des demandes d'assistance technique liée aux investissements.

2. Toutefois, la Communauté peut, en cas de besoin, établir au profit d'un État associé et avec son accord, des projets d'assistance technique liée aux investissements.

Article 2

Les projets sont financés soit par des aides non remboursables, soit par des prêts à conditions spéciales, soit par des prêts accordés par la Banque éventuellement assortis de bonifications d'intérêt, soit simultanément par plusieurs de ces moyens.

Article 3

Les projets sont présentés à la Communauté à l'adresse de la Commission. Toutefois, les projets pour lesquels un prêt de la Banque est demandé sont adressés à la Banque soit directement par les intéressés, soit par l'intermédiaire de la Commission, soit par l'intermédiaire de l'État associé sur le territoire duquel le projet sera réalisé.

Article 4

1. L'assistance technique liée aux investissements est financée par des aides non remboursables.

2. Elle comprend notamment les actions suivantes:
— programmation,
— études spéciales et régionales de développement,

— études techniques et économiques nécessaires à la mise au point de projets d'investissements,

— aide à la préparation des dossiers,

— aide à l'exécution et contrôle technique des travaux,

— aide temporaire pour l'établissement, la mise en route et l'exploitation d'un investissement déterminé ou d'un ensemble d'équipements,

— prise en charge temporaire des techniciens et des biens de consommation nécessaires à la bonne exécution d'un projet d'investissement.

Article 5

Les autorités compétentes des États associés sont responsables de l'exécution des projets présentés par leur gouvernement et financés par la Communauté.

Chapitre II

Coopération technique

Article 6

Le financement des actions visées à l'article 17 paragraphe 2 de la convention est effectué soit sur demande des gouvernements des États associés, présentée de préférence dans le cadre de programmes annuels ou pluri-annuels, soit sur proposition de la Communauté.

Article 7

Les actions de la Communauté dans le domaine de la coopération technique sont financées par des aides non remboursables.

Article 8

Les demandes des États associés sont présentées à la Communauté à l'adresse de la Commission.

Article 9

Les actions de financement de la Communauté dans le domaine de la coopération technique comprennent notamment :

a) Envoi dans les États associés, sur leur demande, d'experts, de conseillers, de techniciens et d'instructeurs pour une mission déterminée et une durée limitée ;

b) Fourniture de matériels d'expérimentation et de démonstration ;

c) Élaboration d'études sur les perspectives de développement et de diversification des économies des États associés ainsi que sur des problèmes intéressant les États associés dans leur ensemble, tels que élaboration et diffusion de plans types pour certains bâtiments ou études de marchés ;

d) Attribution de bourses pour la formation de cadres, dans les universités et instituts spécialisés des États associés ou, à défaut, des États membres ;

e) Formation professionnelle par attribution de bourses ou par stages dans les États associés ou, à défaut, dans les États membres ;

f) Organisation de sessions de formation de courte durée à l'intention des ressortissants des États associés;

g) Information générale et documentation destinées à favoriser le développement économique et social des États associés, le développement des échanges entre ces États et la Communauté ainsi que la bonne réalisation des objectifs du Fonds.

Article 10

Les gouvernements des États associés et, le cas échéant, les instituts ou autres organismes spécialisés des États membres ou des États associés sont responsables de l'exécution des programmes de coopération technique présentés par les gouvernements.

Chapitre III

Prêts à des conditions spéciales

Article 11

Les prêts à des conditions spéciales visés à l'article 16 de la convention servent à financer des projets d'investissement présentant un intérêt général pour l'État bénéficiaire dans la mesure où la rentabilité directe de ces projets ainsi que la capacité d'endettement de l'État intéressé lors de l'octroi du prêt, permettent un tel financement.

Article 12

Ces prêts peuvent être accordés pour une durée maxima de 40 ans et être exonérés d'amortissements pendant une durée allant jusqu'à 10 ans. Ils bénéficient de conditions d'intérêt favorables.

Article 13

La Communauté arrête les conditions d'octroi des prêts ainsi que les modalités de leur exécution et de leur recouvrement.

Chapitre IV

Prêts de la Banque européenne d'investissement

Article 14

L'examen par la Banque de l'admissibilité des projets et l'octroi des prêts aux États associés ou aux entreprises ressortissant de ces États s'effectuent suivant les modalités, conditions et procédures prévues par les statuts de la Banque et compte tenu de la capacité d'endettement de l'État intéressé. La Banque ne finance que ceux des projets auxquels le ou les États associés intéressés ont donné leur avis favorable.

Article 15

La durée de la période d'amortissement de chaque prêt est établie sur la base des caractéristiques économiques du projet à financer; cette période peut atteindre un maximum de 25 ans.

Article 16

Les prêts peuvent être utilisés pour couvrir des dépenses d'importation aussi bien que les dépenses locales nécessaires à la réalisation des projets d'investissement approuvés.

Article 17

Les prêts portent un taux d'intérêt identique à celui pratiqué par la Banque au moment de la signature du prêt. Ils peuvent être assortis à la demande des bénéficiaires de bonifications d'intérêt dans les conditions prévues à l'article 19 de la convention.

Article 18

La décision d'octroi de bonifications d'intérêt est prise par la Communauté. Le montant des bonifications est directement versé à la Banque.

Chapitre V

Avances aux caisses de stabilisation

Article 19

Pour le financement des actions visées à l'article 17 paragraphe 4 de la convention, des avances peuvent être accordées aux caisses de stabilisation existantes ou à créer dans les États associés.

Article 20

Les demandes d'avances sont présentées à la Communauté à l'adresse de la Commission, par les gouvernements des États associés intéressés. Elles sont accompagnées d'un rapport préparé par le conseil d'administration de la caisse de stabilisation intéressée.

Article 21

La Communauté fixe le montant et la durée des avances. Ces avances sont garanties par l'État associé intéressé. Leur terme normal est celui de la convention.

Chapitre VI

Aides à la diversification et à la production

Article 22

Les aides à la production et à la diversification visées aux articles 17 paragraphe 3 et 18 lettre b) de la convention sont réparties et utilisées dans les conditions prévues ci-après.

Article 23

Les aides à la production ont pour objet de faciliter aux producteurs des États associés l'adaptation progressive de leurs productions aux exigences d'une commercialisation aux prix mondiaux.

Les aides à la diversification doivent permettre aux États associés de réformer leur structure et de réaliser les diversifications appropriées dans les domaines agricole, industriel et commercial.

Article 24

Les aides à la production et à la diversification sont réparties comme suit:

1° 183 millions d'unités de compte à titre d'aides à la production et à la diversification aux onze États associés suivants: Cameroun, République centrafricaine, Congo (Brazzaville), Côte-d'Ivoire, Dahomey, Madagascar, Mali, Niger, Sénégal, Tchad et Togo;

2° 32 millions d'unités de compte à titre d'aides à la diversification aux quatre États associés suivants: Burundi, Congo (Léopoldville), Rwanda et Somalie;

3° 15 millions d'unités de compte à titre d'aides à la diversification aux trois États associés suivants: Gabon, Haute-Volta et Mauritanie.

Article 25

Pour le financement des actions visées à l'article 23 ci-dessus et dans la limite du montant dont il bénéficie à ce titre, chaque État associé présente, dans les trois mois de l'entrée en vigueur de la convention, un programme couvrant au maximum la période de validité de celle-ci et prévoyant soit simultanément des aides à la production et des aides à la diversification, soit uniquement des aides à la diversification.

Section A

ÉTATS BÉNÉFICIANT SIMULTANÉMENT D'AIDES A LA DIVERSIFICATION ET A LA PRODUCTION

Article 26

1. Pour chacun des onze États associés bénéficiant simultanément d'aides à la diversification et à la production, la quote-part quinquennale de la somme de 183 millions d'unités de compte servant à l'établissement de son programme, est calculée en fonction de ses exportations des produits suivants: café, arachides en graines, huile d'arachide, huile de palme, coco râpé, coton, poivre, riz, sucre, gomme arabique.

2. Sur la base des dispositions du paragraphe précédent la quote-part quinquennale de chacun de ces États associés est fixée comme suit (en millions d'unités de compte):

Cameroun	15,8
République centrafricaine	6,8
Congo (Brazzaville)	6,4
Côte-d'Ivoire	46,7

Dahomey	5,5
Madagascar	31,6
Mali	5,6
Niger	6,5
Sénégal	46,7
Tchad	5,7
Togo	5,7

Article 27

Chaque État associé recevant simultanément des aides à la production et des aides à la diversification tient compte pour l'établissement de son programme quinquennal des principes suivants:

1. Les aides à la production ne peuvent excéder les trois quarts du montant quinquennal que la Communauté accorde à cet État au titre de l'ensemble des aides à la production et à la diversification;

2. Les aides à la production peuvent être allouées dès la première année de la convention par la Communauté à chaque État associé. Elles deviennent dégressives à partir de la date à laquelle débutera, pour chaque produit, le processus devant conduire à la commercialisation aux prix mondiaux, de manière à parvenir au plus tard à la fin de la période de validité de la convention à la suppression complète de ces aides;

3. Chaque État associé prévoit qu'une partie adéquate du montant alloué au titre des aides à la production sera affectée par les producteurs à l'amélioration structurelle des cultures.

Article 28

La Communauté examine avec chaque État associé si le programme présenté par celui-ci est conforme aux principes établis à l'article 27 ci-dessus. A la suite de cet examen, et si nécessaire après ajustement de ce programme, elle en prend acte et arrête le montant de la première tranche annuelle de son intervention.

Article 29

1. La Communauté examine immédiatement après la fin de chaque année à compter de la date d'entrée en vigueur de la convention, si l'utilisation des aides à la diversification et à la production a été conforme, au cours de l'année écoulée, aux objectifs assignés à ces aides, conformément aux dispositions de la convention et du présent protocole.

2. Cet examen porte notamment sur:

— l'analyse par produit, de l'évolution des cours mondiaux par rapport à ceux ayant servi de base à la détermination de la quote-part de chaque État associé visé à l'article 26;

— la comparaison par produit des niveaux des tonnages effectivement exportés par rapport à ceux ayant servi de base à la détermination de ladite quotepart;

— le montant des aides qui ont été allouées par d'autres sources pour la réalisation des objectifs visés à l'article 23.

3. A la suite de cet examen et après avoir si nécessaire ajusté la tranche annuelle suivante du programme prévu à l'article 25, la Communauté arrête définitivement le montant de cette tranche.

4. Si, à l'issue de cet examen, la Communauté constate que l'aide à la production allouée à l'État associé intéressé au titre de l'année écoulée n'a pas été totalement utilisée, elle décide, après consultation de cet État, de l'affectation à donner à ce solde.

Article 30

1. Les montants de l'aide destinée aux producteurs, tel qu'il est établi en vertu des dispositions des articles 28 et 29 ci-dessus, est versé sous forme d'aides non remboursables à des organismes agréés par la Communauté et les États associés.

2. Le montant annuel et les modalités d'utilisation de l'aide allouée à chaque État pour chaque production font l'objet, à l'intérieur de chaque État associé, d'une publicité appropriée.

Article 31

L'utilisation des montants alloués au titre de l'aide à la production doit être effectuée conformément aux affectations et modalités arrêtées par la Communauté après consultation de l'État associé intéressé.

Les États associés sont responsables chacun en ce qui le concerne des actes qui doivent être accomplis pour l'exécution des dispositions du présent chapitre.

La Communauté veille à l'observation de la prescription de l'alinéa premier et prend, le cas échéant, toutes mesures appropriées.

Article 32

Pour l'application des articles 28 à 30 ci-dessus, chaque État associé présente annuellement un rapport détaillé sur l'utilisation des sommes reçues au titre des aides à la production. Il y joint toutes pièces justificatives et notamment les rapports des organismes agréés.

L'État associé prête son concours à tous contrôles que la Communauté estime utiles d'effectuer notamment auprès desdits organismes.

Article 33

Les sommes que les États associés bénéficiant simultanément d'aides à la production et d'aides à la diversification, consacrent à l'aide à la diversification, sont utilisées conformément aux dispositions des articles 36 à 38.

Section B

ÉTATS BÉNÉFICIANT D'AIDES A LA DIVERSIFICATION

Article 34

1. Les sommes prévues à l'article 24 paragraphe 2 sont réparties comme suit (en millions d'unités de compte):

— Burundi	5,25
— Congo (Léopoldville)	15
— Rwanda	5,25
— Somalie	6,50

2. Les sommes prévues à l'article 24 paragraphe 3 sont réparties comme suit (en millions d'unités de compte):

— Gabon	4
— Haute-Volta	6
— Mauritanie	5

Article 35

Sur la base du programme prévu à l'article 25 ci-dessus, la Communauté examine avec chacun des sept États associés visés à l'article précédent si leurs propositions d'utilisation des aides à la diversification tiennent compte des objectifs assignés à ces aides.

Article 36

Les projets d'aides à la diversification sont financés soit par des aides non remboursables, soit par des prêts à conditions spéciales, soit par des prêts accordés par la Banque avec éventuellement bonifications d'intérêt, soit simultanément par plusieurs de ces moyens.

Article 37

Dans le cadre de son programme, chaque État associé présente à la Communauté des demandes d'aides à la diversification sur la base de projets déterminés.

Article 38

Les dispositions des chapitres I, II, III et IV du présent protocole sont, en tant que de besoin, applicables au financement des projets d'aides à la diversification.

Chapitre VII

Dispositions diverses

Article 39

En vue de permettre une intervention rapide pour l'attribution de secours d'urgence sur les ressources du Fonds à ceux des États associés qui seraient frappés de catastrophes naturelles, il est institué un fonds de réserve, alimenté par un prélèvement de 1% sur la part des aides non remboursables comprises dans le montant visé à l'article 18, lettre *a*) de la convention.

Article 40

Les frais financiers et administratifs résultant de la gestion du Fonds sont imputés sur les ressources destinées aux aides non remboursables.

Article 41

Les importations dans un État associé qui ont fait l'objet d'un marché de fournitures financé par la Communauté, ne sont pas imputées sur les contingents ouverts aux États membres.

Article 42

La Communauté et les États associés collaborent à toutes mesures nécessaires pour assurer que l'utilisation des montants attribués par la Communauté se réalise conformément aux dispositions de l'article 26 de la convention.

Protocol No. 6 regarding the administrative expenses of the institutions of the associations

LES HAUTES PARTIES CONTRACTANTES

SONT CONVENUES des dispositions ci-après qui sont annexées à la convention:

Article premier

Les États membres et la Communauté, d'une part, les États associés, d'autre part, prennent en charge les dépenses qu'ils exposent en raison de leur participation aux sessions du Conseil d'association et des organes qui en dépendent, tant en ce qui concerne les frais de personnel, de voyage et de séjour, qu'en ce qui concerne les frais de postes et de télécommunications.

Les dépenses relatives à l'interprétation en séance ainsi qu'à la traduction et à la reproduction des documents, et les dépenses afférentes à l'organisation matérielle des réunions (local, fournitures, huissiers, etc.) sont supportées par la Communauté ou par les États associés, selon que les réunions ont lieu sur le territoire d'un État membre ou sur celui d'un État associé.

Article 2

La Communauté et les États associés prennent en charge, chacun en ce qui le concerne, les frais de voyage et de séjour de leurs participants aux réunions de la Conférence parlementaire de l'association et de la Commission paritaire.

Dans les mêmes conditions, ils prennent en charge les frais de voyage et de séjour du personnel nécessaire à ces sessions ainsi que les frais de postes et de télécommunications.

Les dépenses relatives à l'interprétation en séance ainsi qu'à la traduction et à la reproduction des documents et les dépenses afférentes à l'organisation matérielle des réunions (local, fournitures et huissiers, etc. . .) sont supportées par la Communauté ou par les États associés selon que les réunions ont lieu sur le territoire d'un État membre ou sur celui d'un État associé.

Article 3

Les membres de la Cour arbitrale ont droit au remboursement de leurs frais de voyage et de leurs frais de séjour. Ces derniers sont fixés à 20 unités de compte pour chaque jour ou les membres de la Cour arbitrale exercent leurs fonctions. Ces sommes leur sont versées par la Cour arbitrale.

Les frais de voyage et de séjour des membres de la Cour arbitrale sont pris en charge par moitié par la Communauté et par moitié par les États associés.

Les dépenses afférentes au greffe de la Cour arbitrale, à l'instruction des différends et à l'organisation matérielle des audiences (local, personnel, interprétation, etc.) sont supportées par la Communauté.

Les dépenses afférentes à des mesures extraordinaires d'instruction sont réglées par la Cour arbitrale avec les autres dépens dans les conditions prévues par son statut et font l'objet d'avances de la part des parties dans les conditions fixées par l'ordonnance de la Cour arbitrale ou de son président dans laquelle ces mesures sont prescrites.

Protocol No. 7 regarding the value of the unit of account

LES HAUTES PARTIES CONTRACTANTES

SONT CONVENUES des dispositions suivantes, qui sont annexées à la convention:

Article premier

La valeur de l'unité de compte utilisée pour exprimer des sommes dans la convention d'association ou dans les dispositions prises en application de celle-ci est de 0,88867088 gramme d'or fin.

Article 2

La parité de la monnaie d'un État membre par rapport à l'unité de compte définie à l'article premier est le rapport entre le poids d'or fin contenu dans cette unité de compte et le poids d'or fin correspondant à la parité de cette monnaie déclarée au Fonds monétaire international. A défaut de parité déclarée ou dans le cas d'application aux paiements courants, de cours s'écartant de la parité d'une marge supérieure à celle qui est autorisée par le Fonds monétaire, le poids d'or fin correspondant à la parité de la monnaie sera calculé sur la base du taux de change appliqué dans l'État membre pour les paiements courants, le jour du calcul, à une monnaie directement ou indirectement définie et convertible en or et sur la base de la parité déclarée au Fonds monétaire de cette monnaie convertible.

Article 3

L'unité de compte, telle que définie à l'article premier ci-dessus, demeurera inchangée pour toute la durée d'exécution de la convention. Toutefois, si avant la date d'expiration de cette dernière devait intervenir une modification uniformément proportionnelle du pair de toutes monnaies par rapport à l'or décidée par le Fonds monétaire international, en application de l'article 4 section 7 de ses statuts, le poids d'or fin de l'unité de compte variera en fonction inverse de cette modification.

Au cas où un ou plusieurs États membres ne mettraient pas en application la décision prise par le Fonds monétaire international visée à l'alinéa ci-dessus, le poids d'or fin de l'unité de compte variera en fonction inverse de la modification décidée par le Fonds monétaire international. Cependant le Conseil de la Communauté économique européenne examinera la situation ainsi créée et prendra, à la majorité qualifiée sur proposition de la Commission et après avis du Comité monétaire, les mesures nécessaires.

EN FOI DE QUOI, les plénipotentiaires des Hautes Parties contractantes ont signé les sept protocoles dont le texte précède.

B. THE TOGO AFFAIR

Resolutions of the Conference of Foreign Ministers of the Inter-African and Malagasay Organisation, Lagos, 26 January 1963[1]

(i) RESOLUTION I

The Council of Ministers of the Inter-African and Malagasy Organization meeting in Lagos on the 24th–26th January, 1963,

1. Condemns and deplores the murder of President Sylvanus Olympio of Togo[2] and energetically condemns political assassination as a means of overthrowing the Government and rising to power, or as a means of settling political conflicts;

2. Requests the Provisional Government of the Republic of Togo, in order to return to a normal situation:—

(*a*) to re-establish very quickly the rule of law with the co-operation of the representatives of all the active forces in the country establishing a Constitution and electoral law;

(*b*) to liberate without delay the political prisoners, notably the Ministers of the Government which has been overthrown;

(*c*) to organize as rapidly as possible free and democratic general elections which would permit the election of a National Assembly and an Executive which would also enable the Republic of Togo to participate in the Assembly of Heads of State and Government in Addis Ababa, in May 1963;

---

[1] *Conference of Foreign Ministers of the Inter-African and Malagasy Organization* (Federal Ministry of Information, Lagos, 1963), pp. 264–6.

[2] President Olympio was assassinated on 13 January 1963. The Foreign Ministers' Conference was convened in an attempt to coordinate the reactions of the states neighbouring Togo to this event.

3. Proposes to the Provisional Government of Togo a mission, the members of which will be chosen from the neighbouring member states:— Dahomey, Ivory Coast, Upper Volta, Niger and Nigeria, to help to clarify the circumstances which surrounded the murder of President Olympio or any external influences which might have incited such a crime and to assist them as necessary in re-establishing democratic institutions. The report of this mission will be circulated to all Member States;[1]

4. Recommends to the provisional Government of Togo that, in accordance with Togolese law, those responsible for this crime should be prosecuted.

(ii) RESOLUTION II

The Council of Ministers of the Inter-African and Malagasy Organisation meeting in Lagos on the 24th–26th January, 1963,

Considering the tragic circumstances of the assassination of President Sylvanus Olympio and further considering his great contributions to the cause of African Unity and independence;

Recommends to the member states that emergency financial and other material assistance be given to the widow and dependent children of the late President Sylvanus Olympio until such time as the Government of the Republic of Togo assumes its lawful responsibility in this regard.

(iii) RESOLUTION III

The Council of Ministers of the Inter-African and Malagasy Organisation meeting in Lagos on the 24th–26th January, 1963,

Recommends to the Provisional Government of Togo to respect the right of political asylum accorded to refugees under international law and conventions.

[1] The Mission which visited Lomé, capital of Togo, on 2 February 1963 failed to achieve its objectives. The substantive part of the Mission's Report reads as follows:

'In view of the fact that the resolutions of the Lagos Conference have been misinterpreted by certain people in Togo, and that some civilians and soldiers have been provoked by the announcement of the Mission's arrival, and since the Mission is determined to be primarily an instrument of assistance rather than be the cause of any more disastrous consequences which could indeed be most unfortunate and regrettable, the Mission therefore considered in compliance with the request of the Togolese Provisional President that it should give Mr. Grunitzky some time to inform his countrymen more fully as to the genuine intentions of the Mission and thereby allaying their anxieties.

'The Head of the Provisional Government and members of the Mission agreed that at the earliest opportune moment, the Mission should be able to return to Togo to discharge its assignment but that in any event the Togo Provisional Government could at any time appeal for assistance from the Mission.

'These talks were held in an atmosphere of complete understanding and were frank and cordial. The Mission returned to Cotonou in the evening and met again on Sunday afternoon February 3, 1963, to adopt the following provisional decisions:

(i) that this report should be circulated to the Heads of States of the Inter-African and Malagasy Organisation;

(ii) that in view of the favourable impression which the Mission got from its visit to Lomé that the Members of the Mission should be in readiness to return to Togo as soon as the time is opportune either to discharge the task of ascertaining information with regard to the recent events in Togo or to provide assistance to the new regime or indeed to perform both functions.'

(iv) Resolution IV

The Council of Ministers of the Inter-African and Malagasy Organization meeting in Lagos on the 24th–26th January, 1963,

Considering the dangers of internal subversion and external aggression which threaten the territorial integrity and the national independence of Member States:

Decides to undertake the study of the question of mutual defence and security between the Member States to implement Article 2 (*f*) of the Charter and requests the Governments of Liberia, Nigeria and Upper Volta to prepare a draft treaty for submission to the Council of Ministers at its meeting in Addis Ababa in May 1963.[1]

(v) Resolution V

The Council of Ministers of the Inter-African and Malagasy Organization, meeting in Lagos on the 24th to 26th January, 1963,

Considering the dangers of internal subversion and external aggression which threaten the territorial integrity and the national independence of Member States:

Recommends to the Assembly of Heads of State and Government's Conference at the next meeting in Addis Ababa to agree that where there is sufficient evidence that internal subversion has been engineered by another state, diplomatic relations with that state be severed by all members of the Inter-African and Malagasy Organization.[2]

C. THE ESTABLISHMENT OF THE ORGANISATION OF AFRICAN UNITY

(a) *The Summit Conference of Independent African States, Addis Ababa, 22–25 May 1963*

Charter of the Organisation of African Unity, 25 May 1963[3]

We, the Heads of African and Malagasy States and Governments assembled in the City of Addis Ababa, Ethiopia;

Convinced that it is the inalienable right of all people to control their own destiny;

Conscious of the fact that freedom, equality, justice and dignity are essential objectives for the achievement of the legitimate aspirations of the African peoples;

---

[1] Although Article II (*f*) of the OAU Charter lists co-operation for defence and security amongst the purposes of the Organization (see below) nothing specific came of this proposal.
[2] Cf. Article III 5 of the OAU Charter. See p. 438 below.
[3] Organization of African Unity, *Basic Documents and Resolutions* (Provisional Secretariat of the OAU, Addis Ababa, 1964), pp. 7–13.

Conscious of our responsibility to harness the natural and human resources of our continent for the total advancement of our peoples in spheres of human endeavour;

Inspired by a common determination to promote understanding and collaboration among our States in response to the aspirations of our peoples for brotherhood and solidarity, in a larger unity transcending ethnic and national differences;

Convinced that, in order to translate this determination into a dynamic force in the cause of human progress, conditions for peace and security must be established and maintained;

Determined to safeguard and consolidate the hard-won independence as well as the sovereignty and territorial integrity of our States, and to resist neo-colonialism in all its forms;

Dedicated to the general progress of Africa;

Persuaded that the Charter of the United Nations and the Universal Declaration of Human Rights, to the principles of which we reaffirm our adherence, provide a solid foundation for peaceful and positive co-operation among States;

Desirous that all African and Malagasy States should henceforth unite so that the welfare and well-being of their peoples can be assured;

Resolved to reinforce the links between our States by establishing and strengthening common institutions;

Have agreed to the present Charter.

Establishment

ARTICLE I

The High Contracting Parties do by the present Charter establish an Organisation to be known as the 'Organisation of African and Malagasy States'.

Purposes

ARTICLE II

1. The Organisation shall have the following purposes:

   a. To promote the unity and solidarity of the African and Malagasy States.

   b. To co-ordinate and intensify their collaboration and efforts to achieve a better life for the peoples of Africa.

   c. To defend their sovereignty, their territorial integrity and independence.

   d. To eradicate all forms of colonialism from the continent of Africa; and

   e. To promote international co-operation, having due regard to the Charter of the United Nations and the Universal Declaration of Human Rights.

2. To these ends, the Member States shall co-ordinate and harmonise their general policies, especially in the following fields:

   a. Political and diplomatic co-operation.

   b. Economic co-operation, including transport and communications.

   c. Educational and cultural co-operation.

   d. Health, sanitation and nutritional co-operation.

    e. Scientific and technical co-operation.

    f. Co-operation for defence and security.[1]

Principles
ARTICLE III

The Member States, in pursuit of the purposes stated in Article II, solemnly affirm and declare their adherence to the following principles:

1. The sovereign equality of all African and Malagasy States.

2. Non-interference in the internal affairs of States.

3. Respect for the sovereignty and territorial integrity of each State and for its inalienable right to independent existence.

4. Peaceful settlement of disputes by negotiation, mediation, conciliation or arbitration.

5. Unreserved condemnation, in all its forms, of political assassination as well as of subversive activities on the part of neighbouring States or any other States.[2]

6. Absolute dedication to the total emancipation of the African territories which are still dependent.

7. Affirmation of a policy of non-alignment with regard to all blocs.

Membership
ARTICLE IV

Each independent sovereign African and Malagasy State shall be entitled to become a Member of the Organisation.

Rights and Duties of Member States
ARTICLE V

All Member States shall enjoy equal rights and have equal duties.

ARTICLE VI

The Member States pledge themselves to observe scrupulously the principles enumerated in Article III of the present Charter.

Institutions
ARTICLE VII

The Organisation shall accomplish its purposes through the following principal institutions:

1. The Assembly of Heads of State and Government.

2. The Council of Ministers.

3. The General Secretariat.

4. The Commission of Mediation, Conciliation and Arbitration.

---

[1] See p. 436 above.   [2] See p. 434 above.

The Assembly of Heads of State and Government

ARTICLE VIII

The Assembly of Heads of State and Government shall be the supreme organ of the Organisation. It shall, subject to the provisions of this Charter, discuss matters of common concern to all Member States with a view to co-ordinating and harmonising the general policy of the Organisation. It may in addition review the structure, functions and acts of all the organs and any specialized agencies which may be created in accordance with the present Charter.

ARTICLE IX

The Assembly shall be composed of the Heads of State and Government or their duly accredited representatives and it shall meet at least once a year (every other year). At the request of any Member State, and approval by the majority of the Member States, the Assembly shall meet in extraordinary session.

ARTICLE X

1. Each Member State shall have one vote.
2. All resolutions shall be determined by a two-thirds majority of those present and voting.
3. Questions of procedure shall require a simple majority. Whether or not a question is one of procedure shall be determined by a simple majority of all Member States present and voting.
4. Two-thirds of the total membership of the Organisation shall form a quorum at any meeting of the Assembly.

ARTICLE XI

The Assembly shall have the power to determine its own rules of procedure.

The Council of Ministers

ARTICLE XII

The Council of Ministers shall consist of Foreign Ministers or such other Ministers as are designated by the Governments of Member States.

The Council of Ministers shall meet at least twice a year. When requested by any Member State and approved by two-thirds of all Member States, it shall meet in extraordinary session.

ARTICLE XIII

The Council of Ministers shall be responsible to the Assembly of Heads of State and Government. It shall be entrusted with the responsibility of preparing conferences of the Assembly.

It shall take cognisance of any matter referred to it by the Assembly. It shall be entrusted with the implementation of the decisions of the Assembly of

Heads of State. It shall co-ordinate inter-African co-operation in accordance with the instructions of the Assembly and in conformity with Article II (2) of the present Charter.

ARTICLE XIV

1. Each Member State shall have one vote.

2. All resolutions shall be determined by a two-thirds majority of those members present and voting.

3. Questions of procedure shall require a simple majority. Whether or not a question is one of procedure shall be determined by a simple majority of all Member States present and voting.

4. Two-thirds of the total membership of the Council shall form a quorum for any meeting of the Council.

ARTICLE XV

The Council shall have the power to determine its own rules of procedure.

General Secretariat

ARTICLE XVI

There shall be an Administrative Secretary-General of the Organisation, who shall be appointed by the Assembly of Heads of State and Government, on the recommendation of the Council of Ministers. The Administrative Secretary-General shall direct the affairs of the Secretariat.

ARTICLE XVII

There shall be one or more Assistant Secretaries-General of the Organisation, who shall be appointed by the Council of Ministers.

ARTICLE XVIII

The functions and conditions of services of the Secretary-General, of the Assistant Secretaries-General and other employees of the Secretariat shall be governed by the provisions of this Charter and the regulations approved by the Council of Ministers.

1. In the performance of their duties the Administrative Secretary-General and his staff shall not seek or receive instructions from any government or from any other authority external to the Organisation. They shall refrain from any action which might reflect on their position as international officials responsible only to the Organisation.

2. Each member of the Organisation undertakes to respect the exclusive character of the responsibilities of the Administrative Secretary-General and the Staff and not seek to influence them in the discharge of their responsibilities.

Commission of Mediation, Conciliation and Arbitration

ARTICLE XIX

Member States pledge to settle all disputes among themselves by peaceful means and, to this end, agree to conclude a separate treaty establishing a Commission of Mediation, Conciliation and Arbitration. Said treaty shall be regarded as forming an integral part of the present Charter.[1]

Specialised Commissions

ARTICLE XX

The Assembly shall establish such Specialised Commissions as it may deem necessary, including the following:

1. Economic and Social Commission.
2. Educational and Cultural Commission.
3. Health, Sanitation and Nutrition Commission.
4. Defence Commission.
5. Scientific, Technical and Research Commission.

ARTICLE XXI

Each Specialised Commission referred to in Article XX shall be composed of the Ministers concerned or other Ministers or Plenipotentiaries designated by the Governments of the Member States.

ARTICLE XXII

The functions of the Specialised Commissions shall be carried out in accordance with the provisions of the present Charter and of the regulations approved by the Council of Ministers.

The Budget

ARTICLE XXIII

The budget of the Organisation prepared by the Administrative Secretary-General shall be approved by the Council of Ministers. The budget shall be provided by contributions from Member States in accordance with the scale of assessment of the United Nations; provided, however, that no Member State shall be assessed an amount exceeding twenty per cent of the yearly regular budget of the Organisation. The Member States agree to pay their respective contributions regularly.

Signature and Ratification of Charter

ARTICLE XXIV

This Charter shall be open for signature to all independent sovereign African and Malagasy States and shall be ratified by the signatory States in accordance with their respective constitutional processes.

[1] The Commission was established by a protocol signed at Cairo on 21 July 1964. For text, see *International Legal Materials, Current Documents*, Volume III, Number 6, November 1964, pp. 1116–24.

The original instrument, done in English and French, both texts being equally authentic, shall be deposited with the Government of Ethiopia which shall transmit certified copies thereof to all independent sovereign African and Malagasy States.

Instruments of ratification shall be deposited with the Government of Ethiopia, which shall notify all signatories of each such deposit.

Entry into Force

ARTICLE XXV

This Charter shall enter into force immediately upon receipt by the Government of Ethiopia of the instruments of ratification from two-thirds of the signatory States.

Registration of the Charter

ARTICLE XXVI

This Charter shall, after due ratification, be registered with the Secretariat of the United Nations through the Government of Ethiopia in conformity with Article 102 of the Charter of the United Nations.

Interpretation of the Charter

ARTICLE XXVII

Any question which may arise concerning the interpretation of this Charter shall be decided by a vote of two-thirds of the Assembly of Heads of State and Government, present and voting.

Adhesion and Accession

ARTICLE XXVIII

1. Any independent sovereign African State may at any time notify the Administrative Secretary-General of its intention to adhere or accede to this Charter.

2. The Administrative Secretary-General shall, on receipt of such notification, communicate a copy of it to all the Member States. Admission shall be decided by a simple majority of the Member States. The decision of each Member State shall be transmitted to the Administrative Secretary-General, who shall, upon receipt of the required number of votes, communicate the decision to the State concerned.

Miscellaneous

ARTICLE XXIX

The working languages of the Organisation and all its institutions shall be English and French.

ARTICLE XXX

The Administrative Secretary-General may accept on behalf of the Organisation gifts, bequests and other donations made to the Organisation, provided that this is approved by the Council of Ministers.

ARTICLE XXXI

The Council of Ministers shall decide on the privileges and immunities to be accorded to the personnel of the Secretariat in the respective territories of the Member States.

Cessation of Membership

ARTICLE XXXII

Any State which desires to renounce its membership shall forward a written notification to the Administrative Secretary-General. At the end of one year from the date of such notification, the Charter shall cease to apply with respect to the renouncing State, which shall thereby cease to belong to the Organisation.

Amendment to the Charter

ARTICLE XXXIII

This Charter may be amended or revised if any Member State makes a written request to the Administrative Secretary-General to that effect; provided, however, that the proposed amendment is not submitted to the Assembly for consideration until all the Member States have been duly notified of it and a period of one year has elapsed. Such an amendment shall not be effective unless approved by at least two-thirds of all the Member States.

In faith whereof, We, the Heads of African and Malagasy State and Government, have signed this Charter.

Done in the City of Addis Ababa, the 25th day of May, 1963.

Algeria	Mali
Burundi	Mauritania
Cameroun	Morocco
Central African Republic	Niger
Chad	Nigeria
Congo (Brazzaville)	Rwanda
Congo (Leopoldville)	Senegal
Dahomey	Sierra Leone
Ethiopia	Somalia
Gabon	Sudan
Ghana	Tanganyika
Guinea	Togo
Ivory Coast	Tunisia
Liberia	Uganda
Libya	United Arab Republic
Madagascar	Upper Volta

Resolutions, 25 May 1963[1]

(i) *Resolution on Decolonization*

The Summit Conference of Independent African States meeting in Addis Ababa, Ethiopia, from 22 May to 25 May 1963;

Having considered all aspects of the question of decolonisation;

Unanimously convinced of the imperious and urgent necessity of coordinating and intensifying their efforts to accelerate the unconditional attainment of national independence by all African territories still under foreign domination;

Reaffirming that it is the duty of all African Independent States to support dependent people in Africa in their struggle for freedom and independence;

Noting with deep concern that most of the remaining dependent territories in Africa are dominated by foreign settlers;

Convinced that the colonial powers by their forcible imposition of the settlers to control the governments and administration of those territories are thus establishing colonial bases in the heart of Africa;

Have agreed unanimously to concert and co-ordinate their efforts and action in this field, and to this end have decided on the following measures:

1. Declares that the forcible imposition by the colonial powers of the settlers to control the governments and administration of the dependent territories is a flagrant violation of the inalienable rights of the legitimate inhabitants of the territories concerned;

2. Invites the colonial powers to take the necessary measures for the immediate application of the Declaration of the Granting of Independence to Colonial Countries and Peoples,[2] and insists that their determination to maintain colonies or semi-colonies in Africa constitutes a menace to the peace of the continent;

3. Invites further, the colonial powers, particularly the United Kingdom, with regard to Southern Rhodesia, not to transfer the powers and attributes of sovereignty to foreign minority governments imposed on African peoples by the use of force and under cover of racial legislation; transfer of power to settler minorities would amount to a violation of the provision of United Nations resolution 1514 (XV) on independence;[2]

4. Reaffirms its support of African nationalists of Southern Rhodesia and solemnly declares that if power in Southern Rhodesia were to be usurped by a racial white minority government, States Members of the Conference would lend their effective moral and practical support to any legitimate measures which the African nationalist leaders may devise for the purpose of recovering such power and restoring it to the African majority; the Conference also *undertakes* henceforth to concert the efforts of its Members to take such measures as the situation demands against any State according recognition to the minority government;

5. Reaffirms further, that the territory of South-West Africa is an African territory under international mandate and that any attempt by the Republic of

---

[1] Organization of African Unity, *Basic Documents and Resolutions* (Provisional Secretariat of the OAU, Addis Ababa, 1964), pp. 17–24.

[2] *Documents, 1960*, pp. 404–6.

South Africa to annex it would be regarded as an act of aggression; Reaffirms also its determination to render all necessary support to the second phase of the South-West Africa case before the International Court of Justice,[1] Reaffirms further the inalienable right of the people of South-West Africa to self-determination and independence;

6. Intervenes expressly with the great powers so that they cease without exception to lend direct or indirect support or assistance to all those colonialist governments which might use such assistance to suppress African national liberation movements, particularly the Portuguese Government which is conducting a real war of genocide in Africa; informs the allies of colonial powers that they must choose between their friendship for the African peoples and their support of powers that oppress African peoples;

7. Decides to send a delegation of Ministers of Foreign Affairs to speak on behalf of all African States at the meeting of the Security Council which will be called to examine the report of the United Nations Committee of 24 on the situation in African territories under Portuguese domination,[2] (The Conference has decided the members of the Delegation to be: Liberia, Tunisia, Madagascar and Sierra Leone);

8. Decides further the breaking off of diplomatic and consular relations between all African States and the Governments of Portugal and South Africa so long as they persist in their present attitude towards decolonisation;

9. Asks for an effective boycott of the foreign trade of Portugal and South Africa by:

(a) prohibiting the import of goods from those two countries;
(b) closing African ports and airports to their ships and planes;
(c) forbidding the planes of those two countries to overfly the territories of all African States;

10. Earnestly invites all national liberation movements to co-ordinate their efforts by establishing common action fronts wherever necessary so as to strengthen the effectiveness of their struggle and the rational use of the concerted assistance given them;

11. Establishes a co-ordinating committee consisting of Algeria, Ethiopia, Guinea, Congo (Leopoldville), Nigeria, Senegal, Tanganyika, United Arab Republic and Uganda, with Headquarters in Dar-es-Salaam, Tanganyika, responsible for harmonising the assistance from African States, and for managing the Special Fund to be set up for that purpose;

12. Establishes a Special Fund to be raised by voluntary contribution of Member States for the current year, the deadline for such contribution being 15 July 1963; Requests the Co-ordinating Committee to propose the necessary fund for the Council of Ministers so as to supply the necessary practical and financial aid to the various African national liberation movements;

---

[1] The first phase ended on 21 December 1962 when the International Court of Justice decided, by eight votes to seven, that it had jurisdiction to adjudicate on the case brought by Ethiopia and Liberia against South Africa alleging that the latter had violated her mandate over South West Africa. For text, see International Court of Justice, *South West Africa, Preliminary Objections, Judgement, I.C.J. Reports 1962*, p. 319.

[2] *G.A.O.R.*, Eighteenth Session, Annexes, A/5446/Rev. 1.

13. Appoints the day of 25 May 1963 as African Liberation Day so as to organise popular demonstrations on that day to disseminate the recommendations of the Summit Conference and to collect sums over and above the national contributions for the special fund; (This year it will be the opening day of the 18th Session of the UN);

14. Decides to receive on the territories of independent African States, nationalists from liberation movements in order to give them training in all sectors, and afford young people all the assistance they need for their education and vocational training;

15. Decides further to promote, in each State, the transition of material aid and the establishment of a body of volunteers in various fields, with a view to providing the various African national liberation movements with the assistance they need in various sectors.

(ii) *Resolution on Apartheid and Racial Discrimination*

Having considered all aspects of the questions of apartheid and racial discrimination;

Unanimously convinced of the imperious and urgent necessity of coordinating and intensifying their efforts to put an end to the South African Government's criminal policy of apartheid and wipe out racial discrimination in all its forms;

Have agreed unanimously to concert and co-ordinate their efforts and action in this field, and to this end have decided on the following measures:

1. To grant scholarships, educational facilities and possibilities of employment in African Government service to refugees from South Africa;

2. To support the recommendations presented to the Security Council and the General Assembly by the special Committee of the United Nations on the apartheid policies of the South African Government;

3. To despatch a delegation of Foreign Ministers to inform the Security Council of the explosive situation existing in South Africa; (The Conference has decided the members of the Delegation to be: Liberia, Tunisia, Madagascar and Sierra Leone);

4. To co-ordinate concerted measures of sanction against the Government of South Africa;

5. Appeals to all States, and more particularly to those which have traditional relations and co-operate with the Government of South Africa, to strictly apply UN resolution 1761 (XVII) of 6 November 1962 concerning apartheid;[1]

6. Appeals to all Governments who still have diplomatic, consular and economic relations with the Government of South Africa to break off those relations and to cease any other form of encouragement for the policy of apartheid;

7. Stresses the great responsibility incurred by the colonial authorities

---

[1] The operative paragraphs of this resolution requested Member States to break diplomatic relations with South Africa, close their ports to ships flying the South African flag, prohibit their own vessels from entering South African ports, boycott South African goods, refrain from exporting goods to South Africa, and refuse landing and passage facilities to South African aircraft. The resolution also established a special committee to keep the racial policies of the Government of South Africa under review and to report to the General Assembly and Security Council.

administering territories neighbouring South Africa in the pursuit of the policy of apartheid;

8. Condemns racial discrimination in all its forms in Africa and all over the world;

9. Expresses the deep concern aroused in all African peoples and governments by the measures of racial discrimination taken against communities of African origin living outside the continent and particularly in the United States of America; Expresses appreciation for the efforts of the Federal Government of the United States of America to put an end to these intolerable mal-practises which are likely seriously to deteriorate relations between the African peoples and governments on the one hand and the people and government of the United States of America on the other.

(iii) *Resolution on Africa and the United Nations*

Believing that the United Nations is an important instrument for the maintenance of peace and security among nations and for the promotion of the economic and social advancement of all peoples;

Reiterating its desire to strengthen and support the United Nations;

Noting with regret that Africa as a region is not equitably represented in the principal organs of the United Nations;

Convinced of the need for closer co-operation and co-ordination among the African States Members of the United Nations:

1. Reaffirms its dedication to the purposes and the principles of the United Nations Charter, and its acceptance of all obligations contained in the Charter, including financial obligations;

2. Insists that Africa as a geographical region should have equitable representation in the principal organs of the United Nations, particularly the Security Council and the Economic and Social Council and its Specialised Agencies;

3. Invites African Governments to instruct their representatives in the United Nations to take all possible steps to achieve a more equitable representation of the African regions;

4. Further invites African Governments to instruct their representatives in the United Nations, without prejudice to their membership in and collaboration with the African-Asian Group, to constitute a more effective African Group, with a permanent secretariat to bring about closer co-operation and better co-ordination in matters of common concern.

(iv) *Resolution on Disarmament*

Having considered all aspects of the question of disarmament;

Unanimously convinced of the imperious and urgent necessity of coordinating and intensifying their efforts to contribute to the achievement of a realistic disarmament programme through the signing, by all States concerned, of a treaty on general and complete disarmament under strict and effective international control;

Have agreed unanimously to concert and co-ordinate their efforts and action in these various fields, and to this end have decided on the following measures:

1. To affirm and respect the principle of declaring Africa a Denuclearised Zone; to oppose all nuclear and thermonuclear tests, as well as the manufacture of nuclear weapons; and to promote the peaceful uses of nuclear energy;

2. The destruction of existing nuclear weapons;

3. To undertake to bring about, by means of negotiation, the end of military occupation of the African continent and the elimination of military bases and nuclear tests, which elimination constitutes a basic element of African Independence and Unity;

4. To appeal to the great powers to:

(*a*) reduce conventional weapons;

(*b*) put an end to the arms race; and

(*c*) sign a general and complete disarmament agreement under strict and effective international control;

5. To appeal to the great powers, in particular to the Soviet Union and the United States of America, to use their best endeavours to secure the objectives stated above.

(v) *Resolution on Areas of Cooperation: Economic Relations*

Concerned with the active share of the developing countries in world trade and at the persistent deterioration of the terms of trade in these external commercial relationships;

Conscious of the fact that owing to its extreme dependence on the export of primary products, Africa more than any other developing region is adversely affected by persistent deteriorations in export earnings;

Convinced of the necessity for concerted action by the African countries in order to ensure a much more remunerative price from the sale of their primary products;

Mindful of the need to eliminate the barriers to trade between the African countries and thereby to strengthen their economies;

Considering that economic development, including the expansion of trade on the basis of fair and remunerative prices, should tend to eliminate the need for external economic aid, and that such external economic aid should be unconditional and should not prejudice the independence of African States;

Considering the imperative necessity for African countries to pool their resources and harmonise their activities in the economic field;

Aware of the necessity for the joint utilisation of river basin resources, the study of the use of Sahara Zones, the co-ordination of means of transport and communication systems, and the provision of research facilities, all of which serve to stimulate economic growth and expansion of trade, both regionally and inter-regionally;

Convinced that the acceleration of the rate of economic and social development of the various African countries lies in the industrialisation of these countries and the diversification of their production;

Considering the serious problems arising from the great shortage of trained and skilled personnel, the lack of qualified staff, scarce capital resources, grossly inadequate infrastructure, limited outlines for industrial products and the far too inadequate participation of Africans in the economic construction of their countries;

Desiring to explore the effects of regional economic groupings of the African economy;

Noting with satisfaction that the Executive Secretary of the Economic Commission for Africa has decided to convene a Conference of African Ministers of Finance, to be held in Khartoum (Sudan) in July 1963, with a view to setting up an African Development Bank;[1]

Resolves to:

1. Appoint, pending the establishment of the economic commission of the organisation, a preparatory economic committee to study in collaboration with governments and in consultation with the Economic Commission for Africa, *inter alia*, the following questions and submit their findings to Member States:

(*a*) the possibility of establishing a free trade area between the various African countries,

(*b*) the establishment of a common external tariff to protect the emergent industries and the setting up of a raw material price stabilisation fund,

(*c*) the restructuralisation of international trade,

(*d*) means for developing trade between African countries by the organisation and participation in African trade fairs and exhibitions and by the granting of transport and transit facilities,

(*e*) the co-ordination of means of transport and the establishment of road, air and maritime companies,

(*f*) the establishment of an African Payments and Clearing Union,

(*g*) a progressive freeing of national currencies from all non-technical external attachments and the establishment of a Pan-African monetary zone,

(*h*) ways and means of effecting the harmonisation of existing and future national development plans;

2. Invite ECA to request its Executive Secretary to give the Commission of Experts all the necessary support and assistance which it may require in the fulfillment of its assignment;

3. Welcome the forthcoming Conference of African Ministers of Finance and give the respective Ministers of Finance instructions to take the necessary measures for the rapid establishment of the African Development Bank;

4. Note with satisfaction the progress achieved by the Economic Commission for Africa in establishing the Dakar Institute of Economic Development and Planning and affirm their profound interest in that institute and their intention of giving it appropriate financial and other support;

---

[1] The conference took place between 31 July–4 August 1963. It was attended by the representatives of thirty-two independent African states and Kenya, and agreed to establish an African Development Bank with an initial capital of $250 million. See also, African Development Bank, *First Annual Report, 1964–65* (Abidjan, 1966).

5. Welcome the forthcoming World Conference on Trade and Development which is to examine international trade problems in relation to the economic development of emerging countries;

6. Urge all States concerned to conduct negotiations, in concert, with a view to obtaining from the consumer countries real price stabilisation and guaranteed outlets on the world market so that the developing countries may derive considerably greater revenue from international trade.

(vi) *Resolution on Areas of Cooperation: the future of the C.C.T.A.*[1]

Considering that at the last C.C.T.A. session in Dar-es-Salaam in January to February, 1963, the final adoption of the new C.C.T.A. convention was deferred until the Heads of African States had had an opportunity to consider and direct on the role of the C.C.T.A. within the overall context of Pan-African Co-operation,

And in view of the fact that Article 23 of this new convention lays down as follows:

'Pending the signature and the ratification of this convention as provided in Article 16, the Parties having initialled this convention agree to apply it provisionally as if it had entered into force as from the date of initialling, subject to any decision which may be taken by the Heads of African and Malagasy States at the Conference at Addis Ababa or at any subsequent conference on the role of the C.C.T.A. within the overall context of Pan-African Co-operation.'

Decides to maintain C.C.T.A. and to reconsider its role in order to bring it eventually within the scope of the organisation of African States which will have, as one of its arms, an organ for technical, scientific and cultural co-operation.

Supplementary Resolutions, 25 May 1963[2]

(i) *Resolution on Social and Labour Matters*

The Summit Conference of Independent African States meeting in Addis Ababa, Ethiopia, from the 22nd to the 25th May 1963:

Realising the importance of social standards for the African peoples and the urgent need for raising such standards;

Considering that co-operation amongst the African States in the social and labour fields is vital and will contribute to the realisation of a sound solidarity amongst their peoples;

Believing that the coming together of youth from African States will create better understanding and contribute to the realisation of the desired African unity;

Believing further that co-operation in the labour field amongst African States is vital for our continent:

[1] Commission for Technical Cooperation in Africa.

[2] Organization of African Unity, *Basic Documents and Resolutions* (Provisional Secretariat of the OAU, Addis Ababa, 1964), pp. 25–7.

Decides that a Committee of Experts be called to convene within three months, pending the setting up of the Economic and Social Commission provided for in Article XX of the Charter of the Organisation of African Unity[1] to submit a report to the above Commission:

With regard to social and labour matters:

1. To conduct extensive studies on social and labour problems in the continent;

2. To lay down detailed programmes with a view to raising the social standard and to strengthen inter-African co-operation through:

(*a*) The exchange of social and labour legislations;

(*b*) The establishment of African Youth Organisation;

(*c*) The organisation of African Scouts Union and an annual continental jamboree;

(*d*) The organisation of an annual African Sport Games;

(*e*) The organisation of vocational training courses in which African workers will participate;

(*f*) The establishment of an African Trade Union.

(ii) *Resolution on Education and Culture*

Desirous of strengthening educational and cultural ties amongst the peoples of Africa;

Considering that the educational and cultural co-operation amongst African States will break down linguistic barriers and promote understanding amongst the peoples of the continent;

Believing that once this co-operation in the educational and cultural fields amongst African States has been organised, co-ordinated and harmonised and fully implemented, it will pave the way to the final goal, namely African Unity;

Realising the lack of information media in various parts of the African continent and the necessity of strengthening exchange of information amongst African States in order to promote better understanding amongst their peoples;

1. Decides that a Committee of Experts be called to convene within three months, pending the setting up of the Educational and Cultural Commission, provided for in Article XX of the Charter of the Organisation of African Unity,[1] to submit a report to the above Commission on educational and cultural matters by taking into account the resolutions which have been adopted by the Conferences of Casablanca and Lagos;

2. Proposes:

(*a*) the establishment of an Institute of African Studies to be a department of the African University proposed by Ethiopia;

(*b*) the introduction, as soon as possible, of programmes in the major African languages in the broadcasting stations of the various African States and the exchanges of radio and television programmes;

(*c*) the establishment of an African News Agency.

---

[1] See p. 441 above.

(iii) *Resolution on Health, Sanitation and Nutrition*

Realising the importance of health standards for the African peoples and the urgent need for raising such standards and improving sanitation and nutrition amongst the peoples;

Considering that the co-operation amongst the African States in health, sanitation and nutrition fields is vital and will contribute to the realisation of stronger solidarity amongst their peoples;

Decides that a Committee of Experts be called to convene within three months, pending the setting up of the Commission on Health, Sanitation and Nutrition provided for in Article XX of the Charter of the Organisation of African Unity[1] to submit a report to the above Commission;

With regard to health:

1. To conduct extensive studies on health problems facing the continent;

2. To lay down detailed programmes with a view to raising health standards among the peoples and to strengthen inter-African co-operation through:

(*a*) The exchange of information about endemic and epidemic diseases and the means to control them;

(*b*) The exchange of health legislations;

(*c*) The exchange of doctors, technicians and nurses;

(*d*) The reciprocal offer of scholarships for medical students and the establishment of training courses on health, sanitation and nutrition;

3. To conduct research in all African States on sanitation and nutrition and to study ways and means to improve them.

Special Resolution, 25 May 1963[2]

The Summit Conference of Independent African States meeting in Addis Ababa, Ethiopia, from 22 May to 25 May 1963;

Having signed the Charter of the Organisation of African Unity:

1. Establishes forthwith a Provisional General Secretariat that will operate until the Charter of the Organisation of African Unity is applied;

2. This Provisional General Secretariat is entrusted to the Ethiopian Government and will essentially perform such common tasks as have been decided by the present Conference; (The expert committee which will assist the provisional Secretariat to be set up by the Ethiopian Government shall be composed of the following countries: Congo (Brazzaville), Ghana, Nigeria, Niger, Uganda and United Arab Republic);

3. Decides to establish the Provisional Headquarters of the General Secretariat in Addis Ababa, Ethiopia;

4. Decides further, that the first meeting of the Council of Ministers of the Organisation of African Unity, shall take place in Dakar, Senegal.

---

[1] See p. 441 above.
[2] OAU, *Basic Documents and Resolutions*, p. 28.

(b) *First Meeting of the Council of Ministers of the Organisation of African Unity, Dakar, 2–11 August 1963*

Draft resolution on regional groupings, submitted by the delegation of Guinea, 10 August 1963[1]

The Council of Ministers of the Organization of African Unity assembled at Dakar from August 2 to 8, 1963,

RECALLING that the African countries, with the aim of liberating Africa from all forms of colonialism, fostering greater solidarity among themselves and an equitable co-operation based on equality, mutual respect and the reciprocity of interests with all countries of the world, were moved to create Groupings of various forms such as the Union of African States in November 1958, the Charter of Casablanca in January 1961, the Conference of Monrovia in May 1961, the A.M.U. in September 1961, etc.;

CONSIDERING the will of African countries to end the division of African States on the basis of different Charters, which conviction was unanimously proclaimed by the Summit Conference of the Heads of State and Government at Addis Ababa;

CONSIDERING that the high aims of unity pursued by these numerous Groupings are met through the creation of the O.A.U. and that the separate maintenance of the institutions of these Groupings would be contrary to the Charter and prejudicial to its smooth and harmonious operation;

CONSCIOUS that this Charter forms, at the present stage, the best instrument of African liberation, solidarity between peoples and co-operation of African States with a view to the co-ordination and harmonization of their general policy, particularly in the following fields:

(*a*) Politics and Diplomacy;
(*b*) Economy, Transport and Communications;
(*c*) Education and Culture;
(*d*) Health, Hygiene and Nutrition;
(*e*) Science and Technology;
(*f*) Defence and Security;

CONSIDERING that the creation of the Organization for African Unity has aroused immense and legitimate hope among African peoples;

RECALLING that the Charter of the Organization of African Unity has provided for specialized institutions of Economic and Social, Scientific, Cultural and Military nature;

CONSIDERING that the creation of Regional and Sub-Regional Groupings can assist the cause of unity defined by the O.A.U.;

CONSIDERING, however, the importance of defining and specifying the criteria and objects of Regional and Sub-Regional Groupings compatible with the aims and principles of the Charter of the O.A.U.

---

[1] OAU, *Council of Ministers Conference, Dakar, 2–11 August 1963, Verbatim Report of Plenary Sessions* (Apapa, 1963), pp. 132–3.

RECOMMENDS

I.   To make the following definition of Regional Groupings:

(1) That the Charter be the sole valid basis for the creation of any Regional and Sub-Regional Grouping;

(2) That geographical realities and economic and social conditions common to neighbouring States be the sole justification for the creation of such Groupings and Sub-Groupings;

(3) That the aim of any such Grouping be the co-ordination of specific, economic, social and cultural activities of the States concerned, in conformity with the objectives of the Charter, as defined in Article 2.

II. To abrogate, effectively and immediately, all charters governing previous Groupings and Sub-Groupings, and to integrate or reorganize their technical bodies within the specialised institutions of the O.A.U.

III. That the statutes of any Regional Grouping be submitted in advance for the approval of the O.A.U. before coming into force.

INVITES

All African Groupings and Sub-Groupings in existence to make the necessary arrangements for the application of the measures provided for above and to keep the Secretary-General of the O.A.U. informed.

REQUESTS

The Secretary-General of the O.A.U. to report on this matter to the next meeting of the Council of Ministers.

Resolution on Regional Groupings, 11 August 1963[1]

The Council of Ministers meeting in Dakar, Senegal, from 2nd to 11th August, 1963;

WHEREAS the setting up of the O.A.U. has given rise to great and legitimate hopes amongst African peoples;

MINDFUL of the will of these peoples to put an end to the division of African States;

WHEREAS this will was unanimously proclaimed by the Heads of State and Government at the Addis Ababa Conference;

WHEREAS furthermore regional groupings have favoured the achievement of African Unity and the development of co-operation amongst Member States;

WHEREAS also the Charter of the O.A.U. has made provision for economic, cultural, scientific, technical and military specialized institutions in order to strengthen solidarity amongst African peoples and co-operation amongst Member States;

[1] OAU, *Basic Documents and Resolutions*, p. 49.

CONSIDERING therefore the need for regional or sub-regional groupings to evolve with a view to their adaptation to the Charter of the O.A.U.;

1. TAKES NOTE of the will of Member States to implement all means in order to bring about this adaptation;

2. RECOMMENDS that any regional groupings or sub-groupings be in keeping with the Charter of the O.A.U. and meet the following criteria:

(a) Geographical realities and economic, social and cultural factors common to the States;

(b) Co-ordination of economic, social and cultural activities peculiar to the States concerned;

3. SUGGESTS to the African States signatories of Charters in existence before the setting up of the O.A.U. that they henceforth refer to the Charter of Addis Ababa;

4. INVITES all African States desiring to constitute regional groupings or sub-groupings to conform with the principles set forth above and to contemplate the integration of already existing bodies into the specialized institutions of the O.A.U.;

5. REQUESTS Member States to deposit the statutes of the said groupings at the seat of the O.A.U. before their entry into force.

D. AFRICA AT THE UNITED NATIONS

Security Council resolution on the 'territories under Portuguese administration', adopted 31 July 1963[1]

The Security Council,

Having examined the situation in the Territories under Portuguese administration as submitted by the thirty-two African Member States,[2]

Recalling its resolution 163 (1961) of 9 June 1961 and General Assembly resolutions 1807 (XVII) of 14 December 1962 and 1819 (XVII) of 18 December 1962,

Recalling General Assembly resolution 1542 (XV) of 15 December 1960, which declares the Territories under Portuguese administration to be Non-Self-Governing Territories within the meaning of Chapter XI of the Charter of the United Nations, as well as resolution 1514 (XV) of 14 December 1960, by which the General Assembly declares *inter alia* that immediate steps shall be taken to transfer all powers to the peoples of those Territories, without any conditions or reservations, in accordance with their freely expressed wishes, without distinction as to race, creed or colour, in order to enable them to enjoy complete freedom and independence,

1. *Confirms* General Assembly resolution 1514 (XV);

2. *Affirms* that the policies of Portugal in claiming the Territories under its

---

[1] *S.C.O.R.*, Eighteenth Session, Supplement for July, August and September, 1963, S/5380.
[2] Ibid., S/5347.

administration as 'overseas territories' and as integral parts of metropolitan Portugal are contrary to the principles of the Charter and the relevant resolutions of the General Assembly and of the Security Council;

3. *Deprecates* the attitude of the Portuguese Government, its repeated violations of the principles of the Charter and its continued refusal to implement the resolutions of the General Assembly and of the Security Council;

4. *Determines* that the situation in the Territories under Portuguese administration is seriously disturbing peace and security in Africa;

5. *Urgently calls upon* Portugal to implement the following:

(*a*) The immediate recognition of the right of the peoples of the Territories under its administration to self-determination and independence;

(*b*) The immediate cessation of all acts of repression and the withdrawal of all military and other forces at present employed for that purpose;

(*c*) The promulgation of an unconditional political amnesty and the establishment of conditions that will allow the free functioning of political parties;

(*d*) Negotiations, on the basis of the recognition of the right to self-determination, with the authorized representatives of the political parties within and outside the Territories with a view to the transfer of power to political institutions freely elected and representative of the peoples, in accordance with General Assembly resolution 1514 (XV);

(*e*) The granting of independence immediately thereafter to all the Territories under its administration in accordance with the aspirations of the peoples;

6. *Requests* that all States should refrain forthwith from offering the Portuguese Government any assistance which would enable it to continue its repression of the peoples of the Territories under its administration, and take all measures to prevent the sale and supply of arms and military equipment for this purpose to the Portuguese Government;

7. *Requests* the Secretary-General to ensure the implementation of the provisions of the present resolution, to furnish such assistance as he may deem necessary and to report to the Security Council by 31 October 1963.

Speech by the Permanent Representative of the United States at the United Nations, Mr. Adlai Stevenson, to the Security Council, 2 August 1963[1]

All of us sitting here today know the melancholy truth about the racial policies of the Government of South Africa. Our task now is to consider what further steps we can take to induce that Government to remove the evil business of apartheid, not only from our agenda but from the continent of Africa. The policy of apartheid denies the worth and the dignity of the human person, and for this very reason we must try to express our feelings with as much restraint as we can muster. Self-righteousness is no substitute for practical results.

It is all too true that there is scarcely a society in the world that is not touched by some form of discrimination. Who among us can cast the first stone or boast that we are free of any semblance of discrimination by colour or religion or in

[1] *S.C.O.R.*, Eighteenth Session, 1052nd meeting, 2 August 1963.

some other form? I take the liberty of quoting to you a few lines from a speech I made in Geneva a couple of weeks ago. I said:

'In my country too many of our negro citizens still do not enjoy their full civil rights because ancient attitudes stubbornly resist change, in spite of the vigorous official policy of the Government. But such indignities are an anachronism that no progressive society can tolerate and the last vestiges must be abolished with all possible speed. Actually, in the last few years we have made more progress in achieving full equality of rights and opportunities for all of our citizens than during any comparable period since Abraham Lincoln's Proclamation of Emancipation freed our Republic and our national conscience from a heavy burden. The very struggles which now call world-wide attention to our shame are themselves signs of a progress that will be increasingly visible in the months ahead. The sound and the fury about racial equality that fills our Press and airwaves are the signs of the great thaw. The log jam of the past is breaking up.'

I wanted to repeat what I said in Geneva so as to leave no doubt that the United States position is not one of self-righteousness or self-satisfaction. The question before us, however, is how and when the log-jam of racial discrimination will be loosened and brought into the mainstream of the United Nations Charter.

We all suffer from the disease of discrimination in various forms, but at least most of us recognize the disease for what it is: a disfiguring blight. The whole point is that, in many countries, governmental policies are dedicated to rooting out this dread syndrome of prejudice and discrimination, while in South Africa we see the anachronistic spectacle of the Government of a great people which persists in seeing the disease as the remedy, prescribing for the malady of racism the bitter toxic of apartheid.

Just as my country is determined to wipe out discrimination in our society, it will support efforts to bring about a change in South Africa. It is in the United States' interest to do this; it is in the interest of South Africa; it is in the interest of a world which has suffered enough from bigotry, prejudice and hatred.

The past two decades have seen an explosion of nationhood unequalled in history. Certainly, the pace of decolonization in Africa has been nothing less than phenomenal, and it offers a record of progress far beyond what the most optimistic among us could have expected in 1945. The new States of Africa are gaining strength, resolutely fighting to build prosperous, dynamic societies, and to do this in co-operation with other African States.

But, as this meeting of the Security Council so graphically emphasizes, the full potential of this new era cannot be realized because of South Africa's self-chosen isolation. Worse yet, progress in Africa is overshadowed by the racial bitterness and resentment caused by the policies of the South African Government; and it is the duty of this Council to do what it can to ensure that this situation does not deteriorate further, and that the injustice of apartheid comes to an end, not in blood and bondage, but in peace and freedom.

What we see and hear, however, offers us at present little hope. Indeed, the situation is worse than it was three years ago, when the Council first met on the question of apartheid. Speakers before me have reviewed the record of previous discussions of apartheid by this Council and the General Assembly. As they have pointed out, we have called repeatedly upon the Government of South Africa to consider world opinion, to co-operate with the United Nations, and to set in motion some meaningful steps toward ending discrimination and the policies and practices that would offend the whole world, wherever they were pursued.

Outside this Organization, many Members—not the least of which is my own Government—have attempted repeatedly to persuade the South African Government to begin moving along the lines of these resolutions. I myself have had something emphatic to say on this score, on two occasions, in the Republic of South Africa—things that it grieved me to say after enjoying so much courtesy and hospitality from the friendly and gracious people of the lovely land. But it is only stating a fact of life to say that the visible result of all these discussions and resolutions here in the United Nations, and all the diplomatic activities so far, is zero. It is only stating the obvious to say that, up until this time, our efforts have yielded no tangible results. It is only calling things by their right name to say that we are confronted for the moment with a deadlock between the overwhelming majority of mankind and the Republic of South Africa. There has been no forward motion; indeed, there has been retrogression—calculated retrogression.

Need I read the bill of particulars? For the past fifteen years, the Government of South Africa has built a barrier between the races, piling new restrictions upon old: all South Africans must carry identity cards indicating racial ancestry; segregation in religion, education and public accommodation is virtually total; freedom of employment is limited; wages rates for the same work and the same responsibility are different, according to the colour of one's skin; freedom of movement is inhibited; strikes by Africans in South Africa are illegal; Africans in South Africa are prohibited from residing, from doing business, or acquiring real property, in most cities and in large areas of the countryside; voters are registered on separate rolls according to race. This is not the whole story; but the point is that these and other measures of discrimination, aimed at the total separation of races into privileged and underprivileged segments of society, do not represent inherited social defects for which remedies are being sought: but injustices, deliberately and systematically imposed, in the recent past.

We are all agreed, and we have proclaimed again and again, in this body and in the General Assembly, and in many other forums of the United Nations, certain basic views about the issue before us. However, we must restate them again and again so that we can sum up where we stand, and deliberate with clarity and with candour on how to move forward.

First, we have affirmed and reaffirmed that apartheid is abhorrent. Our belief in the self-evident truths about human equality is enshrined in the Charter. Apartheid and racism, despite all of the tortured rationalizations that we have heard from the apologists, are incompatible with the moral, social, and constitutional foundations of our societies.

A second basic principle on which we are agreed is that all Members of the Organization have pledged themselves to take action, in co-operation with the Organization, to promote observance of human rights, without distinction as to race.

Thirdly, we continue to believe that this matter is of proper and legitimate concern to the United Nations. We have often stated, in the General Assembly, our belief that the Assembly can properly consider questions of racial discrimination and other violations of human rights where they are a Member's official policy and are inconsistent with the obligations of that Member, under Articles 55 and 56 of the Charter, to promote observance of human rights, without distinction as to race.

Moreover, the apartheid policy of South Africa has clearly led to a situation the continuance of which is likely to endanger international peace and security. We also believe that all Members, in the words of the resolution passed almost unanimously by the sixteenth General Assembly, should take such separate and collective action as is open to them in conformity with the Charter to bring about an abandonment of those policies. The United States supported that resolution and has complied with it.[1]

I should like to take this occasion to bring up to date the record of the measures the United States has taken to carry out this purpose. First, we have continued and indeed have accelerated our official representations to the Government of South Africa on all aspects of apartheid in that country. We have done this through public words and private diplomacy, expressing our earnest hope that the South African Government would take steps to reconsider and to revise its racial policies and to extend the full range of civic rights and opportunities to non-whites in the life of their country. And we have observed to the South African Government that in the absence of an indication of change, the United States would not cooperate in matters that would lend support to South Africa's present racial policies.

We have utilized our diplomatic and our consular establishments in South Africa to demonstrate by words and by deeds our official disapproval of apartheid and, as the United States representative informed the Special Political Committee of the General Assembly on 19 October last,[2] the United States has adopted and is enforcing the policy of forbidding the sale to the South African Government of arms and military equipment whether from Government or commercial sources, which could be used by that Government to enforce apartheid either in South Africa or in the Administration of South West Africa. We have carefully screened both government and commercial shipments of military equipment to make sure that this policy is rigorously enforced.

But I am now authorized to inform the Security Council of still another important step which my Government is prepared to take. We expect to bring to an end the sale of all military equipment to the Government of South Africa by the end of this calendar year, in order further to contribute to a peaceful solution and to avoid any steps which might at this point directly contribute to international friction in the area. There are existing contracts which provide for limited quantities of strategic equipment for defence against external threats, such as air-to-air missiles and torpedoes for submarines. We must honour these contracts. The Council should be aware that in announcing this policy the United States, as a nation with many responsibilities in many parts of the world, naturally reserves the right in the future to interpret this policy in the light of requirements for assuring the maintenance of international peace and security.

[1] Resolution 1598 (xv), *Documents, 1961*, pp. 708–9.
[2] *G.A.O.R.*, Seventeenth Session, Special Political Committee, 334th meeting, para. 30.

If the interests of the world community require the provision of equipment for use in the common defence effort, we would naturally feel able to do so without violating the spirit and the intent of this resolution. We are taking this further step to indicate the deep concern which the Government of the United States feels at the failure of the Republic of South Africa to abandon its policy of apartheid. In pursuing this policy the Republic of South Africa, as we have so often said, is failing to discharge its obligations under Articles 55 and 56 of the Charter whereby Members pledge themselves to take joint and separate action in co-operation with our Organization for the achievement, among other things, of 'universal respect for, and observance of, human rights and fundamental freedoms for all without distinction as to race, sex, language, or religion'.

Stopping the sale of arms to South Africa emphasizes our hope that the Republic will now reassess its attitude towards apartheid in the light of the constantly growing international concern at its failure to heed the numerous appeals made to it by various organs of the United Nations, as well as appeals of Member States such as my Government.

As to the action of the Council in this proceeding, we are prepared to consult with other members and with the African Foreign Ministers present at the table and we will have some suggestions to make. It is clear to my delegation that the application of sanctions under Chapter VII in the situation now before us would be both bad law and bad policy. It would be bad law because the extreme measures provided in Chapter VII were never intended and cannot reasonably be interpreted to apply to situations of this kind. The founders of the United Nations were very careful to reserve the right of the Organization to employ mandatory coercive measures in situations where there was an actuality of international violence or such a clear and present threat to the peace as to leave no reasonable alternative but resort to coercion.

We do not have that kind of situation here. Fortunately for all of us, there is still some time to work out a solution through measures of pacific settlement, and any solution adopted by this Council must be reasonably calculated to promote such settlement. It is bad policy because the application of sanctions in this situation is not likely to bring about the practical result that we seek, that is, the abandonment of apartheid. Far from encouraging the beginning of a dialogue between the Government of South Africa and its African population, punitive measures would only provoke intransigence and harden the existing situation. Furthermore, the result of the adoption of such measures, particularly if compliance is not widespread and sincere, would create doubts about the validity of, and diminish respect, for the authority of the United Nations and the efficacy of the sanction process envisioned in the Charter.

Also, views on this matter differ so widely that we cannot hope to agree on the necessary consensus to make such action effective even if it were legitimate and appropriate. And as for suggestions of diplomatic isolation, persuasion cannot be exercised in a vacuum. Conflicting views cannot be reconciled *in absentia*. Instead, we believe that still further attempts should be made to build a bridge of communication, of discussion and of persuasion. If the human race is going to survive on this earth wisdom, reason and right must prevail. Let us not forget that there are many wise and influential people in that great country who share our views. It is regrettable that the accomplishments in so many fields of human endeavour in South Africa are being obscured by a racial policy repugnant to Africa and to the world. Certainly, one ultimate goal for all of us is to assist South Africa to rejoin the African continent and to assist in the development of all the peoples of Africa. And that is why my Government has looked with such favour on the idea of appointing special representatives of the Security Council who can work energetically and persistently and be free to exercise their own ingenuity and to pursue every prospect and every hint of a useful opening.

We cannot accept the proposition that the only alternative to apartheid is bloodshed. We cannot accept the conclusion that there is no way out, no direction in which to go except the present collision course towards ultimate disaster in South Africa. Certainly there are alternatives and they must be identified and they must be explored before it is too late.

It is a matter of considerable regret to my delegation that the Government of South Africa has chosen to absent itself from these proceedings. But aside from regrets, it is exceedingly difficult in this shrunken interdependent world to live in self-ostracism from international society. In this world of instant communication, it is progressively more hazardous to fly in the face of world opinion. And certainly the obligation to talk about dangerous disputes is too solemn to be ignored by even the most stubborn of leaders today.

There is nothing inherently immutable in any impasse in human affairs. Many a seemingly hopeless cause has prevailed in the course of history. I had occasion just last week to recall here that negotiations over the testing of nuclear weapons looked hopeless for five long, dreary, frustrating years, until the impasse was broken suddenly, to the vast relief of an anxious world. And, as I said, the stalemate was broken because men refused to give up hope, because men declined to give in to despair, because men worked consistently and doggedly to break the deadlock. Manifestly this treaty does not solve all of the problems in connexion with nuclear armaments. But every long journey begins with a single step, and this is a beginning.

So I should like to suggest very emphatically that we approach the problem of apartheid in South Africa as a similar challenge to ingenuity, to the instinct for survival for humankind. As President Kennedy said with reference to the atomic treaty, 'We must not be afraid to test our hopes'. It is in the spirit of testing our hopes that this sad episode will end in reason and not in flame that I, on behalf of my Government, solemnly and earnestly appeal to the Government of South Africa to change course and to embark on a policy of national reconciliation and emancipation.

Security Council resolution on 'apartheid in South Africa', adopted 7 August 1963[1]

The Security Council,

Having considered the question of race conflict in South Africa resulting from the policies of *apartheid* of the Government of the Republic of South Africa, as submitted by the thirty-two African Member States,[2]

---

[1] *S.C.O.R.*, Eighteenth Session, Supplement for July, August, and September 1963, p. 7, S/5386.   [2] Ibid., S/5348.

Recalling its resolution 134 (1960) of 1 April 1960,[1]

Taking into account that world public opinion has been reflected in General Assembly resolution 1761 (XVII) of 6 November 1962, and particularly in its paragraphs 4 and 8,

Noting with appreciation the interim reports adopted on 6 May and 16 July 1963 by the Special Committee on the Policies of *apartheid* of the Government of the Republic of South Africa,[2]

Noting with concern the recent arms build-up by the Government of South Africa, some of which arms are being used in furtherance of that Government's racial policies,

Regretting that some States are indirectly providing encouragement in various ways to the Government of South Africa to perpetuate, by force, its policy of *apartheid*,

Regretting the failure of the Government of South Africa to accept the invitation of the Security Council to delegate a representative to appear before it.

Being convinced that the situation in South Africa is seriously disturbing international peace and security,

1. *Strongly deprecates* the policies of South Africa in its perpetuation of racial discrimination as being inconsistent with the principles contained in the Charter of the United Nations and contrary to its obligations as a Member of the United Nations;

2. *Calls upon* the Government of South Africa to abandon the policies of *apartheid* and discrimination, as called for in Security Council resolution 134 (1960), and to liberate all persons imprisoned, interned or subjected to other restrictions for having opposed the policy of *apartheid*;

3. *Solemnly calls upon* all States to cease forthwith the sale and shipment of arms, ammunition of all types and military vehicles to South Africa;

4. *Requests* the Secretary-General to keep the situation in South Africa under observation and to report to the Security Council by 30 October 1963.

Speech by the Permanent Representative of Great Britain at the United Nations, Sir Patrick Dean, to the Security Council, 7 August 1963[3]

It is a matter of regret to my delegation that we have found ourselves unable to vote on this occasion with the majority of the Council on its resolution on the policy of apartheid. In spite of our very strongly felt opposition to the racial policies of the South African Government, there are certain features of the resolution which the Council has adopted which have made it impossible for us to do so.

I should now like to explain in more detail the position of my delegation on

---

[1] *Documents, 1960*, p. 348.

[2] *G.A.O.R.*, Eighteenth Session, Annexes, addendum to agenda item 30, documents A/5497 and Add. 1, annexes III and IV.

[3] *S.C.O.R.*, Eighteenth Session, 1056th meeting, 7 August 1963.

the vote which the Council has just taken.[1] First, may I draw attention to the preambular paragraph which reads:

Regretting that some States are indirectly providing encouragement in various ways to the Government of South Africa to perpetuate, by force, its policy of apartheid.

In the course of our debates a number of States, including the United Kingdom, have been mentioned in terms which can only suggest that this particular expression of regret may be directed at actions which they have taken, or are taking. Since the charge or the insinuation is wholly without foundation so far as my country is concerned, my delegation could not accept such a paragraph in the resolution. Furthermore, we have some reservation about the terms of the operative paragraph which has now become operative paragraph 3 in the resolution which has just been adopted.

As I stated in my remarks to the Council yesterday [1054th meeting], it is the position of my Government that no arms should be exported to South Africa which would enable the policy of apartheid to be enforced. Our export licensing system will make sure that arms of this nature will not reach South Africa. The resolution as now framed, however, calls on all States to cease to provide military equipment of any type to South Africa. It is the view of my delegation that the right of South Africa to self-defence under Article 51 of the Charter and requirements which may arise from the maintenance of international peace and security must be borne in mind. In view of our arrangements of co-operation with South Africa for the protection of the sea routes[2] we must reserve our position in the light of the requirements regarding the supply of equipment appropriate to these purposes.

In my opening statement I expressed the views of my delegation about the powers of the Council in the present situation. My delegation has listened with close attention to the statement which has just been made by the representative of the United States, in which it was made clear that the resolution which the Council has just adopted and the measures which it calls upon all States to take should not be regarded as being a resolution within Chapter VII of the Charter.

My delegation is in agreement with this statement and in particular with the observations of the representative of the United States on the meaning to be attached to the words 'is seriously disturbing international peace and security' in the eighth preambular paragraph.

The explanations which I have just given will show why my delegation felt unable to join with other members of the Council in voting for the resolution. In spite of this, however, there should be no doubt in the Council's mind or in the mind of anyone in South Africa that we remain strongly opposed to the policies of apartheid and are in agreement with the underlying purpose, in this regard, of the resolution. It is our profound hope—and I believe that there are many of all races in South Africa who share this hope—that the Government of South Africa may heed the unanimous sense of our debate.

---

[1] See pp. 461–2 above.

[2] See *Exchanges of letters on Defence Matters between the Governments of the United Kingdom and the Union of South Africa, June 1955*, Cmd. 9520.

Security Council resolution on 'apartheid in South Africa', adopted 4 December 1963[1]

The Security Council,

Having considered the race conflict in South Africa resulting from the policies of *apartheid* of the Government of the Republic of South Africa,

Recalling previous resolutions of the Security Council and of the General Assembly which have dealt with the racial policies of the Government of the Republic of South Africa, and in particular Security Council resolution 181 (1963) of 7 August 1963,[2]

Having considered the Secretary-General's report contained in document S/5438 and addenda,[3]

Deploring the refusal of the Government of the Republic of South Africa, as confirmed in the reply of the Minister of Foreign Affairs of the Republic of South Africa to the Secretary-General received on 11 October 1963,[4] to comply with Security Council resolution 181 (1963) and to accept the repeated recommendations of other United Nations organs,

Noting with appreciation the replies to the Secretary-General's communication to the Member States on the action taken and proposed to be taken by their Governments in the context of paragraph 3 of that resolution, and hoping that all the Member States as soon as possible will inform the Secretary-General about their willingness to carry out the provisions of that paragraph,

Taking note of the reports of the Special Committee on the Policies of *apartheid* of the Government of the Republic of South Africa,[5]

Noting with deep satisfaction the overwhelming support for resolution 1881 (XVIII) adopted by the General Assembly on 11 October 1963,[6]

Taking into account the serious concern of the Member States with regard to the policy of *apartheid*, as expressed in the general debate in the General Assembly as well as in the discussions in the Special Political Committee,

Being strengthened in its conviction that the situation in South Africa is seriously disturbing international peace and security, and strongly deprecating the policies of the Government of South Africa in its perpetuation of racial discrimination as being inconsistent with the principles contained in the Charter of the United Nations and with its obligations as a Member of the United Nations,

Recognizing the need to eliminate discrimination in regard to basic human rights and fundamental freedoms for all individuals within the territory of the Republic of South Africa without distinction as to race, sex, language or religion,

Expressing the firm conviction that the policies of *apartheid* and racial discrimination as practised by the Government of the Republic of South Africa are

---

[1] *S.C.O.R.*, Eighteenth Session, Supplement for October, November, and December 1963, pp. 103–5, S/5471.

[2] See pp. 461–2 above.

[3] *S.C.O.R.*, Eighteenth Session, Supplement for October, November, and December, 1963, pp. 7–40.

[4] Ibid., S/5438, para. 5.

[5] *G.A.O.R.*, Eighteenth Session, Annexes, addendum to agenda item 30, documents A/5497 and Add. 1.

[6] *G.A.O.R.*, Eighteenth Session, Supplement No. 15, p. 19.

abhorrent to the conscience of mankind and that therefore a positive alternative to these policies must be found through peaceful means,

1. *Appeals* to all States to comply with the provisions of Security Council resolution 181 (1963) of 7 August 1963;

2. *Urgently requests* the Government of the Republic of South Africa to cease forthwith its continued imposition of discriminatory and repressive measures which are contrary to the principles and purposes of the Charter and which are in violation of its obligations as a Member of the United Nations and of the provisions of the Universal Declaration of Human Rights;

3. *Condemns* the non-compliance by the Government of the Republic of South Africa with the appeals contained in the above-mentioned resolutions of the General Assembly and the Security Council;

4. *Again calls upon* the Government of the Republic of South Africa to liberate all persons imprisoned, interned or subjected to other restrictions for having opposed the policy of *apartheid*;

5. *Solemnly calls upon* all States to cease forthwith the sale and shipment of equipment and materials for the manufacture and maintenance of arms and ammunition in South Africa;

6. *Requests* the Secretary-General to establish under his direction and reporting to him a small group of recognized experts to examine methods of resolving the present situation in South Africa through full, peaceful and orderly application of human rights and fundamental freedoms to all inhabitants of the territory as a whole, regardless of race, colour or creed, and to consider what part the United Nations might play in the achievement of that end;

7. *Invites* the Government of the Republic of South Africa to avail itself of the assistance of this group in order to bring about such peaceful and orderly transformation;

8. *Requests* the Secretary-General to continue to keep the situation under observation and to report to the Security Council such new developments as may occur and in any case, not later than 1 June 1964, on the implementation of the present resolution.

Security Council resolution on the 'territories under Portuguese' administration, adopted 11 December 1963[1]

The Security Council,

Having considered the Secretary-General's report as contained in document S/5448 and addendu,[2]

Recalling General Assembly resolution 1541 (XV) of 15 December 1960,[3]

Recalling further Security Council resolution 180 (1963) of 31 July 1963,[4]

Noting with appreciation the efforts of the Secretary-General in establishing

[1] *S.C.O.R.*, Eighteenth Session, Supplement for October, November, and December 1963 pp. 110–11, S/5481.

[2] Ibid., pp. 55–86, S/5448 and Addenda 1–3.

[3] *G.A.O.R.*, Fifteenth Session, Supplement No. 16, pp. 29–30.

[4] See pp. 455–6 above.

contact between representatives of Portugal and representatives of African States,

1. *Regrets* that this contact has not achieved the desired results, because of failure to reach agreement on the United Nations interpretation of self-determination;

2. *Calls upon* all States to comply with paragraph 6 of resolution 180 (1963);

3. *Deprecates* the non-compliance of the Government of Portugal with resolution 180 (1963);

4. *Reaffirms* the interpretation of self-determination laid down in General Assembly resolution 1514 (XV) as follows:

> All peoples have the right to self-determination; by virtue of that right they freely determine their political status and freely pursue their economic, social and cultural development;

5. *Notes* General Assembly resolution 1542 (XV) of 15 December 1960,[1] which enumerated, *inter alia*, Territories under Portuguese administration as falling in the category of Non-Self-Governing Territories within the meaning of Chapter XI of the Charter of the United Nations;

6. *Believes* that action by the Government of Portugal to grant an amnesty to all persons imprisoned or exiled for advocating self-determination in these Territories will be an evidence of its good faith;

7. *Requests* the Secretary-General to continue his efforts and report to the Security Council not later than 1 June 1964.

E. THE MOROCCAN-ALGERIAN BORDER CONFLICT

Communiqué issued at the conclusion of the Conference of Bamako, 30 October 1963[2]

Les 29 et 30 octobre, sa Majesté Impériale l'Empereur Haïlé Selassié, sa Majesté Hassan II, roi du Maroc, son Excellence Ahmed Ben Bella, Président de la République Algérienne, son Excellence Modibo Keïta, Président de la République du Mali se sont réunis à Bamako.

La rencontre avait pour objet la solution du conflit qui oppose deux pays frères.

A l'issue de ces entretiens sa Majesté l'Empereur Haïlé Selassié a annoncé les importantes mesures qui ont été prises et qui sont:

1) Arrêt effectif et immédiat des combats à partir du 2 novembre à 0 heure.

2) Une commission composée d'officiers marocains, éthiopiens et maliens déterminera une zone dans laquelle les troupes engagées seront retirées.

3) Dans chaque zone, les observateurs éthiopiens et maliens vieilleront pour la sécurité et la neutralité militaire.

4) La demande d'une réunion le plus tôt possible des ministres des Affaires

---

[1] *G.A.O.R.*, Fifteenth Session, Supplement No. 16, pp. 30–1.

[2] Algeria, Ministère de L'Orientation Nationale, *De Bamako à Addis-Ababa* (Algiers, 1964), p. 29.

étrangères de l'OUA à Addis-Abéba pour la création d'une commission d'arbitrage pour le règlement définitif du différent frontalier algéro-marocain.

5) Les chefs d'État ont décidé la cessation pour l'Algérie et le Maroc de toute attaque par voie de presse et orale à partir du 1er novembre 1963. L'entretien s'est déroulé dans une atmosphère amicale et fraternelle. Les quatre chefs d'État, sa Majesté Impériale Haïlé Selassié, sa Majesté Hassan II, son Excellence le Président Ben Bella, et son Excellence Modibo Keïta, se félicitent de l'heureux aboutissement de ces entretiens de leur contribution au maintien de la paix et au renforcement de l'unité africaine.

Final resolution of the Extraordinary Session of the Council of Ministers of the Organisation of African Unity, Addis Ababa, 18 November 1963[1]

The Council of Ministers meeting in Extraordinary Session at Addis Ababa from 15 to 18 November 1963, by virtue of Article 12, paragraph 2,[2] of the Charter of the Organization of African Unity and in accordance with the request contained in the joint Bamako Communiqué dated 30 October 1963 with regard to the Algerian-Moroccan difference;[3]

CONSIDERING that all the Member States are bound by Article 6 to respect scrupulously all the principles formulated in Article 3 of the Charter of the Organization of African Unity;[4]

CONSIDERING the imperative need of settling all differences between African States by peaceful means and within a strictly African framework;

HAVING HEARD the statements made respectively by the Ministers for Foreign Affairs of Morocco and Algeria on the question of the dispute between these two brother States;

WELCOMES the Agreements reached at Bamako on 30 October 1963 by His Imperial Majesty Haile Selassie I, Emperor of Ethiopia, His Majesty Hassan II, King of Morocco, His Excellency Ahmed BEN BELLA, President of the Republic of Algeria, His Excellency Modibo KEITA, Prime Minister of the Government of Mali and Head of the State;

REAFFIRMS the unwavering determination of the African States always to seek a peaceful and fraternal solution to all differences that may arise among them by negotiation and within the framework of the principles and the institutions prescribed by the Charter of the Organization of African Unity;

NOTES WITH SATISFACTION the moderate and fraternal tone in which the discussions of the Council have been conducted;

PAYS A WARM TRIBUTE to His Majesty Haile Selassie I, Emperor of Ethiopia, and to His Excellency Modibo KEITA, President of the Government of Mali and Head of the State, for their efforts to obtain a cease-fire between Algeria and Morocco;

CONSIDERING that the Commission of Mediation, Conciliation and Arbitration provided for in Article 19 of the Charter has not yet been set up;[5]

DECIDES therefore to create the *ad hoc* Commission provided for in Article 4

---

[1] Organization of African Unity, *Basic Documents and Resolutions* (Provisional Secretariat of the OAU, Addis Ababa, 1964), p. 61.

[2] See p. 439 above.   [3] See p. 466 above.
[4] See p. 438 above.   [5] See p. 441 above.

of the joint Bamako Communiqué and designates for this purpose the following
countries:—

1. Ethiopia
2. Ivory Coast
3. Mali
4. Nigeria
5. Senegal
6. Sudan
7. Tanganyika

The terms of reference of this *ad hoc* Commission thus constituted are those laid
down in Article 4, sub-paragraphs (a) and (b), of the joint Bamako Communiqué.

In the spirit of the Bamako Communiqué, the Commission shall as soon as
possible establish its own rules of procedure and its working methods in accordance with the principles and the provisions of the Charter of the Organization
of African Unity and of the Rules of Procedure of the Council of Ministers;

REQUESTS further that the *ad hoc* Commission report back to it on the results
of its work;

APPEALS finally to the two parties to refrain from any action likely to
jeopardize the success of the *ad hoc* Commission.

V. THE WESTERN HEMISPHERE

A. RELATIONS BETWEEN CANADA AND THE UNITED STATES

Statement by the Prime Minister of Canada, Mr. Diefenbaker, to the House of Commons, 25 January 1963[1] (extracts)

. . . We shall make our decisions, and have, on the basis of Canada's security and the maintenance of our responsibilities internationally. We have made them and will continue to make them on the basis of no other consideration. I start at once by saying that any suggestion that we have repudiated any undertaking by Canada internationally is false in substance and in fact. Canada does not, has not and will not renege on her responsibilities. Let there be no doubt about that. . . .

Defence is a complex problem, a difficult one not alone for Canada but for all the countries in the free world who are having difficulty in this connection. All of them have made expenditures for weapons and the like which, before they were produced, have had to be put in the scrap heap. Somebody said, and I think this is a slogan that appears on the walls of some of the defence establishments in the United States, if it works it is obsolete. There has been a tremendous expansion in plans for defence and the media for defence. How often it has been found that before the weapons are ready for distribution they have already ceased to have any effect.

I want to point out a few general rules that we in this Government have adopted. We say we shall take adequate steps at all times to protect this country. We have taken these steps. Indeed, as the Secretary of State for External Affairs said on December 17 on his return to the House of Commons from the NATO conference in Paris, the various nations there without exception paid tribute to the degree to which Canada had carried out her responsibilities. There was some suggestion today that in the interest of collective security we should co-operate in things that, for us, would not be effective. The stand we take is this: Canada has co-operated and will co-operate, but she will not be a pawn nor be pushed around by other nations to do those things which, in the opinion of the Canadian people, are not in keeping with her sovereignty and her sovereign position.

Our general purpose has been to do our part to assure Canada's security, to work with our allies in close relationship, and at the same time press forward for disarmament, which is the only hope for peace. This is our purpose, this is our aim and our objective. Regardless of the political consequences, we will act to do those things that will carry out our responsibilities. We will fully co-operate with the countries of the Western Alliance, but with policies in co-operation with them that are made in Canada and not elsewhere. We will maintain Canadian

---

[1] Canada, Department of External Affairs, *Statements and Speeches*, No. 63/6.

sovereignty, regardless of the pressures, of the views, of anyone visiting our country or otherwise. We will have a policy that remains flexible so as to meet changing conditions. We will do nothing to extend the nuclear family. We will do our part to assure the continuance of the contribution of Canada to all UN forces designed to preserve peace.

Fundamental to our policy as it relates to other nations is the desire to be a useful and ever-ready agent for peace and for productive solutions, while at the same time pulling our weight. Some say you should take the advice of generals if they are eminent. This was not the view of President Eisenhower, who had occupied the highest position in the Western world as a general. He did not say this until the last speech he delivered prior to giving up the Presidency. This is what he said at that time:

> In the councils of government, we must guard against acquisitions of unwarranted influence, whether sought or unsought, by the military-industrial complex. The potential for the disastrous rise of misplaced power exists and will persist.
>
> We must never let the weight of this combination endanger our liberties or democratic processes. We should take nothing for granted. Only an alert and knowledgeable citizenry can compel the proper meshing of the huge industrial and military machinery of defence with our peaceful methods and goals, so that security and liberty may prosper together.[1]

This has been the view of Canadian leaders, too. Sir Robert Borden, in 1917, said, 'They advise but the civil authority determines.' . . .

I am going to deal with the question of nuclear weapons. This is a question that arouses in all of us those feelings of fear. I am going to deal with that at some length.

Nuclear weapons have a basis, for all peoples, of power and danger far beyond anything known before. Today, the United States has a preponderance of that power, and that caused Khrushchev to realize there would be no payoff in victory for the Communists if they moved forward. This was the essence of the Cuban question and of the stand taken by the President of the United States. . . .

The United States has today taken over the Herculean responsibilities that Britain carried for a hundred years, and there is resting upon the President of the United States decisions the seriousness of which affect all parts of the world.

We have been confronted with serious difficulties and problems in the defence field since 1957. One of our first acts was to continue an arrangement which our predecessors had made, which permitted United States interceptor aircraft to fly over Canada. A few weeks later we entered into a NORAD[2] agreement to establish a single separate effective control of North American defences. Forces of the United States and Canada were organized to defend our two nations against nuclear attack and, I point out, so far as the 'Bomarc' is concerned, it was simply part of the plan, and was not to defend Canada. That is not its purpose. Its purpose is to preserve the Strategic Air Command from an attack which would prevent the Strategic Air Command from striking out with all its deterrent

[1] Partial text in *Documents, 1960*, pp. 62–3; for full text, see *Public Papers, 1960–1*, pp. 1037–9.
[2] North American Air Defence Command.

power. We organized to defend the bases of the deterrent nuclear force which has protected us, as well as the Western world, for the past half dozen years and more.

That agreement was worked out to the mutual advantage of both countries and Canadian officers have taken a full share of responsibility and have done outstanding work in carrying it out.

The question of defensive nuclear weapons is one that must receive the attention of all the countries. We believe strongly in limiting the spread of nuclear weapons at the independent disposal of national governments. . . .

In December 1957, I was one of those who attended the meeting of the NATO powers in Paris. We agreed to the establishment of stockpiles of nuclear warheads in NATO nations, to be readily available for use by nuclear forces in Europe who were then confronted with the threat of Russian nuclear weapons against them.[1]

During 1958 the Canadian Government studied intensively the arms required by Canadian forces in modern circumstances, and we reached the decision we would provide aircraft for the purposes of NATO. At that time I made it perfectly clear, as I shall point out in a moment, that those forces would have to be equipped, in order to be fully effective, with defensive nuclear weapons if and when the need arose. That was recognized in taking the decision that was announced in September 1958, to install 'Bomarc' anti-aircraft missiles in Canada.

. . . In 1958, when the 'Bomarc' was first laid down as a plan, the great challenge to North America was believed to be bombers carrying bombs. That is what we thought. Today that is changed. More and more there is a phasing out in connection with the bomber threat as more and more intercontinental ballistic missiles are increasing in number. Those are some of the stands we have taken and I set forth the views of the Government on February 20, 1959,[2] as quoted by the Leader of the Opposition. In accordance with that statement, we proceeded to acquire equipment, aircraft, launchers and other items necessary to enable the Canadian forces to be ready to use defensive weapons if and when that became necessary.

In May 1959, the Supreme Commander of NATO forces visited Ottawa and proposed to the Government that the First Canadian Air Division in Europe should undertake a strike-reconnaissance role to protect the NATO forces from the first attack on them. That we placed before the House of Commons. The Government considered the proposal, and early in July announced its decision in the House to accept this role and to equip eight squadrons of the division to discharge it.[3] Our Ambassador informed the NATO Council of this decision.

While nothing was specified about arming the aircraft with nuclear weapons, it was realized by all that this would be desirable and that nuclear weapons should be available as and when required, under joint control, in NATO stockpiles in accordance with the general NATO decision of December 1957, to which I have referred. Similarly, but less important, plans were made in connection with short-range defensive missiles. . . .

We have spent billions of dollars on defence since World War II. Much of

[1] *Documents, 1957*, pp. 405–10.
[2] Canada, House of Commons, *Debates, 1959*, II, pp. 1121–4.
[3] Ibid., V, p. 5352.

what has been spent might be considered by some to have been wasted, but if it had not been for the defences we built up, and those associated with us, our freedom might long since have disappeared. Since the time we entered into these commitments I have referred to things which have changed greatly. It was not a mistake to take measures to ensure the necessary security, on the basis of the information we had then, even though in the light of subsequent events some of the things that were done had been proven, as with every country, to be unnecessary.

I referred a moment ago to the tremendous strength of the United States. In December it was publicly stated that the United States had now 200 nuclear-tipped, intercontinental ballistic missiles in place and that American missiles—these were press reports—now include 126 'Atlas' missiles, 54 'Titans' and 20 'Minutemen'. In other words, they are moving in the direction of a new concept of defensive measures. Those new concepts were the result of the meeting in Nassau, to which I will later make reference.

No one can predict the future. We build today on the basis of information that we have. We provide the weapons today according to our best lights and following collaboration among those associated in this matter of defence. New forms of deterrent are being developed. Military mistakes and changes have been made by all the countries in the Western world. A short resume will give the committee some idea of how easy it is to say what should be done now on the basis of what was done earlier in the face of other circumstances.

Britain had the 'Blue Streak', a long-range missile which cost her some $267 million. She gave it up. Recently the United States decided that the 'Skybolt' would not be used. . . . What they decided was that in view of the uncertainty of this missile there was no real purpose in going on with it. But on the other hand, in Nassau the United States was willing to proceed, provided Britain would put up a corresponding amount of money in order to ascertain whether or not it could be made workable. By the spring of 1960 the United States had spent over $3 billion on various forms of projects, military weapons and the like, that had to be cancelled or ended in their production.

We had to take the same course. Some people talk about courage. Well, we took a stand in reference to the 'Arrow'. No one wanted to take that stand. . . . As I look back on it, I think it was one of the decisions that was right. Here was an instrument beautiful in appearance, powerful, a tribute to Canadian production. But people sometimes say to me, 'How would it have defended Canada?' What is the total area in which it would operate at full speed? The answer is, 325 miles out and back, in a vast country like Canada. We could not get sales for it at all and the cost would have been $7½ million per unit. What a tremendous cost to this nation. This instrument that was otherwise beautiful, magnificent in its concept, would have contributed little, in the changing order of things, to our national defence.

Every now and then some new white hope of rocketry goes into the scrap pile. We established the 'Bomarc', the two units. They are effective over an area of only a few hundred miles. They are effective only against aircraft. People talk about change. Who would have thought three years ago that today the fear would be an attack with intercontinental missiles? This programme cost Canada some $14 million. The United States put up the major portion of the total cost.

I do not want to repeat, but it is necessary to do so, that with the advent more and more into intercontinental ballistic missiles the bomber carrier is less and less the threat that it was.

So what should we do? Should we carry on with what we have done in the past, merely for the purpose saying, 'Well, we started, and, having started and having proceeded, we will continue'? Should we do this in an area where mistakes are made? I am not dealing with those mistakes at the moment; but should we continue with such programmes, in the light of changing circumstances? These were not mistakes in judgment at the time, but the failure to be able to look ahead and read the mind of Khrushchev and those associated with him in the Presidium. More and more the nuclear deterrent is becoming of such a nature that more nuclear arms will add nothing materially to our defences. Greater and greater emphasis must be placed on conventional arms and conventional forces. We in Canada took a lead in that connection. In the month of September 1961 we increased the numbers of our conventional forces. There was criticism at the time.

I was in Nassau. I formed certain ideas. I read the communique that was issued there and I come to certain conclusions based on that communique.[1] Those conclusions are as follows, and these are the views expressed also by the United States Under-Secretary of State, George W. Ball: that nuclear war is indivisible; that there should be no further development of new nuclear power anywhere in the world; that nuclear weapons as a universal deterrent is a dangerous solution. Today an attempt is being made by the United States to have the NATO nations increase their conventional arms. The Nassau agreement seemed to accept these three principles as basic, and to carry them out both countries agreed to assign to NATO part of their existing nuclear force as the nucleus of a multilateral force.

What was the plan? The 'Skybolt', they said, had not been too successful— although it is ironical that the day after the communique the first one was successfully launched into space. The day is rapidly passing when we will have missile sites that are set, firm, on land. The new concept is the 'Polaris' missile, which is delivered from a submarine. When the 'Polaris' missiles are delivered to the United Kingdom as part of the multilateral force, Britain will not have her independent nuclear-deterrent power any more to the same extent, excepting to use these in a case of supranational emergency.

. . . I am going to read the paragraphs in question from the communique. They illustrate in a most striking way the state of flux of the defence of the free world. The communique shows that changes are taking place, and I will read the various paragraphs that set this out:

> The President informed the Prime Minister that for this reason— (That was, that it was very complex, and so on)
> . . . and because of the availability to the United States of alternative weapons systems, he had decided to cancel plans for the production of 'Skybolt' for use by the United States. Nevertheless, recognizing the importance of the 'Skybolt' programme for the United Kingdom and recalling that the purpose of the offer of 'Skybolt' to the United Kingdom in 1960 had been

---

[1] For the text of the Nassau meeting communiqué, see *Documents, 1962*, pp. 482-4.

to assist in improving and extending the effective life of the British V-bombers, the President expressed his readiness to continue the development of the missile as a joint enterprise between the United States and the United Kingdom, with each country bearing equal shares of the future cost of completing development.

Then the Prime Minister of the United Kingdom, while recognizing the value of this offer, decided, after full consideration, not to avail himself of it because of doubts which had been expressed about the prospects of the success of the enterprise. As an alternative, the President offered the 'Hound Dog' missile; but the 'Hound Dog' missile cannot be used on British aircraft because it would put the bottom of the aircraft too close to the ground, causing danger to those operating the planes.

The statement continues:

The Prime Minister then turned to the possibility of provision of the 'Polaris' missile to the United Kingdom by the United States. After careful review, the President and the Prime Minister agreed that a decision on 'Polaris' must be considered in the widest context both of the future defence of the Atlantic Alliance and of the safety of the whole free world. . . . The Prime Minister suggested and the President agreed, that for the immediate future a start could be made by subscribing to NATO some part of the forces already in existence. This could include allocations from United States strategic forces, from United Kingdom Bomber Command, and from tactical nuclear forces now held in Europe. Such forces would be assigned as part of a NATO nuclear force and targeted in accordance with NATO plans.

Finally, they came out in favour of this multilateral NATO nuclear force. Returning to the 'Polaris', the President and the Prime Minister agreed that the purpose of their two governments with respect to the provision of the 'Polaris' missiles must be the development of a multilateral NATO nuclear force in the closest consultation with other NATO allies. Accordingly, they agreed that the United States would make available a contribution of 'Polaris' missiles on a continuing basis for British submarines and that the nuclear warheads for 'Polaris' missiles should also be provided. These forces, and at least equal United States forces, would be made available for inclusion in a NATO multilateral nuclear force. At the same time, while they set up this multilateral force in embryo, the last paragraph points out that the President and the Prime Minister agreed that, in addition to having a nuclear shield, it was important to have a non-nuclear sword. For this reason, the communique concludes, they agreed on the importance of increasing the effectiveness of their conventional forces on a world-wide basis.

That is a tremendous step—a change in the philosophy of defence; a change in the views of NATO, if accepted by the NATO partners. Certainly it represents a change in the views of two nations which play such a large part in the NATO organization. They went further, as I understand it. They concluded that the day of the bomber is phasing out. Britain wanted a striking force of its own. Britain needed a delivery system produced at the lowest cost. Hence, the 'Skybolt'. With the advent of the 'Polaris' missile, the United States believed there was no longer need for the 'Skybolt', and this was agreed to by the Prime Minister of the United Kingdom. Who made the mistake? Are they to be condemned? No less than $600 million was spent on the development of the 'Skybolt', which was believed to be the essence of defence measures for the United Kingdom itself. I point this out because everywhere in the world, as a result of Khrushchev's changing moods, and vast improvements in technology both with respect to defensive and offensive warfare, the decisions of today are often negatived tomorrow.

When we say there has been a change, let me point out this fact. Only today, in a dispatch from Washington, it is reported that President Kennedy called Livingston Merchant, a veteran diplomat, out of retirement to lead a government team which will prepare United States proposals for a nuclear force in Europe. This was announced yesterday in a statement read to the press by the President's Press Secretary.[1] The report says that although United States and British efforts to create a nuclear striking force under NATO have run into stiff resistance from the French, Mr. Salinger . . . said: 'Mr. Merchant and his group will talk with French officials as well as with officials from other NATO countries.' All of us know the kind of man Mr. Merchant is—one of those dedicated servants who, in his period of office, did so much to increase the good relations between our country and the United States.

Concepts are changing. I do not intend to go now into many particulars but I ask Hon. Members who say there is no new strategy to read the article in one of the December issues of the *Saturday Evening Post*. The heading is 'Our New Strategy—the Alternatives to Total War', and the viewpoint given is that of Mr. McNamara, the Secretary of Defence of the United States.

Only on Wednesday, the Turkish Government is reported to have announced that 'Jupiter' missiles were being removed from Turkey and 'Polaris' weapons substituted. A similar announcement was made yesterday, I think, by Premier Fanfani of Italy. As far as these missiles are concerned, the reported proposal to replace the present missiles in Italy and Turkey by submarines mounted with 'Polaris' missiles is an example of the rapid changes of these times. Obsolete missiles in vulnerable positions are being replaced by a relatively invulnerable weapon. . . . Since they are mobile, these 'Polaris' missiles can be put in position or removed as the situation requires. They can be centrally controlled by NATO or another agency. By having the weapons stationed at sea, the provocation of having them mounted on the territory of close U.S.S.R. neighbours is removed. Because they are relatively invulnerable, their effectiveness as a deterrent is all the greater.

I propose to review some of the views expressed by this Government on the question of defence and to go back over some of the various statements which have been made.

I said (Hansard, February 20, 1959, page 1223) that, in keeping with the determination that Canada should carry out its task in a balanced, collective defence:

In keeping with that determination, careful thought is being given to the principles which in our opinion are applicable to the acquisition and control

---

[1] *Current Documents, 1963*, p. 381.

of nuclear weapons. The Government's decisions of last autumn to acquire 'Bomarc' missiles for air defence and 'Lacrosse' missiles for the Canadian Army.

(One doesn't hear anything more about 'Lacrosse' missiles).

. . . were based on the best expert advice available on the need to strengthen Canada's air defence against the threat to this continent and on its determination to continue an effective contribution to the NATO shield.

The full potential of these defensive weapons is achieved only when they are armed with nuclear warheads. The Government is, therefore, examining with the United States Government questions connected with the acquisition of nuclear warheads for 'Bomarc' and other defensive weapons for use by the Canadian forces in Canada, and the storage of warheads in Canada. Problems connected with the arming of the Canadian Brigade in Europe with short-range nuclear weapons for NATO's defence tasks are also being studied.

It set this out in great detail. There is no concealment. There is complete revelation of what we are doing. I could read from *Hansard* year by year. As found at page 1223 of *Hansard* for 1959, I said this:

It is our intention to provide Canadian forces with modern and efficient weapons to enable them to fulfil their respective roles. . . . It is the policy of the Canadian Government not to undertake the production of nuclear weapons in Canada. . . . We must reluctantly admit the need in present circumstances for nuclear weapons of a defensive character.

Then again, . . . on a number of occasions I stated that there was no expectation of an early conclusion of a formal agreement. On January 18, 1960, as found at page 73 of *Hansard*, I said this:

Eventually Canadian forces may require certain nuclear weapons if Canadian forces are to be kept effective.

Then again:

Negotiations are proceeding with the United States in order that the necessary weapons can be made available for Canadian defence units if and when they are required.

That was always of the essence throughout in the stand that we took; I cannot comment in detail on these negotiations but I wish to state that arrangements for the safeguarding and security of all such weapons in Canada will be subject to Canadian approval and consent. Then again on February 9, 1960:

If and when Canada does acquire nuclear weapons, it will be in accordance with our own national policies and with our obligations under the North Atlantic Treaty.

Again on July 4, 1960, I said a similar thing. As found at page 5653 of *Hansard*, I said this:

In so far as general policy is concerned, we are always in this position. On the one hand, we are desirous of achieving disarmament; on the other hand, we have to discharge our responsibility of ensuring to the maximum degree the security of the Canadian people. So far as that is concerned . . .

And so on. Again, in July, I mentioned the matter, and again in August:

. . . We are, therefore, going ahead with the procurement of vehicles which can use these nuclear weapons, but the decision as to the acquisition of the nuclear warheads depends on circumstances which might develop some time in the future.

Throughout we have followed that course. I do not wish to fill the record, but again on November 23, 1960, I was asked to give a report and I said I would refer the Hon. Gentleman to what was said on January 19 and February 20, both in 1959; January 18, 1960; February 9, 1960; July 4, 1960, and July 14, 1960. On November 30 I said this:

. . . The position of Canada is completely unchanged. We have made it perfectly clear that, when and if nuclear weapons are required, we shall not accept them unless we have joint control.

There has been no suggestion at any time of any watering down of that stand. Then again on September 20, 1961:

However, and I emphasize this, in each of the instruments that we have, the 'Bomarc' and the 'Voodoos', nuclear weapons could be used. The defensive weapons requirements of Canada and the need for the preservation of security will be the overriding consideration in the mind of this Government.

And so on throughout the entire piece. Then as well, in various speeches made outside of the House of Commons, I underlined this fact, namely that we were in a position where nuclear weapons could be secured and would be secured in the event that the circumstances at the time made such a course reasonable and necessary. I went further in that connection when I said this:

Would you, in 1961, faced by the overwhelming power of Soviet might in East Germany close to West Berlin, with large divisions fully armed, would you place in the hands of those who guard the portals of freedom nothing but bows and arrows? They would stand against overwhelming power—it is as simple as that.

Throughout the election campaign I followed the same course. In the two speeches I made before the United Nations I asked, as had the Secretary of State for External Affairs . . . for the abolition of nuclear weapons, the end of nuclear weapons, the systematic control of missiles designed to deliver nuclear weapons of mass destruction, the designation and inspection of launching sites for missiles, the abolition of biological and chemical weapons and the outlawing of outer space for military purposes. That has been our course throughout.

During the election campaign, however, with the change in circumstances that had been taking place from the point of view of defence, I outlined the position of this party in a speech which I made in Brockville. It was not too successful, judging by the results, but I spoke there during the campaign and I said this:

> We shall not, so long as we are pursuing the ways of disarmament, allow the extension of the nuclear family into Canada . . . We do not intend to allow the spread of nuclear arms beyond the nations which now have them.

Those, in short, are the views expressed, with one exception. . . . On June 12, 1961, I set out in detail the arrangements that had been arrived at between Canada and the United States (regarding the arming of 60F–101B interceptors with nuclear weapons). I think I had better read from it:

> For some time representatives of the Canadian and United States Governments have been working on an agreement relating to the defence of Canada, more particularly to air defence and to the Canada–United States production-sharing programme. The objective of such an agreement was to reflect the desire of both Governments to ensure more effective use of the productive capacities, skills and resources of each country and at the same time to demonstrate our mutual determination to improve the defensive strength of NATO and particularly of NORAD under it . . .
>
> In consideration of the financial and other benefits which will accrue to the United States as a result of Canada's assumption of additional responsibilities under the Pine Tree agreements, Canada will be furnished with 66 F–101B interceptor aircraft and appropriate support equipment. These aircraft, title to which will be vested in Canada, will be armed with conventional weapons.

. . . That is the background. That is the recital of some of the stands we have taken and which are consistent throughout and which, when read in conjunction one with the other reveal the situation as we saw it. . . .

To summarize our viewpoint, there is a will to peace, as the Secretary of State for External Affairs said yesterday. There is progress being made. We must maintain our defence. We shall not allow Canada to be placed in a subservient or unsovereign position. We shall follow the course that we have been following —one that has been consistent. It has been one of calm consideration of the matters as they arise.

We know . . . that the way to prevent nuclear war is to prevent it. What course should we take at this time? I emphasize what I have already stated, that we shall at all times carry out whatever our responsibilities are. I have said that strategic changes are taking place in the thinking of the Western world, and there is general recognition that the nuclear deterrent will not be strengthened by the expansion of the nuclear family. With these improvements in the international situation, this is no time for hardened decisions that cannot be altered. We must be flexible and fluid, for no one can anticipate what Khrushchev will do.

A meeting is about to take place in Ottawa of the NATO nations. They will meet here on May 21 to 23 and the very fact that they are meeting here indicates the attitude towards Canada and the feeling of the NATO nations towards her....

What shall our attitude be? It will not be one of recklessness, not one of making final decisions in the face of a changing world. I mentioned Nassau a moment ago and, as one examines what took place there, he realizes that we are living in a new and changing world of defence realism. . . .

I have said earlier that all the nations made mistakes, $3 billion worth of mistakes and more, up to 1960, but the fact that a mistake may have been made, or may not have been made, should not be a basis for the continuation of a policy just because to admit it would be wrong. Delivery of the F–104G has commenced, but the strike-reconnaissance role has been placed under doubt by the recent Nassau declaration concerning nuclear arms, as well as other developments both technical and political in the defence field. It will be necessary, therefore, at this meeting in May, for Canada to give consideration to this matter and we will, in co-operation with the nations of NATO, undertake a clarification of our role in NATO defence plans and disposition.

We are united in NATO. We have never and will never consent to Canada breaking any of her pledged words or undertakings. It is at that meeting, where there will be reviewed the entire collective defence policy, that we shall secure from the other member nations their views, and on the basis of that we will be in a position to make a decision, a consistent decision, first to maintain our undertakings and secondly to execute, if that be the view, the maintenance of our collective defence. In the meantime the training of Canadian forces in the use of these weapon systems can continue.

So far as NORAD is concerned I have said at the beginning of my remarks that Canada's sovereignty must be maintained. We shall continue our negotiations. They have been going on quite forcibly for two months or more. . . .

There was never any concealment of the fact. We will negotiate with the United States so that, as I said earlier, in case of need nuclear warheads will be made readily available. In other words, we will be in a position to determine finally, in the interests of Canada and our allies, the course to be followed in the light of changing circumstances in the disarmament field, which have become encouraging recently through Khrushchev's acceptance of even a minimum observation of nuclear testing. We will discuss with the nations of NATO the new concept of a nuclear force for NATO. If that concept at Nassau is carried into effect, much of our planning in the past will pass out of existence.

. . . It is so easy to say what should be done. Conscientiously and honestly we have tried, in the face of changing conditions, to bring about peace. We do not want to do anything at this time to rock the boat. If in the progress of disarmament it is found that we are beginning to approach that new era that all of us look forward to, the NATO nations meeting together can make that determination in agreement that is best for each and all. If, on the other hand, there is going to be set up a multilateral nuclear force, then all our planning to date, or most of it, will be of little or no consequence. I know they say, 'Make decisions. Be concrete; be direct' . . . Recklessness was never evidence of decisiveness. We will, as a result of the fullest discussion and consideration, determine a course which I believe now means a vast alteration in all the defensive techniques that we have accepted in the last few years, and we will come back to Parliament and place before it the considered view of this Government.

. . . All of us should be true Canadians when facing a problem that touches the heartstrings of each and every one of us. My prayer is that we will be directed in this matter. Some may ridicule that belief on my part. I believe that the

Western world has been directed by God in the last few years, or there would have been no survival. I believe that will continue. My prayer is that we shall so live as to maintain not only the integrity of Canada and its high reputation by carrying out our responsibilities, but at the same time that we will be right, that the Canadian people will be able to say that, whatever decision is made, it was made with every consideration being given to all those moral and psychological things that form one's make-up.

I would rather be right . . . so that those who come after may say, 'He refused to be stampeded. He refused to act on the impulse of the moment. He and his colleagues together, with the support of the Canadian Parliament, brought about a policy, in co-operation with their allies and by influence over their allies, that led to the achievement of peace.'

Statement by the United States Department of State, 30 January 1963[1]

The Department has received a number of inquiries concerning the disclosure during a recent debate in the Canadian House of Commons regarding negotiations over the past 2 or 3 months between the United States and Canadian Governments relating to nuclear weapons for Canadian armed forces.[2]

In 1958 the Canadian Government decided to adopt the BOMARC–B weapons systems. Accordingly two BOMARC–B squadrons were deployed to Canada where they would serve the double purpose of protecting Montreal and Toronto as well as the U.S. deterrent force. The BOMARC–B was not designed to carry any conventional warhead. The matter of making available a nuclear warhead for it and for other nuclear-capable weapons systems acquired by Canada has been the subject of inconclusive discussions between the two Governments. The installation of the two BOMARC–B batteries in Canada without nuclear warheads was completed in 1962.

In addition to the BOMARC–B, a similar problem exists with respect to the modern supersonic jet interceptor with which the Royal Canadian Air Force has been provided. Without nuclear air defense warheads, they operate at far less than their full potential effectiveness.

Shortly after the Cuban crisis in October 1962, the Canadian Government proposed confidential discussions concerning circumstances under which there might be provision of nuclear weapons for Canadian armed forces in Canada and Europe. These discussions have been exploratory in nature; the Canadian Government has not as yet proposed any arrangement sufficiently practical to contribute effectively to North American defense.

The discussions between the two Governments have also involved possible arrangements for the provision of nuclear weapons for Canadian NATO forces in Europe, similar to the arrangements which the United States has made with many of our other NATO allies.

During the debate in the House of Commons various references were made to recent discussions at Nassau. The agreements made at Nassau have been fully published.[3] They raise no question of the appropriateness of nuclear weapons for Canadian forces in fulfilling their NATO or NORAD[4] obligations.

[1] *D.S.B.*, 18 February 1963, pp. 243–4.   [2] See pp. 469–80 above.
[3] *Documents, 1962*, pp. 481–4.   [4] North American Air Defence Command.

Reference was also made in the debate to the need of NATO for increased conventional forces. A flexible and balanced defense requires increased conventional forces, but conventional forces are not an alternative to effective NATO or NORAD defense arrangements using nuclear-capable weapons systems. NORAD is designed to defend the North American Continent against air attack. The Soviet bomber fleet will remain at least throughout this decade a significant element in the Soviet strike force. An effective continental defense against this common threat is necessary.

The provision of nuclear weapons to Canadian forces would not involve an expansion of independent nuclear capability, or an increase in the 'nuclear club.' As in the case of other allies, custody of U.S. nuclear weapons would remain with the United States. Joint control fully consistent with national sovereignty can be worked out to cover the use of such weapons by Canadian forces.

Communiqué issued by President Kennedy and the Canadian Prime Minister, Mr. Pearson, Hyannis Port, Massachusetts, 11 May 1963[1]

During the past two days the President and the Prime Minister have met together in this historic State where so many of the currents of the national life of the two countries have mingled from early times.

2. Mr. Pearson's visit to Mr. Kennedy's family home took place in the atmosphere of informality and friendliness which marks so many of the relations between the people of the United States and Canada. There was no agenda for the talks. It was taken for granted that any matter of mutual interest could be frankly discussed in a spirit of goodwill and understanding.

3. In this community on the Atlantic seaboard, the Prime Minister and the President reaffirmed their faith in the North Atlantic Alliance and their conviction that, building upon the present foundations, a true community of the Atlantic peoples will one day be realized. They noted that questions which would be under discussion at the forthcoming NATO Ministerial Meeting in Ottawa[2] would give both countries an opportunity to demonstrate their belief in the Atlantic concept.

4. Their Governments will continue to do everything possible to eliminate causes of dangerous tensions and to bring about peaceful solutions. In this task, they will continue to support the role of the United Nations, and to make every effort to achieve progress in the negotiations on nuclear tests and disarmament.[3]

5. In the face of continuing dangers, the President and the Prime Minister emphasized the vital importance of continental security to the safety of the free world and affirmed their mutual interest in ensuring that bilateral defense arrangements are made as effective as possible and continually improved and adapted to suit changing circumstances and changing roles. The Prime Minister confirmed his government's intention to initiate discussions with the United States Government leading without delay towards the fulfilment of Canada's existing defense commitments in North America and Europe, consistent with Canadian parliamentary procedures.

[1] *D.S.B.*, 27 May 1963, pp. 815–17. The Liberal Party won the election of 17 April 1963 and Mr. Pearson formed a Government on 22 April.

[2] See pp. 31–3 above.   [3] See pp. 170–2 above.

6. President Kennedy and Prime Minister Pearson reaffirmed the desire of the two Governments to cooperate in a rational use of the continent's resources; oil, gas, electricity, strategic metals and minerals, and the use of each other's industrial capacity for defense purposes in the defense production-sharing programs. The two countries also stand to gain by sharing advances in science and technology which can add to the variety and richness of life in North America and in the larger world.

7. The President and the Prime Minister stressed the interest of both countries in the balance of payments between them and with the rest of the world. The Prime Minister drew particular attention to the large United States surplus in the balance of current payments with Canada and noted the importance of allowing for this fact in determining the appropriate policies to be followed by each country. It was agreed that both Governments should always deal in a positive and cooperative manner with developments affecting their international trade and payments.

8. The Prime Minister and the President noted that encouraging discussions had recently taken place between Governor Herter [Christian A. Herter, the President's Special Representative for Trade Negotiations] and Canadian Ministers about the prospects for general trade negotiations and that these talks would be continuing with a large number of other countries in the General Agreement of Tariffs and Trade in Geneva next week. The two Governments will cooperate closely so that these negotiations can contribute to the general advantage of all countries.

9. While it is essential that there should be respect for the common border which symbolizes the independence and national identity of two countries, it is also important that this border should not be a barrier to cooperation which could benefit both of them. Wise cooperation across the border can enhance rather than diminish the sovereignty of each country by making it stronger and more prosperous than before.

10. In this connection the President and the Prime Minister noted especially the desirability of early progress on the cooperative development of the Columbia River. The Prime Minister indicated that if certain clarifications and adjustments in arrangements proposed earlier could be agreed on, to be included in a protocol to the treaty, the Canadian Government would consult at once with the provincial Government of British Columbia, the province in which the Canadian portion of the river is located, with a view to proceeding promptly with the further detailed negotiations required with the United States and with the necessary action for approval within Canada. The President agreed that both Governments should immediately undertake discussions on this subject looking to an early agreement.

11. The two Governments will also initiate discussions shortly on the suitability of present trans-border air travel arrangements from the point of view of the traveling public and of the airlines of the two countries.

12. On the great waters that separate and unite the two countries—the St. Lawrence River and the Great Lakes—it is essential that those who own and sail the ships should be free to go about their lawful business without impediment of harassment. The Prime Minister and President shared a common concern at the consequences which could result from industrial strife on this central

waterway. They urged those directly concerned to work strenuously for improvement in the situation, and to avoid incidents which could lead to further deterioration. To help bring about more satisfactory conditions they have arranged for a meeting to take place in the near future between the Canadian Minister of Labour, Allan J. MacEachen, the United States Secretary of Labor, W. Willard Wirtz, the President of the AFL–CIO, George Meany, and the President of the Canadian Labour Congress, Claude Jodoin.

13. On the oceans that surround the two countries, while there has always been healthy competition, there has also been a substantial similarity of sentiment among those who harvest the sea. The need for some better definitions of the limits of each country's own fishing waters has long been recognized, particularly with respect to the most active fishing areas. The Prime Minister informed the President that the Canadian Government would shortly be taking decisions to establish a 12-mile fishing zone. The President reserved the long-standing American position in support of the 3-mile limit. He also called attention to the historic and treaty fishing rights of the United States. The Prime Minister assured him that these rights would be taken into account.

14. The President and the Prime Minister talked about various situations of common interest in this hemisphere. In particular they expressed a readiness to explore with other interested countries the possibility of a further cooperative effort to provide economic and technical aid to the countries in the Caribbean area which have recently become independent or which are approaching independence, many of which have long had close economic, educational and other relations with Canada and the United States. Such a program could provide a very useful supplement to the resources which those countries are able to raise themselves or to secure from the international agencies which the United States and Canada are already supporting.

15. Our two countries will inevitably have different views on international issues from time to time. The Prime Minister and the President stressed the importance of each country showing regard for the views of the other where attitudes differ. For this purpose they are arranging for more frequent consultation at all levels in order that the intentions of each Government may be fully appreciated by the other, and misunderstandings may be avoided.

16. These preliminary discussions between the President and the Prime Minister will lead to a good deal of additional activity for the two Governments over the next few months. It is expected that there will be almost continuous exchanges of views during that period as work progresses in resolving many matters of concern to the two countries. Then, in the latter part of the year, meetings will be held of the Joint Cabinet-level Committee on Trade and Economic Affairs and on Defense.

17. The Prime Minister and the President look forward to a period of particularly active and productive cooperation between the two countries.

B. LATIN AMERICA

(a) *Cuba in the Inter-American System*

Note from the Representative of the United States, Mr. Morrison, to Sr. Lavalle, Chairman of the Special Committee to study Resolutions II.1 and VIII of the Eighth Meeting of Consultation of Ministers of Foreign Affairs of the O.A.S., 30 January 1963[1] (extract), with Annex

. . . On January 16, 1963, Prime Minister Fidel Castro in a speech at the closing session of the Congress of Women of the Americas made a major policy statement, further defining the Cuban Government's position of encouragement and support for armed insurrection in other countries of the hemisphere. The statement constitutes a declaration of war against the hemisphere. Given in the context of the present dispute between Moscow and Peiping over the strategy and tactics which international communism should follow in its pursuit of world domination, the statement has added significance since Castro clearly advocates the path of violence. There follows the text of the principal sections of what he had to say on this subject.[2]

In the opinion of the United States Government the repeated emphasis placed by high officials of the Castro regime on violence to overthrow established governments, coupled with recent outcroppings of sabotage, terrorism and other forms of subversive activity in several American Republics makes it increasingly important that the governments and the appropriate organs of the OAS redouble their vigilance against Castro-communist subversion. Likewise it becomes of major importance that the member governments develop their capacity of counteracting this threat through individual and cooperative measures.

Because of the importance of the subject matter, I am again taking the liberty of sending a copy of this note to the Chairman of the Council of the Organization with the request that he make it available to the members of the Council.

Annex: Speech by the Prime Minister of Cuba, Fidel Castro, to the Congress of Women of the Americas, Havana, 16 January 1963[3] (extracts)

. . . We must think about how to change that situation [i.e. social and economic conditions in Latin America]. There are persons who are experts on figures, but what is needed are experts on changing the situation, experts on leading peoples on revolutions. That is the art of the revolutionaries, the art that must be learned and developed. How to bring the masses to the struggle?

It is the masses who make history, but for them to make history, the masses must be taken to the battle. That is the duty of leaders and the revolutionary organizations: to make the masses march, to launch the masses into battle. That is what they did in Algeria. And that is what the patriots are doing in South

---

[1] *D.S.B.*, 18 February 1963, pp. 263–4. For texts of resolutions II. 1 and VIII, see *Documents, 1962*, pp. 160–1 and 166–7. The Eighth Ministerial Meeting was held at Punta del Este, 22–31 January 1962.

[2] See Annex, pp. 484–6 below.

[3] Text as printed in *D.S.B.*, 18 February 1963, pp. 263–4.

Vietnam. They have sent the masses into battle with correct methods, correct tactics, and they have brought the greatest amount of the masses into the battle.

That is what we did. The four, five, six, or seven of us who one day were separated did not conquer power. It was the movement of the masses that the struggle against the tyranny unleashed, which culminated in the victory of the people. . . . Those are the historic truths. And we believe that we at least have the right to speak about our historic truths without some long-distance theoreticians telling us what happened here without ever having come here. One does not have to whisper about those things, nor must one say them in low tones. They must be said in a loud voice so that they will be heard, really heard.

And let the peoples hear them, because those false interpretations of history tend to create that conformism that also suits imperialism; it tends to create that resignation and reformism and that policy of waiting for the Greek calends to make revolutions. Those false interpretations of history do not conform with the situation of the majority of the Latin American countries, where objective conditions exist—and the imperialists have clearly seen that objective conditions do exist—but where subjective conditions are missing. Those subjective conditions must be created, and they are created by historic truth, not by falsification of history.

Those subjective conditions are not created by saying that there was a peaceful transition in Cuba. (One of the delegates shouts something about cowards—Ed.) It is not a matter of cowards, but of confused, of mistaken views. We do not deny the possibility of peaceful transition, but we are still awaiting the first case. But we do not deny it, because we are not dogmatists, and we understand the ceaseless change of historic conditions and circumstances.

We do not deny it but we do say that there was no peaceful transition; and we do protest against an attempt to use the case of Cuba to confuse the revolutionaries of other countries where the objective conditions for the revolution exist and where they can do the same thing Cuba did. It is logical that imperialist theoreticians try to prevent revolutions, the imperialists slander the Cuban revolution, sow lies, say the worst horrors, create fear of revolutions among the people. But let no one from a revolutionary position attempt to create conformism or fear of revolutions. That is absurd. Let the imperialist theoreticians preach conformism. Let the revolutionary theoreticians preach revolution without fear.

That is what we think. That was what we said in the Declaration of Havana,[1] which, in some fraternal countries, received from some revolutionary organizations the honors of a desk drawer when it should have received the just publicity it deserved. It would be like locking up everything you have discussed here. Of course, if we do not want the masses to learn about it, we must put it in a drawer. But if we tell the masses what the situation is, they must also be told what the road is. We must bring them to the struggle, because that road is much easier in many Latin American countries than it was in Cuba.

I want to make it clear, so that the theoreticians will not get angry, that we are not making an irresponsible generalization. I want to make it clear that we know that each country has its specific conditions, and that is why we do not generalize. But we say the majority. We know there are exceptions. We know there are

[1] Contained in a speech by Prime Minister Castro of 2 September 1960; for text, see *Documents, 1960*, pp. 597–601.

countries in which those objective conditions do not exist. But they exist in the majority of the Latin American countries. That is our opinion. To say it here is a duty, because we hope that in 40 years we will not meet as today—the grand-daughters of our federated women with your grand-daughters—to discuss the same problems.

Statement by President Kennedy at the Meeting of the Presidents of the Central American Republics, Panama and the United States, San José, Costa Rica, 18 March 1963[1] (extract)

. . . Here in Central America we have already begun to move toward the goals of the *Alianza*.

You have made enormous strides toward the creation of a common market of 13 million people. New regional institutions have been created; a central bank has been established, and centralized planning and direction are going ahead in education, finance, and many other fields. I congratulate you on your effort to reestablish an historic unity to meet new needs; and I pledge my Government's continued assistance to that great effort.

In addition you have begun to formulate the long-range economic development plans essential to the success of the *Alianza*. The organization of the Central American Joint Planning Mission gives new impetus to planning on a regional development scale.

In nearly every country represented here, new land-reform or tax-reform programs have been adopted in an effort to meet the basic pledges of increased social justice contained in the Charter of Punta del Este[2] and demanded by all of our people.

In the 2-year period beginning July 1961, under programs supported by the United States as part of its contribution to the alliance, almost 3,000 new class-rooms will have been built in the nations represented here today; almost a million new books have been distributed; and tomorrow we will begin to distribute more than 2 million more to children hungry for learning. Much more remains to be done.

Some 7,600 new homes will have been built during this 2-year period under *Alianza* programs in these nations—but much more remains to be done.

Three-quarters of a million children will have been fed—but many are still hungry.

Six thousand new teachers have been trained, as well as many thousands of agricultural workers, public-health and other public administrators. Still more are needed.

During the last 18 months almost 3 million people in Central America—farmers, workers, children, and slum dwellers—have received some form of direct benefit under the *Alianza*, and almost $250 million of external resources have been committed in support of the alliance in Central America and Panama, to help strengthen the basic structure of the economy and at the same time meet

---

[1] *D.S.B.*, 8 April 1963, pp. 512–15. The Central American participants were Costa Rica, El Salvador, Guatemala, Honduras, and Nicaragua.
[2] *Documents, 1961*, pp. 810–23.

the basic needs of the people for improved health, education, housing, and institutions.

Finally, a revolutionary worldwide agreement to stabilize the price of coffee[1] has been entered into which we in the United States are determined to make work—to protect your most vital source of export earnings. As every speaker here today has said, every one of these countries sell their agricultural commodities in a sense at wholesale, and buy their manufactured goods at retail, and pay the freight both ways. And we are also willing to move ahead on agreements stabilizing the prices of other commodities, so that your future prosperity will not depend on the often destructive fluctuation of prices beyond your control.

Tomorrow, at El Bosque,[2] we will see with our own eyes how the *Alianza* enters into the lives of citizens of Costa Rica, providing them with new homes in which they and their families can find decent shelter for the first time.

We shall continue under the alliance to build economies more balanced and less dependent on one or two export commodities. To this end we must push forward plans for industrialization, greater crop diversification, stronger educational facilities, and better utilization of resources.

Yet we cannot be, and I know none of us are, satisfied with the progress we have made. Peoples who have waited centuries for opportunity and dignity cannot wait much longer. And unless those of us now making an effort are willing to redouble our efforts, unless the rich are willing to use some of their riches more wisely, unless the privileged are willing to yield up their privileges to the common good, unless the young and the educated are given opportunities to use their education, and unless governments are willing to dedicate themselves tirelessly to the tasks of governing efficiently and developing swiftly, then let us realize our *Alianza* will fail, and with it will fall the society of free nations which our forefathers labored to build.

Unfortunately, while this new endeavor goes forward we are also confronted by one of the oldest of our enemies. For, at the very time that newly independent nations rise in the Caribbean, the people of Cuba have been forcibly compelled to submit to a new imperialism, more ruthless, more powerful, and more deadly in its pursuit of power than any this hemisphere has known. Just when it was hoped that Cuba was about to enter upon a new era of democracy and social justice, the Soviet Union, through its Cuban puppets, absorbed the Cuban nation into its empire—and it now seeks to extend its rule to the shores of the continent itself.

But other foreign powers have discovered that the American hemisphere is not fertile ground for foreign tyranny and that any effort to spread such rule will meet with fierce and unyielding resistance. For Americans will not easily yield up those freedoms which they shed so much blood to achieve.

At the OAS, at this meeting, and wherever Americans gather to consult about the future of their continent, we will continue to strengthen the structure of resistance to subversion. I am hopeful that at this meeting we will again increase our capacity to prevent the infiltration of Cuban agents, money, and propaganda. We will build a wall around Cuba—not a wall of mortar or brick or barbed wire, but a wall of dedicated men determined to protect their freedom and sovereignty.

[1] Summary in *Current Documents, 1963*, pp. 1140–2.
[2] Costa Rican housing project financed under the Alliance for Progress.

And in this effort, as in all the other necessary efforts, I can assure you the United States will play its full part and carry its full burden.

In 1822 Bolívar, the father of the inter-American system, said this:

> United in heart, in spirit and in aims, this Continent . . . must raise its eyes . . . to peer into the centuries which lie ahead. It can then contemplate with pride those future generations of men, happy and free, enjoying to the full the blessings that heaven bestows on this earth, and recalling in their hearts the protectors and liberators of our day.

My friends and colleagues, today we meet, representing seven of the great Republics of America, united in spirit and in aims. We are confident of our ultimate success in protecting our freedom, in raising the living standards of our citizens, in beginning a new era of hope in American history. Secure in that confidence, we too can look forward to future centuries knowing that our descendants may also gratefully recall in their hearts the 'protectors and liberators' of our day.

Declaration of Central America, issued by the Presidents of the Central American Republics, Panama and the United States, San José, Costa Rica, 19 March 1963[1]

The Presidents of the Republics of Central America and Panama are determined to improve the well-being of their peoples, and are aware that such a task demands a dynamic economic and social development program based on the carefully planned use of human, natural and financial resources. It also depends on important changes of the economic, social and administrative structure, within the framework of the principles that govern our democratic institutions. They have met with the President of the United States of America in San José, Costa Rica. to review the difficulties which impede the achievement of these objectives as well as the progress thus far made in the Isthmus since the integration programs began and since the Alliance for Progress was jointly established by the Republics of the Hemisphere in August 1961.

Following an analysis of the situation, the Presidents of the Republics of Central America, convinced that the best hope for the development of the region is through economic integration, and bearing in mind the extraordinary efforts made toward this end in the last decade and of the importance of accelerating over-all economic growth, pledge to their peoples:

—To accelerate establishment of a customs union to perfect the functioning of the Central American Common Market;

—To formulate and implement national economic and social development plans, coordinating them at the Central American level, and progressively to carry out regional planning for the various sectors of the economy;

—To establish a monetary union and common fiscal, monetary and social policies within the program of economic integration;

—To cooperate in programs to improve the prices of primary export commodities;

[1] *D.S.B.*, 8 April 1963, pp. 515–17; see also footnote 1, p. 487 above.

—To complete as soon as possible the reforms needed to achieve the objectives set forth in the Act of Bogotá[1] and the Charter of Punta del Este[2] especially in the fields of agriculture, taxation, education, public administration, and social welfare;

—To take the above measures with a view to achieving the creation of a Central American Economic Community which will establish relationships with other nations or regional groups having similar objectives.

The Central American Presidents affirm that the economic integration movement in itself constitutes an effort which is laying the groundwork for regional planning in which sectoral plans of common interest to the Isthmian Republics serve as a point of departure. Their governments have already taken measures to coordinate national plans so that their execution will aid rather than impede the achievement of the objectives of the economic integration program. It is intended that the first global plan for harmonious regional development be presented as soon as possible for evaluation in accordance with the procedures set forth in the Charter of Punta del Este. Meanwhile, the Central American Presidents declare their resolve to proceed immediately with their sectoral plans and with projects of interest to the Isthmus. The President of the United States agrees to consider a long-term loan to enable the appropriate Central American regional organizations, principally the Central American Bank for Economic Integration, to conduct economic feasibility surveys relative to this program of regional development.

The Presidents of Central America reaffirm their hope that the Republic of Panama will participate more closely in the economic integration movement, and the President of Panama declares that his Government fully reaffirms its support of the program of Central American economic integration. He further declares that his Government is prepared to initiate immediate negotiations with the Governments of the general treaty of economic integration as a whole with a view to concluding a special agreement to facilitate the association of his country with this program.

The President of the United States is impressed by the determination of the Presidents of the Central American Republics to move as rapidly as possible toward the integration of the economies of their countries, and of their intention to formulate a regional economic development plan within which national plans would be coordinated, and he believes that the coordination of their respective monetary, fiscal, economic and social policies is a great step forward in the achievement of this objective as well as toward the achievement of the goals set forth in the Charter of Punta del Este.

The President of the United States is prepared to offer the greatest cooperation in the preparation and implementation of the regional and national development projects of Central America and Panama and declares that his government will intensify its joint efforts with the governments and appropriate regional organizations in order to extend to them increased technical and financial assistance for this purpose within the framework of the broad regional program entitled 'Joint Exposition of the Presidents of Central America' and the development plan being prepared by Panama.

[1] Text in *Documents*, pp. 607–12.   [2] Ibid., pp. 810–23.

To this end he proposes a fund for Central American economic integration, to be made available through the Central American Bank for Economic Integration, to which the United States would make an immediate substantial initial contribution, to assist in carrying out regional development projects in accordance with various sectoral plans now being developed by the regional organizations.

For the longer term, he also declares that as soon as the Central American Republics have formulated an over-all regional development plan, and as soon as this plan has been evaluated favorably in accordance with the procedures established in the Charter of Punta del Este, the United States will enlarge and expand its participation in the fund and will work with the Central American countries in obtaining other Free World resources so that the agreed plan can be effectively implemented.

The Presidents have discussed the fundamental importance to economic development of a vigorous and freely-competitive private sector, and declare their intention of taking the necessary steps to encourage private investment which is prepared to accept the normal responsibilities compatible with the development of a modern economy. These measures include establishment of regional trade and promotion offices for the specific purpose of attracting private foreign investment. They also agree that development banks or corporations should be established in each country as soon as possible to provide credit on reasonable terms for the growth of private industry, the President of the United States offering financial assistance to their operation.

Concurrently they agree that economic and social conditions should be created to assure labor of an improved living standard through a better distribution of national income. Furthermore they agree to encourage and support free democratic labor organizations as a means of contributing toward greater worker participation in the common effort on behalf of the general welfare.

The Presidents also agree that opportunities should be given to the people of Central America to build and purchase their homes. There exist in Central America national savings and loan institutions which have been assisted under the Alliance for Progress, and others are about to be created. In order to give further support for these national efforts, the Presidents of Central America suggest that a regional home loan department, which would be a secondary source of home mortgage funds, should be created as a division within the Central American Bank for Economic Integration and the President of the United States agrees to offer technical and financial assistance to it.

The Isthmian Presidents indicate that Central American institutions should be strengthened as much as possible to enable them to play a major role in training the personnel who will be needed to put into effect the plans for integration of the Isthmus. A large part of the responsibility for training will devolve on the Superior Council of Central American Universities (CSUCA). Recognizing, moreover, that trained manpower at all levels is needed for economic development, they agree to the proposal of the President of the United States to establish a multi-million dollar scholarship fund for vocational training in agriculture and in industry for young people of outstanding ability who can not afford the normal expenses of such training to which the United States will offer substantial financial assistance.

The Presidents note the primary role of coffee in the economies of Central America and the importance of the International Coffee Agreement[1] for the achievement of stable and remunerative prices.

They reiterate the intention of their governments to fully support the agreement so that it will serve as an effective instrument to improve the earnings of exporting countries from coffee and to promote their economic development.

Other primary commodity problems exist and the Isthmian Presidents will hand to President Kennedy studies on these problems.

President Kennedy agrees he will have them reviewed immediately on his return to Washington.

The Presidents, notwithstanding the fact that present conditions are favourable to undertake a solution of the economic and social problems of the Isthmus through joint action of the countries of the area, believe that all of them are faced with an externally provoked political problem, which by its very nature can imperil the exercise of representative democracy and the normal development of the plans in which their respective governments are engaged to attain as rapidly as possible the highest levels of economic and social justice and to bring to full realization the plans for Central American integration. Consequently, the Presidents declare that in order to carry out their programs for social and economic betterment, it is essential to reinforce the measures to meet subversive aggression originating in the focal points of Communist agitation which Soviet imperialism may maintain in Cuba or in any other place in America.

The Presidents note that the Council of the Organization of American States is actively engaged in maintaining vigilance over the continued intervention of Sino-Soviet powers in this Hemisphere as requested by the Eighth Meeting of Consultation of Foreign Ministers.[2] They express special interest in early completion by the Council of the OAS of the studies on Castro-Communist subversion in the Hemisphere, and particularly in early action by the Council on recommendations to the governments for counteracting those activities in these areas.[3]

The Presidents agree that Ministers of Government of the seven countries should meet as soon as possible to develop and put into immediate effect common measures to restrict the movement of their nationals to and from Cuba, and the flow of material, propaganda and funds from that country.

This meeting will take action, among other things, to secure stricter travel and passport controls, including appropriate limitations in passports and other travel documents on travel to Cuba. Cooperative arrangements among not only the countries meeting here but also among all OAS members will have to be sought to restrict more effectively not only these movements of people for subversive purposes but also to prevent insofar as possible the introduction of money, propaganda, materials, and arms. Arrangements for additional sea and air surveillance and interception within territorial waters will be worked out with special cooperation from the United States.

In addition to these measures, a more rapid and complete exchange of intelligence information on the movement of people, propaganda, money and

[1] Text in *U.N. Treaty Series, Vol. 469, 1963, No. 6791*, pp. 170–245.
[2] *Documents, 1962*, pp. 160–1.
[3] Text in *Current Documents, 1962*, pp. 361–6.

arms between Cuba and our countries is to be developed by the Meeting of Ministers.[1]

The Presidents voice their deep sympathy for the people of Cuba, and reaffirm their conviction that Cuba soon will join the family of free nations. The Presidents recall how, in 1959, the Cuban people were fired with the hope of a purely Cuban revolution that was to bring them freedom and social justice; honest government and free elections; fair sharing of goods; opportunities for all; more schools and jobs, better health and housing, and constructive land reform not collectivization of the land. In sum, a progressive republic which, in the words of Martí, would be 'con todos y para todos'. The Presidents declare that they have no doubt that the genuine Cuban revolution will live again, and its betrayers will fall into the shadows of history, and the martyred people of the oppressed isle of the Caribbean will be free from foreign Communist domination, free to choose for themselves the kind of government they wish to have, and free to join their brothers of the Hemisphere in the common undertaking to secure for each individual the liberty, dignity, and well-being which are the objectives of all free societies.

Finally the Presidents solemnly reaffirm their adherence to the principles established by the Treaty of Reciprocal Assistance of Rio de Janeiro,[2] the Charter of the OAS,[3] in the Act of Bogotá and in the Charter of Punta del Este.

Final Act, adopted by the meeting of the Ministers of Government, Interior and Security of Costa Rica, El Salvador, Guatemala, Honduras, Nicaragua, Panama and the United States, Managua, 4 April 1963[4]

RESOLUTION I

The Meeting of Ministers of Government, Interior and Security convoked pursuant to the pertinent section of the Declaration of Central America signed by the Presidents of the seven countries in San José, Costa Rica, on March 19, 1963[5]

AGREES

To recommend to their Governments that they adopt, within the limitations of their respective constitutional provisions, measures to be put into effect immediately, to prohibit, restrict and discourage the movement of their nationals to and from Cuba. To this end, they propose the adoption of the following measures:

1) Provide, as a general rule, that every passport or other travel document which may be issued carry a stamp which indicates that said passport is not valid for travel to Cuba.

2) Declare officially that nationals who are permitted to travel to Cuba should have the permission duly inscribed in their official travel document.

---

[1] See pp. 499–504 below.
[2] 2 September 1947; for text, see *Documents, 1947–1948*, pp. 773–9.
[3] Text in *A Decade of American Foreign Policy: Basic Documents, 1941–1949*, pp. 427–45.
[4] *D.S.B.*, 6 May 1963, pp. 719–21.   [5] See pp. 486–8 above.

3) Promulgate regulations restricting the granting of visas to foreigners who have traveled to Cuba within a stipulated period of time.

4) Notify travel agencies and transport companies of these measures for due compliance; and inform the governments of other countries through the most appropriate means.

5) Request the Governments of the Hemisphere:

a) not to allow the nationals of signatory countries to travel to Cuba unless they possess a valid passport or other document issued by their country of origin valid for such travel;

b) not to accept visas, tourist cards or other documents issued to their nationals for travel to Cuba which do not form an integral (nondetachable) part of their passports or other travel documents;

c) to observe the limitations placed in the passports or other travel documents of the nationals of signatory governments and not allow them to depart for Cuba;

d) to inform the signatory countries through appropriate channels of refusals to allow one of their nationals to depart for Cuba; and

e) to provide the signatory governments the names of their nationals which may appear on the passenger list of any airplane or ship going to or coming from Cuba.

RESOLUTION II

The Meeting of Ministers of Government, Interior and Security convoked pursuant to the pertinent section of the Declaration of Central America signed by the Presidents of the seven countries in San José, Costa Rica, on March 19, 1963

AGREES

To recommend to their Governments that they enlist the cooperation of financial institutions to report on the transfer of funds which persons or groups catalogued as Communist subversive elements make, within their respective countries, for subversive purposes; and to establish surveillance of Communist-controlled businesses and other activities to identify the transfer of funds through such establishments for subversive purposes or activities; and impound such funds, or take preventive measures, compatible with each country's legislation, so that they may not be used for purposes that would tend to destroy democratic governments.

RESOLUTION III

The Meeting of Ministers of Government, Interior and Security convoked pursuant to the pertinent section of the Declaration of Central America signed by the Presidents of the seven countries in San José, Costa Rica on March 19, 1963

AGREES

To recommend that their Governments take action to impede the clandestine movement of arms into the Isthmian countries, including specific instructions to border control forces to intensify port, airfield and border inspection of incoming and outgoing cargo in order to prevent contraband traffic in arms; and establish strict security and accountability with respect to arms and ammunition issued to their armed forces and law enforcement agencies.

RESOLUTION IV

The Meeting of Ministers of Government, Interior and Security convoked pursuant to the pertinent section of the Declaration of Central America signed by the Presidents of seven countries in San José, Costa Rica, on March 19, 1963

AGREES

To recommend to their Governments action to prevent the introduction of subversive propaganda materials into the Isthmian countries from abroad, adopting laws as necessary to provide severe penalties for persons knowingly engaged in the introduction or dissemination of such propaganda; and report to the diplomatic missions of the signatory countries the identity of any person discovered introducing or disseminating such propaganda material in the country.

RESOLUTION V

The Meeting of Ministers of Government, Interior and Security convoked pursuant to the pertinent section of the Declaration of Central America signed by the Presidents of the seven countries in San José, Costa Rica, on March 19, 1963

AGREES

To recommend to their Governments that they adopt as soon as possible for immediate implementation effective measures to prevent subversive activities that may be instigated by Castro-communist propaganda or agents in each of the Central American countries and Panama.

RESOLUTION VI

The Meeting of Ministers of Government, Interior and Security convoked pursuant to the pertinent section of the Declaration of Central America signed by the Presidents of the seven countries in San José, Costa Rica, on March 19, 1963

AGREES

To recommend to their Governments that in order to impede the clandestine movement of persons, propaganda materials and arms for subversive purposes a cooperative system be established involving:

a. surveillance by each country of its own coastal area, and interception of suspicious craft within its territorial waters; and

b. cooperation of the Central American States, Panama and the United States to carry out such surveillance and interception, upon the request of any of the governments concerned.

RESOLUTION VII

The Meeting of Ministers of Government, Interior and Security convoked pursuant to the pertinent section of the Declaration of Central America signed by the Presidents of the seven countries in San José, Costa Rica, on March 19, 1963

AGREES

To recommend to the Governments of Central America and Panama the establishment, as soon as possible, of an organization in each State, with the sole purpose of counteracting Communist subversion in the Central America-Panama area. This organization will be staffed by specialized personnel to whom privileges will be extended for travel in the above-mentioned area. These organizations will be primarily responsible for:

a) detecting, controlling and counteracting actions and objectives of the members, instrumentalities, sympathizers and collaborators of the Communist Party; and

b) lending mutual support to each other and constantly exchanging information regarding movements of persons or groups, propaganda, funds and arms for Communist subversive purposes.

RESOLUTION VIII

The Meeting of Ministers of Government, Interior and Security convoked pursuant to the pertinent section of the Declaration of Central America signed by the Presidents of the seven countries in San José, Costa Rica, on March 19, 1963

AGREES

1. To recommend that their Governments:

a) hold periodic meetings of representatives of Isthmian countries and the United States to review progress made and problems remaining in the control of movements of persons, arms, funds and propaganda, for subversive Communist purposes;

b) hold bilateral discussions among the signatory countries regarding requirements for technical, materiel assistance and training support; and

c) furnish information on a continuing basis to the Council of the Organization of American States on Communist subversive activities in their respective countries.

2. To inform the Organization of American States of the agreements taken at the present meeting requesting of that Organization and the Member

Governments the indispensable backing and support required to achieve their effective implementation, thereby strengthening the inter-American system.

Joint Soviet-Cuban statement, Moscow, 23 May 1963[1] (extract)

. . . Views were exchanged in the course of the meetings and talks between Comrades Nikita Khrushchev and Fidel Castro on the further development of cooperation between the Soviet Union and Cuba and the situation in the area of the Caribbean Sea.

The two sides note that the construction of the new Cuba is being carried out in difficult and complex conditions. From the very first days of the existence of the revolutionary Cuban state, the reactionary circles of the United States have done everything to wipe out the gains of the Cuban people and to impose the yoke of imperialist exploitation on it once again.

Flagrantly flouting the United Nations Charter and the generally acknowledged standards of international law, the United States is trying to interfere in the domestic affairs of the Cuban Republic, organizing and guiding subversive activities against the new social and state system in Cuba, and sending armed bands of counter-revolutionary riff-raff to the Island of Freedom.

The United States is promoting a policy of economic aggression against Cuba and is exerting unprecedented pressure on its allies in military blocs, and on other countries, to try to make them follow their policy.

The United States of America would like to isolate the Cuban Republic politically, especially from the peoples of the Latin American countries. For this purpose, they are using the Organization of American States, basing themselves there on representatives of dictatorial military regimes.

Freedom-loving Cuba, however, did not flinch either before political blackmail and economic pressure, or before direct armed intervention. In April 1961, at Playa Giron, the armed forces of the Cuban Republic routed the army of mercenaries which was equipped with American military material and was trained in military camps on the territory of the United States and its henchmen.

Revolutionary Cuba carried the banner of freedom and independence high in the grim days of October 1962, when having prepared a new armed intervention against the Cuban people, the United States, by its aggressive actions, strained the situation in the area of the Caribbean Sea to the limit, as a result of which an international crisis emerged and the world was placed on the brink of a nuclear-missile world war.

At that tense moment, the leaders of the Revolutionary Government of the Cuban Republic, led by Fidel Castro, and the whole Cuban people displayed unbending determination to uphold the gains of their revolution, and the honour and freedom of Cuba.

True to their heroic traditions, the Cuban people rose to the defence of their country, ready to fight to the last man against the foreign interventionists.

The firm stand of the Soviet Union and the other socialist countries in the cause of defending revolutionary Cuba, the restrained and sober evaluation by the responsible statesmen of the Soviet Union and Cuba of the situation that

---

[1] *Soviet News*, 27 May 1963, pp. 109–13.

resulted, and the support for Cuba from all peace-loving states, averted thermo-nuclear war. The immediate danger of an armed attack on Cuba was removed.

Today, revolutionary Cuba is an example of unbending courage and staunchness in the struggle for independence, and for the right to create a new life without exploiters.

The two sides note that, although the immediate danger of military intervention in Cuba has been removed, the tension in the area of the Caribbean Sea still remains.

This situation could be normalized on the basis of the implementation of the five points advanced by the Prime Minister of the Revolutionary Government of Cuba, Fidel Castro, which include the ending of all measures of economic pressure; the ending of all subversive activities; the ending of attacks from bases situated in the United States and Puerto Rico; the ending of all intrusions by military planes and ships of the United States into the air space and territorial waters of Cuba; and the removal of the United States naval base at Guantánamo from Cuban territory.

The Soviet government emphatically supports these principles, because they are in full accord with the United Nations Charter and reflect the efforts of the Revolutionary Government of Cuba to find a peaceful solution to the outstanding issues that create tension in that part of the world.

The government of the Soviet Union and the government of Cuba proceed from the premise that revolutionary Cuba does not threaten anyone.

The road of development and social change which has been chosen by the Cuban people, is its domestic affair, and no one has the right to interfere in its affairs.

Both governments resolutely state their adherence to the principle of non-interference of states in the internal affairs of other countries, and solemnly confirm that the peace-loving principles of the United Nations, including the principle of respect for the sovereignty of states, have their full support, because they meet the interests of peace and friendship between nations.

The Cuban side declares that the people of Cuba highly appreciate the moral and political support and help rendered by the Soviet Union. The statement of the U.S.S.R. government and its head, Comrade Nikita Khrushchev, the defence by the Soviet Union of Cuba's interests in the United Nations and in other international forums, the action of mass public organizations in the U.S.S.R. in support of Cuba, and the economic and military aid of the Soviet Union, played a very important role in the struggle of the Cuban people for its freedom and independence against the external threat from imperialism.

The Soviet Union has rendered, and is rendering, effective aid to Cuba in strengthening her defence potential. At the request of the Cuban government the Soviet Union helped Cuba to create a strong army, well trained, and equipped with modern military material, capable of administering a rebuff to any attempts at encroachment on the sovereignty and freedom of the Cuban state.

In the course of the talks between Comrades Nikita Khrushchev and Fidel Castro, it was confirmed by the Soviet side that, if an attack was made on Cuba in violation of the commitments undertaken by the President of the United States not to invade Cuba, the Soviet Union would fulfill its international duty to the fraternal Cuban people, and would render it the necessary aid for the defence of freedom and independence of the Cuban republic, with all the means at its disposal.

The organizers of aggression should remember that an invasion of Cuba will confront mankind with a devastating nuclear rocket war.

The two sides considered questions connected with the implementation of the Soviet-Cuban agreements on trade and economic, technical, scientific and cultural co-operation, and noted with satisfaction that these agreements are being successfully implemented.

The Soviet Union is constantly increasing the purchase of goods which constitute Cuba's traditional exports, and, together with other socialist countries, is doing everything to satisfy the pressing requirements of Cuba in equipment and raw materials for her industry, and in goods to supply the country's population.

The Soviet Union is also rendering the necessary aid in transporting the goods purchased or sold by Cuba.

The two sides take note with satisfaction of the fact that economic co-operation between the U.S.S.R. and Cuba is acquiring a more and more extensive and all-around nature. The Soviet Union is rendering Cuba technical assistance in conducting geological prospecting, in expanding and reconstructing three re-smelting metallurgical works, in the construction of a big thermal power station, in the development of the nickel and chemical industries and commercial fishing, and the carrying out of priority irrigation and land improvement projects.

The construction of an engineering plant now under way with the help of the Soviet Union is of great importance.

The Soviet Union is rendering help to the Cuban Republic in creating national cadres, by training Cuban citizens in the U.S.S.R., and by setting up training centres in Cuba.

Co-operation between Soviet and Cuban organizations and institutions in the fields of culture, science, education, public health and sports is developing successfully.

Agreement was reached in the course of the talks on measures for the further development of economic, trade and scientific and cultural links between the U.S.S.R. and the Cuban Republic.

Guided by the desire to help to consolidate the socialist economy of fraternal Cuba, and taking into consideration that in recent years raw sugar prices in the world market have risen considerably, the Soviet government, on its own initiative, proposed to change the existing agreement, and to increase the price of the Cuban raw sugar to be bought in 1963, so as to bring this price into line with the level of world prices.

The Soviet government proceeded from the fact that the production of sugar is one of the staple branches of Cuba's economy, and that an increase of sugar prices will play an effective part in consolidating the economic situation in Cuba.

This proposal by the Soviet government was accepted by the Cuban side. . . .

Report of the Special Committee To Study Resolutions II.1 and VIII of the Eighth Meeting of Consultation of Ministers of Foreign Affairs, Submitted to the Council of the O.A.S., 4 June 1963[1] (extracts)

. . . II. STUDY OF THE TRANSFER OF FUNDS TO THE AMERICAN REPUB-
LICS FOR SUBVERSIVE PROPAGANDA, AND THE UTILIZATION OF
CUBA AS A BASE FOR TRAINING IN TECHNIQUES OF SUBVERSION

A. CUBA AS A BASE FOR TRAINING IN TECHNIQUES OF SUBVERSION

1. *General Considerations* . . .

2. *Recommendations on Control of Travel*

The effective control of travel to Cuba should include both national and international procedures.

a. *National Procedures*

1. To provide that every person who crosses an international border must have in his possession some travel or identification document, and to exercise control over such documentation.

2. To prohibit trips to Cuba, as a general rule, and to regulate those that may be made to those persons who have valid reasons, such as those of an official or humanitarian nature. It would be advisable, in the corresponding stipulations, to consider the following suggestions, among others:

a. To limit the use of passports or other travel documents by means of an inscription stating that these are not valid for travel to Cuba, and to penalize as a violation of law any trip not authorized by the terms of the travel document.

b. To require that every person who desires to travel to Cuba present a request to that effect to the appropriate office and prove that he has a valid reason for making the trip. If the permit is issued, a statement to that effect should be made on the passport itself.

c. To give wide publicity to the laws and regulations of each country in relation to travel to Cuba, and to inform the travel agencies and transport companies of them for due compliance therewith.

3. To provide to the immigration officers at the ports, border crossings, and airports a list of persons known to be agents or members of the communist party, and of those who have traveled to Cuba, for such control action as they deem necessary. For this purpose close cooperation between the police and immigration authorities is required.

4. To record in the passport or other travel documents authorized by the government of the traveler the date of departure, date of entry, destination, and place of origin.

---

[1] O.A.S. doc. OEA/Ser. G/IV/C–i–605 Rev. 3, 3 July 1963; text as printed in *Current Documents, 1963*, pp. 271–6.

b. *International Procedures*

1. To recommend to the governments that, in cooperation with one another, they:

a. Observe the limitations on travel that are noted in the respective documents. For example, a country 'A' should take the steps necessary in order not to permit the departure for Cuba of a national of a country 'B' whose documentation specifies that it is not valid for making such a trip. In relation to this measure, country 'A' should not accept visas, tourist cards, or other documents for travel to Cuba that are not an integral part of the passport or travel document of a national of country 'B'.

b. Supply the other governments with information regarding its laws and regulations on travel.

c. Inform the diplomatic or consular authorities of the respective American country when a national of that country is refused departure for Cuba.

d. Transmit to the diplomatic or consular authorities of any other American country the names of its nationals that appear in the passenger list of every airplane or ship that departs for Cuba or comes from that country.

e. Examine minutely the travel documents of every passenger in order to prevent violations of the terms of those documents.

2. To establish a system for the exchange of information between governments on known communists, subversive agents, and persons who travel to Cuba.

B. The Flow of Subversive Propaganda

1. *General Considerations* . . .

2. *Recommendations*

In connection with the measures employed by communism to spread its subversive propaganda, and based on the foregoing considerations, the Committee makes the following recommendations:

a. *Diplomatic and Consular Missions*

It would be advisable for the American countries to establish, with respect to the members of missions from the communist countries, the same limitations that are imposed on the members of their own missions in the communist countries, particularly in regard to their movement and circulation and the exercise of privileges. It would likewise be advisable to adopt, on a reciprocal basis, measures to equalize the number of members of the missions from the communist countries and of the missions of the American governments to those countries.

b. *Trade and Technical Assistance*

1. To establish strict supervision of the trade and technical missions of the countries of the communist bloc.

2. To keep careful watch over the activities of national organizations for trade with communist countries, to make sure that these activities do not go beyond their legal purposes.

c. *Binational Centers and Associations for Friendship or Culture Organized with Countries of the Communist Bloc*

1. To intensify control over entities of this nature as effectively as possible in order to make sure that they do not carry on subversive activities.

2. To bring to the attention of the public any connections that these entities and their leaders may have with the international communist movement, as well as any of their activities and objectives of a subversive nature.

3. To enforce more effectively the legal provisions intended to repress the activities of these entities and of their members who incite to the use of violence or practice it to disturb public order.

4. To take the most appropriate measures to prevent the holding of international congresses, conferences, or meetings of a communist nature, that are organized or sponsored by these entities. Among such measures we may mention the denial of facilities for holding the meetings and restriction of issuance of visas.

d. *Printed Propaganda*

1. To exercise control of and seize communist printed propaganda of a subversive nature coming from abroad, adopting suitable customs and postal measures for this purpose.

2. To adopt measures on a cooperative basis to prevent or restrict the entry of propaganda through diplomatic and consular missions from countries of the communist bloc.

3. The interested governments should inform the countries that maintain diplomatic relations with countries of the communist bloc regarding subversive propaganda entering the former through communist diplomatic missions, and request their cooperation in controlling this.

4. To prevent in an effective way the circulation of any publication that contains subversive propaganda of a communist nature or that incites to the use of violence to disturb public order.

C. The Transfer of Funds to the American Republics for Subversive Purposes

1. *General Considerations* . . .

2. *Recommendations*

In addition to the recommendations already made with regard to controlling travel, the Committee submits to the Council, for consideration, the following measures, which, if adopted by the governments, may control the transfer of funds to a certain degree:

a. To maintain investigative control of individual communists and communist groups, in order to determine the origin of the funds that makes their subversive activities possible.

b. To intensify control of contraband trade, particularly narcotics.

c. To suggest that, in their respective countries, experts on the subject study means that would make it possible to control the entry of money or securities intended for communist individuals and groups.

III. GENERAL OBSERVATIONS AND RECOMMENDATIONS

The Committee notes that intervention by Sino-Soviet powers in this hemisphere, by way of Cuba, has increased considerably during the past year. This intervention has the following two main characteristics: intensification of Soviet military power in Cuba, and utilization of the island as a base for promoting subversive activities in other countries.

The intensification of Soviet military power is a cause of grave concern to all the governments and peoples of the hemisphere. In view of the events that took place in October, 1962, the Committee considers it essential that the Organization and the member states endeavor to maintain the strictest vigilance over the situation. Military intervention by any extracontinental power creates a situation that gravely affects the peace and security of the hemisphere—a situation that cannot be accepted by the inter-American system as normal or permanent.

The utilization of Cuba as a base for promoting subversive activities imposes on the countries of the hemisphere the task of developing adequate methods to combat subversion. Because of their nature, such techniques of subversion must be opposed principally by individual action on the part of each government. To this end, it would be in order for the American governments to examine their internal security laws and the organizations and means at their disposal, in order to determine whether they are adequate, and to adopt the measures that may be necessary in each case. Individual action on the part of each government is the first line of defense, but cooperation between the governments is also essential in order that the measures taken by the countries individually may be fully effective. In order to strengthen this cooperation, the Committee considers it necessary that meetings of American government officials such as those in charge of security and intelligence services, migration, customs, and communications be held. It should be remembered that the Ministers of Foreign Affairs of the American republics, at the Eighth Meeting of Consultation, in requesting the Council to maintain all necessary vigilance, took into consideration the fact that:

> The American states are firmly united for the common goal of fighting the subversive action of international communism and for the preservation of democracy in the Americas, as expressed in Resolution XXXII of the Ninth International Conference of American States, held in Bogotá, in 1948,[1] and that for such purpose they can and should assist each other, mainly through the use of the institutional resources of the Organization of American States.[2]

It is the duty of the Council of the Organization of American States to observe the situation carefully, with a view to alerting the governments to the dangers,

[1] Text in *Ninth International Conference of American States, Bagotá, Colombia, March 30–May 2, 1948: Report of the United States Delegation and Related Documents* (Department of State publication 3263), pp. 266–7.

[2] For texts of the resolutions of the Eighth Meeting of Consultation, see *Documents, 1962*, pp. 158–67.

and to recommend pertinent measures that should be taken in this respect. The Committee considers that the Council of the Organization, availing itself of the means at its disposal and supported by the full and effective cooperation of the member states, can fulfil the mandate it has been given to serve the security of the continent.

In conclusion, the Committee wishes to make the following recommendations of a general nature:

1. To urge the governments of the member states to give effect to the recommendations on the subversive action of international communism that have been repeatedly agreed upon in resolutions of the various Inter-American Conferences and Meetings of Consultation since 1948.

2. To request the American governments to devote particular attention to the improvement of their intelligence services in order that they may have the means that will enable them to effectively plan, coordinate, and carry out action against communist subversion, and to organize, equip, and train their security forces so that they will be in a position to counteract the subversive activities of international communism.

3. To recommend to the Council of the Organization of American States that it convoke, as soon as possible, a meeting of high-level officials in the security, intelligence, migration, customs, and communications services, for the purpose of establishing the bases for achieving the necessary cooperation in order that the measures taken individually by each country may be fully effective.

4. To point out to the member governments the advisability of utilizing the technical advisory services of the Special Consultative Committee on Security.

5.[1] To recommend to the governments that they promote the holding of symposia in which all the sectors of the country will participate, insofar as possible, and which will be devoted to analyzing and disseminating information on the characteristics of the communist regime, particularly in Cuba, and the systems of life and general level of well-being, comparing them with those in the democratic countries. In particular, the public should be informed that the restrictive measures that it is recommended be adopted against communist infiltration imply suitable regulation of the exercise of civil and political liberties and human rights, in accordance with the provisions of Article 28 of the American Declaration of the Rights and Duties of Man,[2] particularly in comparison to the totalitarian repressive methods employed by the communist police state. Likewise, it is of interest to point out the fallacies of the communist economic and social development plans, which are implemented at the cost of complete sacrifice of the human individual, depriving him of the fruits of his labor and denying him the exercise of civil and political rights, with total disregard for human dignity.

6. To urge the governments of the member states in accordance with the provisions of Paragraph 2 of the declaratory part of Resolution VI of the Eighth Meeting of Consultation, to provide information on communist subversive activities on a continuing basis, in order that the Council of the Organization

---

[1] The change approved on July 3, 1963, by the Special Committee to Study Resolutions II.1 and VIII of the Eighth Meeting of Consultation of Ministers of Foreign Affairs has been incorporated in this text. [Footnote in source text.]

[2] Text in *Ninth International Conference of American States*, p. 265.

may effectively discharge the responsibilities entrusted to it in Resolution II.1, of the same Meeting of Consultation of Ministers of Foreign Affairs.

In view of the foregoing background information, the Special Committee to Study Resolutions II.1 and VIII of the Eighth Meeting of Consultation of Ministers of Foreign Affairs has the honor to submit the following draft resolution to the Council for consideration:

THE COUNCIL OF THE ORGANIZATION OF AMERICAN STATES,

HAVING SEEN the Report of the Special Committee to Study Resolutions II and VIII of the Eighth Meeting of Consultation of Ministers of Foreign Affairs dated June 4, 1963,

RESOLVES:

To transmit the said report to the governments of the member states, urging them to implement to the extent they have not already done so the recommendations contained therein, in accordance with their respective constitutional provisions.[1]

(b) *Creation of the Inter-American Committee on the Alliance for Progress*

Resolution adopted at the Second Annual Meeting of the Inter-American Economic and Social Council at the ministerial level, São Paulo, 15 November 1963[2]

WHEREAS:

The First Annual Meeting of the Inter-American Economic and Social Council adopted Resolution A–8, calling for a study of the inter-American system in order to ascertain whether its present structure meets the requirements of the Alliance for Progress program;[3]

Resolution A–8 begins by recognizing 'that the inter-American system as presently constituted, was in the main established prior to the Alliance for Progress, and, in consequence, may not possess a type of structure permitting of achievement of the objectives of the Charter of Punta del Este in the dynamic and efficient way called for';

That resolution charged two outstanding Latin Americans with studying the structure and activities of those organizations and agencies of the inter-American system that have responsibilities in regard to the Alliance, and empowered them to make, if necessary, recommendations regarding those structural and procedural changes that are required in the system and in its various organs in order that the Alliance for Progress may take on the efficiency and the dynamic qualities called for by the Charter of Punta del Este;

---

[1] This draft resolution was formally approved by the Council of Ministers of the O.A.S. without change at their meeting of 3 July 1963. The voting was 14–1 (Chile) with 4 abstentions (Brazil, Haiti, Mexico, and Venezuela).

[2] O.A.S. doc. OEA/Ser. H/X. 4 (Resolution 1–M/63), pp. 9–15; text as printed in *Current Documents, 1963*, pp. 342–7.

[3] See *Documents, 1962*, esp. p. 173.

The Council of the Organization, after approving resolution A–8, entrusted the former presidents of Brazil and Colombia, Juscelino Kubitschek and Alberto Lleras, with the preparation of a report and conclusions, to be brought to the attention of the governments of the member states and submitted to the Inter-American Economic and Social Council for consideration, if need be, at a special meeting;

Former presidents Kubitschek and Lleras accepted and carried out the mandate of the Inter-American Economic and Social Council, and rendered their conclusions in separate reports presented to the Council of the Organization, for transmittal to the governments at the Special Meeting held on June 15, 1963.[1]

The reports of former presidents Kubitschek and Lleras, which have been presented to the Second Annual Meeting of the Inter-American Economic and Social Council for consideration, are in agreement regarding the need to create a permanent, multilateral body representing the Alliance for Progress, and for this purpose proposed the creation of an inter-American development committee;

The recommendations of the former presidents, which have been examined by the Inter-American Economic and Social Council, suggest ways of organizing the proposed new body so that the Alliance for Progress may have multilateral representation and possess functional mechanisms and sufficient authority to permit it to discharge its responsibilities with the dynamic qualities and efficiency required; and

Consideration has been given to the views expressed in this regard in the Memorandum of the General Secretariat of the Organization of American States (Doc. OEA/Ser.H/X.4, CIES/344), the Report of the Panel of Experts (Doc. OEA/Ser.H/X.4, CIES/370), and the Observations of the Board of Executive Directors of the Inter-American Development Bank.

The Second Annual Meeting of the Inter-American Economic and Social Council at the Ministerial Level,

RESOLVES:

To create an Inter-American Committee on the Alliance for Progress (ICAP),[2] in accordance with the following provisions:

I. NATURE AND PURPOSE

1. The Inter-American Committee on the Alliance for Progress (ICAP) shall be a special, permanent committee of the Inter-American Economic and Social Council for the purpose of representing multilaterally the Alliance for Progress and, in the same way, coordinating and promoting its implementation in accordance with the Charter of Punta del Este,[3] and of carrying out the mandates of this resolution and those it receives from the Council of the Organization of American States or the Inter-American Economic and Social Council.

---

[1] Texts in O.A.S. docs. OEA/Ser. 6/V/c–d–1102 and OEA/Ser. 6/V/c–d–1103.
[2] Usually identified by Spanish initials C.I.A.P.
[3] Text in *Documents, 1961*, pp. 810–23.

II. DUTIES AND FUNCTIONS

2. The Inter-American Committee on the Alliance for Progress shall carry out its duties and functions in keeping with the general orientation and lines of policy established by the Inter-American Economic and Social Council in its meetings at the ministerial level.

3. To fulfill the purpose set forth in the preceding chapter, the Inter-American Committee on the Alliance for Progress shall have the following duties and functions:

a. To study the problems that may arise in connection with the Alliance for Progress and to resolve them or suggest solutions to the competent authority in each case, in accordance with the standards and policies established therefor.

b. To promote continuing improvements in the process of giving the Alliance a more multilateral character.

c. To make an annual estimate of the financing actually needed for Latin American development and of the total funds that may be available from the various domestic and external sources.

d. To make a continuing review of national and regional plans, steps taken, and efforts made within the framework of the Alliance, and to make specific recommendations to the members of the Alliance and to the regional organizations in the Hemisphere concerning those plans, steps and efforts. In discharging this duty, consideration shall be given to the evaluation reports of the ad hoc committees set up under the Charter of Punta del Este or those deriving from steps taken pursuant to paragraph 9 of this resolution.

e. On the basis of the estimates referred to in paragraph 3.c and the review and the recommendations referred to in paragraph 3.d:

(i) To prepare and present proposals on the amount and sort of domestic resources each country would have to utilize to achieve the objectives of the Alliance, and

(ii) To prepare and present annual proposals for determining the distribution among the several countries of public funds under the Alliance for Progress, referred to in Chapter V.7 of Title II of the Charter of Punta del Este, which contribute to the external financing of general plans and specific programs for the development of the Latin American countries, giving special consideration to the progress which, in line with its basic characteristics, each country makes toward reaching the objectives of the Charter of Punta del Este, and being especially mindful of Title I.1 of the Charter.

f. To cooperate with each country and with the Inter-American Development Bank or other financial agents which the country may designate, in their negotiations with governments and with any other source of financing for the purpose of obtaining the external assistance required to finance their development programs and plans.

g. To coordinate those efforts within the Alliance which require multilateral action, such as economic integration, foreign trade policies of the area, and, in general those activities which are related to the economic and social development of Latin America and which are not specifically assigned to any other body.

h. To obtain information on the progress made in multilateral investment programs for integration purposes and, upon request by the countries concerned, to help in obtaining financing for such investments; in accordance with established criteria and procedures.

i. To coordinate the work of the special committees of the Inter-American Economic and Social Council and to decide upon the necessity for their meetings, which shall be convoked by the Chairman of the Inter-American Committee on the Alliance for Progress.

j. To review the budget of the Pan American Union for the Alliance for Progress, the budget of the Program of Technical Cooperation, and that of any other specific multilateral fund, as prepared by the General Secretariat for approval by the Inter-American Economic and Social Council.

k. To review the program and budget prepared by the Secretary General with respect to the regular operations of the Secretariat within the purview of the Inter-American Economic and Social Council—including the items for permanent professional and administrative personnel; for the operation of the Inter-American Economic and Social Council, the Inter-American Committee on the Alliance for Progress, and the Panel of Experts; and for overhead directly related to these operations—for approval by the Inter-American Economic and Social Council, in accordance with Article 19.f of its Statutes.[1]

1. To establish its Regulations and the rules of procedure it considers advisable for the performance of its functions.

2. The member states agree that, when providing financial and technical assistance through their own agencies and when instructing their representatives in the various international organizations that provide such assistance, they shall give special consideration to the recommendations of the Inter-American Committee on the Alliance for Progress, in accordance with paragraph 3. e(ii), regarding the distribution of external public funds under the Alliance for Progress.

III. MEMBERSHIP AND OPERATION

5. The Inter-American Committee on the Alliance for Progress shall be composed of a chairman and seven representatives of the member states of the Organization of American States. Each representative shall be entitled to one vote.

The chairman shall be elected for a three-year period and shall be eligible for re-election for one term only.

The representatives of the countries, proposed thereby, shall be appointed by the Inter-American Economic and Social Council for a two-year period, on the basis of the same distribution agreed upon for electing the Executive Directors of the Inter-American Development Bank (IDB) at the election immediately prior to each period. Such distribution shall not apply to the five countries of Central America, which, as a group, shall propose one representative.

At the time of the first appointment, three of the six members who represent the Latin American countries shall be selected by lot to serve for one year.

---

[1] Text in *Current Documents, 1961*, pp. 418–24.

A member of the Inter-American Committee on the Alliance for Progress may be re-elected only in the event that the countries which proposed their appointment indicate to the Inter-American Economic and Social Council that this be done.

When in the exercise of its functions the Inter-American Committee on the Alliance for Progress is to consider matters specifically concerning a given country, it shall invite that country to appoint an ad hoc representative.

6. The Secretary General of the Organization of American States (OAS), the President of the Inter-American Development Bank (IDB), the Coordinator of the Panel of Experts, and the Principal Director of the Economic Commission for Latin America (ECLA) shall serve as permanent advisors to the Inter-American Committee on the Alliance for Progress and in that capacity may attend its meetings.

7. The Panel of Experts shall be the technical arm of the Inter-American Committee on the Alliance for Progress in carrying out its functions of evaluating development plans and programs, in the spirit of the provisions of Title II, Chapter V.3 of the Charter of Punta del Este, and, in general, it may be consulted by the Inter-American Committee on the Alliance for Progress in relation to other matters relating to its functions. The Inter-American Development Bank shall be the technical arm of the Committee in matters concerning the financing of Latin American development.

The Inter-American Committee on the Alliance for Progress may request the technical advice of the Latin American Free Trade Association (LAFTA) and the Permanent Secretariat of the General Treaty on Central American Economic Integration (SIECA) on matters of economic integration.

8. In conformity with existing provisions, the Inter-American Committee on the Alliance for Progress may invite representatives of governmental and non-governmental agencies, who are recognized international authorities and who may have a particular interest in matters to be taken up at given meetings, to attend these meetings as observers. The Organization for Economic Cooperation and Development (OECD) and the European Economic Community (EEC) shall be among the entities to be so invited.

9. Those countries which have only sectoral programs and those which have national development plans but do not request the formation of an ad hoc committee may come to an agreement with the Inter-American Committee on the Alliance for Progress as to the best way of evaluating their programs or plans in consonance with the aims of the Charter of Punta del Este.

10. In order to ensure more frequent information on the progress of the activities of the Inter-American Committee on the Alliance for Progress, the Chairman of the Inter-American Economic and Social Council, pursuant to Article 20 of its Statutes, shall convoke special meetings of the Inter-American Economic and Social Council at the ministerial level, when such shall be considered necessary.

11. The Inter-American Committee on the Alliance for Progress shall submit to the Inter-American Economic and Social Council for consideration an annual report on the fulfillment of its mandate and the draft resolutions that it may agree upon.

IV. CHAIRMAN

12. The Inter-American Economic and Social Council at the Ministerial Level shall elect an outstanding personality of the nationality of one of its members to be chairman of the Inter-American Committee on the Alliance for Progress. In addition to the functions and powers normal to the position, and to those which may be entrusted to him by the Inter-American Economic and Social Council and, on occasion, by the Council of the Organization of American States, the Chairman shall be the permanent representative of the Inter-American Committee on the Alliance for Progress in actions required for rapid and effective execution of its decisions.

In the discharge of his duties, the Chairman shall be responsible only to the Inter-American Committee on the Alliance for Progress and the Inter-American Economic and Social Council.

The Chairman shall take office at a special ceremony in the presence of the Council of the Organization of American States.

V. SECRETARIAT AND HEADQUARTERS

13. The Executive Secretary of the Inter-American Economic and Social Council shall be the Secretary of the Inter-American Committee on the Alliance for Progress. Secretariat services shall be provided by the General Secretariat. Whenever the Chairman of the Inter-American Committee on the Alliance for Progress considers it indispensable to enlist the services of additional personnel in order to carry out the functions of the Committee more efficiently, he may request the Secretary General of the Organization of American States to take the necessary steps to appoint suitable persons.

14. The Inter-American Committee on the Alliance for Progress shall have its headquarters in Washington, D.C., United States of America, but it may hold meetings in any other city in the member states of the Organization of American States.

CHRONOLOGICAL LIST OF DOCUMENTS
1963

May

July

August

November

December

January 1964